Contents at a Glance

Contents

DAY 10 Creating and Programming Sound 175

DAY 11 Getting Started on Your RPG 211

About the Author

Award-winning author Clayton Walnum started programming computers in 1982, when he traded in an IBM Selectric typewriter to buy an Atari 400 computer (16KB of RAM!). Clay soon learned to combine his interest in writing with his newly acquired programming skills and started selling programs and articles to computer magazines. In 1985, *ANALOG Computing*, a nationally distributed computer magazine, hired him as a technical editor, and, before leaving the magazine business in 1989 to become a freelance writer, Clay worked his way up to Executive Editor. He has since acquired a degree in computer science, as well as worked on more than 40 books (translated into many languages) covering everything from computer gaming to 3D graphics programming. He's also written hundreds of magazine articles and software reviews, as well as countless programs. His recent books include *Windows 2000 Programming Secrets*, *C++ Master Reference*, *The Complete Idiot's Guide to VB.NET*, and *Teach Yourself Game Programming with Visual Basic in 21 Days*. Clay's biggest disappointment in life is that he wasn't one of the Beatles. To compensate, he writes and records rock music in his home studio. You can reach Clay by sending e-mail to `cwalnum@claytonwalnum.com` or by visiting his Web site at `www.claytonwalnum.com`. And don't forget to visit Clay's music page at `www.mp3.com/claywalnum`.

About the Technical Editor

David Franson been a professional in the field of networking, programming, and 2D and 3D computer graphics since 1990. In 2000, he resigned his position as information systems director of one of the largest entertainment law firms in New York City to pursue a full-time career in game development. Currently, he is writing *2D Artwork* and *3D Modeling for Game Artists*, to be published September 2002.

Dedication

To Lynn

Acknowledgments

I would like to thank the many people whose hard work made this book as good as it could be. Thanks to Neil Rowe for signing me up for this book and getting things off on the right track. Thanks also to the team of editors for keeping things rolling and for making sure everything resembled the English language and was technically correct. Specifically, those editors are (in no particular order) Matt Purcell, Mark Renfrow, Michael Dietsch, and David Franson. As always, thanks goes to my family: Lynn, Christopher, Justin, Stephen, and Caitlynn.

We Want to Hear from You!

As the reader of this book, you are our most important critic and commentator. We value your opinion and want to know what we're doing right, what we could do better, what areas you'd like to see us publish in, and any other words of wisdom you're willing to pass our way.

As an executive editor for Sams, I welcome your comments. You can e-mail or write me directly to let me know what you did or didn't like about this book—as well as what we can do to make our books better.

Please note that I cannot help you with technical problems related to the topic of this book. We do have a User Services group, however, where I will forward specific technical questions related to the book.

When you write, please be sure to include this book's title and author as well as your name, e-mail address, and phone number. I will carefully review your comments and share them with the author and editors who worked on the book.

Email: `feedback@samspublishing.com`
Mail: Executive Editor
Sams
201 West 103rd Street
Indianapolis, IN 46290 USA

For more information about this book or another Sams title, visit our Web site at `www.samspublishing.com`. Type the ISBN (excluding hyphens) or the title of a book in the Search field to find the page you're looking for.

Introduction

Few can argue that Windows is the most popular desktop operating system on the planet. Still, when it comes to computer games, it was a DOS world for a long, long time. Thanks to the sluggish graphics library available then in Windows, few games used to run well under Windows. And those games that did run well tended toward less graphically oriented themes such as puzzles or card games.

Microsoft was not unaware of the lack of appeal Windows held out to game developers and was bound and determined to fix up Windows so that it could perform as well as DOS. Microsoft's cure for Windows game programmers is DirectX, and Direct3D specifically.

Using Direct3D, you can write programs under Windows that incorporate the programming techniques that made DOS games so successful. In fact, Direct3D works so well that Windows games have now almost completely taken over from DOS.

In this book, you'll learn the basics of using Direct3D, one of DirectX's graphics libraries, in your 2D game programs. That's right, Direct3D is not just for 3D game programming! With a little know-how, you can use it to create any kind of graphically based program you want. As you learn about using Direct3D for 2D programs, you'll discover how to handle bitmaps, animation, sound, and much more. More importantly, you'll learn to create an old-style role-playing game, along the lines of the early *Ultima* games, and you'll do it all without page after page of complicated math!

Who This Book Is For

This book is not an introductory text for programmers interested in learning Visual C++ Windows game programming. To understand the programming advice that follows, you must have a working knowledge of C++ and be somewhat familiar with the Visual C++ development system. In addition, you should have some knowledge of object-oriented programming concepts. Previous Windows programming experience will also be helpful, although it's not required.

Hardware and Software Requirements

To compile and run the programs on this book's CD, and to get the most out of the upcoming lessons, you must have at least the following:

- An IBM-compatible with a 450 MHz Pentium II processor and 256 megabytes of memory

- Windows XP or Windows 2000
- A monitor and graphics card that supports True Color graphics
- Visual Studio .NET (you may be able to get by with Visual Studio 6, although some project steps will be different)

Compiling the Programs in This Book

The programs in this book were written with Visual C++ .NET, but did not use the .NET Framework. In other words, the source code is straight Visual C++. This book assumes your copy of Visual C++ .NET was installed using the default settings and directories. If you've changed any of the default settings or directories and are not sure how to fix errors that may result from these changes, you should reinstall Visual C++.

The programs that follow are organized on this book's CD-ROM by chapter. Each chapter's programs are found in their own folder on the CD-ROM. That is, the programs for Day 2 are in the Chapter02 folder, the programs for Day 3 are in the Chapter03 folder, and so on. In addition, each program is contained in its own folder, based on the program's name.

To compile a program, copy its folder (and thus all its files) to your main Visual C++ folder. Then start Visual C++, open the program's .sln file, and build the project. Note that you must have the DirectX 8.1 SDK installed in its default directory on drive C. Note also that the CD-ROM includes an executable version of each program. You don't have to compile the programs unless you really want to.

How to Use This Book

This book approaches its programs as hands-on programming projects that you can follow step-by-step. Often, rather than presenting an entire program all at once, you'll build each program version a piece at a time, inserting new code as you advance through the text. Each program version has its own section in the book, including a numbered list of steps you must follow to create that version of the program. There are three approaches you can take toward completing each programming project:

Approach 1: Read each project step and follow the instructions exactly, typing whatever new code is required. Although typing is a lot of work, it's also the best way to learn, because you are forced to focus on each line of code. (Of course, typing code usually adds a bug or two to a program—bugs you'll have to search out on your own.)

Approach 2: Read each project's steps, but, instead of typing source code, use the Visual C++ editor's cut and paste functions to add new code to the project. (You'll find the code snippets you need on the CD-ROM.) This approach saves a lot of time and typing, but at the expense of learning. You'll have to be more careful that you truly understand each step before you move on.

Approach 3: Read each project's steps, but don't bother to build the programs on your own. Instead, run the executable versions of the programs supplied on this book's CD-ROM. This is the easiest way to get through the book, but also the least educational. If you're an expert programmer and are already knowledgeable about Visual C++, then you can probably get away with the easy way out.

Notice that all three approaches to using this book start with *Read each project's steps*. This is important, even if you're not actually building the example programs yourself. Smaller pieces of source code are explained within the steps themselves, whereas larger functions are explained in their own section of the text. In short, you must read all the steps, as well as the regular text, to get a full explanation of the programs.

Hand Me a Sword

You're probably anxious now to dive into Direct3D, not to mention starting to build *The Adventures of Jasper Bookman*, the full-featured role-playing game that makes up much of this book. Not only are you going to learn new techniques for writing successful Windows games, but you're also going to take a trip through a dangerous fantasy world. At the end of your journey, you'll emerge a better game programmer—that is, if the monsters don't eat you first.

Clayton Walnum
May 2002

WEEK 1

At a Glance

This week, you'll be introduced to some introductory game-programming concepts, as well as get started learning how to use Direct3D. In Day 1, your introduction to game programming starts with an overview of the elements of game design, including graphics design, sound effects, user interfaces, animation, and more. In Day 2, you take a look at the various types of tools you need to create games. Then, in Day 3, you start the programming, by learning how to put together a basic Windows application.

Day 4 is your introduction to Direct3D. There you'll see what Direct3D has to offer the developer of 2D games. In Day 5, you start programming Direct3D, by creating devices, setting display modes, and understanding the differences between windowed and full-screen Direct3D applications. Day 6 gets you started with Direct3D surfaces, which are the objects you use to store graphics. Finally, Day 7 gets into some 3D programming concepts that you need to understand even when programming 2D games.

WEEK 1

DAY 1

Introduction to Game Programming

In your first day of studying game programming, you'll examine the reason why you might want to program games and why you might want to use C++ to do it. In addition, you'll take a brief look at the general process of creating a game. That is, you'll learn about the many areas of expertise that work together to enable you to design and create a computer game. In short, today you will learn the following:

- How game programming can make you a better programmer
- Why C++ is a good language for game programming
- The many skills needed to create a quality game

Complex, but Not Too Complex

In my wild-and-wooly youth, I was a guitarist in a semi-professional rock group. I'll never forget the first time I walked into a recording studio to record a demo song with my band. In the control room was a huge mixing board with more buttons and switches than there are teeth in a great white shark. To the right was a patch bay from which snaked dozens of patch cords, each connecting some vital piece of equipment to another. Lights blinked. Reels spun. Sound processing equipment with fancy names like phase shifter, digital delay, and multiband equalizer clicked on and off.

When I looked at all that complex machinery and considered that I was paying $60 an hour (the equivalent of about $150 an hour today) for the privilege of being there, I almost turned around and walked out the door. It seemed to me that just learning my way around this complicated studio would cost me my life savings. I could see myself being ejected penniless from the premises without having recorded even a note. Luckily, like everything else in life (well, almost everything), a recording studio is not really as complicated as it looks.

The same thing can be said about computer games. When you sit down at your computer and play the latest arcade hit or plunge into the newest state-of-the-art adventure game, you may be in awe of the talent and work that went into the glowing pixels that you see before your eyes. (And you should be.) But, just like recording a song in a studio, writing games is not as difficult as you may think.

If you've had some programming experience, you already have much of the knowledge and many of the skills you need to program a computer game. You need only refine those skills with an eye toward games. In this chapter, you get a quick look at some of the skills required to develop and write computer games.

Hidden Benefits of Programming Games

You probably bought this book because you wanted to have a little fun with your computer. There you were in the bookstore, digging through all those very serious programming manuals, when this volume leaped out at you from the stack. But when you were walking to the cash register with this book in hand, you might have felt a little guilty. After all, games aren't serious computing, are they? You should be learning to write spreadsheet programs, databases, and word processors, right?

Let me tell you a quick story.

Way back in the dark ages of home computing (1981, to be exact), I got my first computer. It was an Atari 400, and like everything Atari at that time, this powerful little computer was best known for its game-playing capabilities. 1981 was, after all, the beginning of the golden age of video games, and Atari was the reigning king.

Unfortunately, after a few phenomenally successful years, video games spiraled into rapid decline, taking many companies in the industry down with them. Computers became serious again. Although Atari managed to survive (barely), it would never be regarded as the designer and manufacturer of serious computers, thanks to its status as a game-computer maker. This is a shame, because the Atari ST computer (the Atari 400/800's successor) was—along with the Apple Macintosh and the Commodore Amiga—way ahead of its time. Certainly these products were light years more advanced than the "serious" IBM clones that gained popularity at that time.

The problem was that darn gaming image with which Atari had been saddled. Who wanted to use a game computer to manage a spreadsheet, balance a bank account, or track an investment portfolio? That would be kind of dumb, wouldn't it?

Not really. The irony is that a computer capable of playing sophisticated games is a computer that's capable of just about anything. A good computer game taxes your computer to the maximum, including its capability to process data quickly, to generate graphics and animation, and to create realistic sound effects. Only a state-of-the-art computer can keep up with today's high-powered games, like flight simulators and 3D action games. In fact, there are few business applications in existence that require more computing power than a sophisticated computer game.

Similarly, a programmer who can write commercial-quality computer games can write just about any other type of software as well, especially considering today's focus on graphics and sound in applications. You may have purchased this book to have a little fun with your computer, but before you're done, you will learn valuable lessons in software design and programming—lessons that you can apply to many different kinds of software.

So, why program computer games? Mostly because it's fun! But remember that your game-programming experience will help you with every other program that you ever write.

Why Use C++?

I could probably come up with dozens of reasons why you'd want to use C++ as your language for learning about game programming. I can also easily come up with reasons why you wouldn't. The truth is that there are a lot of factors to consider when choosing a language for game programming, not the least of which is the type of games you want to write. For learning game programming, you may want to choose C++ for the following reasons:

- C++ is one of the most powerful languages in existence.
- Most professional game programmers use C++.

- A C++ programming environment, like Visual C++ .NET, provides all the tools you need to develop, test, and release your software.
- C++'s object-oriented features enable you to organize your source code into logical, self-contained modules.
- C++ is the language of choice for Windows development.

The Elements of Game Programming

As you've already discovered, good computer games push your computer to its limits. In fact, a good computer game must excel in many areas. To write computer games that people will want to play, then, you must gain some expertise in the related areas of programming. These areas represent the elements of game programming:

- Game design
- Graphic design
- Sound generation
- Controls and interfaces
- Image handling
- Animation
- Algorithms
- Artificial intelligence
- Game testing

These game-programming elements overlap to an extent. For example, to learn graphic design for computer games, you need to know how a computer handles graphical images. Moreover, game design draws on all the other elements in the list. After all, you can't design a game unless you know how the graphics, sound, controls, and computer algorithms fit together to form the final product.

In the rest of this chapter, you learn more about each of these game elements.

Game Design

Whether your game is a standard shoot-'em-up, in which the player's only goal is to blast everything on the screen, or a sophisticated war game, requiring sharp wits and clever moves, first and foremost your game must be fun. If a game isn't fun, it doesn't matter how great the graphics are, how realistic the sound effects are, or how well you designed the computer player's algorithms. A boring game will almost certainly get filed away in a closet to gather dust.

Many things determine whether a game is fun. The most important thing, of course, is the game's concept. Often, a game concept is based on some real-world event or circumstance. For example, chess—probably one of the most popular board games of all time—is really a war game. Monopoly, on the other hand, is a financial simulation in which players try to bankrupt their competition.

Computer games are no different from their real-world cousins. They too must have some logical goal for the player and—with rare exceptions—be set in some sort of believable "world." This world can be as simple as an on-screen maze or as complex as an entire planet with continents, countries, and cities. In the insanely addictive computer game Tetris, the player's world is simply a narrow on-screen channel in which the player must stack variously shaped objects. On the other hand, in the fabulous Might & Magic series of role-playing games, the player's world is filled with forests, swamps, cities, monsters, and the other elements that make up a complete fantasy scenario.

Whatever type of computer world you envision for your game, it's imperative that the world have consistent rules that the player can master. For a game to be fun, the player must be able to figure out how to surmount the various obstacles that you place in his path. When a player loses a computer game, it should be only because he has not yet mastered the subtleties of the rules, not because some random bolt out of the blue blasted him into digital bits and pieces.

Of course, to build a logical, fair, and effective gaming world, you must draw on all your skills as a programmer. All the other areas of programming in the previous list come into play here. Graphics, sound, interface design, computer algorithms, and more all help determine whether a game is ultimately fun or just another dime-a-dozen hack job whose compact disc will be used as a Frisbee at the next family picnic.

The topic of consistent rules for your game leads directly to a related topic: a consistent game world. Every element of your game—fonts, graphics, sound, story—contributes to this goal. For example, if you're writing a game in which the player must battle zombies and werewolves, you're probably not going to have much use for those cute little bunny characters you drew (that is, unless the bunnies suddenly grow fangs and horns and develop an unquenchable desire to consume human flesh!). Similarly, your zombie game will need suitably eerie sound effects and spooky music. The Sugarplum Fairies theme just ain't gonna cut it.

Graphic Design

There's a good reason why so many computer game packages are covered with exciting illustrations and awe-inspiring screen shots. In spite of how hard people try to make intelligent buying decisions, everyone is swayed by clever packaging. Although your smart side may tell you to ignore that fabulous wizard on the box cover, your impulsive side sees that wizard as just a hint of the excitement that you'll find in the box. Of course, reality usually falls far short of packaging. Buyer beware.

The lesson here is not that you should make your games look better than they play, but rather that how a game looks is often as important as how well it performs. You want your gaming screens to be neat and uncluttered, logically laid out, and, above all, exciting to look at. Your screens should scream "Play me!" to anyone who comes into viewing distance.

Like anything else, graphic design is a professional skill that takes many years of study and practice to master. Luckily, you don't have to be a graphic-design whiz to create attractive game screens. You can look at other games to get design ideas. You can also experiment with different screen designs to see which are the most attractive and which work best with your game world. Use your favorite paint program to draw different layouts and compare them. Trial and error is not only a powerful technique for devising improved designs, but it's also a great learning tool. The more you experiment, the more you'll learn about what looks good on a computer screen and what doesn't. Figure 1.1 shows Microsoft Paint loaded with an image that you'll be using in this book.

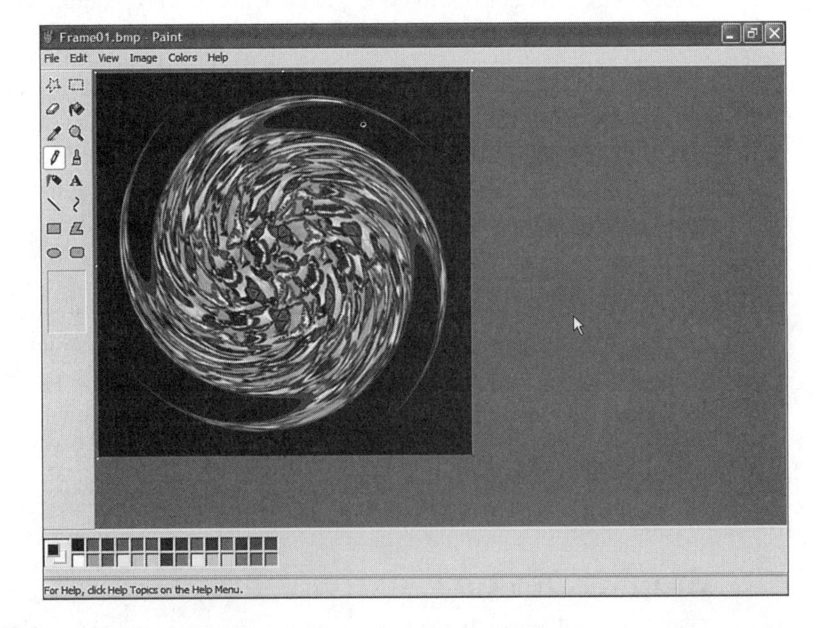

FIGURE 1.1

Using Microsoft Paint to design graphics.

Sound Generation

The word we live in is a noisy place, indeed. There's hardly a moment in our lives when we're not assaulted by hundreds of sounds simultaneously. If your game world is to seem realistic to the player, it too must provide sound. That's not to say that you must re-create the full spectrum of sounds that a player hears in the real world. With today's computers, that task would be impossible.

Although you shouldn't fill your player's ears with unnecessary noise, you should provide as many sound cues as appropriate. When the player selects an on-screen button, she should hear the button click. Similarly, when the player slams a home run, she should hear the crack of the bat and the roar of the crowd.

There's not a computer game on the planet (or, I'd venture to say, in the universe) that could not be improved by better sound effects. Luckily, thanks to powerful sound cards, many of today's games include fabulous digitized sound effects.

Music, although less important than sound effects, can also add much to a computer game. The most obvious place for music is at the beginning of the game, usually accompanying a title screen. You might also want to use music when the player advances to the next level, or when he accomplishes some other important goal in the game.

Adding music to a computer game, however, requires that you have some knowledge of music composition. Bad music in a game is worse than none at all. If you have no musical training, chances are that you have a friend who does. You can work together to compose the music for your computer game magnum opus. If you're lucky, she won't even ask for a share of the royalties! Figure 1.2 shows the sound editing software that I frequently use when working on sound effects or music.

Controls and Interfaces

Everything that happens in a computer game happens inside the computer. Unlike a conventional board game in the real world, the player can't use his hands to pick up pieces and move them around. To enable the player to control the game, the programmer must provide some sort of interface that the player can use to manipulate the data that exists inside the computer. In a computer game, menus and on-screen buttons enable the user to select options and commands. In addition, the keyboard or mouse acts as the player's hands, enabling him to move and otherwise manipulate objects on the screen.

A good game interface makes playing the game as easy as possible. The commands that the player needs to control the game should be logical and readily available. Also, the more you can make your game work like a real-world game, the easier it will be for the player to learn its controls. For example, in a computer chess game, you might enable the player to move a game piece with her mouse pointer instead of forcing her to use her keyboard to type the square to which she wants to move the piece. Figure 1.3 shows the interface for the game editor you'll use later in this book.

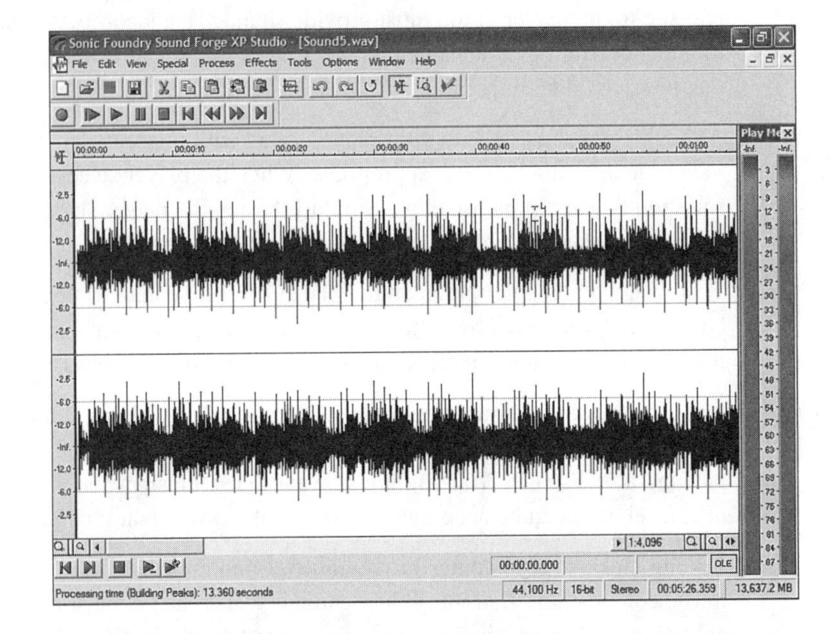

FIGURE 1.2
Sound Forge XP Studio 5.

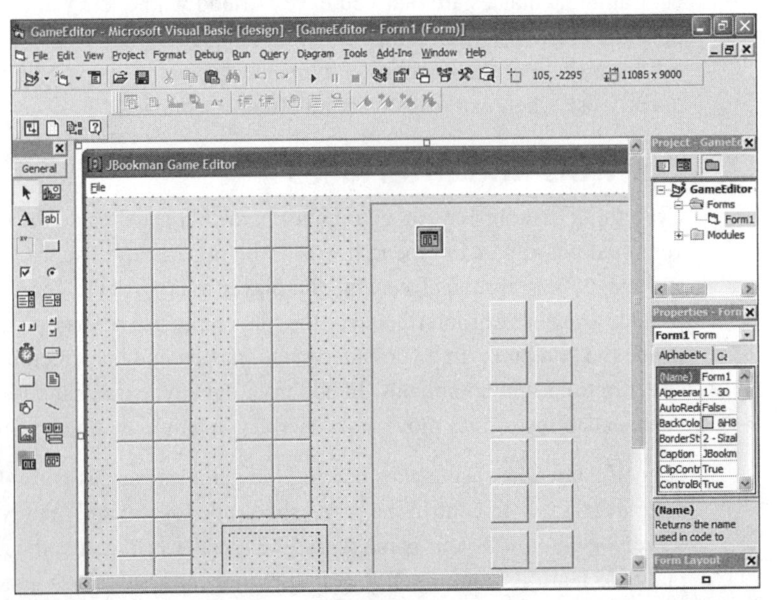

FIGURE 1.3
The interface for a game editor.

Image Handling

Every computer game must deal with various types of images. These images may be full-screen background graphics, icons that represent game commands or game pieces, or tiles that you use to create a map or other complex game screen. When you design your game, you must decide which types of images you need. Should you draw your program's background screen at runtime? Or should you create the screen with a paint program and just load it in your program? If you need to conserve memory, maybe you should create your game screens from small tiles?

New Term In game-programming lingo, a *tile* is a small graphical object that can be used with other similar objects to assemble a complex game screen. For example, several tiles depicting a tree can be used to create an entire forest. Various types of tiles—trees, grass, water, mountains, and so on—can be used to assemble an entire world map.

You must consider questions like these as you design your computer game's graphics. You want your game to use enough quality graphics to look as professional as possible (which means that you may need to find an artist), but you also must consider the amount of memory the graphics will consume and how long it takes to move graphic images from the disk to the computer's memory. Most gamers hate to wait for files to load from a disk. On the other hand, keeping too much data in memory may make your game clunky with computers that have smaller amounts of free memory.

Another important issue is the amount of time it takes to create your game's graphics. You can't spend the next 10 years drawing detailed graphics for every aspect of your game. You need to use shortcuts (such as tiling, which is using small graphical images to piece together a game screen) to speed up the graphic design process. In other words, although every tree in the real world looks different, many trees in a computer game look identical. Figure 1.4 shows a set of tiles that you'll be using in this book.

Animation

Once you've learned to design and manipulate computer graphic images, you're ready to take the next step: animation. Animation is the process of making objects appear to come to life and to move around the computer screen. By using a series of images, you can make a chicken waddle across a road, a rock tumble from a cliff side, or a spaceship blast off from a launch pad.

New Term *Animation* is the process of causing a graphical game object to move or change in some way. For example, a ball that bounces around the screen is an animation, as is a game creature that falls to the ground when shot.

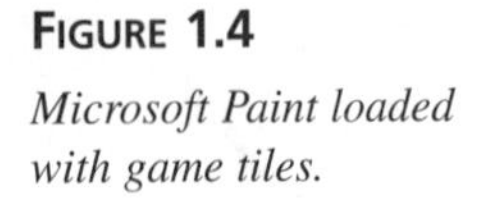

FIGURE 1.4
Microsoft Paint loaded with game tiles.

For example, when a player moves a game piece, instead of having the piece simply disappear from its current location and reappear at its new one, you might make the piece seem to dissolve and then reform itself. Or, if the playing piece represents a human being or an animal, you could have the piece saunter over to its new location.

Such animation effects can make your game much more interesting and even more fun to play. Although animation requires a lot of work on the programmer's part, it's well worth the effort.

Algorithms

Although the term *algorithm* sounds like the most horrid technobabble, it's really a simple word. An algorithm is nothing more than a series of steps that solves a problem. You use algorithms every day of your life. When you make pancakes for breakfast, you must follow an algorithm. When you drive to work, you must follow another algorithm. Algorithms enable you to solve all of life's simple (and sometimes not-so-simple) tasks.

Computer algorithms enable you to solve computing problems. In other words, to write computer games, you need to be able to figure out how to get your computer to do things—things that you may not have tried to do on a computer before. How, for example, can you determine who has the best hand in a poker game, or create a smart computer player? You must write an algorithm. Once you know how to solve a problem with your computer, you can write the specific code in whatever programming language you're using. Throughout this book, you'll see many algorithms for solving game problems.

NEW TERM An *computer algorithm* is a set of program steps that solves a programming problem. For example, a function that determines whether a player has a full house in a computer card game uses an algorithm to analyze the cards in the player's hand.

Artificial Intelligence

Artificial intelligence routines are algorithms that make computers seem smart. By smart, I don't mean the ability to calculate the player's score or process a player's input. I mean instead a computer's ability to act as an opponent. If you want to write a computer game that features computer players, you must create algorithms that enable the computer to compete with human players. How involved this algorithm turns out to be depends on how complex the game is and how well you want the computer to play.

For example, good algorithms for creating a computer chess player can be difficult to write, because winning a game of chess requires a great deal of strategy. On the other hand, an algorithm for a computer chess player can also be easy to write. For example, you can simply have the computer choose a random move each turn, although such an algorithm yields a computer player that's easy to beat. As you can see, the algorithm that you write can determine the difficulty of your game.

Game Testing

After you read this book and learn everything you need to know to design and program your computer game, you'll get to work (I hope) on your own masterpiece. However, after you write your game, you're far from finished, because you then must test it extensively to ensure that it works properly.

The best way to test a game is to give it to a few trusted friends and watch as they play, taking notes about things that don't work quite the way you expect. Remember to watch not only for program bugs (things that make the program do unexpected things and even crash the computer) but also interface bugs, which may make your program confusing to use.

After your friends have played the game for a while, ask them what they liked or didn't like. Find out how they think the game could be improved. You don't have to agree with everything they say, but always be polite, taking their suggestions seriously and writing them down so that you can review them later. Don't be defensive. Your friends aren't criticizing your work so much as helping you to make it better. Remember: There's no such thing as a perfect computer program. There's always room for improvement. After the testing is complete, implement those suggestions that you think are valuable.

The only way to test a game is to have several people play it repeatedly. Of course, before you pass the game on to a few close friends, you should have already played the game so much that you would rather read a phone book from cover to cover than see your opening screen again!

Summary

Writing a computer game requires that you bring into play the best of your programming skills. To create a successful game, you must first design it. This means that you must think about, experiment with, and finally implement the game's graphic design and interface. As you design your game, you need to consider the types of images and sounds that will bring the game to life. Animation and smart algorithms will also help your game be the next best-seller.

In Day 2, "Tools of the Trade," you discover the various tools you need to create computer games that'll wow your players. These tools include not only a programming language, but also things like paint programs and audio software.

Q&A

Q. Why shouldn't I use an easier language like Visual Basic to program my games?

A. Actually, you *can* use Visual Basic to create games, as this popular language is becoming more powerful all the time. C++ is still the language of choice for game programming, though, because it has none of the limitations you may run up against using Visual Basic. Anyway, using DirectX in C++ and in Visual Basic is similar, so if you already know Visual Basic, but don't know C++, maybe you should be reading a Visual Basic DirectX book.

Q. Is it hard to call Windows API functions from C++?

A. Not at all. In fact, the Windows API was originally designed with C and C++ in mind. You do, however, need to understand how all the API functions work together to create a Windows applications. Luckily, Day 3, "Writing a Windows Program," covers just about everything you need to know. You don't need to be an accomplished Windows programmer to understand this book.

Q. How good of a C++ programmer do I need to be to write game programs?

A. The type of programming you do when writing a game is not all that different from the programming you use to write any type of application. The biggest difference is that game programs tend to be more graphically oriented than other types of programs like utilities or productivity applications. However, because this book is about DirectX programming, you'll learn such graphical skills in these pages.

Workshop

The workshop includes quiz questions to help gauge your grasp of the material. You'll find the answers to this quiz at the end of this section. Even if you feel that you totally understand the concepts presented here, you should work through the quiz anyway. The last section is an exercise or two that you might work through to help reinforce your learning.

Quiz

1. Why does programming games make you a better all-around programmer?
2. Name four reasons why C++ is a good language to use for game programming.
3. What is a computer algorithm?
4. How are artificial intelligence and computer algorithms related in game programming?

Exercises

1. Imagine that you're going to write a computer version of checkers. How would you create the main game screen? What type of user interface might you use? What images would you need to design?

Answers for Day 1

Quiz

1. Why does programming games make you a better all-around programmer?

   Because game programs often require that you get the most out of your computer's hardware, an experience that gives you practice solving problems you might encounter in many other programming projects.

2. Name four reasons why C++ is a good language to use for game programming.

   C++ is powerful, object-oriented, and the language of choice for Windows development. Moreover, C++ is the language of choice for game developers.

3. What is a computer algorithm?

   A set of steps for solving a programming problem.

4. How are artificial intelligence and computer algorithms related in game programming?

   Computer algorithms determine how a computer player will play the game. Such algorithms may create easy-to-beat computer players or may create computer players that are difficult to beat, depending on how well the programmer designs the algorithm.

Exercises

1. Imagine that you're going to write a computer version of checkers. How would you create the main game screen? What type of user interface might you use? What images would you need to design?

   Everybody will come up with their own ideas on how best to design this game. For example, one programmer might want to create a screen that looks like a checkers board viewed from an angle, while someone else might be happy with a simple straight-down view. In any case, the user interface will require a way to move the checkers, as well as commands for starting and ending games. You might have the user move a checker by clicking source and destination squares, or you could get fancy and enable the player to drag the checker images around the board. You could use buttons for starting and ending games, but you'll also want these commands in the application's menu bar. As for images, you'll need to draw the checker board. You'll also need images of checkers, as well as a way to indicate when a checker has been "kinged."

WEEK 1

DAY 2

Tools of the Trade

Oddly enough, making software requires using software. You might think this fact leads to a kind of chicken-and-egg conundrum, but we'll leave all that for the philosophers. The fact is that those of us who want to design and create games need to have a minimum set of software tools, including a programming language or two, a paint program, and a sound editor. In this chapter, you'll take a quick look at these important tools. Specifically, today you will learn the following:

- Choosing the appropriate programming language
- Choosing graphics software
- Choosing sound software
- Discovering the right tools for the job

Programming Languages

The first step in writing a program is choosing the best language for the job. In the case of game programming, you can't go wrong with C++. One reason is that C++ is a powerful language that can yield applications that run almost as efficiently as those written with the dreaded assembly language. (In case you don't know, when you use assembly language, you're programming at the hardware level, which is quite a challenge!)

Another good reason to use C++ is that it provides the types of programming constructs, such as classes, that can make programming more convenient and organized. Anyway, because DirectX was designed mostly with C++ in mind, the two make a perfect match. And if none of this convinces you, consider that most professional games are written using C++.

For all of these reasons (and a few more that I haven't thought of yet), this book uses the C++ language to develop its programs. Specifically, all programs in this book—except the map editor—were written with Microsoft's latest version of C++, Visual C++ .NET.

NEW TERM A *map editor* is a program that enables you to easily create the world in which your computer game takes place. Such programs are also sometimes called level editors.

You'll probably be able to get away with using Visual C++ 6, because I've avoided using any of the new .NET stuff, such as the .NET frameworks, in these programs; those of you who aren't too quick to adopt new technologies (or can't afford to, as is often the case) won't get left in the dust. Figure 2.1 shows Visual Studio .NET in action. Visual Studio is the host IDE (integrated development environment) for Visual C++ .NET.

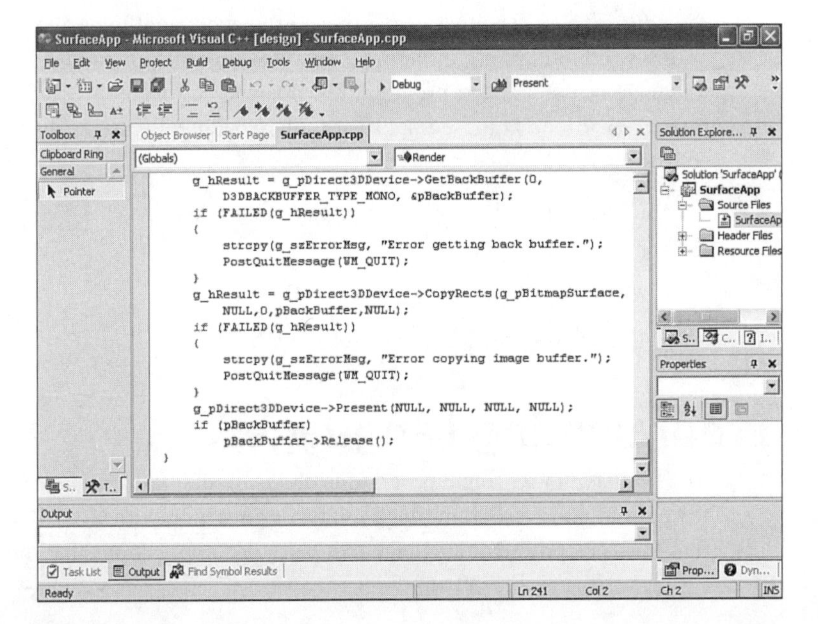

FIGURE 2.1
The Visual C++ .NET IDE.

New Term An *integrated development environment* (IDE) is a set of related programming tools, such as a source code editor, a compiler, a linker, and a debugger, all grouped together so as to appear to be a single application.

C++ notwithstanding, I'm a big believer in using the right tools for the job, so the map editor in this book was written using Visual Basic 6, a higher level programming tool than C++. I didn't use Visual Basic .NET because that language is a huge departure from the VB most of us are used to and, again, I didn't want to leave anyone behind.

New Term A *high-level language* isolates the programmer from the details of how the computer system actually works. For example, assembly language, which is the lowest level programming language, requires that the programmer have intimate knowledge of the smallest details of how a computer works, whereas as high-level language like Visual Basic enables a programmer to program using more easily understood commands. C++ is a higher level language than assembly language, but a lower level language than Visual Basic.

But why did I pick VB at all? Visual Basic is an outstanding language for putting together sophisticated user interfaces very quickly. Because the map editor has a slew of controls, and because the code didn't need to be as efficient as what you'd get with C++, I decided to go with VB. This decision enabled me to put the program together much faster than I could have with C++. Figure 2.2 shows Visual Basic 6 with the level editor project open.

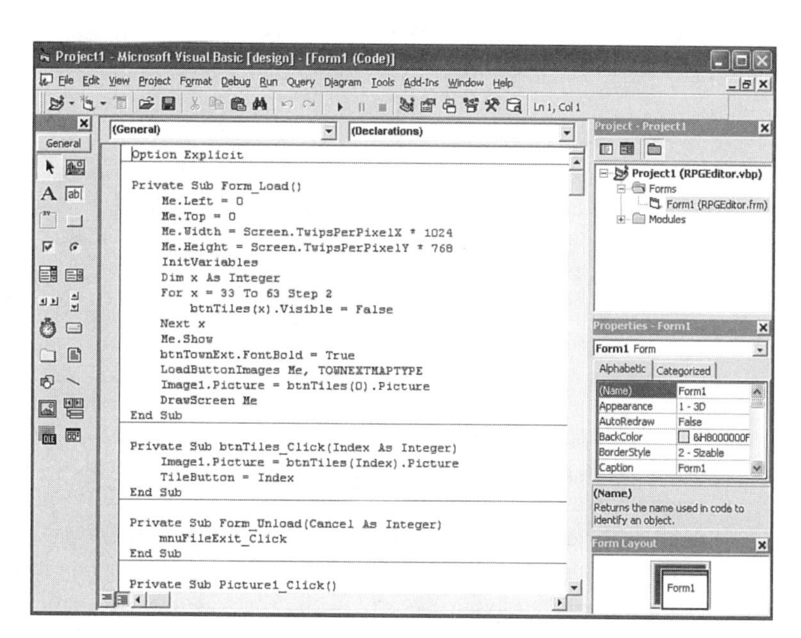

Figure 2.2

The Visual Basic 6 programming environment.

If you don't own VB, don't sweat it. Only an appendix in this book have anything to do with it. Anyway, the complete map editor is ready to go on this book's CD-ROM, and the VB code should be pretty easy to understand for a C++ programmer. In the case of the editor, it's the concepts that are important, not the implementation details.

Paint Programs

Game programs require graphics. Sure, in the old days, you could write text-only games and get away with it, but not now. Trying to make a modern computer game without a paint program would be like trying to build a house without nails. Luckily, paint programs are pretty easy to come by. In fact, you have a pretty decent one included with Windows. This handy application called, appropriately enough, Paint, can handle all the basic functions any paint program must perform, including drawing, cutting and pasting, rotating, and so on. Figure 2.3 shows Paint in action, displaying a bitmap that you'll see again when you get to Day 6, "Understanding Direct3D Surfaces."

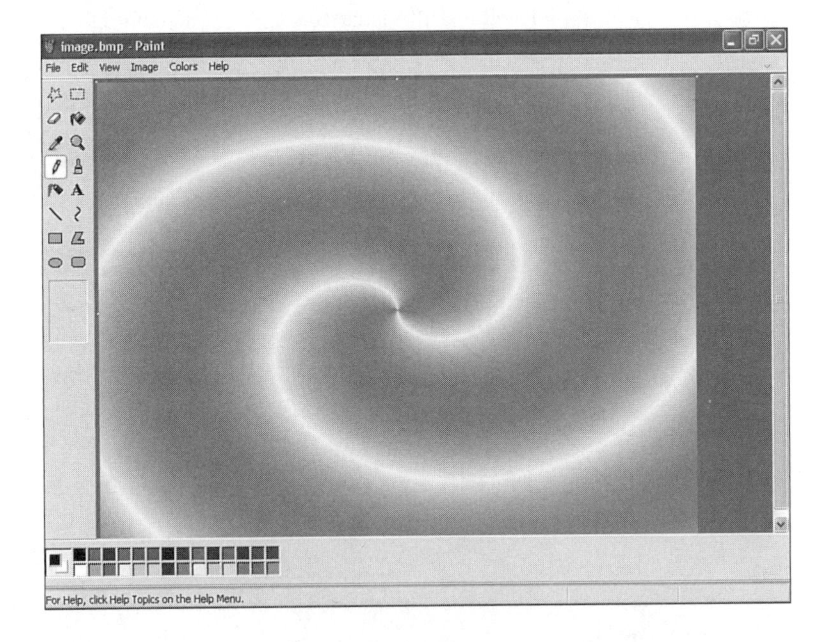

FIGURE 2.3
Microsoft's Paint.

Although Paint is a good enough program to get you started, most game programmers require a more professional paint application. One favorite is Paint Shop Pro, which you can download for a free trial from Jasc Software at `http://www.jasc.com`. Paint Shop Pro can do just about anything you can imagine, from resizing images to manipulating their colors and applying special effects. You can also use a program like Paint Shop Pro to convert between different image file formats. Figure 2.4 shows Paint Shop Pro.

FIGURE 2.4
Paint Shop Pro.

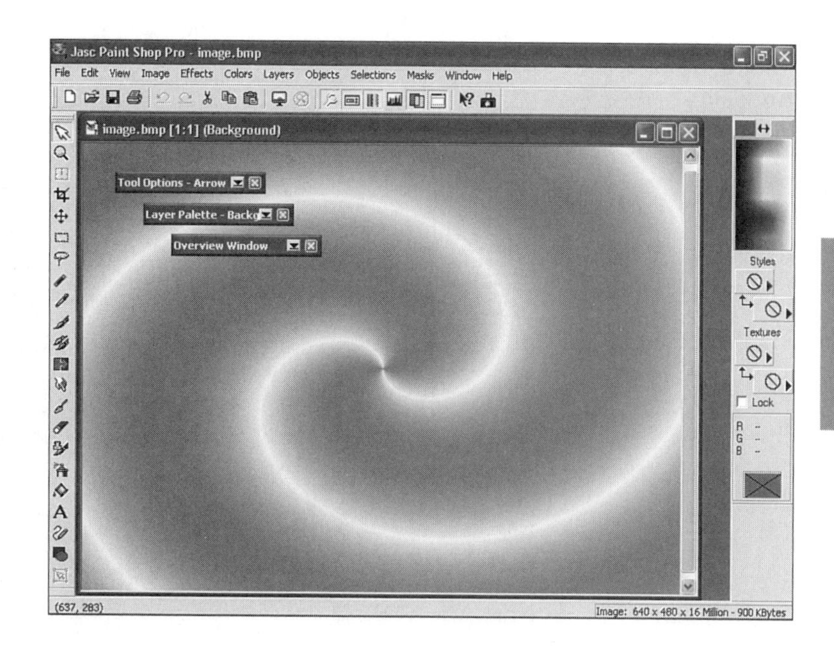

NEW TERM An *image file format* is the form in which an image's data is saved to disk. You can usually determine an image's format by looking at its filename extension. There are several popular image formats, including .BMP, .GIF, and .JPG. Some image formats, such as .GIF and .JPG, use file compression to make an image file smaller, where as others, such as .BMP, do not usually use compression.

Another program that's very handy for generating graphics, especially if you lack any artistic skill, is Microsoft's PhotoDraw. Using this program, you can quickly design very sophisticated graphical objects without having to rely on artistic talent. PhotoDraw can create fancy lettering, add shadows to objects, change 2D objects into 3D, and a whole lot more.

Unfortunately, Microsoft recently discontinued PhotoDraw, so get your copy quickly if you want it. If you can't find it at the software store, try an auction site like eBay. Figure 2.5 shows PhotoDraw applying a special effect to a line of text.

For the stout-hearted—not to mention the rich—there are graphics programs designed for creating all types of 3D images for games. Such programs, like all professional-level tools, tend to be very expensive. A popular choice is 3d Studio MAX, which was used to design the graphics for such games as Max Payne and Starcraft. You should plan to spend over $1,000 for this program! Anyway, this book doesn't deal with 3D applications, so if you're interested in this kind of stuff, you'll need to get another book to go along with this one. Figure 2.6 shows 3D Studio MAX.

FIGURE 2.5
Microsoft's PhotoDraw.

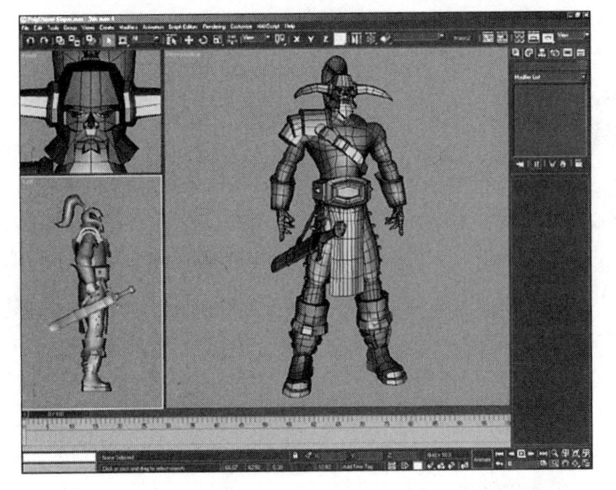

FIGURE 2.6
3D Studio MAX.

Sound Editors

Most people who use computers are familiar with paint programs, but not too many get into sound editors. This is a shame, because sound editors are not only valuable tools, but they are also a blast to use. In the case of a game programmer, a sound editor is an essential tool. Using a sound editor, you can edit, clean up, and apply effects to the sounds you'll use in your game. You can also use a sound editor to record sounds into your computer.

There are dozens of sound editors out there, ranging in price from free to many hundreds of dollars. One of my favorites is Sonic Foundry's Sound Forge XP Studio 5.0. This is an extremely powerful audio editor at a very reasonable price—only about $60.

If you're loaded, you could opt for the full professional version, Sound Forge 5.0, which goes for a list price of $400, but the XP version provides everything you'll need to edit sounds for your game. You can get more information at Sonic Foundry's Web site located at `http://www.sonicfoundry.com`. You can even download a trial version of the software, so you can try before you buy. (The Internet rocks!) Figure 2.7 shows a sound file loaded into Sound Forge XP Studio 5.0.

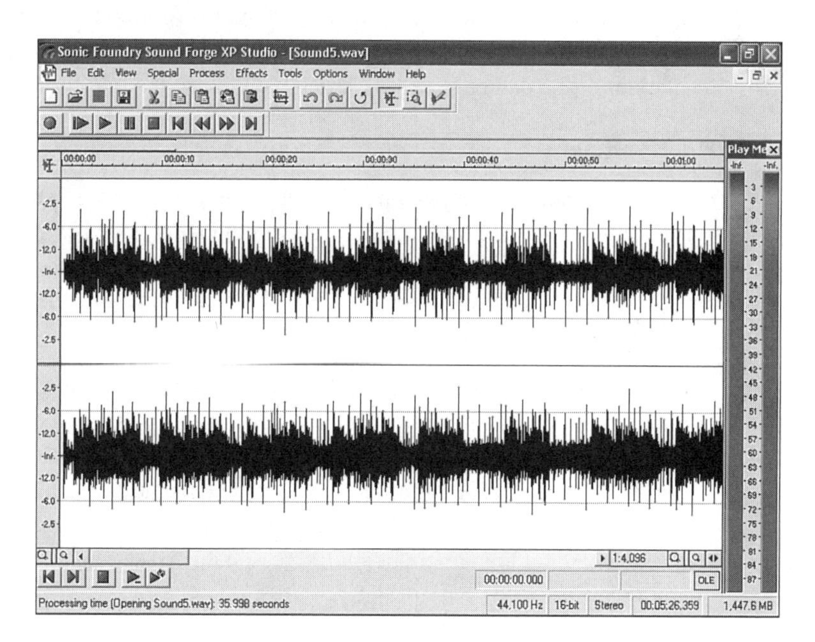

FIGURE 2.7

Sonic Foundry's Sound Forge XP Studio 5.0.

Above and Beyond

Because I'm a musician, dealing with sound is one of the things I'm best prepared to do. Because I write and record music in my home studio, I have a lot of handy tools that are extremely useful to a game programmer. These tools include microphones, recorders, and synthesizers (not to mention my trusty guitar!). While I understand that many of these tools are too expensive for the casual game programmer, they still need to be covered here.

Microphones

The first of these tools, and one that won't require you to mortgage your home to buy, is a decent microphone. The better the microphone, the better the sounds you record. However, for gaming purposes, you shouldn't have to spend more than $100 for a decent mic. You do, however, need to consider what you're going to plug the microphone into so that you end up with the right kind of jack. This isn't too great a problem because you can get adapters that enable you to plug just about any kind of microphone into any sort of input device.

The thing to watch out for is something called *impedance*. High-impedance microphones must be plugged into high-impedance inputs, whereas low-impedance microphones must be plugged into low-impedance inputs. Again, you can buy adapters that enable you to mix and match, but impedance adapters, called *transformers*, can get kind of expensive. You're better off getting the proper mic for the job right from the start. Check the documentation for the device with which you plan to use the mic for impedance information.

Recorder

If you have a microphone, you need to plug it into something that records sound. Duh! What you use for this purpose can be everything from your computer's sound card to a portable DAT recorder. The advantage of your computer's sound card is that you already have it; no additional investment needed. The disadvantage is that it's pretty tough to bring your computer around with you.

If you want to capture the sound of that babbling brook, you're going to need a more portable solution. This means some sort of recorder that's small and runs on batteries. A favorite solution is something called a DAT recorder. DAT stands for Digital Audio Tape. Portable DAT recorders aren't much larger than cassette personal stereos you see so many joggers with. However, they can be pretty pricey, $1000 or more, so you'll probably want to opt for something in a more reasonable price range, unless you're planning on going pro.

You can still do recording by opting for a portable mini disc recorder. A mini disc is similar to the disks you use with your computer, but mini discs are smaller. The average price of one of these puppies is around $200. If you want to opt for a bargain basement solution, you can look for a portable cassette recorder—if they still make them!

Sound Libraries

If recording your own sound effects seems like overkill, you can purchase yourself a sound effects library. Such libraries start at about $100, which includes a license to use the sound effects in your projects without having to pay additional royalties. Sound effects libraries usually come on CDs and include hundreds or even thousands of stereo sound effects you can transfer to your computer and incorporate into your games.

There are even online sound effects libraries where you can browse for the sounds you need and then purchase only those sound effects you want, downloading them directly to your computer. (Did I mention that the Internet rocks?) When you buy sound effects this way, you'll pay more for each individual effect than you would for a comparable effect from a CD collection, so for a single project you might save money, but for the long run, a CD collection is much cheaper. For an example of online sound effects, point your browser to `http://www.sonomic.com`. This company charges $7.95 for each sound effect.

Summary

In this chapter, you discovered that game programming requires more than just programming skills. If you're going to go it alone, you need to be handy with graphics and sound tools, as well. How far you want to go with these kinds of tools depends on what you want to do and what you can afford. In any case, you're not going to be able to avoid a minimal investment—unless you can afford to hire an artist and a sound engineer!

Q&A

Q. Is there a big difference in the sound quality between the cheaper version of a sound editor and the full professional version?

A. Nope. The big difference is features. The professional tools simply do more. Unless you do serious sound recording and studio work, you shouldn't need to invest in a high-end sound editor.

Q. Can I really get away with using just Paint for a graphics editor?

A. Again, it all comes down to features. A more professional package provides piles of extra features that you don't get in a minimal program like Paint. But if you're happy with the end result, that's all that counts.

Q. What's the advantage of recording my own sound effects?

A. By recording your own sound effects, you can create exactly the effect you want. Also, outside of the cost of recording equipment, your own sound effects are free. However, recording sounds can be a meticulous process. Often, the easiest solution is a sound effects library.

Workshop

The workshop includes quiz questions to help gauge your grasp of the material. You'll find the answers to this quiz at the end of this section. Even if you feel that you totally understand the concepts presented here, you should work through the quiz anyway. The last section is an exercise or two that you might work through to help reinforce your learning.

Quiz

1. What is the advantage of using C++ to program games?
2. When might you opt to use a higher level language like Visual Basic?
3. What type of program can you use to create graphics for your games? Give two examples.
4. How can you get sound effects for your games? Name two ways.
5. What type of hardware do you need to record sounds?

Exercises

1. Load up Paint and spend some time exploring its drawing tools and features.
2. Learn how to use your sound card to record sounds directly into your computer.

Answers for Day 2

Quiz

1. What is the advantage of using C++ to program games?

   C++ is a powerful language that yields programs that run almost as efficiently as those created with assembly language.
2. When might you opt to use a higher level language like Visual Basic?

   If you're writing a program that doesn't need the efficiency of C++, you can get away with a higher level language and so be able to develop the program much more quickly.
3. What type of program can you use to create graphics for your games? Give two examples.

   Paint programs are the main tool you need to create graphics. Two popular examples are Paint and Paint Shop Pro.

4. How can you get sound effects for your games? Name two ways.

   You can create your own sound effects by recording and editing sound, or you can purchase a sound effects library.

5. What type of hardware do you need to record sounds?

   You need some kind of recorder and a microphone. Depending upon you needs, you can get away with recording directly into your computer through your sound card, or you may need to purchase a separate, portable recorder.

Exercises

1. Load up Paint and spend some time exploring its drawing tools and features.

   No answer for this exercise.

2. Learn how to use your sound card to record sounds directly into your computer.

   No answer for this exercise.

WEEK 1

DAY 3

Writing a Windows Program

Because DirectX programs must be able to run under Windows, before you can actually dig into DirectX, you need to know how to write a simple Windows program. Luckily, you don't need to know too much about Windows programming. In fact, most of what you need to know, you can learn in this one chapter. Specifically, today you will learn the following:

- How to write the `WinMain()` function
- How to create and register a window class
- How to display a window
- How to process Windows messages
- How to build a Windows application with Visual Studio .NET

Windows the Old-Fashioned Way

When Windows first became popular, sophisticated programming tools were as scarce as roaches in an insecticide factory. Programmers wrote Windows applications in straight C (no C++) and compiled them under DOS, strange as that sounds. There weren't any C compilers that ran under Windows, even though you could program Windows applications with the compilers.

These days, complex libraries like Microsoft's MFC take a lot of the drudgery out of writing Windows applications, but such advantages come with a price. MFC itself has a steep learning curve. Moreover, if you don't understand how a conventional Windows program works, learning MFC is even harder.

When writing DirectX game programs, you're not going to want to be stuck with the significant overhead MFC adds to your programs. For this reason, the first step toward learning to write DirectX game programs is to learn to write a basic Windows application the old-fashioned way. You will, however, use C++ rather than C. There's no need to go back to the dark ages!

The Minimum Windows Application

Listing 3.1 is a simple C++ Windows application called BasicWindowsApp. Figure 3.1 shows BasicWindowsApp when you run it.

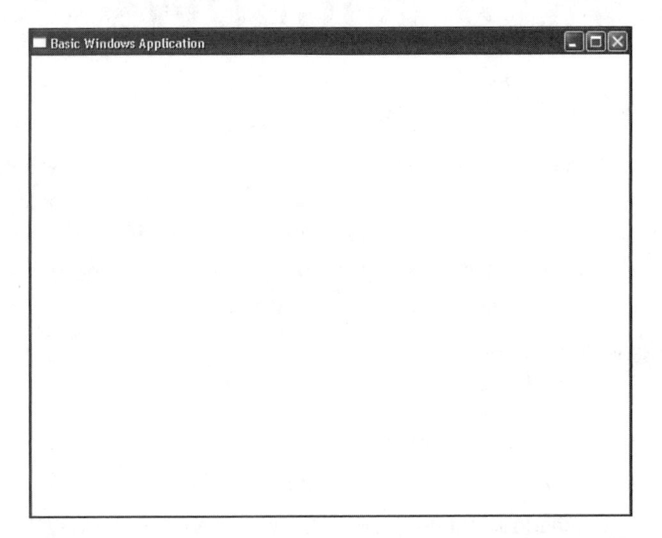

FIGURE 3.1
The running BasicWindowsApp application.

LISTING 3.1 A Basic Windows Application

```
1:  ///////////////////////////////////////////////////////////
2:  // BasicWindowsApp.cpp
3:  ///////////////////////////////////////////////////////////
4:
5:
```

LISTING 3.1 continued

```
6:   #include <windows.h>
7:
8:   // Function prototypes.
9:   LRESULT WINAPI WndProc(HWND hWnd, UINT msg,
10:      WPARAM wParam, LPARAM lParam);
11:  void RegisterWindowClass(HINSTANCE hInstance);
12:  void CreateAppWindow(HINSTANCE hInstance);
13:  WPARAM StartMessageLoop();
14:
15:  // Global variables.
16:  HWND g_hWnd;
17:
18:
19:  ///////////////////////////////////////////////////////
20:  // WinMain()
21:  ///////////////////////////////////////////////////////
22:  INT WINAPI WinMain(HINSTANCE hInstance, HINSTANCE, LPSTR, INT)
23:  {
24:      RegisterWindowClass(hInstance);
25:      CreateAppWindow(hInstance);
26:      ShowWindow(g_hWnd, SW_SHOWDEFAULT);
27:      UpdateWindow(g_hWnd);
28:      INT result = StartMessageLoop();
29:      return result;
30:  }
31:
32:  ///////////////////////////////////////////////////////
33:  // WndProc()
34:  ///////////////////////////////////////////////////////
35:  LRESULT WINAPI WndProc(HWND hWnd, UINT msg, WPARAM wParam, LPARAM lParam)
36:  {
37:      switch(msg)
38:      {
39:      case WM_CREATE:
40:          return 0;
41:
42:      case WM_DESTROY:
43:          PostQuitMessage( 0 );
44:          return 0;
45:
46:      case WM_PAINT:
47:          ValidateRect(g_hWnd, NULL);
48:          return 0;
49:      }
50:      return DefWindowProc(hWnd, msg, wParam, lParam);
51:  }
52:
53:  ///////////////////////////////////////////////////////
54:  // RegisterWindowClass()
55:  ///////////////////////////////////////////////////////
```

LISTING 3.1 continued

```
56:  void RegisterWindowClass(HINSTANCE hInstance)
57:  {
58:      WNDCLASSEX wc;
59:      wc.cbSize = sizeof(WNDCLASSEX);
60:      wc.style = CS_HREDRAW | CS_VREDRAW | CS_OWNDC;
61:      wc.lpfnWndProc = WndProc;
62:      wc.cbClsExtra = 0;
63:      wc.cbWndExtra = 0;
64:      wc.hInstance = hInstance;
65:      wc.hIcon = LoadIcon(NULL, IDI_APPLICATION);
66:      wc.hCursor = (HCURSOR)LoadCursor(NULL, IDC_ARROW);
67:      wc.hbrBackground = (HBRUSH)GetStockObject(WHITE_BRUSH);
68:      wc.lpszMenuName = NULL;
69:      wc.lpszClassName = "WinApp";
70:      wc.hIconSm = NULL;
71:
72:      RegisterClassEx(&wc);
73:  }
74:
75:  ///////////////////////////////////////////////////////
76:  // CreateAppWindow()
77:  ///////////////////////////////////////////////////////
78:  void CreateAppWindow(HINSTANCE hInstance)
79:  {
80:      g_hWnd = CreateWindowEx(
81:          NULL,
82:          "WinApp",
83:          "Basic Windows Application",
84:          WS_OVERLAPPEDWINDOW,
85:          100,
86:          100,
87:          648,
88:          514,
89:          GetDesktopWindow(),
90:          NULL,
91:          hInstance,
92:          NULL);
93:  }
94:
95:  ///////////////////////////////////////////////////////
96:  // StartMessageLoop()
97:  ///////////////////////////////////////////////////////
98:  WPARAM StartMessageLoop()
99:  {
100:     MSG msg;
101:     while(1)
102:     {
103:         if (PeekMessage(&msg, NULL, 0, 0, PM_REMOVE))
104:         {
```

LISTING 3.1 continued

```
105:             if (msg.message == WM_QUIT)
106:                 break;
107:             TranslateMessage(&msg);
108:             DispatchMessage(&msg);
109:         }
110:         else
111:         {
112:             // Use idle time here.
113:         }
114:     }
115:     return msg.wParam;
116: }
```


As you can see, getting a window up on the screen takes a bit of work. For the most part, though, you can use the code in Listing 3.1 as the beginning of just about any Windows application, so most of your work is already done. In the following sections, you'll learn in general how the program works. However, you only need to understand a few important concepts, such as creating a window, defining a Windows procedure, and handling Windows messages.

Digging into the Program

It's time now to discover exactly how a Windows application works. In the following sections, you'll examine Listing 3.1 a little at a time. By the time you reach the end of this chapter, you'll know how to write and compile a basic Windows application.

The Windows Header File

First, Line 6 of the program includes some necessary stuff:

```
#include <windows.h>
```

The windows.h file contains many declarations that all Windows programs require. All Windows programs include this header file.

The Function Prototypes

The next thing to notice is lines 8–16:

```
// Function prototypes.
LRESULT WINAPI WndProc(HWND hWnd, UINT msg,
WPARAM wParam, LPARAM lParam);
void RegisterWindowClass(HINSTANCE hInstance);
void CreateAppWindow(HINSTANCE hInstance);
WPARAM StartMessageLoop();
```

```
// Global variables.
HWND g_hWnd;
```

As a C++ programmer, you will recognize these lines as prototypes for the program's functions, as well as a single global variable. You'll dig into all these functions soon. You'll also see what that single global variable holds.

The `WinMain()` Function

Now, take a look at Listing 3.1's lines 19–30, which are the `WinMain()` function:

```
///////////////////////////////////////////////////////
// WinMain()
///////////////////////////////////////////////////////
INT WINAPI WinMain(HINSTANCE hInstance, HINSTANCE, LPSTR, INT)
{
    RegisterWindowClass(hInstance);
    CreateAppWindow(hInstance);
    ShowWindow(g_hWnd, SW_SHOWDEFAULT);
    UpdateWindow(g_hWnd);
    INT result = StartMessageLoop();
    return result;
}
```

As you can see, the `WinMain()` function's signature looks like the following (although in your version of `WinMain()`, you're not accessing the last three parameters and so have given them no names):

```
INT WINAPI WinMain(HINSTANCE hInstance,
    HINSTANCE hPrevInstance, LPSTR lpszCmdLine,
    int nCmdShow)
```

`WinMain()` is the entry point for all Windows programs, in the same way `main()` is the entry point for DOS C programs. `WinMain()`'s four parameters are as follows:

- *`hInstance`*—The handle of this instance of the program
- *`hPrevInstance`*—The handle of the previous instance
- *`lpszCmdLine`*—A pointer to the command line used to run the program
- *`nCmdShow`*—A set of flags that determine how the application's window should be displayed

Handles are one type of data that you may not be familiar with, if you haven't done much Windows programming. A handle is nothing more than a value that identifies a window or some other object. In a traditional Windows program, you almost always refer to a window by its handle, and most Windows API functions that manipulate windows require a handle as their first argument.

An instance of an application is much the same thing as an instance of a class in object-oriented programming. For example, in most cases, the user can run the same Windows application multiple times, having several separate, but identical, windows on the screen. Each window represents an instance of the program.

In 16-bit Windows programming, all application instances shared the same memory space. By checking the handle to the previous instance, programmers could prevent multiple instances. If `hPrevInstance` was `NULL`, there was no previous instance. If `hPrevInstance` was not `NULL`, the application had already been run, and the programmer could display the already existing window, rather than create a new instance of the application.

In Windows 98 and later versions, however, every application gets its own block of virtual memory. For this reason, the `hPrevInstance` handle in modern Windows programs is always `NULL`.

Getting back to the program, the `WinMain()` function must perform several important functions in order to get a window up on the screen, including:

1. Create and register a class for the window.
2. Create the window.
3. Display the window.
4. Start the application's message loop.

To keep things less confusing, the BasicWindowsApp program performs each of these important steps in a separate function.

Creating the Window Class

The first task in `WinMain()` is to create a class for the application's window, a task that is handled by the `RegisterWindowClass` function, defined in lines 53–73 of Listing 3.1. That function looks like this:

```
///////////////////////////////////////////////////////
// RegisterWindowClass()
///////////////////////////////////////////////////////
void RegisterWindowClass(HINSTANCE hInstance)
{
    WNDCLASSEX wc;
    wc.cbSize = sizeof(WNDCLASSEX);
    wc.style = CS_HREDRAW | CS_VREDRAW | CS_OWNDC;
    wc.lpfnWndProc = WndProc;
    wc.cbClsExtra = 0;
    wc.cbWndExtra = 0;
    wc.hInstance = hInstance;
```

```
    wc.hIcon = LoadIcon(NULL, IDI_APPLICATION);
    wc.hCursor = (HCURSOR)LoadCursor(NULL, IDC_ARROW);
    wc.hbrBackground = (HBRUSH)GetStockObject(WHITE_BRUSH);
    wc.lpszMenuName = NULL;
    wc.lpszClassName = "WinApp";
    wc.hIconSm = NULL;

    RegisterClassEx(&wc);
}
```

Windows defines a structure for holding the values that make up a window class. `RegisterWindowClass()` declares an instance of this structure like this:

```
WNDCLASS wc;
```

`RegisterWindowClass()` also initializes this structure to the values required for the window class. The `WNDCLASS` structure defines the window's style, as well as specifies the window's icons, cursor, background color, and menu. I won't go into great detail about what all these values mean, because you can use the program just as it's shown. Nothing in the code really has much to do with game programming. If you want to know more, you can consult a Windows programming manual. The important thing to know here is that every Windows application must create an instance of this structure and register it with Windows.

Registering the Window Class

The application-defined function `RegisterWindowClass()` registers the new window class with Windows by calling the Windows API function `RegisterClassEx()`, like this:

```
RegisterClassEx(&wc);
```

`RegisterClassEx()`'s single argument is the address of the initialized `WNDCLASS` structure.

Creating an Instance of the Window Class

After creating and registering the window class, `WinMain()` creates an instance of the window class, by calling the function `CreateAppWindow()`, which looks like this:

```
////////////////////////////////////////////////////////
// CreateAppWindow()
////////////////////////////////////////////////////////
void CreateAppWindow(HINSTANCE hInstance)
{
    g_hWnd = CreateWindowEx(
        NULL,
       "WinApp", /* Window class's name */
       "Basic Windows Application", /* Title bar text */
```

```
        WS_OVERLAPPEDWINDOW, /* The window's style */
        100, /* The window's horizontal position */
        100, /* The window's vertical position */
        648, /* The window's width */
        514, /* The window's height */
        GetDesktopWindow(), /* The parent window's handle */
        NULL, /* The window's menu handle */
        hInstance, /* The instance handle */
        NULL);
}
```

The comments I've added to the function briefly describe `CreateWindow()`'s arguments. Again, you don't need to know the specifics in order to create a window for your game program. I'll explain, when the time comes, anything that needs to be different in upcoming programs.

Showing the Window

At this point, the application has defined a window class and created an instance of that window class. But, so far, there is nothing on the screen. To display the new window, `WinMain()` calls the Windows API function `ShowWindow()`:

```
ShowWindow(hWnd, nCmdShow);
```

Finally, to ensure that the window updates its display, the program calls the Windows API function `UpdateWindow()`:

```
UpdateWindow(hWnd);
```

Notice how both functions, like most other window-manipulation functions, take a window handle as the first argument.

The Infamous Message Loop

Now that the window is up on the screen, it can start to process the many messages that Windows will send it. The program does this by setting up a message loop, which BasicWindowsApp does in the `StartMessageLoop()` function, defined in lines 95–116 of Listing 3.1:

```
///////////////////////////////////////////////////////
// StartMessageLoop()
///////////////////////////////////////////////////////
WPARAM StartMessageLoop()
{
    MSG msg;
    while(1)
    {
        if (PeekMessage(&msg, NULL, 0, 0, PM_REMOVE))
```

```
        {
            if (msg.message == WM_QUIT)
            break;
            TranslateMessage(&msg);
            DispatchMessage(&msg);
        }
        else
        {
            // Use idle time here.
        }
    }
    return msg.wParam;
}
```

As you can see, the `while` loop continues indefinitely, gathering up messages from Windows again and again and again until the user quits the program. At that point, when the current Windows message is `WM_QUIT`, a `break` statement ends the loop.

The `PeekMessage()` Windows API function retrieves a message from the window's message queue. As long as `PeekMessage()` returns a nonzero value, the application has messages to handle. If `PeekMessage()` returns 0, the application has no waiting messages and is considered to be idle. As you'll see in upcoming programs, DirectX game programs use this idle time to process graphics and other game elements.

Inside the loop, the call to `TranslateMessage()` handles virtual-key messages (messages that represent keystrokes), translating them into character messages that go back into the message queue. The `DispatchMessage()` function sends the message off to the application's window procedure.

The Window Procedure

When you defined BasicWindowsApp's window class in the `WNDCLASS` structure, you specified the function to which Windows messages should be directed:

```
wc.lpfnWndProc = WndProc;
```

When the program registered the window class, Windows made note of the window procedure passed in the `lpfnWndProc` structure member. So, calls to `DispatchMessage()` result in Windows sending the message to `WndProc()`, where the messages are either handled by the application or sent back to Windows for default processing.

In BasicWindowsApp, `WndProc()`'s signature looks like this:

```
LRESULT WINAPI WndProc(HWND hWnd, UINT msg,
    WPARAM wParam, LPARAM lParam)
```

The function's four parameters are as follows:

- *hWnd*—The handle of the window to which the message is directed
- *msg*—The message ID (for example, WM_CREATE)
- *wParam*—A 32-bit message parameter
- *lParam*—A 32-bit message parameter

The values of the two 32-bit parameters depend on the type of message. For example, when the user selects a menu item from an application's menu bar, the application gets a WM_COMMAND message, with the menu item's ID in the low word of the wParam parameter.

WndProc()'s job is to determine whether the application needs to handle the message or pass it back to Windows for default processing. (All messages must be dealt with in one of these ways.) In most Windows procedures, the programmer sets up a switch statement with case clauses for the messages the application should handle. BasicWindowsApp handles only three Windows messages: WM_CREATE, WM_DESTROY, and WM_PAINT. Its switch statement looks like the following code snippet, taken from lines 37–49 of Listing 3.1:

```
switch(msg)
{
case WM_CREATE:
    return 0;
case WM_DESTROY:
    PostQuitMessage( 0 );
    return 0;
case WM_PAINT:
    ValidateRect(g_hWnd, NULL);
    return 0;
}
```

The following list describes the windows messages used in the program:

- WM_CREATE—This message means that the program is creating its window. You can do certain kinds of initialization here.
- WM_PAINT—This message means that the window must redraw its display. Because you'll eventually be using DirectX to draw the application's display, all you need to do here is call the Windows API function ValidateRect(), which tells windows that the display has been taken care of.
- WM_DESTROY—This message means that the user wants to close the application. All Windows applications must handle WM_DESTROY. The call to the Windows API function PostQuitMessage() ends the program.

Notice that, after handling a message, the function returns a value of zero. Messages that are not handled in the switch statement must be passed back to Windows. Failure to do this could result in the application being incapable of responding to the user. To pass a message back to Windows, the application calls `DefWindowProc()` in line 50 of Listing 3.1:

```
return DefWindowProc(hWnd, msg, wParam, lParam);
```

The function's arguments are the same as the parameters passed to the window procedure. Notice that `WndProc()` returns `DefWindowProc()`'s return value.

Now that you have a general idea of how a "handwritten" Windows application works, you need a little experience building one with Visual C++ .NET. Guess what you're going to do next?

Building a Basic Windows Application

Now that you know most of the theory behind programming a simple Windows application, it's time to build one for yourself. Load up Visual C++ .NET, and perform the following steps:

1. Click the New Project button on Visual Studio .NET's Start page. The New Project dialog box appears, as shown in Figure 3.2.

FIGURE 3.2

The New Project dialog box.

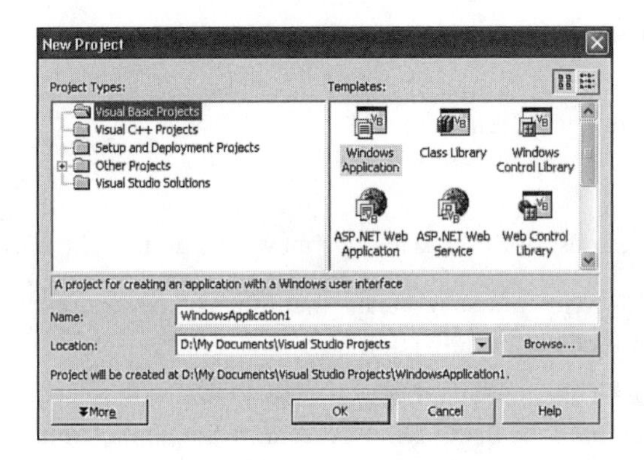

2. In the Project Types box, select Visual C++ Projects, as shown in Figure 3.3.
3. In the Templates box, select Win32 Project, as shown in Figure 3.4.
4. In the Name box, type BasicWindowsApp, as shown in Figure 3.5.
5. In the Location box, enter the location where the project should be saved, or just leave it set to the default, which should be the Visual Studio Projects folder that was created for you when you installed Visual Studio .NET.

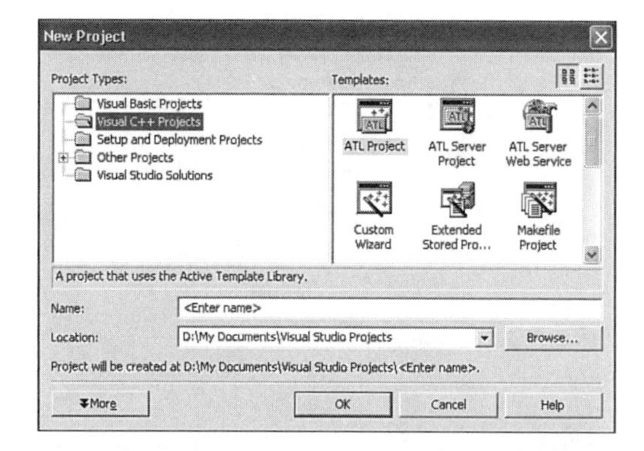

FIGURE 3.3

Selecting the project type.

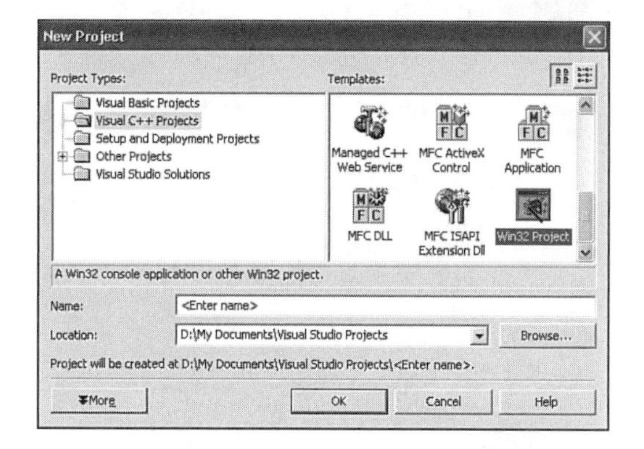

FIGURE 3.4

Selecting the project template.

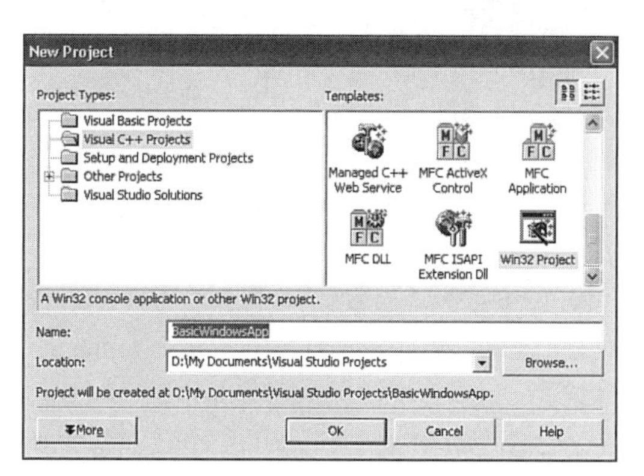

FIGURE 3.5

Entering the project's name.

6. Click the OK button. The Win32 Application Wizard appears, as shown in Figure 3.6.
7. On the left side of the wizard, click the Application Settings selection. The application settings appear in the wizard, as shown in Figure 3.7.

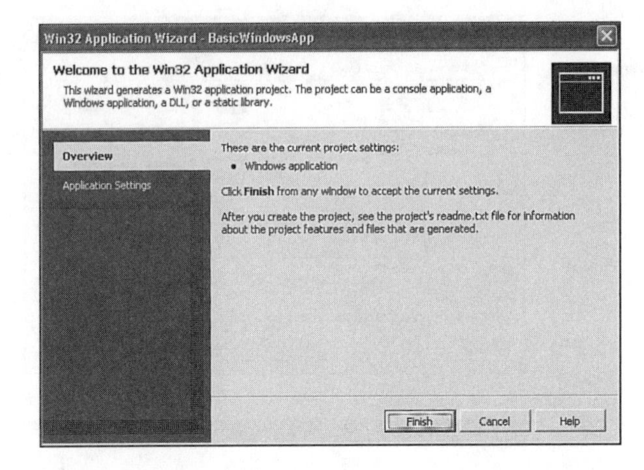

FIGURE 3.6

The Win32 Application Wizard.

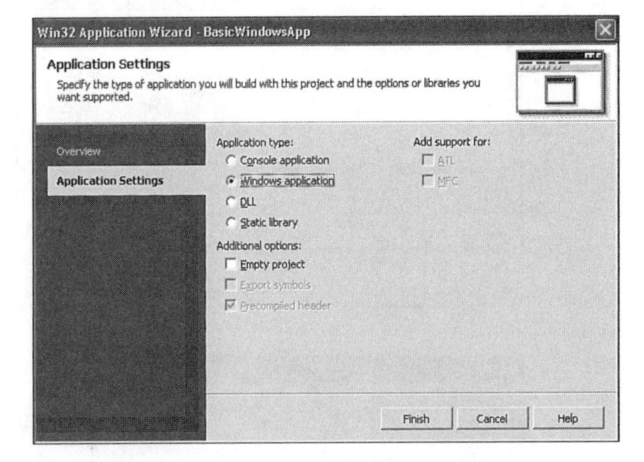

FIGURE 3.7

The application's settings.

8. Select the Empty Project option under the Additional Options heading, as shown in Figure 3.8.
9. Click the Finish button, and Visual Studio .NET creates the project for you.
10. On the Project menu, select the Add New Item command. The Add New Item dialog box appears, as shown in Figure 3.9.
11. In the Templates box, select the C++ File (.cpp) icon, and in the Name box, type BasicWindowsApp.cpp, as shown in Figure 3.10.
12. Click Open. The new, blank file appears, as shown in Figure 3.11.

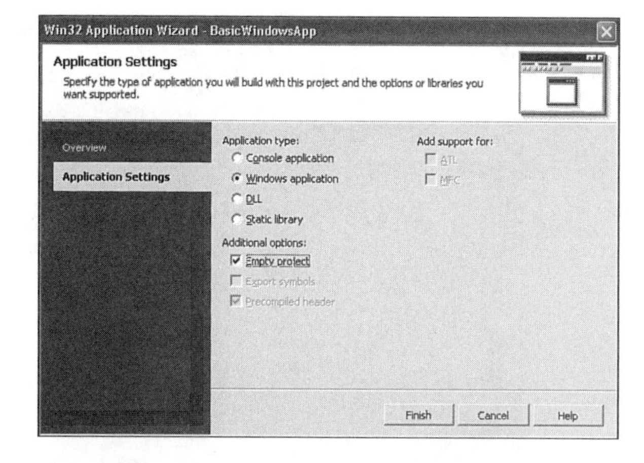

FIGURE 3.8

Choosing the Empty Project option.

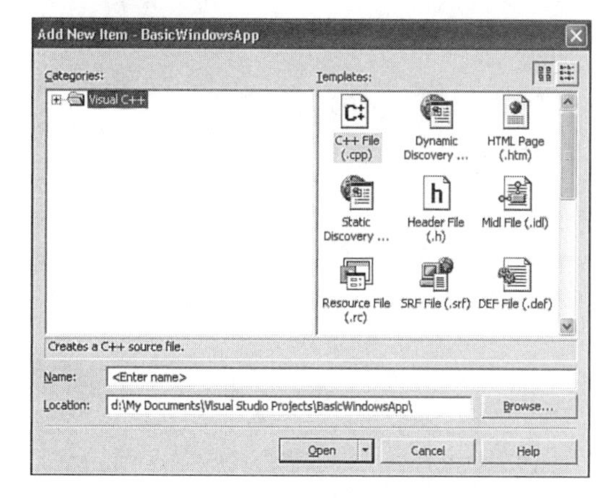

FIGURE 3.9

The Add New Item dialog box.

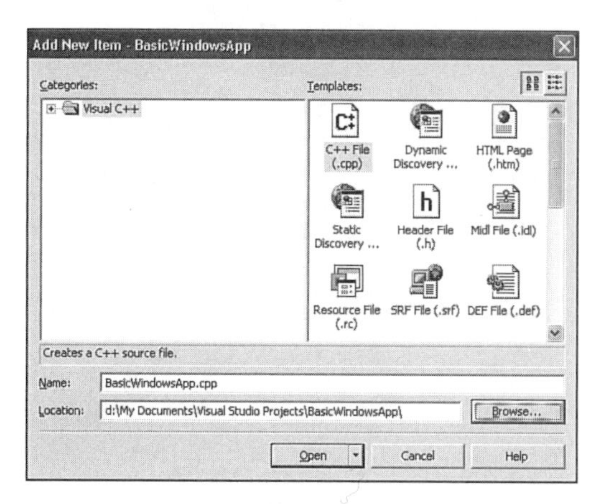

FIGURE 3.10

Entering the file's name.

FIGURE 3.11

The newly created file.

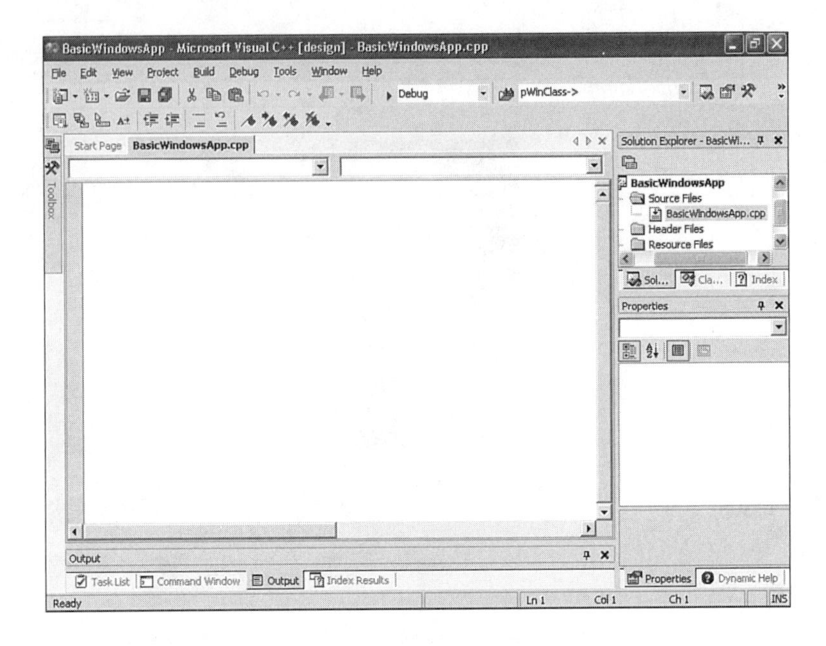

13. Type Listing 3.1 into the new window, or just copy the code from the BasicWindowsApp.cpp file included in the Chapter03/BasicWindowsApp folder on this book's CD-ROM. Figure 3.12 shows the source code in the code window.

FIGURE 3.12

The source code typed or copied into the window.

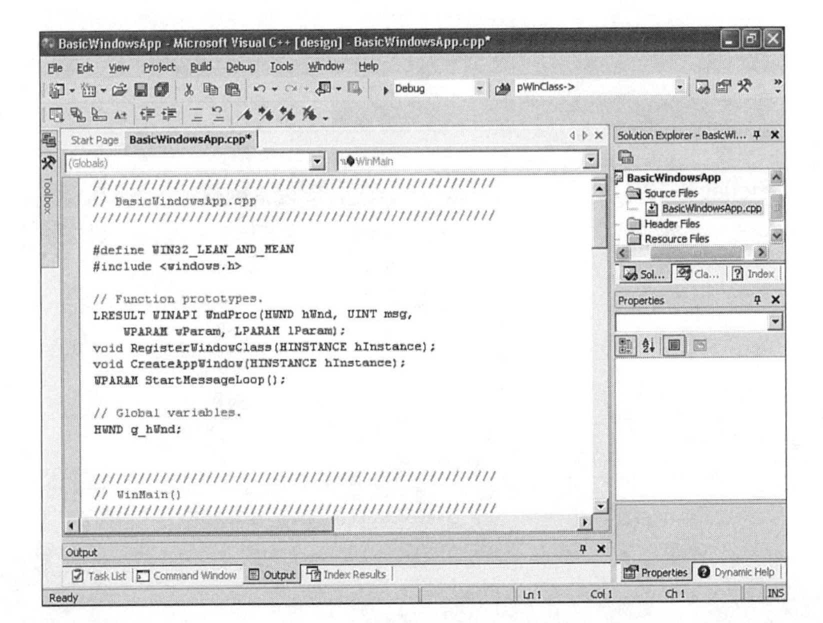

14. Press F5 to compile and run the program. Visual Studio asks whether you want to build the out of date files, as shown in Figure 3.13. Click Yes.

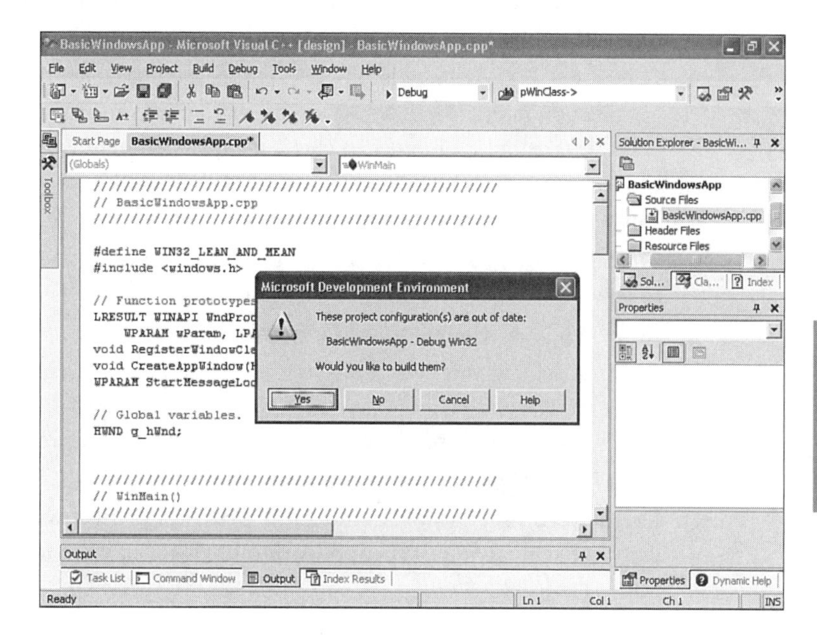

FIGURE 3.13
Visual Studio about to build the project.

After completing these steps, you should see the window shown back in Figure 3.1. If the program doesn't work, recheck each of the steps above. If you typed the program, make sure you're typing is correct. It's easy to make mistakes!

This completes your quick course in writing Windows applications. In future chapters, you'll use a similar program as the basis for the DirectX applications you'll be building. However, because you'll be using DirectX rather than Windows to display stuff on the screen, your application's window provides only the basic functionality of a full Windows application. This basic functionality is all you need for the programs in this book. If you want to write an application like a word processor or a spreadsheet, you're reading the wrong programming book!

Summary

Every DirectX game program starts with a basic Windows application. Although programming a full-fledged Windows application is a complex process, your DirectX games will need to use a few Windows API functions and respond to only a couple Windows messages. Because of this, you can usually use the same basic Windows application as the starting point for any game.

Q&A

Q. The Windows API is so immense that it's overwhelming. Do I need to know all those functions?

A. I doubt that there's a single programmer on the planet who's fluent with every single function in the Windows API. All programmers use Windows reference books when programming in order to check the types of arguments that functions need and to find just the right function for what they want to do. Anyway, as a DirectX game programmer, you'll use the API only occasionally. So don't sweat it!

Q. Most Windows games I've played don't even show a window. Why do I need to learn how to create and display one?

A. Every Windows application has a window. However, not all windows have visible elements such as title bars and menu bars. The simplest window is nothing more than a rectangular area on the screen that's reserved for your application's output. Those so-called full-screen games are associated with a simple window that covers the entire screen.

Q. I've noticed that Visual Studio .NET provides project templates that automatically generate a Windows application for me. So, why do I have to start with a blank project?

A. If you were creating a more conventional Windows application, Visual Studio .NET's various templates can help get you started quickly. However, the templates generate a lot of extra code that your game program won't need. With a game program, you want to keep your programs as lean as possible.

Workshop

The workshop includes quiz questions to help gauge your grasp of the material. You'll find the answers to this quiz at the end of this section. Even if you feel that you totally understand the concepts presented here, you should work through the quiz anyway. The last section is an exercise or two that you might work through to help reinforce your learning.

Quiz

1. Why do all Windows applications need a `WinMain()` function?
2. What's a handle used for?
3. What are the four main steps a program must perform to get a functional window up on the screen?

4. What does a Windows application's message loop do?
5. When does a Windows application enter its idle state, and why is this idle time significant to a DirectX game program?
6. How does Windows know where to send messages for your application?
7. What should an application do with Windows messages it receives but doesn't handle?
8. When does Windows send your application `WM_CREATE`, `WM_PAINT`, and `WM_DESTROY` messages?

Exercises

1. Practice creating a complete project for a Windows application with Visual Studio .NET. It'll be helpful throughout this book if you can learn all the steps so you don't have to look them up.
2. Make the following changes to this chapter's sample program: In the `RegisterWindowClass()` function, change the window class's background color from `(HBRUSH)GetStockObject(WHITE_BRUSH)` to `(HBRUSH)GetStockObject(BLACK_BRUSH)`. Also, in the `CreateAppWindow()` function, change the `WS_OVERLAPPEDWINDOW` constant in the call to `CreateWindowEx()` to `WS_POPUP`. When you run the program, what happens? (To close the application's window, you'll have to press Alt+F4.)
3. Load up your Visual Studio .NET help, and spend a few minutes looking over the many Windows messages an application can receive. To find them, do a search on `WM_`.

Answers for Day 5

Quiz

1. Why do all Windows applications need a `WinMain()` function?

   The `WinMain()` function is where program execution begins.
2. What's a handle used for?

   In Windows programming, a handle is a value that represents some sort of object, such as a window. When you want to refer to an object, you provide the object's handle.

3. What are the four main steps a program must perform to get a functional window up on the screen?

   Create a window class, create an instance of the class, display the window, start the window's message loop.

4. What does a Windows application's message loop do?

   The message loop extracts Windows messages from the application's message queue.

5. When does a Windows application enter its idle state, and why is this idle time significant to a DirectX game program?

   When an application has no messages to process, it's in its idle state. Your game uses this idle time to perform its own processing.

6. How does Windows know where to send messages for your application?

   You register a window procedure when you create your window's class.

7. What should an application do with Windows messages it receives but doesn't handle?

   Windows sends messages to the registered window procedure's message queue. Your application should return unhandled messages to Windows for default processing. You return a message to Windows by calling the `DefWindowProc()` Windows API function.

8. When does Windows send your application `WM_CREATE`, `WM_PAINT`, and `WM_DESTROY` messages?

   When your application's window is created, when the application needs to repaint its display, and when the application is about to close, respectively.

WEEK 1

DAY 4

Introducing Direct3D

You may be wondering why a book that teaches 2D game programming would cover a technology like Direct3D. I use Direct3D in this book for a very good reason: I have no choice! Why? Because if this book is to stay current, its programs must be developed with the latest version of DirectX, which is, as of this writing, DirectX 8.1. When you use DirectX 8.1 to develop 2D games, you have to use Direct3D. In this chapter, you'll discover why. Specifically, in this chapter you learn:

- What happened to DirectDraw
- Why DirectDraw is no longer needed by programmers
- Why 2D graphics are still important
- How Direct3D and DirectDraw work together

The Suddenly Missing DirectDraw

If I had written this book a year or two ago, we wouldn't be having the discussion we're about to have about Direct3D and DirectDraw. Why? Because DirectDraw and Direct3D were separate technologies. Sure, using Direct3D required also using DirectDraw and so there was a link between the two. But a couple of years ago, when you wanted to create a 2D game program you used DirectDraw, and when you wanted to create a 3D program, you used Direct3D. Figure 4.1 shows the connections between these technologies.

FIGURE 4.1

The old DirectDraw/Direct3D architecture.

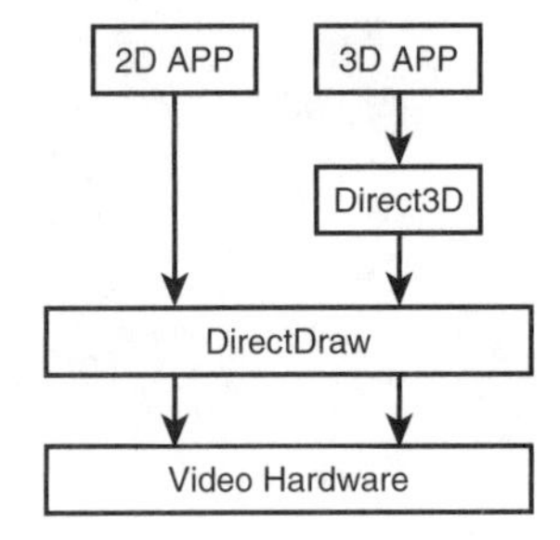

However, Microsoft decided to remove DirectDraw as a separate technology and incorporate it fully into Direct3D. In fact, not only is DirectDraw fully subsumed into Direct3D, with the combined technology being named DirectX Graphics, but it is now not possible to directly access DirectDraw. Direct3D now uses DirectDraw behind the scenes, out of view of the programmer, as shown in Figure 4.2.

FIGURE 4.2

The new DirectDraw/Direct3D architecture.

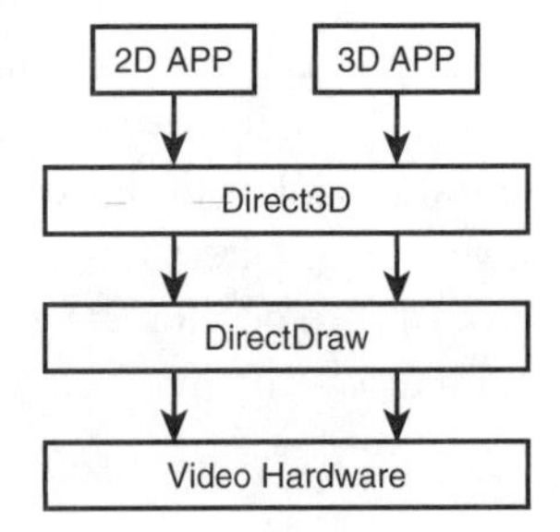

For 3D game programmers, this combining of graphics technology is a good thing, because it makes it easier to write Direct3D programs. Previously, the programmer who wanted to use Direct3D had to deal with DirectDraw as well. Now, Direct3D handles DirectDraw for you.

The downside is that, if you want to write a 2D game, you can no longer use DirectDraw. Instead, you have to use Direct3D, which, although it provides some cool abilities that you don't have in DirectDraw, requires a whole new way to put together your 2D game programs.

> **Note**
> It's actually a bit of a lie to say that you can no longer use DirectDraw. You can still use DirectDraw if you program with a previous version of DirectX. However, DirectX 8.1 does not allow direct access to DirectDraw.

If you know how to use DirectDraw, you already know about important graphics-programming techniques such as handling surfaces, performing animation, and implementing transparency. However, the way you do these things with Direct3D is very different from the way you did them with DirectDraw.

Why Did DirectDraw Go Away?

Microsoft's decision to do away with DirectDraw as a separate technology took a lot of people by surprise. No doubt the DirectX developers were flooded with complaints. DirectDraw provided powerful features that were fairly easy to use, especially for people who didn't need to deal with 3D graphics programming.

The truth is, however, that all major changes are greeted with disdain and suspicion, if not outright anger. After all, in the case of DirectX, many programmers have spent a lot of hours learning to use DirectDraw. To have Microsoft take away this tool was like pulling out the rug. So, why did Microsoft make this decision?

Okay, the real answer to that question is "I don't know." I haven't interviewed anyone from Microsoft on the subject. However, I can take a few informed guesses.

First, in case you haven't noticed, 3D graphics are everywhere. Virtually every game incorporates some form of 3D graphics. Even traditional 2D console games like the Mario series have moved to 3D worlds. The days of 2D games are pretty much numbered, if not gone—at least in the commercial market.

The Story of 2D Graphics

But what about 2D graphics? They will never go away completely. There are many applications that work fine, if not better, with simpler 2D displays. The answer is that, although Direct3D is designed for 3D graphics programming, there's no reason that you can't use it for a 2D application. All the tools you need are there. You just need to learn to use them.

Putting in those extra hours of learning is the real reason a lot of people hated to see DirectDraw go away. There can't be another reason, because you can do pretty much anything with Direct3D that you could do with DirectDraw. Microsoft would argue even further by saying that Direct3D not only does the same stuff, but does it better.

Luckily, kind reader, you don't need to worry about the DirectDraw versus Direct3D controversy. This book will teach you to use Direct3D to create 2D games. If this seems to be like trying to kill a fly with a grenade, well that's just the way it is.

If you've never programmed graphics with DirectX, I'll get you off to a good start. If, on the other hand, you're used to the DirectDraw way of doing things, the lessons that follow will help you make the leap into Direct3D. The truth is that it's not even much of a leap; it's more like a hop.

2D Graphics? We Don't Need No Stinkin' 2D Graphics!

Well…er…actually, you do. For one thing, as I mentioned before, many types of games work perfectly well with 2D graphics, and there's no pressing reason to move such games into a 3D environment. Card games, for example, don't need 3D graphics. A playing card is, for all intents and purposes, a 2D object. Sure, you could use 3D graphics to perform cool effects like spinning cards, but, while such effects may make the game look a bit cooler, they don't change the game play much.

More to the point, though, are role-playing games (RPGs). I say "more to the point" because you'll be designing and writing such a game in this book. Although most RPGs these days are 3D, there's a big difference between the game play experience you get with one of these 3D games (take *Wizardry 8*, for example) and what you get with the more "old-fashioned" console-style RPG (for example, the early *Ultima* games).

While the submersion effect you get from a well-programmed 3D game can be awesome, you end up with a very different type of game than the "old-fashioned" RPGs. There's a good reason why a 2D RPG such as *The Legend of Zelda: A Link to the Past* (commonly known as Zelda III) is still immensely popular in spite of the amazing 3D worlds one gets to explore in *The Legend of Zelda: Majora's Mask*.

Another thing to keep in mind is the learning curve for 3D graphics programming. To give you an example of what I mean, if you took a college-level course on 3D graphics, you'd still have only a basic introduction to this immense subject.

It takes years to become a competent 3D graphics programmer. If all you want to do is learn to program games for your Windows computer, you sure don't need to spend years doing it! Using 2D graphics programming techniques can get you started with game programming quickly. Later, after you understand the basics of game programming, you can start studying 3D graphics.

Direct3D Versus DirectDraw

Obviously, if DirectDraw has been incorporated into Direct3D, it's still an important technology that provides useful, even essential, services to your game programs. What exactly does DirectDraw do? DirectDraw provides Windows with the core functionality required to directly access and manipulate graphical images in memory.

With plain ol' Windows, you're not allowed this type of direct access to memory. As a result, Windows by itself is incapable of running high-performance games. The graphical functions built into the Windows API are just too slow and cumbersome to handle the high frame rates required by today's games.

However, when you add DirectX to the equation—or more specifically DirectDraw—Windows becomes a graphical powerhouse, capable of manipulating and displaying graphics with lightning speed. In fact, libraries like DirectX are the main reason virtually all PC games now run in Windows rather than in DOS. Without such libraries (OpenGL is another example of a graphics library), gaming on a Windows platform would have been limited to the infamous Solitaire and Minesweeper!

Because a Direct3D program must access display memory in exactly the same way as any other graphically intensive application, it requires the type of base services provided by DirectDraw. Specifically, it needs to set aside areas of memory in which to store graphical data, and it requires direct access to that data in order to process graphics efficiently. Direct3D itself provides all the power you need to create 3D worlds for your games. DirectDraw provides the link between Direct3D and your computer's display.

Using Direct3D for 2D Game Programming

Okay, let's get to the bottom line: if you know how to program using DirectDraw, forget about it! While most of the concepts you learned from DirectDraw programming are still valid, the way you apply those concepts programming-wise is going to be very different with Direct3D.

An example of this change is the use of *transparency*. (If you know what I mean by transparency, skip this and the next paragraph.) For those of you new to all this, transparency is a graphics programming technique for displaying images that allow what's already on the screen to show through. A simple example would be when you want to display a round object on the screen. Computers can only handle rectangular objects, so to display something round, you have to place the round image inside a rectangular image and then display the rectangle. Figure 4.3 shows this type of image being edited in Paint.

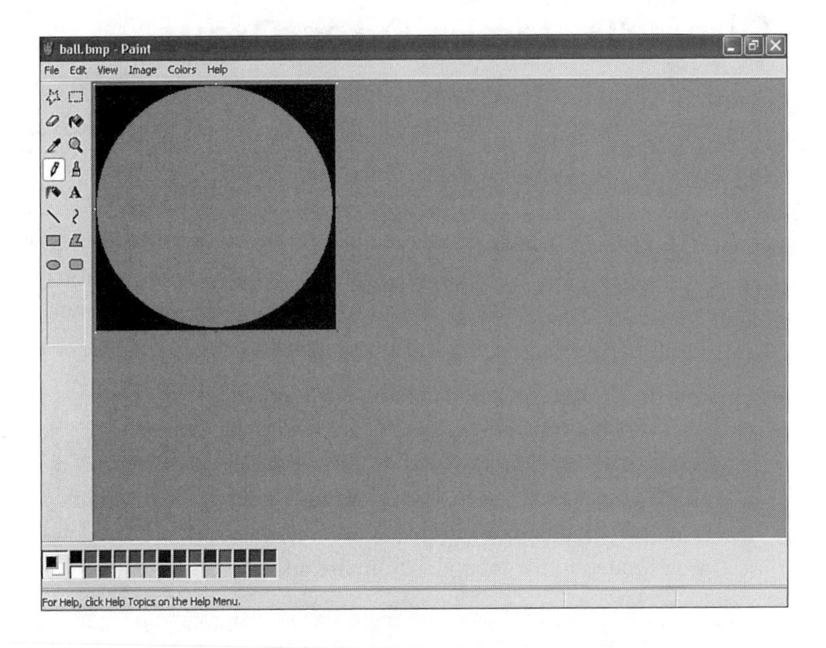

FIGURE 4.3
Preparing a round graphical object.

In your game, if you try to display the object in Figure 4.3 without using transparency, the areas of the rectangular image surrounding the ball will blot out what was on the screen previously, which is not what you want. Figure 4.4 shows you want I mean.

However, by processing those areas of the rectangle you don't need as transparent colors, only the area containing the ball's image gets transferred to the screen, even though the system is actually processing a rectangle. Figure 4.5 shows the result.

In DirectDraw, you could specify a transparent color in an image and DirectDraw would display only areas of the image that didn't match the transparent color. With Direct3D, you need to use texturing and alpha values to get the same effect. The process is a wee bit trickier, but you can use the same techniques for both 2D and 3D graphics programs. So once you learn how to do it, you're all set!

There are many other differences between DirectDraw and Direct3D programs. Even the way you initialize each type of program is different. But we'll leave all that for the next chapter.

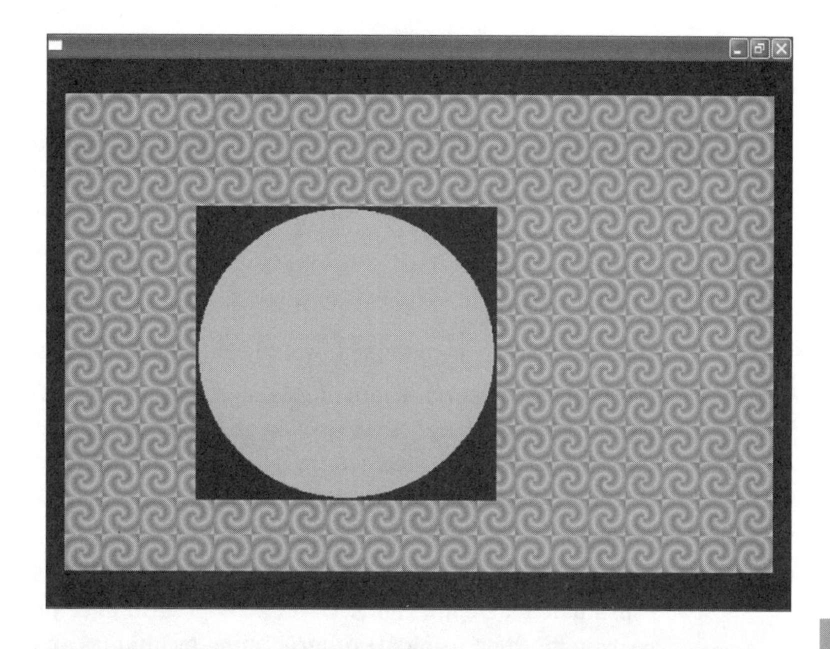

FIGURE 4.4

Displaying a round graphical object without transparency.

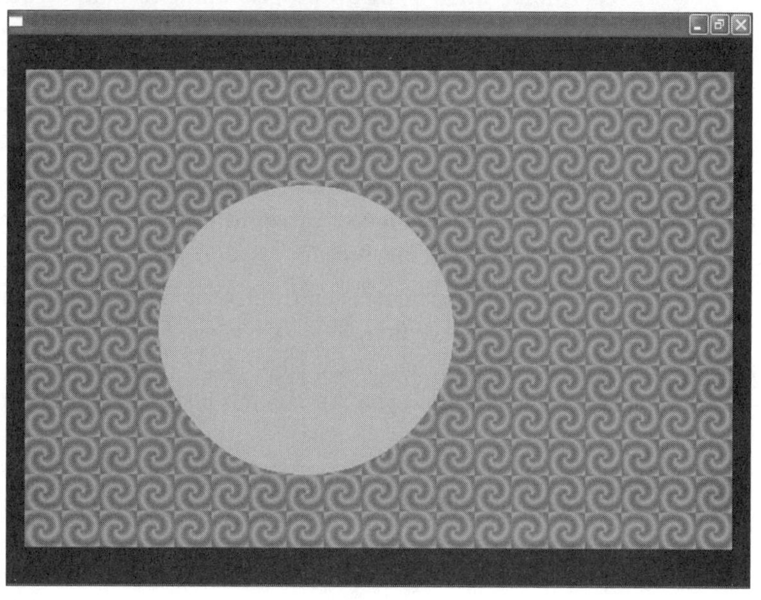

FIGURE 4.5

Displaying a round graphical object with transparency.

Summary

DirectDraw provided a powerful and fairly easy way to write programs that used 2D graphics. However, now that DirectDraw has been merged with Direct3D and is no longer directly accessible, DirectX programmers need to learn new methods for programming 2D games with DirectX. Luckily for you, that's what most of this book is about!

Q&A

Q. If enough people complained, would Microsoft bring back DirectDraw?

A. Not likely. Microsoft has moved its graphics technologies forward and has no intention looking back. However, DirectDraw is still available in DirectX 7. In fact, the help files for the DirectX 8.1 SDK include the full documentation for DirectDraw, so Microsoft isn't expecting all use of DirectDraw to disappear overnight.

Q. Basically, the only difference between a 2D display and a 3D one is a third coordinate for depth, right? Can't a 2D programmer just ignore that third coordinate when using 3D programming techniques and so end up with a 2D program?

A. Writing a 2D program with Direct3D requires a lot more than just dropping the third coordinate. You need to learn about stuff like vertices and textures in order to duplicate the functionality of a 2D library like DirectDraw.

Q. Because Direct3D relies a lot on the abilities of a computer's graphics hardware, won't having to use Direct3D for 2D programming mean my programs will run on fewer machines?

A. Most game programmers don't worry too much about archaic machines. For example, when's the last time you saw a game written for DOS? That may be an extreme example, but almost all of today's video cards can handle the type of Direct3D operations you'll use in this book's programs. Don't sweat it!

Workshop

The workshop includes quiz questions to help gauge your grasp of the material. You'll find the answers to this quiz at the end of this chapter. Even if you feel that you totally understand the concepts presented here, you should work through the quiz anyway.

Quiz

1. Why can't you program directly with DirectDraw anymore?
2. What does DirectDraw do?
3. Why does Direct3D need DirectDraw?
4. What are a couple reasons why merging DirectDraw into Direct3D was a good decision?
5. Why is it a good idea to start learning about game programming with 2D games rather than 3D?
6. Why does Windows need graphics libraries such as Direct3D and OpenGL?

Exercises

No exercises for this chapter.

Answers for Day 5

Quiz

1. Why can't you program directly with DirectDraw anymore?

   Because, as of DirectX 8, DirectDraw has been merged with Direct3D and is no longer directly accessible by programs.

2. What does DirectDraw do?

   DirectDraw provides the basic functionality needed to directly manipulate graphics data in memory.

3. Why does Direct3D need DirectDraw?

   Because Direct3D, just like any other graphically intensive software, needs direct access to graphics data in memory.

4. What are a couple reasons why merging DirectDraw into Direct3D was a good decision?

   First, most game programs these days are 3D. Second, Direct3D provides the same features that DirectDraw did; it just implements these features differently. So combining the two technologies doesn't limit its abilities, but does provide a single library for developing both 2D and 3D programs

5. Why is it a good idea to start learning about game programming with 2D games rather than 3D?

   It takes a long time to become competent with 3D programming techniques, even with a library like Direct3D. By avoiding all those extra details, you can get started with game programming much more quickly.

6. Why does Windows need graphics libraries such as Direct3D and OpenGL?

   Windows on its own is incapable of the type of efficient graphics manipulations required by today's games.

WEEK 1

DAY 5

Programming Direct3D Objects and Devices

Every Direct3D program has a few things it has to do to get started. You'll face this overhead with every Direct3D program you write, so you might as well get it out of the way now. Not only that, until you learn to do this stuff, you can't do anything else with Direct3D! So, in this chapter, you study Direct3D objects and Direct3D devices. Specifically, today you will learn the following:

- How to create a Direct3D object
- How to create a Direct3D device object
- Display modes and pixel formats
- How to check for device availability
- How to clear a Direct3D display

Creating a Direct3D Object

The first step in writing a Direct3D program is to create a Direct3D object, which provides you access to the `IDirect3D8` interface. This interface provides the methods you need to get your Direct3D application up and running, including methods to check for display modes, create Direct3D devices, and more. Later in this chapter, you'll learn to call some of these methods, but for now, here's how you create your Direct3D object:

```
IDirect3D8* g_pDirect3D = NULL;
g_pDirect3D = Direct3DCreate8(D3D_SDK_VERSION);
if (g_pDirect3D == NULL)
    return E_FAIL;
```

Here, the code first declares a pointer to the `IDirect3D8` interface. The pointer is named `g_pDirect3D` and is a global variable in your program. To obtain the pointer to the Direct3D object, you call the `Direct3DCreate8()` method, which is declared in the DirectX API like this:

```
IDirect3D8* Direct3DCreate8(
  UINT SDKVersion
);
```

As you can see, `Direct3DCreate8()` returns a pointer to the `IDirect3D8` interface and requires a single argument. Supplying the value for this argument is easy; you have only one choice: `D3D_SDK_VERSION`.

After calling `Direct3DCreate8()`, you should check the value returned by the method. If the value is `NULL`, the call to `Direct3DCreate8()` failed; otherwise, the return value is the pointer to your Direct3D object.

You might have noticed the constant `E_FAIL` in the previous example of creating a Direct3D object. The DirectX SDK defines this constant for you. Obviously, it represents an error value that you can use to indicate the failure of the call to `Direct3DCreate8()`. The DirectX SDK defines hundreds of such error constants, many of which you'll learn about as you proceed through this book.

You should always check for a `NULL` value in the returned pointer and handle the error if it occurs. Because your Direct3D program will be completely crippled if it's unable to get this pointer, you'd probably handle the error by giving the user a quick message and then terminating the application.

Creating a Direct3D Device

After you create your Direct3D object, it's time to create a Direct3D device, which is an object of the `IDirect3DDevice8` interface. This object provides your program with access to a slew of methods (nearly 100!) for handling graphical resources, drawing shapes, manipulating images and textures, and a whole lot more. In fact, a great deal of the graphical work your Direct3D application performs will be done through the `IDirect3DDevice8` object.

Here's how you use your Direct3D object's pointer to create a device object for your application:

```
IDirect3DDevice8* g_pDirect3DDevice = NULL;
HRESULT hResult = g_pDirect3D->CreateDevice(D3DADAPTER_DEFAULT,
    D3DDEVTYPE_HAL, g_hWnd, D3DCREATE_SOFTWARE_VERTEXPROCESSING,
    &D3DPresentParams, &g_pDirect3DDevice);
if (FAILED(hResult))
    return E_FAIL;
```

As you can see, you first need to declare a pointer to the `IDirect3DDevice8` interface. In this example, the pointer is named `g_pDirect3DDevice` and is initialized to `NULL`, something you should do with all of your pointers. To create the Direct3D device object and obtain a pointer to it, your program must call the Direct3D object's `CreateDevice()` method. The DirectX API declares that method like this:

```
HRESULT CreateDevice(
  UINT Adapter,
  D3DDEVTYPE DeviceType,
  HWND  hFocusWindow,
  DWORD BehaviorFlags,
  D3DPRESENT_PARAMETERS* pPresentationParameters,
  IDirect3DDevice8** ppReturnedDeviceInterface
);
```

5

This method requires six arguments, which are used as follows:

- *`Adapter`*—A number that specifies the adapter for which Direct3D should create the device.
- *`DeviceType`*—Specifies the type of device object to create.
- *`hFocusWindow`*—A handle to the window with which the device will be associated.
- *`BehaviorFlags`*—A set of flags that specify the required behaviors for the device.
- *`pPresentationParameters`*—A pointer to an instance of the `D3DPRESENT_PARAMETERS` structure.
- *`ppReturnedDeviceInterface`*—The address of a pointer to the `IDirect3DDevice8` interface.

Whoa! Obviously, there's a whole lot more going on with the `CreateDevice()` call than there was with the `Direct3DCreate8()` call!

First, let's talk about the adapter, which is the first argument in the call. The adapter referred to here is the graphics hardware that the user has installed in his machine. This hardware is usually a graphics card that was installed in the computer's slots. Most systems have only one adapter, but it's possible to have more than one, which is why the `CreateDevice()` method insists that you specify the adapter to use.

Although a system can have more than one adapter, only one can be the default adapter. Because you're not going to be doing anything too wild and crazy in this book, the default adapter will work fine for everything you need to do. As luck would have it, the DirectX SDK defines a constant, `D3DADAPTER_DEFAULT`, that you can use to specify the default adapter.

That takes care of the first argument. Now take a gander at the second. She's a beauty, huh? This second argument specifies the type of device to create. Direct3D defines three types of devices, each of which has its own constant, defined in the `D3DDEVTYPE` structure, which looks like this:

```
typedef enum _D3DDEVTYPE {
    D3DDEVTYPE_HAL         = 1,
    D3DDEVTYPE_REF         = 2,
    D3DDEVTYPE_SW          = 3,
    D3DDEVTYPE_FORCE_DWORD = 0xffffffff
} D3DDEVTYPE;
```

You can forget that fourth constant in the structure; it's currently unused. Here's what the other three mean:

- `D3DDEVTYPE_HAL`—A device that takes advantage of any 3D hardware installed on the machine.
- `D3DDEVTYPE_REF`—A device in which all Direct3D features are performed by software. This is called the reference device.
- `D3DDEVTYPE_SW`—Currently unsupported.

For the best results, you'll want to use `D3DDEVTYPE_HAL`. If you do that, though, you'll need to query the device to discover what Direct3D features the user's system supports. The advantage of the `D3DDEVTYPE_REF` type of device is that all features of Direct3D can be tested on any machine, because Direct3D will perform all of these features in software. No 3D hardware is required. However, because all the complex processing happens with software, this type of device is much slower than the hardware device. Typically, `D3DDEVTYPE_REF` is used only for testing.

Moving on, the third argument is simply your application's window handle. If you recall from Chapter 3, "Writing a Windows Program," you acquire the handle when you call the Windows API function `CreateWindowEx()`. Nothing more to say about this argument.

The fourth argument is a value containing the flags that specify how the device should behave. There are actually seven of these flags, but in this book, you only need to know two: D3DCREATE_HARDWARE_VERTEXPROCESSING and D3DCREATE_SOFTWARE_VERTEXPROCESSING. The former specifies that Direct3D should process vertices (a fancy word for points in a shape) using hardware and the latter specifies using software for the same purpose. In this book, you'll use D3DCREATE_SOFTWARE_VERTEXPROCESSING, which ensures compatibility with all systems at the cost of slightly less efficiency.

Now we get to the fifth argument, which is a monster. It's not only its name that's intimidating. Don't panic, though. You'll soon master this beast. The fifth argument is the address of a D3DPRESENT_PARAMETERS structure. The DirectX SDK defines the structure like this:

```
typedef struct _D3DPRESENT_PARAMETERS_ {
    UINT                    BackBufferWidth;
    UINT                    BackBufferHeight;
    D3DFORMAT               BackBufferFormat;
    UINT                    BackBufferCount;

    D3DMULTISAMPLE_TYPE     MultiSampleType;

    D3DSWAPEFFECT           SwapEffect;
    HWND                    hDeviceWindow;
    BOOL                    Windowed;
    BOOL                    EnableAutoDepthStencil;
    D3DFORMAT               AutoDepthStencilFormat;
    DWORD                   Flags;

    UINT                    FullScreen_RefreshRateInHz;
    UINT                    FullScreen_PresentationInterval;
} D3DPRESENT_PARAMETERS;
```

Even I'm getting nervous. Okay, not really. This isn't as bad as it looks, especially considering that you can use standard settings and forget about it. In fact, you really need to know only a couple of these settings to get started. You'll run into most of the others throughout this book. For now, just know this:

- *hDeviceWindow*—Your window's handle.
- *Windowed*—TRUE for a windowed application and FALSE for a full-screen application.

The other members of this structure, you can take on faith for now, filling them in with the values supplied here (and ignoring the rest):

```
D3DPRESENT_PARAMETERS D3DPresentParams;
ZeroMemory(&D3DPresentParams, sizeof(D3DPRESENT_PARAMETERS));
D3DPresentParams.Windowed = FALSE;
```

5

```
D3DPresentParams.BackBufferCount = 1;
D3DPresentParams.BackBufferWidth = 800;
D3DPresentParams.BackBufferHeight = 600;
D3DPresentParams.BackBufferFormat = D3DFMT_X8R8G8B8;
D3DPresentParams.SwapEffect = D3DSWAPEFFECT_DISCARD;
D3DPresentParams.hDeviceWindow = g_hWnd;
```

Notice, in this example, how a call to the `ZeroMemory()` function initializes the entire structure to zeroes. Notice also that the example sets `Windowed` to `FALSE` and `hDeviceWindow` to `g_hWnd`, which is a global variable that holds the application's window handle.

It might seem strange to tell Direct3D that you don't want a window and then have to pass along a window handle. Remember, though, that even a full-screen display is actually a window, albeit one without any of the visible elements of a window. In the case of a full-screen application, you can think of `hDeviceWindow` as holding a handle to the full screen.

Finally, you've made it all the way to the last argument in the call to `CreateDevice()`. This argument is named `ppReturnedDeviceInterface` and is nothing more than the address where `CreateDevice()` should store the pointer to your Direct3D device. After the call to `CreateDevice()`, if `ppReturnedDeviceInterface` remains `NULL`, the call to `CreateDevice()` failed.

Releasing Direct3D Objects

If you've been programming for any time at all, you know that when you allocate memory in a program, you need to release it before the application terminates. This is just the way programmers in polite society do things. The same is true of Direct3D objects: When you're through with them, you have to remove them from memory. To do this, you must call each object's `Release()` method. For example, here's how you would release the Direct3D objects you just created:

```
if (g_pDirect3DDevice)
    g_pDirect3DDevice->Release();
if (g_pDirect3D)
    g_pDirect3D->Release();
```

You need to look at a couple of things here. First, notice how the code checks whether the object pointers are `NULL` before trying to release them. This is why it's so important to set these pointers to `NULL` when you first declare them, so that the only time they can contain a value other than `NULL` is when the program successfully creates the Direct3D objects. You don't want to call `Release()` through a bad or `NULL` pointer! If you do, you'll almost certainly crash the program.

The other thing to notice here is that the program releases the objects in the reverse order they were created. Because of this, every Direct3D program always releases the Direct3D object last, since it's always the first to be created. To tell you the truth, nothing bad seems to happen if you don't follow this rule, but the key word here is "seems." You have to figure that they make these rules for a reason.

Your First Direct3D Program

That's enough theory for now. Before your head starts spinning, you should spend a little time being sure you understand what you've just read. To help you toward this goal, you'll now build your first Direct3D program. This program won't do a heck of a lot. In fact, it won't seem to do much of anything. But if it works okay, you should successfully create and release Direct3D and Direct3D device objects.

Creating the Basic Project

Perform the following steps to get the main Windows application up and running:

1. Start a new empty Win32 project named BasicDirect3DApp, as shown in Figures 5.1 and 5.2.

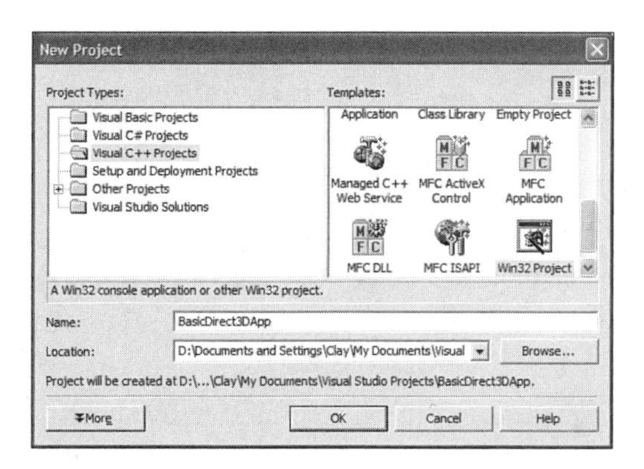

FIGURE 5.1
Creating the BasicDirect3DApp project.

2. On the Project menu, select the Add New Item command. The Add New Item dialog box appears.
3. Add a new C++ File (.cpp) named BasicDirect3DApp.cpp, as shown in Figure 5.3.

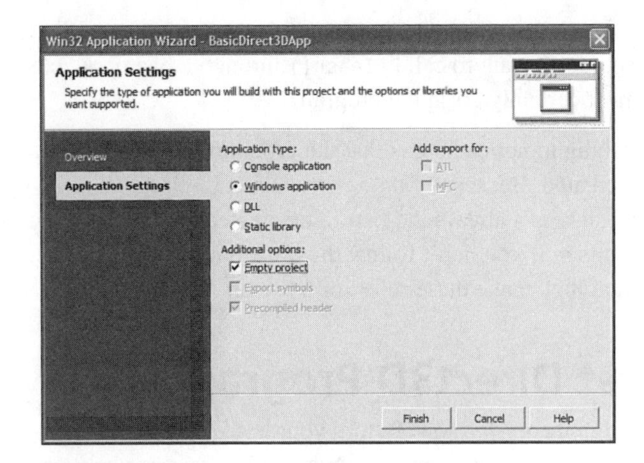

FIGURE 5.2

Be sure to choose the Empty Project setting.

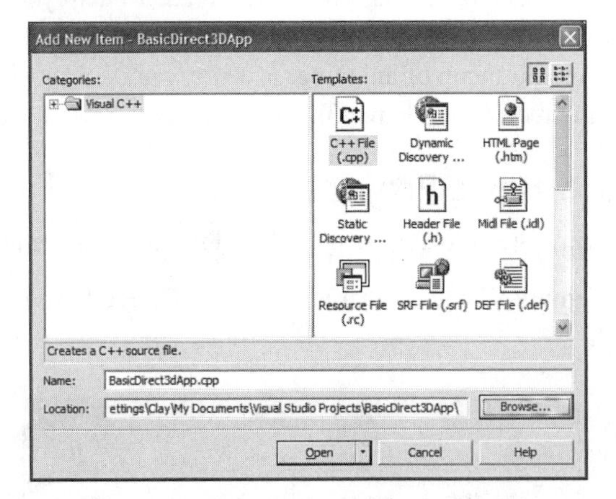

FIGURE 5.3

Creating the main source-code file.

4. Copy the contents of the BasicWindowsApp.cpp file (from Chapter 3) into the new BasicDirect3DApp code window.
5. Change the name in the comment at the top of the file to BasicDirect3DApp.
6. In the `RegisterWindowClass()` function change `wc.lpszClassName = "WinApp"` to `wc.lpszClassName = "Direct3DApp"`.
7. In the `CreateAppWindow()` function, change `"WinApp"` to `"Direct3DApp"`, and then change `"Basic Windows Application"` to `"Basic Direct3D Application"`.
8. Compile and run the application to be sure that it works okay. You should see the window shown in Figure 5.4.

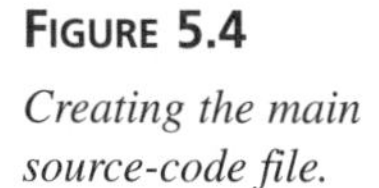

FIGURE 5.4

Creating the main source-code file.

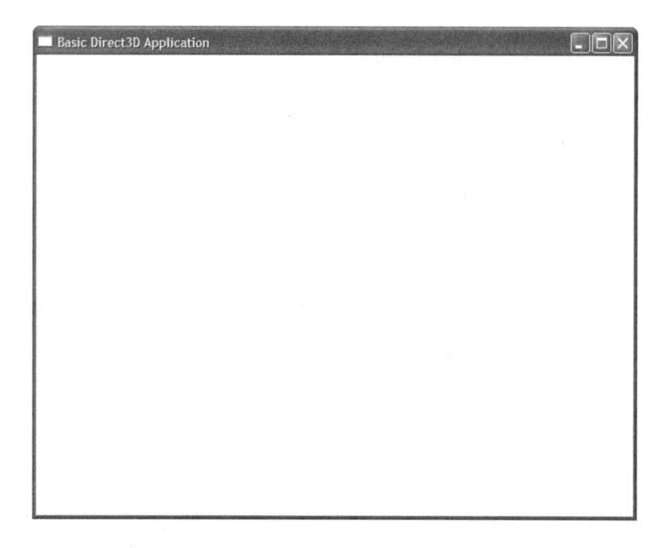

Adding the Direct3D Stuff

You're now ready to start programming your Direct3D application. Perform the following steps:

1. Add the following lines to the program's function prototypes:

```
HRESULT InitFullScreenDirect3D();
void Render();
void CleanUpDirect3D();
```

2. Add the following lines to the program's global variables:

```
IDirect3D8* g_pDirect3D = NULL;
IDirect3DDevice8* g_pDirect3DDevice = NULL;
```

3. In the `WinMain()` function, replace the line `INT result = StartMessageLoop();` with the following:

```
HRESULT hResult = InitFullScreenDirect3D();
if (SUCCEEDED(hResult))
    WPARAM result = StartMessageLoop();
CleanUpDirect3D();
```

4. Change the line `return result;` to `return 0;`

5. Add the following functions to the program:

```
////////////////////////////////////////////////////////
// InitFullScreenDirect3D()
////////////////////////////////////////////////////////
HRESULT InitFullScreenDirect3D()
{
    g_pDirect3D = Direct3DCreate8(D3D_SDK_VERSION);
    if (g_pDirect3D == NULL)
```

```
        return E_FAIL;
    D3DPRESENT_PARAMETERS D3DPresentParams;
    ZeroMemory(&D3DPresentParams, sizeof(D3DPRESENT_PARAMETERS));
    D3DPresentParams.Windowed = FALSE;
    D3DPresentParams.BackBufferCount = 1;
    D3DPresentParams.BackBufferWidth = 800;
    D3DPresentParams.BackBufferHeight = 600;
    D3DPresentParams.BackBufferFormat = D3DFMT_X8R8G8B8;
    D3DPresentParams.SwapEffect = D3DSWAPEFFECT_DISCARD;
    D3DPresentParams.hDeviceWindow = g_hWnd;
    HRESULT hResult = g_pDirect3D->CreateDevice(D3DADAPTER_DEFAULT,
        D3DDEVTYPE_HAL, g_hWnd, D3DCREATE_SOFTWARE_VERTEXPROCESSING,
        &D3DPresentParams, &g_pDirect3DDevice);
    if (FAILED(hResult))
        return E_FAIL;
    return D3D_OK;
}

//////////////////////////////////////////////////////
// CleanUpDirect3D()
//////////////////////////////////////////////////////
void CleanUpDirect3D()
{
    if (g_pDirect3DDevice)
        g_pDirect3DDevice->Release();
    if (g_pDirect3D)
        g_pDirect3D->Release();
}
```

Adding the Required References

If you try to compile the program at this point, you'll end up with a bunch of errors. This is because your project doesn't yet know where to find the Direct3D header and library files it needs to build the application. Go ahead and try to compile. When you get your list of errors, look at the top three. They should look like this:

```
error C2143: syntax error : missing ';' before '*'
error C2501: 'IDirect3D8' : missing storage-class or type specifiers
error C2501: 'g_pDirect3D' : missing storage-class or type specifiers
```

You're getting these errors because the program doesn't recognize the `IDirect3D8*` data type, which, as you now know, is a pointer to the `IDirect3D8` interface. You should also see similar errors for the `IDirect3DDevice8*` data type, like this:

```
error C2143: syntax error : missing ';' before '*'
error C2501: 'IDirect3DDevice8' : missing storage-class or type specifiers
error C2501: 'g_pDirect3DDevice' : missing storage-class or type specifiers
```

There's a slew of other similar errors, where the program doesn't recognize the Direct3D symbols you're using. To resolve these errors, you need to tell the program where these symbols are defined. To do that, first add the line `#include <d3d8.h>` near the top of the program, right after the line `#include <windows.h>` that's already there.

Now, you need to tell your project where to find that header file. Perform the following steps to accomplish this task:

1. Right-click the project's name in the Solution Explorer, and select Properties from the menu that appears. The BasicDirect3DApp Property Pages dialog box appears, as shown in Figure 5.5.

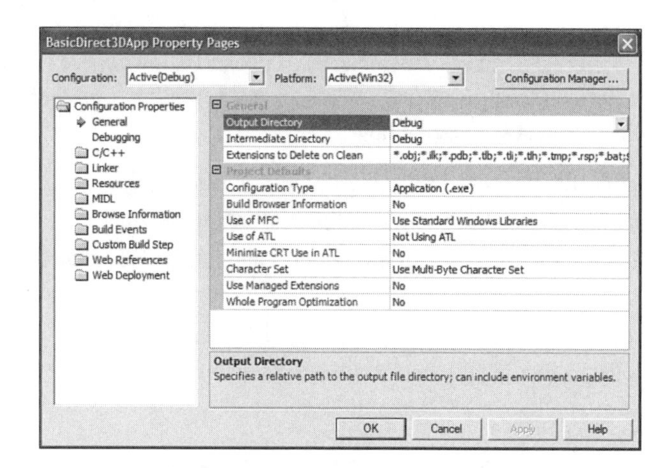

FIGURE 5.5

The project's property pages.

2. Click the C/C++ selection in the left pane, and select General from the displayed choices, as shown in Figure 5.6.
3. In the Additional Include Directories box, enter the path to the DirectX 8.1 SDK's include folder. If you installed the SDK using the default settings, this path should be `C:\DXSDK\include`, as shown in Figure 5.6.

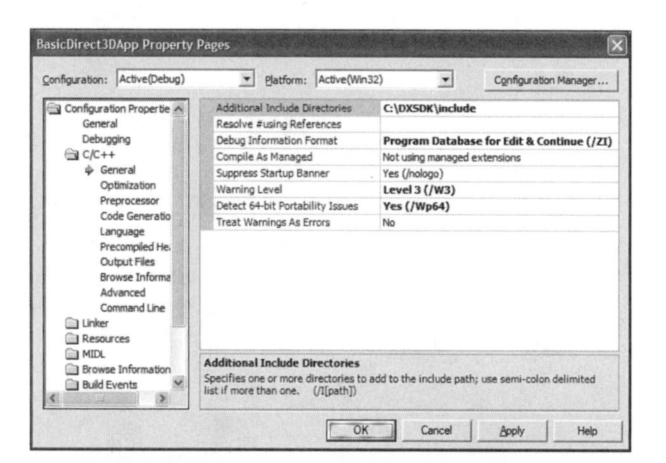

FIGURE 5.6

The general C/C++ settings.

4. Dismiss the dialog box by clicking OK.

Now you should be able to compile the program successfully. However, when the linker gets busy, you get the following errors:

```
error LNK2019: unresolved external symbol _Direct3DCreate8@4 referenced in
    function "long __cdecl InitFullScreenDirect3D(void)"
    (?InitFullScreenDirect3D@@YAJXZ)
BasicDirect3DApp fatal error LNK1120: 1 unresolved externals
```

Why isn't anything easy!? Because this is programming, and if it were easy, anyone could do it. You're getting these errors because, even though the project now knows how all those Direct3D symbols are declared, it doesn't know where the actual code for the objects is defined. In other words, you now need to tell the project where the Direct3D library files are located. Here's how:

1. Right-click the project's name in the Solution Explorer, and bring up the BasicDirect3DApp Property Pages dialog box again.
2. Click the Linker selection in the left pane, and select General from the displayed choices.
3. In the Additional Library Directories box, enter the path to the DirectX 8.1 SDK's library folder. If you installed the SDK using the default settings, this path should be `C:\DXSDK\lib`, as shown in Figure 5.7.

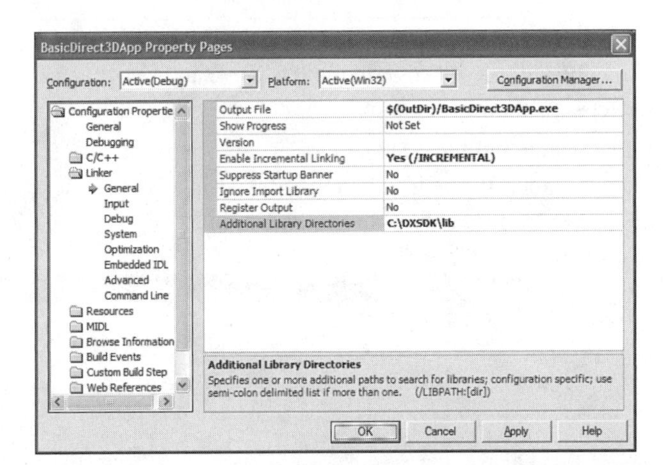

FIGURE 5.7

The general linker settings.

4. Click the Linker's Input selection in the left pane.
5. In the Additional Dependencies box in the right pane, enter `d3d8.lib`—which is the Direct3D 8.1 library file—as shown in Figure 5.8.

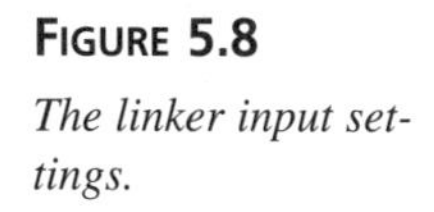

FIGURE 5.8

The linker input settings.

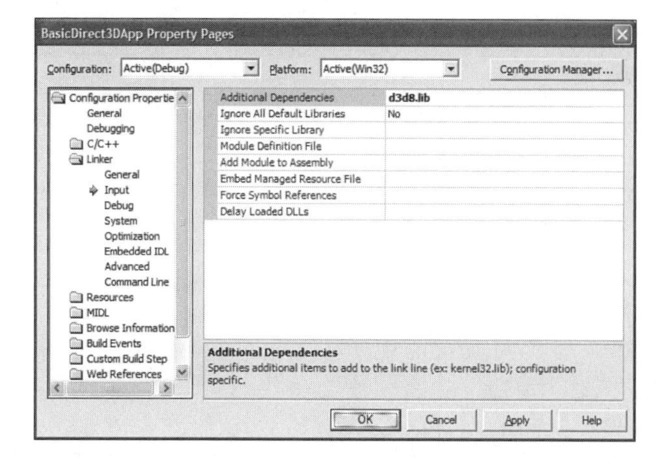

6. Dismiss the dialog box by clicking OK.

Now you should be able to compile, link, and run the application. When you do, your screen will probably flicker a couple of times and then you'll see your full-screen Direct3D window. Unfortunately, because you haven't yet drawn anything in the window, what you see will be a bit of a mess. To get out of the program Alt+Tab back to Visual Studio and then exit the program by clicking the toolbar's Stop Debugging button or by selecting Stop Debugging from the Debug menu.

Understanding Display Modes

To continue programming your first Direct3D program, you need to know about display modes. For the most part, a display mode comprises screen resolution and color depth. For example, most computer displays these days are set to 800×600 resolution with 32-bit color or 1024×768 resolution with 32-bit color. There are dozens of other display modes that you can access as long as the graphics hardware in the computer supports them.

Most supported display modes, however, are archaic and are of no use to you as a Direct3D programmer. For example, we could get into a whole bag of worms here and talk about things like palletized display modes and monochrome display modes and other not-so-cool stuff, but you want to get started with game programming as soon as you can. So, for the purposes of this book, you'll need to know only about the nine most commonly used display modes on today's computers, as shown in Table 5.1.

TABLE 5.1 Common Display Modes

Resolution	*Color Setting*
640×480	16-bit color
640×480	24-bit color
640×480	32-bit color
800×600	16-bit color
800×600	24-bit color
800×600	32-bit color
1024×768	16-bit color
1024×768	24-bit color
1024×768	32-bit color

And when I said these were the only settings you need to know about, I meant that you should understand what these display modes represent and realize that your Direct3D applications will most likely have to deal with them at one time or another.

Now, I think you understand that an 800×600 display is 800 dots horizontally and 600 dots vertically, right? If not, you do now. The tricky part of a display mode is the color depth. To really understand how your computer displays a dot of a particular color, you need to know about pixel formats. A pixel, of course, is one of those tiny dots on your screen. The pixel format determines how the information that represents that dot is stored in the computer's memory.

The first thing to know is that the number of bits in a color determines how much video card memory each pixel on the screen consumes. For example, 16 bits is two bytes, so each pixel of a 16-bit color display requires two bytes. So, if your computer display is set to 800×600 resolution with 16-bit color, your video card requires 800×600×2 bytes of memory, or a total of 960,000 bytes of memory. If the same display uses 32-bit color, the video card memory is 1,920,000 bytes or twice that required by the 16-bit scenario.

But what, you may wonder, is actually stored inside those bytes of screen memory? The answer to that question is what pixel formats are all about.

For your purposes in this book, colors on the screen are created by combining red, green, and blue. These are called RGB color modes. One of the simplest display modes to understand is the 24-bit mode, which uses three bytes for each pixel. One byte represents red intensity, one represents green, and the last represents blue. Because a byte of memory can hold a value from 0 to 255, each of these three color elements can be set to one of 256 intensities, from 0 (none of the color) to 255 (full intensity of the color).

So, if you have a 24-bit pixel with the RGB values 255,0,0, you've got a red dot on the screen. 0,255,0 gives you a green dot, and, as you've undoubtedly already guessed, 0,0,255 is a blue dot. The rest of the colors range from 0,0,0, which is black, to 255,255,255, which is white. If you've ever heard that black is the absence of all color and white is the presence of all color, you now know what that means.

Now that you know about 24-bit color, forget about it. Huh? Yep, you heard right. Forget it. As most programmers know, computers hate to work with odd numbers of bytes, and that's exactly what you have with 24-bit color. Direct3D programs, too, are not too fond of 24-bit color displays and work much better with either 16- or 32-bit displays. In this book, you'll work almost exclusively with 32-bit displays.

The most common 32-bit display mode still uses three bytes for the red, green, and blue color elements, but it adds a fourth byte for something called an alpha value. You don't need to know too much about alpha values yet. Just know that an alpha value specifies a color's transparency. Table 5.2 shows some of the 16-, 24-, and 32-bit pixel formats and the constants that the DirectX SDK defines for them.

TABLE 5.2 Pixel Formats

Format	*Description*
D3DFMT_R5G6B5	16-bit RGB pixel format with 5 bits for red, 6 bits for green, and 5 bits for blue.
D3DFMT_X1R5G5B5	16-bit pixel format with 5 bits for each color.
D3DFMT_A1R5G5B5	16-bit pixel format with 5 bits for each color and 1 bit for alpha.
D3DFMT_A4R4G4B4	16-bit ARGB pixel format with 4 bits for each color and alpha value.
D3DFMT_X4R4G4B4	16-bit RGB pixel format with 4 bits for each color.
D3DFMT_R8G8B8	24-bit RGB pixel format with 8 bits per channel.
D3DFMT_A8R8G8B8	32-bit ARGB pixel format with 8 bits for each color and alpha.
D3DFMT_X8R8G8B8	32-bit RGB pixel format with 8 bits for each color (fourth byte unused).
D3DFMT_A2B10G10R10	32-bit pixel format using 10 bits for each color and 2 bits for alpha.
D3DFMT_G16R16	32-bit pixel format using 16 bits each for green and red.

Checking for Display-Mode Availability

When your Direct3D application first runs, it really should check for the availability of the display mode your application needs. You never know what kind of computer your program will be running on, and although most computers these days can handle any of the display modes you'll need, your program may be unlucky enough to get run on a computer from the Stone Age. In such a case, the program has to know that it can't run properly and must inform the user of this sad fact.

The DirectX API supplies a method to take care of this problem. To discover whether a particular display mode is available, just call the Direct3D object's `CheckDeviceType()` method, which the SDK declares like this:

```
HRESULT CheckDeviceType(
  UINT Adapter,
  D3DDEVTYPE CheckType,
  D3DFORMAT DisplayFormat,
  D3DFORMAT BackBufferFormat,
  BOOL Windowed
);
```

This method requires five arguments, which are described as follows:

- *`Adapter`*—A number that specifies the adapter for which Direct3D should create the device.
- *`CheckType`*—The type of device object for which you're checking.
- *`DisplayFormat`*—The display format for which to check.
- *`BackBufferFormat`*—The back buffer display format for which to check.
- *`Windowed`*—A Boolean value that specifies whether the required device will be used in a windowed (`TRUE`) or full-screen (`FALSE`) application.

In this book, the first argument will always be `D3DADAPTER_DEFAULT`, for the default adapter. The second argument can be either `D3DDEVTYPE_HAL` for a hardware-assisted device or `D3DDEVTYPE_REF` for a software device. The third and fourth arguments are, for your purposes, one of the values from Table 5.2, usually `D3DFMT_X8R8G8B8`. Finally, the fifth argument should be `TRUE` if your application will run in a window or `FALSE` if it's full-screen.

If the call succeeds (that is, the pixel format you want is available), `CheckDeviceType()` returns the value `D3D_OK`. So, a typical call to `CheckDeviceType()` in your programs might look like this:

```
HRESULT hResult = g_pDirect3D->CheckDeviceType(D3DADAPTER_DEFAULT,
    D3DDEVTYPE_REF, D3DFMT_X8R8G8B8, D3DFMT_X8R8G8B8, FALSE);
if (hResult != D3D_OK)
    return E_FAIL;
```

Windowed Versus Full-screen Applications

Checking for a specific pixel format is usually something you do when starting up a full-screen Direct3D application. This is because, with a full-screen application, you can use whatever display mode you want, as long as the hardware supports it. However, if you're running your Direct3D application in a window, you have to share the display with any other applications that might also be running. This means that you're stuck with whatever mode the user has his or her machine set to. Your program must either adapt to the current display mode or ask the user to change it. This is why most Direct3D games run in full-screen mode.

But the windowed mode is cool for quickie types of games that the user may want to switch to from another application. Moreover, windowed games don't seem as isolated to the user as a full-screen game, even though a full-screen game is still a Windows application and the user can switch back and forth with ease (assuming that the Direct3D application has been properly programmed).

When writing a windowed Direct3D application, it makes more sense to check the current display mode than it does to check for the availability of a specific one. After all, only one mode will be available, although you'll probably still want to check for hardware support if your application relies on hardware acceleration.

To check the current display mode, you can call the Direct3D object's `GetAdapterDisplayMode()` method, which the DirectX SDK declares like this:

```
HRESULT GetAdapterDisplayMode(
  UINT Adapter,
  D3DDISPLAYMODE* pMode
);
```

This method's two arguments are the adapter to check and a pointer to a `D3DDISPLAYMODE` structure into which the call will place the information you need about the current display mode. The DirectX SDK declares the structure like this:

```
typedef struct _D3DDISPLAYMODE {
    UINT            Width;
    UINT            Height;
    UINT            RefreshRate;
    D3DFORMAT       Format;
} D3DDISPLAYMODE;
```

The `Width` and the `Height` members of this structure represent the current screen resolution, and the `Format` member represents the current pixel format. You don't need to worry about the `RefreshRate` member. So, if the user's system is set to a resolution of

800×600 with the 32-bit RGB pixel format when your program calls GetAdapterDisplayMode(), you'll end up with Width equal to 800, Height equal to 600, and Format equal to D3DFMT_X8R8G8B8. The actual call would look something like this:

```
D3DDISPLAYMODE d3ddisplaymode;
HRESULT hResult = g_pDirect3D->
    GetAdapterDisplayMode(D3DADAPTER_DEFAULT, &d3ddisplaymode);
if (hResult != D3D_OK)
    return E_FAIL;
```

Once you have the display mode information, you can use it to create the device for your application:

```
D3DPRESENT_PARAMETERS D3DPresentParams;
ZeroMemory(&D3DPresentParams, sizeof(D3DPRESENT_PARAMETERS));
D3DPresentParams.Windowed = TRUE;
D3DPresentParams.BackBufferFormat = d3ddisplaymode.Format;
D3DPresentParams.SwapEffect = D3DSWAPEFFECT_DISCARD;
D3DPresentParams.hDeviceWindow = g_hWnd;
HRESULT hResult = g_pDirect3D->CreateDevice(D3DADAPTER_DEFAULT,
    D3DDEVTYPE_HAL, g_hWnd, D3DCREATE_SOFTWARE_VERTEXPROCESSING,
    &D3DPresentParams, &g_pDirect3DDevice);
if (FAILED(hResult))
    return E_FAIL;
```

That's it. Now, just like the 24-bit pixel format we talked about, you can forget about windowed Direct3D applications. They are too difficult to bother with, which is why most games don't bother with them. From here on out, you'll be concerned only with full-screen Direct3D applications. (Whew. I wiggled out of that one handily. Uh…did I just say that out loud?)

Drawing to the Display

Because you don't want to look at that mess on the screen that you get with your program as it stands now, you need to learn a couple of new Direct3D methods. The first of these is Clear(), which is a method of the Direct3D device object. The DirectX SDK declares Clear() like this:

```
HRESULT Clear(
  DWORD Count,
  CONST D3DRECT* pRects,
  DWORD Flags,
  D3DCOLOR Color,
  float Z,
  DWORD Stencil
);
```

As you can see, this method has quite a few arguments. Here's what they mean:

- *Count*—The number of rectangles in the pRects array or 0 if pRects is NULL.
- *pRects*—A pointer to an array of D3DRECT structures that describe the rectangles to clear or NULL to clear the entire viewport rectangle.
- *Flags*—The flags that specify the surfaces to be cleared. Can be a combination of D3DCLEAR_STENCIL, D3DCLEAR_TARGET, and D3DCLEAR_ZBUFFER.
- *Color*—A 32-bit value that specifies the color to which to clear the rectangles.
- *Z*—A new z value for the depth buffer.
- *Stencil*—The integer value to store in the stencil buffer.

I know this stuff looks pretty advanced, but you don't need to understand all these arguments. In your case, a typical call to Clear() will look like this:

```
g_pDirect3DDevice->Clear(0, 0, D3DCLEAR_TARGET,
    D3DCOLOR_XRGB(0,0,255), 0, 0);
```

The third argument, D3DCLEAR_TARGET, tells Direct3D to clear the surface to the color specified in the fourth argument. The fourth argument is a D3DCOLOR value, which you can create using the XRGB macro. This macro takes the red, green, and blue color intensities as arguments. The remaining four arguments can be all zeroes.

Once you have cleared the surface, you need to display it. All this task requires is a call to the Direct3D device object's Present() method, which the DirectX SDK declares like this:

```
HRESULT Present(
  CONST RECT* pSourceRect,
  CONST RECT* pDestRect,
  HWND hDestWindowOverride,
  CONST RGNDATA* pDirtyRegion
);
```

5

You know, I'm not even going to tell you what these arguments mean, because you're not going to use any of them in this book. For the purposes of the programs you'll be developing in these pages, here's what a call to Present() looks like:

```
g_pDirect3DDevice->Present(NULL, NULL, NULL, NULL);
```

Yep, all NULLs. Makes it all so much easier, eh? Seriously, though, this call to Present() displays the entire surface, overwriting all that nonsense that used to be on the screen.

You're now ready to add to your Direct3D application. When you're done, your full-screen application will present you with a cool blue screen rather than the mess you had before. Just load up the project and follow these steps:

1. Find the `InitFullScreenDirect3D()` function, and add the following lines right after the first `return E_FAIL` line:

```
HRESULT hResult = g_pDirect3D->CheckDeviceType(D3DADAPTER_DEFAULT,
    D3DDEVTYPE_REF, D3DFMT_X8R8G8B8, D3DFMT_X8R8G8B8, FALSE);
if (hResult != D3D_OK)
{
    MessageBox(g_hWnd,
        "Sorry. This program won't\nrun on your system.",
        "DirectX Error", MB_OK);
    return E_FAIL;
}
```

2. Remove the `HRESULT` from in front of the call to `CreateDevice()`.
3. Add the following function to the program:

```
///////////////////////////////////////////////////////
// Render()
///////////////////////////////////////////////////////
void Render()
{
    g_pDirect3DDevice->Clear(0, 0, D3DCLEAR_TARGET,
        D3DCOLOR_XRGB(0,0,255), 0, 0);
    g_pDirect3DDevice->Present(NULL, NULL, NULL, NULL);
}
```

4. Find the `StartMessageLoop()` function, and place the following line after the `// Use idle time` comment that's already there:

```
Render();
```

5. Find the `WndProc()` function and add the following lines right before the `switch` statement's ending brace:

```
case WM_KEYDOWN:
    switch(wParam)
    {
    case VK_ESCAPE:
        PostQuitMessage(WM_QUIT);
        break;
    }
```

Now you're ready to compile and run the application. When you do, you see a bright blue screen. To exit the application, press your keyboard's Escape key.

Summary

As you've learned, the starting point for every Direct3D application is the creation of the Direct3D object. You can then use the Direct3D object to create the application's

Direct3D device, which you'll use a lot to implement much of the Direct3D functionality in your program. Now that you know how to get a Direct3D program up and running, you're ready to experiment with some of the Direct3D programming techniques you need to create 2D game programs. Specifically, in the next chapter, you learn how to manage Direct3D surfaces, which provide a way to store images in memory.

Q&A

Q. What about all those method-call arguments you like to gloss over? Won't I ever need them?

A. Someday, when you're ready to become a DirectX guru, you'll read more advanced texts that will light up every dark corner of the DirectX API. But for now, all you need to know is the basics—how to get your 2D game up and running.

Q. Will I ever need to create anything other than the hardware device?

A. No, except maybe in the case of doing testing. Virtually all of today's graphics hardware supports Direct3D, although not necessarily every feature of Direct3D. The portions of Direct3D you'll use in this book are implemented on pretty much all recent hardware.

Q. How come just calling `Clear()` to fill the screen with a color isn't enough? Why do I also have to call `Present()`?

A. When you call `Clear()`, you're not actually clearing the screen. Instead, you're clearing an area of memory called the back buffer. To make the back buffer show up on the screen, you need to call `Present()`. You learn more about surfaces and back buffers in upcoming chapters, especially Chapter 6, "Understanding Direct3D Surfaces," and Chapter 9, "Programming Direct3D Animation."

Workshop

The workshop includes quiz questions to help gauge your grasp of the material. You'll find the answers to this quiz at the end of this chapter. Even if you feel that you totally understand the concepts presented here, you should work through the quiz anyway. The last section is an exercise or two that you might work through to help reinforce your learning.

Quiz

1. What is the first DirectX object you need to create in a Direct3D application?
2. What function do you call to create a Direct3D object?

3. Why should you check for NULL values in pointers returned from Direct3D methods?
4. What are the two types of Direct3D devices?
5. What method do you call to create a Direct3D device object?
6. What is the D3DPRESENT_PARAMETERS structure used for?
7. Before a Direct3D application terminates, what should it do with the Direct3D objects it created?
8. Where are the Direct3D header files located?
9. Where are the Direct3D library files located?
10. What is a display mode?
11. What is a pixel format?
12. Explain the difference between 24-bit and 32-bit RGB color values?
13. What method do you call to determine whether a specific display mode is available on the system?
14. Why are full-screen Direct3D applications easier to write than windowed ones?
15. What method do you call to clear a Direct3D surface?
16. What method do you call to display the newly cleared surface?

Exercises

1. Modify this chapter's program so that it creates a reference device rather than a hardware device. When you run the program, what happens?
2. Modify the program so that it uses a 640×480, 16-bit display mode, rather than a 800×600, 32-bit one.
3. Modify the program so that it displays a red screen rather than a blue one.
4. Replace the Render() function with the one that follows. When you run the program, why does the screen continually change color from black all the way through to a very bright red?

```
void Render()
{
    static red = 0;
    red = red + 1;
    if (red > 255)
        red = 0;
    g_pDirect3DDevice->Clear(0, 0, D3DCLEAR_TARGET,
        D3DCOLOR_XRGB(red,0,0), 0, 0);
    g_pDirect3DDevice->Present(NULL, NULL, NULL, NULL);
}
```

Answers for Day 5

Quiz

1. What is the first DirectX object you need to create in a Direct3D application?

   An `IDirect3D8` object.

2. What function do you call to create a Direct3D object?

   The `Direct3DCreate8()` function.

3. Why should you check for `NULL` values in pointers returned from Direct3D methods?

   Because a `NULL` value indicates that the method failed and that the returned pointer is invalid.

4. What are the two types of Direct3D devices?

   Hardware devices and reference devices.

5. What method do you call to create a Direct3D device object?

   The Direct3D object's `CreateDevice()` method.

6. What is the `D3DPRESENT_PARAMETERS` structure used for?

   This structure holds the information Direct3D needs to create the required device.

7. Before a Direct3D application terminates, what should it do with the Direct3D objects it created?

   Call each object's `release()` method.

8. Where are the Direct3D header files located?

   In the include subdirectory of the DirectX installation's directory, usually C:\DXSDK\include.

9. Where are the Direct3D library files located?

   In the lib subdirectory of the DirectX installation's directory, usually C:\DXSDK\lib.

10. What is a display mode?

    The display mode comprises the resolution and color depth of a display.

11. What is a pixel format?

    A pixel format describes the way a pixel is represented on the screen.

12. Explain the difference between 24-bit and 32-bit RGB color values?

    A 24-bit RGB color value reserves one byte for each of the red, green, and blue color elements. A 32-bit RGB color value also reserves one byte for each of the color elements, but a fourth byte represents alpha values or is unused.

13. What method do you call to determine whether a specific display mode is available on the system.

    The Direct3D object's `CheckDeviceType()` method.

14. Why are full-screen Direct3D applications easier to write than windowed ones?

    Because your application can use any display mode the user's hardware supports. In a windowed application, you must live with the current display mode.

15. What method do you call to clear a Direct3D surface?

    The Direct3D device object's `Clear()` method.

16. What method do you call to display the newly cleared surface?

    The Direct3D device object's `Present()` method.

Exercises

1. Modify this chapter's program so that it creates a reference device rather than a hardware device. When you run the program, what happens?

   To modify the program, change the second argument of the `CheckDeviceType()` method call from `D3DDEVTYPE_HAL` to `D3DDEVTYPE_REF`. Also, change `D3DDEVTYPE_HAL` in the call to `CreateDevice()` to `D3DDEVTYPE_REF`. The program will run exactly the same because the reference device supports all of Direct3D's features.

2. Modify the program so that it uses a 640×480, 16-bit display mode, rather than an 800×600, 32-bit one. Use the first 16-bit format shown in Table 5.2.

   In the `InitFullScreenDirect3D()` function, change all occurrences of `D3DFMT_X8R8G8B8` in the call to `CheckDeviceType()` to `D3DFMT_R5G6B5`. Also, change the lines

   ```
   D3DPresentParams.BackBufferWidth = 800;
   D3DPresentParams.BackBufferHeight = 600;
   D3DPresentParams.BackBufferFormat = D3DFMT_X8R8G8B8;
   ```

   to

   ```
   D3DPresentParams.BackBufferWidth = 640;
   D3DPresentParams.BackBufferHeight = 480;
   D3DPresentParams.BackBufferFormat = D3DFMT_R5G6B5;
   ```

3. Modify the program so that it displays a red screen rather than a blue one.

   In the call to `Clear()`, change the color value given as the fourth argument to `D3DCOLOR_XRGB(255,0,0)`.

4. Replace the `Render()` function with the one that follows. When you run the program, why does the screen continually change color from black all the way through to a very bright red?

The call to `Render()` is placed in the application's message loop so that it gets called every time through the loop that the program isn't processing a message. In `Render()`, the `Clear()` method's color argument increases with each call to `Render()`, causing the red color element to get brighter and brighter, until it returns to black.

WEEK 1

DAY 6

Understanding Direct3D Surfaces

Surfaces are a hugely important topic to Direct3D programmers, because surfaces enable applications to store and manipulate graphics in a number of ways. In fact, without surfaces, you wouldn't even be able to see what's supposed to be on the screen. In this chapter, you'll see why. Specifically, today you will learn the following:

- What surfaces do for your program
- The different types of surfaces
- How to create and access surfaces
- How to load graphical data into a surface

Understanding Surfaces

Throughout this book and with all of your future Direct3D programs, you'll be working a lot with something called *surfaces*. A surface is really nothing more than an area of memory in which you can store graphical information. For example, the stuff you see on the screen or in a window is stored in a surface, as are the images you may need to build that display. In this book, you'll learn about four different kinds of surfaces:

- The primary surface
- Back-buffer surfaces
- Image surfaces
- Texture surfaces

New Term In Direct3D programming, a *surface* is an area of memory in which the application can store and manipulate graphics.

The Primary Surface

The primary surface, sometimes called the front buffer, is what you're looking at on the screen when you run a Direct3D program. This surface may contain the graphical data for the entire screen, or, in the case of a windowed application, the display you see in the application's window. The primary surface is the only type of surface that every Direct3D application must create and maintain, although the other types of surfaces are important.

You don't have to worry about explicitly creating a primary surface. Because it must always exist, just creating your Direct3D device object automatically creates the primary surface.

New Term The *primary surface* represents what you see on the screen or in a window.

The Back-Buffer Surface

A back buffer is an area of memory where you can draw a display out of view of the user. After you draw onto the back buffer, you call the `Present()` method to make the back buffer the new primary surface. Rendering your display this way prevents nasty stuff like flicker and tearing, problems that plagued graphics programmers until they came up with the idea of back buffers.

The back buffer is so important to rendering smooth animation on a display that you can automatically create a back buffer at the same time that you create the application's Direct3D device. Remember that `D3DPRESENT_PARAMETERS` structure you learned about in the previous chapter? As a reminder, here's what it looks like:

```
typedef struct _D3DPRESENT_PARAMETERS_ {
    UINT                    BackBufferWidth;
    UINT                    BackBufferHeight;
    D3DFORMAT               BackBufferFormat;
    UINT                    BackBufferCount;

    D3DMULTISAMPLE_TYPE     MultiSampleType;

    D3DSWAPEFFECT           SwapEffect;
    HWND                    hDeviceWindow;
    BOOL                    Windowed;
    BOOL                    EnableAutoDepthStencil;
    D3DFORMAT               AutoDepthStencilFormat;
    DWORD                   Flags;

    UINT                    FullScreen_RefreshRateInHz;
    UINT                    FullScreen_PresentationInterval;
} D3DPRESENT_PARAMETERS;
```

You may remember that you had to fill in values for this structure and then had to pass the structure to the `CreateDevice()` method when you created your Direct3D device object. You can see that the first four members of the structure have to do with back buffers. I kind of skipped over these members when you first learned about the `D3DPRESENT_PARAMETERS` structure. So, here's what you use these first four structure members for:

- *`BackBufferWidth`*—The width of the back buffer, which is usually the same as the width of the primary surface.
- *`BackBufferHeight`*—The height of the back buffer, which is usually the same as the height of the primary surface.
- *`BackBufferFormat`*—The pixel format of the back buffer, which is usually the same as the pixel format of the primary surface.
- *`BackBufferCount`*—The number of back buffers to create. In this book, this value will always be 1.

NEW TERM A *back buffer* is a special surface on which you can create a display in memory without the rendering process being visible to the user.

6

Image Surfaces

Most Direct3D applications need a place to store images required by the program. For example, you might have a bitmap that shows a background scene. Before you can use such an image, it needs to be loaded into memory. Specifically, it needs to be placed into an *image surface*. An image surface is something you must create explicitly in your program. To do this, you call the Direct3D device object's `CreateImageSurface()` method, which the DirectX SDK declares like this:

```
HRESULT CreateImageSurface(
  UINT Width,
  UINT Height,
  D3DFORMAT Format,
  IDirect3DSurface8** ppSurface
);
```

Here's what the method's four arguments mean:

- *`Width`*—The desired width of the surface.
- *`Height`*—The desired height of the surface.
- *`Format`*—The surface's pixel format, which is usually the same as the primary surface's pixel format.
- *`ppSurface`*—The address where the method should store the pointer to the new surface object.

So, suppose that you have a 640×480, 32-bit color bitmap that you want to load into memory. You might create a surface for the bitmap with this code:

```
IDirect3DSurface8* g_pBitmapSurface = NULL;
hResult = g_pDirect3DDevice->CreateImageSurface(640, 480,
    D3DFMT_X8R8G8B8, &g_pBitmapSurface);
if (FAILED(hResult))
{
    // Handle error here.
}
```

The first line here declares a pointer to the `IDirect3DSurface8` interface, an object of which is created by `CreateImageSurface()`. If the call to `CreateImageSurface()` fails, it returns an error value. You can easily check whether the method call failed by using the `FAILED()` macro, as shown in the example.

Once you have the surface created, you need to load the bitmap into it. The DirectX SDK provides the `D3DXLoadSurfaceFromFile()` function for exactly this purpose. The SDK declares that function like this:

```
HRESULT D3DXLoadSurfaceFromFile(
  LPDIRECT3DSURFACE8 pDestSurface,
  CONST PALETTEENTRY* pDestPalette,
  CONST RECT* pDestRect,
  LPCTSTR pSrcFile,
  CONST RECT* pSrcRect,
  DWORD Filter,
  D3DCOLOR ColorKey,
  D3DXIMAGE_INFO* pSrcInfo
);
```

That's a lot of arguments! Here's what they mean:

- *pDestSurface*—A pointer to the surface to which to load the image.
- *pDestPalette*—A pointer to the palette to which to load the image's colors. You'll use only `NULL` for this argument, because you won't be dealing with palletized graphics.
- *pDestRect*—The rectangular area of the surface to which to load the image or `NULL` for the entire surface.
- *pSrcFile*—A string holding the path to the file to load.
- *pSrcRect*—The rectangular area of the image to copy or `NULL` for the entire image.
- *Filter*—The type of filtering to use, usually `D3DX_DEFAULT`. You don't have to worry about filtering, since you won't be using it in this book.
- *ColorKey*—The color value that should be changed to transparent black or 0 to disable color keying.
- *pSrcInfo*—A pointer to a `D3DXIMAGE_INFO` structure containing information about the image. Usually, you'll use `NULL` here.

You don't need to deal with most of these arguments. You only need the surface pointer, the file path, and the default filter. So, to load that 640×480, 32-bit color bitmap, you'd write something like this:

```
HRESULT hResult = D3DXLoadSurfaceFromFile(g_pBitmapSurface, NULL, NULL,
    "image.bmp", NULL, D3DX_DEFAULT, 0, NULL);
if (FAILED(hResult))
{
    DXTRACE_ERR("Couldn't load bitmap.", hResult);
}
```

6

Note

The `DXTRACE_ERR()` macro enables you to easily display all the information you need about an error. For example, if this call to `D3DXLoadSurfaceFromFile()` fails, the `DXTRACE_ERR()` macro will display the message box shown in Figure 6.1.

Unfortunately, displaying message boxes in a Direct3D program can be a little tricky. You'll probably need to Alt+Tab away from the application in order to see the dialog box. This is because your Direct3D application continually draws its display, erasing anything that was there before, including message boxes. As you'll soon discover, though, there's a way around this problem.

FIGURE 6.1
Displaying a Direct3D error.

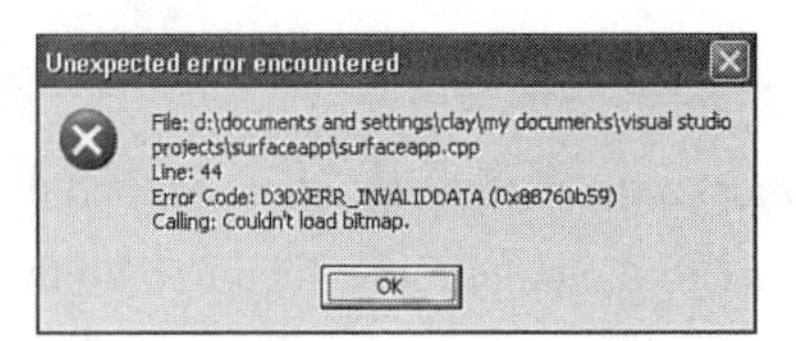

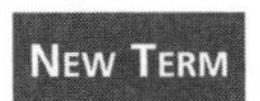

An *image surface* is a storing place for the graphics an application needs to render its display.

Transferring Image Data Between Surfaces

You're cooking now. You've managed to create a surface for an image, and then load the image from disk into the surface. All you have to do now is to show the image. To accomplish this task, you must transfer the image to the back buffer and then call the `Present()` method.

Transferring the image to the back buffer is as easy as a call to the Direct3D device object's `CopyRects()` method. First, though, you need to find a way to access the back buffer. You can get the needed pointer by calling the Direct3D device object's `GetBackBuffer()` method, which the DirectX SDK declares like this:

```
HRESULT GetBackBuffer(
  UINT BackBuffer,
  D3DBACKBUFFER_TYPE Type,
  IDirect3DSurface8** ppBackBuffer
);
```

In this method call, the three arguments are as follows:

- *`BackBuffer`*—The index of the back buffer to get. Unless you're using multiple back buffers, this will be 0.
- *`Type`*—Must be `D3DBACKBUFFER_TYPE_MONO`.
- *`ppBackBuffer`*—The address where the method should store the returned pointer.

A typical call to `GetBackBuffer()` might look like this:

```
IDirect3DSurface8* pBackBuffer = NULL;
HRESULT hResult = g_pDirect3DDevice->GetBackBuffer(0,
```

```
    D3DBACKBUFFER_TYPE_MONO, &pBackBuffer);
if (FAILED(hResult))
{
    // Handle error here.
}
```

Now, you're ready for the `CopyRects()` method, which the DirectX SDK declares like this:

```
HRESULT CopyRects(
  IDirect3DSurface8* pSourceSurface,
  CONST RECT* pSourceRectsArray,
  UINT cRects,
  IDirect3DSurface8* pDestinationSurface,
  CONST POINT* pDestPointsArray
);
```

Here's what all the arguments mean:

- *`pSourceSurface`*—A pointer to the surface from which to copy.
- *`pSourceRectsArray`*—An array containing the coordinates of the rectangles to copy. Use NULL to copy the entire surface.
- *`cRects`*—The number of rectangles in the *`pSourceRectsArray`* array.
- *`pDestinationSurface`*—A pointer to the surface to which to copy the data.
- *`pDestPointsArray`*—An array of points that specify where each rectangle should be copied. Use `NULL` to specify that the destination coordinates are the same as the source coordinates.

In this chapter, you won't worry about all the rectangle stuff, as you'll be copying only the full image surface to the back buffer. Later, when you start working with actual game images, you'll refine your use of this method. Here's what the code looks like:

```
HRESULT hResult = g_pDirect3DDevice->CopyRects(g_pBitmapSurface,
    NULL,0,pBackBuffer,NULL);
if (FAILED(hResult))
{
    // Handle error here.
}
```


At this point, all you need to do is call the Direct3D device object's `Present()` method to view the bitmap you loaded. Want to try it? Build the program presented in the following section to see all this stuff working.

Using Surfaces for Real

In this section, you put together all the stuff you've learned so far in this chapter by building a working Direct3D program that loads and displays a bitmap. I bet you can't wait!

Creating the Basic Project

Perform the following steps to get the main Windows application up and running:

1. Start a new empty Win32 project named SurfaceApp, as shown in Figures 6.2 and 6.3.

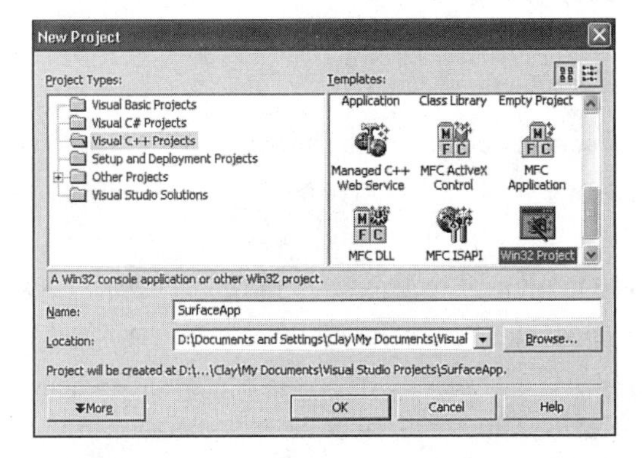

FIGURE 6.2

Creating the SurfaceApp project.

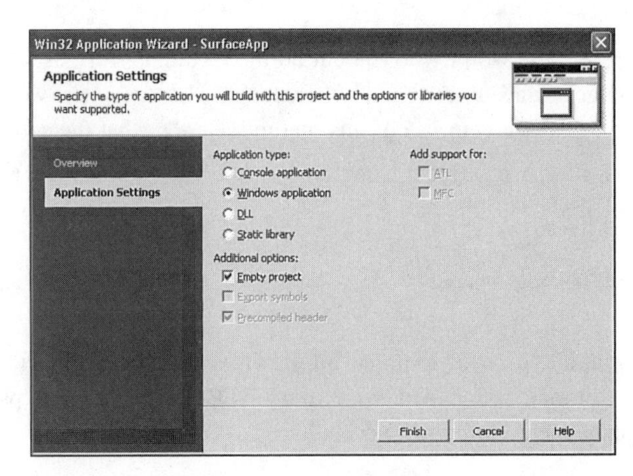

FIGURE 6.3

Choose the Empty Project setting.

2. On the Project menu, select the Add New Item command. The Add New Item dialog box appears.
3. Add a new C++ file (.cpp) named SurfaceApp.cpp, as shown in Figure 6.4.

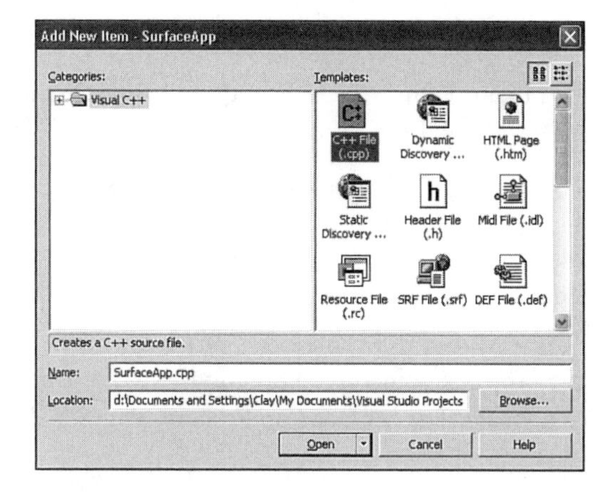

FIGURE 6.4
Creating the SurfaceApp.cpp source-code file.

4. Copy the contents of the BasicWindowsApp.cpp file (from Chapter 3) into the new SurfaceApp code window.
5. Change the name in the comment at the top of the file to SurfaceApp.
6. In the `RegisterWindowClass()` function change `wc.lpszClassName = "WinApp"` to `wc.lpszClassName = "SurfaceApp"`.
7. In the `CreateAppWindow()` function, change `"WinApp"` to `"SurfaceApp"`, and then change `"Basic Windows Application"` to `"Direct3D Surface Application"`.
8. Compile and run the application to be sure that it works okay. You should see the window shown in Figure 6.5.

FIGURE 6.5
The SurfaceApp application's window.

Adding the DirectX References

Next, you need to tell the program where the required DirectX header files and libraries are located. To do that, follow these steps:

1. Near the top of the program, right after the line #include <windows.h>, add the following include directives:

```
#include <d3d8.h>
#include <d3dx8tex.h>
#include <dxerr8.h>
```

2. Right-click the project's name in the Solution Explorer, and select Properties from the menu that appears. The SurfaceApp Property Pages dialog box appears, as shown in Figure 6.6.

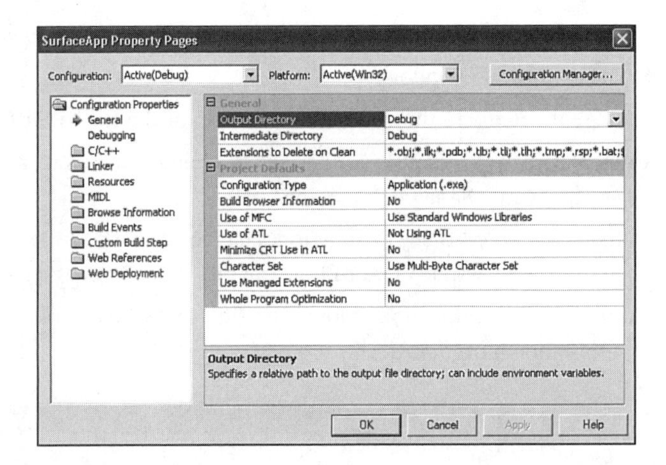

FIGURE 6.6

The project's property pages.

3. Click the C/C++ selection in the left pane, and select General from the displayed choices.
4. In the Additional Include Directories box, enter the path to the DirectX 8.1 SDK's include folder. If you installed the SDK using the default settings, this path should be `C:\DXSDK\include`, as shown in Figure 6.7.
5. Click the Linker selection in the left pane, and select General from the displayed choices.
6. In the Additional Library Directories box, enter the path to the DirectX 8.1 SDK's library folder. If you installed the SDK using the default settings, this path should be `C:\DXSDK\lib`, as shown in Figure 6.8

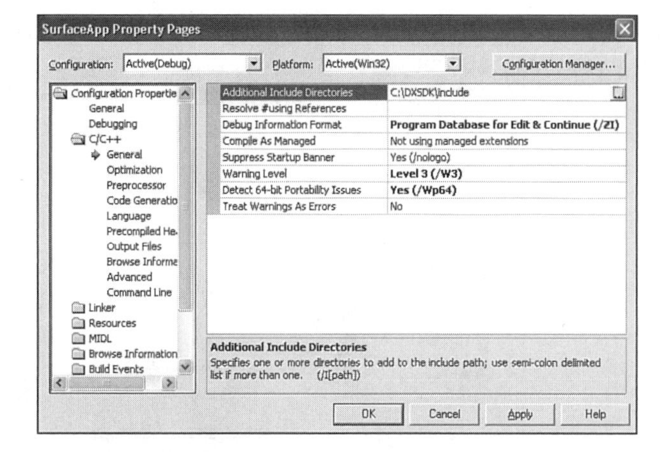

FIGURE 6.7
The general C/C++ settings.

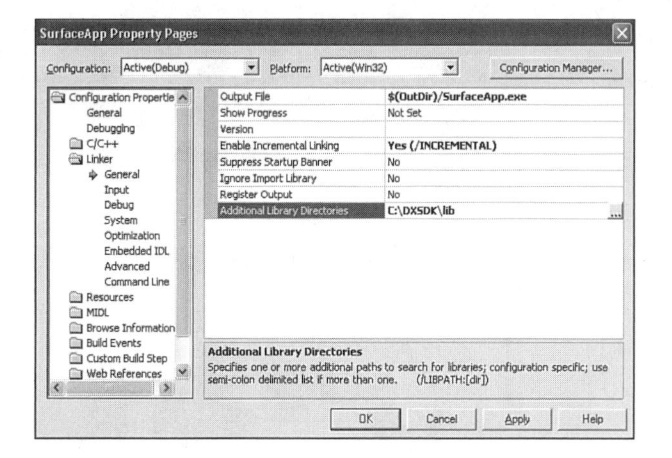

FIGURE 6.8
The general linker settings.

7. Click the Linker's Input selection in the left pane.
8. In the Additional Dependencies box in the right pane, enter `d3d8.lib`, `d3dx8.lib`, and `dxerr8.lib`, as shown in Figure 6.9.
9. Click the Debugging selection in the left pane, and then click inside the Working Directory box.
10. Use the ellipsis button that appears to browse to your project's main directory, and then click Open to select this as the project's working directory, as shown in Figure 6.10. (This enables the project to find additional files, such as the bitmap file you'll be using.)

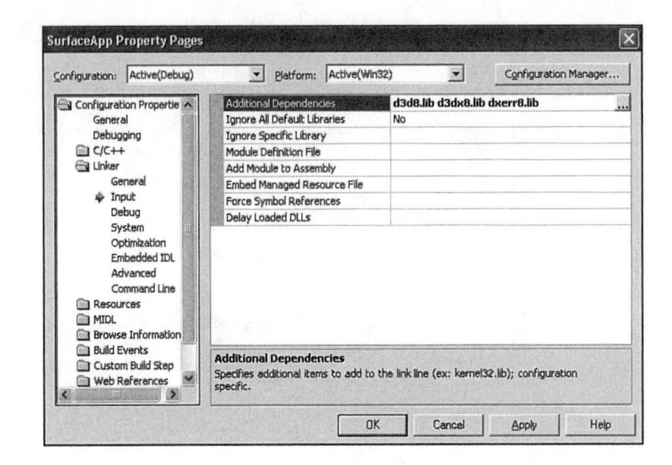

FIGURE 6.9

The linker input settings.

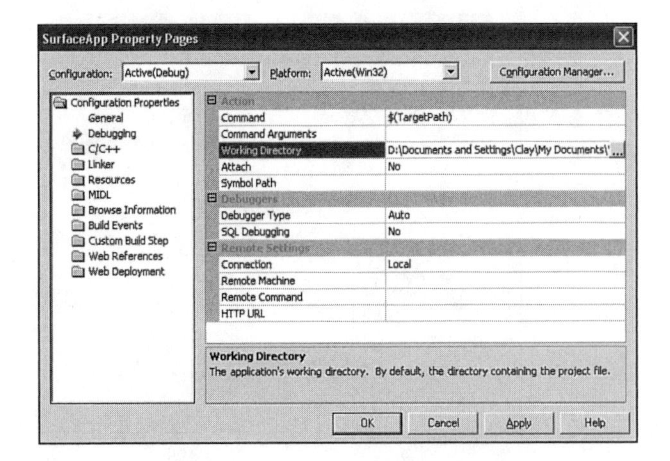

FIGURE 6.10

Setting the working directory.

11. Dismiss the dialog box by clicking OK.

Adding Source Code

Now all you have to do is add the Direct3D code that'll get this project going. Follow these steps to accomplish this task:

1. Add the following lines to the program's function prototypes:

```
HRESULT InitFullScreenDirect3D();
void Render();
void CleanUpDirect3D();
```

2. Add the following lines to the program's global variables:

```
IDirect3D8* g_pDirect3D = NULL;
IDirect3DDevice8* g_pDirect3DDevice = NULL;
IDirect3DSurface8* g_pBitmapSurface = NULL;
HRESULT g_hResult = D3D_OK;
char g_szErrorMsg[256];
```

3. In the `WinMain()` function, replace the line `INT result = StartMessageLoop();` with the following:

```
HRESULT hResult = InitFullScreenDirect3D();
if (SUCCEEDED(hResult))
    WPARAM result = StartMessageLoop();
CleanUpDirect3D();
CloseWindow(g_hWnd);
if (g_hResult != D3D_OK)
    DXTRACE_ERR(g_szErrorMsg, g_hResult);
```

4. Change the line `return result;` to `return 0;`

5. Add the line `Render();` after the idle time comment in the `StartMessageLoop()` function.

6. Find the `WndProc()` function and add the following lines right before the `switch` statement's ending brace:

```
case WM_KEYDOWN:
    switch(wParam)
    {
    case VK_ESCAPE:
        PostQuitMessage(WM_QUIT);
        break;
    }
```

7. Add the following functions to the program. (If you don't want to type all this stuff, you can copy it from the SurfaceApp.cpp file on this book's CD-ROM):

```
///////////////////////////////////////////////////////
// InitFullScreenDirect3D()
///////////////////////////////////////////////////////
HRESULT InitFullScreenDirect3D()
{
    g_pDirect3D = Direct3DCreate8(D3D_SDK_VERSION);
    if (g_pDirect3D == NULL)
    {
        MessageBox(g_hWnd,
            "Couldn't create DirectX object.",
            "DirectX Error", MB_OK);
        return E_FAIL;
    }
```

6

```
    HRESULT hResult = g_pDirect3D->CheckDeviceType(D3DADAPTER_DEFAULT,
        D3DDEVTYPE_HAL, D3DFMT_X8R8G8B8, D3DFMT_X8R8G8B8, FALSE);
    if (hResult != D3D_OK)
    {
        MessageBox(g_hWnd,
            "Sorry. This program won't\nrun on your system.",
            "DirectX Error", MB_OK);
        return E_FAIL;
    }

    D3DPRESENT_PARAMETERS D3DPresentParams;
    ZeroMemory(&D3DPresentParams, sizeof(D3DPRESENT_PARAMETERS));
    D3DPresentParams.Windowed = FALSE;
    D3DPresentParams.BackBufferCount = 1;
    D3DPresentParams.BackBufferWidth = 640;
    D3DPresentParams.BackBufferHeight = 480;
    D3DPresentParams.BackBufferFormat = D3DFMT_X8R8G8B8;
    D3DPresentParams.SwapEffect = D3DSWAPEFFECT_DISCARD;
    D3DPresentParams.hDeviceWindow = g_hWnd;
    hResult = g_pDirect3D->CreateDevice(D3DADAPTER_DEFAULT,
        D3DDEVTYPE_HAL, g_hWnd, D3DCREATE_SOFTWARE_VERTEXPROCESSING,
        &D3DPresentParams, &g_pDirect3DDevice);
    if (FAILED(hResult))
    {
        MessageBox(g_hWnd,
            "Failed to create Direct3D device.",
            "DirectX Error", MB_OK);
        return E_FAIL;
    }

    g_hResult = g_pDirect3DDevice->CreateImageSurface(640, 480,
        D3DFMT_X8R8G8B8, &g_pBitmapSurface);
    if (FAILED(g_hResult))
    {
        strcpy(g_szErrorMsg, "Error creating bitmap surface.");
        PostQuitMessage(WM_QUIT);
    }
    g_hResult = D3DXLoadSurfaceFromFile(g_pBitmapSurface, NULL, NULL,
        "image.bmp", NULL, D3DX_DEFAULT, 0, NULL);
    if (FAILED(g_hResult))
    {
        strcpy(g_szErrorMsg, "Couldn't load bitmap file.");
        PostQuitMessage(WM_QUIT);
    }

    return D3D_OK;
}

//////////////////////////////////////////////////////
// CleanUpDirect3D()
//////////////////////////////////////////////////////
```

```
void CleanUpDirect3D()
{
    if (g_pBitmapSurface)
        g_pBitmapSurface->Release();
    if (g_pDirect3DDevice)
        g_pDirect3DDevice->Release();
    if (g_pDirect3D)
        g_pDirect3D->Release();
}

//////////////////////////////////////////////////////
// Render()
//////////////////////////////////////////////////////
void Render()
{
    IDirect3DSurface8* pBackBuffer = NULL;
    g_hResult = g_pDirect3DDevice->GetBackBuffer(0,
        D3DBACKBUFFER_TYPE_MONO, &pBackBuffer);
    if (FAILED(g_hResult))
    {
        strcpy(g_szErrorMsg, "Error getting back buffer.");
        PostQuitMessage(WM_QUIT);
    }
    g_hResult = g_pDirect3DDevice->CopyRects(g_pBitmapSurface,
        NULL,0,pBackBuffer,NULL);
    if (FAILED(g_hResult))
    {
        strcpy(g_szErrorMsg, "Error copying image buffer.");
        PostQuitMessage(WM_QUIT);
    }
    g_pDirect3DDevice->Present(NULL, NULL, NULL, NULL);
    if (pBackBuffer)
        pBackBuffer->Release();
}
```

8. Copy the image.bmp file from the SurfaceApp directory on this book's CD-ROM to your SurfaceApp project's working directory, or supply a 640×480, 32-bit color bitmap of your own and name it image.bmp.

You can now compile and run the application. When you do, you should see the screen shown in Figure 6.11 (unless you used your own bitmap, in which case the image will be different). Press Esc to exit the program.

The Program Details

This program uses two techniques for error handling, one to handle errors before the program creates the Direct3D device and one for after. In the first case, the program doesn't really need to do anything special, because Direct3D initialization hasn't gotten far enough to affect the display. In that case, this type of error handling works just fine:

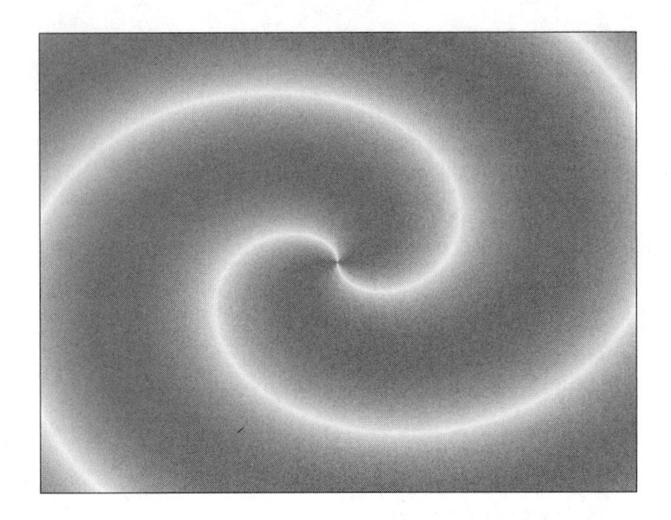

FIGURE 6.11
The running SurfaceApp application.

```
if (hResult != D3D_OK)
{
    MessageBox(g_hWnd,
        "Sorry. This program won't\nrun on your system.",
        "DirectX Error", MB_OK);
    return E_FAIL;
}
```

The message box appears on the screen without difficulty and by returning `E_FAIL` to `WinMain()`, the program never even enters its message loop.

Things get a lot trickier, though, once the application has created its Direct3D device object, because the display mode will have been changed to that required by your program, and, if the program's main loop has started, the `Render()` function will be constantly redrawing the screen.

The solution I came up with is to have two global variables, one for results returned from Direct3D methods and one to hold an error string. The program defines these variables like this:

```
HRESULT g_hResult = D3D_OK;
char g_szErrorMsg[256];
```

The Direct3D code in the program sets these values if an error occurs. It also calls the Windows API function `PostQuitMessage()`, which terminates the message loop and sends program execution back to `WinMain()`:

```
g_hResult = g_pDirect3DDevice->CreateImageSurface(640, 480,
    D3DFMT_X8R8G8B8, &g_pBitmapSurface);
if (FAILED(g_hResult))
{
```

```
        strcpy(g_szErrorMsg, "Error creating bitmap surface.");
        PostQuitMessage(WM_QUIT);
    }
```

All WinMain() has to do is check for the error value and display an error message if an error occurred. A call to the Windows API CloseWindow() ensures that the application's window stays out of the way:

```
CloseWindow(g_hWnd);
if (g_hResult != D3D_OK)
    DXTRACE_ERR(g_szErrorMsg, g_hResult);
```

One other important thing to notice about this program is the way it releases surfaces when it's done with them. In the Render() function, the program must release the back-buffer surface:

```
pBackBuffer->Release();
```

And in the CleanUpDirect3D() function, the program must release the bitmap surface:

```
if (g_pBitmapSurface)
    g_pBitmapSurface->Release();
```

Summary

And that concludes your lesson on Direct3D surfaces. Sure, there's a lot more to know, and you'll get to more of those details as you work your way through this book. For now, though, you should have a good understanding of how surfaces work and how you can use them to display images on the screen.

Q&A

Q. What if I have more than one bitmap I want to load into memory? Can I create more than one image surface?

A. Yes, you can create as many surfaces as your program requires, memory permitting. However, if you have a lot of small bitmaps, it's usually more efficient to group them together into a single bitmap and then transfer the rectangles you need from the bitmap. You'll see how to do this in Chapter 13, "Drawing the Game World."

Q. You hinted that a Direct3D program could have more than one back buffer? Why would I want to do this?

A. Having multiple back buffers can make a Direct3D program run more efficiently for reasons you don't understand yet. But, basically, having multiple back buffers enables the program to render its displays faster. You won't need multiple back buffers for any of the programs in this book. However, you will learn more about how back buffers work in Chapter 9, "Programming Direct3D Animation."

Q. You mentioned texture surfaces in this chapter, but you don't say anything more about them? What are they?

A. Textures are small images often used to provide greater details to objects in a 3D world. Textures are also useful for creating images that have transparent portions, which is how you'll use textures in this book. A texture surface is just a special surface used for holding textures, in the same way an image surface holds other types of images. You'll learn more about textures in Chapter 8, "Using Direct3D Textures."

Workshop

The workshop includes quiz questions to help gauge your grasp of the material. You'll find the answers to this quiz at the end of this chapter. Even if you feel that you totally understand the concepts presented here, you should work through the quiz anyway. The last section is an exercise or two that you might work through to help reinforce your learning.

Quiz

1. What is a surface in Direct3D programming?
2. What are the four types of surfaces you learned about in this chapter?
3. What type of surface does every Direct3D application have?
4. What is a back buffer used for?
5. If you wanted to load a bitmap into memory, what method would you call to create a surface for the image?
6. What Direct3D function loads an image from a disk into a surface?
7. What method do you call to get a pointer to a back buffer?
8. What method do you call to copy image data from one surface to another?
9. Why is it often difficult to display message boxes in a Direct3D application?
10. What does the `DXTRACE_ERR()` macro do?

Exercises

1. Load up this chapter's sample program, and locate the `InitFullScreenDirect3D()` function. Change the first `D3DFMT_X8R8G8B8` in the call to `CheckDeviceType()` to `D3DFMT_A8R8G8B8`. The line should then look like this:

```
HRESULT hResult = g_pDirect3D->CheckDeviceType(D3DADAPTER_DEFAULT,
    D3DDEVTYPE_HAL, D3DFMT_A8R8G8B8, D3DFMT_X8R8G8B8, FALSE);
```

Run the program. Can you explain what happens?

2. Reverse the changes you made in the first exercise. Now change the 640 in the line `D3DPresentParams.BackBufferWidth = 640` to 670. Run the program. What happens? Why?

Answers for Day 5

Quiz

1. What is a surface in Direct3D programming?

   A surface is an area of memory in which a Direct3D application can store graphical data.

2. What are the four types of surfaces you learned about in this chapter?

   The primary, back-buffer, image, and texture surfaces.

3. What type of surface does every Direct3D application have?

   A primary surface, which holds the graphical data displayed on the screen.

4. What is a back buffer used for?

   You use a back buffer to draw a display out of view of the user.

5. If you wanted to load a bitmap into memory, what method would you call to create a surface for the image?

   You would call the Direct3D device object's `CreateImageSurface()` method.

6. What Direct3D function loads an image from disk into a surface?

   The `D3DXLoadSurfaceFromFile()` utility function does the trick.

7. What method do you call to get a pointer to a back buffer?

   You call the Direct3D device object's `GetBackBuffer()` method.

8. What method do you call to copy image data from one surface to another?

   You call the Direct3D device object's `CopyRects()` method.

9. Why is it often difficult to display message boxes in a Direct3D application?

   Because the screen is usually being continually redrawn.

10. What does the `DXTRACE_ERR()` macro do?

    It displays a DirectX error message.

Exercises

1. Load up this chapter's sample program, and locate the `InitFullScreenDirect3D()` function. Change the first `D3DFMT_X8R8G8B8` in the call to `CheckDeviceType()` to `D3DFMT_A8R8G8B8`. The line should then look like this:

   ```
   HRESULT hResult = g_pDirect3D->CheckDeviceType(D3DADAPTER_DEFAULT,
       D3DDEVTYPE_HAL, D3DFMT_A8R8G8B8, D3DFMT_X8R8G8B8, FALSE);
   ```

   Run the program. Can you explain what happens?

   When the program can't create the Direct3D device object, the error-handling routine displays a message box, exits the function, and returns to `WinMain()`, where the application skips the message loop and terminates. (By the way, the reason the call to `CheckDeviceType()` fails is that the device pixel format cannot have an alpha channel, which is what that A in D3DFMT_A8R8G8B8 specifies.)

2. Reverse the changes you made in the first exercise. Now change the 640 in the line `D3DPresentParams.BackBufferWidth = 640` to 670. Run the program. What happens? Why?

   Again, the program causes an error because there is no display mode that is 670 pixels wide. Now, however, the program has to deal with the fact that the Direct3D device has been created and the screen mode has been set by the program. So, the function sets the error string and sends a `WM_QUIT` message to get out of the program's message loop. Back at `WinMain()`, the program closes the window and displays the error message box before terminating.

WEEK 1

DAY 7

Using Points, Vertices, and Graphics Primitives

One of the first things you need to learn when tackling a new graphics library is how to draw simple shapes, such as lines and rectangles. To perform these elementary drawing tasks with Direct3D, you need to know about points and vertices, which are the values that define the way a shape gets drawn, as well as what determines the shape's location in a 3D world. In this chapter, you will get experience using Direct3D to perform simple drawing. Specifically, you will learn:

- How points are expressed as coordinates
- How vertices define shapes
- The different types of primary shapes that Direct3D can draw
- How to create and use a vertex buffer
- How to draw shapes in a Direct3D program

Defining a Point

Everything starts with a point. This is true whether you're talking about a single dot on the screen or you're talking about a fully rendered 3D town in the latest edition of *Might & Magic*. A point is the basic building block for every shape and is the form of data that determines where that shape is located in a 3D world. You may remember, though, that I said that you won't be dealing too much with 3D graphics in this book. Still, because you're using Direct3D, you should understand a few basics.

A *point* is a single location on a graph or in 3D world and is denoted by X,Y coordinates in a 2D display or by X,Y,Z coordinates in a 3D display.

To see how points work, imagine those graphs that you used to deal with in high school math. Such a graph might have looked like Figure 7.1.

FIGURE 7.1

A simple graph from high school math.

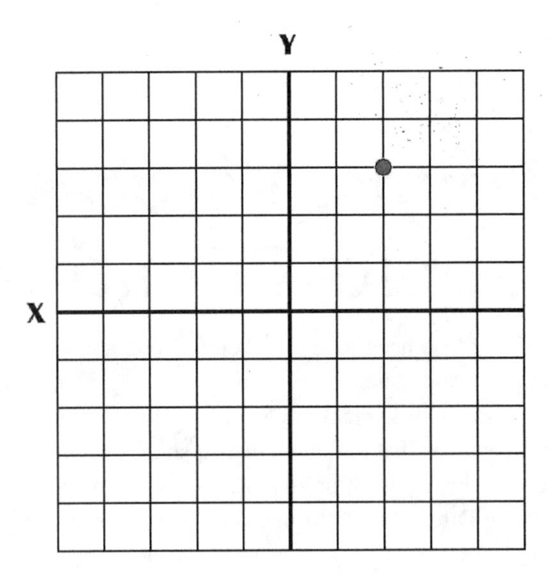

In this graph, the single point shown has a coordinate of 2,3, which means the point is located two units on the X axis and three units on the Y axis. You start counting from the center of the graph where the two axes cross. This location has a coordinate of 0,0 and is called the *origin*.

NEW TERM The *origin* is the location where all axes cross and is denoted by the coordinate 0,0 in a 2D display and by 0,0,0 in a 3D display.

To refresh your memory, points to the right of the origin on the X axis are positive and points to the left of the origin on the X axis are negative. Similarly, points above the origin on the Y axis are positive, and points below the origin on the Y axis are negative. With this in mind, you can see that the point in Figure 7.2 is located at -3,-2.

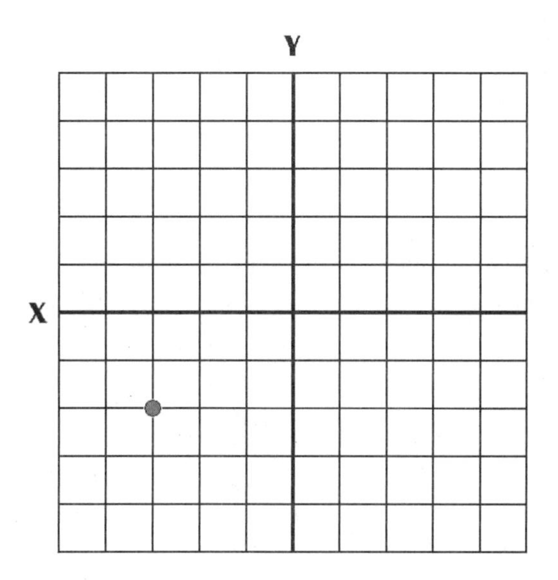

FIGURE 7.2
A point with negative coordinates.

No doubt this is the way you remember graphing points. With 3D graphics, though, things are a little different. First, you'll generally be interested only in positive coordinates, which limits you to the upper right quadrant of the graph. Also, a 3D coordinate system requires three values, not just two. This third value is called Z, and represents depth, by which I mean how far "behind" the screen a point appears to be. For our purposes in this book, the Z value will always be 0. So, you could say that the point in Figure 7.1 is located at 2,3,0.

Defining a Shape with Vertices

A point defines a single location somewhere in 3D space. You'd have a real job on your hand, however, if you had to use nothing but points to draw your displays. This is why 3D programmers use something called a *vertex*. A vertex is a point that defines where two edges of a shape come together. For example, a triangle has three vertices, as shown in Figure 7.3.

NEW TERM A *vertex* is a point located where the edges of a shape come together.

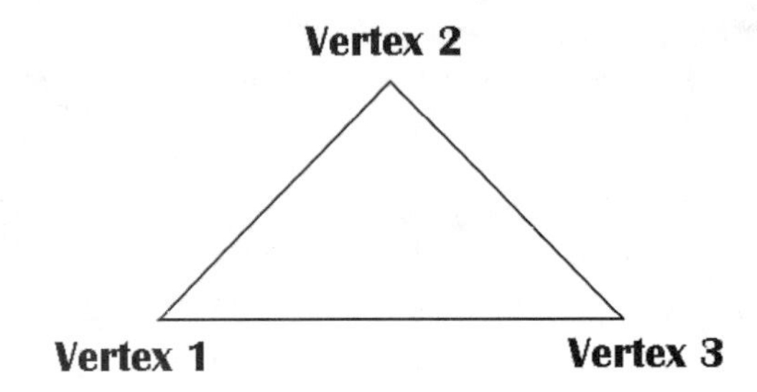

FIGURE 7.3
The vertices of a triangle.

Because a vertex is a special type of point, it's defined just like any other point, with X,Y,Z coordinates. So, if you wanted to draw a triangle on the screen, you might use coordinates like (1,1,0), (3,4,0), and (4,1,0), which would give you the triangle shown in Figure 7.4.

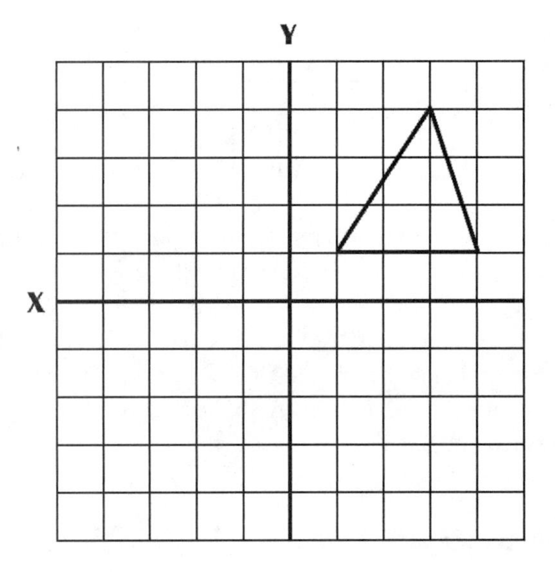

FIGURE 7.4
A triangle with vertices at (1,1,0), (3,4,0), and (4,1,0).

Using Vertex Buffers

All this talk of points and vertices brings us to this chapter's first Direct3D topic: vertex buffers. A *vertex buffer* is a block of memory that contains the vertices needed to draw a shape. For example, if you wanted to draw that triangle we've been talking about, you'd need to create a vertex buffer that holds the triangle's three vertices. Before creating the buffer, though, you need to tell Direct3D what your vertices are like.

NEW TERM A *vertex buffer* is a block of memory that contains the vertices needed to draw a shape.

Defining a Custom Vertex Type

Originally, I said that a vertex was a kind of point, a set of which defines a shape. Up until now, you've been thinking of a vertex as having the same types of values as a point, by which I mean X,Y,Z coordinates. With Direct3D, however, a vertex can be a whole lot more, can include all kinds of information about a point, including its color, texture coordinates, blending information, and more.

These values are managed in Direct3D using what's called *flexible vertex format* (FVF) flags. FVF flags are constants defined by Direct3D that specify the types of information contained in a vertex. When your program provides one or more of these flags, Direct3D can correctly interpret your vertex data and display it on the screen.

As an example, consider the simplest possible vertex, which is the 3D coordinates of a point. Direct3D defines the D3DFVF_XYZ flag to describe this type of vertex. You can represent such a vertex with this simple structure:

```
struct CUSTOMVERTEX
{
    FLOAT x, y, z;
};
```

This structure defines a data type for your vertices. To actually create a set of vertices that describe a shape, you might write something like this:

```
CUSTOMVERTEX triangleVertices[] =
{
    {320.0f,  120.0f, 0.0f,},
    {420.0f, 320.0f, 0.0f,},
    {220.0f, 320.0f, 0.0f,},
};
```

Here, you create an array of CUSTOMVERTEX structures. The three vertices defined here represent a triangle. However, the triangle's coordinates are such that the shape will appear in the center of a 640×480 screen. In other words, the vertices here represent screen coordinates rather than the type of coordinates you used with the graph examples. In the case of the screen, the origin is the upper-left corner, with positive X values going to the right and positive Y values going down, as shown in Figure 7.5.

These types of screen values are called *transformed coordinates*, which are simply values that tell Direct3D the exact screen coordinates at which you want a shape drawn.

FIGURE 7.5

Transformed screen coordinates.

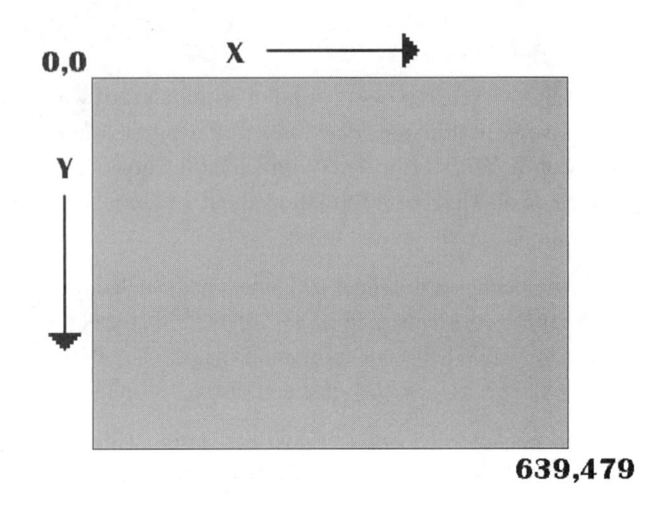

Note

Untransformed coordinates are coordinates that have not yet been processed by Direct3D in order to determine the position, shading, color, and so on of the final point. In other words, untransformed coordinates become transformed coordinates when Direct3D determines how to display a point on the screen using screen coordinates. In this book's programs, you'll never use untransformed coordinates, because you'll always tell Direct3D exactly where and how you want something drawn. 3D graphics programmers don't usually have this convenience, because they have to perform calculations on points that do things like rotate and stretch shapes.

Unfortunately, the simplest vertex type of `D3DFVF_XYZ` describes untransformed coordinates, so we need to specify a different type. In this case, a suitable vertex type would be `D3DFVF_XYZRHW`, which tells Direct3D that every vertex is represented by X,Y,Z values, as well as an RHW value.

What the heck is an RHW value? Believe me, until you get into actual 3D graphics programming, you don't want to know. (Still curious? RHW stands for "reciprocal of homogeneous W." Had enough yet?) For your purposes in this book, the RHW value will always be 1.0. So, here's what your new vertex data type looks like:

```
struct CUSTOMVERTEX
{
    FLOAT x, y, z, rhw;
};
```

And here's how you'd describe the vertices for the triangle:

```
CUSTOMVERTEX triangleVertices[] =
{
    {320.0f,  120.0f, 0.0f,, 1.0f},
    {420.0f, 320.0f, 0.0f, 1.0f},
    {220.0f, 320.0f, 0.0f, 1.0f},
};
```

You're getting close to defining the complete vertex type you need. You're missing only one thing: color. If Direct3D were to draw the shape you've defined here, you'd get a plain, white triangle. To use color, you need to add a color value to your vertex data type, like this:

```
struct CUSTOMVERTEX
{
    FLOAT x, y, z, rhw;
    DWORD color;
};
```

Now, you need to add a color value to your array of vertices. An easy way to do this is to use Direct3D's `D3DCOLOR_XRGB()` macro, which enables you to specify a color using its RGB values. Here's the end result:

```
CUSTOMVERTEX triangleVertices[] =
{
    {320.0f,  120.0f, 0.0f, 1.0f, D3DCOLOR_XRGB(255,0,0),},
    {420.0f, 320.0f, 0.0f, 1.0f, D3DCOLOR_XRGB(0,255,0),},
    {220.0f, 320.0f, 0.0f, 1.0f, D3DCOLOR_XRGB(0,0,255),},
};
```

Each vertex of this triangle has been assigned a color, either red, green, or blue. To describe this type of vertex to Direct3D, you need two FVF flags ORed together, like this:

```
D3DFVF_XYZRHW | D3DFVF_DIFFUSE
```

The `D3DFVF_DIFFUSE` flag tells Direct3D that you're using color values along with the X, Y, Z, and RHW values.

Creating the Vertex Buffer

You now have your custom vertex data type defined, and you have created an array of vertices that represent a triangle with red, green, and blue points. The next step is to create a vertex buffer into which to store the values of the vertices. Your Direct3D device object defines the `CreateVertexBuffer()` method for exactly this task. Here's how Direct3D declares this method:

```
HRESULT CreateVertexBuffer(
  UINT Length,
  DWORD Usage,
  DWORD FVF,
  D3DPOOL Pool,
  IDirect3DVertexBuffer8** ppVertexBuffer
);
```

Here's what the method's five arguments mean:

- `Length`—The desired size of the buffer.
- `Usage`—Flags that specify how the buffer is to be used. In this book, you'll always use 0.
- `FVF`—The vertex format. This is where you use the values such as `D3DFVF_XYZRHW` and `D3DFVF_DIFFUSE`.
- `Pool`—A value that specifies memory usage for the buffer. In this book, you'll always use `D3DPOOL_DEFAULT`.
- `ppVertexBuffer`—The address where the method should store the pointer to the new vertex-buffer object.

In your programs, an actual call to `CreateVertexBuffer()` will look something like this:

```
IDirect3DVertexBuffer8* pVertexBuf = NULL;
HRESULT hResult = g_pDirect3DDevice->CreateVertexBuffer(
    3*sizeof(CUSTOMVERTEX), 0, D3DFVF_XYZRHW | D3DFVF_DIFFUSE,
    D3DPOOL_DEFAULT, &pVertexBuf);
if(FAILED(hResult))
{
    DXTRACE_ERR("Error creating vertex buffer", hResult);
    return;
}
```

As you can see, the type of pointer returned by `CreateVertexBuffer()` is `IDirect3DVertexBuffer8`. This is the interface that represents vertex-buffer objects.

Loading the Vertex Buffer

The last step in creating your vertex buffer is loading the vertex data into the buffer. Before you can do that, though, you must lock the buffer so that Direct3D knows to leave it alone while you're working with it. You lock the buffer by calling the vertex-buffer object's `Lock()` method, which Direct3D declares like this:

```
HRESULT Lock(
  UINT OffsetToLock,
  UINT SizeToLock,
  BYTE** ppbData,
  DWORD Flags
);
```

Here's what the method's four arguments mean:

- *OffsetToLock*—Index of the first byte to lock. In this book, you'll always use 0.
- *SizeToLock*—The number of bytes to lock. In this book, you'll always use 0, which tells Direct3D to lock the entire buffer, no matter its size.
- *ppbData*—The address where the method should store the pointer to the vertex buffer's data.
- *Flags*—A set of flags that specify how to lock the buffer. In this book, you'll always use 0.

Putting this all together, your own call to `Lock()` might look like this:

```
VOID* pVertices;
hResult = pVertexBuf->Lock(0, 0, (BYTE**)&pVertices, 0);
if(FAILED(hResult))
{
    DXTRACE_ERR("Error locking vertex buffer", hResult);
    return;
}
```

With the vertex buffer locked, a quick call to `memcpy()` is all you need to transfer the data from your program into the buffer:

```
memcpy(pVertices, triangleVertices, sizeof(triangleVertices));
```

Last but not least, don't forget to unlock the vertex buffer by calling the buffer object's `Unlock()` method:

```
pVertexBuf->Unlock();
```

Drawing Graphics Primitives

You're finally ready to draw your triangle. To do so, you need to know about something called *graphics primitives*. The word *primitive* describes something in its most elementary state. A graphics primitive, then, is an elementary shape, such as a point, line, or triangle. 3D displays are made up of many thousands of graphics primitives that combine to create the illusion of one or more 3D objects.

NEW TERM A *graphics primitive* is an elementary shape, such as a point, line, or triangle.

Types of Graphics Primitives

Direct3D can draw six types of graphics primitives in sets called a list:

- Point lists—A list of individual points
- Line lists—A list of individual lines

- Line strips—A list of connected lines
- Triangle lists—A list of individual triangles
- Triangle strips—A list of connected triangles
- Triangle fans—A list of triangles connected into a fan shape

Believe it or not, using just these six graphics primitives, a Direct3D application can render any type of display it needs, from a simple cube to a detailed underground dungeon filled with horrific creatures.

However, because this is a book on using DirectX to program 2D games, you don't need to know about all these different graphics primitives. You'll need to use only one: a triangle list.

Rendering a Triangle List

This is where things get really tricky, where you're going to run into some new terms and discover that drawing a shape with Direct3D is nowhere as simple as it might be using traditional drawing functions such as the .NET Framework's `DrawRectangle()` method.

Direct3D can't just throw a shape up onto the screen, because it has a lot of work to do as it calculates how a 3D object will look on the screen. In order to perform these calculations, Direct3D needs some information from your application. In the case of drawing a graphics primitive, Direct3D must know at least the following:

- Where the vertices are stored
- How to shade the shape
- What type of shape to draw

To tell Direct3D where the vertices are stored, your program calls the Direct3D device object's `SetStreamSource()` method, which Direct3D declares like this:

```
HRESULT SetStreamSource(
  UINT StreamNumber,
  IDirect3DVertexBuffer8* pStreamData,
  UINT Stride
);
```

Here's what the method's three arguments mean:

- *`StreamNumber`*—The data stream to use. You'll usually provide 0 for this argument.
- *`pStreamData`*—A pointer to the vertex-buffer object that contains the vertices to render.
- *`Stride`*—The size of each set of vertex data.

So, in your program, the call to `SetStreamSource()` might look like this:

```
g_pDirect3DDevice->SetStreamSource(0, pVertexBuf,
    sizeof(CUSTOMVERTEX));
```

Next, you need to tell Direct3D how to apply shading to the graphics primitive. You do this by calling the Direct3D device object's `SetVertexShader()` method, which Direct3D declares like this:

```
HRESULT SetVertexShader(
  DWORD FVF
);
```

The `FVF` argument is the value that holds the vertex-format flags. The actual call in your program, then, will look something like this:

```
g_pDirect3DDevice->SetVertexShader(D3DFVF_XYZRHW | D3DFVF_DIFFUSE);
```

Finally, you're ready to draw the shape. To do this, call the Direct3D device object's `DrawPrimitive()` method, which Direct3D declares as follows:

```
HRESULT DrawPrimitive(
  D3DPRIMITIVETYPE PrimitiveType,
  UINT StartVertex,
  UINT PrimitiveCount
);
```

Here's what the method's three arguments mean:

- *`PrimitiveType`*—One of the constants that specify primitive types. For a triangle list, use `D3DPT_TRIANGLELIST`.
- *`StartVertex`*—The vertex at which to start drawing. In this book, you'll always use 0 for this argument.
- *`PrimtiveCount`*—The number of shapes to draw. In a triangle list, each shape is represented by three vertices, so if you had to draw two rectangles, your vertex buffer would have six vertices, and you'd set this argument to 2.

To draw a single triangle, the call to `DrawPrimitive()` might look like this:

```
g_pDirect3DDevice->DrawPrimitive(D3DPT_TRIANGLELIST, 0, 1);
```

There's only one last detail to consider. Before you start drawing a Direct3D display, you must call the Direct3D device object's `BeginScene()` method, and when you're finished drawing, you must call the `EndScene()` method, after which you call `Present()`. Here's what the whole process looks like:

```
g_pDirect3DDevice->SetStreamSource(0, pVertexBuf,
    sizeof(CUSTOMVERTEX));
g_pDirect3DDevice->SetVertexShader(D3DFVF_XYZRHW | D3DFVF_DIFFUSE);
```

```
g_pDirect3DDevice->BeginScene();
g_pDirect3DDevice->DrawPrimitive(D3DPT_TRIANGLELIST, 0, 1);
g_pDirect3DDevice->EndScene();
g_pDirect3DDevice->Present( NULL, NULL, NULL, NULL );
```

Building the TriangleApp Application

You're now ready to build a complete program that demonstrates the concepts you've learned in this chapter. Follow the steps outlined in the following sections to complete this process.

Creating the Basic Project

Perform the following steps to get the main Direct3D application project started:

1. Start a new empty Win32 project named TriangleApp.
2. On the Project menu, select the Add New Item command. The Add New Item dialog box appears.
3. Add a new C++ File (.cpp) named TriangleApp.cpp.
4. Copy the contents of the BasicDirect3D.cpp file (from Chapter 5) into the new TriangleApp code window.
5. Change the name in the comment at the top of the file to TriangleApp.
6. In the `RegisterWindowClass()` function change `wc.lpszClassName = "Direct3DApp"` to `wc.lpszClassName = "TriangleApp"`.
7. In the `CreateAppWindow()` function, change "Direct3DApp" to "TriangleApp", and then change "Basic Direct3D Application" to "Triangle Application".

Adding the DirectX References

Next, you need to tell the program where the required DirectX header files and libraries are located. To do that, follow these steps:

1. Near the top of the program, right after the line `#include <d3d8.h>`, add the following include directives:
   ```
   #include <d3dx8tex.h>
   #include <dxerr8.h>
   ```
2. Right-click the project's name in the Solution Explorer, and select Properties from the menu that appears. The TriangleApp Property Pages dialog box appears.
3. Click the C/C++ selection in the left pane, and select General from the displayed choices.

3. In the Additional Include Directories box, enter the path to the DirectX 8.1 SDK's include folder. If you installed the SDK using the default settings, this path should be C:\DXSDK\include.
4. Click the Linker selection in the left pane, and select General from the displayed choices.
5. In the Additional Library Directories box, enter the path to the DirectX 8.1 SDK's library folder. If you installed the SDK using the default settings, this path should be C:\DXSDK\lib.
6. Click the Linker's Input selection in the left pane.
7. In the Additional Dependencies box in the right pane, enter `d3d8.lib`, `d3dx8.lib`, and `dxerr8.lib`.
8. Compile and run the application to be sure it works. When the blue screen appears, press Escape to exit the application.

Adding Source Code

Now all you have to do is add the Direct3D code that'll get your triangle up on the screen. Most of the changes you need to make are in the `Render()` function, so just replace the current `Render()` with this one:

```
//////////////////////////////////////////////////////
// Render()
//////////////////////////////////////////////////////
void Render()
{
    CUSTOMVERTEX triangleVertices[] =
    {
        {400.0f,  180.0f, 0.0f, 1.0f, D3DCOLOR_XRGB(255,0,0),},
        {500.0f, 380.0f, 0.0f, 1.0f, D3DCOLOR_XRGB(0,255,0),},
        {300.0f, 380.0f, 0.0f, 1.0f, D3DCOLOR_XRGB(0,0,255),},
    };

    IDirect3DVertexBuffer8* pVertexBuf = NULL;
    HRESULT hResult = g_pDirect3DDevice->CreateVertexBuffer(
        3*sizeof(CUSTOMVERTEX), 0, D3DFVF_XYZRHW | D3DFVF_DIFFUSE,
        D3DPOOL_DEFAULT, &pVertexBuf);

    if(FAILED(hResult))
    {
        DXTRACE_ERR("Error creating vertex buffer", hResult);
        return;
    }

    VOID* pVertices;
    hResult = pVertexBuf->Lock(0, 0, (BYTE**)&pVertices, 0);
```

```
    if(FAILED(hResult))
    {
        DXTRACE_ERR("Error locking vertex buffer", hResult);
        return;
    }
    memcpy(pVertices, triangleVertices, sizeof(triangleVertices));
    pVertexBuf->Unlock();

    g_pDirect3DDevice->Clear(0, NULL, D3DCLEAR_TARGET,
        D3DCOLOR_XRGB(0,0,0), 1.0f, 0 );
    g_pDirect3DDevice->SetStreamSource(0, pVertexBuf,
        sizeof(CUSTOMVERTEX));
    g_pDirect3DDevice->SetVertexShader(D3DFVF_XYZRHW | D3DFVF_DIFFUSE);

    g_pDirect3DDevice->BeginScene();
    g_pDirect3DDevice->DrawPrimitive(D3DPT_TRIANGLELIST, 0, 1);
    g_pDirect3DDevice->EndScene();

    g_pDirect3DDevice->Present( NULL, NULL, NULL, NULL );

    if (pVertexBuf)
        pVertexBuf->Release();
}
```

Finally, add the declaration for the `CUSTOMVERTEX` structure near the top of the program, right after the global variables:

```
struct CUSTOMVERTEX
{
    FLOAT x, y, z, rhw;
    DWORD color;
};
```

You can now compile and run the application. When you do, you should see the screen shown in Figure 7.6. Press Esc to exit the program.

There's not much to discuss in this program. Everything you need to know has already been covered. However, why do you suppose that the colors of the triangle's three vertices blend together toward the center of the triangle? The truth is that these are more than colors. They're actually a lighting effect. Specifically, it's as if you are shining red, green, and blue lights on the triangle, one color on each point of the triangle. Direct3D uses its shading engine to determine how the three lights blend across the surface of the shape. Pretty cool, huh?

One other thing: notice how the program calls the vertex-buffer object's `Release()` method when it's through with it. Most Direct3D objects require that you release them in this way.

FIGURE 7.6
The TriangleApp application.

Summary

When you want to draw shapes using Direct3D, you need to define vertices and then combine those vertices into shapes. You then tell Direct3D where each vertex is located in 3D space, so that it can draw the shape properly. When you start working on this book's main game program, you'll use these techniques as the basis for displaying objects with transparent areas. To do this, you also need to know about textures, which is the subject of the next chapter.

Q&A

Q. What kinds of operations does Direct3D perform on a vertex when it processes untransformed coordinates into transformed coordinates?

A. There are tons of operations that must be performed, but the most obvious ones are the major 3D transformations named translation, rotation, and scaling. Translation is the process of moving a point from one location to another, rotation is the process of rotating a point around the origin, and scaling is the process of changing the size of a object (or, more accurately, changing the distances between vertices). Direct3D must also perform a number of projections. For example, the perspective projection determines how a 3D object looks when viewed from a given position and angle. Relax, though: You don't need to know any of that 3D stuff for this book.

Q. So, a vertex can hold not only a set of coordinates, but also color information? What other types of vertex data will I need to use in this book?

A. The only other type of vertex data you'll learn about is texture coordinates, which determine how Direct3D applies a texture to a shape. A texture is nothing more than an image that Direct3D can paint onto a shape's surface to make the shape look more detailed.

Q. How can a system that can draw only points, lines, and triangles possible create the great 3D displays that many of today's games have?

A. Easy! Okay, maybe not easy. Every shape can be created by a set of polygons, of which triangles are the simplest example. The trick is that these polygons are very small, and a program uses thousands, or even millions, of them to create a detailed image. You know that your screen's display is made up of many rectangular dots called pixels, right? Well, a rectangle is a polygon. The big difference between your screen and a 3D world is that third dimension, which means that polygons are not always drawn on the same plane as your 2D screen, but rather can be rotated with respect to any of the three axes, X, Y, and Z.

Q. Exactly why does a program have to lock a vertex buffer before loading data into it?

A. Direct3D, just like Windows, likes to fool around with stuff behind your back. When you create an object like a vertex buffer, you have no idea where in memory the buffer is located. Worse, you never know when Direct3D may decide to move the buffer somewhere else. When you lock the buffer, you're telling Direct3D to leave it alone until you unlock the buffer. Anyway, locking the buffer is the only way to get the buffer's actual address in memory.

Workshop

The workshop includes quiz questions to help gauge your grasp of the material. You'll find the answers to this quiz at the end of this chapter. Even if you feel that you totally understand the concepts presented here, you should work through the quiz anyway. The last section is an exercise or two that you might work through to help reinforce your learning.

Quiz

1. What is a point?
2. What is a vertex?
3. How do vertices define shapes?
4. What is a vertex buffer?

5. What are two types of information that you can store in a vertex?
6. What are transformed coordinates?
7. What method do you call to create a vertex buffer?
8. What do you have to do to load a vertex buffer with data?
9. What is a graphics primitive? Give three examples supported by Direct3D.
10. What is a vertex stream source?
11. What method do you call to tell Direct3D how you want a shape shaded?
12. What method do you call to tell draw one or more graphics primitives?
13. What methods do you call before and after rendering a display?

Exercises

1. Modify this chapter's program so that it displays a completely red triangle.
2. Modify the program so that it displays its triangle as far into the upper-left corner of the screen as it can, without any of the triangle being off the screen. Figure 7.7 shows the results.

FIGURE 7.7
A triangle in the upper-left corner.

3. Here's an extra-hard challenge for you: Modify the program so that it draws three triangles on the screen. One triangle should be red and located in the screen's

upper-left corner, one should be green and located in the center of the screen, and the last should be blue and located in the lower-right corner. Figure 7.8 shows the results.

FIGURE 7.8
Three triangles on the screen.

Answers for Day 5

Quiz

1. What is a point?

   A point specifies an exact location in a graph or a 3D world. For your purposes in this book, you define a point with X, Y, and Z coordinates.

2. What is a vertex?

   A vertex is a point that defines where the edges of a shape come together.

3. How do vertices define shapes?

   The vertices define the locations between which Direct3D draws the edges of a shape.

4. What is a vertex buffer?

   An area of memory in which a program stores the vertices that define a set of shapes. In Direct3D programming, a vertex buffer is an object of the `IDirect3DVertexBuffer8` interface.

5. What are two types of information that you can store in a vertex?

   Coordinates and color. A vertex can also hold other types of information, such as the texture coordinates you learn about in Chapter 8.

6. What are transformed coordinates?

   Transformed coordinates represent the exact screen locations at which Direct3D should draw the components of a display.

7. What method do you call to create a vertex buffer?

   The Direct3D device object's `CreateVertexBuffer()` method.

8. What do you have to do to load a vertex buffer with data?

   Lock the buffer with the vertex-buffer object's `Lock()` method, copy the data into the buffer, and then unlock the buffer with the vertex-buffer object's `Unlock()` method.

9. What is a graphics primitive? Give three examples supported by Direct3D.

   A graphics primitive is an elementary shape. Direct3D can draw points, lines, and triangles.

10. What is a vertex stream source?

    A stream is just a flow of data, so a vertex stream is a flow of vertex data. The vertex stream source is the vertex-buffer object that Direct3D will use to draw a shape.

11. What method do you call to tell Direct3D how you want a shape shaded?

    The Direct3D device object's `SetVertexShader()` method.

12. What method do you call to tell Direct3D to draw one or more graphics primitives?

    The Direct3D device object's `DrawPrimitive()` method.

13. What methods do you call before and after rendering a display?

    The Direct3D device object's `BeginScene()` and `EndScene()` methods.

Exercises

1. Modify this chapter's program so that it displays a completely red triangle.

   Just change the color values of the vertices so that all three are red. Here's what the vertex array will look like:

```
CUSTOMVERTEX triangleVertices[] =
{
    {400.0f,  180.0f, 0.0f, 1.0f, D3DCOLOR_XRGB(255,0,0),},
    {500.0f, 380.0f, 0.0f, 1.0f, D3DCOLOR_XRGB(255,0,0),},
    {300.0f, 380.0f, 0.0f, 1.0f, D3DCOLOR_XRGB(255,0,0),},
};
```

2. Modify the program so that it displays its triangle as far into the upper-left corner of the screen as it can, without any of the triangle being off the screen.

   Again, you have to modify the vertex array, this time giving it new coordinates for each of the vertices. The result should look like this:

```
CUSTOMVERTEX triangleVertices[] =
{
    {100.0f,  0.0f, 0.0f, 1.0f, D3DCOLOR_XRGB(255,0,0),},
    {200.0f, 200.0f, 0.0f, 1.0f, D3DCOLOR_XRGB(255,0,0),},
    {0.0f, 200.0f, 0.0f, 1.0f, D3DCOLOR_XRGB(255,0,0),},
};
```

3. Here's an extra-hard challenge for you: Modify the program so that it draws three triangles on the screen. One triangle should be red and located in the screen's upper-left corner, one should be green and located in the center of the screen, and the last should be blue and located in the lower-right corner.

   First, you need to define vertices for three triangles. Your vertex array will look like this:

```
CUSTOMVERTEX triangleVertices[] =
{
    {100.0f,  0.0f, 0.0f, 1.0f, D3DCOLOR_XRGB(255,0,0),},
    {200.0f, 200.0f, 0.0f, 1.0f, D3DCOLOR_XRGB(255,0,0),},
    {0.0f, 200.0f, 0.0f, 1.0f, D3DCOLOR_XRGB(255,0,0),},
    {400.0f,  180.0f, 0.0f, 1.0f, D3DCOLOR_XRGB(0,255,0),},
    {500.0f, 380.0f, 0.0f, 1.0f, D3DCOLOR_XRGB(0,255,0),},
    {300.0f, 380.0f, 0.0f, 1.0f, D3DCOLOR_XRGB(0,255,0),},
    {700.0f,  380.0f, 0.0f, 1.0f, D3DCOLOR_XRGB(0,0,255),},
    {800.0f, 580.0f, 0.0f, 1.0f, D3DCOLOR_XRGB(0,0,255),},
    {600.0f, 580.0f, 0.0f, 1.0f, D3DCOLOR_XRGB(0,0,255),},
};
```

   Next, you must change the call to `CreateVertexBuffer()` so that it creates a buffer of the right size:

```
HRESULT hResult = g_pDirect3DDevice->CreateVertexBuffer(
   9*sizeof(CUSTOMVERTEX), 0, D3DFVF_XYZRHW | D3DFVF_DIFFUSE,
   D3DPOOL_DEFAULT, &pVertexBuf);
```

   Finally, you must change the call to `DrawPrimitive()` so that it draws three shapes instead of just one:

```
g_pDirect3DDevice->DrawPrimitive(D3DPT_TRIANGLELIST, 0, 3);
```

WEEK 1

In Review

As a game-programming language, you may want to choose C++ for several reasons. First, C++ is one of the most powerful languages in existence. Also, most professional game programmers use C++. Moreover, a C++ programming environment, like Visual C++ .NET, provides all the tools you need to develop, test, and release your software. C++'s object-oriented features enable you to organize your source code into logical, self-contained modules. Finally, C++ is the language of choice for Windows development.

To write computer games that people will want to play, you must gain some expertise in the related areas of programming. These areas represent the elements of game programming: game design, graphic design, sound generation, controls and interfaces, image handling, animation, algorithms, artificial intelligence, and game testing.

To create games, you need to have some expertise with several development tools. These include a programming language and development environment, a paint program, and a sound editor. You may also need additional hardware, such as recorders and microphones.

Every DirectX game program starts with a basic Windows application. Although programming a full-fledged Windows application is a complex process, your DirectX games will need to use only a few Windows API functions and respond to only a couple Windows messages. Because of this, you can usually use the same basic Windows application as the starting point for any game. About all you need to know about

Windows programming is how to write the `WinMain()` function, how to create and register a window class, how to display a window, how to process Windows messages, and how to build a Windows application with Visual Studio .NET.

Microsoft decided to remove DirectDraw from DirectX as a separate technology and instead incorporate it fully into Direct3D. In fact, not only is DirectDraw fully subsumed into Direct3D, with the combined technology being named DirectX Graphics, but it is now not possible to directly access DirectDraw. Direct3D now uses DirectDraw behind the scenes, out of view of the programmer. So, if you want to write a 2D game, you have to use Direct3D, which, although it provides some cool abilities that you don't have in DirectDraw, requires a whole new way to put together your 2D game programs.

Every Direct3D program has a few things it has to do to get started. You'll face this overhead with every Direct3D program you write. Until you learn to do this stuff, you can't do anything else with Direct3D. Specifically, you must know how to create a Direct3D object, how to create a Direct3D device object, how to manage display modes and pixel formats, how to check for device availability, and how to clear a Direct3D display.

Surfaces are an important topic to Direct3D programmers, because surfaces enable applications to store and manipulate graphics in a number of ways. A surface is nothing more than an area of memory in which you can store graphical information. For example, the stuff you see on the screen or in a window is stored in a surface, as are the images you may need to build that display. To handle surfaces, you need to know the different types of surfaces, how to create and access surfaces, and how to load graphical data into a surface.

One of the first things you need to learn when tackling a new graphics library is how to draw simple shapes, such as lines and rectangles. To perform these elementary drawing tasks with Direct3D, you need to know about points and vertices, which are the values that define the way a shape gets drawn, as well as what determines the shape's location in a 3D world. Specifically, you need to learn how points are expressed as coordinates, how vertices define shapes, about the different types of primary shapes that Direct3D can draw, how to create and use a vertex buffer, and how to draw shapes in a Direct3D program.

WEEK 2

At a Glance

In Week 2, you study a few more Direct3D topics before getting started on this book's big project, an old-style role-playing game named The Adventures of Jasper Bookman. You start off in Day 8 by learning how to use textures in your programs to create graphical images with transparent areas. Day 9 continues with some study of the art of animation using Direct3D back buffers. Day 10 introduces you to various ways of creating sound in your games. Most importantly, you learn to use DirectSound to play sound effects.

In Day 11, you start putting together the role-playing game, *The Adventures of Jasper Bookman*. Your first step is to create the JBookman project. Then, you program the main Windows application and add a couple of classes for the game engine and Direct3D. In Day 12, you continue the JBookman project by exploring the data used in the program. Day 13 gets the game up on the screen, as you learn to draw a game world using small images called tiles. Finally, in Day 14, you add animation to the game.

WEEK 2

DAY 8

Using Direct3D Textures

Now that you can draw graphics primitives, you need to know how to liven them up by applying textures. This enables you to take advantage of a handy graphics programming technique called transparency. Guess what you'll be doing in this chapter? Specifically, in this chapter you will learn:

- What a texture is
- How textures implement transparency
- What alpha values do
- How to handle texture coordinates
- How to load and display textures

What the Heck Is a Texture?

Back in the early days of game programming, developers had to explicitly draw every graphical detail of their game's display. Because the graphical tools of the time were rudimentary (compared to today's), the realism of the game world suffered. A brick wall, for example, ended up looking only like a vague representation of a real brick wall.

This lack of realism was further complicated when programmers started to develop 3D games. Why? Because in a 3D world, every image on the screen needs to be twisted and turned, not to mention scaled, depending on the viewpoint of the player. Such manipulations require some hefty math and more complicated drawing procedures when having to render something like that aforementioned brick wall.

Then someone had a brilliant idea: Enable the programmer to draw a brick wall by just creating the basic shape of the wall (probably a rectangle) and then adding the details by applying a bitmap to the rectangle. Functions of the graphics library could be responsible for applying the bitmap, much like a decal, so that the bitmap would always look right from any angle in the 3D world.

Today, this decal-like bitmap is called a *texture*. The technique of using textures is immensely important in today's games, especially games of the 3D variety, because it enables game programmers to create extremely detailed game worlds, without having to do much more than provide a shape and a texture image to apply to the shape.

NEW TERM A *texture* is a bitmap image that's applied much like a decal to a shape in a 3D world in order to give the shape greater graphical detail.

Direct3D, Textures, and Transparency

As you can guess, Direct3D provides extensive support for texturing. However, you may recall that this is not a book on 3D game programming. It's a book on 2D game programming using Direct3D. You still need to know about textures, though, because it's through the abilities of textures that you can create images with transparent areas.

Transparency is important because it enables a graphics application to display bitmaps that appear to be non-rectangular or that have areas that allow the background to show through. That is, the transparent areas of the bitmap don't appear on the screen. The process goes something like this:

1. You create a rectangular bitmap, using a specific color (pure black, with an RGB value of 0,0,0 is typical) to indicate the areas of the bitmap that you want to be transparent.
2. You tell Direct3D the transparent color you've chosen.
3. You tell Direct3D to draw the bitmap using transparency.
4. Direct3D draws the bitmap on the screen, ignoring every pixel in the bitmap that matches the transparent color.

With Direct3D and textures, though, the process is actually a little more complicated. This is because transparency is implemented through the use of *alpha values*. An alpha value is a value that tells Direct3D exactly how transparent a color is. Here are the rules:

- An alpha value of 255 specifies that the color is opaque and any pixel drawn in that color will completely obliterate the pixel over which it's drawn.
- An alpha value of 0 specifies that the color is completely transparent and any pixel of that color won't be drawn at all.
- Alpha values between 0 and 255 specify varying degrees of transparency and determine how the colors of the source color (the color that you're drawing) and destination color (the color over which you're drawing the source color) are mixed together.

NEW TERM An *alpha value* specifies the amount of transparency associated with a pixel.

Alpha values make transparency an even more powerful feature, enabling you to do very cool things. For example, you could have a rectangle that represents a window in your game world, and to give the effect of looking through glass, you could use alpha values to specify that you want most of the source colors (in this case, the scene outside the window) to show through the window, but with a slight blue tint.

In this book, though, you'll be concerned only with two types of transparency: fully opaque or fully transparent. Still, learning about textures is the first step towards implementing this important graphics programming technique.

Creating a Texture Surface

The first step in using a texture is, of course, to create in a paint program the bitmap you'll use for the texture. Once you do that, however, you must load the texture into your memory. You've already learned how to create image surfaces and how to load bitmaps into those surfaces. You follow a similar procedure to get a texture into memory. Specifically, you call the DirectX utility function `D3DXCreateTextureFromFileEx()`, which Direct3D declares like this:

```
HRESULT D3DXCreateTextureFromFileEx(
  LPDIRECT3DDEVICE8 pDevice,
  LPCTSTR pSrcFile,
  UINT Width,
  UINT Height,
  UINT MipLevels,
  DWORD Usage,
  D3DFORMAT Format,
  D3DPOOL Pool,
  DWORD Filter,
  DWORD MipFilter,
  D3DCOLOR ColorKey,
  D3DXIMAGE_INFO* pSrcInfo,
  PALETTEENTRY* pPalette,
  LPDIRECT3DTEXTURE8* ppTexture
);
```

Here's what all the arguments mean:

- *pDevice*—A pointer to the Direct3D device that's associated with the texture.
- *pSrcFile*—The path to the texture.
- *Width*—The width of the texture. Use D3DX_DEFAULT to use width specified in the file.
- *Height*—The height of the texture. Use D3DX_DEFAULT to use height specified in the file.
- *MipLevels*—The number of mip levels, something you won't need to worry about in this book. Just use the value 1 here.
- *Usage*—For your purposes in this book, always 0.
- *Format*—The texture's pixel format.
- *Pool*—The texture's memory class. For this book, you'll always use D3DPOOL_MANAGED.
- *Filter*—The type of filtering to use. You'll be using D3DX_DEFAULT.
- *MipFilter*—Another filtering setting for which you'll use D3DX_DEFAULT.
- *ColorKey*—The 32-bit color value that specifies the transparent color. This is in the format ARGB, so for solid black, you'd use the value 0xFF000000. (The FF is the alpha value, which is required here.)
- *pSrcInfo*—In this book, you'll always use NULL here.
- *pPalette*—Again, in this book, you'll always use NULL here.
- *ppTexture*—The address of a pointer to the texture object.

Are you scared yet? I'm quaking in my boots! Here's what a real call to D3DXCreateTextureFromFileEx() might look like in your program, along with the required error handling:

```
IDirect3DTexture8* g_pTexture;
g_hResult = D3DXCreateTextureFromFileEx(g_pDirect3DDevice,
    "Texture.bmp", D3DX_DEFAULT, D3DX_DEFAULT, 1, 0, D3DFMT_A8R8G8B8,
    D3DPOOL_MANAGED, D3DX_DEFAULT, D3DX_DEFAULT, 0xFF000000,
    NULL, NULL, &g_pTexture);
if(FAILED(g_hResult))
{
    strcpy(g_szErrorMsg, "Couldn't load texture file.");
    PostQuitMessage(WM_QUIT);
    return g_hResult;
}
```

If the call goes okay, the last argument will hold a pointer to a texture object, which, as you can see from the example, is an object of the IDirect3DTexture8 interface.

Understanding Texture Coordinates

A texture can be applied to any object (from now on, I will call such an object a *primitive*), no matter what the object's size compared with the texture. For this reason, textures need to be mapped onto their parent primitives. For example, suppose you have a texture bitmap that represents a section of that brick wall you read about earlier. Further, suppose that the texture bitmap's size in pixels is 512×256. Finally, suppose that the rectangle onto which you want to apply the texture is 1024×512, twice as big as the texture.

NEW TERM *Mapping* is the process of converting from one type of value to another. In this section, you're learning about converting texture coordinates to a destination primitive's coordinates.

Obviously, if you want the rectangle completely covered by the texture, Direct3D will have to stretch the texture as it applies it. In this case, the zeroth pixel will be mapped to the zeroth pixel of the rectangle, and the 512th pixel will be mapped to the 1024th pixel of the rectangle, with all the other pixels being somewhere in between.

You can think of this as meaning that 100% of the width and height of the texture will be applied to the rectangle. Another way to express percentages is with decimal numbers. For example, the decimal number 0.5 equals 50%, 0.75 equals 75%, 1.0 equals 100%, and so on. This is exactly the way that you tell Direct3D how to map your textures onto their primitives. These types of percentage values are called *texture coordinates*, and they are associated with each vertex of the object you want to texture.

NEW TERM *Texture coordinates* are expressed as decimal percentages that indicate the portion of the texture to be mapped to the primitive.

Vertices That Contain Texture Coordinates

Thinking back to what you leaned about vertex data, if you wanted to define a type of vertex that provided transformed X,Y,Z coordinates and texture coordinates, you'd define something like this:

```
struct CUSTOMVERTEX
{
    float x, y, z, rhw;
    float tu,tv;
};
```

Here, tu and tv are the texture coordinates associated with the vertex. Each vertex you define from this data type will have its own 3D coordinates and texture coordinates, which work together to tell Direct3D where to draw the primitive and what part of the texture to apply to the primitive. Of course, just as a single vertex doesn't define a primitive, neither does a single texture coordinate tell Direct3D how much of a texture to apply to the primitive. You might, then, define the vertices of a triangle like this:

```
CUSTOMVERTEX triangleVertices[] =
{
    {250.0f,  400.0f, 0.0f, 1.0f, 0.0f, 1.0f,},
    {250.0f, 200.0f, 0.0f, 1.0f, 0.0f, 0.0f,},
    {550.0f, 200.0f, 0.0f, 1.0f, 1.0f, 0.0f,},
};
```

Here, the first vertex is located at the transformed coordinate 250,400,0; the second is located at 250,200,0; and the third is located at 550,200,0. On an 800×600 screen, this gives you the triangle shown in Figure 8.1.

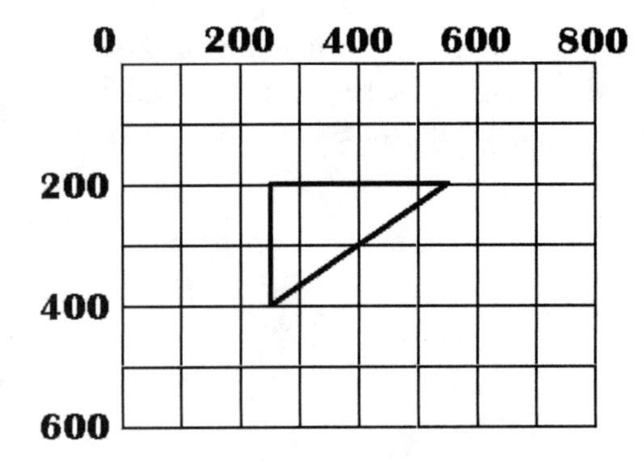

FIGURE 8.1

A transformed triangle on an 800×600 screen.

Now, look again at the defined vertices in the `triangleVertices[]` array. Notice that the first vertex is associated with a texture coordinate of 0.0,1.0. Moreover, notice that the second vertex has texture coordinates of 0.0,0.0; and the third vertex has texture coordinates of 1.0,0.0. Figure 8.2 illustrates how these texture coordinates relate to the triangle on the screen.

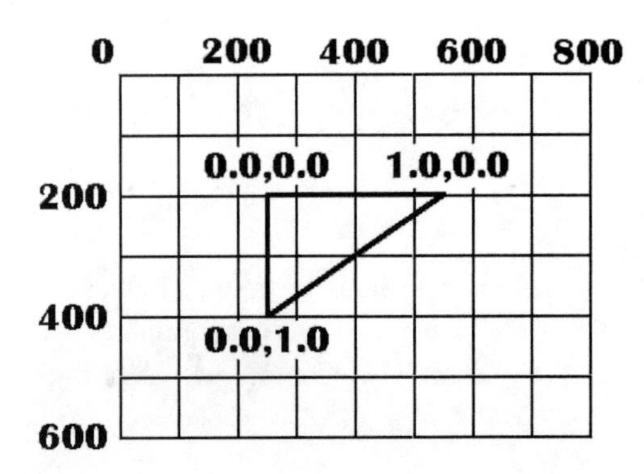

FIGURE 8.2

A transformed triangle showing texture coordinates.

The Texture Bitmap

Now, let's look at the texture bitmap that you want to apply to the triangle. Figure 8.3 shows the bitmap with its texture coordinates.

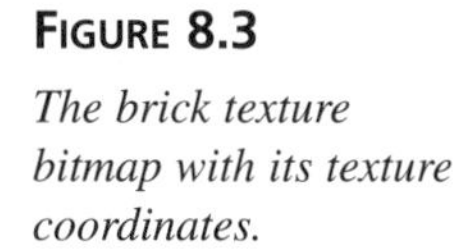

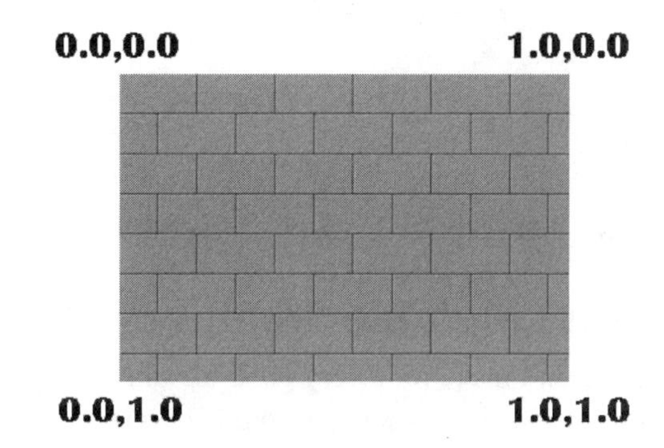

FIGURE 8.3
The brick texture bitmap with its texture coordinates.

When Direct3D gets the texture coordinates for your vertices, it can compare them to the texture and determine how to apply the texture to the shape defined by the vertices. Figure 8.4 shows the relationship the vertices have with the texture bitmap.

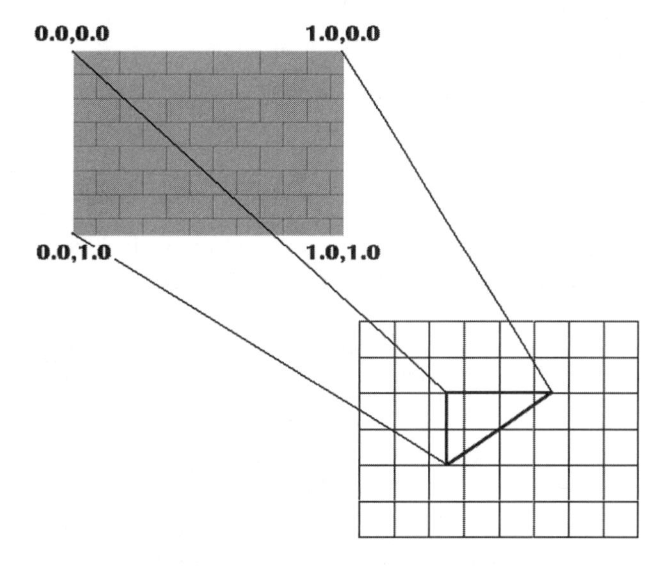

FIGURE 8.4
Mapping the texture using texture coordinates.

When Direct3D gets done with the fancy math, you end up with the image shown in Figure 8.5.

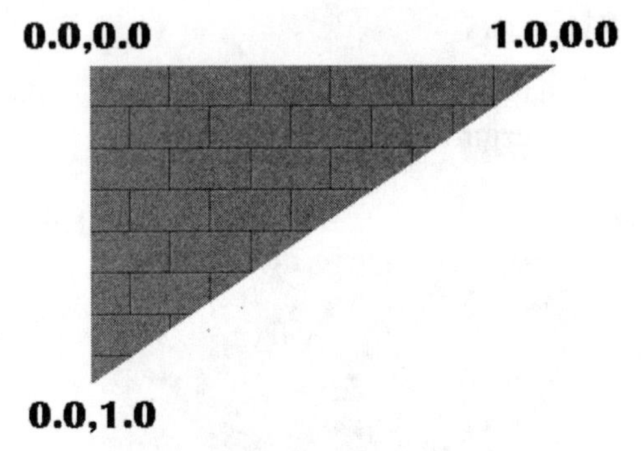

FIGURE 8.5
The final, textured triangle.

Texturing Across Multiple Primitives

Of course, a triangle doesn't make for a very good-looking wall. What you need is a rectangle. Luckily, it's easy to make a rectangle from two triangles. Here's what the vertices for the two rectangles look like:

```
CUSTOMVERTEX triangleVertices[] =
{
    {250.0f,  400.0f, 0.0f, 1.0f, 0.0f, 1.0f,},
    {250.0f, 200.0f, 0.0f, 1.0f, 0.0f, 0.0f,},
    {550.0f, 200.0f, 0.0f, 1.0f, 1.0f, 0.0f,},
    {250.0f,  400.0f, 0.0f, 1.0f, 0.0f, 1.0f,},
    {550.0f, 200.0f, 0.0f, 1.0f, 1.0f, 0.0f,},
    {550.0f,  400.0f, 0.0f, 1.0f, 1.0f, 1.0f,},
};
```

Figure 8.6 shows the two triangles as they appear on the screen, along with their texture coordinates. When Direct3D finishes rendering the two triangles, you get the image shown in Figure 8.7, except that in the figure I've overlaid the triangles so you can see how it all fits together. In the actual image, the black lines would not appear.

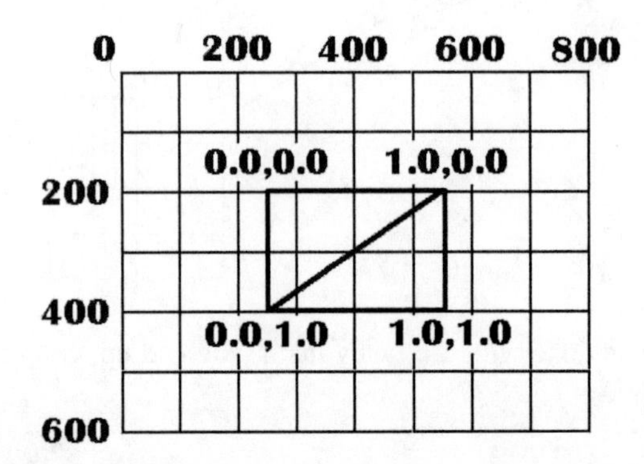

FIGURE 8.6
A rectangle made from two triangles.

FIGURE 8.7

The textured rectangle.

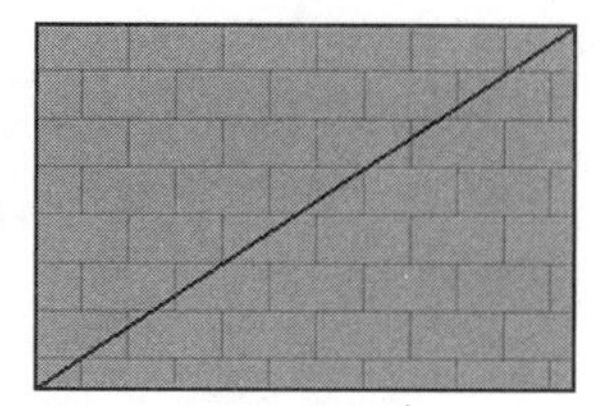

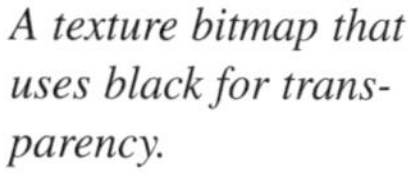

You may have noticed that two of the six vertices defined for the triangles are exactly the same. Direct3D provides a primitive type called a *triangle strip* that enables you to define two or more attached triangles without duplicating vertices. However, because none of the programs in this book have to render huge numbers of rectangles, the simpler rectangle-list primitive works just fine.

A Texture with a Transparent Area

The brick wall shown in Figure 8.7 looks pretty cool, but it doesn't prove anything about transparency. To see how transparency works, you need to replace part of the wall bitmap with pure black. (Actually, you can use any color, but all the examples of transparency in this book use black.) Figure 8.8 shows the new texture bitmap.

FIGURE 8.8

A texture bitmap that uses black for transparency.

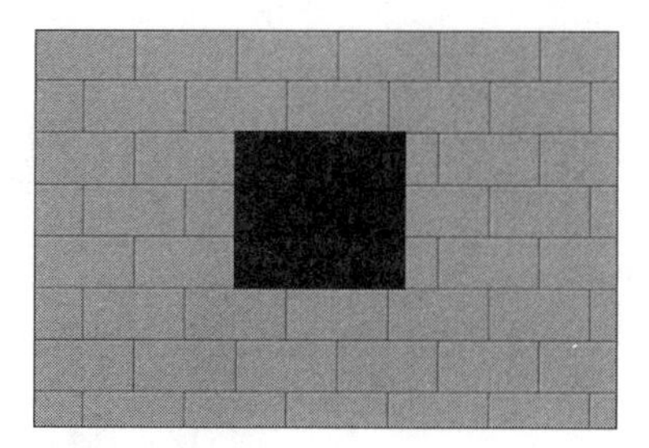

Once you get everything set up in your program correctly, when Direct3D draws the texture, it skips the black parts, allowing the background to show through. Figure 8.8 shows what you get when the texture is drawn over a background image.

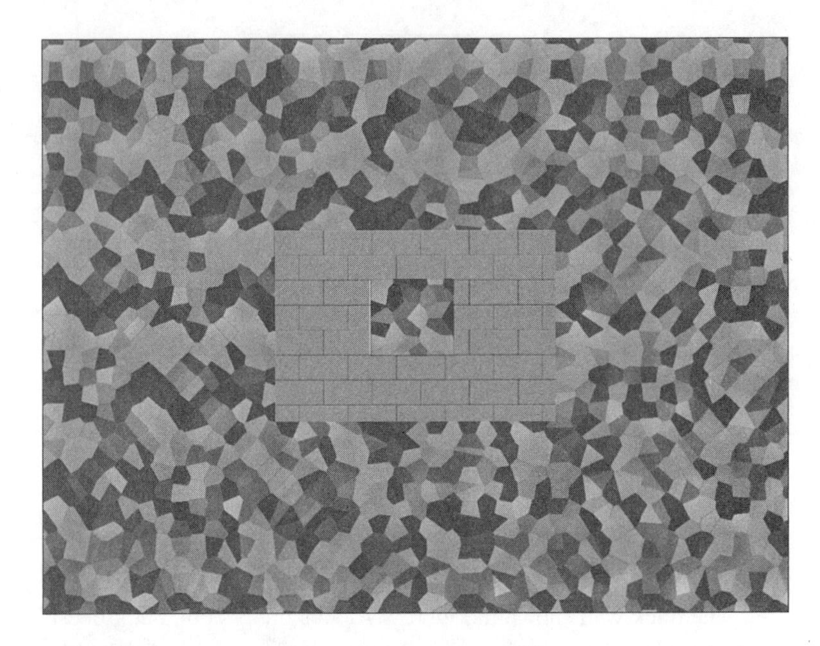

FIGURE 8.9
The textured rectangle with a transparent area.

Rendering a Texture onto a Primitive

Now that you understand texture coordinates, you can examine how you do all this texturing stuff in your program. You already saw how to load your texture, which includes specifying the transparent color. The rest of the process is kind of a complicated one, but because all you need to do for this book is one specific type of texturing, I can limit the discussion a great deal. Specifically, you need to perform the following tasks:

1. Set the texture-stage state.
2. Set the render state.
3. Set the vertex shader.
4. Set the stream source.
5. Set the texture.
6. Render the scene.

Yeah, I know that all sounds overly technical, and when you decide to pursue Direct3D graphics beyond this book, you'll have to spend a lot of time understanding all this stuff. But in this book, all you need to do is know how to call a few methods to get things set up correctly for texturing.

Setting the Texture-Stage State

To understand this step, you need to first understand two things:

- Texture stages
- Texture states

Neither of these topics is as spooky as it sounds. A texture stage is nothing more than the current texture layer you want to work with. Direct3D enables you to layer up to eight textures onto an object, and you identify each layer with a texture stage number, from 0 to 7. In your case, you need only a single texture stage, which will be given the number 0.

A state, on the other hand, is the way that Direct3D is currently set up to perform some task. Direct3D keeps many state variables that you set in order to tell Direct3D how to render your displays. To set a texture-state variable, you call the Direct3D device object's `SetTextureStageState()` method, which Direct3D declares like this:

```
HRESULT SetTextureStageState(
  DWORD Stage,
  D3DTEXTURESTAGESTATETYPE Type,
  DWORD Value
);
```

Here's what the arguments mean:

- *`Stage`*—This is the stage number for which you want to set the variable.
- *`Type`*—This is a constant that identifies the stage variable to set.
- *`Value`*—This is a constant that defines the value to which to set the stage variable.

The first thing to do with `SetTextureStageState()` is set the state's first color argument, which, for our purposes in this book, you do like this:

```
g_pDirect3DDevice->SetTextureStageState(0,
    D3DTSS_COLORARG1, D3DTA_TEXTURE);
```

Basically, this call tells Direct3D that the first color argument for this texture stage is the texture.

Next, you tell Direct3D to use the first color argument (the one you just set) in the color-blending operation:

```
g_pDirect3DDevice->SetTextureStageState(0,
    D3DTSS_COLOROP, D3DTOP_SELECTARG1);
```

Now you tell Direct3D that the first color argument is also to be used for the alpha-blending operation:

```
g_pDirect3DDevice->SetTextureStageState(0,
    D3DTSS_ALPHAOP, D3DTOP_SELECTARG1);
```

Another call to `SetTextureStageState()` tells Direct3D that the texture is the first alpha argument for the stage:

```
g_pDirect3DDevice->SetTextureStageState(0,
    D3DTSS_ALPHAARG1, D3DTA_TEXTURE);
```

And that's it for the texture stage. I know I went through this stuff pretty quickly, but you really don't need to know all the hairy details just to get a texture with transparent areas up on the screen. You want to get to actual game programming sometime in this book! You can use this code verbatim whenever you need to display a 2D texture with (or without) transparent areas.

Setting the Render State

Now you have to tell Direct3D how to set up the rendering state. You do this with the Direct3D device object's `SetRenderState()` method, which Direct3D declares like this:

```
HRESULT SetRenderState(
  D3DRENDERSTATETYPE State,
  DWORD Value
);
```

Here's what the arguments mean:

- *`State`*—A constant that specifies the state variable to set.
- *`Value`*—A constant that specifies the value to which to set the state variable.

The first call to `SetRenderState()` looks like this:

```
g_pDirect3DDevice->SetRenderState(D3DRS_ALPHABLENDENABLE, TRUE);
```

This call tells Direct3D to enable alpha blending, which is just a fancy term for transparency.

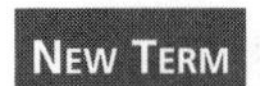

Alpha blending is the process of combining colors into a final color that will appear on the screen.

Next, you set the source and destination blending operations:

```
g_pDirect3DDevice->SetRenderState(D3DRS_SRCBLEND,
    D3DBLEND_SRCALPHA);
g_pDirect3DDevice->SetRenderState(D3DRS_DESTBLEND,
    D3DBLEND_INVSRCALPHA);
```

Again, the full explanation of this stuff is way beyond the scope of this book. If none of this makes sense to you, just use the code verbatim. It should always work for the tasks to which you put it in this book.

Setting the Vertex Shader

In the previous chapter, you got some experience with the Direct3D device object's `SetVertexShader()` method. At that time, you used the argument `D3DFVF_XYZRHW | D3DFVF_DIFFUSE` with the method to tell Direct3D that your vertices held transformed coordinates with color information. Now, you need to tell Direct3D that your vertices contain transformed coordinates with texture coordinates, which you do like this:

```
g_pDirect3DDevice->SetVertexShader(D3DFVF_XYZRHW|D3DFVF_TEX1);
```

Setting the Stream Source

In the previous chapter, you also got experience with the `SetStreamSource()` method, which you use to tell Direct3D where your vertices are stored. The process is exactly the same for rendering the shape on which your texture will be overlaid:

```
g_pDirect3DDevice->SetStreamSource(0, g_pVertexBuf,
    sizeof(CUSTOMVERTEX));
```

Setting the Texture

Finally, the last step before rendering is to give Direct3D the texture you want to use. You do this with the Direct3D device object's `SetTexture()` method, which Direct3D declares like this:

```
HRESULT SetTexture(
  DWORD Stage,
  IDirect3DBaseTexture8* pTexture
);
```

Here's what the arguments mean:

- *`Stage`*—The texture stage for which you're setting the texture.
- *`pTexture`*—A pointer to the `IDirect3DTexture8` object associated with your texture image.

An actual call to the method in your program would look something like this:

```
g_pDirect3DDevice->SetTexture(0, g_pTexture);
```

Rendering the Scene

At last you're ready to draw the textured primitive, which you do exactly as you learned in the previous chapter:

```
if(SUCCEEDED(g_pDirect3DDevice->BeginScene()))
{
    g_pDirect3DDevice->DrawPrimitive(D3DPT_TRIANGLELIST,0,2);
```

```
    g_pDirect3DDevice->EndScene();
    g_pDirect3DDevice->Present( NULL, NULL, NULL, NULL );
}
```

Because of all the state variables you set, Direct3D knows that the shape should be textured and will do it for you automatically when you draw the shape. Also because of the state variables, Direct3D knows how to handle the transparent areas.

And that's enough studying for one day! Now, have some fun in the following section by building an application that demonstrates texturing with transparency.

Building the TextureApp Application

You're now ready to build a complete program that demonstrates the concepts you've learned in this chapter. Follow the steps outlined in the following sections to complete this process.

Creating the Basic TextureApp Project

Perform the following steps to get the main Direct3D application project started:

1. Start a new empty Win32 project named TextureApp. (Don't forget to set the Additional Options to Empty Project.)
2. On the Project menu, select the Add New Item command. The Add New Item dialog box appears.
3. Add a new C++ File (.cpp) named TextureApp.cpp.
4. Copy the contents of the TriangleApp.cpp file (from Chapter 7) into the new TextureApp code window.
5. Change the name in the comment at the top of the file to TextureApp.
6. In the `RegisterWindowClass()` function change `wc.lpszClassName = "TriangleApp"` to `wc.lpszClassName = "TextureApp"`.
7. In the `CreateAppWindow()` function, change "TriangleApp" to "TextureApp", and then change "Triangle Application" to "Texture Application".

Adding the DirectX References

Next, you need to tell the program where the required DirectX header files and libraries are located. To do that, follow these steps:

1. Right-click the project's name in the Solution Explorer, and select Properties from the menu that appears. The TextureApp Property Pages dialog box appears.

2. Click the C/C++ selection in the left-hand pane, and select General from the displayed choices.
3. In the Additional Include Directories box, enter the path to the DirectX 8.1 SDK's include folder. If you installed the SDK using the default settings, this path should be C:\DXSDK\include.
4. Click the Linker selection in the left-hand pane, and select General from the displayed choices.
5. In the Additional Library Directories box, enter the path to the DirectX 8.1 SDK's library folder. If you installed the SDK using the default settings, this path should be C:\DXSDK\lib.
6. Click the Linker's Input selection in the left-hand pane.
7. In the Additional Dependencies box in the right-hand pane, enter **d3d8.lib**, **d3dx8.lib**, and **dxerr8.lib**.
8. Compile and run the application to be sure it works. When the triangle screen appears, press Escape to exit the application.

Adding Source Code

Now all you have to do is add the Direct3D code that'll get your texture up on the screen. Because this program is more complex than any of the others you've written, you'll create some extra functions that enable you to break down the program into logical chunks. Follow these steps to complete the source code:

1. Near the top of the program, add the following lines to the function prototypes. If you don't want to do the typing, you can copy the code from the Code01.txt file in the Chapter08 directory of this book's CD-ROM.

```
void PaintBackground();
void PaintTexture();
HRESULT InitDirect3D();
HRESULT CreateSurfaces();
HRESULT CreateVertices();
```

   These lines declare the new functions you'll be adding to the program.

2. Again, near the top of the program, add the following lines to the global variables. If you don't want to do the typing, you can copy the code from the Code02.txt file in the Chapter08 directory of this book's CD-ROM.

```
IDirect3DSurface8* g_pBitmapSurface = NULL;
IDirect3DTexture8* g_pTexture;
IDirect3DVertexBuffer8* g_pVertexBuf = NULL;
HRESULT g_hResult = D3D_OK;
char g_szErrorMsg[256];
```

These are the new global variables you'll be using in this program, including pointers to the required Direct3D interfaces.

3. Right after the global variables, replace the current `CUSTOMVERTEX` structure declaration with this one:

```
struct CUSTOMVERTEX
{
    float x, y, z, rhw;
    float tu,tv;
};
```

This structure creates a vertex data type that holds not only the vertex's coordinates, but also the associated texture coordinates.

4. In the `WinMain()` function, add the following lines *between* the `CleanUpDirect3D()` and `return 0` lines already there:

```
CloseWindow(g_hWnd);
if (g_hResult != D3D_OK)
    DXTRACE_ERR(g_szErrorMsg, g_hResult);
```

These lines close the window and display a message in the case of an error.

5. Replace the current `InitFullScreenDirect3D()` function with this new one. If you don't want to do the typing, you can copy the code from the Code03.txt file in the Chapter08 directory of this book's CD-ROM.

```
//////////////////////////////////////////////////////
// InitFullScreenDirect3D()
//////////////////////////////////////////////////////
HRESULT InitFullScreenDirect3D()
{
    g_hResult = InitDirect3D();
    if (FAILED(g_hResult))
        return g_hResult;
    g_hResult = CreateSurfaces();
    if (FAILED(g_hResult))
        return g_hResult;
    g_hResult = CreateVertices();
    if (FAILED(g_hResult))
        return g_hResult;

    return D3D_OK;
}
```

As you can see, this version breaks up the Direct3D initialization into several steps, each of which is implemented in its own function.

6. Add the following `InitDirect3D()` function to the program. If you don't want to do the typing, you can copy the code from the Code04.txt file in the Chapter08 directory of this book's CD-ROM.

```
///////////////////////////////////////////////////////
// InitDirect3D()
///////////////////////////////////////////////////////
HRESULT InitDirect3D()
{
    g_pDirect3D = Direct3DCreate8(D3D_SDK_VERSION);
    if (g_pDirect3D == NULL)
    {
        MessageBox(g_hWnd,
            "Couldn't create DirectX object.",
            "DirectX Error", MB_OK);
        return E_FAIL;
    }

    HRESULT hResult = g_pDirect3D->CheckDeviceType(D3DADAPTER_DEFAULT,
        D3DDEVTYPE_HAL, D3DFMT_X8R8G8B8, D3DFMT_X8R8G8B8, FALSE);
    if (hResult != D3D_OK)
    {
        MessageBox(g_hWnd,
            "Sorry. This program won't\nrun on your system.",
            "DirectX Error", MB_OK);
        return E_FAIL;
    }

    D3DPRESENT_PARAMETERS D3DPresentParams;
    ZeroMemory(&D3DPresentParams, sizeof(D3DPRESENT_PARAMETERS));
    D3DPresentParams.Windowed = FALSE;
    D3DPresentParams.BackBufferCount = 1;
    D3DPresentParams.BackBufferWidth = 800;
    D3DPresentParams.BackBufferHeight = 600;
    D3DPresentParams.BackBufferFormat = D3DFMT_X8R8G8B8;
    D3DPresentParams.SwapEffect = D3DSWAPEFFECT_DISCARD;
    D3DPresentParams.hDeviceWindow = g_hWnd;
    hResult = g_pDirect3D->CreateDevice(D3DADAPTER_DEFAULT,
        D3DDEVTYPE_HAL, g_hWnd, D3DCREATE_SOFTWARE_VERTEXPROCESSING,
        &D3DPresentParams, &g_pDirect3DDevice);
    if (FAILED(hResult))
    {
        MessageBox(g_hWnd,
            "Failed to create Direct3D device.",
            "DirectX Error", MB_OK);
        return E_FAIL;
    }

    return D3D_OK;
}
```

This function takes care of creating the Direct3D object and the Direct3D device object.

7. Add the following `CreateSurfaces()` function to the program. If you don't want to do the typing, you can copy the code from the Code05.txt file in the Chapter08 directory of this book's CD-ROM.

```
///////////////////////////////////////////////////////
// CreateSurfaces()
///////////////////////////////////////////////////////
HRESULT CreateSurfaces()
{
    g_hResult = g_pDirect3DDevice->CreateImageSurface(800, 600,
        D3DFMT_X8R8G8B8, &g_pBitmapSurface);
    if (FAILED(g_hResult))
    {
        strcpy(g_szErrorMsg, "Error creating bitmap surface.");
        PostQuitMessage(WM_QUIT);
        return g_hResult;
    }
    g_hResult = D3DXLoadSurfaceFromFile(g_pBitmapSurface, NULL, NULL,
        "image02.bmp", NULL, D3DX_DEFAULT, 0, NULL);
    if (FAILED(g_hResult))
    {
        strcpy(g_szErrorMsg, "Couldn't load bitmap file.");
        PostQuitMessage(WM_QUIT);
        return g_hResult;
    }
    g_hResult = D3DXCreateTextureFromFileEx(g_pDirect3DDevice,
        "Texture.bmp",
        D3DX_DEFAULT, D3DX_DEFAULT, 1, 0, D3DFMT_A8R8G8B8,
        D3DPOOL_MANAGED, D3DX_DEFAULT, D3DX_DEFAULT, 0xFF000000,
        NULL, NULL, &g_pTexture);
    if(FAILED(g_hResult))
    {
        strcpy(g_szErrorMsg, "Couldn't load texture file.");
        PostQuitMessage(WM_QUIT);
        return g_hResult;
    }

    return D3D_OK;
}
```

This function creates and loads surfaces for the application's background image and texture image.

8. Add the following `CreateVertices()` function to the program. If you don't want to do the typing, you can copy the code from the Code06.txt file in the Chapter08 directory of this book's CD-ROM.

```
///////////////////////////////////////////////////////
// CreateVertices()
///////////////////////////////////////////////////////
HRESULT CreateVertices()
```

```
{
    CUSTOMVERTEX triangleVertices[] =
    {
        {250.0f,  400.0f, 0.0f, 1.0f, 0.0f, 1.0f,},
        {250.0f, 200.0f, 0.0f, 1.0f, 0.0f, 0.0f,},
        {550.0f, 200.0f, 0.0f, 1.0f, 1.0f, 0.0f,},
        {250.0f,  400.0f, 0.0f, 1.0f, 0.0f, 1.0f,},
        {550.0f, 200.0f, 0.0f, 1.0f, 1.0f, 0.0f,},
        {550.0f,  400.0f, 0.0f, 1.0f, 1.0f, 1.0f,},
    };

    HRESULT g_hResult = g_pDirect3DDevice->CreateVertexBuffer(
        6*sizeof(CUSTOMVERTEX), 0, D3DFVF_XYZRHW | D3DFVF_TEX1,
        D3DPOOL_DEFAULT, &g_pVertexBuf);
    if (FAILED(g_hResult))
    {
        strcpy(g_szErrorMsg, "Error creating vertex buffer.");
        PostQuitMessage(WM_QUIT);
        return g_hResult;
    }

    VOID* pVertices;
    g_hResult = g_pVertexBuf->Lock(0, 0, (BYTE**)&pVertices, 0);
    if (FAILED(g_hResult))
    {
        strcpy(g_szErrorMsg, "Error locking vertex buffer.");
        PostQuitMessage(WM_QUIT);
        return g_hResult;
    }
    memcpy(pVertices, triangleVertices, sizeof(triangleVertices));
    g_pVertexBuf->Unlock();

    return D3D_OK;
}
```

This function creates the vertex buffer used by the program to draw the rectangle over which Direct3D will apply the texture.

9. Replace the current `CleanUpDirect3D()` function with the following new one. If you don't want to do the typing, you can copy the code from the Code07.txt file in the Chapter08 directory of this book's CD-ROM.

```
//////////////////////////////////////////////////////
// CleanUpDirect3D()
//////////////////////////////////////////////////////
void CleanUpDirect3D()
{
    if (g_pBitmapSurface)
        g_pBitmapSurface->Release();
    if (g_pTexture)
        g_pTexture->Release();
```

```
    if (g_pVertexBuf)
        g_pVertexBuf->Release();
    if (g_pDirect3DDevice)
        g_pDirect3DDevice->Release();
    if (g_pDirect3D)
        g_pDirect3D->Release();
}
```

This function releases all the Direct3D objects created in the program.

10. Replace the current `Render()` function with this one. If you don't want to do the typing, you can copy the code from the Code08.txt file in the Chapter08 directory of this book's CD-ROM.

```
//////////////////////////////////////////////////////
// Render()
//////////////////////////////////////////////////////
void Render()
{
    g_pDirect3DDevice->Clear(0, NULL, D3DCLEAR_TARGET,
        D3DCOLOR_XRGB(0,0,0), 1.0f, 0 );
    PaintBackground();
    PaintTexture();
}
```

This function breaks the rendering process down into three steps, two of which are implemented in their own functions.

11. Add the following `PaintBackground()` function to the program. If you don't want to do the typing, you can copy the code from the Code09.txt file in the Chapter08 directory of this book's CD-ROM.

```
//////////////////////////////////////////////////////
// PaintBackground()
//////////////////////////////////////////////////////
void PaintBackground()
{
    IDirect3DSurface8* pBackBuffer = NULL;
    g_hResult = g_pDirect3DDevice->GetBackBuffer(0,
        D3DBACKBUFFER_TYPE_MONO, &pBackBuffer);
    if (FAILED(g_hResult))
    {
        strcpy(g_szErrorMsg, "Error getting back buffer.");
        PostQuitMessage(WM_QUIT);
    }
    g_hResult = g_pDirect3DDevice->CopyRects(g_pBitmapSurface,
        NULL,0,pBackBuffer,NULL);
    if (FAILED(g_hResult))
    {
        strcpy(g_szErrorMsg, "Error copying image buffer.");
        PostQuitMessage(WM_QUIT);
    }
}
```

This function copies the background bitmap to the back buffer.

12. Add the following `PaintTexture()` function to the program. If you don't want to do the typing, you can copy the code from the Code10.txt file in the Chapter08 directory of this book's CD-ROM.

```
///////////////////////////////////////////////////////
// PaintTexture()
///////////////////////////////////////////////////////
void PaintTexture()
{
    g_pDirect3DDevice->SetTextureStageState(0,
        D3DTSS_COLOROP, D3DTOP_SELECTARG1);
    g_pDirect3DDevice->SetTextureStageState(0,
        D3DTSS_COLORARG1, D3DTA_TEXTURE);
    g_pDirect3DDevice->SetTextureStageState(0,
        D3DTSS_ALPHAOP, D3DTOP_SELECTARG1);
    g_pDirect3DDevice->SetTextureStageState(0,
        D3DTSS_ALPHAARG1, D3DTA_TEXTURE);
    g_pDirect3DDevice->SetRenderState(D3DRS_SRCBLEND,
        D3DBLEND_SRCALPHA);
    g_pDirect3DDevice->SetRenderState(D3DRS_DESTBLEND,
        D3DBLEND_INVSRCALPHA);
    g_pDirect3DDevice->SetRenderState(D3DRS_ALPHABLENDENABLE, TRUE);
    g_pDirect3DDevice->SetVertexShader(D3DFVF_XYZRHW|D3DFVF_TEX1);
    g_pDirect3DDevice->SetStreamSource(0, g_pVertexBuf,
        sizeof(CUSTOMVERTEX));
    g_pDirect3DDevice->SetTexture(0, g_pTexture);

    if(SUCCEEDED(g_pDirect3DDevice->BeginScene()))
    {
        g_pDirect3DDevice->DrawPrimitive(D3DPT_TRIANGLELIST,0,2);
        g_pDirect3DDevice->EndScene();
        g_pDirect3DDevice->Present( NULL, NULL, NULL, NULL );
    }
}
```

This function displays the texture on top of the background image.

13. Place an 800×600 bitmap named Image02.bmp in the application's main directory. You can supply your own bitmap or just use the one in the TextureApp directory of this book's CD-ROM.
14. Copy the Texture.bmp file from the TextureApp directory of this book's CD-ROM and place the file in your application's main directory.

And that's it. You can now compile and run the program. When you do, you should see the window in Figure 8.10 (or something similar if you used your own bitmap for the background image). You can see that Direct3D does not draw the solid black area of the texture, allowing the background to show through the wall.

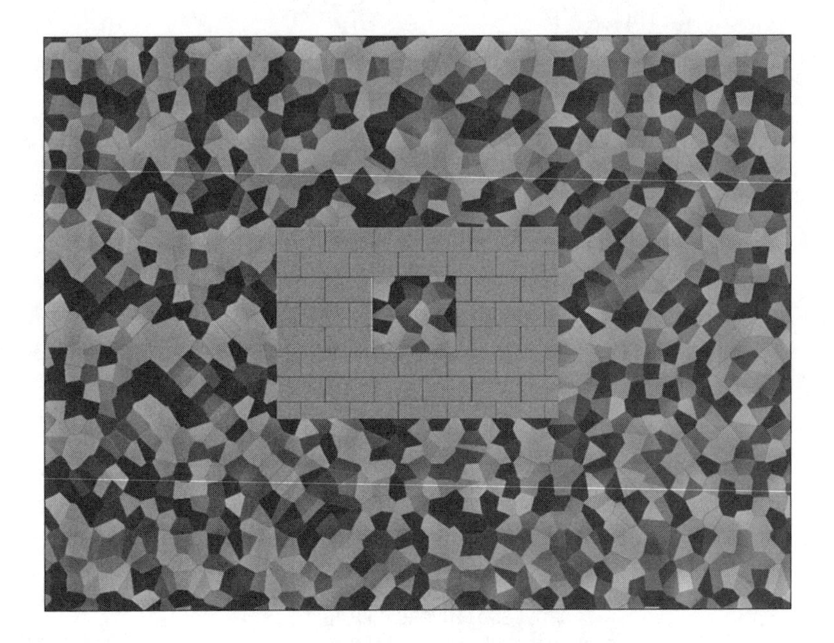

FIGURE 8.10
The running TextureApp application.

Summary

Textures provide programmers with a lot of power, enabling them to render graphical details that would be difficult to accomplish in another way. However, in this book, you use textures only to implement transparency when displaying bitmaps.

In the next chapter, you learn another important programming technique for your games: animation.

Q&A

Q. When I try to create a 32-bit bitmap with my paint program, the best I can do is 24-bit. What's up?

A. Even though the surfaces you use in your Direct3D programs usually have 32-bit color depth, paint programs don't need to bother with more than 24-bit color. This is because, when it comes to just color, 32-bit and 24-bit images are the same. The extra byte in 32-bit images is usually used for alpha values, which is more a programming thing than a paint thing.

Q. Then, where does the alpha value in the bitmap come from?

When Direct3D loads a 24-bit bitmap into a 32-bit surface, it takes care of the alpha values for you. In the case of loading a texture, for example, Direct3D uses the alpha value you specify in the color-key argument.

Q. What if I want to use black in my texture image as both a regular color and a transparent color?

A. You can't do that. However, remember that, with 24-bit color, you have millions of colors to choose from. You could always use an RGB value of 0,0,0 for your transparent color and an RGB value of 1,1,1 for your black color. No one will be able to see the difference.

Q. Can't textures do more than just be drawn onto a 2D rectangle? I mean, I thought I could do stuff like wrap a texture around curved objects.

A. You *can* wrap textures around non-flat surfaces. However, now you're getting into advanced 3D graphics techniques that are beyond the scope of this book.

Q. What if, after setting everything up to draw a texture on a rectangle, I then draw two rectangles?

A. Direct3D will draw the texture on the second rectangle, too. In fact, every primitive you draw will be textured until you change the state of the renderer to either turn texturing off or to provide a different texture. See this chapter's exercises for examples of this.

Workshop

The workshop includes quiz questions to help gauge your grasp of the material. You'll find the answers to this quiz at the end of this chapter. Even if you feel that you totally understand the concepts presented here, you should work through the quiz anyway. The last section is an exercise or two that you might work through to help reinforce your learning.

Quiz

1. What is a texture?
2. What is transparency?
3. What is an alpha value?
4. What function do you call to create and load a texture surface?
5. What are texture coordinates?
6. Where do you define texture coordinates?
7. What method do you call to set texture-state variables?
8. What method do you call to set render-state variables?
9. What method do you call to give Direct3D the texture you want to use for rendering?

Exercises

1. Modify this chapter's program so that it uses only half the texture, both horizontally and vertically. (Make a copy of the program, so that you don't change the original.)
2. Modify this chapter's original program so that it displays two rectangles. What happens with regard to the texture?

Answers for Day 8

Quiz

1. What is a texture?

   A texture is a bitmap image that's applied much like a decal to a shape in a 3D world in order to give the shape greater graphical detail.
2. What is transparency?

   Transparency enables a graphics application to display bitmaps that appear to be non-rectangular or that have areas that allow the background to show through. That is, the transparent areas of the bitmap don't appear on the screen.
3. What is an alpha value?

   An alpha value specifies the amount of transparency associated with a pixel.
4. What function do you call to create and load a texture surface?

   The DirectX utility function `D3DXCreateTextureFromFileEx()`.
5. What are texture coordinates?

   Texture coordinates are expressed as decimal percentages that indicate the portion of the texture to be mapped to a primitive.
6. Where do you define texture coordinates?

   In your vertex data.
7. What method do you call to set texture-state variables?

   To set a texture-state variable, you call the Direct3D device object's `SetTextureStageState()` method.
8. What method do you call to set render-state variables?

   The Direct3D device object's `SetRenderState()` method.
9. What method do you call to give Direct3D the texture you want to use for rendering?

   The Direct3D device object's `SetTexture()` method.

Exercises

1. Modify this chapter's program so that it uses only half the texture, both horizontally and vertically. (Make a copy of the program, so that you don't change the original.)

   All you have to do is change all the 1.0 texture coordinates to 0.5. You do this in the array that defines the vertices, like this:

```
CUSTOMVERTEX triangleVertices[] =
{
    {250.0f,  400.0f, 0.0f, 1.0f, 0.0f, 0.5f,},
    {250.0f, 200.0f, 0.0f, 1.0f, 0.0f, 0.0f,},
    {550.0f, 200.0f, 0.0f, 1.0f, 0.5f, 0.0f,},
    {250.0f,  400.0f, 0.0f, 1.0f, 0.0f, 0.5f,},
    {550.0f, 200.0f, 0.0f, 1.0f, 0.5f, 0.0f,},
    {550.0f,  400.0f, 0.0f, 1.0f, 0.5f, 0.5f,},
};
```

   Now when you run the program, you see the screen shown in Figure 8.11. Notice how Direct3D automatically scales the texture to fit the rectangle.

FIGURE 8.11

Using only 50% of the texture.

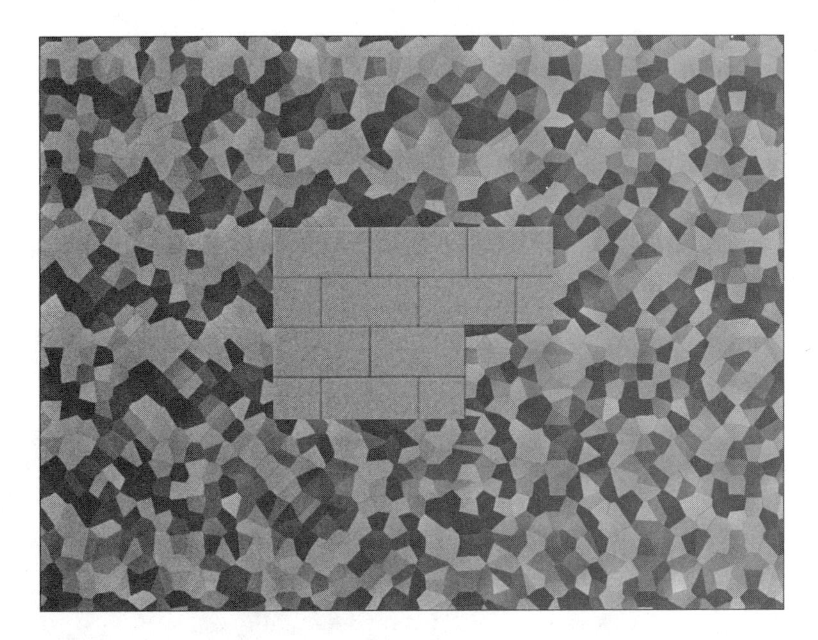

2. Modify this chapter's original program so that it displays two rectangles. What happens with regard to the texture?

   First, in the `CreateVertices()` function, you need to add two more triangles to your vertices. Here's what the final array might look like:

```
CUSTOMVERTEX triangleVertices[] =
{
    {250.0f,  400.0f, 0.0f, 1.0f, 0.0f, 1.0f,},
    {250.0f, 200.0f, 0.0f, 1.0f, 0.0f, 0.0f,},
    {550.0f, 200.0f, 0.0f, 1.0f, 1.0f, 0.0f,},
    {250.0f,  400.0f, 0.0f, 1.0f, 0.0f, 1.0f,},
    {550.0f, 200.0f, 0.0f, 1.0f, 1.0f, 0.0f,},
    {550.0f,  400.0f, 0.0f, 1.0f, 1.0f, 1.0f,},

    {450.0f,  500.0f, 0.0f, 1.0f, 0.0f, 1.0f,},
    {450.0f, 300.0f, 0.0f, 1.0f, 0.0f, 0.0f,},
    {750.0f, 300.0f, 0.0f, 1.0f, 1.0f, 0.0f,},
    {450.0f,  500.0f, 0.0f, 1.0f, 0.0f, 1.0f,},
    {750.0f, 300.0f, 0.0f, 1.0f, 1.0f, 0.0f,},
    {750.0f,  500.0f, 0.0f, 1.0f, 1.0f, 1.0f,},
};
```

Next, you need to change the 6 in the call to `CreateVertexBuffer()` to 12:

```
HRESULT g_hResult = g_pDirect3DDevice->CreateVertexBuffer(
    12*sizeof(CUSTOMVERTEX), 0, D3DFVF_XYZRHW | D3DFVF_TEX1,
    D3DPOOL_DEFAULT, &g_pVertexBuf);
```

Finally, in the `PaintTexture()` function, change the 2 in the call to `DrawPrimitive()` to a 4:

```
g_pDirect3DDevice->DrawPrimitive(D3DPT_TRIANGLELIST,0,4);
```

Now, when you run the program, the texture gets applied to both rectangles. Figure 8.12 shows the results.

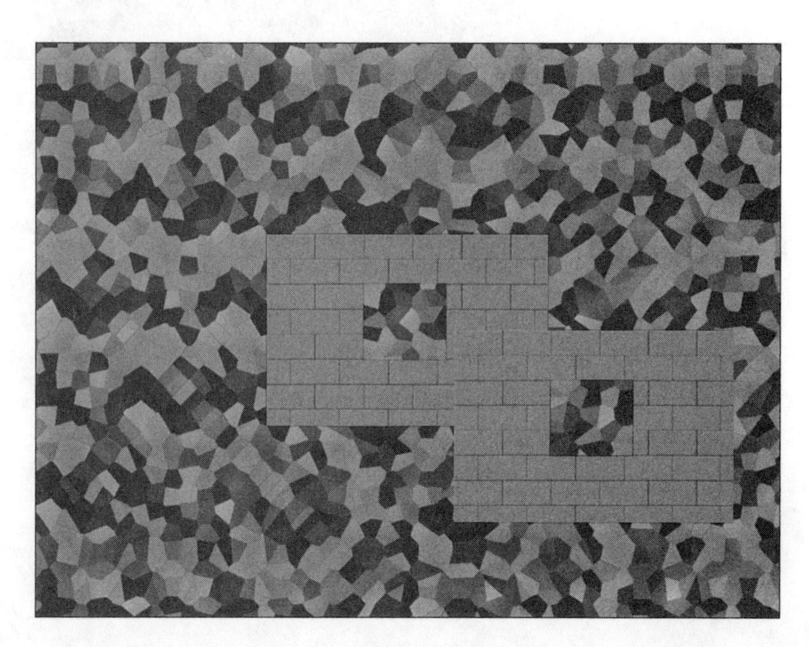

FIGURE 8.12

Drawing two rectangles with textures.

WEEK 2

DAY 9

Programming Direct3D Animation

There are only two more basic game-programming techniques you need to learn before you get started on actually programming a game. Those techniques are animation and sound programming. In this chapter, you learn the basics of animation. Specifically, today you will learn the following:

- How all types of animation work
- The general process needed to perform computer animation
- How to use Direct3D to create an animation sequence
- Timing animation sequences

The Mechanics of Animation

The world is filled with all kinds of animation, including everything from a child's simple flip book to cartoons and feature films. Every form of animation has one thing in common: The appearance of movement comes from rapidly projecting a series of images one after the other.

The simplest form of animation is that flip book I mentioned, which is a small pad of paper with an image on each page. To create the animation effect, you look at the pad while you flip the pages. Because each image is slightly different than the one before, your eyes and brain interpret the changing images as smooth motion.

Feature films work exactly the same way, except that each image in the animation sequence is projected on a screen rather than drawn in a book. Still, if you examine a reel of movie film, you'll see a series of images, each slightly different than the one before.

Computer animation is different only in the details. When you see some sort of movie-like effect on your computer's screen, it's nothing more than a series of images being drawn one after the other on your computer's screen. How the computer draws those images are the details you learn about in this chapter.

As an example, look at Figure 9.1, which shows four images that make up part of an animation sequence. In this sequence, an arrow rotates from an upward position to a downward position. If you were rapidly to display these images one after another, the arrow would appear to rotate.

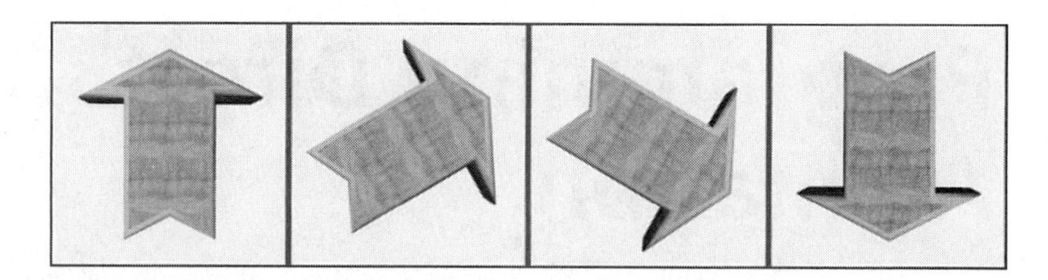

FIGURE 9.1

Four images of an animation sequence.

Computer Animation Details

How, you're probably asking, do you use DirectX to display the animation sequence? Believe it or not, you already know just about everything you need to know to get the job done. In short, here are the steps you need to complete:

1. Load the animation images into memory.
2. Draw an animation image onto the back buffer.
3. Display the back buffer.
4. Go back to Step 2.

Loading the Animation Frames

Up to this point, I've been calling the pictures that make up an animation sequence "animation images." But the real name for such an image is a *frame*. An animation sequence is made up of a series of frames, each of which is displayed one after the other.

NEW TERM A *frame* is a single image of an animation sequence.

The animation sequence with the arrow, then, has four frames. Each frame needs to be loaded into memory. The simplest way to do this is to create a surface for each frame and then load each image into its respective surface. Here's how you might create the surfaces:

```
IDirect3DSurface8* g_pBitmapSurfaces[4];
for (int x=0; x<4; ++x)
{
    g_pBitmapSurfaces[x] = NULL;
    g_hResult = g_pDirect3DDevice->CreateImageSurface(400, 400,
        D3DFMT_X8R8G8B8, &g_pBitmapSurfaces[x]);
    if (FAILED(g_hResult))
    {
        strcpy(g_szErrorMsg, "Error creating bitmap surface.");
        PostQuitMessage(WM_QUIT);
        break;
    }
}
```

Here, you've created an array of pointers, named `g_pBitmapSurfaces[4]`. This array will hold the pointers to each of the frame surfaces, four in all. In the `for` loop, the program creates each surface and stores its pointer in the array.

Now you can load the surfaces with their images, which are the four animation frames, the filenames of which are Frame01.bmp through Frame04.bmp:

```
for (int x=0; x<4; ++x)
{
    char filename[15];
    wsprintf(filename, "%s%d%s", "Frame0", x+1, ".bmp");
    g_hResult = D3DXLoadSurfaceFromFile(g_pBitmapSurfaces[x], NULL, NULL,
        filename, NULL, D3DX_DEFAULT, 0, NULL);
    if (FAILED(g_hResult))
    {
        strcpy(g_szErrorMsg, "Couldn't load bitmap file.");
        PostQuitMessage(WM_QUIT);
        break;
    }
}
```

Note

In most professional applications, the animation frames wouldn't be in separate files and loaded into separate surfaces. Instead, the entire animation sequence would be stored in a single bitmap, which itself would be loaded into a single surface. The application would then use a little math to determine which parts of the bitmap to display for each frame of the animation. This is the method you will use when you build the role-playing game featured later in this book.

Drawing Frames on the Back Buffer

At this point, you've got your animation frames loaded into memory and ready to go. Now you need to display each frame, one after the other, on the screen. All this happens in your application's rendering function, where you must perform the following tasks:

1. Check whether it's time to display the next frame.
2. Update the frame counter.
3. Get access to the back buffer.
4. Copy the appropriate animation frame to the back buffer.

Checking the Timer

The speed at which the animation runs depends on how fast you display the frames. The faster the *frame rate*, the faster the action looks on the screen. To control the speed, then, your program needs some sort of timer.

NEW TERM The *frame rate* is the speed at which an animation sequence runs. This is often expressed as the number of frames per second.

There are several ways to implement a timer, some more crude than others. To keep things simple for this example, we'll use nothing more than a `for` loop as a timer. For example, here's what such a timer function might look like:

```
BOOL IsTimeForNextFrame()
{
    static DWORD count = 0;
    count = count + 1;
    if (count > 100000)
    {
        count = 0;
        return TRUE;
    }
    else
        return FALSE;
}
```

This function returns `TRUE` if it's time to display the next frame, and `FALSE` otherwise. In this case, the timer variable `count` must reach 100,000 between each frame of the animation.

Frankly, this is a horrible way to time animation sequences, because the speed of the animation will depend on the speed of the computer on which it's running. When you build this book's role-playing game, you'll learn a better way to time your animations. But for right now, we're keeping things as simple as possible.

Updating the Frame Counter

Your application must display the animation frames in order, and then loop back to the start of the sequence after displaying the last frame. To know which frame is next to display, you need to keep track of a frame counter. Here's how to do that:

```
static frameNum = 0;
frameNum = frameNum + 1;
if (frameNum == 4)
    frameNum = 0;
```


Here, the variable `frameNum` counts from 0 to 3 and then starts over again. The variable gets incremented once for each frame of the animation, so you can use this counter to determine which frame to display.

Getting Access to the Back Buffer

When it's time to display the next frame of the animation, you need to draw the correct image on the back buffer. Obviously, then, you need to have access to the back buffer. You already know how to get this access, by calling the `GetBackBuffer()` method:

```
IDirect3DSurface8* pBackBuffer = NULL;
g_hResult = g_pDirect3DDevice->GetBackBuffer(0,
    D3DBACKBUFFER_TYPE_MONO, &pBackBuffer);
if (FAILED(g_hResult))
{
    strcpy(g_szErrorMsg, "Error getting back buffer.");
    PostQuitMessage(WM_QUIT);
    return;
}
```

Copying a Frame to the Back Buffer

Copying an animation frame to the back buffer is no different than copying any other image from one surface to another. You already know how to do this by using the `CopyRects()` method of the Direct3D device object. However, in this chapter, you're going to use `CopyRects()` a little differently. In previous chapters, you provided `NULL` for the arguments that specify source and destination coordinates for the copy operation. Now, you'll supply these arguments. So, a call to `CopyRects()` now looks something like this:

```
RECT SrcRect;
SrcRect.left = 0;
SrcRect.right = 399;
SrcRect.top = 0;
SrcRect.bottom = 399;
POINT DstPoint;
DstPoint.x = 200;
DstPoint.y = 100;
```

```
g_hResult = g_pDirect3DDevice->CopyRects(
    g_pBitmapSurfaces[frameNum],
    &SrcRect, 1, pBackBuffer, &DstPoint);
if (FAILED(g_hResult))
{
    strcpy(g_szErrorMsg, "Error copying image buffer.");
    PostQuitMessage(WM_QUIT);
    return;
}
```

Here, the code first defines a `RECT` structure to hold the size and position of the source rectangle, which is the area of the image you want to copy to the back buffer. In this program, you want to copy the entire 400×400 image, so the left, right, top, and bottom members of the `RECT` structure are set as shown.

Next, the code defines a `POINT` structure to hold the destination coordinate to which the source rectangle should be copied. This is the location in the back buffer to which the program will start copying the upper-left corner of the image. Figure 9.2 illustrates how these values translate to the surfaces.

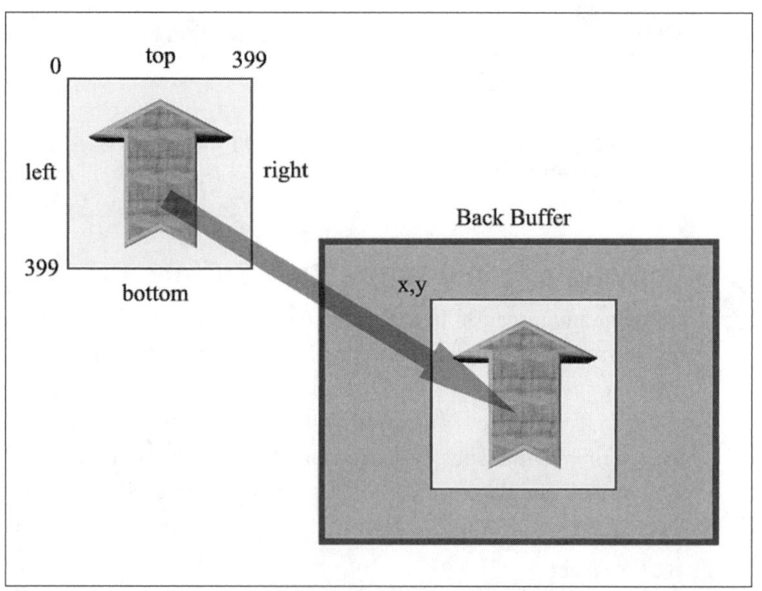

FIGURE 9.2
Copying an image to the back buffer.

With the source and destination structures initialized, a quick call to `CopyRects()`, giving the structures as the appropriate arguments, copies the animation frame to the back buffer.

Displaying the Back Buffer

At this point, you've managed to get the image data for the next animation frame copied to the back buffer. However, as you no doubt recall, the back buffer is hidden away in memory, out of sight of the user. You may also recall that you bring the back buffer into view by calling the Direct3D device object's `Present()` method:

```
g_pDirect3DDevice->Present(NULL, NULL, NULL, NULL);
```

Building the AnimationApp Application

Enough of the theory! You're now ready to build a complete program that demonstrates the concepts you've learned in this chapter. Follow the steps outlined in the following sections to complete the AnimationApp program.

Creating the Basic AnimationApp Project

Perform the following steps to get the main Direct3D application project started:

1. Start a new empty Win32 project named AnimationApp. (Don't forget to set the Application Settings to Empty Project.)
2. On the Project menu, select the Add New Item command. The Add New Item dialog box appears.
3. Add a new C++ File (.cpp) named AnimationApp.cpp.
4. Copy the contents of the SurfaceApp.cpp file (from Chapter 6) into the new AnimationApp code window.
5. Change the name in the comment at the top of the file to AnimationApp.
6. In the `RegisterWindowClass()` function change `wc.lpszClassName = "SurfaceApp"` to `wc.lpszClassName = "AnimationApp"`.
7. In the `CreateAppWindow()` function, change "SurfaceApp" to "AnimationApp", and then change "Direct3D Surface Application" to "Direct3D Animation Application".

Adding the DirectX References

Next, you need to tell the program where the required DirectX header files and libraries are located. To do that, follow these steps:

1. Right-click the project's name in the Solution Explorer, and select Properties from the menu that appears. The AnimationApp Property Pages dialog box appears.

2. Click the C/C++ selection in the left pane, and select General from the displayed choices.
3. In the Additional Include Directories box, enter the path to the DirectX 8.1 SDK's include folder. If you installed the SDK using the default settings, this path should be `C:\DXSDK\include`.
4. Click the Linker selection in the left pane, and select General from the displayed choices.
5. In the Additional Library Directories box, enter the path to the DirectX 8.1 SDK's library folder. If you installed the SDK using the default settings, this path should be `C:\DXSDK\lib`.
6. Click the Linker's Input selection in the left pane.
7. In the Additional Dependencies box in the right pane, enter `d3d8.lib`, `d3dx8.lib`, and `dxerr8.lib`. (Just enter the library names separated by spaces. Don't enter the commas or the word *and*.)
8. Copy the image.bmp file into the AnimationApp main directory. You can find this file in Chapter 6's SurfaceApp directory.
9. Compile and run the application to be sure it works. When the main screen appears, press Escape to exit the application.
10. You can now delete the image.bmp file you copied to the AnimationApp directory. You will no longer need it.

Adding Source Code

Now it's time to add the source code. Follow these steps to complete this task:

1. Near the top of the program, add the following line to the function prototypes:

   ```
   BOOL IsTimeForNextFrame();
   ```

   This declares a new function that will control the speed of the animation.
2. Again near the top of the program, in the global variables, replace the line

   ```
   IDirect3DSurface8* g_pBitmapSurface = NULL;
   ```

   with

   ```
   IDirect3DSurface8* g_pBitmapSurfaces[8];
   ```

   This array will hold pointers to the bitmaps that make up the animation sequence.
3. Right at the beginning of the `WinMain()` function, add the following lines:

   ```
   for (int x=0; x<8; ++x)
       g_pBitmapSurfaces[x] = NULL;
   ```

   These lines ensure that the members of the pointer array start off all `NULL`.

4. In the `InitFullScreenDirect3D()` function, change the lines

```
D3DPresentParams.BackBufferWidth = 640;
D3DPresentParams.BackBufferHeight = 480;
```

to

```
D3DPresentParams.BackBufferWidth = 800;
D3DPresentParams.BackBufferHeight = 600;
```

These lines set up the screen to the 800×600 resolution.

5. In the same function, replace the lines

```
g_hResult = g_pDirect3DDevice->CreateImageSurface(640, 480,
    D3DFMT_X8R8G8B8, &g_pBitmapSurface);
if (FAILED(g_hResult))
{
    strcpy(g_szErrorMsg, "Error creating bitmap surface.");
    PostQuitMessage(WM_QUIT);
}
g_hResult = D3DXLoadSurfaceFromFile(g_pBitmapSurface, NULL, NULL,
    "image.bmp", NULL, D3DX_DEFAULT, 0, NULL);
if (FAILED(g_hResult))
{
    strcpy(g_szErrorMsg, "Couldn't load bitmap file.");
    PostQuitMessage(WM_QUIT);
}
```

with these lines:

```
for (int x=0; x<8; ++x)
{
    g_hResult = g_pDirect3DDevice->CreateImageSurface(400, 400,
        D3DFMT_X8R8G8B8, &g_pBitmapSurfaces[x]);
    if (FAILED(g_hResult))
    {
        strcpy(g_szErrorMsg, "Error creating bitmap surface.");
        PostQuitMessage(WM_QUIT);
        break;
    }
    char filename[15];
    wsprintf(filename, "%s%d%s", "Frame0", x+1, ".bmp");
    g_hResult = D3DXLoadSurfaceFromFile(g_pBitmapSurfaces[x], NULL, NULL,
        filename, NULL, D3DX_DEFAULT, 0, NULL);
    if (FAILED(g_hResult))
    {
        strcpy(g_szErrorMsg, "Couldn't load bitmap file.");
        PostQuitMessage(WM_QUIT);
        break;
    }
}
g_pDirect3DDevice->Clear(0, NULL, D3DCLEAR_TARGET,
    D3DCOLOR_XRGB(0,0,0), 1.0f, 0);
```

If you don't want to do all that typing, copy the code from the Code01.txt file in the Chapter09 directory of this book's CD-ROM. These lines load eight bitmaps into the image surfaces, storing pointers to the surfaces in the pointer array.

6. In the `CleanUpDirect3D()` function, replace the lines

```
if (g_pBitmapSurface)
    g_pBitmapSurface->Release();
```

with the lines

```
for (int x=0; x<8; ++x)
{
    if (g_pBitmapSurfaces[x])
        g_pBitmapSurfaces[x]->Release();
}
```

These lines release all the surfaces whose pointers are stored in the pointer array.

7. Replace the current `Render()` function with the following one. If you don't want to do the typing, copy the code from the Code02.txt file in the Chapter09 directory of this book's CD-ROM.

```
//////////////////////////////////////////////////////
// Render()
//////////////////////////////////////////////////////
void Render()
{
    if (IsTimeForNextFrame())
    {
        static frameNum = 0;
        frameNum = frameNum + 1;
        if (frameNum == 8)
            frameNum = 0;

        IDirect3DSurface8* pBackBuffer = NULL;
        g_hResult = g_pDirect3DDevice->GetBackBuffer(0,
            D3DBACKBUFFER_TYPE_MONO, &pBackBuffer);
        if (FAILED(g_hResult))
        {
            strcpy(g_szErrorMsg, "Error getting back buffer.");
            PostQuitMessage(WM_QUIT);
            return;
        }
        g_pDirect3DDevice->Clear(0, NULL, D3DCLEAR_TARGET,
            D3DCOLOR_XRGB(0,0,0), 1.0f, 0);
        RECT SrcRect;
        SrcRect.left = 0; SrcRect.right = 399;
        SrcRect.top = 0; SrcRect.bottom = 399;
```

```
        POINT DstPoint;
        DstPoint.x = 200;
        DstPoint.y = 100;
        g_hResult = g_pDirect3DDevice->CopyRects(
            g_pBitmapSurfaces[frameNum],
            &SrcRect, 1, pBackBuffer, &DstPoint);
        if (FAILED(g_hResult))
        {
            strcpy(g_szErrorMsg, "Error copying image buffer.");
            PostQuitMessage(WM_QUIT);
            return;
        }
        g_pDirect3DDevice->Present(NULL, NULL, NULL, NULL);
        if (pBackBuffer)
            pBackBuffer->Release();
    }
}
```

This performs the animation by displaying the different bitmaps one after the other.

8. Add the following `IsTimeForNextFrame()` function to the program. If you don't want to do the typing, copy the code from the Code03.txt file in the Chapter09 directory of this book's CD-ROM.

```
//////////////////////////////////////////////////////
// IsTimeForNextFrame()
//////////////////////////////////////////////////////
BOOL IsTimeForNextFrame()
{
    static DWORD count = 0;
    count = count + 1;
    if (count > 100000)
    {
        count = 0;
        return TRUE;
    }
    else
        return FALSE;
}
```

This function acts as a timer for the animation sequence.

9. Copy the image files Frame01.bmp through Frame08.bmp from the AnimationApp directory of this book's CD-ROM to your own AnimationApp directory.

You can now compile and run the program. When you do, you see the screen shown in Figure 9.3, except on your screen, the star shape should be spinning. Exactly how fast it's spinning will depend on the speed of your computer.

FIGURE 9.3
The AnimationApp program.

Summary

Creating computer animation is an important part of game programming. Luckily, the process is fairly easy to implement, once you know the Direct3D method calls you need to use. To make the process even easier, you already knew most of these method calls; you only needed to learn a new way to apply them.

At this point, you've got only one more programming technique to learn before you'll be ready to start programming this book's game. So, the next chapter covers using DirectSound to add sound effects to your programs.

Q&A

Q. You mentioned that, later in the book, we'll be using math to locate portions of a bitmap to display. I'm not exactly a math wizard. How tough is this going to be?

A. When I say "math" in this context, I'm talking about little more than plain old arithmetic, albeit at maybe a high-school level. Anyway, even if you don't understand the formulas you'll use, you can just apply them as is in your own programs. You don't need to be a math wizard or even know how they work.

Q. In this chapter, we used the `CopyRects()` method with source and destination rectangles. Still, the source rectangle ended up being the entire bitmap. What if I wanted only part of the bitmap?

A. To do this, you would simply provide different values for the `left`, `right`, `top`, and `bottom` members of the source `RECT` structure. You can copy any part of a source bitmap to any part of a destination surface. Check out this chapter's exercises for some practice using this technique.

Q. Where the heck am I supposed to get all the images I need for an animation sequence?

A. Just like any other images you use in your programs, you're going to have to create your animation frames using some sort of paint program. If you have little artistic skill, you'll probably need to hire an artist. By the way, I used Microsoft's PhotoDraw to create the animation frames for this chapter.

Workshop

The workshop includes quiz questions to help gauge your grasp of the material. You'll find the answers to this quiz at the end of this chapter. Even if you feel that you totally understand the concepts presented here, you should work through the quiz anyway. The last section is an exercise or two that you might work through to help reinforce your learning.

Quiz

1. What does every form of animation have in common?
2. What are the four general steps required to display an animation sequence?
3. What are the four steps you must perform to draw an animation frame to the back buffer?
4. What does the animation's frame rate have to do with how fast the animation runs?
5. What does the frame counter have to do with how the animation is displayed?
6. What form of data do you use to specify the source rectangle in a call to the `CopyRects()` method?
7. What form of data do you use to specify the destination rectangle in a call to the `CopyRects()` method?

Exercises

1. Modify this chapter's example program so that it displays the animation at half the speed.

2. Modify this chapter's program so that it displays only a 200×200 image from the center of each animation frame. Display this new animation sequence at the location 150,300 on the screen. Figure 9.4 shows what the running program will look like.

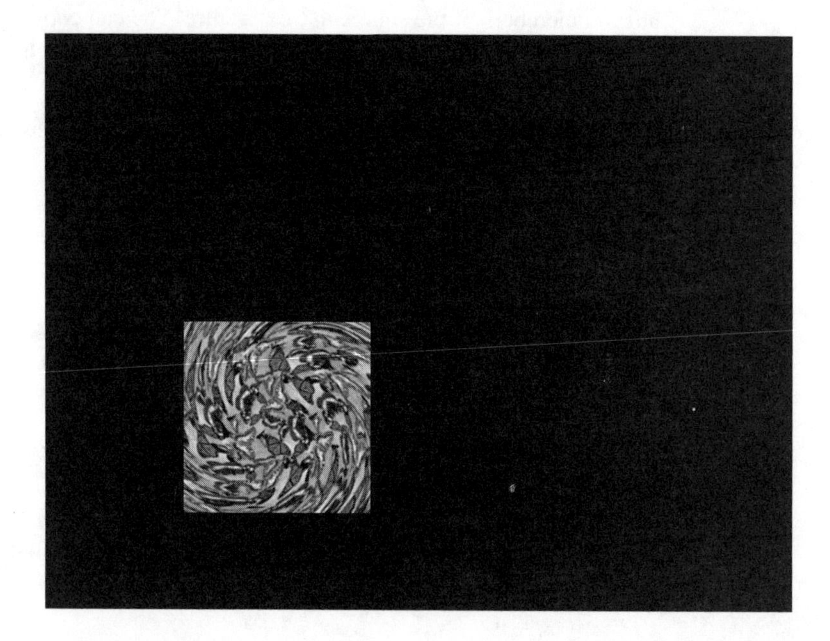

FIGURE 9.4
The modified AnimationApp program.

Answers for Day 9

Quiz

1. What does every form of animation have in common?

   The appearance of movement comes from rapidly projecting a series of images one after the other.

2. What are the four general steps required to display an animation sequence?

   Load the animation images into memory, draw an animation image onto the back buffer, display the back buffer, go back to step 2.

3. What are the four steps you must perform to draw an animation frame to the back buffer?

   Check whether it's time to display the next frame, update the frame counter, get access to the back buffer, and copy the appropriate animation frame to the back buffer.

4. What does the animation's frame rate have to do with how fast the animation runs?

   The faster the frame rate, the faster the action looks on the screen.

5. What does the frame counter have to do with how the animation is displayed?

   The frame counter holds the number of the next frame to display.

6. What form of data do you use to specify the source rectangle in a call to the `CopyRects()` method?

   A `RECT` structure, whose `left`, `right`, `top`, and `bottom` members give the size and location of the rectangle.

7. What form of data do you use to specify the destination rectangle in a call to the `CopyRects()` method?

   A `POINT` structure, whose `x` and `y` members give the location where Direct3D will start drawing the source rectangle's upper-left corner.

Exercises

1. Modify this chapter's example program so that it displays the animation at half the speed.

   All you have to do is change one line in the `IsTimeForNextFrame()` function. Specifically, change the line

   ```
   if (count > 100000)
   ```

   to

   ```
   if (count > 200000)
   ```

2. Modify this chapter's program so that it displays only a 200×200 image from the center of each animation frame. Display this new animation sequence at the location 150,300 on the screen. Figure 9.4 shows what the running program will look like.

   To do this, you need to change the values to which you set the `RECT` and `POINT` structures that you use as arguments to the `CopyRects()` method, like this:

   ```
   RECT SrcRect;
   SrcRect.left = 100;
   SrcRect.right = 299;
   SrcRect.top = 100;
   SrcRect.bottom = 299;
   POINT DstPoint;
   DstPoint.x = 150;
   DstPoint.y = 300;
   ```

WEEK 2

DAY 10

Creating and Programming Sound

The real world is overflowing with sound. There's barely a moment of our lives that we're not barraged with hundreds of different sounds simultaneously. A computer game, of course, can't hope to compete with the real world in the aural department. But, luckily, it doesn't have to. A few well-placed sound effects are often all it takes to bring a game alive.

In this chapter, then, you'll add the final tool to your game-programming tool belt, by learning how to add sound effects to a game. Specifically, today you'll learn the following:

- How to record and edit your own sound effects
- How to use the Windows API to play sound effects
- How to use the DirectSound component of DirectX to play sound effects.

Recording Sound

If you've never recorded sound effects under Windows before, you're in for a treat. Not only is the job easy, it's also fun. Most sound cards come with all the software you need to create sound effects for any game that can handle .WAV files. Moreover, many of these sound-recording programs can also edit sounds in various ways, from clipping unwanted noise to adding echo or even reversing a sound effect.

Because I'm a musician, I have a bit of an upper hand when it comes to recording sound, thanks to my small home studio. If you have home-recording equipment, as well as an electronic instrument like a synthesizer, you can create all sorts of cool sound effects for your game. Add to that some sound manipulation software for your computer, and you're ready to become a sound-effect professional. Still, if you're just starting off, your computer system probably already has the basic programs you need. If not, jump onto the Internet and look for freeware or shareware sound editors. Figure 10.1 shows WaveLab, one of the sound-editing programs I have on my computer.

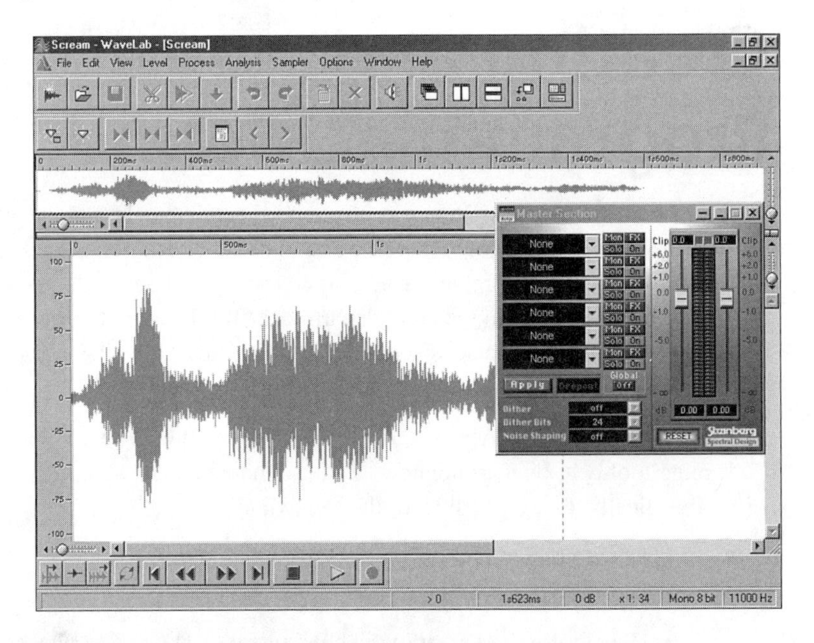

FIGURE 10.1
The WaveLab sound application.

No matter what sound card you have and what software you'll be using to record and edit sound effects, the first step is to plug a microphone into the sound card. Then, whatever sounds the microphone picks up are transmitted to the sound card and on to whatever sound-editing program you're running.

Once you have the microphone plugged in, start up your sound-editing program and turn on the recording function. (You'll need to consult your sound program's documentation for specific instructions on recording sound.) Then, the sounds the microphone picks up are converted to .WAV file format and saved to disk.

For example, suppose you want to record the words "Welcome, soldier, to Battle Blondes" to be used as a greeting when the player first runs your game. After plugging in your microphone and starting your sound program's record feature, just speak into the microphone (using a suitably impressive voice, of course). When you're done speaking, turn off the record feature and save your spoken words to a .WAV file. You can now play back those words with any program that can play .WAV files.

Editing Sounds

Once you have a sound effect recorded, you'll almost always need to edit it somehow. Different sound programs have different editing features, but most of them let you delete various portions of the sound, as well as change the volume of the sound or add special effects such as reverb, echo, phasing, and so on.

One type of editing you'll almost certainly have to do is delete part of the beginning and end of the sound. This is because you're going to have a second or two of silence before the actual sound wave you want. Why? It takes a second or two to go from turning on the sound program's record function to actually creating the sound you want to record.

Figure 10.2 shows WaveLab ready to delete a silent area from the front of a sound effect. The user marked the dark rectangular area with his mouse, in much the same way you'd highlight text in a word processor. Then, selecting the program's Delete function, the user deletes the extraneous sound data, as shown in Figure 10.3.

Another thing you might have to do is increase the volume of the sound effect. For some reason, they never seem to record loud enough. WaveLab has a Change Gain function that multiplies the amplitude of a sound wave by a percentage that the user selects in the Gain Change dialog box (see Figure 10.4).

Your sound-editing program may have many other features, as well. Some typical extra sound-editing functions include echo and reverse. You should also be able to cut and paste pieces of different sound effects together into one WAV file. Using this technique, you can come up with some pretty strange stuff! Figure 10.5 shows some of WaveLab's effects open and ready to use.

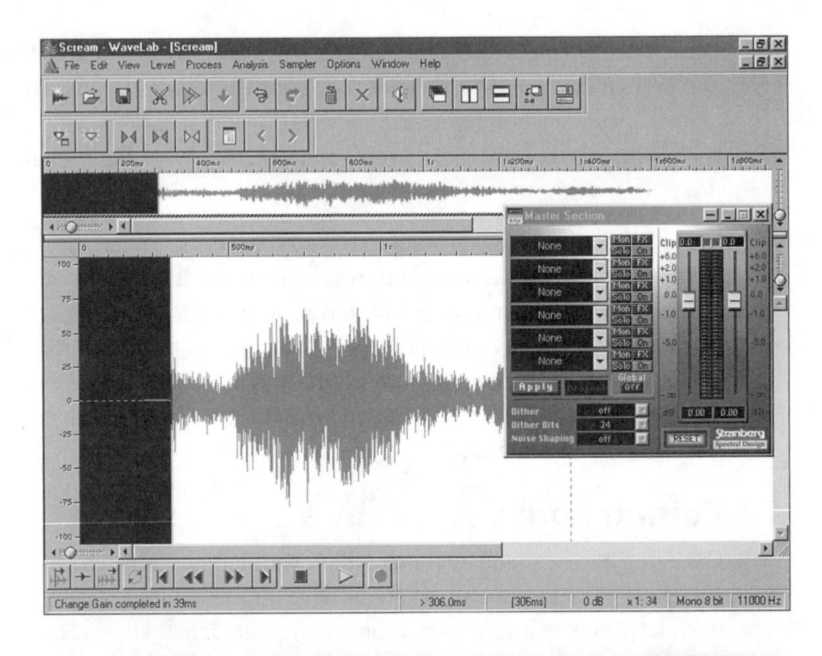

FIGURE 10.2

Deleting part of a sound effect.

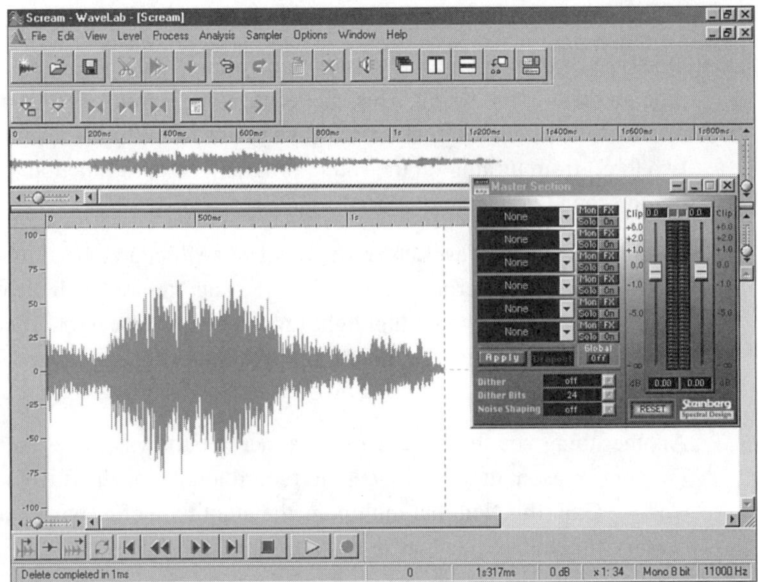

FIGURE 10.3

After deleting the leading silent area of the sound effect.

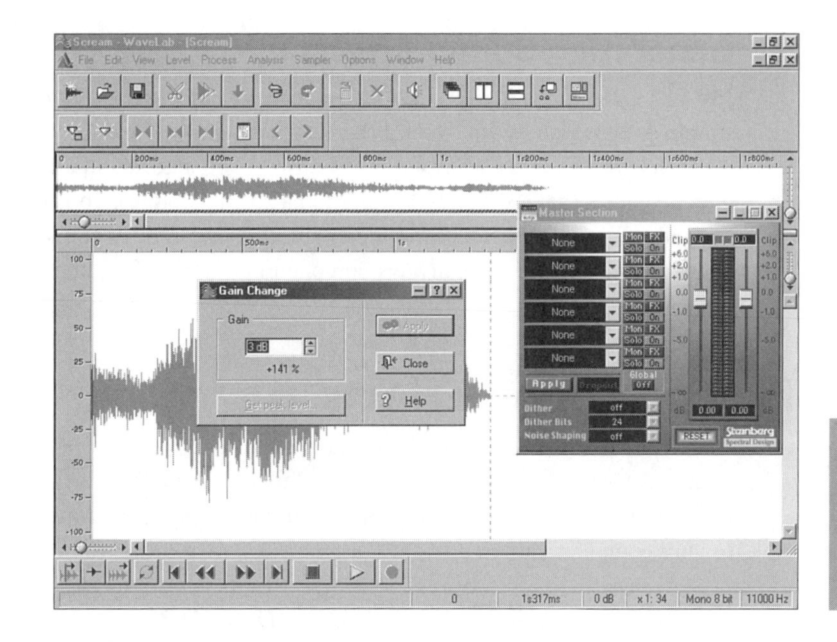

FIGURE 10.4

Scaling a sound effect's volume.

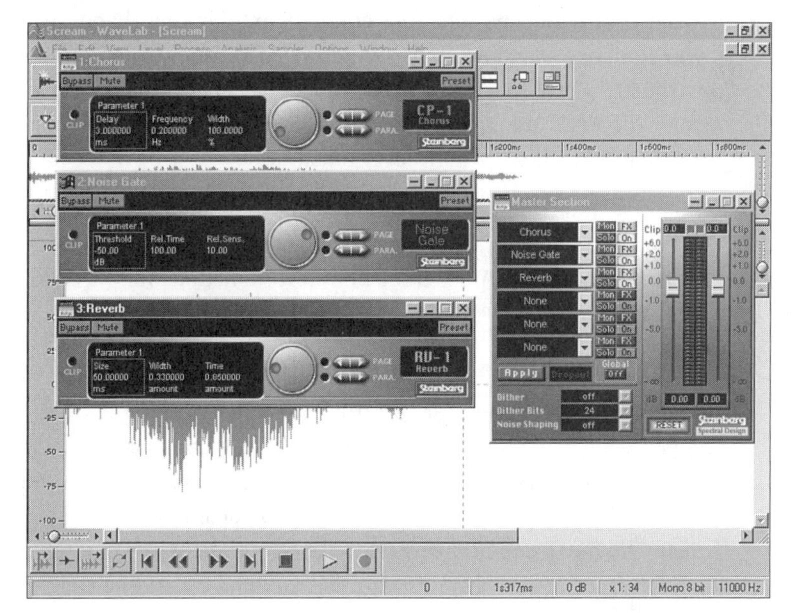

FIGURE 10.5

Most sound editors include special effects.

Generating Sound Effects

Just like most things in life, the sound effects you create for a game can be as simple or elaborate as you want. For most "homegrown" games, you can use items that you have laying around the house to generate sound effects. For commercial games (games that will be sold in a software store), you'll need a full-fledged studio and probably a sound engineer, as well. Now you know why the major game companies are always complaining (or boasting) about their development costs!

Playing Sound Effects

Once you have your sound effects, you need to set up your game program to play the effects. There are a couple of ways to do this, using the Windows API or using the DirectSound component of DirectX. You'll now examine both methods of playing sound in your computer games.

Windows API Waveform Functions

Windows multimedia functions come in both high-level and low-level forms. The easiest way to play a sound using the Windows API from within your application is to call one of the high-level functions. These functions enable you to do everything from play a wave file to record and create MIDI files. Unfortunately, it would take an entire book to cover all of the MCI's high-level functions.

In this section, you get a look at how to use the multimedia high-level functions to control waveform audio, which is the type of audio you'll use most of the time in your games. Windows supplies three high-level functions for playing waveform sounds: `MessageBeep()`, `sndPlaySound()`, and `PlaySound()`.

Using the `MessageBeep()` Function

You can use the `MessageBeep()` function whenever you want to play a sound that's associated with an alert level in Windows. These sounds include the ubiquitous "ding" and other system sounds that inform you of various events. For example, if you click outside of a dialog box that's waiting for input, you hear a bell that reminds you that you must deal with the dialog box before you can continue with your application.

In a program, the various sounds associated with the alert levels are defined by constants, including `MB_ICONASTERISK`, `MB_ICONEXCLAMATION`, `MB_ICONHAND`, `MB_ICONQUESTION`, and `MB_OK`.

When you use one of these constants in a call to MessageBeep(), the system plays the associated sound effect.

A typical call to MessageBeep() looks something like this:

```
MessageBeep(MB_ICONEXCLAMATION);
```

The function returns a zero if it fails and a non-zero value if it succeeds.

Using the sndPlaySound() Function

Whereas the MessageBeep() function limits you to only those sounds associated with system alert levels, the sndPlaySound() function can play any waveform sound you like, including alert sounds. The Windows API declares sndPlaySound() as shown here:

```
BOOL sndPlaySound(
  LPCSTR lpszSound,
  UINT fuSound
);
```


The sndPlaySound() function requires two parameters. The first is the name of the sound or .WAV file that you want to play. The function first searches the system registry for the sound. The sound names found there are not the names of waveform files, but rather names assigned to specific Windows events.

The second parameter for sndPlaySound() is the sound-play option, which, for normal use, you'd set to SND_SYNC or SND_ASYNC.

To play the SystemAsterisk sound, you provide sndPlaySound() with the string SystemAsterisk as its first parameter, like this:

```
sndPlaySound("SystemAsterisk", SND_SYNC);
```

If sndPlaySound can't find the sound represented by the string, the function assumes that the sound string is the name of a waveform file. Then sndPlaySound searches for the file in the current directory, the main Windows directory, the Windows system directory, or directories included in the user's PATH environment variable. If the function can't find the file, it tries to play the SystemDefault sound. Finally, if it can't find this sound, it returns an error.

A typical call to sndPlaySound() that plays a wave file looks like this:

```
sndPlaySound("sound.wav", SND_SYNC);
```

The function returns 0 if it fails and a non-zero number if it succeeds.

Using the `PlaySound()` Function

The last high-level waveform function is `PlaySound`. It's a little more flexible than its cousin `sndPlaySound`, as you can see by its Windows API declaration:

```
BOOL PlaySound(
  LPCSTR pszSound,
  HMODULE hmod,
  DWORD fdwSound
);
```

Like `sndPlaySound()`, there are a number of flags you can use with `PlaySound()`, the most common of which are `SND_ASYNC`, `SND_FILENAME`, and `SND_LOOP`. A typical call to `PlaySound()`looks like this:

```
PlaySound("sound.wav", 0, SND_ASYNC | SND_FILENAME | SND_LOOP)
```

The arguments for the function are the sound name (system name, resource name, or filename), the handle of the module that owns the resource (if the `SND_RESOURCE` flag is used), and the appropriate flags. The function returns 0 if it fails and a non-zero number if it succeeds.

Building the APISoundApp Application

There is still a lot more to learn about programming sound, but before you go any further, how about some hands-on experience with the Windows API sound functions? Just follow the steps in this section to build the first of this chapter's sample programs.

Creating the Basic APISoundApp Project

Perform the following steps to get the main application project started:

1. Start a new empty Win32 project named APISoundApp. (Don't forget to set the Application Settings to Empty Project.)
2. On the Project menu, select the Add New Item command. The Add New Item dialog box appears.
3. Add a new C++ File (.cpp) named APISoundApp.cpp.
4. Copy the contents of the BasicWindowsApp.cpp file (from Chapter 3) into the new APISoundApp.cpp code window.
5. Change the name in the comment at the top of the file to APISoundApp.
6. In the `RegisterWindowClass()` function change `wc.lpszClassName = "WinApp"` to `wc.lpszClassName = "APISoundApp"`.

7. In the `CreateAppWindow()` function, change "WinApp" to "APISoundApp", and then change "Basic Windows Application" to "API Sound Application".

Adding the API Multimedia References

Next, you need to tell the program where the required header files and libraries are located. To do that, follow these steps:

1. Right-click the project's name in the Solution Explorer, and select Properties from the menu that appears. The APISoundApp Property Pages dialog box appears.
2. Click the Linker selection in the left pane, and select Input from the displayed choices.
3. In the Additional Dependencies box in the right pane, enter **Winmm.lib**.

   This is the library that contains the `sndPlaySound()` and `PlaySound()` function implementations.
4. Compile and run the application to be sure it works. When the main screen appears, just close the window and proceed with the next section.

Adding Source Code

Now it's time to add the source code. Follow these steps to complete this task:

1. Near the top of the program, add the following line after the line `#include <windows.h>` that's already there:

   ```
   #include <Mmsystem.h>
   ```

   This is the header file that declares the `sndPlaySound()` and `PlaySound()` functions.
2. Near the top of the program, add the following lines to the function prototypes:

   ```
   void PlaySound1();
   void PlaySound2();
   void PlaySound3();
   ```

   This declares three functions for playing sound effects.
3. In the `WndProc()` function, add the following lines shown in bold to the `switch` statement:

   ```
       switch(msg)
       {
       case WM_CREATE:
           return 0;

       case WM_DESTROY:
   ```

```
            PostQuitMessage( 0 );
            return 0;

        case WM_PAINT:
            ValidateRect(g_hWnd, NULL);
            return 0;

        case WM_KEYDOWN:
            switch(wParam)
            {
            case VK_F1:
                PlaySound1();
                break;
            case VK_F2:
                PlaySound2();
                break;
            case VK_F3:
                PlaySound3();
                break;
            }
    }
```

These new lines enable the user to press the keys F1, F2, or F3 to play a sound effect.

4. Add the following functions to the program:

```
//////////////////////////////////////////////////////////
// PlaySound1()
//////////////////////////////////////////////////////////
void PlaySound1()
{
    MessageBeep(MB_ICONEXCLAMATION);
}

//////////////////////////////////////////////////////////
// PlaySound2()
//////////////////////////////////////////////////////////
void PlaySound2()
{
    sndPlaySound("FunkyLoop.wav", SND_ASYNC);
}

//////////////////////////////////////////////////////////
// PlaySound3()
//////////////////////////////////////////////////////////
void PlaySound3()
{
    PlaySound("FunkyLoop.wav", 0,
        SND_ASYNC | SND_FILENAME | SND_LOOP);
}
```

These functions play sounds using the Windows API sound functions.

5. Copy the sound file FunkyLoop.wav from the APISoundApp directory of this book's CD-ROM to your own APISoundApp directory. (Or you can place any wave file you want in your APISoundApp directory and rename it FunkyLoop.wav.)

You can now compile and run the program. Press F1 to play a sound with `MessageBeep()`, F2 to play a sound with `SndPlaySound()`, or F3 to play a sound with `PlaySound()`. In the case of `PlaySound()`, the FunkyLoop.wav file loops again and again until you close the program or until you press F2 to play the loop a final time.

The FunkyLoop.wav file is a sound loop that I wrote and recorded in my home studio and so is copyright 2002 by Clayton Walnum. This file is for use only with this book's programs. Any other use constitutes a breach of my copyright. Sorry about that.

Dealing with Wave Files

Probably the best way to play sound effects in your programs is with the DirectSound component of DirectX. Soon, you'll learn to use DirectSound, but first you need to know how to load a wave file. Wave files are the most common form of storage for digitized sound effects under Windows. You can usually identify a wave file by its .WAV file extension. A wave file, however, is actually a little more than just sound data; it's a special type of multimedia data known as a RIFF (Resource Interchange File Format) file.

A RIFF file is constructed from a series of chunks, which are data structures that contain three fields of information. The first field is a four-character code, called `ckid`, that specifies the chunk type; the second field is a double word, called `cksize`, that contains the size of the data chunk; and the third field is the data itself.

A RIFF chunk is the granddaddy of chunks in that it contains all the other chunks in the file. The RIFF file's `ckid` field contains the letters "RIFF," which, of course, identifies the file as a RIFF file. The `cksize` field in the RIFF chunk contains the size of the RIFF file's data chunk, which, because the RIFF chunk contains all the other chunks in the file, is the size of all those chunks put together. That is, a RIFF file's data chunk comprises all the remaining chunks in the file.

Although I said a chunk contains three fields of information, a RIFF chunk actually has one extra field, called `fccType`, which specifies the type of data stored in the file. For a wave file, `fccType` is set to the four characters "WAVE."

In a wave file, you'll normally find two other types of chunks tucked away inside the main RIFF chunk. These chunks are the format chunk and the data chunk. The format chunk contains format information about the wave file. Just like all chunks, the format chunk begins with its `ckid`, which is the characters "fmt" followed by a space. The space character is needed because all `ckid` fields must be four characters in length. Following the `ckid` is the format chunk's `cksize` field, which is 16, indicating that the chunk's data field contains sixteen bytes of information.

The sixteen bytes are the actual wave-file format information, which includes the wave format, the number of channels, the sampling rate, the average number of bytes of data per second of sound, and the block alignment (which is the number of bytes per sample times the number of channels). Because you must read this information from the file in order to get the wave file's attributes, it's no surprise that there's a special type of structure into which you can read this data. That structure is called `WAVEFORMATEX` and is declared like this:

```
typedef struct {
    WORD  wFormatTag;
    WORD  nChannels;
    DWORD nSamplesPerSec;
    DWORD nAvgBytesPerSec;
    WORD  nBlockAlign;
    WORD  wBitsPerSample;
    WORD  cbSize;
} WAVEFORMATEX;
```

Notice that all the fields in this structure match up with the data described in the previous paragraph—all, that is, except the last field, called `cbSize`. The `cbSize` field was added to this structure (the previous version of the structure was called `WAVEFORMAT`) in order to accommodate extra information needed by some types of RIFF files. Currently, for wave files, you can just ignore the information stored in `cbSize`.

The last chunk in a wave file is the data chunk, which contains the usual `ckid` and `cksize` fields, followed by the actual audio data. As you may have guessed, the data chunk's `ckid` is the four characters "data." The `cksize` field contains the number of bytes of sound data that follow.

Reading a Wave File

The Windows API includes many multimedia functions that the programmer can use to manipulate various types of files. To load a wave file, you need five of the multimedia I/O functions. Those functions are `mmioOpen()`, `mmioDescend()`, `mmioAscend()`, `mmioRead()`, and `mmioClose()`. In the following section, you see how to use these functions to not only load sound data, but also to obtain information about that data.

Opening a Wave File

The first step is to open the wave file. You do this with the `mmioOpen()` function, which Windows declares like this:

```
HMMIO mmioOpen(
  LPSTR szFilename,
  LPMMIOINFO lpmmioinfo,
  DWORD dwOpenFlags
);
```

Here's what the three arguments mean:

- `szFilename`—The name of the file to open.
- `lpmmioinfo`—The address of the parent chunk's `MMCKINFO` structure (or, in this case, just `NULL`, since a RIFF chunk has no parent).
- `dwOpenFlags`—The flags that indicate how the file should be opened. The flags `MMIO_READ` and `MMIO_ALLOCBUF` open the file as a read-only, buffered file.

If successful, the `mmioOpen()` function returns a handle to the newly opened file; otherwise, it returns zero. Here's what an actual call to mmioOpen() might look like:

```
HMMIO hMMIO = mmioOpen("sound.wav", NULL, MMIO_READ | MMIO_ALLOCBUF);
```

Reading the RIFF Chunk

Once the file is open, you need to read the RIFF header, which you do by calling the `mmioDescend()` function. Windows declares this function like this:

```
MMRESULT mmioDescend(
  HMMIO hmmio,
  LPMMCKINFO lpck,
  LPMMCKINFO lpckParent,
  UINT wFlags
);
```

Here's what the four arguments mean:

- `hmmio`—The file's handle.
- `lpck`—The address of an `MMCKINFO` structure.
- `lpckParent`—The address of the parent chunk's `MMCKINFO` structure (or `NULL`).
- `wFlags`—A search flag. (In this case, the search flag is `MMIO_FINDRIFF` because you're trying to read the RIFF chunk.)

Here's what an actual call to `mmioDescend()` looks like:

```
MMCKINFO mmCkInfoRIFF;
```

```
mmCkInfoRIFF.fccType = mmioFOURCC('W', 'A', 'V', 'E');
MMRESULT result = mmioDescend(hMMIO, &mmCkInfoRIFF, NULL, MMIO_FINDRIFF);
```

Here, the program first defines an MMCKINFO structure, which contains information about a chunk. The MMCKINFO structure is declared by Windows as shown here:

```
typedef struct {
    FOURCC ckid;
    DWORD  cksize;
    FOURCC fccType;
    DWORD  dwDataOffset;
    DWORD  dwFlags;
} MMCKINFO;
```

Before calling mmioDescend(), you must initialize the fccType field of the MMCKINFO structure, so that the function knows what type of chunk it's looking for. Notice that fccType is defined as a FOURCC data type. FOURCC stands for "four-character code" and is actually single 32-bit value with the four characters crammed into it. To create the correct 32-bit value from four characters, you call the mmioFOURCC() macro, as shown in the sample function call above.

After setting up the MMCKINFO structure by initializing its fccType field, you call mmioDescend() to descend into (read) the first chunk in the wave file. The first chunk, as you know, is the RIFF chunk.

After mmioDescend() does its thing, the RIFF chunk's MMCKINFO structure is filled in with information about the RIFF chunk, which is the parent chunk for the other chunks in the file. The information returned in the MMCKINFO structure is as follows:

- ckid—The chunk identifier
- cksize—The size of the data field
- fccType—The file type, which should be "WAVE" for a wave file
- dwDataOffset—The file offset of the beginning of the chunk's data field
- dwFlags—Unused, always 0

Reading the Format Chunk

The next part of the file to read is the format chunk. Because the format chunk is a child chunk to the RIFF chunk, you call mmioDescend() again to read the format chunk's header, as shown here:

```
MMCKINFO mmCkInfoChunk;
mmCkInfoChunk.ckid = mmioFOURCC('f', 'm', 't', ' ');
result = mmioDescend(hMMIO, &mmCkInfoChunk,
    &mmCkInfoRIFF, MMIO_FINDCHUNK);
```

Here, again, you first define an MMCKINFO structure, this time for the child chunk into which you're about to descend. Now, though, you don't initialize the fccType field, but rather the ckid field as shown above. This ckid tells the function that you're looking for the format chunk. After this call, the mmCkInfoChunk structure will be filled in with information about the format chunk, in the same way that the mmCkInfoRIFF structure was filled in for the RIFF chunk. Notice that, in the above call to mmioDescend(), the third argument is the address of the parent chunk's MMCKINFO structure and the search flag is now MMIO_FINDCHUNK.

At this point, you're ready to read the format data into a WAVEFORMATEX structure, which you do with the mmioRead() function. Windows declares mmioRead() like this:

```
LONG mmioRead(
  HMMIO hmmio,
  HPSTR pch,
  LONG cch
);
```


Here's what the arguments mean:

- hmmio—The file handle
- pch—The address of the WAVEFORMATEX structure
- cch—The number of bytes to read

The function returns the number of bytes read or zero if unsuccessful. Here's what a real call looks like:

```
WAVEFORMATEX waveFormatEx;
LONG bytesRead = mmioRead(hMMIO, (char*)&waveFormatEx,
    sizeof(WAVEFORMATEX));
```

The first line above defines a WAVEFORMATEX structure to hold the information about to be read. You already learned about this structure previously in this chapter. The mmioRead() function reads the chunk's data field into the WAVEFORMATEX structure.

Reading the Data Chunk

Now that you have the format information tucked safely away in your WAVEFORMATEX structure, it's time to read the sound data itself. But before you can do that, you must ascend out from the format chunk, which you do with the mmioAscend() function. Windows declares that function like this:

```
MMRESULT mmioAscend(
  HMMIO hmmio,
  LPMMCKINFO lpck,
  UINT wFlags
);
```

Here's what the three arguments mean:

- `hmmio`—The file handle
- `lpck`—The address of the chunk's `MMCKINFO` structure
- `wFlags`—A flag that should always be 0

The actual call in your program might look like this:

```
MMRESULT result = mmioAscend(hMMIO, &mmCkInfoChunk, 0);
```

You must call `mmioAscend()` because the format and data chunks are siblings with respect to the parent RIFF chunk. Calling `mmioAscend()` positions the file at the beginning of the next chunk following the format chunk, which, of course, happens to be the data chunk.

You're now at the beginning of the data chunk. As you can probably figure out, the next step is to call `mmioDescend()` to descend into the data chunk:

```
mmCkInfoChunk.ckid = mmioFOURCC('d', 'a', 't', 'a');
result = mmioDescend(hMMIO, &mmCkInfoChunk,
    &mmCkInfoRIFF, MMIO_FINDCHUNK);
```

The only thing new here is that, this time, you set the `ckid` field of the `MMCKINFO` structure to "data" in order to tell the function which chunk you want.

At last you're ready to dig out the actual sound data. First, you must allocate some memory in which to store the data:

```
pWave = (char*)GlobalAllocPtr(GMEM_MOVEABLE, mmCkInfoChunk.cksize);
```

As you can see, the amount of memory you need to allocate is found in the `MMCKINFO` structure's `cksize` field.

With memory in hand, you can call `mmioRead()` to read in the sound data:

```
bytesRead = mmioRead(hMMIO, (char*)pWave, mmCkInfoChunk.cksize);
```

Finally, you close the file by calling `mmioClose()`, like this:

```
mmioClose(hMMIO, 0);
```

This function's two arguments are the file handle and a close flag, which is usually just zero.

Introducing the CWave Class

With the sound data safely stored in memory, you can create a DirectSound buffer and copy the sound data into it. But, before you get to dealing with that problem, this section of the book takes the functions and techniques you just learned and uses them to put together a class for reading wave files into memory. This class will enable you to forget about all this wave-file structure stuff and just load the darn things!

The CWave Class's Interface

The `CWave` class's interface is represented by its header file, which is shown in Listing 10.1.

LISTING 10.1 CWAVE.H—The CWave Class's Header File

```
///////////////////////////////////////////////////////////
// CWAVE.H: Header file for the WAVE class.
///////////////////////////////////////////////////////////

#ifndef __CWAVE_H
#define __CWAVE_H

#include <windows.h>
#include <mmsystem.h>

class CWave
{
protected:
    DWORD m_dwWaveSize;
    BOOL m_bWaveOK;
    char* m_pWave;
    WAVEFORMATEX m_waveFormatEx;

public:
    CWave(char* fileName);
    ~CWave();

    DWORD GetWaveSize();
    LPWAVEFORMATEX GetWaveFormatPtr();
    char* GetWaveDataPtr();
    BOOL WaveOK();

protected:
    BOOL LoadWaveFile(char* fileName);
};

#endif
```

The class's four protected data members are the size of the sound data (`m_dwWaveSize`), a flag indicating whether the wave file loaded successfully (`m_bWaveOK`), a pointer to the sound data (`m_pWave`), and a `WAVEFORMATEX` structure containing the wave file's format information (`m_waveFormatEx`).

Like most classes, `CWave` has both a constructor and destructor:

```
CWave(char* fileName);
~CWave();
```

As you can see, you create a `CWave` object by passing to the `CWave` constructor the filename of the wave file you want to load.

The `CWave` class is fairly small, containing only four public member functions that you can call from your programs in order to obtain information about the wave object. These four member functions are described in Table 10.1.

TABLE 10.1 The CWave Class's Public Member Functions

Name	*Description*
GetWaveSize()	Returns the size in bytes of the sound data.
GetWaveFormatPtr()	Returns a pointer to the wave file's WAVEFORMATEX structure.
GetWaveDataPtr()	Returns a pointer to the sound data.
WaveOK()	Returns a Boolean value indicating whether the wave file loaded successfully.

Programming the CWave Class

The code that defines the `CWave` class is found in the CWAVE.CPP file, which is shown in Listing 10.2. This file defines each of the functions in the `CWave` class.

LISTING 10.2 CWAVE.CPP—The Implementation of the CWave Class

```
///////////////////////////////////////////////////////////////
// CWAVE.CPP: Implementation file for the WAVE class.
///////////////////////////////////////////////////////////////

#include "windowsx.h"
#include "cwave.h"

///////////////////////////////////////////////////////////////
// CWave::CWave()
///////////////////////////////////////////////////////////////
CWave::CWave(char* fileName)
{
```

LISTING 10.2 continued

```
        m_dwWaveSize = 0;
        m_bWaveOK = FALSE;
        m_pWave = NULL;
        m_bWaveOK = LoadWaveFile(fileName);
    }

    ///////////////////////////////////////////////////////////
    // CWave::~CWave()
    ///////////////////////////////////////////////////////////
    CWave::~CWave()
    {
        GlobalFreePtr(m_pWave);
    }

    ///////////////////////////////////////////////////////////
    // CWave::LoadWaveFile()
    ///////////////////////////////////////////////////////////
    BOOL CWave::LoadWaveFile(char* fileName)
    {
        MMCKINFO mmCkInfoRIFF;
        MMCKINFO mmCkInfoChunk;
        MMRESULT result;
        HMMIO hMMIO;
        long bytesRead;

        // Open the wave file.
        hMMIO = mmioOpen(fileName, NULL, MMIO_READ | MMIO_ALLOCBUF);
        if (hMMIO == NULL)
            return FALSE;

        // Descend into the RIFF chunk.
        mmCkInfoRIFF.fccType = mmioFOURCC('W', 'A', 'V', 'E');
        result = mmioDescend(hMMIO, &mmCkInfoRIFF, NULL, MMIO_FINDRIFF);
        if (result != MMSYSERR_NOERROR)
            return FALSE;

        // Descend into the format chunk.
        mmCkInfoChunk.ckid = mmioFOURCC('f', 'm', 't', ' ');
        result = mmioDescend(hMMIO, &mmCkInfoChunk,
            &mmCkInfoRIFF, MMIO_FINDCHUNK);
        if (result != MMSYSERR_NOERROR)
            return FALSE;

        // Read the format information into the WAVEFORMATEX structure.
        bytesRead = mmioRead(hMMIO, (char*)&m_waveFormatEx,
            sizeof(WAVEFORMATEX));
        if (bytesRead == -1)
            return FALSE;
```

LISTING 10.2 continued

```
    // Ascend out of the format chunk.
    result = mmioAscend(hMMIO, &mmCkInfoChunk, 0);
    if (result != MMSYSERR_NOERROR)
        return FALSE;

    // Descend into the data chunk.
    mmCkInfoChunk.ckid = mmioFOURCC('d', 'a', 't', 'a');
    result = mmioDescend(hMMIO, &mmCkInfoChunk,
        &mmCkInfoRIFF, MMIO_FINDCHUNK);
    if (result != MMSYSERR_NOERROR)
        return FALSE;

    // Save the size of the wave data.
    m_dwWaveSize = mmCkInfoChunk.cksize;

    // Allocate a buffer for the wave data.
    m_pWave = (char*)GlobalAllocPtr(GMEM_MOVEABLE, m_dwWaveSize);
    if (m_pWave == NULL)
        return FALSE;

    // Read the wave data into the buffer.
    bytesRead = mmioRead(hMMIO, (char*)m_pWave, m_dwWaveSize);
    if (bytesRead == -1)
        return FALSE;
    mmioClose(hMMIO, 0);

    return TRUE;
}

////////////////////////////////////////////////////////////
// CWave::GetWaveSize()
////////////////////////////////////////////////////////////
DWORD CWave::GetWaveSize()
{
    return m_dwWaveSize;
}

////////////////////////////////////////////////////////////
// CWave::GetWaveFormatPtr()
////////////////////////////////////////////////////////////
LPWAVEFORMATEX CWave::GetWaveFormatPtr()
{
    return &m_waveFormatEx;
}

////////////////////////////////////////////////////////////
// CWave::GetWaveDataPtr()
////////////////////////////////////////////////////////////
char* CWave::GetWaveDataPtr()
{
```

LISTING 10.2 continued

```
    return m_pWave;
}

//////////////////////////////////////////////////////////
// CWave::WaveOK()
//////////////////////////////////////////////////////////
BOOL CWave::WaveOK()
{
    return m_bWaveOK;
}
```

As you can see, there's nothing too unfamiliar in the source code for the `CWave` class. The class opens and loads a file exactly as described earlier in this chapter. The only difference is that the class retains some information about the wave file in its data members. These values are the sound data's size and address, as well as the address of the wave file's `WAVEFORMATEX` structure.

Using DirectSound

There are several programming steps required to take advantage of DirectSound in a Windows program. You should keep the following steps in mind as you develop the DirectSoundApp application that you create later in this chapter:

1. Call `DirectSoundCreate()` to create a DirectSound object.
2. Call the DirectSound object's `SetCooperativeLevel()` method to set the program's priority level for the sound hardware.
3. Call the DirectSound object's `CreateSoundBuffer()` method to create a secondary sound buffer for each of your program's sound effects.
4. Call the secondary DirectSound buffer object's `Lock()` method to obtain a pointer to the buffer's memory.
5. Copy the sound data to the buffer's memory.
6. Call the secondary DirectSound buffer object's `Unlock()` method to tell DirectSound that the program is done with the buffer.
7. Call the secondary DirectSound buffer object's `Play()` method to mix the secondary buffer's sound data into the primary sound buffer and play the sound.

The preceding steps are a basic outline for implementing DirectSound in a program. The following sections describe each step in detail.

Creating a DirectSound Object

You need to create a DirectSound object in order to gain access to DirectSound's interface, which enables you to call DirectSound's methods. To create a DirectSound object, you must call the `DirectSoundCreate8()` function, which DirectX declares like this:

```
HRESULT WINAPI DirectSoundCreate8(
  LPCGUID lpcGuidDevice,
  LPDIRECTSOUND8 * ppDS8,
  LPUNKNOWN pUnkOuter
);
```

Here's a description of the three arguments:

- `lpcGuidDevice`—A pointer to the driver's GUID (globally unique identifier). Use the value `NULL` to select the default driver.
- `ppDS8`—The address of a `LPDIRECTSOUND` pointer variable.
- `pUnkOuter`—`NULL`.

If the function succeeds, it returns `DS_OK`; otherwise, it returns an error code. An actual call to `DirectSoundCreate8()` in your program, including error handling, might look like this:

```
IDirectSound8* pDirectSoundObj = NULL;
g_hResult = DirectSoundCreate8(NULL, &pDirectSoundObj, NULL);
if (FAILED(g_hResult))
{
    strcpy(g_szErrorMsg, "Error creating DirectSound object.");
    PostQuitMessage(WM_QUIT);
}
```

Setting the Priority Level

Because the Windows environment allows multitasking, many applications may be running simultaneously. In order to keep things running smoothly, different aspects of the operating system are assigned priority levels. For this reason, the DirectSound object provides the `SetCooperativeLevel()` function, which enables a program to request a priority level for the sound hardware. DirectX declares `SetCooperativeLevel()` like this:

```
HRESULT SetCooperativeLevel(
  HWND hwnd,
  DWORD dwLevel
);
```

Here's a description of the two arguments:

- hwnd—The handle of the window requesting a priority level
- dwLevel—The flags representing the requested level (DSSCL_NORMAL for normal multitasking)

Your program might call SetCooperativeLevel() like this:

```
g_hResult = pDirectSoundObj->SetCooperativeLevel(g_hWnd, DSSCL_NORMAL);
if (FAILED(g_hResult))
{
    strcpy(g_szErrorMsg, "Could not set the cooperative level.");
    PostQuitMessage(WM_QUIT);
}
```

Creating DirectSound Buffer Objects

The next step is to create secondary DirectSound buffer objects for the sound effects in your program. To do this, you first must have some information about the wave file that you'll be loading into this buffer. You get that information by using your trusty CWave class to load the wave file into memory:

```
CWave* pWave = new CWave("FunkyLoop.wav");
if (!pWave->WaveOK())
{
    MessageBox(g_hWnd, "Could not load wave file.", "Error", MB_OK);
    PostQuitMessage(WM_QUIT);
    return;
}
```

With the wave file in memory, you can use the CWave class's methods to get the information you need about the file:

```
LPWAVEFORMATEX pWaveFormatEx = pWave->GetWaveFormatPtr();
char* pWaveData = pWave->GetWaveDataPtr();
DWORD dwWaveSize = pWave->GetWaveSize();
```

The information you're getting here is a pointer to the wave file's WAVEFORMATEX structure, a pointer to the actual sound data, and the size of the sound data.

With this information in hand, you can initialize an instance of the DSBUFFERDESC structure:

```
DSBUFFERDESC dsBufferDesc;
memset(&dsBufferDesc, 0, sizeof(DSBUFFERDESC));
dsBufferDesc.dwSize = sizeof(DSBUFFERDESC);
dsBufferDesc.dwBufferBytes = dwWaveSize;
dsBufferDesc.lpwfxFormat = (LPWAVEFORMATEX) pWaveFormatEx;
```

The second line above clears the structure to all zeroes. The third line fills in the dwSize field with the size of the structure. The remaining lines set the size of the requested buffer (dwBufferBytes) to the size of the sound data and sets the lpwfxFormat pointer to the address of the wave file's WAVEFORMATEX structure.

How about a closer look at the DSBUFFERDESC structure? This structure holds information about DirectSound buffer objects and is declared by DirectX as shown here:

```
typedef struct _DSBUFFERDESC
{
    DWORD           dwSize;        // size, in bytes, of this structure
    DWORD           dwFlags;       // see below
    DWORD           dwBufferBytes; // see below
    DWORD           dwReserved;    // reserved. must be zero
    LPWAVEFORMATEX  lpwfxFormat;   // see below
} DSBUFFERDESC, *LPDSBUFFERDESC;
```

You transfer information to and from DirectSound by using structures such as DSBUFFER-DESC. Some of the information in the structure you fill in before calling certain DirectSound member functions, while DirectSound fills in other structure members to provide information back to your program.

Getting back to the programming, after initializing the DSBUFFERDESC structure, the program calls the DirectSound method CreateSoundBuffer() to create the secondary DirectSound buffer object. DirectX declares this method as follows:

```
HRESULT CreateSoundBuffer(
  LPCDSBUFFERDESC pcDSBufferDesc,
  LPDIRECTSOUNDBUFFER * ppDSBuffer,
  LPUNKNOWN pUnkOuter
);
```

Here's what the arguments mean:

- pcDSBufferDesc—The address of the DSBUFFERDESC structure
- ppDSBuffer—The address of a variable of the LPDIRECTSOUNDBUFFER type
- pUnkOuter—NULL

If the method creates the buffer successfully, it returns DS_OK, as well as fills in ppDSBuffer with a pointer to the secondary DirectSound buffer object.

Writing to the Sound Buffer

Once your program has its secondary buffers created, it must copy sound data to those buffers. You start off by defining a few variables:

```
LPVOID pSoundBlock1;
LPVOID pSoundBlock2;
```

```
DWORD dwBytesSoundBlock1;
DWORD dwBytesSoundBlock2;
```

These lines define two pointers to blocks in the sound buffer and two variables that'll contain the number of bytes stored in those blocks.

Before your program can manipulate a sound buffer, the buffer must be locked, which generates pointers to the buffer's memory blocks. You lock a buffer by calling the DirectSound buffer object's `Lock()` member function, which DirectX declares like this:

```
HRESULT Lock(
  DWORD dwOffset,
  DWORD dwBytes,
  LPVOID * ppvAudioPtr1,
  LPDWORD pdwAudioBytes1,
  LPVOID * ppvAudioPtr2,
  LPDWORD pdwAudioBytes2,
  DWORD dwFlags
);
```


Here's what the arguments mean:

- `dwOffset`—The position within the buffer at which you want to start the lock
- `dwBytes`—The number of bytes to lock
- `ppvAudioPtr1`—The address of a pointer to the first sound block
- `pdwAudioBytes1`—The address of a variable that'll contain the number of bytes in the first block
- `ppvAudioPtr2`—The address of a pointer to the second sound block
- `pdwAudioBytes2`—The address of a variable that'll contain the number of bytes in the second block
- `dwFlags`—Usually 0

An actual call to `Lock()` in a program might look as follows:

```
g_hResult = g_pSoundBuffer->Lock(0, dwWaveSize,
    &pSoundBlock1, &dwBytesSoundBlock1,
    &pSoundBlock2, &dwBytesSoundBlock2, 0);
if (FAILED(g_hResult))
{
    strcpy(g_szErrorMsg, "Could not lock sound buffer.");
    PostQuitMessage(WM_QUIT);
    return;
}
```

Notice that `Lock()` is called through a pointer to a DirectSound buffer object, not through a pointer to a DirectSound object. The `Lock()` method may return `DS_OK` or an error code.

If `Lock()` returns `DS_OK`, the buffer has been successfully locked, and DirectSound has stored a pointer to the buffer's memory area in `pSoundBlock1`. Your program can then copy the sound data into the buffer like this:

```
memcpy((void*)pSoundBlock1, pWaveData, dwWaveSize);
```

Finally, after copying the sound data, the program must tell DirectSound that it's done with the buffer. It does this by calling the DirectSound buffer object's `Unlock()` method. DirectX declares that method like this:

```
HRESULT Unlock(
  LPVOID pvAudioPtr1,
  DWORD dwAudioBytes1,
  LPVOID pvAudioPtr2,
  DWORD dwAudioBytes2
);
```

The method's four arguments are used as follows:

- `pvAudioPtr1`—A pointer to the first sound block
- `dwAudioBytes1`—The number of bytes in the first block
- `pvAudioPtr2`—A pointer to the second sound block
- `dwAudioBytes2`—The number of bytes in the second block

An actual call to `Unlock()` might look like this:

```
g_pSoundBuffer->Unlock(pSoundBlock1, dwBytesSoundBlock1,
    pSoundBlock2, dwBytesSoundBlock2);
```

Playing the Sound

Once you have the sound data loaded, playing the sound is a trivial task. First, you set the playback position within the sound buffer:

```
g_hResult = g_pSoundBuffer->SetCurrentPosition(0);
if (FAILED(g_hResult))
{
    strcpy(g_szErrorMsg, "Could not set sound cursor position.");
    PostQuitMessage(WM_QUIT);
    return;
}
```

The call to `SetCurrentPosition()` ensures that the buffer will play from its beginning. The method's single argument is the byte at which to set the playing cursor. The function can return `DS_OK` or an error code.

The `Play()` method actually plays the sound:

```
g_hResult = g_pSoundBuffer->Play(0, 0, DSBPLAY_LOOPING);
```

```
if (FAILED(g_hResult))
{
    strcpy(g_szErrorMsg, "Could not play sound buffer.");
    PostQuitMessage(WM_QUIT);
    return;
}
```

`Play()` takes three arguments. The first two are always zero. The third argument is either 0 or the `DSBPLAY_LOOPING` flag, which causes DirectSound to continue playing the sound effect until it is explicitly stopped.

Releasing DirectSound Objects

Just as with any DirectX objects, DirectSound objects must be released before your program terminates:

```
if (g_pSoundBuffer)
    g_pSoundBuffer->Release();
if (g_pDirectSoundObj)
    g_pDirectSoundObj->Release();
```


Building the DirectSoundApp Application

It's time to put everything you've learned about DirectSound to the test. In the following sections, you build the DirectSoundApp application, which uses DirectSound to play that funky music loop you've come to love so much.

Creating the Basic DirectSoundApp Project

Perform the following steps to get the main DirectSound application project started:

1. Start a new empty Win32 project named DirectSoundApp. (Don't forget to set the Application Settings to Empty Project.)
2. On the Project menu, select the Add New Item command. The Add New Item dialog box appears.
3. Add a new C++ File (.cpp) named DirectSoundApp.cpp.
4. Copy the contents of the BasicWindowsApp.cpp file (from Chapter 3) into the new DirectSoundApp.cpp code window.
5. Change the name in the comment at the top of the file to DirectSoundApp.
6. In the `RegisterWindowClass()` function change `wc.lpszClassName = "WinApp"` to `wc.lpszClassName = "DirectSoundApp"`.
7. In the `CreateAppWindow()` function, change "WinApp" to `"DirectSoundApp"`, and then change "Basic Windows Application" to "DirectSound Application".

Adding the Multimedia and DirectSound References

Next, you need to tell the program where the required header files and libraries are located. To do that, follow these steps:

1. Right-click the project's name in the Solution Explorer, and select Properties from the menu that appears. The DirectSoundApp Property Pages dialog box appears.
2. Click the C/C++ selection in the left pane, and select General from the displayed choices.
3. In the Additional Include Directories box, enter the path to the DirectX 8.1 SDK's include folder. If you installed the SDK using the default settings, this path should be `C:\DXSDK\include`.
4. Click the Linker selection in the left pane, and select General from the displayed choices.
5. In the Additional Library Directories box, enter the path to the DirectX 8.1 SDK's library folder. If you installed the SDK using the default settings, this path should be `C:\DXSDK\lib`.
6. Click the Linker's Input selection in the left pane.
7. In the Additional Dependencies box in the right pane, enter `dxerr8.lib`, `dsound.lib`, and `winmm.lib`. (Just enter the library names separated by spaces. Don't enter the commas or the word *and*.)
8. Compile and run the application to be sure it works. When the main screen appears, just close the window and proceed with the next section.

Adding Source Code

Now it's time to add the source code. Follow these steps to complete this task:

1. Near the top of the program, add the following line after the line `#include <windows.h>` that's already there:

   ```
   #include <dsound.h>
   #include <dxerr8.h>
   #include "CWave.h"
   ```

   These are the header files for DirectSound, DirectX errors, and the `CWave` class.
2. Near the top of the program, add the following lines to the function prototypes:

   ```
   void InitDirectSound();
   void PlaySound();
   ```

3. Near the top of the program, add the following lines to the global variables:

   ```
   HRESULT g_hResult = DS_OK;
   ```

```
char g_szErrorMsg[256];
IDirectSound8* g_pDirectSoundObj = NULL;
IDirectSoundBuffer* g_pSoundBuffer = NULL;
```

The third and fourth of these variables are a pointer to a DirectSound object and a pointer to a DirectSound buffer, respectively.

4. Replace the current `WinMain()` function with this one:

```
////////////////////////////////////////////////////////
// WinMain()
////////////////////////////////////////////////////////
INT WINAPI WinMain(HINSTANCE hInstance, HINSTANCE, LPSTR, INT)
{
    RegisterWindowClass(hInstance);
    CreateAppWindow(hInstance);
    ShowWindow(g_hWnd, SW_SHOWDEFAULT);
    UpdateWindow(g_hWnd);
    InitDirectSound();
    INT result = StartMessageLoop();
    CloseWindow(g_hWnd);
    if (g_hResult != DS_OK)
    {
        DXTRACE_ERR(g_szErrorMsg, g_hResult);
        MessageBox(g_hWnd, g_szErrorMsg, "Error",
            MB_OK | MB_ICONEXCLAMATION);
    }
    if (g_pSoundBuffer)
        g_pSoundBuffer->Release();
    if (g_pDirectSoundObj)
        g_pDirectSoundObj->Release();

    return result;
}
```

5. In the `WndProc()` function, add the following lines shown in bold to the `switch` statement:

```
    switch(msg)
    {
    case WM_CREATE:
        return 0;

    case WM_DESTROY:
        PostQuitMessage( 0 );
        return 0;

    case WM_PAINT:
        ValidateRect(g_hWnd, NULL);
        return 0;

    case WM_KEYDOWN:
```

10

```
        switch(wParam)
        {
        case VK_SPACE:
            PlaySound();
            break;
        }
    }
```

These new lines enable the user to press the spacebar to play a sound effect.

6. Add the following functions to the program:

```
///////////////////////////////////////////////////////
// InitDirectSound()
///////////////////////////////////////////////////////
void InitDirectSound()
{
    g_hResult = DirectSoundCreate8(NULL, &g_pDirectSoundObj, NULL);
    if (FAILED(g_hResult))
    {
        strcpy(g_szErrorMsg, "Error creating DirectSound object.");
        PostQuitMessage(WM_QUIT);
        return;
    }

    g_hResult = g_pDirectSoundObj->SetCooperativeLevel(g_hWnd, DSSCL_NOR-
MAL);
    if (FAILED(g_hResult))
    {
        strcpy(g_szErrorMsg, "Could not set the cooperative level.");
        PostQuitMessage(WM_QUIT);
        return;
    }

    CWave* pWave = new CWave("FunkyLoop.wav");
    if (!pWave->WaveOK())
    {
        MessageBox(g_hWnd, "Could not load wave file.", "Error", MB_OK);
        PostQuitMessage(WM_QUIT);
        return;
    }

    LPWAVEFORMATEX pWaveFormatEx = pWave->GetWaveFormatPtr();
    char* pWaveData = pWave->GetWaveDataPtr();
    DWORD dwWaveSize = pWave->GetWaveSize();

    DSBUFFERDESC dsBufferDesc;
    memset(&dsBufferDesc, 0, sizeof(DSBUFFERDESC));
    dsBufferDesc.dwSize = sizeof(DSBUFFERDESC);
    dsBufferDesc.dwBufferBytes = dwWaveSize;
    dsBufferDesc.lpwfxFormat = (LPWAVEFORMATEX) pWaveFormatEx;
```

```
    g_hResult = g_pDirectSoundObj->
        CreateSoundBuffer(&dsBufferDesc, &g_pSoundBuffer, NULL);
    if (FAILED(g_hResult))
    {
        strcpy(g_szErrorMsg, "Could not create sound buffer.");
        PostQuitMessage(WM_QUIT);
        return;
    }

    LPVOID pSoundBlock1;
    LPVOID pSoundBlock2;
    DWORD dwBytesSoundBlock1;
    DWORD dwBytesSoundBlock2;
    g_hResult = g_pSoundBuffer->Lock(0, dwWaveSize,
        &pSoundBlock1, &dwBytesSoundBlock1,
        &pSoundBlock2, &dwBytesSoundBlock2, 0);
    if (FAILED(g_hResult))
    {
        strcpy(g_szErrorMsg, "Could not lock sound buffer.");
        PostQuitMessage(WM_QUIT);
        return;
    }
    memcpy((void*)pSoundBlock1, pWaveData, dwWaveSize);

    g_pSoundBuffer->Unlock(pSoundBlock1, dwBytesSoundBlock1,
            pSoundBlock2, dwBytesSoundBlock2);

    delete pWave;
}

///////////////////////////////////////////////////////
// PlaySound()
///////////////////////////////////////////////////////
void PlaySound()
{
    g_hResult = g_pSoundBuffer->SetCurrentPosition(0);
    if (FAILED(g_hResult))
    {
        strcpy(g_szErrorMsg, "Could not set sound cursor position.");
        PostQuitMessage(WM_QUIT);
        return;
    }

    g_hResult = g_pSoundBuffer->Play(0, 0, DSBPLAY_LOOPING);
    if (FAILED(g_hResult))
    {
        strcpy(g_szErrorMsg, "Could not play sound buffer.");
        PostQuitMessage(WM_QUIT);
        return;
    }
}
```

7. On the Project menu, select the Add New Item command. The Add New Item dialog box appears.
8. Add a new C++ file (.cpp) named CWave.cpp.
9. Copy the contents of the CWave.cpp file (you can find it in the DirectSoundApp directory of this book's CD-ROM) into the new CWave.cpp code window.
10. On the Project menu, select the Add New Item command. The Add New Item dialog box appears.
11. Add a new header file (.h) named CWave.h.
12. Copy the contents of the CWave.h file (you can find it in the DirectSoundApp directory of this book's CD-ROM) into the new CWave.h code window.
13. Copy the sound file FunkyLoop.wav from the DirectSoundApp directory of this book's CD-ROM to your own DirectSoundApp directory. (Or you can place any wave file you want in your DirectSoundApp directory and rename it FunkyLoop.wav.)

You can now compile and run the program. When you do, you see the screen press the spacebar to play the wave file.

Summary

Creating sound effects for Windows games is easier than you might expect. Just plug a microphone into your sound card and run a sound-recording program. Every sound that the microphone picks up is recorded by the sound program and stored on disk as a .WAV (waveform) file. After recording the sound, you can edit it in various ways, including deleting parts of the sound, increasing the sound's volume, adding echo, and even reversing the sound. To play your sound effects, use the DirectSound routines provided in this chapter.

Q&A

Q. Can I use commercial sound-effect recordings in my games?

A. If you go to a large CD store, you'll probably find libraries of sound effects on CD. Whether you can use these sound effects in your games depends upon the licensing agreement that comes with the CD. In most cases, the lower-priced (around $15) collections are for personal use only. To get a sound-effect library that you can use legally in your games, you usually have to pay $50 or more.

Q. How much do I have to spend to set up a simple studio for creating sound effects?

A. You've already got the most important part of that studio: your computer. You can get fairly powerful sound-editing software for between $50 and $100, or you can get professional software for around $350. To get a decent synthesizer for creating sound effects, you'll probably have to spend at least $500, and more likely around $1,000. A decent microphone (say, a Shure SM-57, which is a great all-around mic) goes for around $90. But don't forget, household items and a microphone may be all you need (outside of a sound-editing program and your sound card) to get started.

Q. It seems like it's a heck of a lot easier to use a Windows function like `sndPlaySound()` to play sound effects than it is to use DirectSound. Why bother with DirectSound at all?

A. First, DirectSound provides a more efficient way to play sounds, making it easier to synchronize sound effects with events in a game. More importantly, though, DirectSound is a powerful library that provides an immense amount of control over your sound effects. Believe me, you've only scratched the surface in this chapter! It'd take an entire book to dig into DirectSound thoroughly.

Q. Is DirectSound really as "simple" to use as it's described in this chapter?

A. Yes and no. If all you want to do is play sound effects from beginning to end, the simple routines I've provided should do the trick nicely. However, DirectSound provides a great deal of control over sound devices. If you're looking for that greater control and are interested in digging deeper into DirectSound, look it up in your DirectX online help.

Workshop

The workshop includes quiz questions to help gauge your grasp of the material. Even if you feel that you totally understand the concepts presented here, you should work through the quiz anyway. The last section is an exercise or two that you might work through to help reinforce your learning.

Quiz

1. What's the minimum hardware and software you need for creating sound effects?
2. What are two general ways of playing sound effects in your programs?
3. What would you use a sound editor for?

4. Compare the `MessageBeep()` API function with the `PlaySound()` API function.
5. What two DirectX objects does a program need in order to play a sound effect?
6. Describe the two objects referred to in question 6.
7. What method do you call to play a sound effect with DirectSound?

Exercises

1. Use your computer and audio software to record and edit a sound effect.
2. Write a short program that plays the sound effect using the Windows API. (Don't use the routines provided in this chapter. Instead, just use this chapter as a reference.)
3. Write a short program that plays the sound effect using DirectSound. (You can use the `CWave` class, but don't use any other routines provided in this chapter. Instead, just use this chapter as a reference.)

Answers for Day 10

Quiz

1. What's the minimum hardware and software you need for creating sound effects?

   You need a sound card, a microphone, and a sound editor.
2. What are two general ways of playing sound effects in your programs?

   Using Windows API MCI functions or using DirectSound.
3. What would you use a sound editor for?

   A sound editor enables you to remove silences from before and after recorded sound effects, as well as to change the effect's volume and add special effects such as echo.
4. Compare the `MessageBeep()` API function with the `PlaySound()` API function.

   The `MessageBeep()` function only allows you to play system sound effects, whereas the `PlaySound()` function can play any wave file.
5. What two DirectX objects does a program need in order to play a sound effect?

   `IDirectSound8` and `IDirectSoundBuffer` objects.
6. Describe the two objects referred to in question 5.

The `IDirectSound8` object provides access to the DirectSound libraries, enabling you to set priority levels and create sound buffers. The `IDirectSoundBuffer` object represents a sound effect, and provides the methods needed for manipulating the sound.

7. What method do you call to play a sound effect with DirectSound?

   The `Play()` method.

WEEK 2

DAY 11

Getting Started on Your Role-Playing Game

Good news: Most of the theoretical stuff is now behind you, and you're ready to start programming a game! You've traveled a long road to get this far, but you'll use everything you've learned—and then some—as you program an old-fashioned role-playing game (RPG) named *The Adventures of Jasper Bookman*. In this chapter, you create the program's guts. Specifically, today you'll learn the following:

- How to create the basic Windows application
- How to start putting together a game engine
- How to use classes to organize the game's various modules

Creating the Basic JBookman Project

You're going to be putting together a lot of code in this chapter, as well as learning to take advantage of object-oriented programming (OOP) techniques to keep your source code organized and easier to understand. Specifically, you'll be creating classes for the game engine and for all of your Direct3D routines.

Just as with every Windows application, though, you must start with the Windows program that holds the `WinMain()` function, the entry point for every Windows application. In this section, you create the basic JBookman project. Just perform the following steps to get the main application project started:

1. Start a new empty Win32 project named JBookman. (Don't forget to set the application settings to Empty Project, as shown in Figure 11.1.)

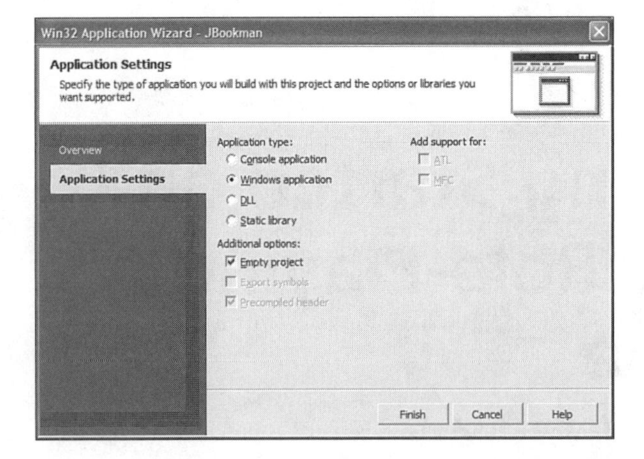

FIGURE 11.1
Choosing to create an empty project.

2. On the Project menu, select the Add New Item command. The Add New Item dialog box appears.
3. Add a new C++ file (.cpp) named JBookman.cpp, as shown in Figure 11.2.
4. Copy the contents of the BasicWindowsApp.cpp file (from Chapter 3) into the new JBookman.cpp code window.
5. Change the name in the comment at the top of the file to JBookman.cpp.
6. In the `RegisterWindowClass()` function change `wc.lpszClassName = "WinApp"` to `wc.lpszClassName = "JBookman"`.
7. In the `CreateAppWindow()` function, change "WinApp" to "JBookman", and then change "Basic Windows Application" to "The Adventures of Jasper Bookman".
8. Compile and run the program to ensure that your changes were correctly applied.

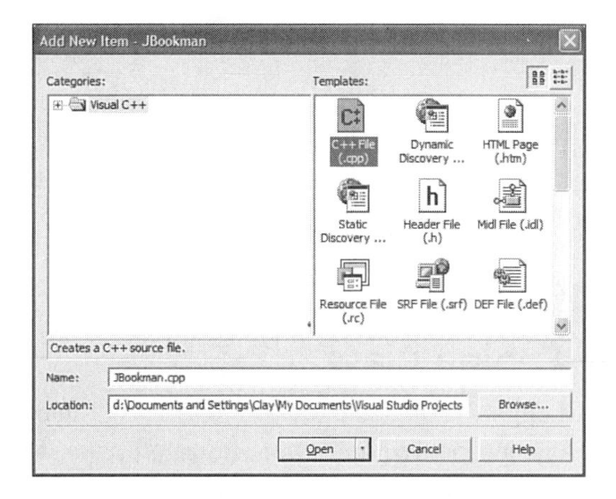

FIGURE 11.2
Creating the JBookman source code file.

Understanding Game Engines

Way back in the early days of computer games, programmers typically created a single program that contained all the game's logic, as well as the data upon which that logic worked. As games became more complex, however, it became necessary to separate the part of the code that powered the game from the part of the code that contained the specific data that supplied the game-play details.

The part of the program that powered the game has come to be known as the *engine*. Typically, developers program a game engine such that it can be used for more than one game. That is, take the game engine and add a new set of data, and you have a new game, albeit a new game that shares the functionality and look of other games that use the same engine.

If you're a computer gamer, you've no doubt noticed games that boast that they run on the Quake engine or the Unreal engine. This shows another advantage of separating the game's engine from the rest of the code: The engine can be licensed to other developers who want to create games without having to develop all the underlying code. Of course, if you want to license one of these commercial 3D engines, you'd better have a lot of money in the bank!

The Bookman Game Engine

The Adventures of Jasper Bookman will run on a game engine, too. The difference is that you don't have to license the engine. Instead, you have to program it from scratch! This engine won't be as sophisticated (by a long shot) as the commercial game engines, but you'll be able to use it to create not only *The Adventures of Jasper Bookman*, but also other RPG games. All you need to do is supply new graphics and data, and *presto!* you have a new game.

Actually, because RPGs take a huge amount of development time, not to mention tons of code, you'll build only part of *The Adventures of Jasper Bookman*, enough so that you can play the first part of the game and see how the engine works with the game data to create the full gaming experience. It'll be up to you to complete the game on your own. Or you might just want to start your own game from scratch using the Bookman engine.

Adding the Engine Class

The Bookman game engine is implemented as a C++ class named `CEngine` and will handle all the general functionality required by the game program. This means that the engine will handle Direct3D for you, as well as do everything from draw game screens to animate characters.

As you can guess, the game engine is going to be pretty big. For that reason, you'll be adding to it little by little as you work your way through the rest of this book. In any case, the first step is to add the class to your JBookman project. Perform the following steps to complete this task:

1. On the Project menu, select the Add Class command. The Add Class dialog box appears.
2. In the Templates box, select Generic C++ Class, as shown in Figure 11.3.

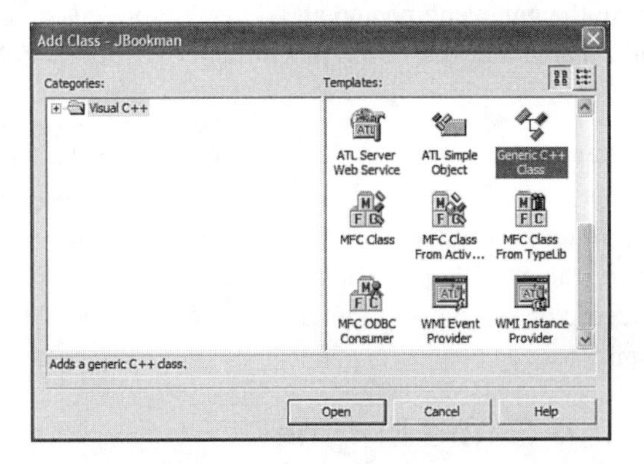

FIGURE 11.3
The Add Class dialog box.

3. Click Open, and the Generic C++ Class Wizard appears.
4. Enter **CEngine** into the Class Name box. The wizard automatically fills in the names for the header and code files, as shown in Figure 11.4.

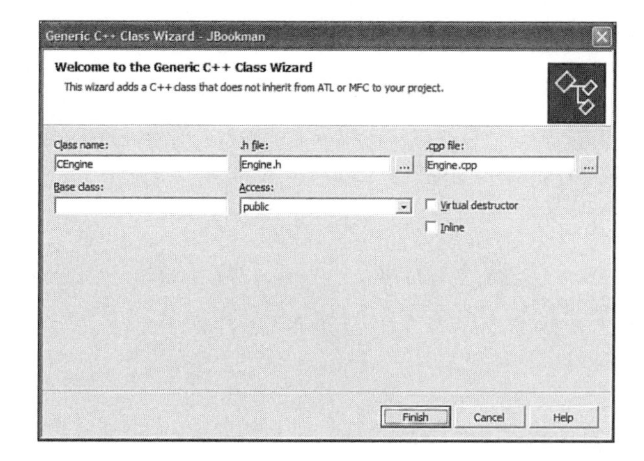

FIGURE 11.4

The Generic C++ Class Wizard.

5. Click Finish to add the class files to the project.
6. In the Engine.h file, modify the code so that it looks like this. If you don't want to do the typing, you can copy the Code01.txt file from the Chapter11 directory on this book's CD-ROM.

```
///////////////////////////////////////////////////////
// Engine.h
///////////////////////////////////////////////////////

#pragma once

#include <windows.h>

class CEngine
{
protected:
    HWND m_hWnd;

public:
    CEngine(void);
    ~CEngine(void);
    void SetWindowHandle(HWND hWnd);
    void ProcessGame();
    void HandleKeys(WPARAM wParam);
};
```

7. In the Engine.cpp file, modify the code so that it looks as follows. If you don't want to do the typing, you can copy the Code02.txt file from the Chapter11 directory on this book's CD-ROM.

```
///////////////////////////////////////////////////////
// Engine.cpp
///////////////////////////////////////////////////////
```

```
#include "engine.h"

//////////////////////////////////////////////////////
// CEngine()
//////////////////////////////////////////////////////
CEngine::CEngine(void)
{
}

//////////////////////////////////////////////////////
// ~CEngine()
//////////////////////////////////////////////////////
CEngine::~CEngine(void)
{
}

//////////////////////////////////////////////////////
// SetWindowHandle()
//////////////////////////////////////////////////////
void CEngine::SetWindowHandle(HWND hWnd)
{
    m_hWnd = hWnd;
}

//////////////////////////////////////////////////////
// ProcessGame()
//////////////////////////////////////////////////////
void CEngine::ProcessGame(void)
{
}

//////////////////////////////////////////////////////
// HandleKeys()
//////////////////////////////////////////////////////
void CEngine::HandleKeys(WPARAM wParam)
{
    switch(wParam)
    {
    }
}
```

8. Compile and run the application to be sure everything works okay. (Ignore the warning about the `switch` statement.) All you should see at this point is the application's window.

Exploring the CEngine Class

This isn't much of a game engine at this point. After all, the darn thing does next to nothing. As I mentioned before, though, you'll be adding to the engine throughout the rest of the book. For now, take a look at Table 11.1, which describes each of the class's members. You'll see how to use the class later in this chapter.

TABLE 11.1 Members of the CEngine class

Member	*Type*	*Description*
m_hWnd	Data	Holds the application's window handle
HandleKeys	Public method	Handles keystrokes for the application
ProcessGame	Public Method	Processes game data during the application's idle time
SetWindowHandle	Public Method	Sets the class's copy of the window handle

Adding the Direct3D Class

I mentioned that the game engine would handle all the Direct3D stuff for you, and, being the honest guy that I am, I wasn't making it up. However, the Direct3D stuff will itself be enclosed in a class named `CDirect3D`. The game engine will create an instance of this class and use that instance to manage Direct3D for you. As always, the first step is to add the class files to the project. Follow these steps to do that:

1. On the Project menu, select the Add Class command. The Add Class dialog box appears.
2. In the Templates box, select Generic C++ class.
3. Click Open, and the Generic C++ Class Wizard appears.
4. Enter **CDirect3D** into the Class Name box. The wizard automatically fills in the names for the header and code files, as shown in Figure 11.5.

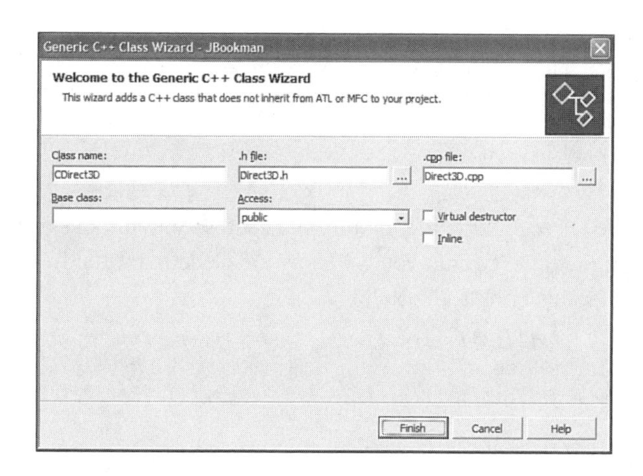

FIGURE 11.5
Adding the CDirect3D class.

5. Click OK to add the class files to the project.

6. In the Direct3D.h file, modify the code so that it looks as follows. If you don't want to do the typing, you can copy the Code03.txt file from the Chapter11 directory on this book's CD-ROM.

```
///////////////////////////////////////////////////////
// Direct3D.h
///////////////////////////////////////////////////////

#pragma once

#include <d3d8.h>

class CDirect3D
{
protected:
    LPDIRECT3D8 m_pD3D;
    LPDIRECT3DDEVICE8 m_pD3DDevice;
    IDirect3DSurface8* m_pBackBuffer;
    HWND m_hWnd;
    char m_szErrorMsg[256];

public:
    CDirect3D(void);
    ~CDirect3D(void);
    void SetWindowHandle(HWND hWnd);
    HRESULT InitD3D(void);
    LPDIRECT3DDEVICE8 GetDevice(void);
    IDirect3DSurface8* GetBackBuffer(void);
    char* GetErrorString(void);

private:
    HRESULT CreateD3DObject(void);
    HRESULT CheckDisplayMode(void);
    HRESULT CreateD3DDevice(void);
    HRESULT CreateSurfaces(void);
    void CleanUp(void);
};
```

7. In the Direct3D.cpp file, modify the code so that it looks as follows. If you don't want to do the typing, you can copy the Code04.txt file from the Chapter11 directory on this book's CD-ROM.

```
///////////////////////////////////////////////////////
// Direct3D.cpp
///////////////////////////////////////////////////////

#include "direct3d.h"

///////////////////////////////////////////////////////
// CDirect3D()
```

```
/////////////////////////////////////////////////////
CDirect3D::CDirect3D(void)
{
    m_pD3D = NULL;
    m_pD3DDevice = NULL;
    m_pBackBuffer = NULL;
    strcpy(m_szErrorMsg, "No Error");
}

/////////////////////////////////////////////////////
// ~CDirect3D()
/////////////////////////////////////////////////////
CDirect3D::~CDirect3D(void)
{
    CleanUp();
}

/////////////////////////////////////////////////////
// SetWindowHandle()
/////////////////////////////////////////////////////
void CDirect3D::SetWindowHandle(HWND hWnd)
{
    m_hWnd = hWnd;
}

/////////////////////////////////////////////////////
// InitD3D()
/////////////////////////////////////////////////////
HRESULT CDirect3D::InitD3D()
{
    HRESULT hResult = CreateD3DObject();
    if (hResult != D3D_OK)
        return hResult;
    hResult = CheckDisplayMode();
    if (hResult != D3D_OK)
        return hResult;
    hResult = CreateD3DDevice();
    if (hResult != D3D_OK)
        return hResult;
    hResult = CreateSurfaces();
    if (hResult != D3D_OK)
        return hResult;
    hResult = m_pD3DDevice->GetBackBuffer(0,
        D3DBACKBUFFER_TYPE_MONO, &m_pBackBuffer);
    m_pD3DDevice->Clear(0, 0, D3DCLEAR_TARGET,
        D3DCOLOR_XRGB(0,0,255), 0, 0);
    m_pD3DDevice->Present(NULL, NULL, NULL, NULL);
    return hResult;
}

/////////////////////////////////////////////////////
```

11

```
// CreateD3DObject()
//////////////////////////////////////////////////////
HRESULT CDirect3D::CreateD3DObject()
{
    m_pD3D = Direct3DCreate8(D3D_SDK_VERSION);
    if (m_pD3D == NULL)
    {
        MessageBox(m_hWnd, "Couldn't create DirectX object.",
            "DirectX Error", MB_OK);
        strcpy(m_szErrorMsg, "CreateD3DObject()");
        return E_FAIL;
    }
    return D3D_OK;
}

//////////////////////////////////////////////////////
// CheckDisplayMode()
//////////////////////////////////////////////////////
HRESULT CDirect3D::CheckDisplayMode()
{
    HRESULT hResult = m_pD3D->CheckDeviceType(D3DADAPTER_DEFAULT,
        D3DDEVTYPE_HAL, D3DFMT_X8R8G8B8, D3DFMT_X8R8G8B8, FALSE);
    if (hResult != D3D_OK)
    {
        MessageBox(m_hWnd, "The required display mode is \
not available on this system.",
            "DirectX Error", MB_OK);
        strcpy(m_szErrorMsg, "CheckDisplayMode()");
        return hResult;
    }
    return D3D_OK;
}

//////////////////////////////////////////////////////
// CreateD3DDevice()
//////////////////////////////////////////////////////
HRESULT CDirect3D::CreateD3DDevice()
{
    D3DPRESENT_PARAMETERS D3DPresentParams;
    ZeroMemory(&D3DPresentParams, sizeof(D3DPRESENT_PARAMETERS));
    D3DPresentParams.Windowed = FALSE;
    D3DPresentParams.BackBufferCount = 1;
    D3DPresentParams.BackBufferWidth = 640;
    D3DPresentParams.BackBufferHeight = 480;
    D3DPresentParams.BackBufferFormat = D3DFMT_X8R8G8B8;
    D3DPresentParams.SwapEffect = D3DSWAPEFFECT_DISCARD;
    D3DPresentParams.hDeviceWindow = m_hWnd;
    HRESULT hResult = m_pD3D->CreateDevice(D3DADAPTER_DEFAULT,
```

```
        D3DDEVTYPE_HAL, m_hWnd, D3DCREATE_SOFTWARE_VERTEXPROCESSING,
        &D3DPresentParams, &m_pD3DDevice);
    if (FAILED(hResult))
    {
        MessageBox(m_hWnd, "Failed to create Direct3D device.",
            "DirectX Error", MB_OK);
        strcpy(m_szErrorMsg, "CreateD3DDevice()");
        return hResult;
    }
    return hResult;
}

//////////////////////////////////////////////////////
// CreateSurfaces()
//////////////////////////////////////////////////////
HRESULT CDirect3D::CreateSurfaces()
{
    return D3D_OK;
}

//////////////////////////////////////////////////////
// CleanUp()
//////////////////////////////////////////////////////
void CDirect3D::CleanUp()
{
    if (m_pBackBuffer)
        m_pBackBuffer->Release();

    if (m_pD3DDevice)
        m_pD3DDevice->Release();

    if (m_pD3D)
        m_pD3D->Release();
}

//////////////////////////////////////////////////////
// GetBackBuffer()
//////////////////////////////////////////////////////
IDirect3DSurface8* CDirect3D::GetBackBuffer()
{
    return m_pBackBuffer;
}

//////////////////////////////////////////////////////
// Getdevice()
//////////////////////////////////////////////////////
LPDIRECT3DDEVICE8 CDirect3D::GetDevice()
{
    return m_pD3DDevice;
}
```

```
///////////////////////////////////////////////////////////
// GetErrorString()
///////////////////////////////////////////////////////////
char* CDirect3D::GetErrorString(void)
{
    return m_szErrorMsg;
}
```

Exploring the CDirect3D Class

Now that looks more like a useful class! You'll still be adding more stuff to it as you go along, but this puppy sure has more guts than the current version of the CEngine class. Table 11.2 describes each of the class's members. You'll see how to use these members as you continue to program the game.

TABLE 11.2 Members of the CDirect3D Class

Member	*Type*	*Description*
m_hWnd	Data	Holds the application's window handle
m_pBackBuffer	Data	Holds a pointer to the application's back buffer
m_pD3D	Data	Holds a pointer to the class's Direct3D object
m_pD3DDevice	Data	Holds a pointer to the application's Direct3D device
m_szErrorMsg[256]	Data	Holds the current error message
CreateSurfaces	Private method	Creates the application's image and texture surfaces
CheckDisplayMode	Private method	Verifies that the user's system supports the required display
CleanUp	Private method	Releases all Direct3D objects
CreateD3DDevice	Private method	Creates the application's Direct3D device
CreateD3DObject	Private method	Creates the application's Direct3D object
GetBackBuffer	Public method	Returns a pointer to the application's back buffer
GetDevice	Public method	Returns a pointer to the application's Direct3D device
GetErrorString	Public method	Returns the current error message
InitD3D	Public method	Initializes Direct3D for the application, including creating the Direct3D object, checking the display mode, creating the Direct3D device object, and creating the various required surfaces
SetWindowHandle	Public method	Sets the class's copy of the application's window handle

Adding the DirectX References

If you try to compile the program at this point, you're going to get a lot of errors. And, by now, you should know why you're getting those errors: you haven't yet added the Direct3D headers and library references to the project. To do that, follow these steps:

1. Right-click the project's name in the Solution Explorer, and select Properties from the menu that appears. The JBookman Property Pages dialog box appears.
2. Click the C/C++ selection in the left pane, and select General from the displayed choices.
3. In the Additional Include Directories box, enter the path to the DirectX 8.1 SDK's include folder, as shown in Figure 11.6. If you installed the SDK using the default settings, this path should be `C:\DXSDK\include`.

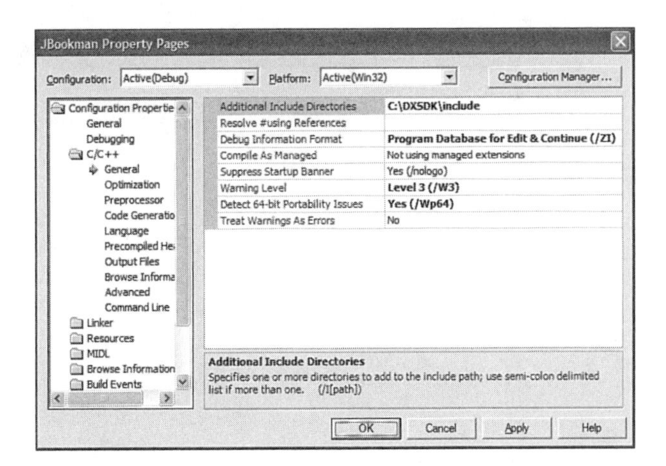

FIGURE 11.6

Adding the Direct3D include directory.

4. Click the Linker selection in the left pane, and select General from the displayed choices.
5. In the Additional Library Directories box, enter the path to the DirectX 8.1 SDK's library folder, as shown in Figure 11.7. If you installed the SDK using the default settings, this path should be `C:\DXSDK\lib`.
6. Click the Linker's Input selection in the left pane.
7. In the Additional Dependencies box in the right pane, enter `d3d8.lib`, `d3dx8.lib`, and `dxerr8.lib`, as shown in Figure 11.8. (Enter the library names separated by spaces. Don't enter the commas or the word *and*.)
8. Compile and run the application to be sure it works. (Again, ignore the warning about the `switch` statement.) When you see the application's window, just close it.

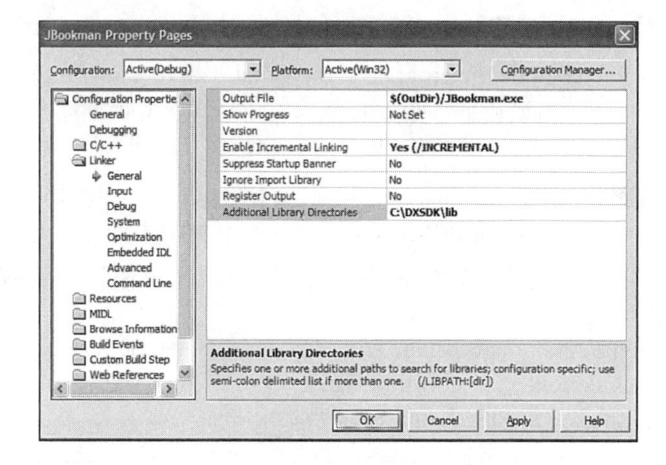

FIGURE 11.7 *Adding the Direct3D library directory.*

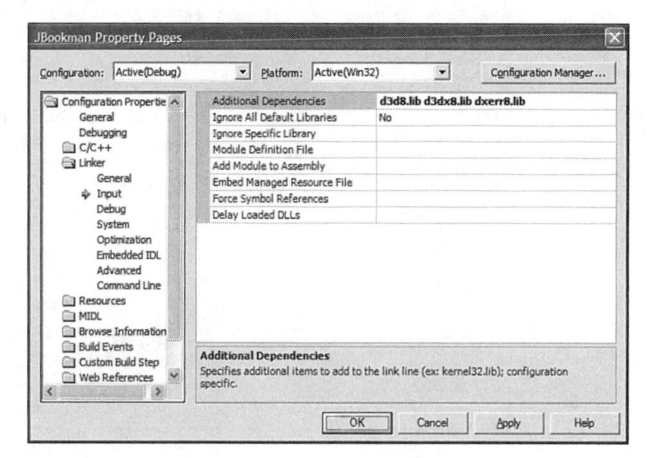

FIGURE 11.8 *Adding the Direct3D libraries to the project.*

Plugging In the Classes

Cool! You've now got the main application, the `CEngine` class, and the `CDirect3D` class all compiled and ready to go. There's just one problem: although the classes are part of your project, they haven't yet been plugged into each other.

Before the main program can take advantage of the game engine, it must create an instance of the `CEngine` class and call a couple of its methods. Also, the `CEngine` class has to create an instance of the `CDirect3D` class in order to handle Direct3D for you. Guess what you do in the following steps?

1. Add the following lines to the Engine.h file, right after the `#include <windows.h>` line that's already there:

```
#include <d3d8.h>
#include "Direct3D.h"
```

These lines include the header files for the Direct3D library and for the `CDirect3D` class.

2. Add the following line to the Engine.h file's data members, right after the `HWND m_hWnd` line that's already there:

```
CDirect3D m_Direct3D;
```

This line creates an instance of the `CDirect3D` class.

3. Add the following line to the Engine.h file's public methods, right after line `void HandleKeys(WPARAM wParam)` that's already there:

```
CDirect3D* GetCDirect3DObj();
```

This line declares a new public method that returns a pointer to the class's `CDirect3D` object (not to be confused with a Direct3D object).

4. Add the following method implementation to the Engine.cpp file:

```
//////////////////////////////////////////////////////
// GetCDirect3DObj()
//////////////////////////////////////////////////////
CDirect3D* CEngine::GetCDirect3DObj()
{
    return &m_Direct3D;
}
```

5. Add the following line to the `SetWindowHandle()` method in the Engine.cpp file:

```
m_Direct3D.SetWindowHandle(hWnd);
```

This line sets the `CDirect3D` object's copy of the application's window handle.

6. Add the following lines to the JBookman.cpp file's include section, right after line `#include <windows.h>` that's already there:

```
#include <dxerr8.h>
#include "Engine.h"
```

These lines include the header files for the Direct3D error-handling library and for the `CEngine` class.

7. Add the following line to the JBookman.cpp file's global variables, right after line `HWND g_hWnd` that's already there:

```
CEngine g_Engine;
```

This line creates a global `CEngine` object for the application.

8. In the JBookman.cpp file, replace the current `WinMain()` function with the one that follows. If you don't want to do the typing, you can copy the Code05.txt file from the Chapter11 directory on this book's CD-ROM.

11

```
///////////////////////////////////////////////////////
// WinMain()
///////////////////////////////////////////////////////
INT WINAPI WinMain(HINSTANCE hInstance, HINSTANCE, LPSTR, INT)
{
    RegisterWindowClass(hInstance);
    CreateAppWindow(hInstance);
    g_Engine.SetWindowHandle(g_hWnd);
    HRESULT hResult = g_Engine.GetCDirect3DObj()->InitD3D();
    if (hResult == D3D_OK)
    {
        ShowWindow(g_hWnd, SW_SHOWDEFAULT);
        UpdateWindow(g_hWnd);
        StartMessageLoop();
    }
    else
    {
        char* msg = g_Engine.GetCDirect3DObj()->GetErrorString();
        DXTRACE_ERR(msg, hResult);
    }
    return 0;
}
```

9. Compile and run the application. If everything works okay, you should see a solid blue screen. To close the application, Alt+Tab back to Visual Studio and select the Stop debugging command.

Understanding the Program

If you're fluent with C++ and OOP techniques, you should already have a good idea of what's going on in the program. Still, how about a quick overview just to make sure everything's clear? Follow through this overview of program execution to be sure you understand everything:

1. Program execution starts with the code in the JBookman.cpp file, which not only defines the global `g_hWnd` variable, but also creates the global `CEngine` object. The `CEngine` class's constructor currently does nothing.
2. Creating the `CEngine` object also creates the `CDirect3D` object, because that object is a data member of the `CEngine` class. The `CDirect3D` constructor initializes the Direct3D pointers and the error string.
3. The `WinMain()` function starts. The function creates the application's window and gives the `CEngine` object the resultant window handle, by calling that object's `SetWindowHandle()` method.

4. The CEngine SetWindowHandle() method passes the window handle on to the CDirect3D object, by calling that object's own SetWindowHandle() method.
5. WinMain() initializes Direct3D through the CEngine object's CDirect3D object, by calling that object's InitD3D() method.
6. The InitD3D() method initializes Direct3D by calling the private helper methods CreateD3DObject(), CheckDisplayMode(), CreateD3DDevice(), and CreateSurfaces().
7. The InitD3D() method also gets a pointer to the application's back buffer, clears the buffer to solid blue, and displays the buffer.
8. Back in WinMain(), if the call to InitD3D() goes okay, the program starts the message loop. Otherwise, the program gets the current error string and displays it with the DXTRACE_ERR() macro.
9. When the program terminates, the CEngine and CDirect3D objects' destructors get called. The CEngine destructor currently does nothing, but the CDirect3D destructor releases the Direct3D objects that the class created.

That wasn't so bad, right? If you're still not clear about what the code is doing so far, print the source code out and follow through the program as you read the previous nine points. Repeat as necessary!

Summary

The first step in programming any game is to get the basic, skeleton application up and running. This includes writing the code required to initialize and start up not only the application's window, but also libraries such as Direct3D. Then, you can move forward with the project, adding the specific code needed to create the game you want. You can save this chapter's project as reusable code for other Direct3D projects you may want to write.

Q&A

Q. This sure was a lot of work just to end up with a functional clone to one of the first Direct3D examples we programmed in the book. Aren't we kind of going backward here?

A. No, not at all. First, you're getting a little more practice at getting Windows applications with Direct3D support up and running. But more importantly, you've put together a more refined and organized version of that earlier program, one that'll be easier to extend into a full-scale game. Just the use of classes alone goes a long way toward refining the code and preparing it for the extensive programming to come.

Q. So, let me get this straight. Once I finish building the game engine for *The Adventures of Jasper Bookman*, I can charge other people to use it?

A. Uh…no. First, this game engine belongs to your humble author and his publisher. Second, if you tried to license the use of such a small engine commercially, you'd get laughed off the planet. Make that the universe. This game engine is just a small example of how you might create such a project. If you want to spend a couple of years with a dozen of your buddies programming the end-all game engine, *then* you can charge other people to use that engine. As for the Jasper Bookman engine, you can use it to create your own RPG games.

Workshop

The workshop includes quiz questions to help gauge your grasp of the material. Even if you feel that you totally understand the concepts presented here, you should work through the quiz anyway. The last section is an exercise or two that you might work through to help reinforce your learning.

Quiz

1. Why must every one of your Windows games start with a basic Windows application?
2. What do you call the part of the program that powers the game? This is the code that reads in and manipulates the game data.
3. What are a couple of advantages of creating a games engine?
4. Why use classes to separate the different parts of the program?
5. What's a fast way to add a new class to your program, using Visual Studio's commands?
6. How does the CEngine class get plugged into the main program?
7. What class in the program contains the code needed to manage Direct3D?
8. What class creates an object of the CDirect3D class and so provides Direct3D support for the main program?

Exercises

1. Use Visual Studio's debugging commands, particularly breakpoints and the Trace Into (F11) and Trace Over (F10) commands to trace through the execution flow of the JBookman application. Start by placing a breakpoint on the line:

```
CEngine g_Engine;
```

in the JBookman.cpp file, because this is where the program constructs the first class object. Then press F11 to start the program, which will start program execution, after which it will pause on the breakpoint. As you step through the program, take special note of how and where the program creates instances of its classes.

2. Add a class called `CMessage` to the JBookman program. This class should display a message box whenever the user presses the F1 key. *Before you make any changes, however, copy the JBookman project and work only on the copy!*

   Hint: The line in the `CMessage` class that actually displays the message box might look something like this:

```
MessageBox(m_hWnd, "F1 pressed.", "CMessage Class", MB_OK);
```

Answers for Day 11

Quiz

1. Why must every one of your Windows games start with a basic Windows application?

   First, because that's where the `WinMain()` function, which is the entry point of every Windows application, is located. Also, the main program creates the application's window, as well as holds the message loop that receives and dispatches Windows messages.

2. What do you call the part of the program that powers the game? This is the code that reads in and manipulates the game data.

   The game engine.

3. What are a couple of advantages of creating a game's engine?

   Creating a game engine enables you to keep the game's main logic separate from the data that drives the game. Also, by creating a game engine that can handle the general data processing required by a game, you can easily create a new game just by supplying new data.

4. Why use classes to separate the different parts of the program?

   Using classes helps you keep your source code organized, so that you can more easily find the sections of the program you need to work on. More importantly, classes enable you to create modules that group related functions and data.

5. What's a fast way to add a new class to your program, using Visual Studio's commands?

   On the Project menu, select the Add Class command.

6. How does the CEngine class get plugged into the main program?

   Mostly through the `ProcessGame()` method, which the main program calls whenever the application has no messages to process.

7. What class in the program contains the code needed to manage Direct3D?

   The `CDirect3D` class.

8. What class creates an object of the CDirect3D class and so provides Direct3D support for the main program?

   The `CEngine` class.

Exercises

1. No answer required.

2. There are, of course, several ways you might complete this exercise. Here's just one way. First, you need to add the `CMessage` class to the program using Visual Studio's Add Class command. Then you might fill out the class so that its header and implementation files look as follows:

   Header file:

```
#pragma once

#include <windows.h>

class CMessage
{
protected:
    HWND m_hWnd;

public:
    CMessage();
    ~CMessage(void);
    void SetWindowHandle(HWND hWnd);
    void ShowMessage(void );
};
```

   Implementation file:

```
#include "message.h"

CMessage::CMessage()
{
    m_hWnd = 0;
}

CMessage::~CMessage(void)
{
}
```

```
void CMessage::SetWindowHandle(HWND hWnd)
{
    m_hWnd = hWnd;
}

void CMessage::ShowMessage(void)
{
    MessageBox(m_hWnd, "F1 pressed.", "CMessage Class", MB_OK);
}
```

To hook the class into the main program, you first need to add the class's header file to the main program's include section:

```
#include "Message.h"
```

Then you need to create a global object of the class (where the program already creates the global `CEngine` class), like this:

```
CMessage g_msg;
```

Next, after the application creates its window, you can pass the handle on to the class object:

```
g_Engine.SetWindowHandle(g_hWnd);
```

Finally, the program needs to respond to the F1 key, something you might implement by adding the following lines to the `WndProc()` function:

```
case WM_KEYDOWN:
    switch(wParam)
    {
    case VK_F1:
        g_msg.ShowMessage();
        break;
    }
```

A modification of this solution might do away with the `m_hWnd` data member and the `SetWindowHandle()` method and just pass the window handle to the `ShowMessage()` method:

```
void CMessage::ShowMessage(HWND hWnd)
{
    MessageBox(hWnd, "F1 pressed.", "CMessage Class", MB_OK);
}
```

Note that, because the JBookman application gets Direct3D up and running, you won't be able to see the message box right away when you press F1. To solve this problem, run the program, and when the blue screen appears, press F1. Then, Alt+Tab back to Windows and bring up the application's window, which will look something like Figure 11.9.

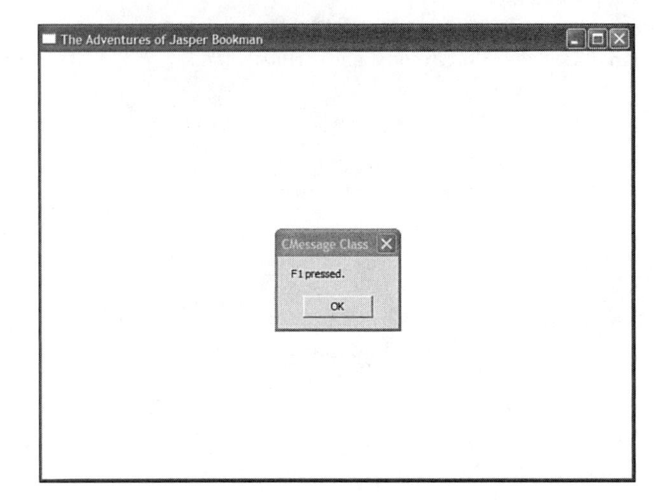

FIGURE 11.9
Displaying the `CMessage` *class's message box.*

WEEK 2

DAY 12

Initializing Game Data

Just as with any type of computer program, a game's state at any point in time is represented by the state of its data, which is stored in various types of variables. Obviously, at the beginning of a game, these values must be initialized to the values that represent the starting game state. In this chapter, you write the part of the game that accomplishes this task. Specifically, today you'll learn the following:

- How to organize related data with classes
- How to plug new classes into the game engine
- How to load game data from disk files

Manipulating Data in Classes

Game programmers have at their beck and call many types of variables in which to store game data. These include everything from integers to floating-point numbers and strings. However, although *The Adventures of Jasper Bookman* will store game data in such types of variables, you'll also create many special data types in the form of classes.

Classes are a great way of dealing with game data, because they enable you to group together data and the functions that manipulate that data. For example, as you'll soon see, the JBookman project uses a class to represent the many doors in the game world. In the class are data members that specify whether the door is locked and whether it's visible. Methods of the class enable the main program to set and retrieve these values as needed.

The JBookman project will, in fact, use many classes to represent various objects in the game, including not only doors, but also containers, people, and the player herself. Table 12.1 lists these classes and their descriptions.

TABLE 12.1 Some Classes Used in the JBookman Project

Class	*Description*
CContainer	Represents a treasure chest, barrel, or other type of container that can hold items of value to the player
CContainers	Represents a group of containers
CDoor	Represents a door
CDoors	Represents a group of doors
CPerson	Represents a non-player character (NPC) in the game
CPeople	Represents a group of NPCs
CPlayer	Represents the player's character

Adding the `CContainer` Class

As the player roams through Jasper Bookman's game world, she will come across many objects with which she can interact. One type of object in the game is a container, which usually comes in the form of a chest or a barrel. As their name suggests, containers can hold other objects, including keys, gold, armor, weapons, and potions.

In the game, a container looks just like a chest or a barrel. However, in the program code, a container is represented by a class. This class, named `CContainer`, provides data members for storing the types of objects hidden inside the container. The class also includes methods for setting and retrieving the values of these data members.

Besides being able to hold items, a container can also be locked. To explore an unlocked container, the player need only move his character so that it bumps into a container. However, a locked container cannot be opened unless the player has a key.

Load up the latest version of *The Adventures of Jasper Bookman*, and perform the following steps to add the `CContainer` class to the program.

1. On the Project menu, select the Add Class command. The Add Class dialog box appears.
2. In the Templates box, select Generic C++ class, as shown in Figure 12.1.

FIGURE 12.1
The Add Class dialog box.

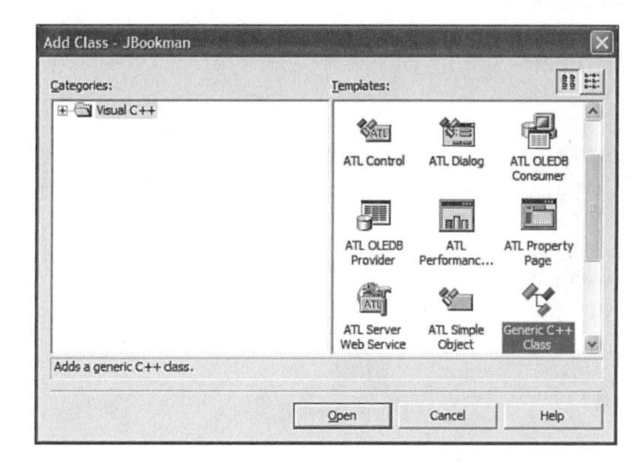

3. Click Open, and the Generic C++ Class Wizard appears.
4. Enter `CContainer` into the Class Name box. The wizard automatically fills in the names for the header and implementation files, as shown in Figure 12.2.

FIGURE 12.2
The Generic C++ Class Wizard.

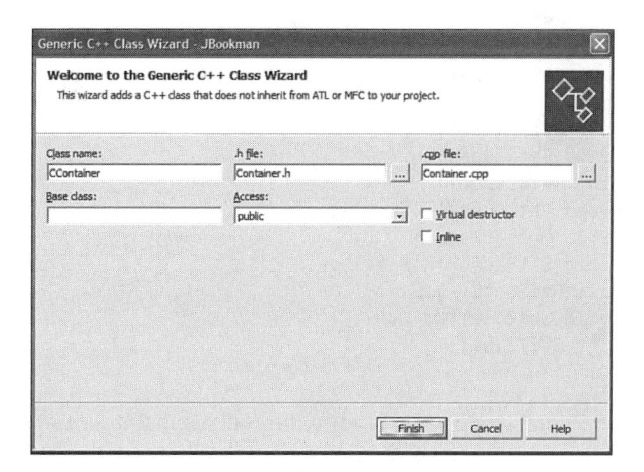

5. Click Finish to add the class files to the project.
6. In the Container.h file, modify the code so that it looks like this. If you don't want to do the typing, you can copy the Code01.txt file from the Chapter 12 directory on this book's CD-ROM.

```
///////////////////////////////////////////////////////
// Container.h
///////////////////////////////////////////////////////

#pragma once

#include <windows.h>

class CContainer
{
protected:
    int m_iGold;
    int m_iKeys;
    int m_iPotion;
    int m_iArmor;
    int m_iWeapon;
    BOOL m_bLocked;
    int m_iSector;
    int m_iTile;

public:
    CContainer(void);
    ~CContainer(void);

    void SetGold(int num);
    int GetGold();
    void SetKeys(int num);
    int GetKeys();
    void SetPotion(int num);
    int GetPotion();
    void SetArmor(int num);
    int GetArmor();
    void SetWeapon(int num);
    int GetWeapon();
    void SetLocked(BOOL val);
    BOOL GetLocked();
    void SetSector(int val);
    int GetSector();
    void SetTile(int num);
    int GetTile();
};
```

7. In the Container.cpp file, modify the code so that it looks as follows. If you don't want to do the typing, you can copy the Code02.txt file from the Chapter 12 directory on this book's CD-ROM.

```
///////////////////////////////////////////////////////
// Container.cpp
///////////////////////////////////////////////////////

#include "container.h"

///////////////////////////////////////////////////////
// CContainer()
///////////////////////////////////////////////////////
CContainer::CContainer(void)
{
    m_iGold = 0;
    m_iKeys = 0;
    m_iPotion = 0;
    m_iArmor = 0;
    m_iWeapon = 0;
    m_bLocked = FALSE;
    m_iSector = 0;
    m_iTile = 0;
}

///////////////////////////////////////////////////////
// ~CContainer()
///////////////////////////////////////////////////////
CContainer::~CContainer(void)
{
}

///////////////////////////////////////////////////////
// SetGold()
///////////////////////////////////////////////////////
void CContainer::SetGold(int num)
{
    m_iGold = num;
}

///////////////////////////////////////////////////////
// GetGold()
///////////////////////////////////////////////////////
int CContainer::GetGold()
{
    return m_iGold;
}

///////////////////////////////////////////////////////
// SetKeys()
///////////////////////////////////////////////////////
void CContainer::SetKeys(int num)
{
    m_iKeys = num;
}
```

```
/////////////////////////////////////////////////////
// GetKeys()
/////////////////////////////////////////////////////
int CContainer::GetKeys()
{
    return m_iKeys;
}

/////////////////////////////////////////////////////
// SetPotion()
/////////////////////////////////////////////////////
void CContainer::SetPotion(int num)
{
    m_iPotion = num;
}

/////////////////////////////////////////////////////
// GetPotion()
/////////////////////////////////////////////////////
int CContainer::GetPotion()
{
    return m_iPotion;
}

/////////////////////////////////////////////////////
// SetArmor()
/////////////////////////////////////////////////////
void CContainer::SetArmor(int num)
{
    m_iArmor = num;
}

/////////////////////////////////////////////////////
// GetArmor()
/////////////////////////////////////////////////////
int CContainer::GetArmor()
{
    return m_iArmor;
}

/////////////////////////////////////////////////////
// SetWeapon()
/////////////////////////////////////////////////////
void CContainer::SetWeapon(int num)
{
    m_iWeapon = num;
}

/////////////////////////////////////////////////////
// GetWeapon()
/////////////////////////////////////////////////////
```

```
int CContainer::GetWeapon()
{
    return m_iWeapon;
}

////////////////////////////////////////////////////////
// SetLocked()
////////////////////////////////////////////////////////
void CContainer::SetLocked(BOOL val)
{
    m_bLocked = val;
}

////////////////////////////////////////////////////////
// GetLocked()
////////////////////////////////////////////////////////
BOOL CContainer::GetLocked()
{
    return m_bLocked;
}

////////////////////////////////////////////////////////
// SetSector()
////////////////////////////////////////////////////////
void CContainer::SetSector(int num)
{
    m_iSector = num;
}

////////////////////////////////////////////////////////
// GetSector()
////////////////////////////////////////////////////////
int CContainer::GetSector()
{
    return m_iSector;
}

////////////////////////////////////////////////////////
// SetTile()
////////////////////////////////////////////////////////
void CContainer::SetTile(int num)
{
    m_iTile = num;
}

////////////////////////////////////////////////////////
// GetTile()
////////////////////////////////////////////////////////
int CContainer::GetTile()
{
    return m_iTile;
}
```

8. Make sure that the Container.cpp file is visible in the code window, and then select the Build menu's Compile command (or just press Ctrl+F7) to compile the class in order to verify that the code is okay. Here, you're compiling just the class, not the entire project.

As you can see from the source code, this class is pretty straightforward, containing nothing more than a group of data members and the member functions that access them. Table 12.2 lists and describes each of the `CContainer` class's members.

TABLE 12.2 Members of the `CContainer` Class

Member	*Type*	*Description*
m_bLocked	Data	Whether the container is locked
m_iArmor	Data	The type of armor in the container
m_iGold	Data	The amount of gold in the container
m_iKeys	Data	The number of keys in the container
m_iPotion	Data	The number of potions in the container
m_iSector	Data	The container's location
m_iTile	Data	The tile that represents the container
m_iWeapon	Data	The type of weapon in the container
GetArmor()	Public method	Sets the m_iArmor data member
GetGold()	Public method	Gets the m_iGold data member
GetKeys()	Public method	Gets the m_iKeys data member
GetLocked()	Public method	Gets the m_bLocked data member
GetPotion()	Public method	Gets the m_iPotion data member
GetSector()	Public method	Gets the m_iSector data member
GetTile()	Public method	Gets the m_iTile data member
GetWeapon()	Public method	Gets the m_iWeapon data member
SetArmor()	Public method	Sets the m_iArmor data member
SetGold()	Public method	Sets the m_iGold data member
SetKeys()	Public method	Sets the m_iKeys data member
SetLocked()	Public method	Sets the m_bLocked data member
SetPotion()	Public method	Sets the m_iPotion data member
SetSector()	Public method	Sets the m_iSector data member
SetTile()	Public method	Sets the m_iTile data member
SetWeapon()	Public method	Sets the m_iWeapon data member

Adding the CContainers Class

A specific location in the game can have more than one container. In fact, thanks to the MAXCONTAINERS constant, which is defined in the Constants.h file, each location in the game can have up to 100 containers. (You'll add the Constants.h file to the project in this section.)

The CContainers class represents an array of CContainer objects, but also supplies the methods needed to retrieve information about the array. For example, the GetContainer() method enables your program to get a pointer to any single CContainer object contained in the array. Perform the following steps to add the CContainers class to the program.

1. On the Project menu, select the Add Class command. The Add Class dialog box appears.
2. In the Templates box, select Generic C++ class.
3. Click Open, and the Generic C++ Class Wizard appears.
4. Enter CContainers into the Class Name box. The wizard automatically fills in the names for the header and implementation files.
5. Click Finish to add the class files to the project.
6. In the Containers.h file, modify the code so that it looks like this. If you don't want to do the typing, you can copy the Code03.txt file from the Chapter 12 directory on this book's CD-ROM.

```
///////////////////////////////////////////////////////
// Containers.h
///////////////////////////////////////////////////////

#pragma once

#include "constants.h"
#include "Container.h"

class CContainers
{
protected:
    int m_iContainerCount;
    CContainer m_Containers[MAXCONTAINERS];

public:
    CContainers(void);
    ~CContainers(void);

    CContainer* GetContainer(int num);
    void SetContainerCount(int count);
```

```
    int GetContainerCount();
};
```

7. In the Containers.cpp file, modify the code so that it looks as follows. If you don't want to do the typing, you can copy the Code04.txt file from the Chapter 12 directory on this book's CD-ROM.

```
///////////////////////////////////////////////////////
// Containers.cpp
///////////////////////////////////////////////////////

#include "containers.h"

///////////////////////////////////////////////////////
// CContainers()
///////////////////////////////////////////////////////
CContainers::CContainers(void)
{
    m_iContainerCount = 0;
}

///////////////////////////////////////////////////////
// ~CContainers()
///////////////////////////////////////////////////////
CContainers::~CContainers(void)
{
}

///////////////////////////////////////////////////////
// GetContainer()
///////////////////////////////////////////////////////
CContainer* CContainers::GetContainer(int num)
{
    return &m_Containers[num];
}

///////////////////////////////////////////////////////
// SetContainerCount()
///////////////////////////////////////////////////////
void CContainers::SetContainerCount(int count)
{
    m_iContainerCount = count;
}

///////////////////////////////////////////////////////
// GetContainerCount()
///////////////////////////////////////////////////////
int CContainers::GetContainerCount()
```

```
{
    return m_iContainerCount;
}
```

8. Add a new header file to the project (Ctrl+Shift+A) named Constants.h. Type the following lines into the file. If you don't want to do the typing, you can copy the Code05.txt file from the Chapter 12 directory on this book's CD-ROM.

```
///////////////////////////////////////////////////////
// Constants.h
///////////////////////////////////////////////////////

#pragma once

const MAPSECTORCOUNT = 1764;
const MAXPEOPLE = 100;
const MAXCONTAINERS = 100;
const MAXDOORS = 100;

enum g_iLocationEnum
{
    FIRSTTOWN,
    FIRSTTOWNHOUSE01ROOM01,
    FIRSTTOWNHOUSE01ROOM02,
    FIRSTTOWNHOUSE02ROOM01,
    FIRSTTOWNHOUSE02ROOM02,
    FIRSTTOWNINNROOM01,
    FIRSTTOWNINNROOM02,
    FIRSTTOWNINNROOM03,
    FIRSTTOWNINNROOM04,
    FIRSTTOWNINNROOM05,
    FIRSTTOWNINNROOM06,
    FIRSTTOWNINNROOM07,
    FIRSTTOWNARMORER,
    FIRSTTOWNPOTIONS,
    GANJEKWILDS
};
```

9. Make sure that the Containers.cpp file is visible in the code window, and then select the Build menu's Compile command (or just press Ctrl+F7) to compile the class in order to verify that the code is okay.

This class is again very straightforward, containing just a group of data members and the member functions that access them. Notice, however, that the `m_Containers` data member uses the constant `MAXCONTAINERS` to specify the array's size. This constant, along with others you'll need in this chapter, is defined in the Constants.h header file. You can see that the Containers.h file includes Constants.h into the class. Table 12.3 lists and describes each of the `CContainers` class's members.

TABLE 12.3 Members of the `CContainers` Class

Member	*Type*	*Description*
m_iContainerCount	Data	The number of containers in the group
m_Containers[]	Data	An array of CContainer objects
GetContainer()	Public method	Gets the specified CContainer object
GetContainerCount()	Public method	Gets the m_iContainerCount data member
SetContainerCount()	Public method	Sets the m_iContainerCount data member

Adding the `CDoor` Class

Just as in the real world, every town in *The Adventures of Jasper Bookman* is loaded with doors. The player needs to go through a door to get into a building and usually needs to go through a door to enter a room. Moreover, some doors can be passed through freely, whereas others are locked. In fact, some doors may not even be visible unless the player searches for them.

With all the different attributes associated with doors, it makes perfect sense to represent a door with a class. This class, named `CDoor`, defines data members to hold the values of a door's attributes, as well as defines methods for setting and retrieving the values of these attributes. Perform the following steps to add the `CDoor` class to the program.

1. On the Project menu, select the Add Class command. The Add Class dialog box appears.
2. In the Templates box, select Generic C++ class.
3. Click Open, and the Generic C++ Class Wizard appears.
4. Enter `CDoor` into the Class Name box. The wizard automatically fills in the names for the header and implementation files.
5. Click Finish to add the class files to the project.
6. In the Door.h file, modify the code so that it looks like this. If you don't want to do the typing, you can copy the Code06.txt file from the Chapter 12 directory on this book's CD-ROM.

```
///////////////////////////////////////////////////////////
// Door.h
///////////////////////////////////////////////////////////

#pragma once

#include "windows.h"
```

```
class CDoor
{
protected:
    BOOL m_bSecret;
    BOOL m_bLocked;
    int m_iSector;
    int m_iTile;

public:
    CDoor(void);
    ~CDoor(void);

    void SetSecret(BOOL val);
    BOOL GetSecret();
    void SetLocked(BOOL val);
    BOOL GetLocked();
    void SetSector(int num);
    int GetSector();
    void SetTile(int num);
    int GetTile();
};
```

7. In the Door.cpp file, modify the code so that it looks as follows. If you don't want to do the typing, you can copy the Code07.txt file from the Chapter 12 directory on this book's CD-ROM.

```
///////////////////////////////////////////////////////
// Door.cpp
///////////////////////////////////////////////////////

#include "door.h"

///////////////////////////////////////////////////////
// CDoor()
///////////////////////////////////////////////////////
CDoor::CDoor(void)
{
}

///////////////////////////////////////////////////////
// ~CDoor()
///////////////////////////////////////////////////////
CDoor::~CDoor(void)
{
}

///////////////////////////////////////////////////////
// SetSecret()
///////////////////////////////////////////////////////
void CDoor::SetSecret(BOOL val)
```

```
{
    m_bSecret = val;
}

////////////////////////////////////////////////////////
// GetSecret()
////////////////////////////////////////////////////////
BOOL CDoor::GetSecret()
{
    return m_bSecret;
}

////////////////////////////////////////////////////////
// SetLocked()
////////////////////////////////////////////////////////
void CDoor::SetLocked(BOOL val)
{
    m_bLocked = val;
}

////////////////////////////////////////////////////////
// GetLocked()
////////////////////////////////////////////////////////
BOOL CDoor::GetLocked()
{
    return m_bLocked;
}

////////////////////////////////////////////////////////
// SetSector()
////////////////////////////////////////////////////////
void CDoor::SetSector(int num)
{
    m_iSector = num;
}

////////////////////////////////////////////////////////
// GetSector()
////////////////////////////////////////////////////////
int CDoor::GetSector()
{
    return m_iSector;
}

////////////////////////////////////////////////////////
// SetTile()
////////////////////////////////////////////////////////
void CDoor::SetTile(int num)
{
    m_iTile = num;
}
```

```
///////////////////////////////////////////////////////
// GetTile()
///////////////////////////////////////////////////////
int CDoor::GetTile()
{
    return m_iTile;
}
```

8. Make sure that the Door.cpp file is visible in the code window, and then select the Build menu's Compile command (or just press Ctrl+F7) to compile the class in order to verify that the code is okay.

Table 12.4 lists and describes each of the `CDoor` class's members.

TABLE 12.4 Members of the `CDoor` Class

Member	*Type*	*Description*
m_bLocked	Data	Specifies whether this is a locked door
m_bSecret	Data	Specifies whether this is a secret (initially invisible) door
m_iSector	Data	Specifies the location of the door
m_iTile	Data	Specifies the tile used to represent the door
GetLocked()	Public method	Gets the m_bLocked data member
GetSecret()	Public method	Gets the m_bSecret data member
GetSector()	Public method	Gets the m_iSector data member
GetTile()	Public method	Gets the m_iTile data member
SetLocked()	Public method	Sets the m_bLocked data member
SetSecret()	Public method	Sets the m_bSecret data member
SetSector()	Public method	Sets the m_iSector data member
SetTile()	Public method	Sets the m_iTile data member

Adding the `CDoors` Class

As mentioned in the previous section, towns in the game have lots of doors. You've now defined a class for a single door, but now it's time to put together a class for a group of doors. Each location in the game will have an instance of this class, which represents an array of `CDoor` objects. The class defines not only the array, but methods to access the array.

For example, if your program needs to know about a particular door, it can call the `GetDoor()` method to retrieve a pointer to the door's `CDoor` object. Using the `CDoor` object, the program can then discover all the door's attributes, such as whether it's locked or secret. Perform the following steps to add the `CDoors` class to the program:

1. On the Project menu, select the Add Class command. The Add Class dialog box appears.
2. In the Templates box, select Generic C++ class.
3. Click Open, and the Generic C++ Class Wizard appears.
4. Enter `CDoors` into the Class Name box. The wizard automatically fills in the names for the header and implementation files.
5. Click Finish to add the class files to the project.
6. In the Doors.h file, modify the code so that it looks like this. If you don't want to do the typing, you can copy the Code08.txt file from the Chapter 12 directory on this book's CD-ROM.

```
///////////////////////////////////////////////////////
// Doors.h
///////////////////////////////////////////////////////

#pragma once

#include "constants.h"
#include "Door.h"

class CDoors
{
protected:
    int m_iDoorCount;
    CDoor m_Doors[MAXDOORS];

public:
    CDoors(void);
    ~CDoors(void);

    CDoor* GetDoor(int num);
    void SetDoorCount(int count);
    int GetDoorCount();
};
```

7. In the Doors.cpp file, modify the code so that it looks as follows. If you don't want to do the typing, you can copy the Code09.txt file from the Chapter 12 directory on this book's CD-ROM.

```
///////////////////////////////////////////////////////
// Doors.cpp
```

```
///////////////////////////////////////////////////////

#include "doors.h"

///////////////////////////////////////////////////////
// CDoors()
///////////////////////////////////////////////////////
CDoors::CDoors(void)
{
    m_iDoorCount = 0;
}

///////////////////////////////////////////////////////
// ~CDoors()
///////////////////////////////////////////////////////
CDoors::~CDoors(void)
{
}

///////////////////////////////////////////////////////
// GetDoor()
///////////////////////////////////////////////////////
CDoor* CDoors::GetDoor(int num)
{
    return &m_Doors[num];
}

///////////////////////////////////////////////////////
// SetDoorCount()
///////////////////////////////////////////////////////
void CDoors::SetDoorCount(int count)
{
    m_iDoorCount = count;
}

///////////////////////////////////////////////////////
// GetDoorCount()
///////////////////////////////////////////////////////
int CDoors::GetDoorCount()
{
    return m_iDoorCount;
}
```

8. Make sure that the Doors.cpp file is visible in the code window, and then select the Build menu's Compile command (or just press Ctrl+F7) to compile the class in order to verify that the code is okay.

Table 12.5 lists and describes each of the `CDoors` class's members.

TABLE 12.5 Members of the `CDoors` Class

Member	*Type*	*Description*
m_iDoorCount	Data	The number of doors in the m_Doors array
m_Doors[]	Data	An array of CDoor objects
GetDoor()	Public method	Gets the specified CDoor object
GetDoorCount()	Public method	Gets the m_iDoorCount data member
SetDoorCount()	Public method	Sets the m_iDoorCount data member

Adding the `CPerson` Class

Anyone who has played a computer RPG game knows that the game's world is usually full of people. Some of these people can be very helpful to the player, whereas others do little more than roam around their town. In any case, in an RPG, a character with which the player can interact is called a non-player character, or an NPC for short.

Usually, it's a game's NPCs that provide the bulk of information that the player needs in order to finish a particular quest or even to get assigned a quest to start with. Non-player characters can also add a lot of…well…*character* to a game, by filling an area of the game world with colorful folks.

Obviously, a person can have a lot of attributes, including not only a name, but also a job, a family, a residence, various skills, and a whole lot more. In full-featured commercial games, an NPC can be almost as complex of a character as the player himself. Keeping track of such NPCs, however, takes a lot of program code, so you'll keep things simpler as you build the JBookman project. Perform the following steps to add the `CPerson` class to the game:

1. On the Project menu, select the Add Class command. The Add Class dialog box appears.
2. In the Templates box, select Generic C++ class.
3. Click Open, and the Generic C++ Class Wizard appears.
4. Enter `CPerson` into the Class Name box. The wizard automatically fills in the names for the header and implementation files.
5. Click Finish to add the class files to the project.
6. In the Person.h file, modify the code so that it looks like this. If you don't want to do the typing, you can copy the Code10.txt file from the Chapter 12 directory on this book's CD-ROM.

```
////////////////////////////////////////////////////////
// Person.h
////////////////////////////////////////////////////////

#pragma once

#include "windows.h"

class CPerson
{
protected:
    char m_pstrName[256];
    int m_iSector;
    BOOL m_bCanMove;
    int m_iTile;

public:
    CPerson(void);
    ~CPerson(void);

    void SetName(char* n);
    char* GetName();
    void SetSector(int num);
    int GetSector();
    void SetCanMove(BOOL val);
    BOOL GetCanMove();
    void SetTile(int num);
    int GetTile();
};
```

7. In the Person.cpp file, modify the code so that it looks as follows. If you don't want to do the typing, you can copy the Code11.txt file from the Chapter 12 directory on this book's CD-ROM.

```
////////////////////////////////////////////////////////
// Person.cpp
////////////////////////////////////////////////////////

#include "person.h"

////////////////////////////////////////////////////////
// CPerson()
////////////////////////////////////////////////////////
CPerson::CPerson(void)
{
}

////////////////////////////////////////////////////////
// ~CPerson()
////////////////////////////////////////////////////////
CPerson::~CPerson(void)
```

```
{
}

///////////////////////////////////////////////////////
// SetName()
///////////////////////////////////////////////////////
void CPerson::SetName(char* n)
{
    strcpy(m_pstrName, n);
}

///////////////////////////////////////////////////////
// GetName()
///////////////////////////////////////////////////////
char* CPerson::GetName()
{
    return m_pstrName;
}

///////////////////////////////////////////////////////
// SetSector()
///////////////////////////////////////////////////////
void CPerson::SetSector(int num)
{
    m_iSector = num;
}

///////////////////////////////////////////////////////
// GetSector()
///////////////////////////////////////////////////////
int CPerson::GetSector()
{
    return m_iSector;
}

///////////////////////////////////////////////////////
// SetTile()
///////////////////////////////////////////////////////
void CPerson::SetTile(int num)
{
    m_iTile = num;
}

///////////////////////////////////////////////////////
// GetTile()
///////////////////////////////////////////////////////
int CPerson::GetTile()
```

```
{
    return m_iTile;
}

///////////////////////////////////////////////////////
// SetCanMove()
///////////////////////////////////////////////////////
void CPerson::SetCanMove(BOOL val)
{
    m_bCanMove = val;
}

///////////////////////////////////////////////////////
// GetCanMove()
///////////////////////////////////////////////////////
BOOL CPerson::GetCanMove()
{
    return m_bCanMove;
}
```

8. Make sure that the Person.cpp file is visible in the code window, and then select the Build menu's Compile command (or just press Ctrl+F7) to compile the class in order to verify that the code is okay.

Table 12.6 lists and describes each of the `CPerson` class's members.

TABLE 12.6 Members of the `CPerson` Class

Member	*Type*	*Description*
m_pstrName[]	Data	A string holding the person's name
m_bCanMove	Data	Specifies whether this person can walk around or must stay in one place
m_iSector	Data	Specifies the location of the person
m_iTile	Data	Specifies the tile used to represent the person
GetCanMove()	Public method	Gets the m_bCanMove data member
GetName()	Public method	Gets the m_pstrName data member
GetSector()	Public method	Gets the m_iSector data member
GetTile()	Public method	Gets the m_iTile data member
SetCanMove()	Public method	Sets the m_bCanMove data member
SetName()	Public method	Sets the m_pstrName data member
SetSector()	Public method	Sets the m_iSector data member
SetTile()	Public method	Sets the m_iTile data member

Adding the `CPeople` Class

They say no man is an island. (That goes for women, too!) Every location in *The Adventures of Jasper Bookman* is populated with people, and just as with the other objects in the game, there is a class that represents an array of `CPerson` objects. This class is named `CPeople`, and you can add it to your project by following these steps:

1. On the Project menu, select the Add Class command. The Add Class dialog box appears.
2. In the Templates box, select Generic C++ class.
3. Click Open, and the Generic C++ Class Wizard appears.
4. Enter `CPeople` into the Class Name box. The wizard automatically fills in the names for the header and implementation files.
5. Click Finish to add the class files to the project.
6. In the People.h file, modify the code so that it looks like this. If you don't want to do the typing, you can copy the Code12.txt file from the Chapter 12 directory on this book's CD-ROM.

```
///////////////////////////////////////////////////////
// People.h
///////////////////////////////////////////////////////

#pragma once

#include "Constants.h"
#include "Person.h"

class CPeople
{
protected:
    int m_iPersonCount;
    CPerson m_People[MAXPEOPLE];
public:
    CPeople(void);
    ~CPeople(void);

    CPerson* GetPerson(int num);
    void SetPersonCount(int count);
    int GetPersonCount();
};
```

7. In the People.cpp file, modify the code so that it looks as follows. If you don't want to do the typing, you can copy the Code13.txt file from the Chapter 12 directory on this book's CD-ROM.

```
////////////////////////////////////////////////////////
// People.cpp
////////////////////////////////////////////////////////

#include "people.h"

////////////////////////////////////////////////////////
// CPeople()
////////////////////////////////////////////////////////
CPeople::CPeople(void)
{
    m_iPersonCount = 0;
}

////////////////////////////////////////////////////////
// ~CPeople()
////////////////////////////////////////////////////////
CPeople::~CPeople(void)
{
}

////////////////////////////////////////////////////////
// GetPerson()
////////////////////////////////////////////////////////
CPerson* CPeople::GetPerson(int num)
{
    return &m_People[num];
}

////////////////////////////////////////////////////////
// SetPersonCount()
////////////////////////////////////////////////////////
void CPeople::SetPersonCount(int count)
{
    m_iPersonCount = count;
}

////////////////////////////////////////////////////////
// GetPersonCount()
////////////////////////////////////////////////////////
int CPeople::GetPersonCount()
{
    return m_iPersonCount;
}
```

8. Make sure that the People.cpp file is visible in the code window, and then select the Build menu's Compile command (or just press Ctrl+F7) to compile the class in order to verify that the code is okay.

Table 12.7 lists and describes each of the `CPeople` class's members.

TABLE 12.7 Members of the `CPeople` Class

Member	*Type*	*Description*
m_iPersonCount	Data	The number of people in the m_People[] array
m_People[]	Data	An array of CPerson objects
GetPerson()	Public method	Gets the specified CPerson object
GetPersonCount()	Public method	Gets the m_iPersonCount data member
SetPersonCount()	Public method	Sets the m_iPersonCount data member

Adding the `CPlayer` Class

The most important person in the game is, of course, the player. Because he's so important, he has more attributes than NPCs in the game. This means that you need a heftier class to represent the player. In the JBookman project, that class is `CPlayer`. Perform the following steps to add the `CPlayer` class to the program.

1. On the Project menu, select the Add Class command. The Add Class dialog box appears.
2. In the Templates box, select Generic C++ class.
3. Click Open, and the Generic C++ Class Wizard appears.
4. Enter **`CPlayer`** into the Class Name box. The wizard automatically fills in the names for the header and implementation files.
5. Click Finish to add the class files to the project.
6. In the Player.h file, modify the code so that it looks like this. If you don't want to do the typing, you can copy the Code14.txt file from the Chapter 12 directory on this book's CD-ROM.

```
///////////////////////////////////////////////////////////
// Player.h
///////////////////////////////////////////////////////////

#pragma once

class CPlayer
{
protected:
    int m_iSector;
    int m_iHitPoints;
    int m_iMaxHitPoints;
```

```
    int m_iArmor;
    int m_iWeapon;
    int m_iGold;
    int m_iKeys;
    int m_iPotions;
    int m_iExperience;

public:
    CPlayer(void);
    ~CPlayer(void);
    void SetSector(int num);
    int GetSector();
    void SetHitPoints(int num);
    int GetHitPoints();
    void SetMaxHitPoints(int num);
    int GetMaxHitPoints();
    void SetArmor(int num);
    int GetArmor();
    void SetWeapon(int num);
    int GetWeapon();
    void SetGold(int num);
    int GetGold();
    void SetKeys(int num);
    int GetKeys();
    void SetPotions(int num);
    int GetPotions();
    void SetExperience(int num);
    int GetExperience();
};
```

7. In the Player.cpp file, modify the code so that it looks as follows. If you don't want to do the typing, you can copy the Code15.txt file from the Chapter 12 directory on this book's CD-ROM.

```
///////////////////////////////////////////////////////
// Player.cpp
///////////////////////////////////////////////////////

#include "player.h"

///////////////////////////////////////////////////////
// CPlayer()
///////////////////////////////////////////////////////
CPlayer::CPlayer(void)
{
    m_iSector = 0;
    m_iHitPoints = 0;
```

```
    m_iMaxHitPoints = 0;
    m_iArmor = 0;
    m_iWeapon = 0;
    m_iGold = 0;
    m_iKeys = 0;
    m_iPotions = 0;
    m_iExperience = 0;
}

///////////////////////////////////////////////////////
// ~CPlayer()
///////////////////////////////////////////////////////
CPlayer::~CPlayer(void)
{
}

///////////////////////////////////////////////////////
// SetSector()
///////////////////////////////////////////////////////
void CPlayer::SetSector(int num)
{
    m_iSector = num;
}

///////////////////////////////////////////////////////
// GetSector()
///////////////////////////////////////////////////////
int CPlayer::GetSector()
{
    return m_iSector;
}

///////////////////////////////////////////////////////
// SetHitPoints()
///////////////////////////////////////////////////////
void CPlayer::SetHitPoints(int num)
{
    m_iHitPoints = num;
}

///////////////////////////////////////////////////////
// GetHitPoints()
///////////////////////////////////////////////////////
int CPlayer::GetHitPoints()
{
    return m_iHitPoints;
```

```
}

////////////////////////////////////////////////////////
// SetMaxHitPoints()
////////////////////////////////////////////////////////
void CPlayer::SetMaxHitPoints(int num)
{
    m_iMaxHitPoints = num;
}

////////////////////////////////////////////////////////
// GetMaxHitPoints()
////////////////////////////////////////////////////////
int CPlayer::GetMaxHitPoints()
{
    return m_iMaxHitPoints;
}

////////////////////////////////////////////////////////
// SetArmor()
////////////////////////////////////////////////////////
void CPlayer::SetArmor(int num)
{
    m_iArmor = num;
}

////////////////////////////////////////////////////////
// GetArmor()
////////////////////////////////////////////////////////
int CPlayer::GetArmor()
{
    return m_iArmor;
}

////////////////////////////////////////////////////////
// SetWeapon()
////////////////////////////////////////////////////////
void CPlayer::SetWeapon(int num)
{
    m_iWeapon = num;
}

////////////////////////////////////////////////////////
// GetWeapon()
////////////////////////////////////////////////////////
int CPlayer::GetWeapon()
{
```

```
    return m_iWeapon;
}

/////////////////////////////////////////////////////////
// SetGold()
/////////////////////////////////////////////////////////
void CPlayer::SetGold(int num)
{
    m_iGold = num;
}

/////////////////////////////////////////////////////////
// GetGold()
/////////////////////////////////////////////////////////
int CPlayer::GetGold()
{
    return m_iGold;
}

/////////////////////////////////////////////////////////
// SetKeys()
/////////////////////////////////////////////////////////
void CPlayer::SetKeys(int num)
{
    m_iKeys = num;
}

/////////////////////////////////////////////////////////
// GetKeys()
/////////////////////////////////////////////////////////
int CPlayer::GetKeys()
{
    return m_iKeys;
}

/////////////////////////////////////////////////////////
// SetPotions()
/////////////////////////////////////////////////////////
void CPlayer::SetPotions(int num)
{
    m_iPotions = num;
}

/////////////////////////////////////////////////////////
// GetPotions()
/////////////////////////////////////////////////////////
int CPlayer::GetPotions()
```

```
{
    return m_iPotions;
}

////////////////////////////////////////////////////////
// SetExperience()
////////////////////////////////////////////////////////
void CPlayer::SetExperience(int num)
{
    m_iExperience = num;
}

////////////////////////////////////////////////////////
// GetExperience()
////////////////////////////////////////////////////////
int CPlayer::GetExperience()
{
    return m_iExperience;
}
```

8. Make sure that the Player.cpp file is visible in the code window, and then select the Build menu's Compile command (or just press Ctrl+F7) to compile the class in order to verify that the code is okay.

Table 12.8 lists and describes each of the `CPlayer` class's members.

TABLE 12.8 Members of the `CPlayer` Class

Member	*Type*	*Description*
m_iArmor	Data	Holds the player's armor (defense) value
m_iExperience	Data	Holds the player's experience value
m_iGold	Data	Holds the amount of gold in the player's possession
m_iHitPoints	Data	Holds the player's remaining hit points
m_iKeys	Data	Holds the number of keys in the player's possession
m_iMaxHitPoints	Data	Holds the player's maximum hit points
m_iPotions	Data	Holds the number of potions in the player's possession
m_iSector	Data	Holds the location of the person
m_iWeapon	Data	Holds the player's weapon (attack) value
GetArmor()	Public method	Gets the m_iArmor data member
GetExperience()	Public method	Gets the m_iExperience data member

TABLE 12.8 Continued

Member	Type	Description
GetGold()	Public method	Gets the m_iGold data member
GetHitPoints()	Public method	Gets the m_iHitPoints data member
GetKeys()	Public method	Gets the m_iKeys data member
GetMaxHitPoints()	Public method	Gets the m_iMaxHitPoints data member
GetPotions()	Public method	Gets the m_iPotions data member
GetSector()	Public method	Gets the m_iSector data member
GetWeapon()	Public method	Gets the m_iWeapon data member
SetArmor()	Public method	Sets the m_iArmor data member
SetExperience()	Public method	Sets the m_iExperience data member
SetGold()	Public method	Sets the m_iGold data member
SetHitPoints()	Public method	Sets the m_iHitPoints data member
SetKeys()	Public method	Sets the m_iKeys data member
SetMaxHitPoints()	Public method	Sets the m_iMaxHitPoints data member
SetPotions()	Public method	Sets the m_iPotions data member
SetSector()	Public method	Sets the m_iSector data member
SetWeapon()	Public method	Sets the m_iWeapon data member

Plugging In the New Classes

Now that you have all these extra classes, you need to get the program to do something with them. As you can probably guess, a lot of what happens with these classes happens in the `CEngine` class. Follow these steps to plug the classes into the program:

1. Add the following lines to the Engine.h file, right after the `#include <Direct3D.h>` line that's already there. If you don't want to type, you can copy the lines from the Code16.txt file in the Chapter 12 directory of this book's CD-ROM.

```
#include <time.h>
#include <fstream>
#include "constants.h"
#include "Player.h"
#include "Person.h"
#include "People.h"
#include "Door.h"
#include "Doors.h"
```

```
#include "Container.h"
#include "Containers.h"
```

These lines include the header files for the new classes, as well as the header files for a couple of libraries you'll be using in the new source code coming up.

2. Add the following lines to the Engine.h file's protected data members, right after the `CDirect3D m_Direct3D` line that's already there. If you don't want to type, you can copy the lines from the Code17.txt file in the Chapter 12 directory of this book's CD-ROM.

```
CPlayer m_Player;
CPeople m_People;
CDoors m_Doors;
CContainers m_Containers;
BYTE m_byMapType;
int m_iCurrentMap;
char m_Sectors[MAPSECTORCOUNT];
char m_pstrFirstMap[_MAX_PATH];
int m_iFirstMapType;
int m_iStartSector;
```

These lines add new member variables to the `CEngine` class, including instances of the classes you added to the program in the previous sections of this chapter. Later in this section, you'll see exactly what these data members do in the class.

3. Replace the constructor's declaration with this one:

```
CEngine(char* pstrMap, int iMapType, int iSector);
```

The new constructor takes several arguments that you'll learn about later in this section.

12

4. Add the following lines to the Engine.h file's public methods, right after line `CDirect3D* GetCDirect3DObj()` that's already there. If you don't want to type, you can copy the lines from the Code18.txt file in the Chapter 12 directory of this book's CD-ROM.

```
char* GetSectors();
int GetCurrentMap();
void SetCurrentMap(int map);
void OpenMapFiles(char* pstrFileName);
void InitGame();
CPlayer* GetPlayer();
```

These lines declare new public methods for the class. You'll see what these methods do later in this section.

5. Add the following private methods to the class, by placing these lines right after line `CPlayer* GetPlayer()` that's already there. If you don't want to type, you can copy the lines from the Code19.txt file in the Chapter 12 directory of this book's CD-ROM.

```
private:
    void ReadMapFile(char* FileName);
    void ConstructFileName(char* fileName);
    void ReadPeopleFile(char* fileName);
    void ReadContainerFile(char* fileName);
    void ReadDoorFile(char* fileName);
    void GetStringFromFile(std::ifstream& str, char* buf);
```

These lines declare new private methods for the class. As you'll see later in the chapter, these methods deal with the file handling required to read game data in from the player's hard disk.

6. In the Engine.cpp implementation file, replace the current constructor definition with the following one. If you don't want to type, you can copy the lines from the Code20.txt file in the Chapter 12 directory of this book's CD-ROM.

```
CEngine::CEngine(char* pstrMap, int iMapType, int iSector)
{
    strcpy(m_pstrFirstMap, pstrMap);
    m_iFirstMapType = iMapType;
    m_iStartSector = iSector;
    InitGame();
}
```

The new constructor accepts several parameters and copies them into data members of the class.

7. Add the following method implementations to the Engine.cpp file. If you don't want to type, you can copy the lines from the Code21.txt file in the Chapter 12 directory of this book's CD-ROM.

```
///////////////////////////////////////////////////////
// InitGame()
///////////////////////////////////////////////////////
void CEngine::InitGame()
{
    OpenMapFiles(m_pstrFirstMap);
    m_iCurrentMap = m_iFirstMapType;
    m_Player.SetGold(25);
    m_Player.SetHitPoints(10);
    m_Player.SetMaxHitPoints(10);
    m_Player.SetKeys(1);
    m_Player.SetSector(m_iStartSector);
    srand((unsigned)time(NULL));
}

///////////////////////////////////////////////////////
// GetPlayer()
///////////////////////////////////////////////////////
CPlayer* CEngine::GetPlayer()
{
```

```
    return &m_Player;
}

/////////////////////////////////////////////////////////
// GetCurrentMap()
/////////////////////////////////////////////////////////
int CEngine::GetCurrentMap()
{
    return m_iCurrentMap;
}

/////////////////////////////////////////////////////////
// SetCurrentMap()
/////////////////////////////////////////////////////////
void CEngine::SetCurrentMap(int map)
{
    m_iCurrentMap = map;
}

/////////////////////////////////////////////////////////
// GetSectors()
/////////////////////////////////////////////////////////
char* CEngine::GetSectors()
{
    return (char*)&m_Sectors;
}

/////////////////////////////////////////////////////////
// OpenMapFiles()
/////////////////////////////////////////////////////////
void CEngine::OpenMapFiles(char* fName)
{
    char fileName[_MAX_PATH];
    strcpy(fileName, fName);
    ConstructFileName(fileName);
    ReadMapFile(fileName);
    ReadPeopleFile(fileName);
    ReadContainerFile(fileName);
    ReadDoorFile(fileName);
}

/////////////////////////////////////////////////////////
// ConstructFileName()
/////////////////////////////////////////////////////////
void CEngine::ConstructFileName(char* fileName)
{
    char NewMapFileName[_MAX_PATH];
    strcpy(NewMapFileName, "Maps\\");
    strcpy(&NewMapFileName[5], fileName);
    strcpy(fileName, NewMapFileName);
```

```
}

/////////////////////////////////////////////////////////
// ReadPeopleFile()
/////////////////////////////////////////////////////////
void CEngine::ReadPeopleFile(char*fileName)
{
    char m_peopleFileName[_MAX_PATH];
    char buf[256];
    strcpy(m_peopleFileName, fileName);
    strcpy(&m_peopleFileName[strlen(m_peopleFileName)], ".peo");
    std::ifstream m_peopleFile(m_peopleFileName, std::ios::binary);

    // Get the number of people in the file.
    GetStringFromFile(m_peopleFile, buf);
    m_People.SetPersonCount(atoi(buf));

    for (int person=0; person<m_People.GetPersonCount(); ++person)
    {
        // Get the person's name.
        GetStringFromFile(m_peopleFile, buf);
        m_People.GetPerson(person)->SetName(buf);

        // Get the person's location.
        GetStringFromFile(m_peopleFile, buf);
        m_People.GetPerson(person)->SetSector(atoi(buf));

        // Get the person's move capability.
        GetStringFromFile(m_peopleFile, buf);
        if (buf[1] == 'F')
            m_People.GetPerson(person)->SetCanMove(FALSE);
        else
            m_People.GetPerson(person)->SetCanMove(TRUE);

        // Get the person's tile number.
        GetStringFromFile(m_peopleFile, buf);
        m_People.GetPerson(person)->SetTile(atoi(buf));
    }
    m_peopleFile.close();
}

/////////////////////////////////////////////////////////
// ReadContainerFile()
/////////////////////////////////////////////////////////
void CEngine::ReadContainerFile(char* fileName)
{
    char ContainerFileName[_MAX_PATH];
    char buf[256];
    strcpy(ContainerFileName, fileName);
    strcpy(&ContainerFileName[strlen(ContainerFileName)], ".itm");
```

```
    std::ifstream ContainerFile(ContainerFileName, std::ios::binary);

    // Get the number of containers in the file.
    GetStringFromFile(ContainerFile, buf);
    m_Containers.SetContainerCount(atoi(buf));

    for (int iContainer=0; iContainer<m_Containers.GetContainerCount();
            ++iContainer)
    {
        // Get the amount of gold.
        GetStringFromFile(ContainerFile, buf);
        m_Containers.GetContainer(iContainer)->SetGold(atoi(buf));

        // Get the number of keys.
        GetStringFromFile(ContainerFile, buf);
        m_Containers.GetContainer(iContainer)->SetKeys(atoi(buf));

        // Get the number of potions.
        GetStringFromFile(ContainerFile, buf);
        m_Containers.GetContainer(iContainer)->SetPotion(atoi(buf));

        // Get the armor type.
        GetStringFromFile(ContainerFile, buf);
        m_Containers.GetContainer(iContainer)->SetArmor(atoi(buf));

        // Get the weapon type.
        GetStringFromFile(ContainerFile, buf);
        m_Containers.GetContainer(iContainer)->SetWeapon(atoi(buf));

        // Get the locked setting.
        GetStringFromFile(ContainerFile, buf);
        if (buf[1] == 'F')
            m_Containers.GetContainer(iContainer)->SetLocked(FALSE);
        else
            m_Containers.GetContainer(iContainer)->SetLocked(TRUE);

        // Get the item's sector.
        GetStringFromFile(ContainerFile, buf);
        m_Containers.GetContainer(iContainer)->SetSector(atoi(buf));

        // Get the item's tile number.
        GetStringFromFile(ContainerFile, buf);
        m_Containers.GetContainer(iContainer)->SetTile(atoi(buf));
    }
    ContainerFile.close();
}

//////////////////////////////////////////////////////
// ReadDoorFile()
//////////////////////////////////////////////////////
void CEngine::ReadDoorFile(char*fileName)
```

```
{
    char doorFileName[_MAX_PATH];
    char buf[256];
    strcpy(doorFileName, fileName);
    strcpy(&doorFileName[strlen(doorFileName)], ".dor");
    std::ifstream doorFile(doorFileName, std::ios::binary);

    // Get the number of doors in the file.
    GetStringFromFile(doorFile, buf);
    m_Doors.SetDoorCount(atoi(buf));

    for (int door=0; door<m_Doors.GetDoorCount(); ++door)
    {
        // Get the secret setting.
        GetStringFromFile(doorFile, buf);
        if (buf[1] == 'F')
            m_Doors.GetDoor(door)->SetSecret(FALSE);
        else
            m_Doors.GetDoor(door)->SetSecret(TRUE);

        // Get the locked setting.
        GetStringFromFile(doorFile, buf);
        if (buf[1] == 'F')
            m_Doors.GetDoor(door)->SetLocked(FALSE);
        else
            m_Doors.GetDoor(door)->SetLocked(TRUE);

        // Get the item's sector.
        GetStringFromFile(doorFile, buf);
        m_Doors.GetDoor(door)->SetSector(atoi(buf));

        // Get the item's tile number.
        GetStringFromFile(doorFile, buf);
        m_Doors.GetDoor(door)->SetTile(atoi(buf));
    }
    doorFile.close();
}

///////////////////////////////////////////////////////
// ReadMapFile()
///////////////////////////////////////////////////////
void CEngine::ReadMapFile(char* fileName)
{
    std::ifstream mapFile(fileName, std::ios::binary);
    mapFile.read((char*)&m_byMapType, 1);
    mapFile.read(m_Sectors, sizeof m_Sectors);
    mapFile.close();
```

```
}

//////////////////////////////////////////////////////////
// GetStringFromFile()
//////////////////////////////////////////////////////////
void CEngine::GetStringFromFile(std::ifstream& str, char* buf)
{
    int i = 0;
    char c;
    str.read(&c, 1);
    while (c != 13)
    {
        buf[i++] = c;
        str.read(&c, 1);
    }
    str.read(&c, 1);
    buf[i] = 0;
}
```

You'll look at these methods in greater detail later in this section.

8. Load the JBookman.cpp file, and near the top of the program replace the line

   ```
   CEngine g_Engine;
   ```

   with this:

   ```
   CEngine g_Engine("FirstTown.map", FIRSTTOWN, 1485);
   ```

   This line initializes the game data by creating an instance of the class `CEngine`.

9. In your main JBookman project directory, create a subdirectory named Maps, as shown in Figure 12.3.

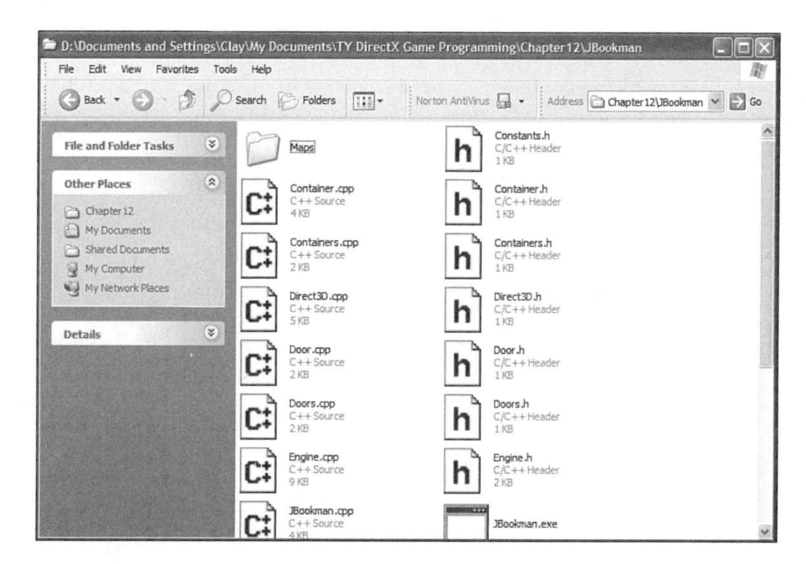

FIGURE 12.3
The Maps subdirectory.

10. Copy the files FirstTown.map, FirstTown.map.dor, FirstTown.map.itm, and FirstTown.map.peo from this book's Chapter 12 folder to your new Maps folder.
11. Compile and run the application. If everything works okay, you should see that familiar blue screen. To close the application, Alt+Tab back to Visual Studio and select the Stop debugging command.

Understanding the Program

In this chapter, you've added tons of code to the JBookman project. You should have a pretty good understanding of the new classes you added, but you haven't yet dug into the new methods you added to the `CEngine` class. Because this code is where the program reads the data needed to initialize the game data, it's pretty important stuff to understand. In this section, you'll explore the new code.

The `CEngine` Class's Constructor

The initialization of the game data begins when the main program creates an instance of the `CEngine` class, like this:

```
CEngine g_Engine("FirstTown.map", FIRSTTOWN, 1485);
```

The `CEngine` class's constructor requires three arguments. Those arguments are described as follows:

- The name of the map file that holds the data for the game's starting location.
- The starting location's ID.
- The sector in which the player character is located.

The map file contains the data required to draw the current location, as well as lists of the items in the current location. The map file is actually four separate, but related files. In the case of First Town, the town's map data is in the file FirstTown.map. However, there are three other files—FirstTown.map.dor, FirstTown.map.itm, and FirstTown.map.peo—that contain information about the location's doors, items, and people, respectively. These files were created by the game editor, which you'll learn about in Appendix A of this book. For now, you'll be using pre-made map files.

The `CEngine` constructor takes the arguments passed to it and initializes several of the class's data members, as well as calls `InitGame()` to initialize the rest:

```
CEngine::CEngine(char* pstrMap, int iMapType, int iSector)
{
    strcpy(m_pstrFirstMap, pstrMap);
    m_iFirstMapType = iMapType;
```

```
    m_iStartSector = iSector;
    InitGame();
}
```

The `InitGame()` Method

The `InitGame()` method's first task is to open and read in the game data, which it does with this method call:

```
OpenMapFiles(m_pstrFirstMap);
```

Then `InitGame()` sets several of the player's attributes to their starting values:

```
m_Player.SetGold(25);
m_Player.SetHitPoints(10);
m_Player.SetMaxHitPoints(10);
m_Player.SetKeys(1);
m_Player.SetSector(m_iStartSector);
```

These lines give the player 25 gold pieces, 10 hit points, and one key. The CPlayer class automatically sets the other attributes to 0, so you only need to set the ones that are non-zero.

What does all this have to do with the game? The one thing more than any other that makes an RPG an RPG is the player's attributes. As the player progresses through the game, he's able to improve these attributes and slowly build a more powerful character. Modern RPGs give player characters dozens of attributes, but for *The Adventures of Jasper Bookman*, I need to keep things simple. Otherwise, I'd never be able to fit the game into this book! Table 12.9 lists the player attributes and their descriptions.

TABLE 12.9 Player Character Attributes

Attribute	*Description*
Armor	The character's defensive abilities. The higher this value, the less damage sustained by enemy attacks.
Experience	The amount of experience earned by the character. The higher the experience, the higher the character's level.
Gold	The amount of gold carried by the character.
Hit points	The maximum amount of damage the player character can sustain before he dies.
Keys	The number of keys in the character's inventory.
Max hit points	The maximum number of hit points the player can have. This value increases as the player becomes more experienced.

TABLE 12.9 Continued

Attribute	*Description*
Potions	The number of potions in the player's inventory. Potions act to heal the character, restoring all or part of the character's hit points.
Weapon	The character's offensive abilities. The higher this value, the more damage the character can do to an enemy during combat.

The last thing `InitGame()` does is seed the random-number generator, which ensures that every game will get a different set of random numbers:

```
srand((unsigned)time(NULL));
```

Reading the Map Files

Reading the map files is a fairly complicated process, but is still, nonetheless, just standard file processing. The `OpenMapFiles()` method calls the various helper functions that get the job done:

```
void CEngine::OpenMapFiles(char* fName)
{
    char fileName[_MAX_PATH];
    strcpy(fileName, fName);
    ConstructFileName(fileName);
    ReadMapFile(fileName);
    ReadPeopleFile(fileName);
    ReadContainerFile(fileName);
    ReadDoorFile(fileName);
}
```

The first three lines here put together the path to the requested file. For example, if the file to be loaded is named FirstTown.map, the path is Maps\FirstTown.map. The last four lines read the four data files required for the current location.

Reading the Location Map

The location map is the data that tells the program what images to display in order to show the player's current location on the screen. This data is found in the file with the .map file extension. In the case of First Town, then, the location map file name is FirstTown.map.

The location map has the simplest file format of all the map files, being nothing more than a leading byte specifying the map-type ID followed by an array of byte values for the map data. The `ReadMapFile()` method gets the easy task of reading in this data, which it does like this:

```
std::ifstream mapFile(fileName, std::ios::binary);
mapFile.read((char*)&m_byMapType, 1);
mapFile.read(m_Sectors, sizeof m_Sectors);
mapFile.close();
```

Here, the program opens the file, reads the map ID into the `m_byMapType` data member, reads the map array into the `m_Sectors` data member, and then closes the file. Figure 12.4 shows the format of a location-map file. In the next chapter, you'll see how these values determine what gets drawn on the screen.

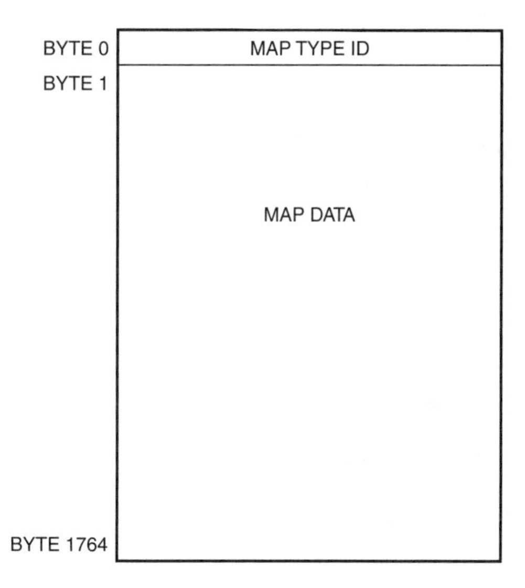

FIGURE 12.4

The structure of the location-map file.

Reading the Door File

You may recall from the `CDoor` class that a door object has three attributes: its location, its tile number, and whether it's locked. You don't have to be a rocket scientist to figure out that these attributes are what is stored in a location's door file. The door file, which in the current example is named FirstTown.map.dor, is in fact an array of doors, with the first value in the file being the number of doors in the array. To keep things simple, every value in this file is a string.

The `ReadDoorFile()` method reads the door file into the game. This method first constructs the file's name and then opens the file:

```
char doorFileName[_MAX_PATH];
char buf[256];
strcpy(doorFileName, fileName);
strcpy(&doorFileName[strlen(doorFileName)], ".dor");
std::ifstream doorFile(doorFileName, std::ios::binary);
```

Next, the method reads the number of doors in the file, passing this value on to the m_Doors object:

```
GetStringFromFile(doorFile, buf);
m_Doors.SetDoorCount(atoi(buf));
```

The method then starts a for loop that iterates through each of the doors in the file, setting the various door attributes, like this:

```
for (int door=0; door<m_Doors.GetDoorCount(); ++door)
{
    // Get the secret setting.
    GetStringFromFile(doorFile, buf);
    if (buf[1] == 'F')
        m_Doors.GetDoor(door)->SetSecret(FALSE);
    else
        m_Doors.GetDoor(door)->SetSecret(TRUE);

    // Get the locked setting.
    GetStringFromFile(doorFile, buf);
    if (buf[1] == 'F')
        m_Doors.GetDoor(door)->SetLocked(FALSE);
    else
        m_Doors.GetDoor(door)->SetLocked(TRUE);

    // Get the item's sector.
    GetStringFromFile(doorFile, buf);
    m_Doors.GetDoor(door)->SetSector(atoi(buf));

    // Get the item's tile number.
    GetStringFromFile(doorFile, buf);
    m_Doors.GetDoor(door)->SetTile(atoi(buf));
}
```

The GetStringFromFile() method called inside the loop does nothing more than read a single string from the file.

If you load the FirstTown.map.dor door file into a text editor, this is what you see:

```
5
#FALSE#
#FALSE#
895
15
#FALSE#
#FALSE#
321
15
#FALSE#
#TRUE#
868
```

```
15
#FALSE#
#FALSE#
1160
15
#FALSE#
#FALSE#
1412
15
```

Figure 12.5 summarizes this file structure.

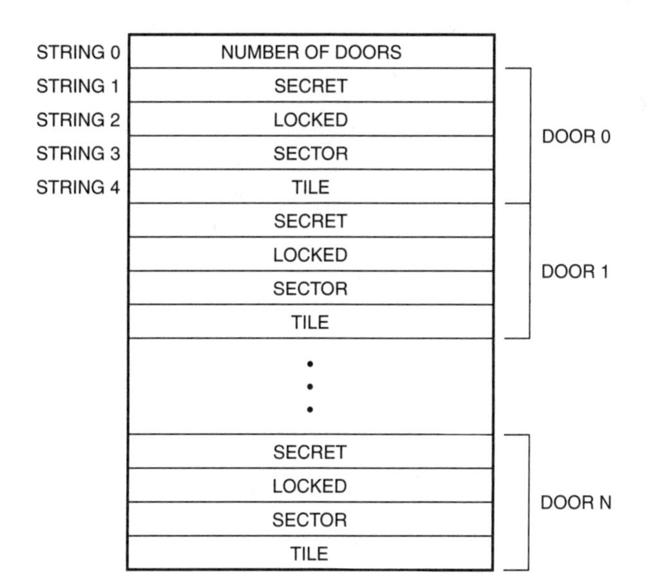

FIGURE 12.5
The structure of the door file.

Reading the People File

People in a location aren't much different from doors, at least as far as attributes go. Each person has four attributes: name, location, whether the person can move, and the tile that represents the person. Reading the people file, then, is a lot like reading the door file, so we'll just skip the details and go right to the file format.

Again, all the values in the people file are stored as strings. Here's what the file would look like if you loaded it into a text editor:

```
3
"Red Frenex"
1619
#FALSE#
60
```

```
"Jon Renfred"
1615
#FALSE#
60
"Denny Green"
86
#TRUE#
58
```

Figure 12.6 summarizes the structure of the people file.

FIGURE 12.6

The structure of the people file.

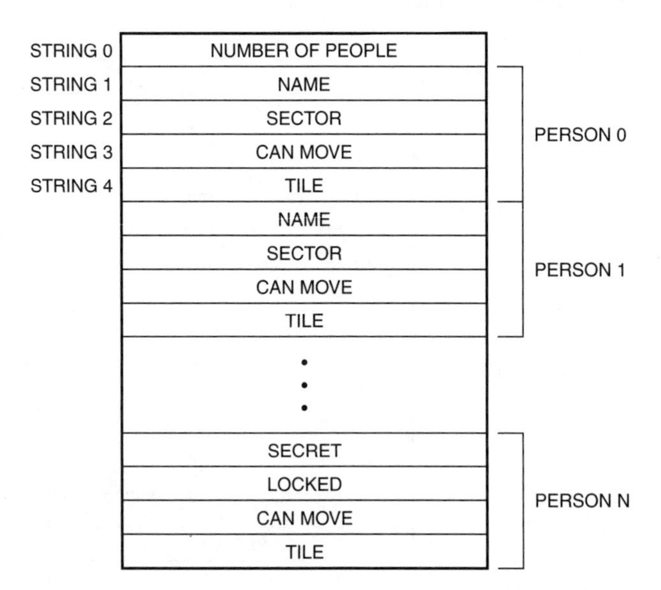

Reading the Item File

The item file contains an array of containers and the items stored in the containers. This file has the most complex structure of all the game-data files, but still is very similar to the door and people files. The main difference is that it takes more information to describe a container than it does to describe an object like a door. If you were to load an item file into a text editor, you'd see something like this:

```
3
20
10
2
3
2
1
#TRUE#
1245
```

```
18
0
34
0
0
0
0
#FALSE#
1119
18
23
0
1
0
0
0
#FALSE#
1165
18
```

Figure 12.7 shows how to interpret the data in the item file.

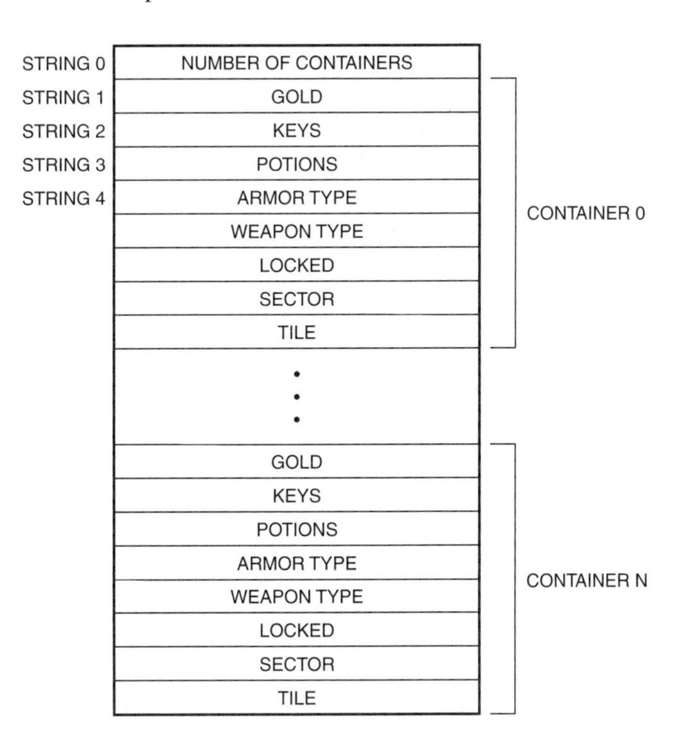

FIGURE 12.7
The structure of the item file.

New Members of the CEngine Class

Now you should have a good idea of how the program loads and initializes its data. In the next chapter, you'll examine this data in greater detail to see how much of it is used in the game. The rest of the source code that you added to the program in this chapter should be pretty easy to understand. However, in order to keep up to date with `CEngine`, Table 12.10 describes the new members you added to the class.

TABLE 12.10 New `CEngine` Members

Member	*Type*	*Description*
m_byMapType	Data	The map type ID for the current location
m_Containers	Data	The class's CContainers object
m_Doors	Data	The class's CDoors object
m_iCurrentMap	Data	The map type ID for the current map
m_iFirstMapType	Data	The map type ID for the starting map
m_iStartSector	Data	The sector in which the player character begins
m_People	Data	The class's CPeople object
m_Player	Data	The class's CPlayer object
m_pstrFirstMap	Data	Name of the first map to display in the game
m_Sectors[]	Data	Array of tile numbers for the current location
GetCurrentMap()	Public method	Returns the map type ID for the current map
GetPlayer()	Public method	Returns a pointer to the class's CPlayer object
GetSectors()	Public method	Returns a pointer to the tile values for the current map
InitGame()	Public method	Initializes all game data at the start of a game
OpenMapFiles()	Public method	Loads all game data from disk
SetCurrentMap()	Public method	Sets the map type ID for the current map
ConstructFileName()	Private method	Creates the path for the file to load
GetStringFromFile()	Private method	Reads a string from the current file
ReadContainerFile()	Private method	Reads the item file into the class's CContainers object
ReadDoorFile()	Private method	Reads the door file into the class's CDoors object
ReadMapFile()	Private method	Reads the location map into the m_Sectors[] array
ReadPeopleFile()	Private method	Reads the people file into the class's CPeople objects

That's a lot of new stuff! You still have a long way to go, though. Luckily, things are going to start to get fun, because in the next chapter, you learn to display the player's current location, as well as enable him to move around in the game world.

Summary

Every computer game, no matter how simple or complex, starts off with its data set to the default values for the beginning of the game. What happens after that is up to the player. Because of the large amounts of data that must be maintained in an RPG, using classes is a great way to organize data into logical objects, along with the methods that operate on the data.

Q&A

Q. In this chapter, I added a lot of classes with a lot of variables, but I'm not very clear about how all this stuff is going to be used in the game.

A. This is one of the problems an author runs into when trying to write a programming book. Some topics are kind of circular in nature. For example, you can't draw the game screen until you initialize the appropriate game variables, but you can't completely understand the variables until you see how they're used to draw the screen. Just take it on faith that, if you're not clear about how the data you added to the game in this chapter is used, you will be as you continue forward with the JBookman project.

Q. The player character in this game seems kind of lightweight. I mean what happened to all the RPG stuff like skills, nationality, character class, food, and so on?

A. It all comes down to whether you want to read—and pay for!—a 3,000-page book. *The Adventures of Jasper Bookman* is only meant to demonstrate how to program a 2D RPG, and as such, gives you a taste of the problems you'll run into when creating such a game. When you're done with the book, feel free to fill out the game with as complex a character system as you like.

Q. How come one of the map files uses binary data as its storage format, but the other related files are all string data?

A. Because the location map data (such as that stored in the FirstTown.map file) is all numbers, it doesn't really make sense to use strings to store the information. (Of course, you could if you wanted to.) The other files contain some string information, such as a person's name or the values #TRUE# and #FALSE#, so it seemed logical to use strings for all the data in these files. The advantage of string files is that they're easy to edit.

Workshop

The workshop includes quiz questions to help gauge your grasp of the material. Even if you feel that you totally understand the concepts presented here, you should work through the quiz anyway. The last section is an exercise or two that you might work through to help reinforce your learning.

1. Why are classes a good way to manage game data?
2. In the JBookman project, what does the `CContainer` class represent?
3. What's the difference between the `CContainer` and `CContainers` classes?
4. Name and describe the four attributes of a door represented by the `CDoor` class.
5. In all the classes in the JBookman project, how do you access the data members that represent the attributes of an object?
6. Describe how the hit point, armor, and weapon attributes of the game's player character determine the outcome of a battle.
7. What is an NPC?
8. In what part of the program do objects of classes such as `CContainers` and `CDoors` get created?
9. Name and describe the purpose of the four files that represent that data needed to create the First Town location in the game.
10. What's the biggest difference between the data formats of the location map file (such as FirstTown.map) and the other map data files?

Exercises

1. Use a text editor, such as Windows Notepad, to create a door file that contains three doors. The doors can be located wherever you want, but the first door should be locked and visible, the second should be unlocked and visible, and the third door should be unlocked and invisible. All doors use tile #10 as their graphical image.
2. Use Visual Studio's debugging commands, particularly breakpoints and the Trace Into (F11) and Trace Over (F10) commands to trace through the creation of the various objects in the game. Start by placing a breakpoint on the line

   ```
   CEngine g_Engine("FirstTown.map", FIRSTTOWN, 1485);
   ```

   in the JBookman.cpp file, because this is where the program constructs the first class object. Then press F11 to start the program, which will start program execution, after which it will pause on the breakpoint. As you step through the program, take special note of how and where the program creates instances of the new classes such as CContainers and CContainer. For example, you'll see that CEngine creates an object of the CContainers class, but it's CContainers that creates objects of the CContainer class.

Answers for Day 12

Quiz

1. Why are classes a good way to manage game data?

   Because they enable you to group together data and the functions that manipulate that data.

2. In the JBookman project, what does the CContainer class represent?

   It represents a container such as a chest or a barrel. Containers can hold other objects, including keys, gold, armor, weapons, and potions.

3. What's the difference between the CContainer and CContainers classes?

   The CContainer class represents a single container object, whereas the CContainers class represents an array of CContainer objects.

4. Name and describe the four attributes of a door represented by the CDoor class.

   The locked attribute, stored in the m_bLocked data member, specifies whether the door is locked. The secret attribute, stored in the m_bSecret data member, determines whether the door is initially visible. The sector attribute, stored in the m_iSector data member, specifies the door's location. Finally, the tile attribute, stored in the m_iTile data member, specifies the image used to represent the door.

5. In all the classes in the JBookman project, how do you access the data members that represent the attributes of an object?

   Every data member has a Get and Set method. For example, the CDoor class defines the methods GetLocked() and SetLocked() for manipulating the m_bLocked data member.

6. Describe how the hit point, armor, and weapon attributes of the game's player character determine the outcome of a battle.

   Hit points represent the player's health; when they are gone, the player character dies. The armor and weapon attributes represent the players defensive (shield) and offensive (attack) values.

7. What is an NPC?

NPC stands for non-player character and is a person or creature with which the player can interact in the game.

8. In what part of the program do objects of classes such as `CContainers` and `CDoors` get created?

   They are data members of the `CEngine` class and so are created when an object of the `CEngine` class is created.

9. Name and describe the purpose of the four files that represent that data needed to create the First Town location in the game.

   The file FirstTown.map holds the data needed to draw the location map. The file FirstTown.map.dor contains information about all doors in the location, whereas the file FirstTown.map.peo contains information about the NPCs in the location. Finally, the FirstTown.map.itm file contains information about containers and the items they hold.

10. What's the biggest difference between the data formats of the location map file (such as FirstTown.map) and the other map data files?

    The location map file is binary, whereas the other files contain a list of strings.

Exercises

1. Use a text editor, such as Windows Notepad, to create a door file that contains three doors. The doors can be located wherever you want, but the first door should be locked and visible, the second should be unlocked and visible, and the third door should be unlocked and invisible. All doors use tile #10 as their graphical image.

   Your file should look as shown here, except you can have different values for the sector fields (where I have the 100, 200, and 300):

```
3
#FALSE#
#TRUE#
100
10
#FALSE#
#FALSE#
200
10
#TRUE#
#FALSE#
300
10
```

Week 2

Day 13

Drawing the Game World

In the previous day, you learned how to load a file of values that represent a game world. You've also read a little bit about how you can build a graphical representation of that game world using rectangular images called tiles. In this chapter, you put all that information together as you finally get your game's first images up on the screen. When you complete this chapter, you'll even be able to explore the game's first town. Specifically, in this day you learn how to:

- Draw a game world using tiles
- Represent a game map in memory
- Use Direct3D to draw the game world
- Move a player character through the game world

Creating Worlds One Square at a Time

The world around us is filled with objects of a virtually infinite variety of shapes and sizes. Not only is a lake very different from a tree, but also no two lakes or two trees look alike, either. They say, in fact, that no two snowflakes have ever looked the same, though how you'd go about proving that is beyond me!

When it comes time to create the world in which your game is set, the huge diversity of the real world becomes a problem. Obviously, a computer game must find some way to simplify the world, streamlining it to the point that it can be represented on the screen. There are a lot of ways to do this, but most old-style RPGs (that is, the ones that were around before everything went 3D), use a technique called *tiling*.

A tile is nothing more than a small bitmap that represents an object in your game world. When I say object, I don't mean just stuff like treasure chests and potions. I also mean grass, water, desert, trees, walls and anything else you want to include in your virtual world. Often, a tile is designed such that several can be put together to create a seamless surface of some kind.

For example, look at Figure 13.1. On the left is a single tile that represents an area of grass, and on the right is a larger grassy area created by putting 36 of the grass tiles together. The grass tile is just a 32×32 bitmap that a game designer created in a paint program, such as Microsoft Paint.

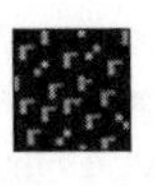

FIGURE 13.1

Representing grass with a tile.

You can do the same thing with an object like a tree. What if you want to add a small forest to your grassy area? Load up your paint program and draw a single tree tile. Then use a bunch of them to create the forest, as shown in Figure 13.2. Sure, every tree looks alike, but your tree tile is meant to be more of a symbol for a tree than an actual tree. Anyway, if you want a little variety, you can always create several different tree tiles and use them all to make your forest.

FIGURE 13.2
Adding a small forest to the grassy area.

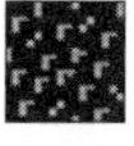

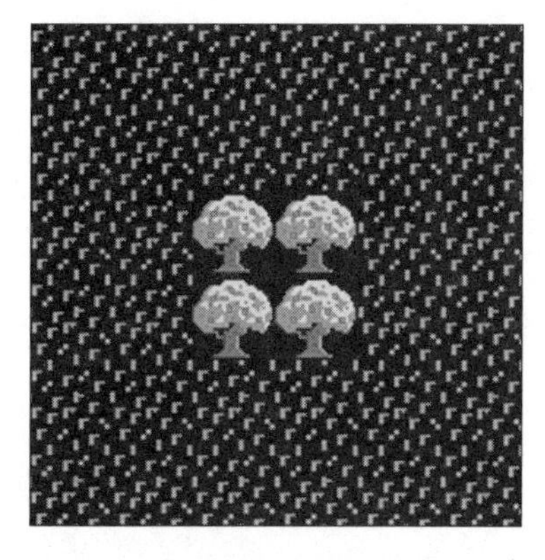

What if you want a wall around your forest? No problem! Break out your paint program, create a wall tile, and use it multiple times to create any size wall you want, as shown in Figure 13.3. The figure also shows a tile that represents a signpost.

FIGURE 13.3
Surrounding the forest with a wall.

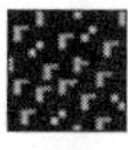

By adding more and more tiles, you can make your game world as detailed as you like. Of course, creating tons of tiles is a lot of work. Moreover, computer memory is not unlimited (at least, not yet), so you have certain limitations on the number of tiles you can use with your game. But that limit is pretty high.

Representing a World Map with Computer Data

So, now you know how you can use small, rectangular images to create the world in which your game takes place. How, though, does your program know where to place what tile? To tell your program how to draw your game world, first you need to give each tile an ID number. Then, you need to create an array of values that contain the tile ID values in the order required to draw the game screen.

Continuing with the grass-forest-wall-signpost example (refer to Figure 13.3), you might assign the ID 0 to the grass tile, 1 to the tree tile, 2 to the wall tile, and 3 to the signpost. Using these values would give you the map data shown in Figure 13.4.

FIGURE 13.4

Using tile IDs to represent a map.

0	0	0	0	0	0
0	2	2	2	2	0
0	2	1	1	2	0
0	2	1	1	2	0
0	2	0	2	2	0
0	0	0	0	0	3

Starting in the upper corner of the map and working your way across and down, you would place the map values into an array. Your program can then read through the array, using the IDs and their position in the array to draw the game screen. In your program, such as array might look like this:

```
char g_Sectors[] =
    {0,0,0,0,0,0,
     0,2,2,2,2,0,
     0,2,1,1,2,0,
     0,2,1,1,2,0,
     0,2,0,2,2,0,
     0,0,0,0,0,3};
```

As you can see here, by breaking up the array values into several lines, you can more easily see the map that it represents. You could also go with a two-dimensional array, but I just went with the straight array.

Organizing Tiles into a Bitmap

The next question is how you store the tiles in memory. You could create a surface for each one, but that would be a lot of unnecessary work and would also be an inefficient use of memory. The best way to handle your tiles is to put them all into a single bitmap. Then you can use a little math to figure out the location of the tile you want. (Don't worry, I've already done the math for you!) Figure 13.5 shows what I mean, by grouping the four tiles you've seen so far into a single bitmap.

FIGURE 13.5
Grouping tiles into a single bitmap.

Unfortunately, you're not going to get away with having only four tiles in your game. You're going to need dozens—maybe even hundreds. With that in mind, Figure 13.6 shows what the real thing might look like. This is a set of tiles from *The Adventures of Jasper Bookman*. There are actually four sets of tiles like this in the whole game.

FIGURE 13.6
A full set of tiles grouped into a bitmap.

Seeing Tiling in Action

Just like anything else in programming, the best way to understand the tiling technique is to do it for real. Perform the following steps to write a program that creates the field with the forest, walls, and signposts.

Creating the Basic TileApp Project

Perform the following steps to get the main Direct3D application project started:

1. Start a new empty Win32 project named TileApp. (Don't forget to set the Additional Options to Empty Project.)
2. Add to the project a new C++ File (.cpp) named TileApp.cpp.

3. Copy the contents of the SurfaceApp.cpp file (from Chapter 6) into the new TileApp code window.
5. Change the name in the comment at the top of the file to TileApp.
6. In the `RegisterWindowClass()` function change `wc.lpszClassName = "SurfaceApp"` to `wc.lpszClassName = "TileApp"`.
7. In the `CreateAppWindow()` function, change "SurfaceApp" to "TileApp", and then change "Direct3D Surface Application" to "Tile Application".

Adding the DirectX References

Next, you need to tell the program where the required DirectX header files and libraries are located. To do that, follow these steps:

1. Right-click the project's name in the Solution Explorer, and select Properties from the menu that appears. The TileApp Property Pages dialog box appears.
2. Click the C/C++ selection in the left-hand pane, and select General from the displayed choices.
3. In the Additional Include Directories box, enter the path to the DirectX 8.1 SDK's include folder. If you installed the SDK using the default settings, this path should be `C:\DXSDK\include`.
4. Click the Linker selection in the left-hand pane, and select General from the displayed choices.
5. In the Additional Library Directories box, enter the path to the DirectX 8.1 SDK's library folder. If you installed the SDK using the default settings, this path should be `C:\DXSDK\lib`.
6. Click the Linker's Input selection in the left-hand pane.
7. In the Additional Dependencies box in the right-hand pane, enter `d3d8.lib`, `d3dx8.lib`, and `dxerr8.lib`.
8. Build the application (Ctrl+Shift+B) to be sure everything is okay. Don't try to run it yet, though, as you'll just get an error.

Adding Source Code

The final step is to add the source code that'll get everything up and running. Follow these steps to get that task done:

1. Near the top of the program, add the following lines to the function prototypes. If you don't want to do the typing, you can copy the source code from the Code01.txt file in the Chapter 13 directory of this book's CD-ROM.

```
void PaintBackground();
int ColumnRow2Sector(int c, int r, int numCols);
HRESULT PlaceTile(IDirect3DSurface8* pBackBuffer,
    IDirect3DSurface8* pTileSurface, int TileNumber,
    int DstCol, int DstRow, int numTileCols, int numMapCols,
    int tileSize, int xOffset, int yOffset);
int TileNumber2SourceX(int TileNumber, int numCols, int tileSize);
int TileNumber2SourceY(int TileNumber, int numCols, int tileSize);
int Column2X(int col, int tileSize, int numCols);
int Row2Y(int r, int tileSize);
```

These lines declare the new functions you'll be adding to the program.

2. Again, near the top of the program, add the following lines to the global variables. If you don't want to do the typing, you can copy the source code from the Code02.txt file in the Chapter 13 directory of this book's CD-ROM.

```
IDirect3DSurface8* g_pBackBuffer = NULL;
char g_Sectors[] =
    {0,0,0,0,0,0,
     0,2,2,2,2,0,
     0,2,1,1,2,0,
     0,2,1,1,2,0,
     0,2,0,2,2,0,
     0,0,0,0,0,3};
```

These are the new global variables you'll be using in this program, including a pointer to the application's back buffer and the location map.

3. Add the following lines right after the program's includes. If you don't want to do the typing, you can copy the source code from the Code03.txt file in the Chapter 13 directory of this book's CD-ROM.

```
// Constants.
const COLUMNSINTILEFILE = 2;
const TILESIZE = 32;
const MAPCOLUMNCOUNT = 6;
const MAPROWCOUNT = 6;
const XOFFSET = 220;
const YOFFSET = 120;
```

You'll see what these constants do a little later in the chapter, when you explore the source code in detail.

4. Go to the `InitFullScreenDirect3D()` function, and in the call to `CreateImageSurface()`, change the 640 and 480 to 64 and 64.

The tile bitmap is much smaller than the image the original application loaded.

5. Add the following lines to the `InitFullScreenDirect3D()`, right before the final return statement. If you don't want to do the typing, you can copy the source code from the Code04.txt file in the Chapter 13 directory of this book's CD-ROM.

```
g_hResult = g_pDirect3DDevice->GetBackBuffer(0,
    D3DBACKBUFFER_TYPE_MONO, &g_pBackBuffer);
if (FAILED(g_hResult))
{
    strcpy(g_szErrorMsg, "Couldn't get back buffer.");
    PostQuitMessage(WM_QUIT);
}
```

These lines get a pointer to the application's back buffer, which the program needs in order to draw images on the back buffer.

6. Add the following lines to the beginning of the `CleanUpDirect3D()` function:

```
if (g_pBackBuffer)
    g_pBackBuffer->Release();
```

These lines release the back buffer when the program is through with it.

7. Replace the current `Render()` function with the one that follows:

```
void Render()
{
    PaintBackground();
    g_pDirect3DDevice->Present(NULL, NULL, NULL, NULL);
}
```

This function calls the helper function that draws the map on the back buffer. The call to `Present()` makes the back buffer visible to the user.

8. Add the following `PaintBackground()` function to the program. If you don't want to do the typing, you can copy the source code from the Code05.txt file in the Chapter 13 directory of this book's CD-ROM.

```
/////////////////////////////////////////////////////////
// PaintBackground()
/////////////////////////////////////////////////////////
void PaintBackground()
{
    g_pDirect3DDevice->Clear(0, NULL, D3DCLEAR_TARGET,
        D3DCOLOR_XRGB(0,0,0), 1.0f, 0);
    for (int Row = 0; Row < MAPROWCOUNT; ++Row)
    {
        for (int Col = 0; Col < MAPCOLUMNCOUNT; ++Col)
        {
            int iSector = ColumnRow2Sector(Col, Row, MAPCOLUMNCOUNT);
            int TileNumber = g_Sectors[iSector];
            g_hResult = PlaceTile(g_pBackBuffer, g_pBitmapSurface,
              TileNumber, Col, Row,COLUMNSINTILEFILE, MAPCOLUMNCOUNT,
              TILESIZE, XOFFSET, YOFFSET);
```

```
            if (FAILED(g_hResult))
            {
                strcpy(g_szErrorMsg, "Error drawing tiles.");
                PostQuitMessage(WM_QUIT);
            }
        }
    }
}
```

This function iterates through the map data, drawing the appropriate tile for each value in the map.

9. Add the following `PlaceTile()` function to the program. If you don't want to do the typing, you can copy the source code from the Code06.txt file in the Chapter 13 directory of this book's CD-ROM.

```
///////////////////////////////////////////////////////
// PlaceTile()
///////////////////////////////////////////////////////
HRESULT PlaceTile(IDirect3DSurface8* pBackBuffer,
    IDirect3DSurface8* pTileSurface, int TileNumber,
    int DstCol, int DstRow, int numTileCols, int numMapCols,
    int tileSize, int xOffset, int yOffset)
{
    RECT SrcTileRect;
    POINT DstPoint;
    SrcTileRect.left = TileNumber2SourceX(TileNumber,
        numTileCols, tileSize);
    SrcTileRect.right = SrcTileRect.left + tileSize;
    SrcTileRect.top = TileNumber2SourceY(TileNumber,
        numTileCols, tileSize);
    SrcTileRect.bottom = SrcTileRect.top + tileSize;
    DstPoint.x = Column2X(DstCol, tileSize, numMapCols) + xOffset;
    DstPoint.y = Row2Y(DstRow, tileSize) + yOffset;
    HRESULT hResult = g_pDirect3DDevice->
        CopyRects(g_pBitmapSurface, &SrcTileRect,
        1, pBackBuffer, &DstPoint);
    return hResult;
}
```

This function draws a single tile on the back buffer.

10. Add the following functions to the program. If you don't want to do the typing, you can copy the source code from the Code07.txt file in the Chapter 13 directory of this book's CD-ROM.

```
///////////////////////////////////////////////////////
// ColumnRow2Sector()
///////////////////////////////////////////////////////
```

```
int ColumnRow2Sector(int c, int r, int numCols)
{
    return r * numCols + c;
}
/////////////////////////////////////////////////////////
// TileNumber2SourceX()
/////////////////////////////////////////////////////////
int TileNumber2SourceX(int TileNumber, int numCols, int tileSize)
{
    return (TileNumber - ((int)(TileNumber / numCols))
        * numCols) * tileSize;
}
/////////////////////////////////////////////////////////
// TileNumber2SourceY()
/////////////////////////////////////////////////////////
int TileNumber2SourceY(int TileNumber, int numCols, int tileSize)
{
    return ((int)(TileNumber / numCols)) * tileSize;
}
/////////////////////////////////////////////////////////
// Column2X()
/////////////////////////////////////////////////////////
int Column2X(int col, int tileSize, int numCols)
{
    return (col - ((int)((col / numCols)) *
        numCols)) * tileSize;
}
/////////////////////////////////////////////////////////
// Row2Y()
/////////////////////////////////////////////////////////
int Row2Y(int r, int tileSize)
{
    return r * tileSize;
}
```

These functions contain the math needed to locate and display a tile. After you finish building the program, you'll explore these functions in greater detail.

11. Copy the Image.bmp file from the Chapter13 directory of this book's CD-ROM and place the file in your application's main directory.

    This is the bitmap file that contains the tiles.

And that's it. You can now compile and run the program. When you do, you should see the window in Figure 13.7. *Presto!* Your walled forest springs into life.

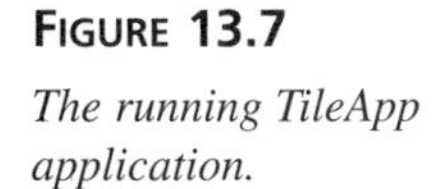

FIGURE 13.7
The running TileApp application.

Digging into the Program

Now that you've built the program and seen it run, how about taking a tour through the source code? You don't need to look at the Windows stuff. You should already have that down pat. The following sections fill you in on the rest of the details.

Loading the Tiles and Getting the Back Buffer

The first source code of interest is where the program loads the tiles:

```
g_hResult = g_pDirect3DDevice->CreateImageSurface(64, 64,
    D3DFMT_X8R8G8B8, &g_pBitmapSurface);
if (FAILED(g_hResult))
{
    strcpy(g_szErrorMsg, "Error creating the Tile surface.");
    PostQuitMessage(WM_QUIT);
}
g_hResult = D3DXLoadSurfaceFromFile(g_pBitmapSurface, NULL, NULL,
    "image.bmp", NULL, D3DX_DEFAULT, 0, NULL);
if (FAILED(g_hResult))
{
    strcpy(g_szErrorMsg, "Couldn't load the tile file.");
    PostQuitMessage(WM_QUIT);
}
```


This part of the program creates a 64x64 surface and loads the Image.bmp file, which holds the tiles into it.

After getting the tiles loaded into memory, the program gets a pointer to the back buffer, which it needs in order to draw the tile map:

```
g_hResult = g_pDirect3DDevice->GetBackBuffer(0,
    D3DBACKBUFFER_TYPE_MONO, &g_pBackBuffer);
if (FAILED(g_hResult))
{
    strcpy(g_szErrorMsg, "Couldn't get back buffer.");
    PostQuitMessage(WM_QUIT);
}
```

Rendering During Idle Time

With all the initialization complete, the program enters its message loop. Whenever there are no messages to process (which is most of the time), the program calls the `Render()` function:

```
void Render()
{
    PaintBackground();
    g_pDirect3DDevice->Present(NULL, NULL, NULL, NULL);
}
```

Here, a call to the `PaintBackground()` function draws the tile map, and the call to `Present()` makes the back buffer visible.

Drawing the Map

The `PaintBackground()` function is where the program draws each tile in its proper location. First the function clears the back buffer:

```
g_pDirect3DDevice->Clear(0, NULL, D3DCLEAR_TARGET,
    D3DCOLOR_XRGB(0,0,0), 1.0f, 0);
```

The function then processes each tile in a nested loop:

```
for (int Row = 0; Row < MAPROWCOUNT; ++Row)
{
    for (int Col = 0; Col < MAPCOLUMNCOUNT; ++Col)
    {
            .
            .
            .
    }
}
```

Inside the loop, the program first calculates the sector at which to place the current tile:

```
int iSector = ColumnRow2Sector(Col, Row, MAPCOLUMNCOUNT);
```

The `ColumnRow2Sector()` function takes the current column and row in the map, along with the number of columns in the map, and returns the sector number at which to draw the tile.

I use the word *sector* to mean a specific square in the map. For example, the first square in the map, the one in the upper-left corner, is sector 0. The sectors are then numbered from left to right across each row. The sector in the lower-right corner of the map is the sector with the highest number.

Figure 13.8 shows how the columns and rows in the map relate to the sector numbers. The column numbers are across the top of the map, whereas the row numbers run down the left side. The sector numbers are inside each of the squares in the map.

FIGURE 13.8

A map showing column, row, and sector numbers.

	0	1	2	3	4	5
0	0	1	2	3	4	5
1	6	7	8	9	10	11
2	12	13	14	15	16	17
3	18	19	20	21	22	23
4	24	25	26	27	28	29
5	30	31	32	33	34	35

Once the program has the sector number, it can use it to index the map array and so get the tile ID for that sector:

```
int TileNumber = g_Sectors[iSector];
```

Finally, a call to the application-defined `PlaceTile()` function draws the tile on the back buffer:

```
g_hResult = PlaceTile(g_pBackBuffer, g_pBitmapSurface, TileNumber, Col, Row,
    COLUMNSINTILEFILE, MAPCOLUMNCOUNT, TILESIZE, XOFFSET, YOFFSET);
if (FAILED(g_hResult))
{
    strcpy(g_szErrorMsg, "Error drawing tiles.");
    PostQuitMessage(WM_QUIT);
}
```

Drawing a Single Tile

The `PlaceTile()` function is where all the Direct3D stuff happens. You may recall that when copying image data from one surface to another, you don't need to copy an entire surface. Instead, you can copy any part of one surface and copy it to any part of another surface. To do this, you first need to declare the `RECT` and `POINT` structures that will hold the source rectangle and the destination location. The `PlaceTile()` function takes care of that detail like this:

```
RECT SrcTileRect;
POINT DstPoint;
```

The next task is to fill the RECT structure with the coordinates of the tile the program needs to copy to the back buffer. Because the tiles are all in one bitmap, the program needs to use a little math to get the job done. To get the left edge of the required tile, the program calls the application-defined TileNumber2SourceX() function:

```
SrcTileRect.left = TileNumber2SourceX(TileNumber,
    numTileCols, tileSize);
```

The TileNumber2SourceX() function takes a tile number and returns the pixel location of the tile's left edge within the bitmap. The function requires the following arguments:

- The tile number
- The number of columns in the tile bitmap (that is, how many tiles across in the bitmap)
- The size of a tile (the width, which should be the same as the height)

You can use this function (and the others you'll soon see) with any size tile bitmap as long as you provide the correct values for the arguments. For example, if you had a tile bitmap that was 10 tiles across with each tile being 64 pixels square, you'd use 10 and 64, respectively, for the function's second and third arguments.

The location of the tile's right edge is just the location of the left edge plus the tile's width:

```
SrcTileRect.right = SrcTileRect.left + tileSize;
```

The program gets the location of the tile's top edge by calling the application-defined TileNumber2SourceY() function, which works similarly to its counterpart, TileNumber2SourceX():

```
SrcTileRect.top = TileNumber2SourceY(TileNumber,
    numTileCols, tileSize);
```

The location of the tile's bottom edge is simply the location of the top edge plus the tile's height:

```
SrcTileRect.bottom = SrcTileRect.top + tileSize;
```

Now that the source RECT structure is filled in, it's time to tackle the destination POINT structure. To get the pixel X coordinate for the tile's upper-left corner, the program calls the application-defined function Column2X():

```
DstPoint.x = Column2X(DstCol, tileSize, numMapCols) + xOffset;
```

The Column2X() function takes the map column in which the tile needs to be drawn and returns the pixel X coordinate for that column. It requires the following arguments:

- The destination column in the map
- The tile's size (that is, the tile's width, which should be the same as its height)
- The number of columns in the map, by which I mean the number of tiles across in the final image that will be displayed on the screen

Notice that the program sums the value returned by Column2X() with xOffset. The xOffset value determines how far to the right the map's left edge gets drawn. If you left off xOffset, the map would be drawn on the screen's left edge.

To get the Y coordinate for the tile's upper-left corner, the program calls the application-defined function Column2Y():

```
DstPoint.y = Row2Y(DstRow, tileSize) + yOffset;
```

The Column2Y() function takes the map row in which the tile needs to be drawn and returns the pixel Y coordinate for that column. It requires the following arguments:

- The destination row in the map
- The tile's size

Finally, a call to the Direct3D device object's CopyRects() method draws the tile on the back buffer:

```
HRESULT hResult = g_pDirect3DDevice->
    CopyRects(g_pBitmapSurface, &SrcTileRect,
    1, pBackBuffer, &DstPoint);
```

The Game Map Versus the Viewport

Now that you understand how to draw a game map from a set of tiles, it's time to complicate matters a little further. In many games, including *The Adventures of Jasper Bookman*, the full map for a location is much larger than the part of the map that appears onscreen. For example, the JBookman project uses location maps that are 42 tiles wide and 42 tiles high. However, the game screen displays an area only 19 tiles wide and 13 tiles high.

13

This window onto the game world is called the *viewport* and can make programming a game like *The Adventures of Jasper Bookman* a little complicated and confusing. You always have to keep in mind that you're actually dealing with two maps: the full location map and the viewport map. Figure 13.9 shows the relationship between these two types of maps.

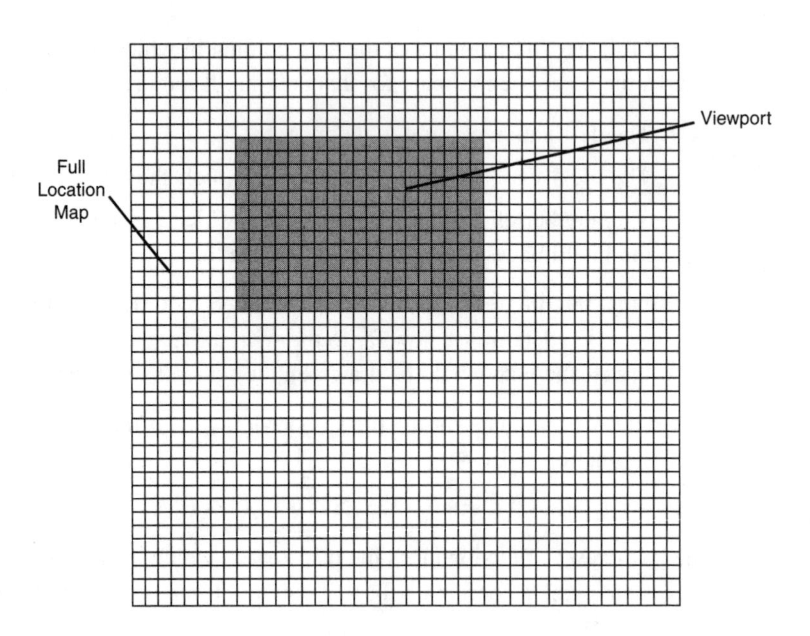

FIGURE 13.9

The viewport within the full location map.

NEW TERM You can think of a *viewport* as a kind of window into the game world. That is, it's as if you were looking through the viewport and seeing only the part of the game world that's visible through the viewport.

As the player moves through the game world, the viewport moves with him. For example, Figure 13.10 shows the location of the viewport within the full location map after the player has moved his character down toward the lower-right corner.

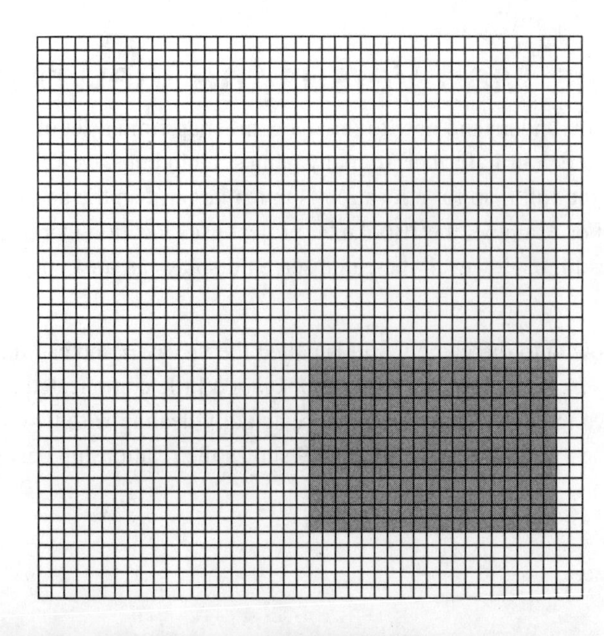

FIGURE 13.10

The viewport after the player moves.

JBookman: Drawing the Map

It's time to put everything you've learned about drawing a game world to work, as you add more to the JBookman project. In this section, you add the code needed to enable the JBookman project to display its game map. Load up the JBookman project from the previous chapter, and perform the steps that follow (broken into several parts).

Adding Code to the Game Engine

First, you need to make changes to the game engine. Here's what to do:

1. Add the following lines to the Engine.h file's public methods, right after line `CPlayer* GetPlayer()` that's already there. If you don't want to type, you can copy the lines from the Code08.txt file in the Chapter13 directory of this book's CD-ROM.

```
void PaintBackBuffer();
HRESULT PlaceTile(IDirect3DSurface8* pBackBuffer,
    IDirect3DSurface8* pTileSurface, int TileNumber,
    int DstCol, int DstRow, int numTileCols, int numMapCols,
    int tileSize, int xOffset, int yOffset);
int ColumnRow2Sector(int c, int r, int colCount);
int TileNumber2SourceX(int TileNumber, int numCols, int tileSize);
int TileNumber2SourceY(int TileNumber, int numCols, int tileSize);
int Column2X(int col, int tileSize, int numCols);
int Row2Y(int r, int tileSize);
int Sector2Column(int iSector, int numCols);
int Sector2Row(int iSector, int numCols);
```

   These lines declare new public methods for the class. You'll see what these methods do later in this section.

2. Add the following private methods to the class, by placing these lines right after line `void GetStringFromFile(std::ifstream& str, char* buf)` that's already there. If you don't want to type, you can copy the lines from the Code09.txt file in the Chapter13 directory of this book's CD-ROM.

```
void PaintBackground();
void SetVisibleColsRows(int& LowVisibleCol, int& HiVisibleCol,
    int& LowVisibleRow, int& HiVisibleRow);
void PaintPlayer(IDirect3DSurface8* pBackBuffer);
```

   These lines declare new private methods for the class. You'll explore these methods later in this chapter.

3. Add the following method implementations to the Engine.cpp file. If you don't want to type, you can copy the lines from the Code10.txt file in the Chapter13 directory of this book's CD-ROM.

13

```
//////////////////////////////////////////////////////
// PaintBackBuffer()
//////////////////////////////////////////////////////
void CEngine::PaintBackBuffer()
{
    PaintBackground();
    PaintPlayer(m_Direct3D.GetBackBuffer());
    m_Direct3D.GetDevice()->Present(NULL, NULL, NULL, NULL);
}
//////////////////////////////////////////////////////
// PaintBackground()
//////////////////////////////////////////////////////
void CEngine::PaintBackground()
{
    int LowVisibleCol;
    int HiVisibleCol;
    int LowVisibleRow;
    int HiVisibleRow;
    SetVisibleColsRows(LowVisibleCol, HiVisibleCol,
        LowVisibleRow, HiVisibleRow);
    m_Direct3D.GetDevice()->Clear(0, NULL, D3DCLEAR_TARGET,
        D3DCOLOR_XRGB(0,0,0), 1.0f, 0);
    int DstRow = 0;
    for (int SrcRow = LowVisibleRow; SrcRow <= HiVisibleRow; ++SrcRow)
    {
        int DstCol = 0;
        for (int SrcCol = LowVisibleCol; SrcCol <= HiVisibleCol; ++SrcCol)
        {
            int iSector = ColumnRow2Sector(SrcCol, SrcRow, MAPCOLUMNCOUNT);
            int TileNumber = m_Sectors[iSector];
            IDirect3DSurface8* backbuf = m_Direct3D.GetBackBuffer();
            PlaceTile(m_Direct3D.GetBackBuffer(),
                m_Direct3D.GetCurrentTileSurface(), TileNumber, DstCol,
DstRow,
                COLUMNSINTILEFILE, MAPCOLUMNCOUNT, TILESIZE, XOFFSET, YOFF-
SET);
            ++DstCol;
        }
        DstRow = DstRow + 1;
    }
}
//////////////////////////////////////////////////////
// PlaceTile()
//////////////////////////////////////////////////////
HRESULT CEngine::PlaceTile(IDirect3DSurface8* pBackBuffer,
    IDirect3DSurface8* pTileSurface, int TileNumber,
    int DstCol, int DstRow, int numTileCols, int numMapCols,
    int tileSize, int xOffset, int yOffset)
{
    RECT SrcTileRect;
    POINT DstPoint;
```

```
    SrcTileRect.left = TileNumber2SourceX(TileNumber,
        numTileCols, tileSize);
    SrcTileRect.right = SrcTileRect.left + tileSize;
    SrcTileRect.top = TileNumber2SourceY(TileNumber,
        numTileCols, tileSize);
    SrcTileRect.bottom = SrcTileRect.top + tileSize;
    DstPoint.x = Column2X(DstCol, tileSize, numMapCols) + xOffset;
    DstPoint.y = Row2Y(DstRow, tileSize) + yOffset;
    HRESULT hResult = m_Direct3D.GetDevice()->
        CopyRects(pTileSurface, &SrcTileRect,
        1, pBackBuffer, &DstPoint);
    return hResult;
}
//////////////////////////////////////////////////////
// SetVisibleColsRows()
//////////////////////////////////////////////////////
void CEngine::SetVisibleColsRows(int& LowVisibleCol, int& HiVisibleCol,
         int& LowVisibleRow, int& HiVisibleRow)
{
    int PlayerMapCol = Sector2Column(m_Player.GetSector(), MAPCOLUMNCOUNT);
    int PlayerMapRow = Sector2Row(m_Player.GetSector(), MAPCOLUMNCOUNT);
    LowVisibleCol = PlayerMapCol - NORMALVISIBLEPLAYERCOL;
    HiVisibleCol = PlayerMapCol + NORMALVISIBLEPLAYERCOL;
    LowVisibleRow = PlayerMapRow - NORMALVISIBLEPLAYERROW;
    HiVisibleRow = PlayerMapRow + NORMALVISIBLEPLAYERROW;
    if (PlayerMapCol < NORMALVISIBLEPLAYERCOL)
    {
        LowVisibleCol = 0;
        HiVisibleCol = 18;
    }
    else if (PlayerMapCol > 32)
    {
        LowVisibleCol = 23;
        HiVisibleCol = 41;
    }
    if (PlayerMapRow < NORMALVISIBLEPLAYERROW)
    {
        LowVisibleRow = 0;
        HiVisibleRow = 12;
    }
    else if (PlayerMapRow > 34)
    {
        LowVisibleRow = 29;
        HiVisibleRow = 41;
    }
}
//////////////////////////////////////////////////////
// PaintPlayer()
//////////////////////////////////////////////////////
void CEngine::PaintPlayer(IDirect3DSurface8* pBackBuffer)
{
    int PlayerMapCol = Sector2Column(m_Player.GetSector(), MAPCOLUMNCOUNT);
```

```
    int PlayerMapRow = Sector2Row(m_Player.GetSector(), MAPCOLUMNCOUNT);
    int FinalVisiblePlayerCol = NORMALVISIBLEPLAYERCOL;
    int FinalVisiblePlayerRow = NORMALVISIBLEPLAYERROW;
    if (PlayerMapCol < NORMALVISIBLEPLAYERCOL)
    {
        FinalVisiblePlayerCol = NORMALVISIBLEPLAYERCOL -
            (NORMALVISIBLEPLAYERCOL - PlayerMapCol);
    }
    else if (PlayerMapCol > 32)
    {
        FinalVisiblePlayerCol =
            VISIBLECOLUMNCOUNT -((MAPCOLUMNCOUNT-1)-PlayerMapCol)-1;
    }
    if (PlayerMapRow < NORMALVISIBLEPLAYERROW)
    {
        FinalVisiblePlayerRow = NORMALVISIBLEPLAYERROW -
            (NORMALVISIBLEPLAYERROW - PlayerMapRow);
    }
    else if (PlayerMapRow > 34)
    {
        FinalVisiblePlayerRow =
            VISIBLEROWCOUNT -((MAPROWCOUNT-1)-PlayerMapRow)-1;
    }
    RECT SrcTileRect;
    SrcTileRect.left = 0;
    SrcTileRect.right = 32;
    SrcTileRect.top = 0;
    SrcTileRect.bottom = 32;
    POINT DstPoint;
    DstPoint.x = Column2X(FinalVisiblePlayerCol,
        TILESIZE, MAPCOLUMNCOUNT) + XOFFSET;
    DstPoint.y = Row2Y(FinalVisiblePlayerRow, TILESIZE) + YOFFSET;
    HRESULT hResult = m_Direct3D.GetDevice()->
        CopyRects(m_Direct3D.GetPlayerTile(), &SrcTileRect,1,
        pBackBuffer,&DstPoint);
}
///////////////////////////////////////////////////////
// ColumnRow2Sector()
///////////////////////////////////////////////////////
int CEngine::ColumnRow2Sector(int c, int r, int numCols)
{
    return r * numCols + c;
}
///////////////////////////////////////////////////////
// Column2X()
///////////////////////////////////////////////////////
int CEngine::Column2X(int col, int tileSize, int numCols)
{
    return (col - ((int)((col / numCols)) *
        numCols)) * tileSize;
}
```

```
////////////////////////////////////////////////////////
// Row2Y()
////////////////////////////////////////////////////////
int CEngine::Row2Y(int r, int tileSize)
{
    return r * tileSize;
}
////////////////////////////////////////////////////////
// TileNumber2SourceX()
////////////////////////////////////////////////////////
int CEngine::TileNumber2SourceX(int TileNumber, int numCols, int tileSize)
{
    return (TileNumber - ((int)(TileNumber / numCols))
        * numCols) * tileSize;
}
////////////////////////////////////////////////////////
// TileNumber2SourceY()
////////////////////////////////////////////////////////
int CEngine::TileNumber2SourceY(int TileNumber, int numCols, int tileSize)
{
    return ((int)(TileNumber / numCols)) * tileSize;
}
////////////////////////////////////////////////////////
// Sector2Column()
////////////////////////////////////////////////////////
int CEngine::Sector2Column(int iSector, int numCols)
{
    int result = iSector % numCols;
    return result;
}
////////////////////////////////////////////////////////
// Sector2Row()
////////////////////////////////////////////////////////
int CEngine::Sector2Row(int iSector, int numCols)
{
    return (int)(iSector / numCols);
}
```

4. Replace the current `HandleKeys()` method with the one that follows. If you don't want to type, you can copy the lines from the Code11.txt file in the Chapter13 directory of this book's CD-ROM.

```
void CEngine::HandleKeys(WPARAM wParam)
{
    switch(wParam)
    {
    case VK_ESCAPE:
        PostQuitMessage(WM_QUIT);
        break;
    }
}
```

These lines enable you to quit the program with the escape key, rather than having to Alt+Tab back to Visual Studio.

5. Add the following line to the `ProcessGame()` method:

```
PaintBackBuffer();
```

Adding Code to the CDirect3D Class

Next, you need to beef up the `CDirect3D` class so that it can manage the tile surfaces needed by *The Adventures of Jasper Bookman*. Here's what to do:

1. Add the following line to the Direct3D.h file, right after the `#include <d3d8.h>` line that's already there.

```
#include <D3dx8tex.h>
```

This is the header file for the Direct3D utility library.

2. Add the following lines to the Direct3D.h file's protected data members, right after the `char m_szErrorMsg[256]` line that's already there. If you don't want to type, you can copy the lines from the Code12.txt file in the Chapter13 directory of this book's CD-ROM.

```
IDirect3DSurface8* m_pTownExtTileSurface;
IDirect3DSurface8* m_pTownIntTileSurface;
IDirect3DSurface8* m_pDungeonTileSurface;
IDirect3DSurface8* m_pWildernessTileSurface;
IDirect3DSurface8* m_pCurrentTileSurface;
IDirect3DSurface8* m_pPlayerTile;
```

These lines add new member variables to the `CDirect3D` class, including pointers to the various tile surfaces used in the program. Later in this section, you'll see exactly what these data members do in the class.

3. Add the following lines to the Direct3D.h file's public methods, right after line `char* GetErrorString(void)` that's already there. If you don't want to type, you can copy the lines from the Code13.txt file in the Chapter13 directory of this book's CD-ROM.

```
IDirect3DSurface8* GetTownExtTileSurface();
IDirect3DSurface8* GetTownIntTileSurface();
IDirect3DSurface8* GetDungeonTileSurface();
IDirect3DSurface8* GetWildernessTileSurface();
IDirect3DSurface8* GetCurrentTileSurface();
IDirect3DSurface8* GetPlayerTile();
```

These lines declare new public methods that return pointers to the game's surfaces.

4. In the Direct3D.cpp file, add the following lines to the class's constructor, right after the line `m_pBackBuffer = NULL` that's already there. If you don't want to type, you can copy the lines from the Code14.txt file in the Chapter13 directory of this book's CD-ROM.

```
m_pTownExtTileSurface = NULL;
m_pTownIntTileSurface = NULL;
m_pDungeonTileSurface = NULL;
m_pWildernessTileSurface = NULL;
m_pCurrentTileSurface = NULL;
m_pPlayerTile = NULL;
```

   These lines ensure that the surface pointers all start off as `NULL`.

5. Add the following line to the `InitD3D()` method, right after the call to `m_pD3DDevice->GetBackBuffer()` that's already there.

```
m_pCurrentTileSurface = m_pTownExtTileSurface;
```

   This line initializes a pointer that will always point to the surface that contains the currently needed tiles. Which tiles the program needs depends on whether the player is exploring the exterior of a town, the interior of a town, a dungeon, or the wilderness.

6. Replace the current `CreateSurfaces()` method with the one that follows. If you don't want to type, you can copy the lines from the Code15.txt file in the Chapter13 directory of this book's CD-ROM.

```
///////////////////////////////////////////////////////
// CreateSurfaces()
///////////////////////////////////////////////////////
HRESULT CDirect3D::CreateSurfaces()
{
    HRESULT hResult = m_pD3DDevice->CreateImageSurface(256, 256,
        D3DFMT_X8R8G8B8, &m_pTownExtTileSurface);
    if (FAILED(hResult))
    {
        strcpy(m_szErrorMsg, "Town ext tile surface not created.");
        return hResult;
    }
    hResult = D3DXLoadSurfaceFromFile(m_pTownExtTileSurface, NULL, NULL,
        "Graphics\\Town01Ext.bmp", NULL, D3DX_DEFAULT, 0, NULL);
    if (FAILED(hResult))
    {
        strcpy(m_szErrorMsg, "Error loading ext town surface.");
        return hResult;
    }
    hResult = m_pD3DDevice->CreateImageSurface(256, 256,
        D3DFMT_X8R8G8B8, &m_pTownIntTileSurface);
    if (FAILED(hResult))
    {
```

```
        strcpy(m_szErrorMsg, "Town int tile surface not created.");
        return hResult;
    }
    hResult = D3DXLoadSurfaceFromFile(m_pTownIntTileSurface, NULL, NULL,
        "Graphics\\Town01Int.bmp", NULL, D3DX_DEFAULT, 0, NULL);
    if (FAILED(hResult))
    {
        strcpy(m_szErrorMsg, "Error loading int town surface.");
        return hResult;
    }
    hResult = m_pD3DDevice->CreateImageSurface(256, 256,
        D3DFMT_X8R8G8B8, &m_pDungeonTileSurface);
    if (FAILED(hResult))
    {
        strcpy(m_szErrorMsg, "Dungeon tile surface not created.");
        return hResult;
    }
    hResult = D3DXLoadSurfaceFromFile(m_pDungeonTileSurface, NULL, NULL,
        "Graphics\\Dungeon01.bmp", NULL, D3DX_DEFAULT, 0, NULL);
    if (FAILED(hResult))
    {
        strcpy(m_szErrorMsg, "Error loading dungeon surface.");
        return hResult;
    }
    hResult = m_pD3DDevice->CreateImageSurface(256, 256,
        D3DFMT_X8R8G8B8, &m_pWildernessTileSurface);
    if (FAILED(hResult))
    {
        strcpy(m_szErrorMsg, "Wilderness tile surface not created.");
        return hResult;
    }
    hResult = D3DXLoadSurfaceFromFile(m_pWildernessTileSurface, NULL, NULL,
        "Graphics\\Wilderness.bmp", NULL, D3DX_DEFAULT, 0, NULL);
    if (FAILED(hResult))
    {
        strcpy(m_szErrorMsg, "Error loading wilderness surface.");
        return hResult;
    }
    hResult = m_pD3DDevice->CreateImageSurface(32, 32,
        D3DFMT_X8R8G8B8, &m_pPlayerTile);
    if (FAILED(hResult))
    {
        strcpy(m_szErrorMsg, "Player tile surface not created.");
        return hResult;
    }
    hResult = D3DXLoadSurfaceFromFile(m_pPlayerTile, NULL, NULL,
        "Graphics\\Player.bmp", NULL, D3DX_DEFAULT, 0, NULL);
    if (FAILED(hResult))
    {
        strcpy(m_szErrorMsg, "Error loading player tile surface.");
        return hResult;
```

```
    }
    return hResult;
}
```

The `CreateSurfaces()` function now creates and loads surfaces for the new images, including the tiles, needed by the program.

7. Add the following lines to the beginning of the `CleanUp()` method. If you don't want to type, you can copy the lines from the Code16.txt file in the Chapter13 directory of this book's CD-ROM.

```
if (m_pTownExtTileSurface)
    m_pTownExtTileSurface->Release();
if (m_pTownIntTileSurface)
    m_pTownIntTileSurface->Release();
if (m_pDungeonTileSurface)
    m_pDungeonTileSurface->Release();
if (m_pWildernessTileSurface)
    m_pWildernessTileSurface->Release();
if (m_pPlayerTile)
    m_pPlayerTile->Release();
```

These lines release the new surfaces you've added to the program.

8. Add the following method implementations to the Direct3D.cpp file. If you don't want to type, you can copy the lines from the Code17.txt file in the Chapter13 directory of this book's CD-ROM.

```
///////////////////////////////////////////////////////
// GetCurrentTileSurface()
///////////////////////////////////////////////////////
IDirect3DSurface8* CDirect3D::GetCurrentTileSurface()
{
    return m_pCurrentTileSurface;
}
///////////////////////////////////////////////////////
// GetPlayerTile()
///////////////////////////////////////////////////////
IDirect3DSurface8* CDirect3D::GetPlayerTile()
{
    return m_pPlayerTile;
}
```

These methods return pointers to the surfaces that hold the currently used tile file and the player image.

9. Load the Constants.h file, and add the following lines right after the line `const MAXDOORS = 100` that's already there. If you don't want to type, you can copy the lines from the Code18.txt file in the Chapter13 directory of this book's CD-ROM.

```
const TILESIZE = 32;
```

```
const XOFFSET = 16;
const YOFFSET = 30;
const NORMALVISIBLEPLAYERCOL = 9;
const NORMALVISIBLEPLAYERROW = 6;
const VISIBLECOLUMNCOUNT = 19;
const VISIBLEROWCOUNT = 13;
const MAPCOLUMNCOUNT = 42;
const MAPROWCOUNT = 42;
const COLUMNSINTILEFILE = 8;
```

These lines define constants for some important values used in the program. By using constants with descriptive names, the program code will be easier to read and understand.

Adding Code to the Main Program

The last step is hooking everything into the main Windows program, which is in the JBookman.cpp file. Because almost everything happens in the program's various class objects, especially the `CEngine` object, there's not much to do here. To complete this part of the project, here's what to do:

1. Add the following lines to the `WndProc()` function, right before the `switch` statement's closing brace:

   ```
   case WM_KEYDOWN:
       g_Engine.HandleKeys(wParam);
       return 0;
   ```

   This line sends all keystrokes to the `CEngine` object for processing.

2. Add the following line to the `StartMessageLoop()` function, right after the `Use idle time here` comment that's already there:

   ```
   g_Engine.ProcessGame();
   ```

   This line enables the program to run the game during the Windows application's idle time.

3. In your main JBookman project directory, create a subdirectory named Graphics, as shown in Figure 13.11.

4. Copy the files Dungeon01.bmp, Player.bmp, Town01Ext.bmp, Town01Int.bmp, and Wilderness.bmp from this book's Chapter13 folder to your new Graphics folder.

   All of these files, except Player.bmp, contain the tile sets for the game. The Player.bmp file contains the image used to represent the player character.

5. Compile and run the application. If everything works okay, you should see the screen shown in Figure 13.12.

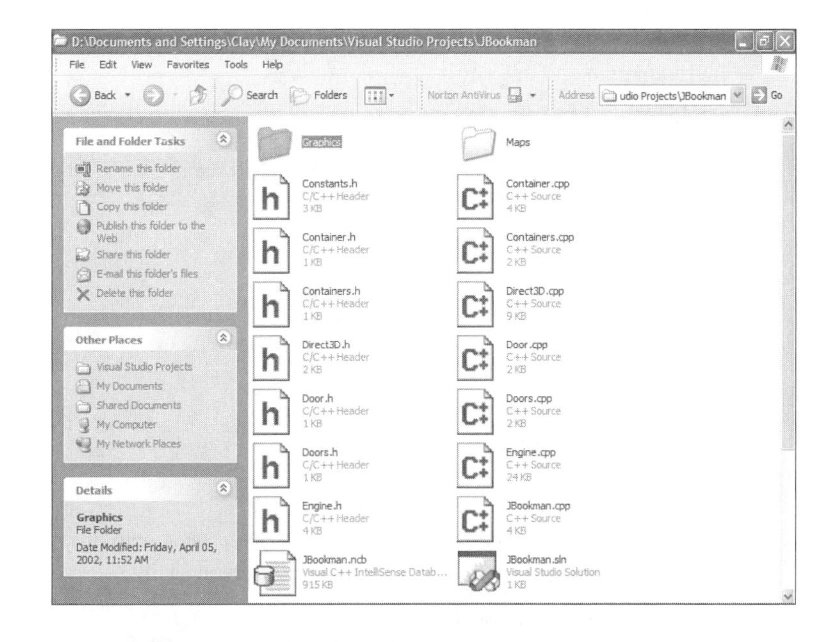

FIGURE 13.11
Creating the Graphics subdirectory.

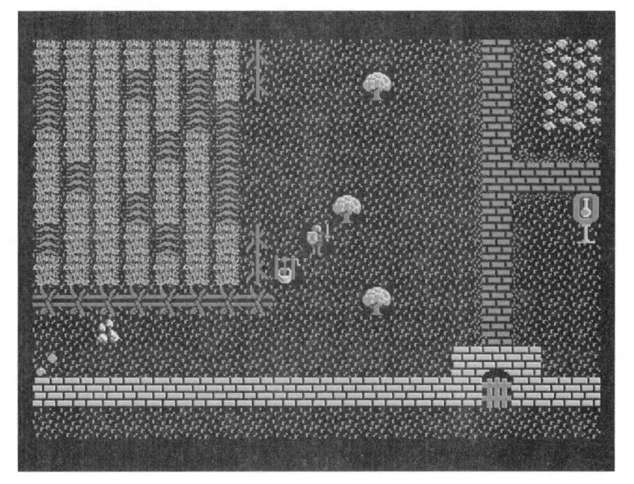

FIGURE 13.12
The current version of The Adventures of Jasper Bookman.

Examining the Project So Far

This version of the JBookman project displays the location map for the game's starting location. It does this very similarly to the sample program, TileApp, but with the added complication of viewing the game world through a viewport.

Within its message loop, the main application calls the `CEngine` object's `ProcessGame()` method again and again:

```
while(1)
{
    if (PeekMessage(&msg, NULL, 0, 0, PM_REMOVE))
    {
        if (msg.message == WM_QUIT)
            break;
        TranslateMessage(&msg);
        DispatchMessage(&msg);
    }
    else
    {
        // Use idle time here.
        g_Engine.ProcessGame();
    }
}
```

The `ProcessGame()` method in turn draws the game screen and the player, and then calls the device's `Present()` method to make the screen visible:

```
void CEngine::PaintBackBuffer()
{
    PaintBackground();
    PaintPlayer(m_Direct3D.GetBackBuffer());
    m_Direct3D.GetDevice()->Present(NULL, NULL, NULL, NULL);
}
```

Notice how this code calls methods of the `CDirect3D` object to get pointers to the back buffer and to the device.

The `PaintBackground()` method is where all the tricky stuff happens. First, the method must figure out which sectors are visible on the screen:

```
int LowVisibleCol;
int HiVisibleCol;
int LowVisibleRow;
int HiVisibleRow;
SetVisibleColsRows(LowVisibleCol, HiVisibleCol,
    LowVisibleRow, HiVisibleRow);
```

These visible sectors represent the viewport and are based on where the player character is located in the full location map. That is, a certain number of sectors are always visible around the player character, and, except for when the character moves close to the edge of full location map, the player character is always shown in the center of the viewport.

You'll look at these calculations in detail when we get to the `SetVisibleColsRows()` method discussion.

After getting the columns and rows for the location of the viewport, `PaintBackground()` uses nested `for` loops to cycle through all the tiles that need to be displayed:

```
int DstRow = 0;
for (int SrcRow = LowVisibleRow; SrcRow <= HiVisibleRow; ++SrcRow)
{
    int DstCol = 0;
    for (int SrcCol = LowVisibleCol; SrcCol <= HiVisibleCol; ++SrcCol)
    {
        int iSector = ColumnRow2Sector(SrcCol, SrcRow, MAPCOLUMNCOUNT);
        int TileNumber = m_Sectors[iSector];
        IDirect3DSurface8* backbuf = m_Direct3D.GetBackBuffer();
        PlaceTile(m_Direct3D.GetBackBuffer(),
            m_Direct3D.GetCurrentTileSurface(), TileNumber, DstCol, DstRow,
            COLUMNSINTILEFILE, MAPCOLUMNCOUNT, TILESIZE, XOFFSET, YOFFSET);
        ++DstCol;
    }
    DstRow = DstRow + 1;
}
```

This loop works very much like the one in the TileApp application you built earlier in this chapter. The difference is that the method must keep track of not only the source columns and rows (the area of the full map to draw into the viewport), but also the destination column and rows (where in the viewport to draw the tiles).

Things can get very confusing here because you have three different grids of tiles to consider:

- The tiles in the full location map, which is a grid 42 tiles across and 42 tiles down. The column numbers go from 0 to 41, as do the row numbers.
- The area of the full location map that must be copied to the viewport. This is the visible area surrounding the player character and is 19 tiles horizontally and 13 tiles vertically. The column and row numbers are based on the full map numbers and the player's location. For example, if the player character is standing in column 20 and row 50, the visible area of the location map goes from column 11 to column 29, and from row 44 to 56.
- The tiles in the viewport, which is a grid 19 tiles horizontally and 13 tiles vertically. The column numbers go from 0 to 18, and the row numbers go from 0 to 12.

Figure 13.13 illustrates the relationship between these different grids of tiles.

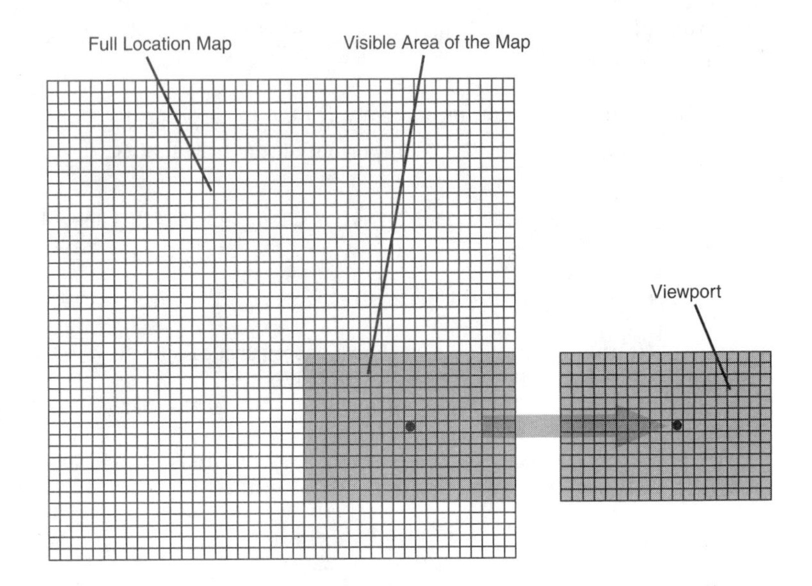

FIGURE 13.13
The three tile grids used to create the display.

The `SetVisibleColsRows()` Method

The `SetVisibleColsRows()` method figures out what part of the location map is visible around the player character. Here's what the returned values mean:

- `LowVisibleCol`—The first visible column in the viewport
- `HiVisibleCol`—The last visible column in the viewport
- `LowVisibleRow`—The first visible row in the viewport
- `HiVisibleRow`—The last visible row in the viewport

If this is a little confusing, take a look at Figure 13.14, which shows you how these values relate to the viewport and the full location map.

The tricky part of calculating the viewport is the fact that there are times when the player character won't appear exactly in the center of the screen. This occurs when the player moves close to one of the edges of the current location, so that the screen can no longer scroll with the character. When this happens, the program repaints the player in a new location, but does not change what's visible in the viewport.

For example, take another look at Figure 13.14 and imagine that the player moves two tiles to the right. You then have the situation shown in Figure 13.15.

Everything is fine in Figure 13.15. Even though the viewport is now right on the edge of the location map, the player is still in the center of the visible area. But what happens if the player moves two more tiles to the right? You then have a situation like Figure 13.16.

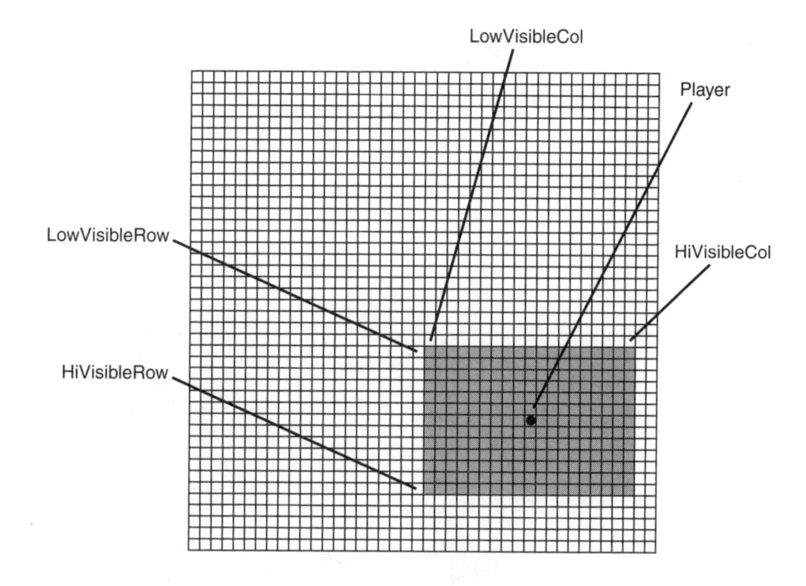

FIGURE 13.14
Calculating the viewport.

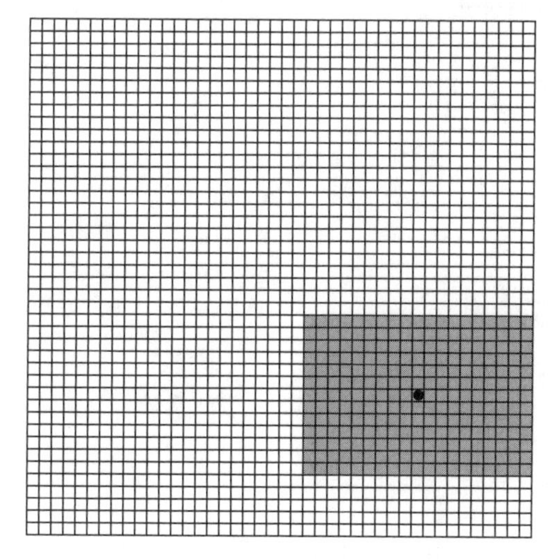

FIGURE 13.15
Moving toward the edge of the location map.

Now the viewport has moved too far and is out of bounds. This is no good. To avoid this problem, when the player is near the edge of the location map, the player's character moves on the screen, but the viewport stays put. The situation shown in Figure 13.16 then ends up looking like Figure 13.17.

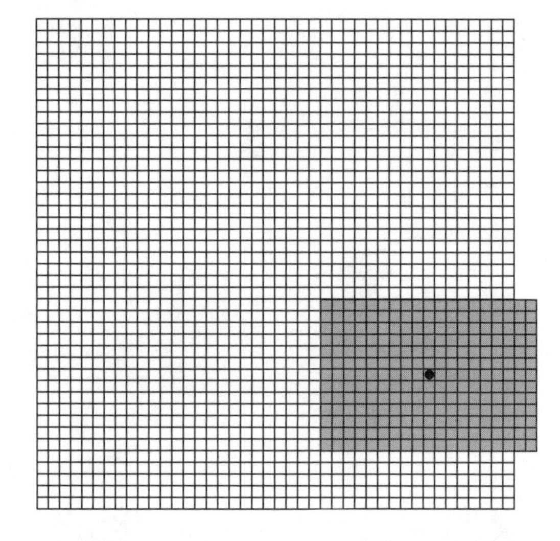

FIGURE 13.16
The viewport moving off the location map.

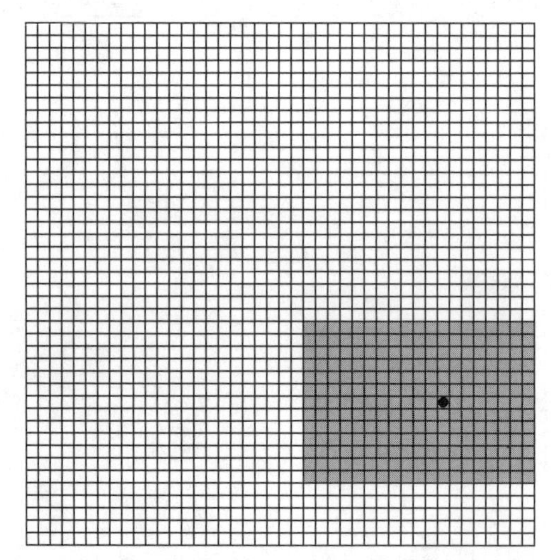

FIGURE 13.17
Moving the player figure instead of the viewport.

As long as the player keeps moving to the right, the viewport doesn't change. Finally, the player can go no farther, as shown in Figure 13.18.

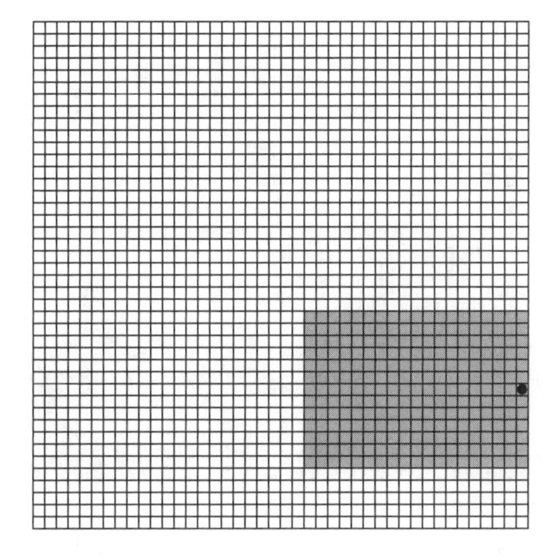

FIGURE 13.18

The player on the edge of the location map.

As a final example, look at Figure 13.19, which is the actual game screen representing the situation in Figure 13.15 and compare it with Figure 13.20, which is the game screen representing the situation shown in Figure 13.18.

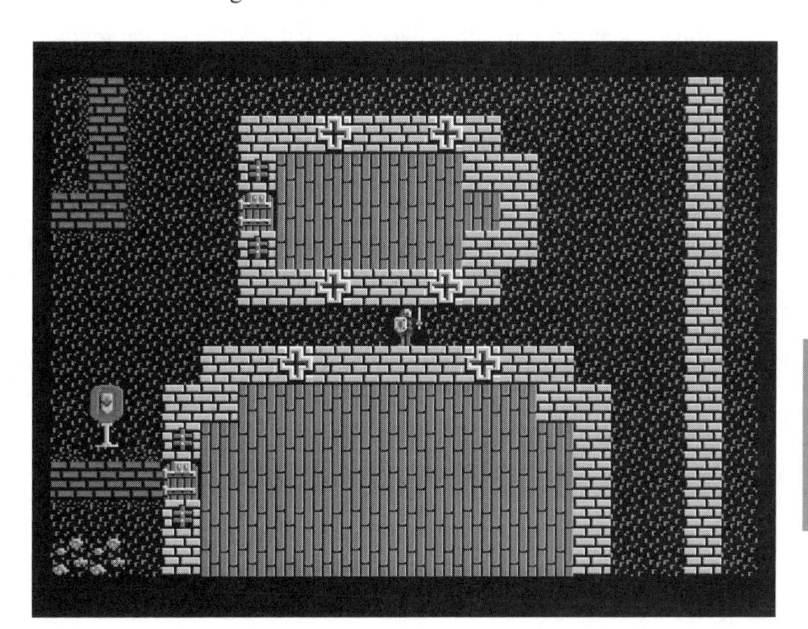

FIGURE 13.19

The player near the edge of the game screen.

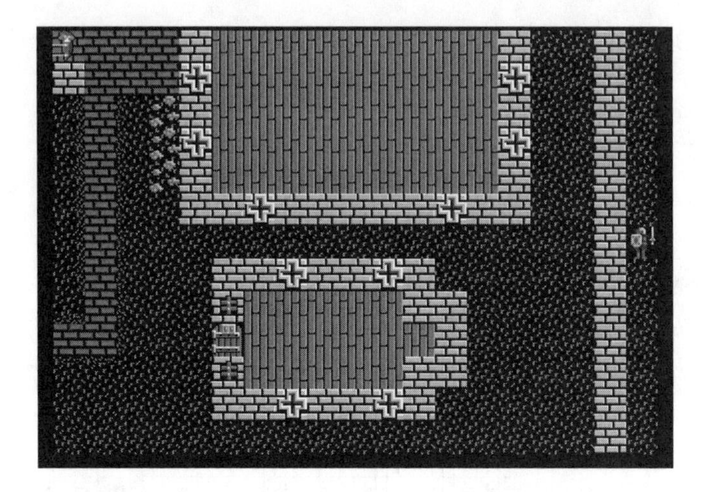

FIGURE 13.20
The player on the edge of the game screen.

Getting back to the `SetVisibleColsRows()` method, the method first gets the player's current column and row in the map:

```
int PlayerMapCol = Sector2Column(m_Player.GetSector(), MAPCOLUMNCOUNT);
int PlayerMapRow = Sector2Row(m_Player.GetSector(), MAPCOLUMNCOUNT);
```

If the player isn't near the edge of the game screen, figuring out the size of the viewport is easy:

```
LowVisibleCol = PlayerMapCol - NORMALVISIBLEPLAYERCOL;
HiVisibleCol = PlayerMapCol + NORMALVISIBLEPLAYERCOL;
LowVisibleRow = PlayerMapRow - NORMALVISIBLEPLAYERROW;
HiVisibleRow = PlayerMapRow + NORMALVISIBLEPLAYERROW;
```

The `NORMALVISIBLEPLAYERCOL` constant is the number of columns to the left and right of the player, and the `NORMALVISIBLEPLAYERROW` constant is the number of rows above and below the player.

When the player is near the edge of the game screen, however, the program must be sure not to move the viewport out of the map area. Here's how the `SetVisibleColsRows()` method handles this problem for columns:

```
if (PlayerMapCol < NORMALVISIBLEPLAYERCOL)
{
    LowVisibleCol = 0;
    HiVisibleCol = 18;
}
else if (PlayerMapCol > 32)
{
    LowVisibleCol = 23;
    HiVisibleCol = 41;
}
```

If you were to translate this code into English, it would say "If the player is too close to the left edge, then show columns 0 through 18, but if the player is too close to the right edge, then show columns 23 through 41." The program handles the rows similarly:

```
if (PlayerMapRow < NORMALVISIBLEPLAYERROW)
{
    LowVisibleRow = 0;
    HiVisibleRow = 12;
}
else if (PlayerMapRow > 34)
{
    LowVisibleRow = 29;
    HiVisibleRow = 41;
}
```

Displaying the Player Character

The last thing you need to examine is how the program displays the tile that represents the player character on the screen. This happens in the `PaintPlayer()` method of the `CEngine` object.

That method first calculates the player's location (the column and row) in the full location map:

```
int PlayerMapCol = Sector2Column(m_Player.GetSector(), MAPCOLUMNCOUNT);
int PlayerMapRow = Sector2Row(m_Player.GetSector(), MAPCOLUMNCOUNT);
```

The method also needs to calculate where the player character will be drawn in the viewport. In most cases, the player character will appear in the center of the viewport, represented by the `NORMALVISIBLEPLAYERCOL` and `NORMALVISIBLEPLAYERROW` constants. The method starts the player at this location:

```
int FinalVisiblePlayerCol = NORMALVISIBLEPLAYERCOL;
int FinalVisiblePlayerRow = NORMALVISIBLEPLAYERROW;
```

Now, the method needs to determine whether the player is too close to an edge of the full location map. As you know, in this case, the viewport doesn't move. Instead, the player gets drawn somewhere other than the center of the screen. Here's how the `PaintPlayer()` method handles the columns:

```
if (PlayerMapCol < NORMALVISIBLEPLAYERCOL)
{
    FinalVisiblePlayerCol = NORMALVISIBLEPLAYERCOL -
        (NORMALVISIBLEPLAYERCOL - PlayerMapCol);
}
else if (PlayerMapCol > 32)
{
    FinalVisiblePlayerCol =
        VISIBLECOLUMNCOUNT - ((MAPCOLUMNCOUNT-1)-PlayerMapCol)-1;
}
```

Translated to English, this source code says, "If the player is too close to the full map's left edge, set the player's destination column to the appropriate value near the left edge, or else if the player is too close to the full map's right edge, set the player's destination column to the appropriate value near the right edge.

The method handles the player's destination row in a similar way:

```
if (PlayerMapRow < NORMALVISIBLEPLAYERROW)
{
    FinalVisiblePlayerRow = NORMALVISIBLEPLAYERROW -
        (NORMALVISIBLEPLAYERROW - PlayerMapRow);
}
else if (PlayerMapRow > 34)
{
    FinalVisiblePlayerRow =
        VISIBLEROWCOUNT -((MAPROWCOUNT-1)-PlayerMapRow)-1;
}
```

With the player's location in the viewport figured out, the method sets the source rectangle for the player's tile image:

```
RECT SrcTileRect;
SrcTileRect.left = 0;
SrcTileRect.right = 32;
SrcTileRect.top = 0;
SrcTileRect.bottom = 32;
```

The method must also set the destination point in the back-buffer surface:

```
POINT DstPoint;
DstPoint.x = Column2X(FinalVisiblePlayerCol,
    TILESIZE, MAPCOLUMNCOUNT) + XOFFSET;
DstPoint.y = Row2Y(FinalVisiblePlayerRow, TILESIZE) + YOFFSET;
```

Finally, the method can draw the player character's image:

```
HRESULT hResult = m_Direct3D.GetDevice()->
    CopyRects(m_Direct3D.GetPlayerTile(), &SrcTileRect,1,
    pBackBuffer,&DstPoint);
```

Moving Through the Game World

You now have the game's world up on the screen. What could be cooler? How about moving the player through the game world? Accomplishing this task is easier than you might expect. Pretty much all you have to do is respond to the player's input by changing the player character's location in the full world map.

Because the program is constantly redrawing the screen, just changing the player character's position is all you have to do. Then, the next time the program draws the game screen, it'll automatically draw the appropriate viewport and position the player character's image where it belongs in the viewport.

Honest, it's that easy! So easy, in fact, that we're all done with the theory and are ready to add the code to *The Adventures of Jasper Bookman*.

Adding Code to the Game Engine

If you don't have it ready to go, load up the latest version of the JBookman project. Then, perform the following steps to enable the player to explore the game's first location, which is a comfy little place appropriately named First Town.

1. Load the Engine.h file, and add the following lines to the class's public methods, right after the line `int Sector2Row(int iSector, int numCols)` that's already there:

   ```
   void HandleUpArrow();
   void HandleDownArrow();
   void HandleLeftArrow();
   void HandleRightArrow();
   ```

   These are declarations for the new class methods that will handle keyboard input from the player.

2. Add the following lines to the class's private methods, right after the line `void PaintPlayer(IDirect3DSurface8* pBackBuffer)` that's already there. If you don't want to type, you can copy the lines from the Code19.txt file in the Chapter13 directory of this book's CD-ROM.

   ```
   void MovePlayerUp();
   void MovePlayerDown();
   void MovePlayerLeft();
   void MovePlayerRight();
   BOOL CharacterCanMove(int direction, int curSector);
   BOOL PlayerBlocked(int g_iPlayerSector, int direction);
   ```

   These are declarations for the class methods that move the player character throughout the game world.

3. Load the Engine.cpp file, and add the following method implementations. If you don't want to type, you can copy the lines from the Code20.txt file in the Chapter13 directory of this book's CD-ROM.

   ```
   ///////////////////////////////////////////////////////
   // HandleUpArrow()
   ///////////////////////////////////////////////////////
   void CEngine::HandleUpArrow()
   {
       MovePlayerUp();
   }
   ```

13

```
///////////////////////////////////////////////////////
// HandleDownArrow()
///////////////////////////////////////////////////////
void CEngine::HandleDownArrow()
{
    MovePlayerDown();
}
///////////////////////////////////////////////////////
// HandleLeftArrow()
///////////////////////////////////////////////////////
void CEngine::HandleLeftArrow()
{
    MovePlayerLeft();
}
///////////////////////////////////////////////////////
// HandleRightArrow()
///////////////////////////////////////////////////////
void CEngine::HandleRightArrow()
{
    MovePlayerRight();
}
///////////////////////////////////////////////////////
// MovePlayerUp()
///////////////////////////////////////////////////////
void CEngine::MovePlayerUp()
{
    if (CharacterCanMove(NORTH, m_Player.GetSector()))
        m_Player.SetSector(m_Player.GetSector() - MAPCOLUMNCOUNT);
}
///////////////////////////////////////////////////////
// MovePlayerDown()
///////////////////////////////////////////////////////
void CEngine::MovePlayerDown()
{
    if (CharacterCanMove(SOUTH, m_Player.GetSector()))
        m_Player.SetSector(m_Player.GetSector() + MAPCOLUMNCOUNT);
}
///////////////////////////////////////////////////////
// MovePlayerLeft()
///////////////////////////////////////////////////////
void CEngine::MovePlayerLeft()
{
    if (CharacterCanMove(WEST, m_Player.GetSector()))
        m_Player.SetSector(m_Player.GetSector() - 1);
}
///////////////////////////////////////////////////////
// MovePlayerRight()
///////////////////////////////////////////////////////
void CEngine::MovePlayerRight()
{
    if (CharacterCanMove(EAST, m_Player.GetSector()))
```

```
        m_Player.SetSector(m_Player.GetSector() + 1);
}
//////////////////////////////////////////////////////
// CharacterCanMove()
//////////////////////////////////////////////////////
BOOL CEngine::CharacterCanMove(int direction, int curSector)
{
    BOOL move = TRUE;
    if (direction == NORTH)
    {
        if (Sector2Row(curSector, MAPCOLUMNCOUNT) < 1) move = FALSE;
        if (PlayerBlocked(curSector, direction)) move = FALSE;
    }
    else if (direction == SOUTH)
    {
        if (Sector2Row(curSector, MAPCOLUMNCOUNT) > 40) move = FALSE;
        if (PlayerBlocked(curSector, direction)) move = FALSE;
    }
    else if (direction == EAST)
    {
        if (Sector2Column(curSector, MAPCOLUMNCOUNT) > 40) move = FALSE;
        if (PlayerBlocked(curSector, direction)) move = FALSE;
    }
    else if (direction == WEST)
    {
        if (Sector2Column(curSector, MAPCOLUMNCOUNT) < 1) move = FALSE;
        if (PlayerBlocked(curSector, direction)) move = FALSE;
    }
    return move;
}
//////////////////////////////////////////////////////
// PlayerBlocked()
//////////////////////////////////////////////////////
BOOL CEngine::PlayerBlocked(int iPlayerSector, int direction)
{
    BOOL blocked = FALSE;
    int iSector = iPlayerSector;
    if (direction == NORTH)
        iSector = iSector - MAPCOLUMNCOUNT;
    else if (direction == SOUTH)
        iSector = iSector + MAPCOLUMNCOUNT;
    else if (direction == EAST)
        iSector = iSector + 1;
    else if (direction == WEST)
        iSector = iSector - 1;
    int item = m_Sectors[iSector];
    switch (m_byMapType)
    {
        case TOWNEXTERIOR:
            if (item == BRICKWALL_EXT || item == VERTFENCE_EXT
                  || item == HORZFENCE_EXT || item == ANGLEFENCE_EXT
```

```
                        || item == TREE_EXT || item == WINDOW1_EXT
                        || item == WINDOW2_EXT || item == WELL_EXT
                        || item == FOUNTAIN_EXT || item == FOUNTAIN_EXT + 1
                        || item == STONEWALL_EXT
                        || (item >= WATER01_EXT && item <= WATER02_EXT))
                      blocked = TRUE;
                      break;
        }
        return blocked;
    }
```

4. Replace the `HandleKeys()` method with the one that follows. If you don't want to type, you can copy the lines from the Code21.txt file in the Chapter13 directory of this book's CD-ROM.

```
void CEngine::HandleKeys(WPARAM wParam)
{
    switch(wParam)
    {
    case VK_UP:
        HandleUpArrow();
        break;
    case VK_DOWN:
        HandleDownArrow();
        break;
    case VK_LEFT:
        HandleLeftArrow();
        break;
    case VK_RIGHT:
        HandleRightArrow();
        break;
    case VK_ESCAPE:
        PostQuitMessage(WM_QUIT);
        break;
    }
}
```

The `HandleKeys()` method now responds not only to the escape key, but also the four arrow keys.

5. Load the Constants.h file, and add the following lines, right after the line `const COLUMNSINTILEFILE = 8` that's already there. If you don't want to type, you can copy the lines from the Code22.txt file in the Chapter13 directory of this book's CD-ROM.

```
// Impassable Objects in the town exterior.
const BRICKWALL_EXT = 6;
const VERTFENCE_EXT = 16;
const HORZFENCE_EXT = 17;
const ANGLEFENCE_EXT = 18;
```

```
const TREE_EXT = 3;
const FOUNTAIN_EXT = 50;
const WELL_EXT = 29;
const STONEWALL_EXT = 30;
const WINDOW1_EXT = 8;
const WINDOW2_EXT = 9;
const WATER01_EXT = 32;
const WATER02_EXT = 49;
// Movement directions.
const NORTH = 0;
const SOUTH = 1;
const EAST = 2;
const WEST = 3;
// Map types.
enum g_byMapTypeEnum
{
    TOWNEXTERIOR,
    TOWNINTERIOR,
    DUNGEON,
    WILDERNESS
};
```

These constants represent the tile values for the various types of tiles that the program must deal with specifically. The constants also define values for directions and for the different types of tile maps.

Compile and run the application. If everything works okay, you should see the same screen you saw when you ran the previous version of the program. Now, however, you can move the player character around the screen and explore the starting town. Figure 13.21, for example, shows the player character standing in front of the town's inn.

FIGURE 13.21

Exploring the First Town map.

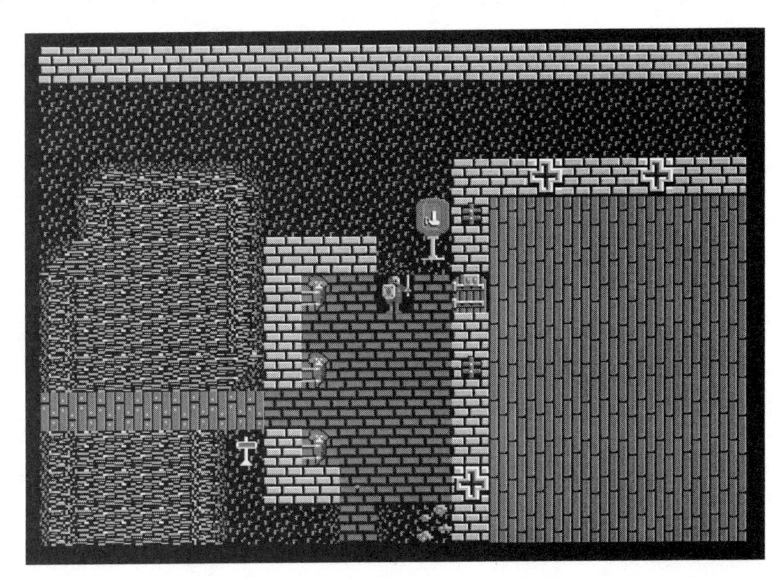

Understanding the Source Code

I know I said that moving the player character on the screen is as simple as giving the character a new position. However, I have to admit that there is one minor complication and that is ensuring that the player can move to the requested location. For example, what if the player character's requested location contains a wall? In most cases, people can't move into or through walls, and the same is true in *The Adventures of Jasper Bookman*.

So before doing anything with the player character's location, the program must first verify that the character can move there. To see how this works, look at the `MovePlayerUp()` method, which gets called whenever the player presses the up arrow on her keyboard:

```
void CEngine::MovePlayerUp()
{
    if (CharacterCanMove(NORTH, m_Player.GetSector()))
        m_Player.SetSector(m_Player.GetSector() - MAPCOLUMNCOUNT);
}
```

Here, the `CharacterCanMove()` method checks whether the player character can move upward. If he can, a call to the `CPlayer` object's `SetSector()` method repositions the player character one row up, which, mathematically, means subtracting the number of columns in the map (which is also the number of sectors in a single row) from the player character's current location.

The `MovePlayerDown()` method works similarly, except it adds the number of sectors in a row to the player's current position:

```
void CEngine::MovePlayerDown()
{
    if (CharacterCanMove(SOUTH, m_Player.GetSector()))
        m_Player.SetSector(m_Player.GetSector() + MAPCOLUMNCOUNT);
}
```

Moving the player character left or right is even easier. The program just subtracts (to go left) or adds (to go right) 1 to the player's current location:

```
void CEngine::MovePlayerLeft()
{
    if (CharacterCanMove(WEST, m_Player.GetSector()))
        m_Player.SetSector(m_Player.GetSector() - 1);
}

void CEngine::MovePlayerRight()
{
    if (CharacterCanMove(EAST, m_Player.GetSector()))
        m_Player.SetSector(m_Player.GetSector() + 1);
}
```

Now it's time to take a look at the CharacterCanMove() method, which starts off by setting a flag to TRUE:

```
BOOL move = TRUE;
```

If this flag remains TRUE when program execution reaches the end of the method, the player character can move in the requested direction. But, first, there's a lot of checking to do. Two things prevent the player character from moving. The first is if the player is already at the edge of the map, and the second is if the player is trying to move into an impassable object, such as a wall or a locked door.

Suppose the player is trying to move up (north), here's how CharacterCanMove() works:

```
if (direction == NORTH)
{
    if (Sector2Row(curSector, MAPCOLUMNCOUNT) < 1) move = FALSE;
    if (PlayerBlocked(curSector, direction)) move = FALSE;
}
```

Here, the first if statement checks whether the player's new location is off the north edge of the map. If it is, no move allowed! The second if statement checks whether the sector to which the player wants to move is blocked by an impassable object.

The method handles the other directions similarly:

```
else if (direction == SOUTH)
{
    if (Sector2Row(curSector, MAPCOLUMNCOUNT) > 40) move = FALSE;
    if (PlayerBlocked(curSector, direction)) move = FALSE;
}
else if (direction == EAST)
{
    if (Sector2Column(curSector, MAPCOLUMNCOUNT) > 40) move = FALSE;
    if (PlayerBlocked(curSector, direction)) move = FALSE;
}
else if (direction == WEST)
{
    if (Sector2Column(curSector, MAPCOLUMNCOUNT) < 1) move = FALSE;
    if (PlayerBlocked(curSector, direction)) move = FALSE;
}
```


The last piece of the puzzle is the PlayerBlocked() method, which looks hairy, but is actually pretty simple. First, the method sets a flag and then calculates the sector to which the player wants to move:

```
BOOL blocked = FALSE;
int iSector = iPlayerSector;
if (direction == NORTH)
    iSector = iSector - MAPCOLUMNCOUNT;
else if (direction == SOUTH)
```

```
    iSector = iSector + MAPCOLUMNCOUNT;
else if (direction == EAST)
    iSector = iSector + 1;
else if (direction == WEST)
    iSector = iSector - 1;
```

The method can then use the target sector as an index into the map array and so get the ID of the object in that sector:

```
int item = m_Sectors[iSector];
```

Because there are four different map types (town exterior, town interior, dungeon, and wilderness), the method uses a `switch` statement to jump to the section of the code appropriate for the current location:

```
switch (m_byMapType)
{
    .
    .
    .
}
```

Within the `switch` statement, the program merely compares the ID of the target sector with a list of IDs of impassable objects. For example, here's the `case` clause for the town exterior:

```
case TOWNEXTERIOR:
    if (item == BRICKWALL_EXT || item == VERTFENCE_EXT
          || item == HORZFENCE_EXT || item == ANGLEFENCE_EXT
          || item == TREE_EXT || item == WINDOW1_EXT
          || item == WINDOW2_EXT || item == WELL_EXT
          || item == FOUNTAIN_EXT || item == FOUNTAIN_EXT + 1
          || item == STONEWALL_EXT
          || (item >= WATER01_EXT && item <= WATER02_EXT))
        blocked = TRUE;
        break;
```

The constants make it easy to see which items are impassable. (The `EXT` means that the item is in the town exterior tiles.) See the constants that are compared directly, as well as compared by adding 1? Those are animated objects. For example, the water fountain is an impassable, animated object:

```
item == FOUNTAIN_EXT || item == FOUNTAIN_EXT + 1
```

As you'll see in the next chapter on animation, the animated objects have two tiles in the tile bitmap, one next to the other, which is why the program not only checks for the impassable object `FOUNTAIN_EXT`, but also `FOUNTAIN_EXT + 1`.

And that's the end of that story!

New Members of the `CEngine` Class

So here you are again, at the point in the chapter where you get to review the members you've added to the game-engine class. If you're going to use the engine to expand *The Adventures of Jasper Bookman* or to write your own game from scratch, you especially need to know how to use the public methods of the class. Table 13.1 describes the new members you added to the `CEngine` class.

TABLE 13.1 New `CEngine` Members

Member	*Type*	*Description*
Column2X()	Public method	Returns the pixel X coordinate for a specified sector in a grid
ColumnRow2Sector()	Public method	Returns the sector number for a specified column and row in a grid
HandleDownArrow()	Public method	Handles the down arrow key
HandleLeftArrow()	Public method	Handles the left arrow key
HandleRightArrow()	Public method	Handles the right arrow key
HandleUpArrow()	Public method	Handles the up arrow key
PaintBackBuffer()	Public method	Calls the helper functions that render the current scene to the back buffer
PlaceTile()	Public method	Draws a single tile onto the back buffer
Row2Y()	Public method	Returns the row in a grid given the pixel Y coordinate
Sector2Column()	Public method	Returns the column in a grid given the sector number
Sector2Row()	Public method	Returns the row in a grid given the sector number
TileNumber2SourceX()	Public method	Returns the pixel X coordinate of a given tile in the tile's tile file
TileNumber2SourceY()	Public method	Returns the pixel Y coordinate of a given tile in the tile's tile file
CharacterCanMove()	Private method	Checks whether the player character can move to the requested sector
MovePlayerDown()	Private method	Moves the player character's location down one row in the map grid
MovePlayerLeft()	Private method	Moves the player character's location left one sector in the map grid

TABLE 13.1 Continued

Member	*Type*	*Description*
MovePlayerRight()	Private method	Moves the player character's location right one sector in the map grid
MovePlayerUp()	Private method	Moves the player character's location up one row in the map grid
PaintBackground()	Private method	Draws the tiles that make up the current scene in the viewport
PaintPlayer()	Private method	Draws the player character's image in the viewport
PlayerBlocked()	Private method	Determines whether the player's requested target location is blocked by an impassable object
SetVisibleColsRows()	Private method	Calculates the columns and rows of the map grid that need to be drawn in the viewport

Summary

Your RPG game is really starting to come together now. Not only can you display the game world, but you can also manipulate your on-screen player character with your keyboard and so explore the first town in the game. In the next chapter, you add animation to the project, which goes a long way toward making the game world a little more realistic.

Q&A

Q. What if I have an object I want to add to my game world, but the object's image won't fit into a single tile?

A. There's nothing to say that you can't use multiple tiles to represent a single object. In fact, some of the objects you'll see when you get to the JBookman project's town interior tiles—objects like tables, for example—use several tiles to depict the complete image.

Q. What if I want the player to be able to move through something like a wall?

A. Currently the JBookman project's game engine can't handle this eventuality, but it will be able to before you get to the end of the book. Specifically, when you learn to create and respond to game events in Chapters 15, 16, and 17, you'll see how to hook your own special goodies into the engine.

Q. It's really a pain in the posterior to plug all the tile IDs into a map array in the source code. Isn't there a better way to get those values into the program?

A. Sure. In fact, if you think about it you already have a better way. Remember how the JBookman project loads map data from a disk file? You don't have to write out the array values in the program's source code at all. In fact, at the end of this book, you get a game editor that creates these files for you. All you have to do is point and click to place the tiles where you want them, and the editor does the rest, including placing people and objects like chests and barrels.

Workshop

The workshop includes quiz questions to help gauge your grasp of the material. Even if you feel that you totally understand the concepts presented here, you should work through the quiz anyway. The last section is an exercise or two that you might work through to help reinforce your learning.

1. What is meant by the term *tiling*?
2. How do you represent the grid of tiles in your program's source code?
3. Why is it a good idea to organize your game tiles into a single bitmap rather than load each tile into its own surface?
4. Generally, how does your program display the tiles specified in the tile array?
5. Explain the relationship between the full game map for a location and the viewport.
6. When the player character moves, what happens to the viewport?
7. When does the player character's image not appear in the center of the display, and what happens to the viewport in these situations?
8. When might a player character not be allowed to move at all?

Exercises

1. Make a copy of the TileApp project and modify it so that it displays a map 10 sectors wide and 10 sectors high. When you run the program, you should see the screen shown in Figure 13.22.
2. Further modify your copy of the TileApp project so that it creates the display shown in Figure 13.23. Hint: You need to add two tiles to the tile file. You can change the color of two existing tiles to create the new ones.

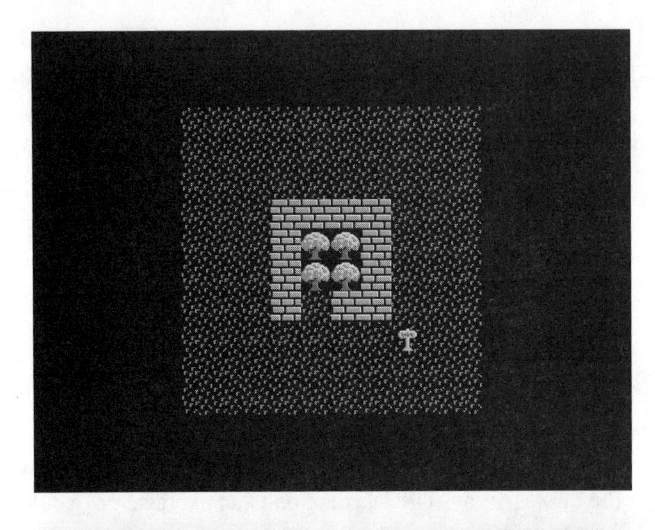

FIGURE 13.22
The TileApp project displaying a 10×10 map.

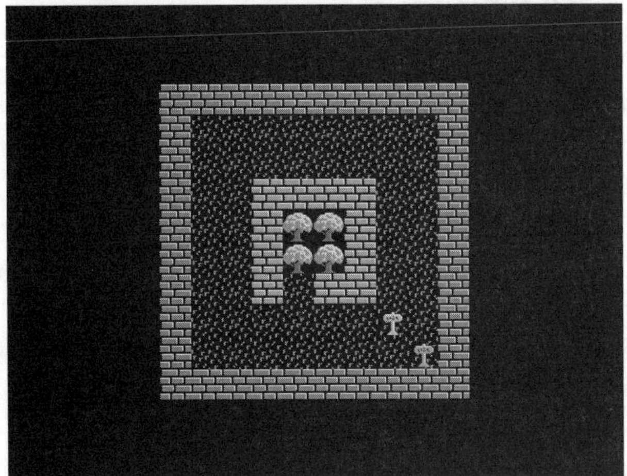

FIGURE 13.23
The TileApp project after the second modification.

Answers for Day 13

Quiz

1. What is meant by the term *tiling*?

   Tiling is when you draw a game world using small, rectangular images organized into a grid.

2. How do you represent the grid of tiles in your program's source code?

   You assign each tile an ID based on its position in the tile file, and then you plug the IDs into an array that represents the tile grid.

3. Why is it a good idea to organize your game tiles into a single bitmap rather than load each tile into its own surface?

   First, this technique cuts down on a lot of source code where you have to create and load a surface for each tile. Second, using this technique is a much better use of memory. Finally, having the tiles organized this way makes it easy to find the tile you need based on the tile's ID.

4. Generally, how does your program display the tiles specified in the tile array?

   The program loops through the array, using the values contained in the array to locate and display each tile from the tile bitmap. The program can use the array index to calculate the column and row in the viewport at which to draw each tile.

5. Explain the relationship between the full game map for a location and the viewport.

   The full game map for a location represents an area that is too large to display in the game. Instead, the viewport shows the area of the full game map that's currently visible to the player.

6. When the player character moves, what happens to the viewport?

   The viewport moves with the player character, so that the player character's image usually appears in the center of the display.

7. When does the player character's image not appear in the center of the display, and what happens to the viewport in these situations?

   When the player character moves close to the edge of the full location map, the viewport cannot move with him, because it would then move off the edge of the game world. In this case, the viewport stays put, and instead the player character moves across the viewport, away from the center of the display.

8. When might a player character not be allowed to move at all?

   When the player character is on the very edge of the game map and is trying to move off the map, or when the player character is trying to move through an impassable object such as a wall or a locked door.

Exercises

1. Make a copy of the TileApp project and modify it so that it displays a map 10 sectors wide and 10 sectors high. When you run the program, you should see the screen shown in Figure 13.22.

   Amazingly, thanks to the way the program uses constants rather than hard-coded values, you only need to make two changes to the program's source code. First, change the lines

```
const MAPCOLUMNCOUNT = 6;
const MAPROWCOUNT = 6;
const XOFFSET = 220;
const YOFFSET = 120;
```

to

```
const MAPCOLUMNCOUNT = 10;
const MAPROWCOUNT = 10;
const XOFFSET = 160;
const YOFFSET = 80;
```

Next, change the lines

```
char g_Sectors[] =
    {0,0,0,0,0,0,
     0,2,2,2,2,0,
     0,2,1,1,2,0,
     0,2,1,1,2,0,
     0,2,0,2,2,0,
     0,0,0,0,0,3};
```

to

```
char g_Sectors[] =
    {0,0,0,0,0,0,0,0,0,0,
     0,0,0,0,0,0,0,0,0,0,
     0,0,0,0,0,0,0,0,0,0,
     0,0,0,2,2,2,2,0,0,0,
     0,0,0,2,1,1,2,0,0,0,
     0,0,0,2,1,1,2,0,0,0,
     0,0,0,2,0,2,2,0,0,0,
     0,0,0,0,0,0,0,3,0,0,
     0,0,0,0,0,0,0,0,0,0,
     0,0,0,0,0,0,0,0,0,0};
```

2. Further modify your copy of the TileApp project so that it creates the display shown in Figure 13.23. Hint: You need to add two tiles to the tile file. You can change the color of two existing tiles to create the new ones.

   The first step is to create a tile file that looks like Figure 13.24.

FIGURE 13.24
The new tile file.

Then, make these changes to the program's source code. First, change the line

```
const COLUMNSINTILEFILE = 2;
```

to

```
const COLUMNSINTILEFILE = 3;
```

Next, change the lines

```
char g_Sectors[] =
    {0,0,0,0,0,0,0,0,0,0,
     0,0,0,0,0,0,0,0,0,0,
     0,0,0,0,0,0,0,0,0,0,
     0,0,0,2,2,2,2,0,0,0,
     0,0,0,2,1,1,2,0,0,0,
     0,0,0,2,1,1,2,0,0,0,
     0,0,0,2,0,2,2,0,0,0,
     0,0,0,0,0,0,0,3,0,0,
     0,0,0,0,0,0,0,0,0,0,
     0,0,0,0,0,0,0,0,0,0};
```

to

```
char g_Sectors[] =
    {2,2,2,2,2,2,2,2,2,2,
     2,0,0,0,0,0,0,0,0,2,
     2,0,0,0,0,0,0,0,0,2,
     2,0,0,3,3,3,3,0,0,2,
     2,0,0,3,1,1,3,0,0,2,
     2,0,0,3,1,1,3,0,0,2,
     2,0,0,3,0,3,3,0,0,2,
     2,0,0,0,0,0,0,4,0,2,
     2,0,0,0,0,0,0,0,5,2,
     2,2,2,2,2,2,2,2,2,2};
```

Finally, change the lines

```
g_hResult = g_pDirect3DDevice->CreateImageSurface(64, 64,
    D3DFMT_X8R8G8B8, &g_pBitmapSurface);
```

to

```
g_hResult = g_pDirect3DDevice->CreateImageSurface(96, 64,
    D3DFMT_X8R8G8B8, &g_pBitmapSurface);
```

WEEK 2

DAY 14

Adding Animation to the Game

At this point, the game world in *The Adventures of Jasper Bookman* is a pretty unlively place. All the graphics are static, which means that everything just sits there on the screen with no movement. And that's just no fun at all! As you know, Direct3D provides all the tools you need to create everything from the simplest animation to the spectacular worlds you see in today's computer games. It would take an entire book (and then some!) to cover the animation techniques used by today's commercial games. But here in Day 14, you'll get a look at how to add simple animation sequences to the game. Specifically, you learn how to:

- Add animated tiles to a tile file
- Start and stop a Windows timer
- Respond to timer events
- Update animated tiles in the map array
- Create three speeds of animation with one timer

Organizing Animated Tiles

In Day 9, "Programming Direct3D Animation," you learned to use Direct3D to perform animation in a program. In that chapter's sample program, you created an eight-frame animation sequence, but for *The Adventures of Jasper Bookman*, you won't be doing anything that fancy. Instead, you'll be using two-frame animation sequences, with a choice of three different speeds.

Performing a two-frame animation sequence with your tiles means having two versions of each tile you want to animate. Luckily, the tile files you've been using so far are already set up for animation.

For example, Figure 14.1 shows the tile set for town exteriors. The first four rows hold single, non-animated tiles. However, if you look closely at the last four rows, you'll see that the tiles there come in pairs. These are the animated tiles.

FIGURE 14.1
Organizing animated tiles in the tile file.

During animation, the program switches between each tile in an animated pair, which gives the illusion of movement on the screen.

Timing the Animation

As you learned when you studied animation in Day 9, any animation sequence requires a timer to control when and how fast the program switches between the animation frames. In the case of *The Adventures of Jasper Bookman*, the program needs a timer that can trigger an animation event every tenth of a second. It turns out that Windows has a perfect timer mechanism for this purpose.

The Windows API enables you to create a timer that sends `WM_TIMER` messages to your program at a specified interval. Creating and using the timer is actually pretty easy. The entire process goes like this:

1. Call the Windows API function `SetTimer()` to start the timer.
2. Respond to `WM_TIMER` events in the application's message loop.
3. Call the Windows API function `KillTimer()` to destroy the timer when it's no longer needed.

> **Note**
>
> A Windows timer is a low-resolution solution to timing problems. By low resolution, I mean that a Windows timer can't handle timings any faster than about one-tenth of a second. As it turns out, this works just fine for games like *The Adventures of Jasper Bookman*, but other types of game programs may require higher resolution timers.

Setting the Timer

To start a Windows timer, you call the `SetTimer()` Windows API function. Windows declares the function like this:

```
UINT_PTR SetTimer(
  HWND hWnd,
  UINT_PTR nIDEvent,
  UINT uElapse,
  TIMERPROC lpTimerFunc
);
```

The function's four arguments are used as follows:

- `hWnd`—The handle for the window that will own the timer.
- `nIDEvent`—The timer's ID. Usually, you'll use 1 for the first timer, 2 for the second, and so on.
- `uElapse`—The number of milliseconds between timer events (there are 1,000 milliseconds in a second).
- `lpTimerFunc`—A pointer to the function that should receive the timer events. Normally, you supply `NULL` for this argument, which indicates that the timer events should be sent to the application's Windows procedure.

So, if you want to receive timer events every two seconds, you'd write something like this:

```
SetTimer(g_hWnd, 1, 2000, NULL);
```

Responding to the Timer

After the call to `SetTimer()`, timer events start arriving at your application's message loop. To capture and respond to those events, you must handle the `WM_TIMER` event. This is no different than handling any other kind of event. All you have to do is add a `case` clause for `WM_TIMER` to your event loop. Here's an example of a Windows procedure that catches `WM_TIMER` messages:

```
LRESULT WINAPI WndProc(HWND hWnd, UINT msg, WPARAM wParam, LPARAM lParam)
{
    switch(msg)
    {
    case WM_CREATE:
        return 0;

    case WM_DESTROY:
        PostQuitMessage(0);
        return 0;

    case WM_PAINT:
        ValidateRect(g_hWnd, NULL);
        return 0;

    case WM_TIMER:
        // Handle timer events here.
        return 0;
    }
    return DefWindowProc(hWnd, msg, wParam, lParam);
}
```

Destroying the Timer

When your application is finished with the timer, the timer must be destroyed. You do this by calling the `KillTimer()` Windows API function, which Windows declares like this:

```
BOOL KillTimer(
  HWND hWnd,
  UINT_PTR uIDEvent
);
```

The function's two arguments are used as follows:

- `hWnd`—The handle for the window that owns the timer
- `nIDEvent`—The timer's ID

So, the actual call in your program might look like this:

```
KillTimer(g_hWnd, 1);
```

Using Windows Timers for Real

To see a Windows timer in action, build the following sample application:

1. Start a new empty Win32 project named TimerApp. (Don't forget to set the Additional Options to Empty Project.)
2. Add to the project a new C++ File (.cpp) named TimerApp.cpp.
3. Copy the contents of the BasicWindowsApp.cpp file (from Day 3, "Writing a Windows Program") into the new TimerApp code window.
4. Change the name in the comment at the top of the file to TimerApp.
5. In the `RegisterWindowClass()` function change `wc.lpszClassName = "WinApp"` to `wc.lpszClassName = "TimerApp"`.
6. In the `CreateAppWindow()` function, change "WinApp" to "TimerApp", and then change "Basic Windows Application" to "Timer Application".
7. In the `WinMain()` function, add the following line right after the line `UpdateWindow(g_hWnd)` that's already there:

   ```
   SetTimer(g_hWnd, 1, 5000, NULL);
   ```
8. Also in the `WinMain()` function, add the following line right after the line `StartMessageLoop()` that's already there:

   ```
   KillTimer(g_hWnd, 1);
   ```
9. Finally, in the `WndProc()` function, add the following `case` clause to the `switch` statement:

   ```
   case WM_TIMER:
       MessageBox(0, "Timer event arrived.", "Timer", MB_OK);
       return 0;
   ```

Now, go ahead and compile and run the application. When you do, the main window appears. Five seconds later, a message box appears (see Figure 14.2), telling you that a timer event has occurred. The message boxes continue to appear every five seconds until you close the application.

Notice how the call to `MessageBox()` in TimerApp uses 0 as the first argument, which is the handle of the window that owns the message box. Using 0 specifies the desktop window as the owner. By doing this, you can close the TimerApp application without having to close all message boxes that have appeared in response to the timer events. If you were to use the application's window handle, every message box would have to be closed before you could close the application's window. Try it and see!

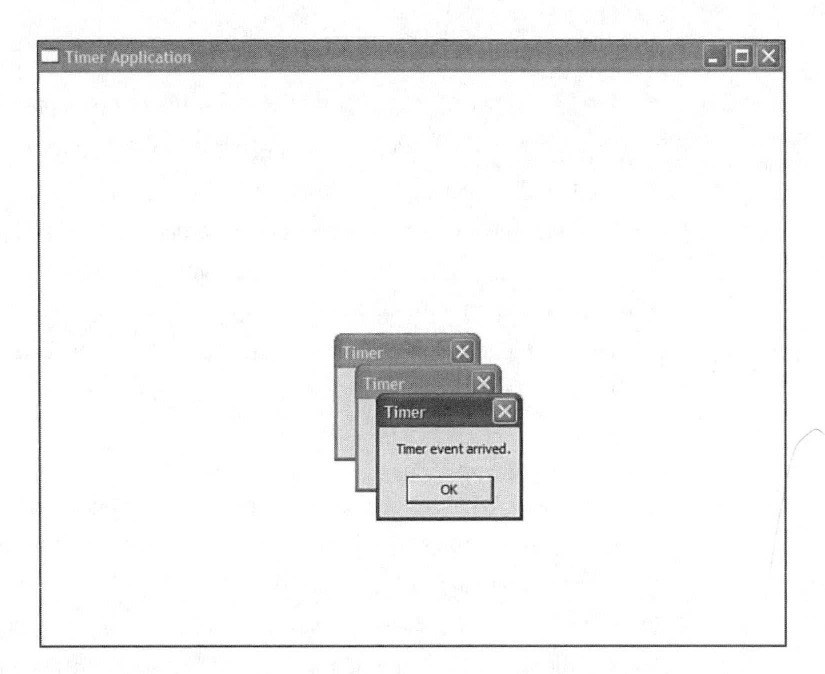

FIGURE 14.2
The TimerApp application receiving timer events.

Getting Tiled Animation Up and Running

You know that in order to change a tile that appears in the game screen, you plug a new value into the program's map array. Once you do that, the game engine automatically displays the requested tile, because the engine is continually redisplaying the game screen, drawing whatever tiles have their IDs in the map array. For example, if you wanted to change the upper-left corner of the display to the grass tile, you'd simply do this:

```
m_Sectors[0] = 0;
```

Here, the 0 array index specifies the first sector in the map, and the 0 tile ID specifies the grass tile (using the tiles you've been using with the JBookman project).

To perform the tile animation, then, you must update the map array every time a timer event occurs—or at least after a specific number of timer events have occurred, depending upon how you're using the timer.

Trying Animation for Yourself

We could, at this point, just jump in and add the animation code to the JBookman project, but there are several complications that would make doing that kind of confusing.

It's best if you first see tile animation in action, without a lot of other code and complications getting in the way. To that end, you should build the following sample application, which puts everything we've discussed so far to the test.

Creating the Basic `TileAnimationApp` Project

The first step is to create the main application to which you'll add the animation features. This is just a plain ol' Windows application just like the others you've used to start a project. To get this application going, follow these steps:

1. Start a new empty Win32 project named TileAnimationApp. (Don't forget to set the Additional Options to Empty Project.)
2. Add to the project a new C++ file (.cpp) named TileAnimationApp.cpp.
3. Copy the contents of the TileApp.cpp file (from Day 13) into the new TileAnimationApp code window.
4. Change the name in the comment at the top of the file to TileAnimationApp.
5. In the `RegisterWindowClass()` function change `wc.lpszClassName = "TileApp"` to `wc.lpszClassName = "TileAnimationApp"`.
6. In the `CreateAppWindow()` function change "TileApp" to "TileAnimationApp" and change "Tile Application" to "Tile Animation Application".

Adding the DirectX References

As you've learned, in order to use Direct3D, you have to tell the compiler where to find the required header and library files. To complete this task, follow these steps:

1. Right-click the project's name in the Solution Explorer, and select Properties from the menu that appears. The TileApp Property Pages dialog box appears.
2. Click the C/C++ selection in the left-hand pane, and select General from the displayed choices.
3. In the Additional Include Directories box, enter the path to the DirectX 8.1 SDK's include folder. If you installed the SDK using the default settings, this path should be `C:\DXSDK\include`.
4. Click the Linker selection in the left-hand pane, and select General from the displayed choices.
5. In the Additional Library Directories box, enter the path to the DirectX 8.1 SDK's library folder. If you installed the SDK using the default settings, this path should be `C:\DXSDK\lib`.
6. Click the Linker's Input selection in the left-hand pane.

7. In the Additional Dependencies box in the right-hand pane, enter `d3d8.lib`, `d3dx8.lib`, and `dxerr8.lib`.

Adding Source Code

With all the overhead out of the way, you can now add the source code that implements the application's animation features. Just follow these steps to get the job done:

1. Add the following lines to the constant definitions near the top of the program:

```
const GRASS = 0;
const TREE = 1;
```

2. Add the following line to the function prototypes near the top of the program:

```
void PerformAnimation();
```

3. In the `WinMain()` function, add the following line right after the line `UpdateWindow(g_hWnd)` that's already there:

```
SetTimer(g_hWnd, 1, 1000, NULL);
```

4. Also in the `WinMain()` function, add the following line right after the line `CloseWindow(g_hWnd)` that's already there:

```
KillTimer(g_hWnd, 1);
```

5. In the `WndProc()` function, add the following `case` clause to the `switch` statement:

```
case WM_TIMER:
    PerformAnimation();
    return 0;
```

6. Add the following function to the end of the program:

```
//////////////////////////////////////////////////////
// PerformAnimation()
//////////////////////////////////////////////////////
void PerformAnimation()
{
    int iNewTile;
    if (g_Sectors[14] == GRASS)
        iNewTile = TREE;
    else
        iNewTile = GRASS;

    g_Sectors[14] = iNewTile;
    g_Sectors[15] = iNewTile;
    g_Sectors[20] = iNewTile;
    g_Sectors[21] = iNewTile;
}
```

7. Copy the image.bmp file from Day 13, "Drawing the Game World," into your TileAnimationApp project's main directory.

Now, go ahead and compile and run the application. When you do, the main display appears, as shown in Figure 14.3. One second later, the trees appear, as shown in Figure 14.4. The trees keep appearing and disappearing until you terminate the program.

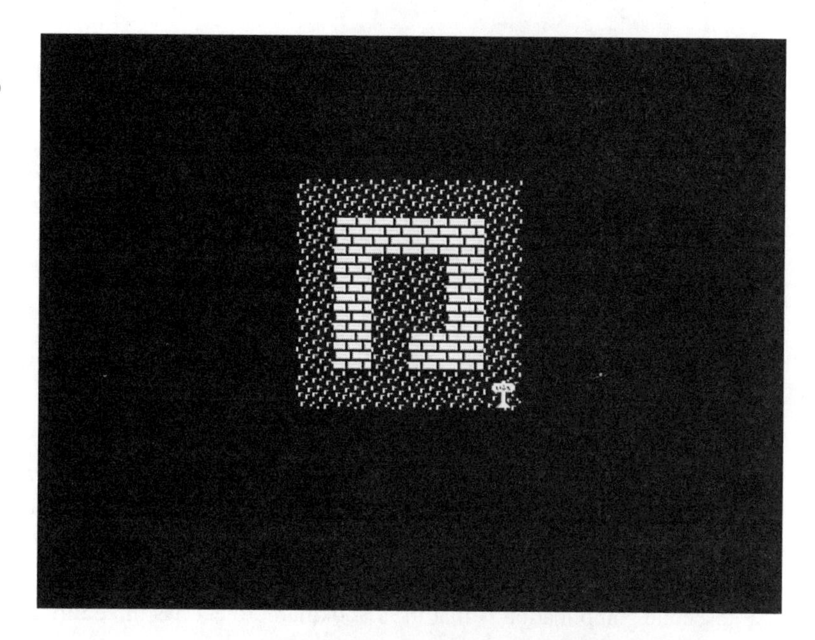

FIGURE 14.3

The `TileAnimationApp` *application when it first runs.*

FIGURE 14.4

The `TileAnimationApp` *application after the trees appear.*

There's really not too much to explain in this program. Setting up the animation is really easy. Whenever a timer event arrives, the program calls the `PerformAnimation()` function. That function first figures out which tile needs to be displayed, the grass or the tree:

```
int iNewTile;
if (g_Sectors[14] == GRASS)
    iNewTile = TREE;
else
    iNewTile = GRASS;
```

Then, it's just a matter of plugging the new tile's ID into the map array wherever the change is to take place:

```
g_Sectors[14] = iNewTile;
g_Sectors[15] = iNewTile;
g_Sectors[20] = iNewTile;
g_Sectors[21] = iNewTile;
```

Animation and Jasper Bookman

While it's easy to get tile animation up and running, *The Adventures of Jasper Bookman*'s animation features are a bit more complicated than those you've experimented with so far. The first complication is that there are 16 tiles that need to be animated in each tile set, and those tiles can appear anywhere in the full 42×42 tile location map. The second complication is that the JBookman project has three different speeds of animation:

- Slow—One second between frames
- Fast—One-fifth of a second between frames
- Fastest—One-tenth of a second between frames

Moreover, the program manages all these different animation speeds using only a single timer.

Handling Timer Events in the JBookman Project

A single timer for three animation speeds? Yep. Here's how it works. First, the program starts the timer such that it sends timer events at the fastest animation speed, which is ten times a second:

```
SetTimer(m_hWnd, 1, 100, NULL);
```

The 100 in this call to `SetTimer()` tells Windows to send timer events every 100 milliseconds. Because there are 1,000 milliseconds in a second, 100 milliseconds represents one-tenth of a second.

Every time a timer event arrives, the program calls the `HandleTimer()` method of the `CEngine` class. (You haven't added this method yet.) The first thing that method does is call `HandleFastestAnimation()`, which, as you can guess from its name, handles those tiles that are animated at ten frames a second.

Then, the method increments a timer-event counter:

```
++m_iAnimationTimerCount;
```

When this counter is an even number (2, 4, 6, 8, or 10), one-fifth of a second has elapsed, and it's time to do the fast animation tiles:

```
if (m_iAnimationTimerCount % 2 == 0)
{
    HandleFastAnimation();
}
```

Finally, if the counter is at 10, a full second has elapsed, and it's time to do the slow animation. It's also time to set the counter back to 0:

```
if (m_iAnimationTimerCount == 10)
{
    m_iAnimationTimerCount = 0;
    HandleSlowAnimation();
}
```

That takes care of three animation speeds with one timer, but the program still has to deal with updating the map array with the proper tile IDs for each animation speed.

Updating the JBookman Map for Animation

In the previous sample program, you used hard-coded values as indexes into the map array. That is, to check the contents of a sector, you wrote this:

```
g_Sectors[14] == GRASS
```

This won't work with *The Adventures of Jasper Bookman* because you can never know which sectors of the map will be animated. Instead, to find animated sectors, the program must search through the entire map array to locate tile IDs that represent animated tiles. These IDs will always be between 32 and 63 because the last four rows of a tile file always contain animated tiles.

To make this search a little tougher, the animated tiles in the map will be animated at one of three available speeds.

Handling the Slow Animation

Here's how the JBookman project will handle the slowest animation. First, the program must scan through the map array, looking for animated tiles. It does this with a `for` loop:

```
for (int x=0; x<MAPSECTORCOUNT; ++x)
{
    .
    .
    .
}
```

Inside the loop, the program checks whether the tile ID is 32 or higher (meaning it's an animated tile) and whether the tile is meant for fast animation or fastest animation:

```
if (m_Sectors[x] > 31 && !IsFastAnimationTile(m_Sectors[x]) &&
    !IsFastestAnimationTile(m_Sectors[x]))
```

This part of the program does not handle the fast or fastest animation, only the slow. If the sector being checked is slated for fast or fastest animation, the `if` statement ends without doing anything.

Once the program finds a sector slated for slow animation, it must check whether the sector is on the first animation frame or the second. The program uses a flag to keep track of this. If the flag is `TRUE`, the second animation frame is currently displayed, and it's time to go back to the first:

```
if (m_bAnimationTilesUpdated)
    m_Sectors[x] = m_Sectors[x] - 1;
```

Otherwise, it's time to go to the second frame:

```
else
    m_Sectors[x] = m_Sectors[x] + 1;
```

After updating the sector with the appropriate tile, the program reverses the flag's setting:

```
m_bAnimationTilesUpdated = !m_bAnimationTilesUpdated;
```

Handling the Fast Animation

The fast animation works similarly to the slow, except that the fast animation has its own flag, named `m_bFastAnimationTilesUpdated`:

```
for (int x=0; x<MAPSECTORCOUNT; ++x)
{
    if (IsFastAnimationTile(m_Sectors[x]))
    {
        if (m_bFastAnimationTilesUpdated)
            m_Sectors[x] = m_Sectors[x] - 1;
        else
            m_Sectors[x] = m_Sectors[x] + 1;
    }
}
m_bFastAnimationTilesUpdated = !m_bFastAnimationTilesUpdated;
```

Handling the Fastest Animation

And, no surprises here, the fastest animation also works similarly to the slow, except that the fastest animation, like the fast animation, has its own flag, this time named m_bFastestAnimationTilesUpdated:

```
for (int x=0; x<MAPSECTORCOUNT; ++x)
{
    if (IsFastestAnimationTile(m_Sectors[x]))
    {
        if (m_bFastestAnimationTilesUpdated)
            m_Sectors[x] = m_Sectors[x] - 1;
        else
            m_Sectors[x] = m_Sectors[x] + 1;
    }
}
m_bFastestAnimationTilesUpdated = !m_bFastestAnimationTilesUpdated;
```

Determining Which Animation Speed to Use

As you've seen in the previous source code, the program uses two methods, IsFastAnimationTile() and IsFastestAnimationTile() to determine what speed of animation to use for a specific animated tile. (Animated tiles that aren't fast or fastest are slow.)

These two methods do nothing more than check for specific tile IDs. For example, here's the IsFastAnimationTile() method:

```
BOOL CEngine::IsFastAnimationTile(int iTileNum)
{
    BOOL bFastAnimated = FALSE;
    switch (iTileNum)
    {
        case FOUNTAIN_EXT:
        case FOUNTAIN_EXT + 1:
        case LEFTTORCH + 1:
        case LEFTTORCH:
        case RIGHTTORCH:
        case RIGHTTORCH + 1:
     bFastAnimated = TRUE;
     break;
    }
    return bFastAnimated;
}
```

You'll be adding more tile IDs to this and other CEngine methods as you progress with the building of the JBookman project.

Adding Code to the Game Engine

Now that you know how the JBookman project handles its animated tiles, it's time to complete the next step in the project. First, you need to make changes to the game engine. So load up the latest version of the project, and follow these steps:

1. Add the following lines to the Engine.h file's protected data members, right after line `int m_iStartSector` that's already there. If you don't want to type, copy the lines from the Code01.txt file in the Chapter14 directory of this book's CD-ROM.

```
int m_iAnimationTimerCount;
BOOL m_bAnimationTilesUpdated;
BOOL m_bFastAnimationTilesUpdated;
BOOL m_bFastestAnimationTilesUpdated;
```

2. Add the following lines to the Engine.h file's public methods, right after line `void HandleRightArrow()` that's already there.

```
void StartAnimationTimer();
void HandleTimer();
```

3. Add the following lines to the Engine.h file's private methods, right after line `BOOL PlayerBlocked(int g_iPlayerSector, int direction)` that's already there. If you don't want to type, copy the lines from the Code02.txt file in the Chapter14 directory of this book's CD-ROM.

```
BOOL IsFastAnimationTile(int iSectorNum);
BOOL IsFastestAnimationTile(int iTileNum);
void HandleSlowAnimation();
void HandleFastAnimation();
void HandleFastestAnimation();
```

4. Add the following method implementations to the `Engine.cpp` file. If you don't want to type, you can copy the lines from the Code03.txt file in the Chapter14 directory of this book's CD-ROM.

```
///////////////////////////////////////////////////////
// StartAnimationTimer()
///////////////////////////////////////////////////////
void CEngine::StartAnimationTimer()
{
    SetTimer(m_hWnd, 1, 100, NULL);
}

///////////////////////////////////////////////////////
// HandleTimer()
///////////////////////////////////////////////////////
void CEngine::HandleTimer()
{
```

```
    HandleFastestAnimation();
    ++m_iAnimationTimerCount;
    if (m_iAnimationTimerCount % 2 == 0)
    {
        HandleFastAnimation();
    }
    if (m_iAnimationTimerCount == 10)
    {
        m_iAnimationTimerCount = 0;
        HandleSlowAnimation();
    }
}

///////////////////////////////////////////////////////
// HandleSlowAnimation()
///////////////////////////////////////////////////////
void CEngine::HandleSlowAnimation()
{
    for (int x=0; x<MAPSECTORCOUNT; ++x)
    {
        if (m_Sectors[x] > 31 && !IsFastAnimationTile(m_Sectors[x]) &&
            !IsFastestAnimationTile(m_Sectors[x]))
        {
            if (m_bAnimationTilesUpdated)
                m_Sectors[x] = m_Sectors[x] - 1;
            else
                m_Sectors[x] = m_Sectors[x] + 1;
        }
    }
    m_bAnimationTilesUpdated = !m_bAnimationTilesUpdated;
}

///////////////////////////////////////////////////////
// HandleFastAnimation()
///////////////////////////////////////////////////////
void CEngine::HandleFastAnimation()
{
    for (int x=0; x<MAPSECTORCOUNT; ++x)
    {
        if (IsFastAnimationTile(m_Sectors[x]))
        {
            if (m_bFastAnimationTilesUpdated)
                m_Sectors[x] = m_Sectors[x] - 1;
            else
                m_Sectors[x] = m_Sectors[x] + 1;
        }
    }
    m_bFastAnimationTilesUpdated = !m_bFastAnimationTilesUpdated;
}
```

```
/////////////////////////////////////////////////////////
// HandleFastestAnimation()
/////////////////////////////////////////////////////////
void CEngine::HandleFastestAnimation()
{
    for (int x=0; x<MAPSECTORCOUNT; ++x)
    {
        if (IsFastestAnimationTile(m_Sectors[x]))
        {
            if (m_bFastestAnimationTilesUpdated)
                m_Sectors[x] = m_Sectors[x] - 1;
            else
                m_Sectors[x] = m_Sectors[x] + 1;
        }
    }
    m_bFastestAnimationTilesUpdated = !m_bFastestAnimationTilesUpdated;
}

/////////////////////////////////////////////////////////
// IsFastAnimationTile()
/////////////////////////////////////////////////////////
BOOL CEngine::IsFastAnimationTile(int iTileNum)
{
    BOOL bFastAnimated = FALSE;
    switch (iTileNum)
    {
        case FOUNTAIN_EXT:
        case FOUNTAIN_EXT + 1:
        case LEFTTORCH:
        case LEFTTORCH + 1:
        case RIGHTTORCH:
        case RIGHTTORCH + 1:
            bFastAnimated = TRUE;
            break;
    }
    return bFastAnimated;
}

/////////////////////////////////////////////////////////
// IsFastestAnimationTile()
/////////////////////////////////////////////////////////
BOOL CEngine::IsFastestAnimationTile(int iTileNum)
{
    BOOL bFastestAnimated = FALSE;
    switch (iTileNum)
    {
        case STREETLIGHT_EXT:
        case STREETLIGHT_EXT + 1:
```

```
                bFastestAnimated = TRUE;
                break;
        }
        return bFastestAnimated;
}
```

5. Add the following lines to the end of the class's constructor. If you don't want to type, you can copy the lines from the Code04.txt file in the Chapter14 directory of this book's CD-ROM.

```
m_iAnimationTimerCount = 0;
m_bAnimationTilesUpdated = FALSE;
m_bFastAnimationTilesUpdated = FALSE;
m_bFastestAnimationTilesUpdated = FALSE;
```

6. Add the following line to the class's destructor:

```
KillTimer(m_hWnd, 1);
```

7. Add the following lines to the Constants.h file, after the line `const WATER02_EXT = 49` that's already there:

```
// Fast animation objects in the town exterior.
const RIGHTTORCH = 54;
const LEFTTORCH = 56;

// Fastest animation objects in the town exterior.
const STREETLIGHT_EXT = 52;
```

Adding Code to the Main Program

1. Add the following line to the `WinMain()` function, right after the line `g_Engine.SetWindowHandle(g_hWnd)` that's already there:

```
g_Engine.StartAnimationTimer();
```

2. Add the following lines to the `WndProc()` function, right before the `switch` statement's closing break:

```
case WM_TIMER:
    g_Engine.HandleTimer();
    return 0;
```

Now, go ahead and compile and run the application. When the main screen appears, move the player character straight north until you see the screen shown in Figure 14.5. In this scene, the street lights flicker at the fastest animation speed (ten times a second), while the water in the fountain goes at the fast animation speed (five times a second).

Move a little further north, and you'll run into a small lake, as shown in Figure 14.6. The water in the lake is animated at the slowest speed (once a second).

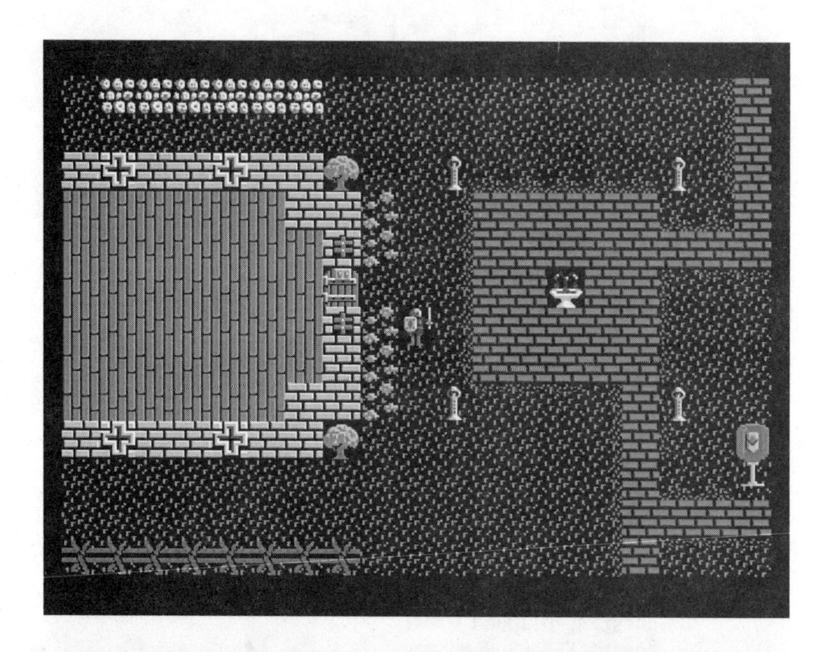

FIGURE 14.5
The animated street lights and fountain.

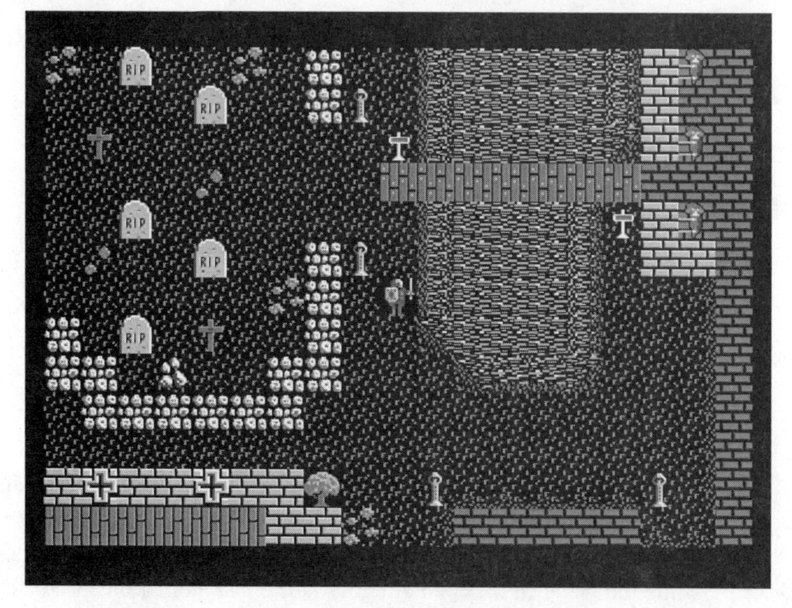

FIGURE 14.6
The animated water.

New Members of the `CEngine` Class

The `CEngine` class, which represents the game engine, keeps getting bigger and bigger! With any luck (not to mention a little studying), you'll understand everything that's been covered so far. To get you up to date, Table 13.1 describes the new members you added to the `CEngine` class in this chapter.

TABLE 13.1 New `CEngine` Members

Member	*Type*	*Description*
`m_bAnimationTilesUpdated`	Data	Flag for determining whether slow animation tiles are on their first or second frame
`m_bFastAnimationTilesUpdated`	Data	Flag for determining whether fast animation tiles are on their first or second frame
`m_bFastestAnimationTilesUpdated`	Data	Flag for determining whether fastest animation tiles are on their first or second frame
`m_iAnimationTimerCount`	Data	Holds the number of timer events that have occurred in the last second
`HandleTimer()`	Public method	Handles `WM_TIMER` events
`StartAnimationTimer()`	Public method	Starts the game engine's animation timer
`HandleFastAnimation()`	Private method	Performs the fast animation sequences
`HandleFastestAnimation()`	Private method	Performs the fastest animation sequences
`HandleSlowAnimation()`	Private method	Performs the slow animation sequences
`IsFastAnimationTile()`	Private method	Returns `TRUE` of the specified tile is a fast animation til
`IsFastestAnimationTile()`	Private method	Returns `TRUE` of the specified tile is a fastest animation tile

Summary

The game world in *The Adventures of Jasper Bookman* is starting to get pretty lively. A little animation goes a long way toward accomplishing that goal. Sure, the animation isn't exactly going to put the creators of *Morrowind* into a sweat, but, hey, it's a start. Still, it's amazing how even simple animation effects can bring a game to life. In the next chapter, you'll liven things up even more, as you add game events and new locations to the JBookman project. Specifically, you'll learn how to hook your own customized routines into the game engine, enabling the player to move from one location to another.

Q&A

Q. What if I want to use more detailed animation with, say, four frames, or even eight frames in the JBookman game engine?

A. Then you have your work cut out for you. First, you'll need to change the format of the tile files. Then, you'll need to rewrite not only the animation routines, but also the way the program deals with the tiles in the last four rows of the tile set. Have fun!

Q. Wouldn't it just be easier to use three different Windows timers for the three different animation speeds than to fudge it with one?

A. First, providing three animation speeds with one timer is a pretty easy thing to do. The complications are minor, amounting to little more than providing a variable to count timer events. Second, Windows timers are system resources, and you should always strive to limit your use of those resources as much as possible.

Q. I've always thought of animation being a bit more than just objects sitting in one place and blinking. What about objects that move around the screen?

A. Just be patient. In Day 17, you add people to the game world. These people will not only be animated in the same way as the objects you animated in this chapter are, but they will also move around whatever location they happen to be in.

Workshop

The workshop includes quiz questions to help gauge your grasp of the material. Even if you feel that you totally understand the concepts presented here, you should work through the quiz anyway. The last section is an exercise or two that you might work through to help reinforce your learning.

1. In the tile sets for the JBookman project, what's significant about the final four rows of tiles in the file?
2. How do you create and start a Windows timer?
3. What type of Windows message does the timer send to your program?
4. How do you catch the `WM_TIMER` message in a Windows application?
5. What do you do with a Windows timer when you're finished with it?
6. How does the JBookman project manage to handle three speeds of animation with one timer?
7. How does the program know which tile of the pair to display for a particular animation sequence?

Exercises

1. Make a copy of the TileAnimationApp project and modify it so that the animation occurs twice as fast.
2. Make a copy of the latest version of the JBookman project, and modify it so that the grass tile alternates, at the fastest animation speed, with the tile that follows the grass in the tile file.
3. Now modify the program so that the water in the fountain animates only twice a second.

Answers for Day 14

Quiz

1. In the tile sets for the JBookman project, what's significant about the final four rows of tiles in the file?

   These are the pairs of animated tiles.
2. How do you create and start a Windows timer?

   By calling the Windows API function `SetTimer()`.
3. What type of Windows message does the timer send to your program?

   The `WM_TIMER` message.
4. How do you catch timer messages in a Windows application?

   In the application's message loop, you add a `case` clause for the event.
5. What do you do with a Windows timer when you're finished with it?

   You call the `KillTimer()` function to destroy the timer.
6. How does the JBookman project manage to handle three speeds of animation with one timer?

   The program sets the timer for the fastest speed and then uses a counter to determine how many timer events have occurred in the last second. The value of the counter then determines which type of animation needs to be performed.
7. How does the program know which tile of the pair to display for a particular animation sequence?

   The program has a flag for each of the animation speeds. If the flag is `TRUE`, the program needs to display the first tile in the pair. If the flag is `FALSE`, the program needs to display the second.

Exercises

1. Make a copy of the TileAnimationApp project and modify it so that the animation occurs twice as fast.

   All you have to do is change the line

   ```
   SetTimer(g_hWnd, 1, 1000, NULL);
   ```

   to

   ```
   SetTimer(g_hWnd, 1, 500, NULL);
   ```

2. Make a copy of the latest version of the JBookman project, and modify it so that the grass tile alternates, at the fastest animation speed, with the tile that follows the grass in the tile file.

   This exercise demonstrates how you can get a whole lot of animation going with very little effort. First, add this constant to the Constant.h file:

   ```
   const GRASS_EXT = 0;
   ```

   Then, in the CEngine.cpp file, add these lines to the `IsFastestAnimationTile()` method, right after the line case `STREETLIGHT_EXT + 1` that's already there:

   ```
   case GRASS_EXT:
   case GRASS_EXT + 1:
   ```

   Now when you run the program, the grass will go crazy!

3. Now modify the program so that the water in the fountain animates only twice a second.

   All you have to do is change the 2 in the line

   ```
   if (m_iAnimationTimerCount % 2 == 0)
   ```

   to a 5. *Presto!* A new animation speed.

WEEK 2

In Review

Direct3D textures enable you to take advantage of a handy graphics programming technique called transparency. Transparency is important because it enables a graphics application to display bitmaps that appear to be non-rectangular or that have areas that allow the background to show through. That is, the transparent areas of the bitmap don't appear on the screen. A texture is a bitmap image that's applied much like a decal to a shape in a 3D world in order to give the shape greater graphical detail. To use textures effectively, you must know how textures implement transparency, what alpha values do, about texture coordinates, and how to load and display textures.

Creating computer animation is an important part of game programming. Luckily, the process is fairly easy to implement, once you know the Direct3D method calls you need to use. When you see some sort of movie-like effect on your computer's screen, it's nothing more than a series of images being drawn one after the other on your computer's screen. To use DirectX to display an animation sequence, you must load the animation images into memory, draw an animation image onto the back buffer, display the back buffer, and then load the next image into memory. You repeat this process again and again, probably for as long as your program runs.

The real world is overflowing with sound. A computer game can't hope to compete with the real world in the aural department. Still, a few well-placed sound effects are often all it takes to bring a game alive. To accomplish this task you must know how to record and edit sound effects, as well as how to play back the sound effects in your game.

Most sound cards come with all the software you need to create sound effects for any game that can handle .WAV files. Moreover, many of these sound-recording programs can also edit sounds in various ways, from clipping unwanted noise to adding echo or even reversing a sound effect. Once you have your sound effects, you need to set up your game program to play the effects. There are a couple of ways to do this, using the Windows API or using the DirectSound component of DirectX.

By this point, you had learned what you need to get started on programming *The Adventures of Jasper Bookman*, an old-style role-playing game. You put your knowledge to the test to create the game's basic Windows application. You also created classes for the program's game engine and for the Direct3D routines the application uses.

A game's state at any point in time is represented by the state of its data, which is stored in various types of variables. Obviously, at the beginning of a game, these values must be initialized to the values that represent the starting game state. Every computer game, no matter how simple or complex, starts off with its data set to the default values for the beginning of the game. What happens after that is up to the player. Because of the large amounts of data that must be maintained in a role-playing game, classes can help simplify the program.

Classes are a great way of dealing with game data, because they enable you to group together data and the functions that manipulate that data. For example, the JBookman project uses a class to represent the many doors in the game world. There are data members in the class that specify whether the door is locked and whether it's visible. Methods of the class enable the main program to set and retrieve these values as needed. The JBookman project uses many classes to represent various objects in the game, including not only doors, but also containers, people, and the player herself.

You can build a graphical representation of your game's world using rectangular images called tiles. A tile is nothing more than a small bitmap that represents an object in your game world. When I say object, I don't mean just stuff like treasure chests and potions. I also mean grass, water, desert, trees, walls and anything else you want to include in your virtual world. Often, a tile is designed such that several can be put together to create a seamless surface of some kind. To continue building the JBookman project, you needed to know how to draw a game world using tiles, how to represent a game map in memory, how to use Direct3D to draw the game world, and how to move a player character through the game world.

Performing a two-frame animation sequence with your tiles means having two versions of each tile you want to animate. During animation, the program switches between each tile in an animated pair, which gives the illusion of movement on the screen. To get animation working, you had to learn how to add animated tiles to a tile file, how to start and stop a Windows timer, how to respond to timer events, how to update animated tiles in the map array, and how to create three speeds of animation with one timer.

WEEK 3

At a Glance

Week 3 continues the JBookman project, applying everything you've learned toward the completion of this major project. In Day 15, you learn to move the player character around the game world, as well as start to understand how to trigger game events. In Day 16, you discover how to add even more game events, by handling objects such as doors and containers. Day 17 introduces you to the inhabitants of your game world, as you learn to add speaking non-player characters (NPCs) to the game.

In Day 18, you have the exciting job of programming combat sequences for the game. Here, you learn not only how to display enemy creatures, but also how to animate the battle. Day 19 introduces you to the important task of saving and loading games, whereas in Day 20, you add sound effects to *The Adventures of Jasper Bookman*. Finally, in Day 21, you complete the game, by adding some finishing touches, such as manipulating player attributes and enabling the player to purchase items from shops.

WEEK 3

DAY 15

Traveling Through a Virtual World

Having a game engine that draws game locations on the screen and moves a player character through those locations is all well and good, but it doesn't give you much of a game. To have an enjoyable RPG, you need to trigger game events that give the player the ability not only to interact with game objects, but also to move from one map to another.

When it comes right down to it, the bulk of your game will deal with the events that create the game's story. In this chapter, you learn to handle one kind of event: moving from one map to another. Specifically, in this chapter you learn how to:

- Customize the game engine for events
- Trigger and respond to game events
- Add new locations to the game

Understanding Game Events

Up until now, you've been working hard on getting the game engine up and running. As you know, the game engine represents the general elements of the game that must be performed in a specific way. For example, the game engine handles the drawing of the game screens, animating specific tiles, moving the player character through the game world, and so on. These actions must happen in any RPG game such as *The Adventures of Jasper Bookman*.

Now, however, it's time to talk about the game's events. These events are what make your game unique and unable to be managed by the game engine, which deals only with general game-processing tasks. A good example of such an event is when the player decides to go through a door. The game engine has no idea what you want to have happen when the player goes through that door. It's up to you to tell the game engine what to do.

You can think of this process as taking the general game engine and adding your own customized game code. You don't, though, want to change the game engine itself in any way. Now that you have it working, you don't want to take a chance of breaking something!

Luckily, OOP techniques give you exactly the tools you need to handle this situation. All you have to do is create a new class that inherits from the `CEngine` class. Then, you can use the game engine as it is in its current form (although you will still be working on it a bit throughout the book) and add your own code to the game, without the fear of ruining any of the hard work you've already put into the game.

You do have to install some sort of hook between the `CEngine` class and your specialized class. There are a couple of ways to do this. The first is to create a virtual method in the `CEngine` class. This method's implementation in the `CEngine` class would do nothing. Your inherited class would override the virtual method and so provide the special functions your game needs.

A better way, considering that this virtual method will do nothing at all in the base `CEngine` class, is to make the method a *pure* virtual method. For those whose OOP knowledge is a little rusty, a pure virtual method is a virtual method that has no implementation in the base class. The implementation must be provided by the derived class. The base `CEngine` class then calls the method in your derived class whenever it needs to know what to do.

When does the base class need to ask your specialized class what to do? Pretty much constantly! In *The Adventures of Jasper Bookman*, it's mostly the player character's location—or the location to which he's trying to move—that determines any events that might occur. For example, when the player character moves toward a door, you need to program the specialized source code that will enable the player to walk through the door.

In fact, this chapter deals almost entirely with what happens whenever the player goes through an entrance to a new area, which includes not only buildings, but also dungeons, rooms inside buildings, and even wilderness areas. Day 16, "Manipulating Game Objects," discusses other types of events, such as when the player wants to open a chest or search for a secret door.

Adding Your Specialized Engine Class to the Game

You're going to be writing a lot of code in this chapter. Probably nothing takes more code in the game than managing the many locations that the player can explore. This is especially true when you consider how many of such areas a full game features. The truth is that the source code you're about to add to the game deals with only a few locations. It'll be up to you, once you work through this book, to expand the game's world to any size you like.

To see how to respond to events, especially those that deal with area entrances, load up the latest version of the JBookman project and perform the following steps. First, you'll install your specialized game-engine class:

1. In the Engine.h file, add the following line to the public method declarations, right after the line `void HandleTimer()` that's already there:

   ```
   virtual void RespondToPlayerLocation() = 0;
   ```

   This is the pure virtual method that provides the link between the `CEngine` class and the class you'll derive from `CEngine`.

2. In the Engine.cpp file, add the following line to the beginning of the `ProcessGame()` method, right before the line `PaintBackBuffer()` that's already there.

   ```
   RespondToPlayerLocation();
   ```

   This is where the `CEngine` class calls your derived class's implementation of the pure virtual method `RespondToPlayerLocation()`.

3. Create a new class named `CMyEngine` that uses CEngine as a base class, as shown in Figures 15.1 and 15.2.

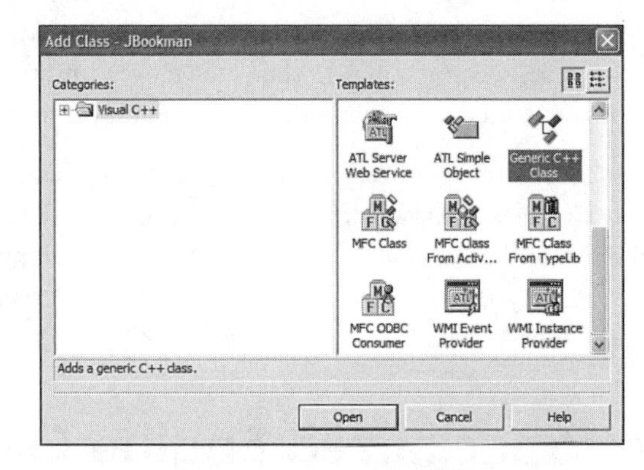

FIGURE 15.1
Creating a generic class.

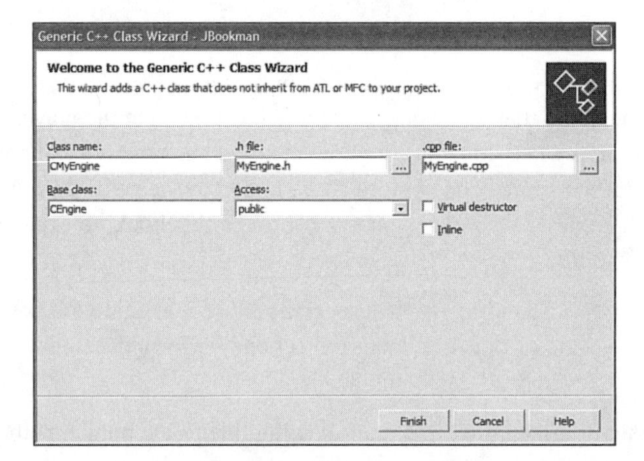

FIGURE 15.2
Creating the `CMyEngine` *class.*

4. Replace the contents of the MyEngine.h file with the following lines. If you don't want to type, you can copy the lines from the Code01.txt file in the Chapter15 directory of this book's CD-ROM.

```
///////////////////////////////////////////////////////
// MyEngine.h
///////////////////////////////////////////////////////

#pragma once

#include "Engine.h"

class CMyEngine : public CEngine
{
public:
    CMyEngine(char* pstrMap, int iMapType, int iSector);
    ~CMyEngine(void);

    void RespondToPlayerLocation();
};
```

5. Replace the contents of the MyEngine.cpp file with the following lines. If you don't want to type, you can copy the lines from the Code02.txt file in the Chapter15 directory of this book's CD-ROM.

```
///////////////////////////////////////////////////////
// MyEngine.cpp
///////////////////////////////////////////////////////

#include "myengine.h"

///////////////////////////////////////////////////////
// CMyEngine()
///////////////////////////////////////////////////////
CMyEngine::CMyEngine(char* pstrMap, int iMapType, int iSector) :
    CEngine(pstrMap, iMapType, iSector)
{
}

///////////////////////////////////////////////////////
// ~CMyEngine()
///////////////////////////////////////////////////////
CMyEngine::~CMyEngine(void)
{
}

///////////////////////////////////////////////////////
// RespondToPlayerLocation()
///////////////////////////////////////////////////////
void CMyEngine::RespondToPlayerLocation()
{
    static int count = 0;
    ++count;
    if (count == 1000)
    {
        count = 0;
        MessageBox(0, "Hello from RespondToPlayerLocation.","", MB_OK);
    }
}
```

6. Near the top of the JBookman.cpp file, change the line

```
#include "Engine.h"
```

to

```
#include "MyEngine.h"
```

7. Also near the top of the JBookman.cpp file, change the line

```
CEngine g_Engine("FirstTown.map", FIRSTTOWN, 1485);
```

to

```
CMyEngine g_Engine("FirstTown.map", FIRSTTOWN, 1485);
```

The main program now creates an object of the `CMyEngine` class instead of the `CEngine` class.

You can now compile and run the application. As soon as the game screen appears, Alt+Tab back to the desktop and minimize all windows. You'll soon see a message box with the greeting "Hello from RespondToPlayerLocation." Dismiss the message box, and a couple of seconds later another appears. To close the application, bring its window up and press Escape (or just click the window's close box).

What's going on here? The main program continually calls the `CEngine` object's `ProcessGame()` method. That method in turn continually calls the `CMyEngine` class's `RespondToPlayerLocation()` method. This gives your specialized game-engine class plenty of opportunities to make the game do what you want it to.

Adding Your Own Events

Now that you have the opportunity to add events to the game, what might such events be? One of the most important events is moving the player character from one location to another. By this, I don't mean moving the player character around the screen, which the game engine already handles for you. Instead, I mean moving the player character into buildings and even to entirely new areas and towns.

To accomplish this task, you must check where the player is located in the current map with every move. If the player's current sector is a place that must trigger an event—for example, an entrance to a building—the program must handle the event appropriately. In the case of an entrance to a building, handling the event means loading a new location map and positioning the player character within it.

In this next part of the JBookman project, you add a new location to the game. Specifically, you'll be adding the interior of a house with two rooms. With the latest version of the JBookman project, perform the following steps to add this new location to the game:

1. Add a new header file named FirstTown.h, and then add the following lines to it. If you don't want to type, you can copy the lines from the Code03.txt file in the Chapter15 directory of this book's CD-ROM.

```
///////////////////////////////////////////////////////////
//// FirstTown.h
///////////////////////////////////////////////////////////

void HandleFirstTown();
void HandleFirstTownHouse01Room01();
void HandleFirstTownHouse01Room02();
```

2. Add a new source code file named FirstTown.cpp, and then add the following lines to it. If you don't want to type, you can copy the lines from the Code04.txt file in the Chapter15 directory of this book's CD-ROM.

```
///////////////////////////////////////////////////////////
// FirstTown.cpp
///////////////////////////////////////////////////////////

#include <d3d8.h>
#include "constants.h"
#include "MyEngine.h"
#include "FirstTown.h"

extern CMyEngine g_Engine;

const HOUSE01FRONTDOOR = 895;
const HOUSE01ROOM01DOOR = 975;

///////////////////////////////////////////////////////////
// HandleFirstTown()
///////////////////////////////////////////////////////////
void HandleFirstTown()
{
    switch (g_Engine.GetPlayer()->GetSector())
    {
    case HOUSE01FRONTDOOR:
        g_Engine.GetPlayer()->SetSector(HOUSE01FRONTDOOR - 1);
        g_Engine.OpenMapFiles("FirstTownHouse01Room01.map");
        g_Engine.SetCurrentMap(FIRSTTOWNHOUSE01ROOM01);
        g_Engine.GetCDirect3DObj()->SetCurrentTileSurface
            (g_Engine.GetCDirect3DObj()->GetTownIntTileSurface());
        break;
    }
}

///////////////////////////////////////////////////////////
// HandleFirstTownHouse01Room01()
///////////////////////////////////////////////////////////
void HandleFirstTownHouse01Room01()
{
    switch (g_Engine.GetPlayer()->GetSector())
    {
    case HOUSE01FRONTDOOR:
        g_Engine.GetPlayer()->SetSector(HOUSE01FRONTDOOR + 1);
        g_Engine.OpenMapFiles("FirstTown.map");
        g_Engine.SetCurrentMap(FIRSTTOWN);
        g_Engine.GetCDirect3DObj()->SetCurrentTileSurface
            (g_Engine.GetCDirect3DObj()->GetTownExtTileSurface());
        break;
    case HOUSE01ROOM01DOOR:
        g_Engine.GetPlayer()->SetSector(HOUSE01ROOM01DOOR - 1);
```

```
            g_Engine.OpenMapFiles("FirstTownHouse01Room02.map");
            g_Engine.SetCurrentMap(FIRSTTOWNHOUSE01ROOM02);
            break;
        }
}

//////////////////////////////////////////////////////////
// HandleFirstTownHouse01Room02()
//////////////////////////////////////////////////////////
void HandleFirstTownHouse01Room02()
{
    if (g_Engine.GetPlayer()->GetSector() == HOUSE01ROOM01DOOR)
    {
        g_Engine.GetPlayer()->SetSector(HOUSE01ROOM01DOOR + 1);
        g_Engine.OpenMapFiles("FirstTownHouse01Room01.map");
        g_Engine.SetCurrentMap(FIRSTTOWNHOUSE01ROOM01);
    }
}
```

The source code in this file will handle all events in the town First Town.

3. Add the following line to the MyEngine.h file, right after the line `#include "Engine.h"` that's already there:

```
#include "FirstTown.h"
```

4. In the MyEngine.cpp file, replace the current `RespondToPlayerLocation()` method with the one that follows. If you don't want to type, you can copy the lines from the Code05.txt file in the Chapter15 directory of this book's CD-ROM.

```
void CMyEngine::RespondToPlayerLocation()
{
    switch (m_iCurrentMap)
    {
        case FIRSTTOWN:
            HandleFirstTown();
            break;
        case FIRSTTOWNHOUSE01ROOM01:
            HandleFirstTownHouse01Room01();
            break;
        case FIRSTTOWNHOUSE01ROOM02:
            HandleFirstTownHouse01Room02();
            break;
    }
}
```

These lines route program execution to the appropriate method for the player's current location.

5. In the Direct3D.h file, add the following line to the public method declarations, right after the line `IDirect3DSurface8* GetPlayerTile()` that's already there:

```
void SetCurrentTileSurface(IDirect3DSurface8* pSurface);
```

This method sets the image bitmap that the program will use to draw the player's current location.

6. Add the following method definitions to the end of the Direct3D.cpp file. If you don't want to type, you can copy the lines from the Code06.txt file in the Chapter15 directory of this book's CD-ROM.

```
///////////////////////////////////////////////////////
// SetCurrentTileSurface()
///////////////////////////////////////////////////////
void CDirect3D::SetCurrentTileSurface(IDirect3DSurface8* pSurface)
{
    m_pCurrentTileSurface = pSurface;
}

///////////////////////////////////////////////////////
// GetTownExtTileSurface()
///////////////////////////////////////////////////////
IDirect3DSurface8* CDirect3D::GetTownExtTileSurface()
{
    return m_pTownExtTileSurface;
}

///////////////////////////////////////////////////////
// GetTownIntTileSurface()
///////////////////////////////////////////////////////
IDirect3DSurface8* CDirect3D::GetTownIntTileSurface()
{
    return m_pTownIntTileSurface;
}
```

These methods simply return pointers to the current tile surface in use, as well as to the surfaces that hold the tiles for the town exterior and town interior.

7. Copy the following files from the Chapter15 directory of this book's CD-ROM to the Maps directory of your JBookman project.

```
FirstTownHouse01Room01.map
FirstTownHouse01Room01.map.dor
FirstTownHouse01Room01.map.item
FirstTownHouse01Room01.map.peo
FirstTownHouse01Room02.map
FirstTownHouse01Room02.map.dor
FirstTownHouse01Room02.map.item
FirstTownHouse01Room02.map.peo
```

These files are the maps for the interior of First Town's house #1. There is a map for each of the house's rooms and, of course, each map file also includes a set of files for doors, items, and people.

You can now compile and run the program. When the game screen appears, head directly north until you get to the house shown in Figure 15.3.

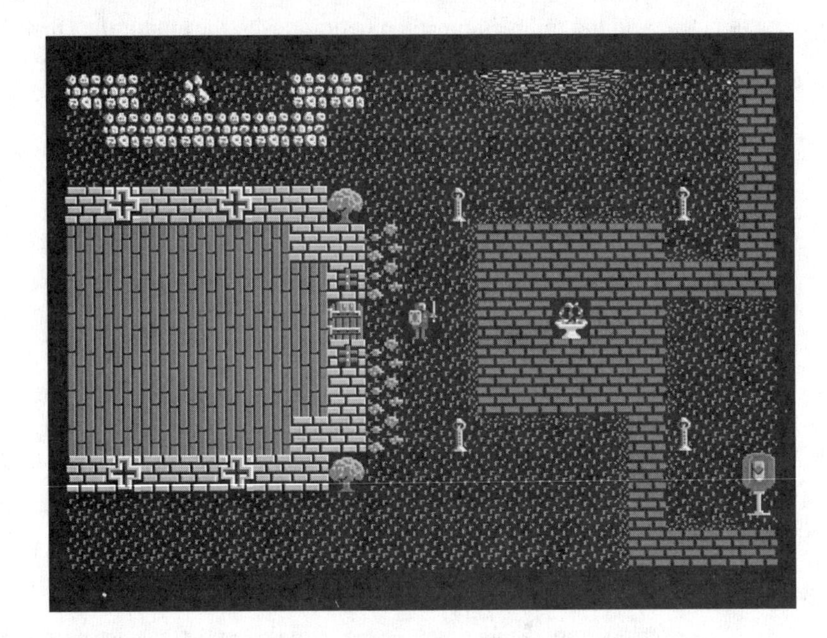

FIGURE 15.3
This is First Town's house #1.

Walk through the door and you should find yourself in the house's first room, shown in Figure 15.4.

If the animated fireplace is doing weird stuff, don't worry about it for now. Instead, head for the door to the house's other room, and go through it. You should then be in the house's second room, as shown in Figure 15.5.

While you're at it, see whether you can walk through the house's walls. Whoops! Either your player character has gained supernatural powers or something is wrong with the program. You'll fix this problem in the next section.

Now, head back to the front door, and go back out into the town. Do the fountains and the streetlights look weird? If not, go back in and out of the house until you see something like Figure 15.6, where the streetlights have suddenly been replaced with fountains. What's going on here?

You'll find out what's wrong with the animation and why your player character can walk through walls in the next section. But, for now, let's examine the source code you added.

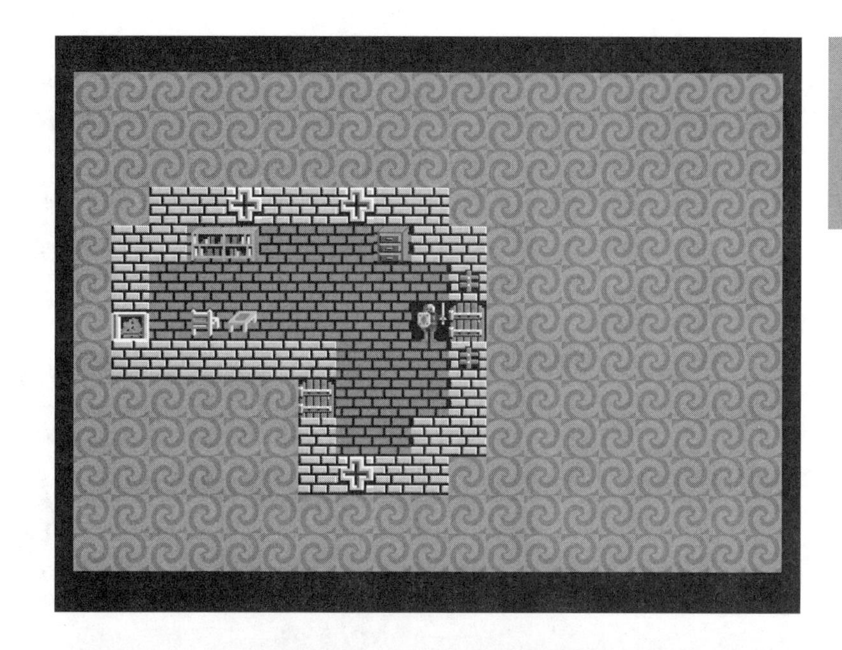

FIGURE 15.4

In the house's first room.

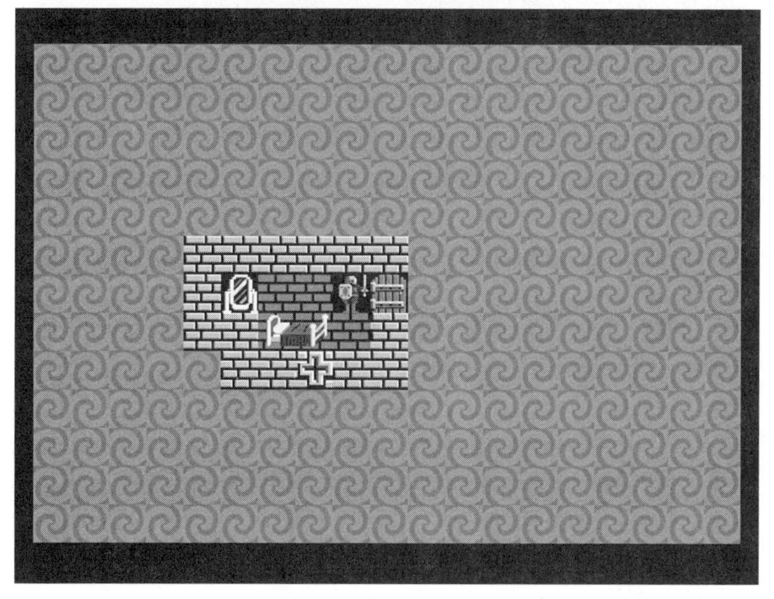

FIGURE 15.5

In the house's second room.

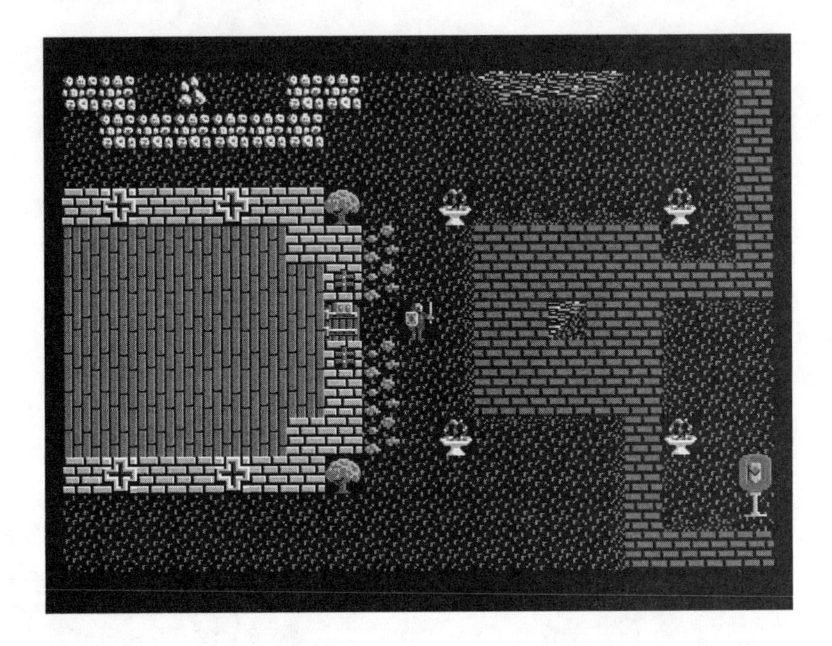

FIGURE 15.6
Something's wrong here!

Every time the player moves, the program checks the player's current sector for an event. For the sake of this discussion, assume that the player character is in the First Town area and has just stepped into house #1's front door. Here's what happens in detail:

1. The player moves to a new sector.
2. The `CEngine` object calls the `CMyEngine` object's `RespondToPlayerLocation()` method:

```
void CEngine::ProcessGame(void)
{
    RespondToPlayerLocation();
    PaintBackBuffer();
}
```

3. The `RespondToPlayerLocation()` method checks to see in which map the player is currently located and calls the method that handles that location. In this case, `RespondToPlayerLocation()` calls the `HandleFirstTown()` method located in the FirstTown.cpp file:

```
void CMyEngine::RespondToPlayerLocation()
{
    switch (m_iCurrentMap)
    {
        case FIRSTTOWN:
            HandleFirstTown();
            break;
```

```
                    .
                    .
                    .
                case FIRSTTOWNINNROOM07:
                    HandleFirstTownInnRoom07();
                    break;
            }
        }
```

4. The `HandleFirstTown()` method retrieves the player's current sector inside a `switch` statement:

   ```
   switch (g_Engine.GetPlayer()->GetSector())
   ```

5. The program executes the `case` clause for the house's front door:

   ```
   case HOUSE01FRONTDOOR:
   ```

6. In the `case` clause, the program first moves the player to the sector on the other side of the door:

   ```
   g_Engine.GetPlayer()->SetSector(HOUSE01FRONTDOOR - 1);
   ```

7. Next, the program loads the map file needed for the new location (the first room in the house):

   ```
   g_Engine.OpenMapFiles("FirstTownHouse01Room01.map");
   g_Engine.SetCurrentMap(FIRSTTOWNHOUSE01ROOM01);
   ```

8. To display the new area, the program must switch to the correct tile file, which it does next:

   ```
   g_Engine.GetCDirect3DObj()->SetCurrentTileSurface
       (g_Engine.GetCDirect3DObj()->GetTownIntTileSurface());
   ```

Now, when the program draws the game screen, the player will be located inside the house. You may recall, though, that switching locations wreaked havoc with the animation. Also, the program now lets the player character walk through walls. Time to fix that stuff.

Fixing the Animation

The reason your animated tiles are doing weird things has to do with the way the program loads new map files for the three areas in which you can now travel (First Town, House Room 1, and House Room 2). Every time the player enters a new location, the program loads a new area map. However, currently the program doesn't consider what frame of animation the program may be on. If the program is on the first animation frame, everything in the new area will look fine. If the program is on the second animation frame, the animated tiles will look all wrong.

Here's what happens:

1. The animation starts on frame 1, displaying the first tile of an animated pair on the screen. The animation flags (m_bAnimationTilesUpdated, m_bFastAnimationTilesUpdated, and m_bFastestAnimationTilesUpdated) start off set to FALSE.
2. The animation switches to frame 2, loading the second tile for each animated pair into the area map. The program sets the animation flags to TRUE.
3. The player enters a new area. The program loads the area's map, which means all the animated tiles are reset to the first of the pair. However, the animation flags are still set to TRUE. Trouble!
4. On the next animation frame, the program thinks (because of the setting of the animation flags) that it's moving from the second animation frame to the first. In reality, it should be moving from the first to the second. As a result, the program selects the wrong tiles to display.

The reason you can walk through walls is simply that you haven't yet added the code that handles impassable objects for town interior locations. To solve the animation and walk-through-walls problems, perform the following steps:

1. Add the following line to the Engine.h file's public method declarations, right after line virtual void RespondToPlayerLocation() = 0 that's already there.

   ```
   void ResetAnimation();
   ```

2. Add the following method implementation to the end of the Engine.cpp file. If you don't want to type, you can copy the lines from the Code07.txt file in the Chapter15 directory of this book's CD-ROM.

   ```
   ///////////////////////////////////////////////////////////
   // ResetAnimation()
   ///////////////////////////////////////////////////////////
   void CEngine::ResetAnimation()
   {
       m_iAnimationTimerCount = 0;
       m_bAnimationTilesUpdated = FALSE;
       m_bFastAnimationTilesUpdated = FALSE;
       m_bFastestAnimationTilesUpdated = FALSE;
   }
   ```

3. Add the following lines to the PlayerBlocked() method, right before the switch statement's closing brace. If you don't want to type, you can copy the lines from the Code08.txt file in the Chapter15 directory of this book's CD-ROM.

   ```
   case TOWNINTERIOR:
       if (item == BRICKWALL_INT || item == WINDOW1_INT
           || item == WINDOW2_INT || item == CUPBOARD_INT
   ```

```
            || item == TABLE01_INT || item == TABLE02_INT
            || item == TABLE03_INT
            || item == BED01_INT || item == BED02_INT
            || item == BED03_INT || item == BED04_INT
            || item == FIREPLACE_INT || item == FIREPLACE_INT + 1
            || item == MANINCHAIR01_INT || item == MANINCHAIR01_INT + 1
            || item == MANINCHAIR02_INT || item == MANINCHAIR02_INT + 1
            || item == MANINCHAIR03_INT || item == MANINCHAIR03_INT + 1
            || item == MANINCHAIR04_INT || item == MANINCHAIR04_INT + 1
            || item == MANINBED01_INT || item == MANINBED01_INT + 1
            || item == MANINBED02_INT || item == MANINBED02_INT + 1)
        blocked = TRUE;
        break;
```

4. Replace the `IsFastAnimationTile()` and `IsFastestAnimationTile()` methods with the versions that follow. If you don't want to type, you can copy the lines from the Code09.txt file in the Chapter15 directory of this book's CD-ROM.

```
///////////////////////////////////////////////////////
// IsFastAnimationTile()
///////////////////////////////////////////////////////
BOOL CEngine::IsFastAnimationTile(int iTileNum)
{
    BOOL bFastAnimated = FALSE;
    if (m_byMapType == TOWNEXTERIOR)
    {
        switch (iTileNum)
        {
            case FOUNTAIN_EXT:
            case FOUNTAIN_EXT + 1:
            case LEFTTORCH:
            case LEFTTORCH + 1:
            case RIGHTTORCH:
            case RIGHTTORCH + 1:
                bFastAnimated = TRUE;
                break;
        }
    }
    else if (m_byMapType == TOWNINTERIOR)
    {
        switch (iTileNum)
        {
            case STAIRSUP_INT:
            case STAIRSUP_INT + 1:
            case STAIRSDOWN_INT:
            case STAIRSDOWN_INT + 1:
                bFastAnimated = TRUE;
                break;
        }
    }
    return bFastAnimated;
```

```
}

/////////////////////////////////////////////////////////
// IsFastestAnimationTile()
/////////////////////////////////////////////////////////
BOOL CEngine::IsFastestAnimationTile(int iTileNum)
{
    BOOL bFastestAnimated = FALSE;
    if (m_byMapType == TOWNEXTERIOR)
        {
        switch (iTileNum)
        {
            case STREETLIGHT_EXT:
            case STREETLIGHT_EXT + 1:
                bFastestAnimated = TRUE;
                break;
        }
    }
    else if (m_byMapType == TOWNINTERIOR)
        {
        switch (iTileNum)
        {
            case BRASIER_INT:
            case BRASIER_INT + 1:
            case STOVE_INT:
            case STOVE_INT + 1:
            case FIREPLACE_INT:
            case FIREPLACE_INT + 1:
                bFastestAnimated = TRUE;
                break;
        }
    }
    return bFastestAnimated;
}
```

5. In the FirstTown.cpp file, add the following line right before every `break` statement in the file. Also, add the line to the `HandleFirstTownHouse01Room02()` method, right before the `if` statement's closing brace:

   ```
   g_Engine.ResetAnimation();
   ```

6. Add the following lines to the Constants.h file, after the line `const STREET-LIGHT_EXT = 52` that's already there. If you don't want to type, you can copy the lines from the Code10.txt file in the Chapter15 directory of this book's CD-ROM.

   ```
   // Impassable Objects in the town interior.
   const BRICKWALL_INT = 1;
   const WINDOW1_INT = 2;
   const WINDOW2_INT = 3;
   const CUPBOARD_INT = 6;
   const TABLE01_INT = 13;
   ```

```
const TABLE02_INT = 14;
const TABLE03_INT = 15;
const BED01_INT = 24;
const BED02_INT = 25;
const BED03_INT = 26;
const BED04_INT = 27;
const FIREPLACE_INT = 38;
const MANINCHAIR01_INT = 44;
const MANINCHAIR02_INT = 46;
const MANINCHAIR03_INT = 48;
const MANINCHAIR04_INT = 50;
const MANINBED01_INT = 52;
const MANINBED02_INT = 54;

// Fast animation objects in the town interior.
const STAIRSUP_INT = 40;
const STAIRSDOWN_INT = 42;

// Fastest animation objects in the town interior.
const BRASIER_INT = 34;
const STOVE_INT = 36;
```

When you compile and run the program now, you'll find that you can no longer walk through walls. Also, you can move back and forth between the interior of the house and the town without the animation going flaky on you.

Adding the Inn

Now, how about trying something a little more challenging? In this section, you add an inn to First Town. This inn has seven rooms, lots of doors, and even a staircase. You'll need to add quite a few events to the program to handle all this stuff. Perform the following steps to install the inn:

1. In MyEngine.cpp, add the following lines to the `RespondToPlayerLocation()` method, right before the `switch` statement's closing brace. If you don't want to type, you can copy the lines from the Code11.txt file in the Chapter15 directory of this book's CD-ROM.

```
case FIRSTTOWNINNROOM01:
    HandleFirstTownInnRoom01();
    break;
case FIRSTTOWNINNROOM02:
    HandleFirstTownInnRoom02();
    break;
case FIRSTTOWNINNROOM03:
    HandleFirstTownInnRoom03();
    break;
case FIRSTTOWNINNROOM04:
```

```
        HandleFirstTownInnRoom04();
        break;
    case FIRSTTOWNINNROOM05:
        HandleFirstTownInnRoom05();
        break;
    case FIRSTTOWNINNROOM06:
        HandleFirstTownInnRoom06();
        break;
    case FIRSTTOWNINNROOM07:
        HandleFirstTownInnRoom07();
        break;
```

These lines route program execution to the appropriate method for the player's current location for each room in the inn.

2. In the FirstTown.h file, add the following function declarations. If you don't want to type, you can copy the lines from the Code12.txt file in the Chapter15 directory of this book's CD-ROM.

```
void HandleFirstTownInnRoom01();
void HandleFirstTownInnRoom02();
void HandleFirstTownInnRoom03();
void HandleFirstTownInnRoom04();
void HandleFirstTownInnRoom05();
void HandleFirstTownInnRoom06();
void HandleFirstTownInnRoom07();
```

3. Near the top of the FirstTown.cpp file, add the following constant definitions, right after the line `const HOUSE01ROOM01DOOR = 975` that's already there. If you don't want to type, you can copy the lines from the Code13.txt file in the Chapter15 directory of this book's CD-ROM.

```
const FIRSTTOWNINNFRONTDOOR = 321;
const FIRSTTOWNINNROOM02DOOR = 493;
const FIRSTTOWNINNROOM03DOOR = 495;
const FIRSTTOWNINNROOM04DOOR = 619;
const FIRSTTOWNINNROOM05DOOR = 621;
const FIRSTTOWNINNROOM06STAIRS = 662;
const FIRSTTOWNINNROOM07DOOR = 368;
```

These lines define constants for the sectors in the inn that trigger events. Using constants makes the code easier to read and understand.

4. Again in the FirstTown.cpp file, add the following lines to the `HandleFirstTown()` method, right before the `switch` statement's closing brace. If you don't want to type, you can copy the lines from the Code14.txt file in the Chapter15 directory of this book's CD-ROM.

```
case FIRSTTOWNINNFRONTDOOR:
    g_Engine.GetPlayer()->SetSector(FIRSTTOWNINNFRONTDOOR + 1);
    g_Engine.OpenMapFiles("FirstTownInnRoom01.map");
```

```
    g_Engine.SetCurrentMap(FIRSTTOWNINNROOM01);
    g_Engine.GetCDirect3DObj()->SetCurrentTileSurface
        (g_Engine.GetCDirect3DObj()->GetTownIntTileSurface());
    g_Engine.ResetAnimation();
    break;
```

These lines handle the event that occurs when the player walks through the inn's front door.

5. Add the following method definitions to the end of the FirstTown.cpp file. If you don't want to type, you can copy the lines from the Code15.txt file in the Chapter15 directory of this book's CD-ROM.

```
///////////////////////////////////////////////////////////
// HandleFirstTownInnRoom01()
///////////////////////////////////////////////////////////
void HandleFirstTownInnRoom01()
{
    switch (g_Engine.GetPlayer()->GetSector())
    {
    case FIRSTTOWNINNFRONTDOOR:
        g_Engine.GetPlayer()->SetSector(FIRSTTOWNINNFRONTDOOR - 1);
        g_Engine.OpenMapFiles("FirstTown.map");
        g_Engine.SetCurrentMap(FIRSTTOWN);
        g_Engine.GetCDirect3DObj()->SetCurrentTileSurface
            (g_Engine.GetCDirect3DObj()->GetTownExtTileSurface());
        g_Engine.ResetAnimation();
        break;
    case FIRSTTOWNINNROOM02DOOR:
        g_Engine.GetPlayer()->SetSector(FIRSTTOWNINNROOM02DOOR - 1);
        g_Engine.OpenMapFiles("FirstTownInnRoom02.map");
        g_Engine.SetCurrentMap(FIRSTTOWNINNROOM02);
        g_Engine.ResetAnimation();
        break;
    case FIRSTTOWNINNROOM03DOOR:
        g_Engine.GetPlayer()->SetSector(FIRSTTOWNINNROOM03DOOR + 1);
        g_Engine.OpenMapFiles("FirstTownInnRoom03.map");
        g_Engine.SetCurrentMap(FIRSTTOWNINNROOM03);
        g_Engine.ResetAnimation();
        break;
    case FIRSTTOWNINNROOM04DOOR:
        g_Engine.GetPlayer()->SetSector(FIRSTTOWNINNROOM04DOOR - 1);
        g_Engine.OpenMapFiles("FirstTownInnRoom04.map");
        g_Engine.SetCurrentMap(FIRSTTOWNINNROOM04);
        g_Engine.ResetAnimation();
        break;
    case FIRSTTOWNINNROOM05DOOR:
        g_Engine.GetPlayer()->SetSector(FIRSTTOWNINNROOM05DOOR + 1);
        g_Engine.OpenMapFiles("FirstTownInnRoom05.map");
        g_Engine.SetCurrentMap(FIRSTTOWNINNROOM05);
        g_Engine.ResetAnimation();
```

```
            break;
        case FIRSTTOWNINNROOM06STAIRS:
            g_Engine.GetPlayer()->SetSector(FIRSTTOWNINNROOM06STAIRS -
                MAPCOLUMNCOUNT);
            g_Engine.OpenMapFiles("FirstTownInnRoom06.map");
            g_Engine.SetCurrentMap(FIRSTTOWNINNROOM06);
            g_Engine.ResetAnimation();
            break;
        }
}

///////////////////////////////////////////////////////////
// HandleFirstTownInnRoom02()
///////////////////////////////////////////////////////////
void HandleFirstTownInnRoom02()
{
    switch (g_Engine.GetPlayer()->GetSector())
    {
    case FIRSTTOWNINNROOM02DOOR:
        g_Engine.GetPlayer()->SetSector(FIRSTTOWNINNROOM02DOOR + 1);
        g_Engine.OpenMapFiles("FirstTownInnRoom01.map");
        g_Engine.SetCurrentMap(FIRSTTOWNINNROOM01);
        g_Engine.ResetAnimation();
        break;
    }
}

///////////////////////////////////////////////////////////
// HandleFirstTownInnRoom03()
///////////////////////////////////////////////////////////
void HandleFirstTownInnRoom03()
{
    switch (g_Engine.GetPlayer()->GetSector())
    {
    case FIRSTTOWNINNROOM03DOOR:
        g_Engine.GetPlayer()->SetSector(FIRSTTOWNINNROOM03DOOR - 1);
        g_Engine.OpenMapFiles("FirstTownInnRoom01.map");
        g_Engine.SetCurrentMap(FIRSTTOWNINNROOM01);
        g_Engine.ResetAnimation();
        break;
    }
}

///////////////////////////////////////////////////////////
// HandleFirstTownInnRoom04()
///////////////////////////////////////////////////////////
void HandleFirstTownInnRoom04()
{
    switch (g_Engine.GetPlayer()->GetSector())
    {
    case FIRSTTOWNINNROOM04DOOR:
```

```
        g_Engine.GetPlayer()->SetSector(FIRSTTOWNINNROOM04DOOR + 1);
        g_Engine.OpenMapFiles("FirstTownInnRoom01.map");
        g_Engine.SetCurrentMap(FIRSTTOWNINNROOM01);
        g_Engine.ResetAnimation();
        break;
    }
}

///////////////////////////////////////////////////////////
// HandleFirstTownInnRoom05()
///////////////////////////////////////////////////////////
void HandleFirstTownInnRoom05()
{
    switch (g_Engine.GetPlayer()->GetSector())
    {
    case FIRSTTOWNINNROOM05DOOR:
        g_Engine.GetPlayer()->SetSector(FIRSTTOWNINNROOM05DOOR - 1);
        g_Engine.OpenMapFiles("FirstTownInnRoom01.map");
        g_Engine.SetCurrentMap(FIRSTTOWNINNROOM01);
        g_Engine.ResetAnimation();
        break;
    }
}

///////////////////////////////////////////////////////////
// HandleFirstTownInnRoom06()
///////////////////////////////////////////////////////////
void HandleFirstTownInnRoom06()
{
    switch (g_Engine.GetPlayer()->GetSector())
    {
    case FIRSTTOWNINNROOM07DOOR:
        g_Engine.GetPlayer()->SetSector(FIRSTTOWNINNROOM07DOOR -
            MAPCOLUMNCOUNT);
        g_Engine.OpenMapFiles("FirstTownInnRoom07.map");
        g_Engine.SetCurrentMap(FIRSTTOWNINNROOM07);
        g_Engine.ResetAnimation();
        break;
    case FIRSTTOWNINNROOM06STAIRS:
        g_Engine.GetPlayer()->SetSector(FIRSTTOWNINNROOM05DOOR - 1);
        g_Engine.OpenMapFiles("FirstTownInnRoom01.map");
        g_Engine.SetCurrentMap(FIRSTTOWNINNROOM01);
        g_Engine.ResetAnimation();
        break;
    }
}

///////////////////////////////////////////////////////////
// HandleFirstTownInnRoom07()
///////////////////////////////////////////////////////////
void HandleFirstTownInnRoom07()
```

```
{
    switch (g_Engine.GetPlayer()->GetSector())
    {
    case FIRSTTOWNINNROOM07DOOR:
        g_Engine.GetPlayer()->SetSector(FIRSTTOWNINNROOM07DOOR +
            MAPCOLUMNCOUNT);
        g_Engine.OpenMapFiles("FirstTownInnRoom06.map");
        g_Engine.SetCurrentMap(FIRSTTOWNINNROOM06);
        g_Engine.ResetAnimation();
        break;
    }
}
```

These methods handle the events for all the rooms inside the inn.

6. Copy the following files from the Chapter15 directory of this book's CD-ROM to the Maps directory of your JBookman project.

```
FirstTownInnRoom01.map
FirstTownInnRoom01.map.dor
FirstTownInnRoom01.map.item
FirstTownInnRoom01.map.peo
FirstTownInnRoom02.map
FirstTownInnRoom02.map.dor
FirstTownInnRoom02.map.item
FirstTownInnRoom02.map.peo
FirstTownInnRoom03.map
FirstTownInnRoom03.map.dor
FirstTownInnRoom03.map.item
FirstTownInnRoom03.map.peo
FirstTownInnRoom04.map
FirstTownInnRoom04.map.dor
FirstTownInnRoom04.map.item
FirstTownInnRoom04.map.peo
FirstTownInnRoom05.map
FirstTownInnRoom05.map.dor
FirstTownInnRoom05.map.item
FirstTownInnRoom05.map.peo
FirstTownInnRoom06.map
FirstTownInnRoom06.map.dor
FirstTownInnRoom06.map.item
FirstTownInnRoom06.map.peo
FirstTownInnRoom07.map
FirstTownInnRoom07.map.dor
FirstTownInnRoom07.map.item
FirstTownInnRoom07.map.peo
```

You can now compile and run the application. When the game's screen appears, head north to the inn, as shown in Figure 15.7. Step through the inn's door, and you'll find yourself in the inn's lobby (see Figure 15.8).

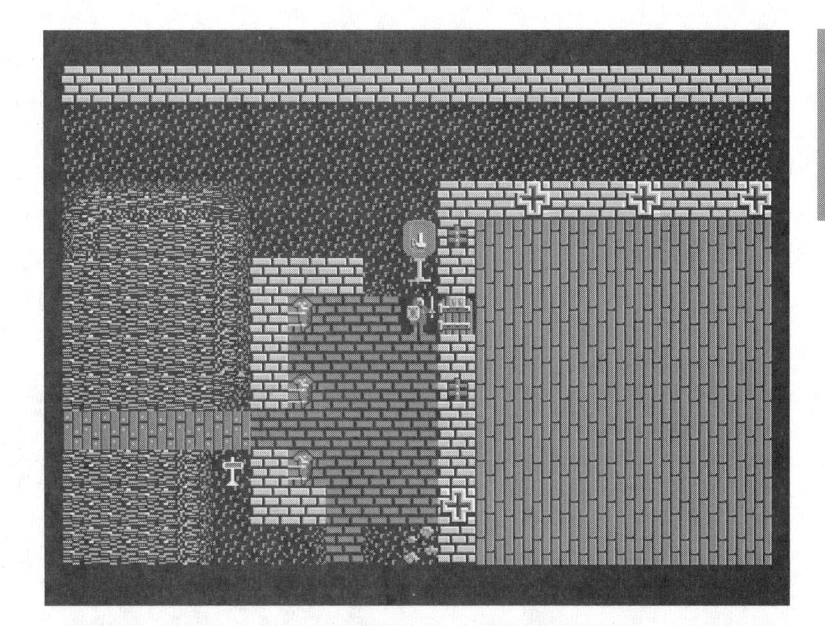

FIGURE 15.7
Standing in front of the inn.

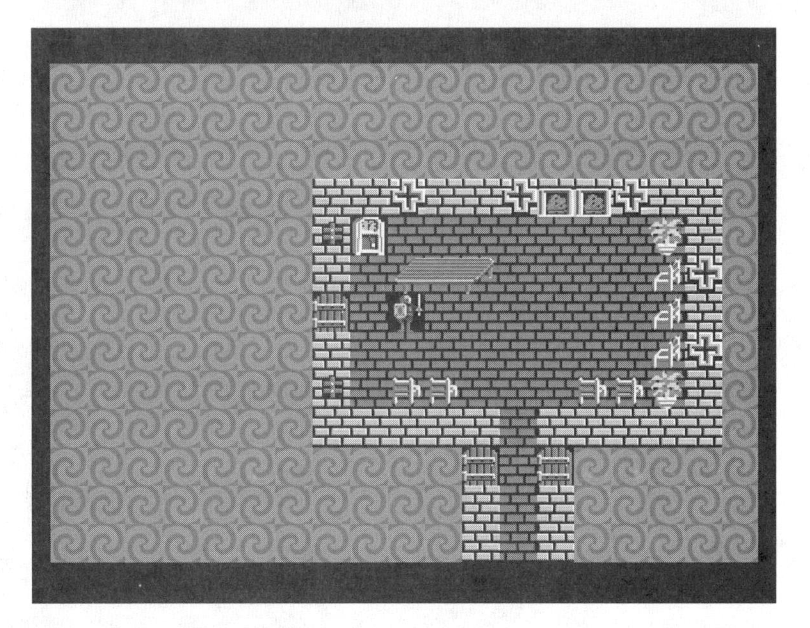

FIGURE 15.8
Standing in the inn's lobby.

To the south, you'll find a short hallway lined with doors. Take a walk down there and check out the rooms on the other side of those doors. Figure 15.9 shows the first room on your left as you go down the hall.

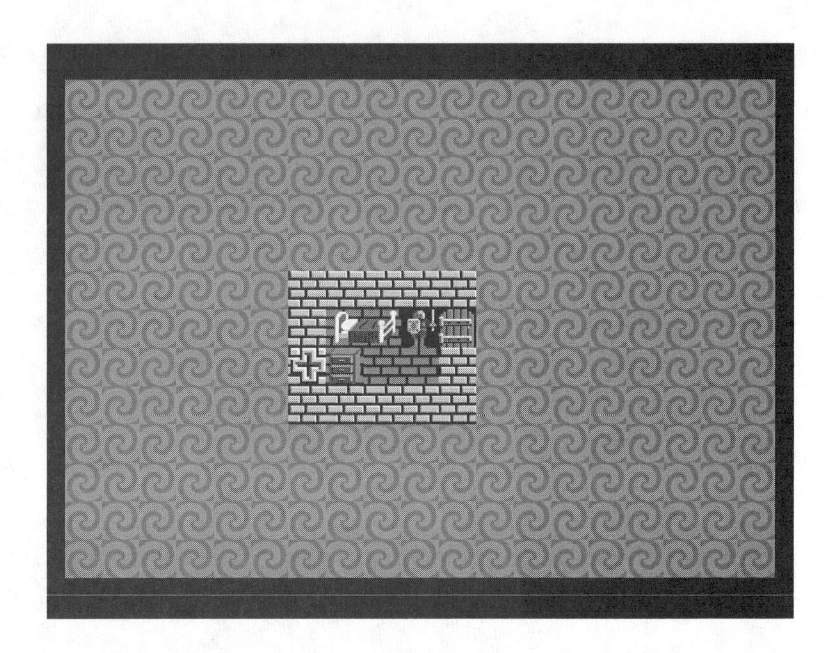

FIGURE 15.9
One of the inn's bedrooms.

At the end of the stairs, you'll find a ladder with a blinking arrow pointing up. This is the symbol for a staircase. When you move your player character onto the stairs, you go to the second floor and end up in the room shown in Figure 15.10. This is the inn's general sleeping area, which is cheaper than the private rooms.

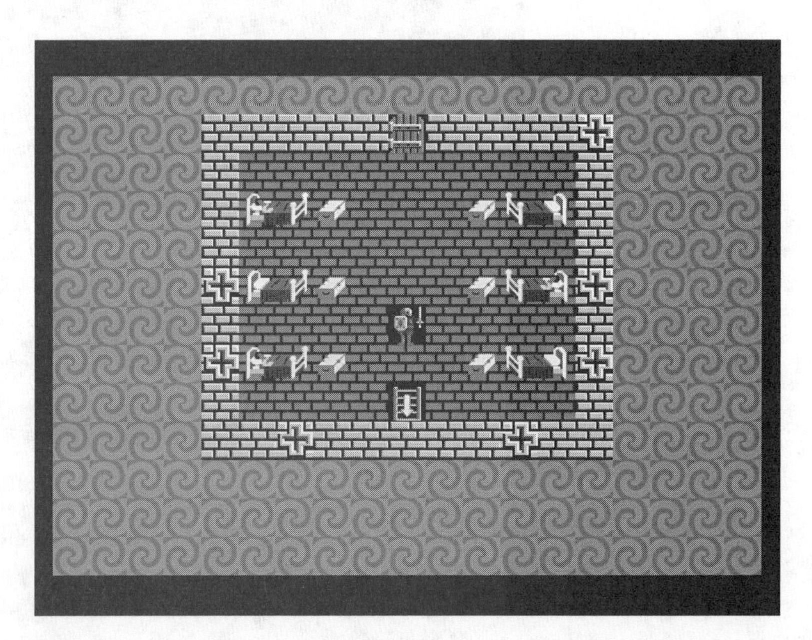

FIGURE 15.10
The inn's upper floor.

There's a supply room at the other side of the general sleeping area. See the door? Go through the door, and you end up in the supply room, shown in Figure 15.11.

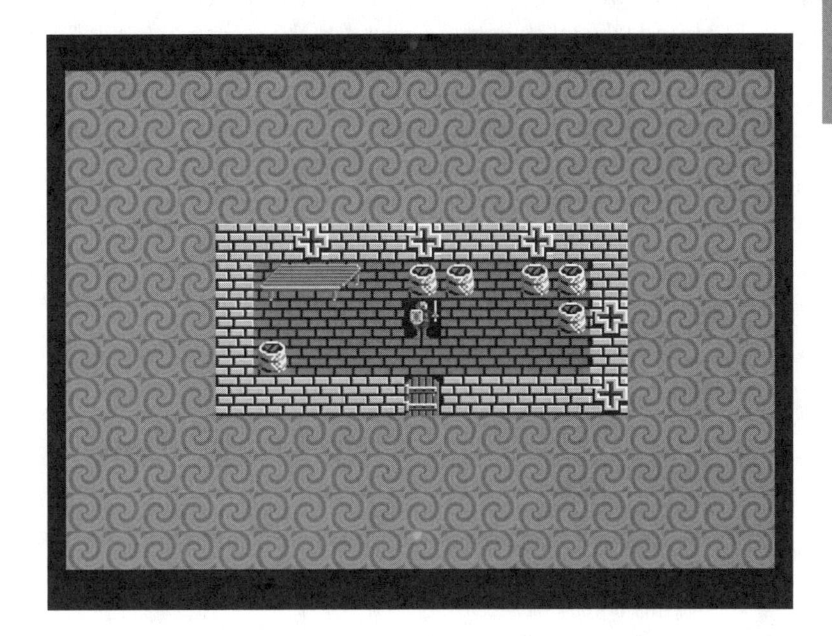

FIGURE 15.11
The inn's supply room.

There are still a few more locations to add to *The Adventures of Jasper Bookman*. However, before you do that, how about reviewing exactly what you need to do to add a location to First Town? Then, you'll be able to modify the town any way you like. (Modify only a copy of the JBookman project, though, because you're still not finished with the original.) Here are the steps you must perform:

1. Add a `case` clause for the new location to the `RespondToPlayerLocation()` method.
2. In the FirstTown.h file, add a function prototype for the new location's "Handle" function.
3. In the FirstTown.cpp file, add the "Handle" function's implementation.
4. Also in FirstTown.cpp, define constants for the sectors that trigger events.
5. Again in FirstTown.cpp, add a case clause for the new location. This case clause must set the player's new location, load the appropriate map, set the current map ID, switch to the appropriate tile set, and reset the animation.
6. Add the appropriate map files to the Maps directory.

Keeping these steps in mind, perform the following to add the final location events to First Town. Each of these steps is in the same order as the previous numbered list:

1. Add the following `case` clauses to the `RespondToPlayerLocation()` method in the MyEngine.cpp file. If you don't want to type, you can copy the lines from the Code16.txt file in the Chapter15 directory of this book's CD-ROM.

```
case FIRSTTOWNHOUSE02ROOM01:
    HandleFirstTownHouse02Room01();
    break;
case FIRSTTOWNARMORER:
    HandleFirstTownArmorer();
    break;
case FIRSTTOWNPOTIONS:
    HandleFirstTownPotions();
    break;
```

2. Add the following function prototypes to FirstTown.h:

```
void HandleFirstTownHouse02Room01();
void HandleFirstTownArmorer();
void HandleFirstTownPotions();
```

3. Add the following method implementations to FirstTown.cpp. If you don't want to type, you can copy the lines from the Code17.txt file in the Chapter15 directory of this book's CD-ROM.

```
///////////////////////////////////////////////////////////
// HandleFirstTownHouse02Room01()
///////////////////////////////////////////////////////////
void HandleFirstTownHouse02Room01()
{
    switch (g_Engine.GetPlayer()->GetSector())
    {
    case HOUSE02FRONTDOOR:
        g_Engine.GetPlayer()->SetSector(HOUSE02FRONTDOOR - 1);
        g_Engine.OpenMapFiles("FirstTown.map");
        g_Engine.SetCurrentMap(FIRSTTOWN);
        g_Engine.GetCDirect3DObj()->SetCurrentTileSurface
            (g_Engine.GetCDirect3DObj()->GetTownExtTileSurface());
        g_Engine.ResetAnimation();
        break;
    }
}

///////////////////////////////////////////////////////////
// HandleFirstTownArmorer()
///////////////////////////////////////////////////////////
void HandleFirstTownArmorer()
```

```
{
    switch (g_Engine.GetPlayer()->GetSector())
    {
    case ARMORERFRONTDOOR:
        g_Engine.GetPlayer()->SetSector(ARMORERFRONTDOOR - 1);
        g_Engine.OpenMapFiles("FirstTown.map");
        g_Engine.SetCurrentMap(FIRSTTOWN);
        g_Engine.GetCDirect3DObj()->SetCurrentTileSurface
            (g_Engine.GetCDirect3DObj()->GetTownExtTileSurface());
        g_Engine.ResetAnimation();
        break;
    }
}

///////////////////////////////////////////////////////////
// HandleFirstTownPotions()
///////////////////////////////////////////////////////////
void HandleFirstTownPotions()
{
    switch (g_Engine.GetPlayer()->GetSector())
    {
    case POTIONSFRONTDOOR:
        g_Engine.GetPlayer()->SetSector(POTIONSFRONTDOOR - 1);
        g_Engine.OpenMapFiles("FirstTown.map");
        g_Engine.SetCurrentMap(FIRSTTOWN);
        g_Engine.GetCDirect3DObj()->SetCurrentTileSurface
            (g_Engine.GetCDirect3DObj()->GetTownExtTileSurface());
        g_Engine.ResetAnimation();
        break;
    }
}
```

4. Add the following constants to FirstTown.cpp:

```
const HOUSE02FRONTDOOR = 868;
const ARMORERFRONTDOOR = 1160;
const POTIONSFRONTDOOR = 1412;
```

5. Add the following case clauses to the `HandleFirstTown()` method. If you don't want to type, you can copy the lines from the Code18.txt file in the Chapter15 directory of this book's CD-ROM.

```
case HOUSE02FRONTDOOR:
    g_Engine.GetPlayer()->SetSector(HOUSE02FRONTDOOR + 1);
    g_Engine.OpenMapFiles("FirstTownHouse02Room01.map");
    g_Engine.SetCurrentMap(FIRSTTOWNHOUSE02ROOM01);
    g_Engine.GetCDirect3DObj()->SetCurrentTileSurface
        (g_Engine.GetCDirect3DObj()->GetTownIntTileSurface());
    g_Engine.ResetAnimation();
    break;
```

```
case ARMORERFRONTDOOR:
    g_Engine.GetPlayer()->SetSector(ARMORERFRONTDOOR + 1);
    g_Engine.OpenMapFiles("FirstTownArmorer.map");
    g_Engine.SetCurrentMap(FIRSTTOWNARMORER);
    g_Engine.GetCDirect3DObj()->SetCurrentTileSurface
        (g_Engine.GetCDirect3DObj()->GetTownIntTileSurface());
    g_Engine.ResetAnimation();
    break;
case POTIONSFRONTDOOR:
    g_Engine.GetPlayer()->SetSector(POTIONSFRONTDOOR + 1);
    g_Engine.OpenMapFiles("FirstTownPotions.map");
    g_Engine.SetCurrentMap(FIRSTTOWNPOTIONS);
    g_Engine.GetCDirect3DObj()->SetCurrentTileSurface
        (g_Engine.GetCDirect3DObj()->GetTownIntTileSurface());
    g_Engine.ResetAnimation();
    break;
```

6. Copy the following map files from this book's Chapter15 directory to the Maps folder in your main JBookman directory:

```
FirstTownHouse02Room01.map
FirstTownHouse02Room01.map.dor
FirstTownHouse02Room01.map.item
FirstTownHouse02Room01.map.peo
FirstTownArmorer.map
FirstTownArmorer.map.dor
FirstTownArmorer.map.item
FirstTownArmorer.map.peo
FirstTownPotions.map
FirstTownPotions.map.dor
FirstTownPotions.map.item
FirstTownPotions.map.peo
```

That finishes up the six steps you need to perform to add new locations to the First Town area of the game (or to any other areas, for that matter). You can now compile and run the program. When the game starts up, you should be able to explore any of the buildings in the town. For example, Figure 15.12 shows the potions vender, and Figure 15.13 shows the inside of the tiny house just south of the inn. Notice how the inside of the house seems so much smaller than the outside. That's a clue to a hidden secret you'll discover in the next chapter.

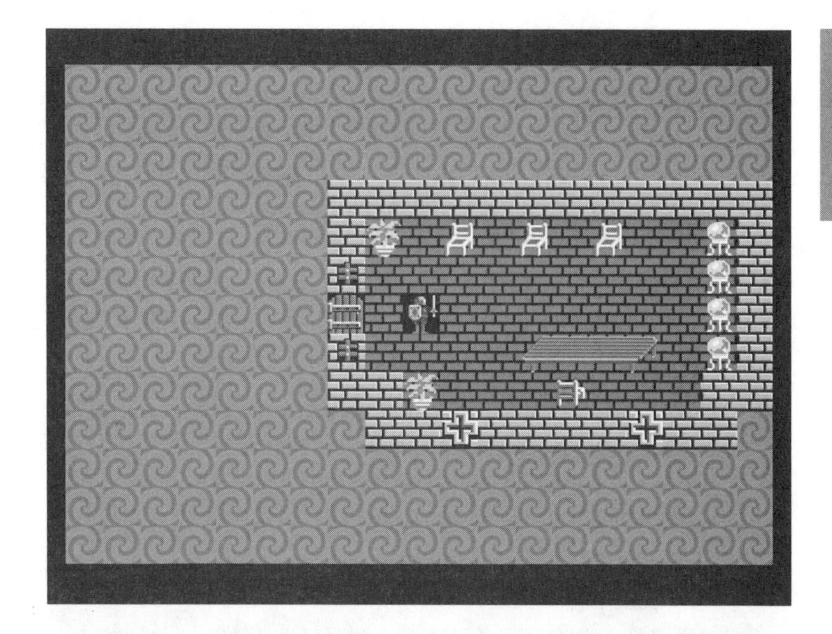

FIGURE 15.12

First Town's potion vender.

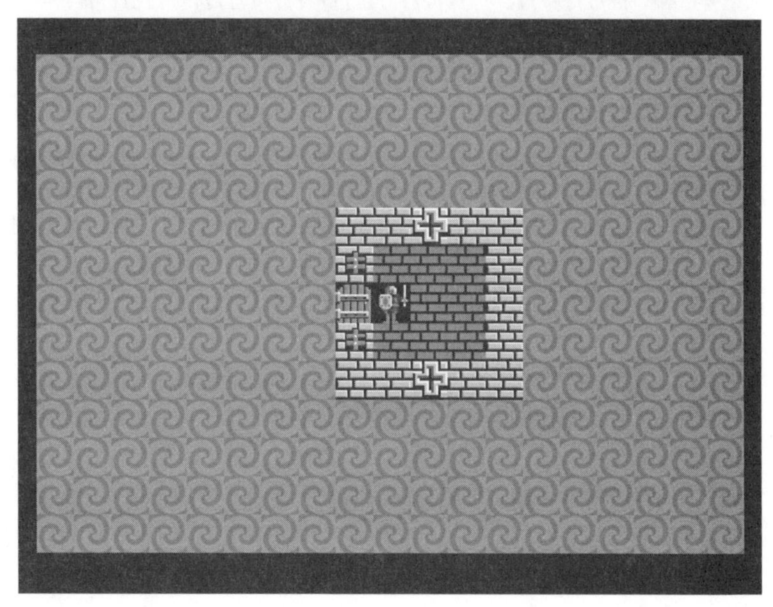

FIGURE 15.13

A mysterious, empty house.

Adding a New Major Location

I tend to think of locations in *The Adventures of Jasper Bookman* as coming in two varieties: major locations and minor locations. A major location is a town or a wilderness area, a place that's large enough to hold many other smaller locations. It's these smaller locations that I think of being minor locations.

So far in this game, you've seen only one major location: First Town. Every other location—such as the houses and the rooms in the houses—has been a minor location. The game would be pretty boring if there were only one major location. That's why you're now going to see how to add new major locations to the game.

This task isn't all that different from adding minor locations. The biggest difference is that you need to (or at least should, in order to keep everything organized) supply a separate header and implementation file for each major location. For example, the First Town location has the files FirstTown.h and FirstTown.cpp.

1. Add a new header file to the program named Ganjek.h. Place the following source code into the file:

```
//////////////////////////////////////////////////////////
//// Ganjek.h
//////////////////////////////////////////////////////////

void HandleGanjek();
```

2. Add a new implementation file to the program named Ganjek.cpp. Place the following source code into the file. If you don't want to type, you can copy the lines from the Code19.txt file in the Chapter15 directory of this book's CD-ROM.

```
//////////////////////////////////////////////////////////
// Ganjek.cpp
//////////////////////////////////////////////////////////

#include <d3d8.h>
#include "constants.h"
#include "MyEngine.h"
#include "Ganjek.h"

extern CMyEngine g_Engine;

const FIRSTTOWNENTRANCE = 860;
```

```
//////////////////////////////////////////////////////
// HandleGanjek()
//////////////////////////////////////////////////////
void HandleGanjek()
{
    switch (g_Engine.GetPlayer()->GetSector())
    {
    case FIRSTTOWNENTRANCE:
        g_Engine.GetPlayer()->SetSector(1701);
        g_Engine.OpenMapFiles("FirstTown.map");
        g_Engine.SetCurrentMap(FIRSTTOWN);
        g_Engine.GetCDirect3DObj()->SetCurrentTileSurface
            (g_Engine.GetCDirect3DObj()->GetTownExtTileSurface());
        g_Engine.ResetAnimation();
        break;
    }
}
```

3. Add the following include directive to MyEngine.h, right after the line `#include "FirstTown.h"` that's already there:

```
#include "Ganjek.h"
```

4. Add the following `case` clause to the `RespondToPlayerLocation()` method in the MyEngine.cpp file:

```
case GANJEKWILDS:
    HandleGanjek();
    break;
```

5. Add the following `case` clause to the `HandleFirstTown()` method in the FirstTown.cpp file. If you don't want to type, you can copy the lines from the Code20.txt file in the Chapter15 directory of this book's CD-ROM.

```
case GANJEKENTRANCE:
    g_Engine.GetPlayer()->SetSector(902);
    g_Engine.OpenMapFiles("GanjekWilds.map");
    g_Engine.SetCurrentMap(GANJEKWILDS);
    g_Engine.GetCDirect3DObj()->SetCurrentTileSurface
        (g_Engine.GetCDirect3DObj()->GetWildernessTileSurface());
    g_Engine.ResetAnimation();
    break;
```

6. Add the following constant to FirstTown.cpp, right after the line `const POTIONS-FRONTDOOR = 1412` that's already there:

```
const GANJEKENTRANCE = 1743;
```

7. Add the following method to the Direct3D.cpp file. If you don't want to type, you can copy the lines from the Code21.txt file in the Chapter15 directory of this book's CD-ROM.

```
///////////////////////////////////////////////////////////
// GetWildernessIntTileSurface()
///////////////////////////////////////////////////////////
IDirect3DSurface8* CDirect3D::GetWildernessTileSurface()
{
    return m_pWildernessTileSurface;
}
```

8. Add the following constants to the Constants.h file, right after the line `const STOVE_INT = 36` that's already there. If you don't want to type, you can copy the lines from the Code22.txt file in the Chapter15 directory of this book's CD-ROM.

```
// Impassable objects in the Wilderness.
const MOUNTAIN01_WLD = 8;
const MOUNTAIN02_WLD = 9;
const MOUNTAIN03_WLD = 10;
const MOUNTAIN04_WLD = 11;
const WATER_WLD = 32;
```

9. In the Engine.cpp file, add the following case clause to the `PlayerBlocked()` method. If you don't want to type, you can copy the lines from the Code23.txt file in the Chapter15 directory of this book's CD-ROM.

```
case WILDERNESS:
    if (item == MOUNTAIN01_WLD || item == MOUNTAIN02_WLD
        || item == MOUNTAIN03_WLD || item == MOUNTAIN04_WLD
        || item == WATER_WLD || item == WATER_WLD + 1)
    blocked = TRUE;
    break;
```

10. Copy the following map files from this book's Chapter15 directory to the Maps folder in your main JBookman directory:

```
GanjekWilds.map
GanjekWilds.map.dor
GanjekWilds.map.item
GanjekWilds.map.peo
```

Go ahead now and compile and run the program. When the program starts, move the player character until he's standing in the town's main gate, as shown in Figure 15.14.

Now take a single step forward and *presto!*, you're in a new location, this one named the Ganjek Wilds. Figure 15.15 shows this new location.

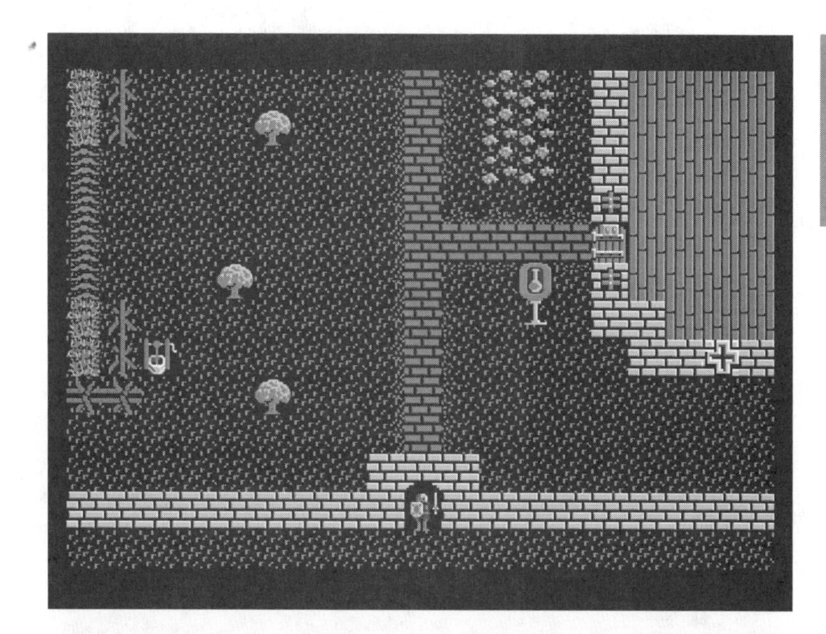

FIGURE 15.14

The way out of town.

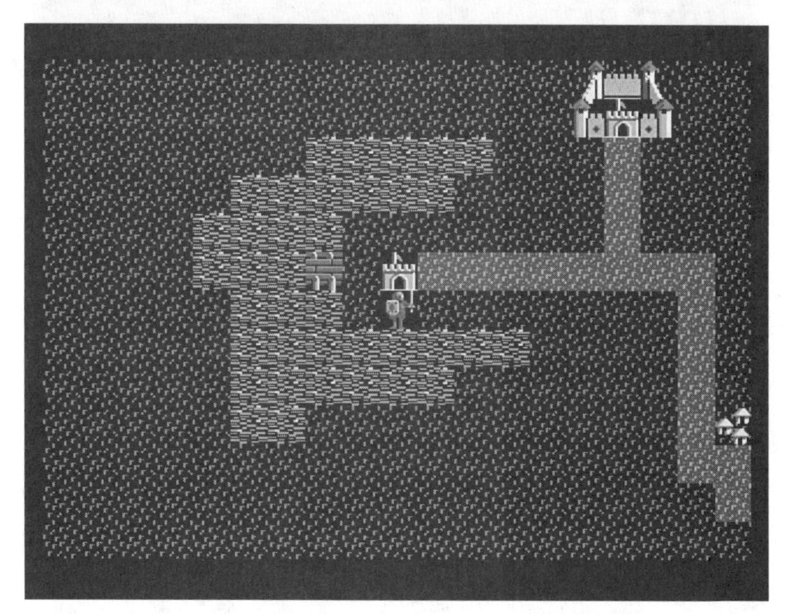

FIGURE 15.15

Entering the Ganjek Wilds.

New Members of the `CEngine` Class

In this chapter, you didn't do as much work on the game engine as you have in some other chapters. This is because much of the game engine's functionality is complete. You did, however, add two new methods. Table 15.1 describes these new class members.

TABLE 15.1 New `CEngine` Members

Member	*Type*	*Description*
ResetAnimation()	Public method	Ensures that the animation sequence remains properly synchronized after the game loads a new area map.
RespondToPlayerLocation()	Pure virtual method	This method, which must be implemented in any class that derives from CEngine, continually checks the player's current location for game-event triggers.

Summary

Being able to handle game events is the one thing more than any other that makes *The Adventures of Jasper Bookman* a game. After all, the entire storyline, including travel, battles, exploring, and more, relies on the triggering of game events.

In this chapter, you learned to manage just one type of game event, the movement from one map to another, whether that be between the rooms of a house or between a town and the wilderness. In the next chapter, you'll discover how to customize the game engine even more, to install your game's story elements.

Q&A

Q. We sure added tons of source code in order to get a very small part of the game going. How much more source code will it take to make *Jasper Bookman*'s game world as big as those in commercial RPGs?

A. Not to discourage you, but to reach that goal will require more source code than you've probably ever seen in your life! Now you know why RPG programs tend to be so huge and take so long for even the biggest companies to program. The game engine is the smallest part of the program. Creating a solid story in a believable world is what takes the most time and effort. This book can only give you a start in that direction.

Q. How can I make one area of the game look significantly different from another?

A. Currently, the JBookman project's game engine allows you to use four types of tile files: town exterior, town interior, dungeon, and wilderness. However, there's no reason you can't use as many tile files of these four basic types as you want. You could, for example, have three different sets of town exterior tiles, switching between them as needed. You just have to be sure that the individual tiles in each file are located in the same place in the file. If you wanted a different color grass in a town, for example, just create a new tile file from the original file and replace the grass tile with the new one. The more tiles you replace with different ones, the more the town will look different.

Q. In one version of this chapter's JBookman project, the player character could walk through walls. Now, I know that that was actually something that had to be fixed, but what if I want the character to be able to walk through walls?

A. In the next chapter, you'll learn to extend your `MyEngine` class to provide specialized behavior like walking through walls and searching for hidden items.

Workshop

The workshop includes quiz questions to help gauge your grasp of the material. Even if you feel that you totally understand the concepts presented here, you should work through the quiz anyway. The last section is an exercise or two that you might work through to help reinforce your learning.

1. Why did it become necessary to create the `CMyEngine` class?
2. How does the `CEngine` class request game-event handling from your `CMyEngine` class?
3. How does the JBookman program know when to respond to an event? That is, what actually triggers a game event?
4. Why is it a good idea to provide separate header and source-code files for each major location in the game?

Exercises

1. Make a copy of the JBookman project and modify it that when the player character steps on the sector immediately south of the fountain (see Figure 15.16), he is magically transported to the sector right in front of the inn's door (see Figure 15.17). Hint: The required sector numbers are 943 and 320.

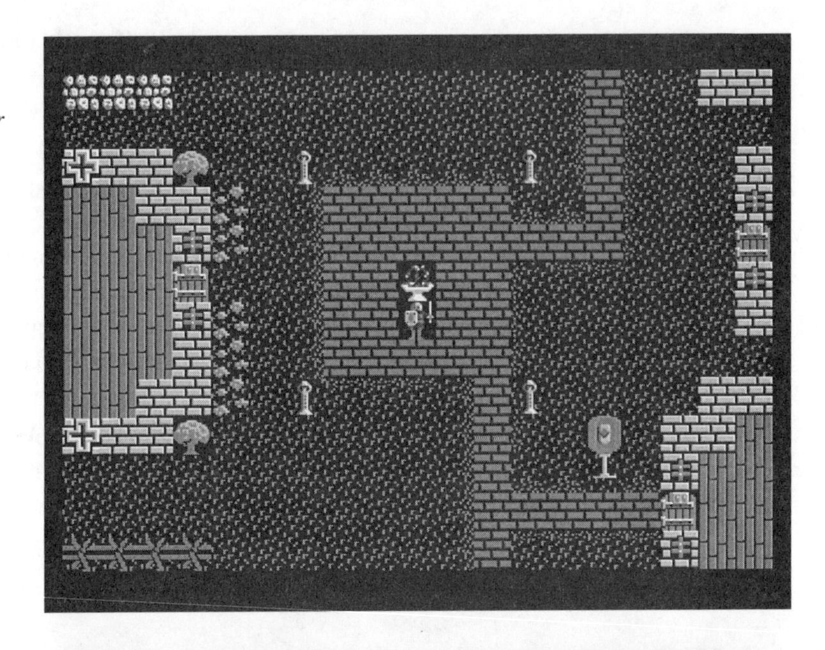

FIGURE 15.16

Here, the player is standing on the trigger sector.

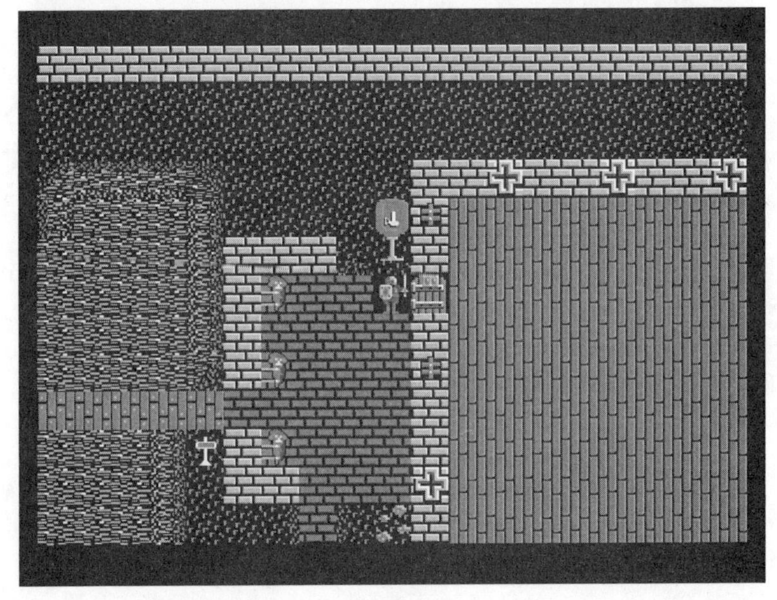

FIGURE 15.17

Here, the player is standing on the destination sector.

2. Next, modify the program so that when the player character steps on the sector immediately north of the fountain, he is magically transported into the inn's lobby. Hint: The required sector numbers are 859 and 322.

Answers for Day 15

Quiz

1. Why did it become necessary to create the `CMyEngine` class?

   Because you needed a way to modify the game engine to handle the game's many events. However, in order to avoid actually changing the working `CEngine` class, you created a new class that derived from `CEngine`. You can add all the code you want to `CMyEngine` without fear of breaking the `CEngine` class.

2. How does the `CEngine` class request game-event handling from your `CMyEngine` class?

   Through the `RespondToPlayerLocation()` pure virtual method. Any class that derives from `CEngine` must implement the `RespondToPlayerLocation()` method. In the next chapter, you'll learn other ways to communicate between the classes.

3. How does the JBookman program know when to respond to an event? That is, what actually triggers a game event?

   For the most part, game events are associated with sectors in the current map. When the player moves, the program checks whether the target sector is associated with an event. If so, the program performs the required action.

4. Why is it a good idea to provide separate header and source-code files for each major location in the game?

   Because doing so helps keep the source code from becoming too unwieldy. Each major location in the game is likely to require a lot of source code to implement its many game events. If all that code were squished into a single file, you'd really have a mess on your hands!

Exercises

1. Make a copy of the JBookman project and modify it that when the player character steps on the sector immediately south of the fountain (see Figure 15.16), he is magically transported to the sector right in front of the inn's door (see Figure 15.17). Hint: The required sector numbers are 943 and 944.

   This is very easy to accomplish. All you have to do is add the following `case` clause to the `HandleFirstTown()` method's `switch` statement:

```
case 943:
    g_Engine.GetPlayer()->SetSector(320);
    break;
```

Because you're not moving the player character to another map, you don't need to worry about loading map files and resetting the animation.

2. Next, modify the program so that when the player character steps on the sector immediately north of the fountain, he is magically transported into the inn's lobby. Hint: The required sector numbers are 859 and 322.

   This is a little more complicated, but still pretty easy. Just add the following `case` clause to the `HandleFirstTown()` method's `switch` statement:

```
case 859:
    g_Engine.GetPlayer()->SetSector(322);
    g_Engine.OpenMapFiles("FirstTownInnRoom01.map");
    g_Engine.SetCurrentMap(FIRSTTOWNINNROOM01);
    g_Engine.GetCDirect3DObj()->SetCurrentTileSurface
        (g_Engine.GetCDirect3DObj()->GetTownIntTileSurface());
    g_Engine.ResetAnimation();
    break;
```

WEEK 3

DAY 16

Manipulating Game Objects

In the previous chapter, you learned to handle game events that move the player from one location in the game to another. There are other types of events that the game must handle, as well. For example, what should the program do when the player attempts to open a treasure chest or to go through a locked door? Moreover, while many of these types of events can be handled by the main game engine, you will often need to customize the event handling to handle special occurrences unique to your particular game. In this day, you discover how to handle such game events, both the standard and custom types. Specifically, in this day you learn how to:

- Display text on the screen
- Manage both locked, unlocked, and secret doors
- Enable the player to open containers and retrieve their contents

Displaying Text

When you start programming game events, a problem arises. Often, you need to display text that describes the outcome of an event. For example, if the player opens a treasure chest, you have to tell him what he found. Similarly, if the player tries to go through a locked door, you have to tell him he needs a key.

Displaying text in a Direct3D program isn't much more difficult than displaying text in any other Windows program. However, the process is a little different. Also, while you can just throw a bunch of text anywhere on the screen, it's a better idea to have some sort of text box in which to display your messages to the player.

To display a line of text on the screen, you must perform the following steps:

1. Create an `ID3DXFont` object.
2. Calculate the size of a rectangle that can hold the text.
3. Call the Direct3D device's `BeginScene()` method.
4. Draw the text.
5. Call the Direct3D device's `EndScene()` method.
6. Release the `ID3DXFont` object.

Creating a Font Object

In order to display text on the screen, you need to call the `DrawText()` method of an `ID3DXFont` object. Obviously, before you can call that method, you need to create the object. Accomplishing this task requires a few steps. First, you need to declare a pointer to an `ID3DXFont` object:

```
LPD3DXFONT pFont = NULL;
```

Next, you need to define a `LOGFONT` structure, which is the structure the Windows API uses to describe a font. Here's how you would define the structure for an Arial font of height 16:

```
LOGFONT LogFont = {16, 0, 0, 0, FW_NORMAL, false, false, false,
    DEFAULT_CHARSET, OUT_TT_PRECIS, CLIP_DEFAULT_PRECIS,
    PROOF_QUALITY, DEFAULT_PITCH, "Arial"};
```

If you've never worked with fonts before, this is pretty scary stuff. Windows declares the `LOGFONT` structure like this:

```
typedef struct tagLOGFONT {
  LONG lfHeight;
  LONG lfWidth;
  LONG lfEscapement;
```

```
  LONG lfOrientation;
  LONG lfWeight;
  BYTE lfItalic;
  BYTE lfUnderline;
  BYTE lfStrikeOut;
  BYTE lfCharSet;
  BYTE lfOutPrecision;
  BYTE lfClipPrecision;
  BYTE lfQuality;
  BYTE lfPitchAndFamily;
  TCHAR lfFaceName[LF_FACESIZE];
} LOGFONT, *PLOGFONT;
```


Yep, this is some serious structure. Luckily, you really don't need to know what all of its members mean. You can just use the `LOGFONT` definition I gave you in the example for an Arial font. All you need to know is that the first member of the structure sets the height of the font and the last member is the font's name. So, if you wanted to create a Times Roman font with a height of 24, you'd write this:

```
LOGFONT LogFont = {24, 0, 0, 0, FW_NORMAL, false, false, false,
    DEFAULT_CHARSET,OUT_TT_PRECIS, CLIP_DEFAULT_PRECIS,
    PROOF_QUALITY, DEFAULT_PITCH, "Times New Roman"};
```

If you want to know more about the `LOGFONT` structure, go ahead and look it up in your Windows programming documentation.

Note

> When you create fonts, keep in mind that the fonts you have on your machine may be different from the fonts the player has on her machine. If you request a font that doesn't exist on the user's machine, you'll end up with a default font. To be safe, you should choose fonts that are installed with Windows. These fonts include Arial, Times New Roman, and Courier New, to name just a few

Once you have the `LOGFONT` structure ready to go, you create your `ID3DXFont` object by calling the Direct3D utility function `D3DXCreateFontIndirect()`, which Direct3D defines like this:

```
HRESULT D3DXCreateFontIndirect(
  LPDIRECT3DDEVICE8 pDevice,
  CONST LOGFONT* pLogFont,
  LPD3DXFONT* ppFont
);
```

Here's how the function's three arguments are used:

- `pDevice`—A pointer to the Direct3D device.
- `pLogFont`—A pointer to the `LOGFONT` structure that contains information about the requested font.
- `ppFont`—The address of the pointer into which the function will place the pointer to the `ID3DXFont` object.

The actual call looks something like this:

```
D3DXCreateFontIndirect(pDirect3DDevice, &LogFont, &pFont);
```

Calculating the Text Rectangle

The next task is to determine the size of a rectangle that can contain the text. You do that by calling the `ID3DXFont` object's `Drawtext()` method with the `DT_CALCRECT` flag. First, however, you need to define a `RECT` structure that will hold the results of the calculation:

```
RECT r;
r.left = 0;
r.top = 0;
r.right = 0;
r.bottom = 0;
```

With the `RECT` structure defined, you can call `DrawText()`. Direct3D declares the `DrawText()` method like this:

```
INT DrawText(
  LPCSTR pString,
  INT Count,
  LPRECT pRect,
  DWORD Format,
  D3DCOLOR Color
);
```

Here's what the arguments are used for:

- `pString`—The address of the string to display.
- `Count`—The number of characters to display. For a null-terminated string, just use –1 for this argument.
- `pRect`—A pointer to the `RECT` structure into which the method will place the results of its calculations.
- `Format`—One or more format flags that describe how to display the text. You use `DT_CALCRECT` to specify that you want to calculate the text rectangle.
- `Color`—The color with which to display the text.

To calculate the text rectangle, the actual call to `DrawText()` looks something like this:

```
pFont->DrawText(pstrMsg, -1, &r, DT_CALCRECT, 0xff000000);
```

After the call to `DrawText()`, the `RECT` structure will contain the size of the rectangle needed to display the text. The left and top members of the `RECT` structure will be the same as you originally set them. However, the right and bottom members will have been adjusted to the appropriate sizes to contain the text. You can get the width and height of this rectangle by using the following calculations:


```
int iWidth = r.right - r.left;
int iHeight = r.bottom - r.top;
```

Next, you need to use this information to position the rectangle exactly on the screen where you want the text to appear. For example, say that you want to display the text in the center of a 640×480 screen. You'd use calculations similar to this:

```
r.left = (640 - iWidth) / 2;
r.right = r.left + iWidth;
r.top = (480 - iHeight) / 2;
r.bottom = r.top + iHeight;
```

Drawing the Text

Finally, you're ready to actually draw the text on the screen. You do this with another call to `DrawText()`, this time with a different set of flags. There are a ton of these flags, but Table 16.1 shows the most useful to you at this point.

TABLE 16.1 Most Useful `DrawText()` Flags

Flag	*Description*
DT_BOTTOM	Formats the text to the bottom of the rectangle. Must be combined with DT_SINGLELINE.
DT_CALCRECT	Calculates the width and height of the text rectangle.
DT_CENTER	Horizontally centers the text in the rectangle.
DT_LEFT	Formats text to the left in the rectangle.
DT_RIGHT	Formats text to the right in the rectangle.
DT_SINGLELINE	Formats text on a single line.
DT_TOP	Formats single-line text to the top of the rectangle.
DT_VCENTER	Vertically centers a single line of text in the rectangle.

This time the call to `DrawText()` must be sandwiched between calls to `BeginScene()` and `EndScene()`, like this:

```
pDirect3DDevice()->BeginScene();
pFont->DrawText("This is a test", -1, &r, DT_CENTER, 0xff000000);
pDirect3DDevice()->EndScene();
```

Last, but not least, you must release the `ID3DXFont` object:

```
pFont->Release();
```

Adding Text Drawing to the JBookman Project

Okay, that's enough yakking about fonts and text. It's time to put your new knowledge to work, as you add the ability to display text to *The Adventures of Jasper Bookman*. This task will involve not only displaying text, but also displaying a texture that contains the image of the text box in which your messages to the player will appear. Perform the following steps to complete this part of the project:

1. Add the following lines to the Engine.h file, right after the `#include` statements. If you don't want to type this source code, you can copy it from the Code01.txt file in the Chapter16 directory of this book's CD-ROM.

   ```
   // Define a custom vertex type and structure.
   #define D3D8T_CUSTOMVERTEX (D3DFVF_XYZRHW|D3DFVF_TEX1)
   struct vertex
   {
       float x, y, z, rhw;
       float tu,tv;
   };
   ```

   These lines define the custom vertex type and the vertex structure the program will use when displaying a texture.

2. Add the following lines to the class's protected data members, right after the line `BOOL m_bFastestAnimationTilesUpdated` that's already there:

   ```
   BOOL m_bShowingPlaque;
   char m_pstrPlaqueMsg[1024];
   ```

   These variables are a flag that indicates whether the text box is currently displayed on the screen and a string that contains the message to display in the text box.

3. Add the following lines to the class's public method declarations, right after the line `void ResetAnimation()` that's already there. If you don't want to type this source code, you can copy it from the Code02.txt file in the Chapter16 directory of this book's CD-ROM.

```
BOOL IsShowingPlaque();
void TurnOnPlaque(char* msg);
void TurnOffPlaque();
void PaintPlaque();
```

4. In the Engine.cpp file, add the following line to the end of the class's constructor, right after the line `m_bFastestAnimationTilesUpdated = FALSE` that's already there:

```
m_bShowingPlaque = FALSE;
```


5. In the Engine.cpp file, add the following `case` clause to the `switch` statement in the `HandleKeys()` method. If you don't want to type this source code, you can copy it from the Code03.txt file in the Chapter16 directory of this book's CD-ROM.

```
case VK_SPACE:
    if (IsShowingPlaque())
        TurnOffPlaque();
    else
        TurnOnPlaque("This is a test\nof multi-line text\ndisplay.");
    break;
```

These lines display or hide the text box in response to the keyboard's spacebar.

6. Add the following lines to the `PaintBackBuffer()` method, right after the line `PaintPlayer(m_Direct3D.GetBackBuffer())` that's already there:

```
if (m_bShowingPlaque)
    PaintPlaque();
```

These lines cause the program to draw the text box whenever the `m_bShowingPlaque` flag is `TRUE`.

7. Add the following methods to the end of the Engine.cpp file. If you don't want to type this source code, you can copy it from the Code04.txt file in the Chapter16 directory of this book's CD-ROM.

```
//////////////////////////////////////////////////////
// IsShowingPlaque()
//////////////////////////////////////////////////////
BOOL CEngine::IsShowingPlaque()
{
    return m_bShowingPlaque;
}

//////////////////////////////////////////////////////
// PaintPlaque()
//////////////////////////////////////////////////////
```

```
void CEngine::PaintPlaque()
{
    unsigned char *vb_vertices;
    IDirect3DVertexBuffer8* pSquare;
    vertex m_square_vertices[] =
    {
      {192.0f, 340.0f, 0.0f, 1.0f, 0.0f, 1.0f }, /* Lower left corner */
      {192.0f, 152.0f, 0.0f, 1.0f, 0.0f, 0.0f }, /* Upper left corner */
      {448.0f, 340.0f, 0.0f, 1.0f, 1.0f, 1.0f }, /* Lower right corner*/
      {448.0f, 152.0f, 0.0f, 1.0f, 1.0f, 0.0f }  /* Upper right corner*/
    };

    // Create a font.
    LPD3DXFONT pFont = NULL;
    LOGFONT LogFont = {16, 0, 0, 0, FW_NORMAL, false, false, false,
        DEFAULT_CHARSET,OUT_TT_PRECIS, CLIP_DEFAULT_PRECIS,
        PROOF_QUALITY, DEFAULT_PITCH, "Times New Roman"};
    D3DXCreateFontIndirect(m_Direct3D.GetDevice(), &LogFont, &pFont);
    // Calculate the size of a rectangle that can hold the text.
    RECT r;
    r.left = 0;
    r.top = 0;
    r.right = 0;
    r.bottom = 0;
    pFont->DrawText(m_pstrPlaqueMsg, -1, &r, DT_CALCRECT, 0xff000000);
    int iWidth = r.right - r.left;
    int iHeight = r.bottom - r.top;
    r.left = (640 - iWidth) / 2;
    r.right = r.left + iWidth;
    r.top = (480 - iHeight) / 2;
    r.bottom = r.top + iHeight;

    // Create and load the vertex buffer.
    HRESULT hResult = m_Direct3D.GetDevice()->
        CreateVertexBuffer(4*sizeof(vertex),D3DUSAGE_WRITEONLY,
        D3D8T_CUSTOMVERTEX, D3DPOOL_MANAGED, &pSquare);
    hResult = pSquare->Lock(0, 0, &vb_vertices, 0);
    memcpy(vb_vertices, m_square_vertices, sizeof(m_square_vertices));
    pSquare->Unlock();
    // Display the plaque texture.
    m_Direct3D.GetDevice()->SetTextureStageState(0,
        D3DTSS_COLOROP, D3DTOP_SELECTARG1);
    m_Direct3D.GetDevice()->SetTextureStageState(0,
        D3DTSS_COLORARG1, D3DTA_TEXTURE);
```

```
    m_Direct3D.GetDevice()->SetTextureStageState(0,
        D3DTSS_ALPHAOP, D3DTOP_SELECTARG1);
    m_Direct3D.GetDevice()->SetTextureStageState(0,
        D3DTSS_ALPHAARG1, D3DTA_TEXTURE);
    m_Direct3D.GetDevice()->SetRenderState(D3DRS_SRCBLEND,
        D3DBLEND_SRCALPHA);
    m_Direct3D.GetDevice()->SetRenderState(D3DRS_DESTBLEND,
        D3DBLEND_INVSRCALPHA);
    m_Direct3D.GetDevice()->SetRenderState(D3DRS_ALPHABLENDENABLE, TRUE);
        if(SUCCEEDED(m_Direct3D.GetDevice()->BeginScene()))
    {
        m_Direct3D.GetDevice()->SetVertexShader(D3D8T_CUSTOMVERTEX);
        m_Direct3D.GetDevice()->SetStreamSource(0, pSquare, sizeof
          (vertex));
        m_Direct3D.GetDevice()->SetTexture(0, m_Direct3D.GetTexture());
        m_Direct3D.GetDevice()->DrawPrimitive(D3DPT_TRIANGLESTRIP,0,2);
        pFont->DrawText(m_pstrPlaqueMsg, -1, &r, DT_CENTER, 0xff000000);
        m_Direct3D.GetDevice()->EndScene();
    }
    pSquare->Release();
    pFont->Release();
}

//////////////////////////////////////////////////////
// TurnOnPlaque()
//////////////////////////////////////////////////////
void CEngine::TurnOnPlaque(char* msg)
{
    strcpy(m_pstrPlaqueMsg, msg);
    m_bShowingPlaque = TRUE;
}

//////////////////////////////////////////////////////
// TurnOffPlaque()
//////////////////////////////////////////////////////
void CEngine::TurnOffPlaque()
{
    m_bShowingPlaque = FALSE;
}
```

8. In the Direct3D.h file, add the following line to the class's protected data members, right after the line `IDirect3DSurface8* m_pPlayerTile` that's already there:

   ```
   IDirect3DTexture8* m_pTexture;
   ```

9. Again in the Direct3D.h file, add the following line to the class's public method declarations, right after the line `void SetCurrentTileSurface(IDirect3DSurface8* pSurface)` that's already there:

   ```
   IDirect3DTexture8* GetTexture();
   ```

10. In the Direct3D.cpp file, add the following lines to the end of the `CreateSurfaces()` method, right before the method's `return` statement. If you don't want to type this source code, you can copy it from the Code05.txt file in the Chapter16 directory of this book's CD-ROM.

```
hResult = D3DXCreateTextureFromFileEx(m_pD3DDevice, "Graphics\\Plaque.bmp",
    D3DX_DEFAULT, D3DX_DEFAULT, 1, 0, D3DFMT_A8R8G8B8,
    D3DPOOL_MANAGED, D3DX_DEFAULT, D3DX_DEFAULT, 0xFF000000,
    NULL, NULL, &m_pTexture);
if (FAILED(hResult))
{
    strcpy(m_szErrorMsg, "Error loading texture surface.");
    return hResult;
}
```

These lines create and load the texture surface for the text box's image.

11. Add the following lines to the beginning of the `CleanUp()` method:

```
if (m_pTexture)
    m_pTexture->Release();
```

12. Add the following line to the end of the class's constructor, right after the line `strcpy(m_szErrorMsg, "No Error")` that's already there:

```
m_pTexture = NULL;
```

13. Add the following method to the end of the Direct3D.cpp file. If you don't want to type this source code, you can copy it from the Code06.txt file in the Chapter16 directory of this book's CD-ROM.

```
///////////////////////////////////////////////////////
// GetTexture()
///////////////////////////////////////////////////////
IDirect3DTexture8* CDirect3D::GetTexture()
{
    return m_pTexture;
}
```

14. Copy the Plaque.bmp file from the Chapter16 directory of this book's CD-ROM to the Graphics directory of your main JBookman project directory.

You can now compile and run the application. When the game screen appears, press the spacebar on your keyboard, and you should see the screen shown in Figure 16.1. Press the spacebar again to dismiss the text box.

FIGURE 16.1
Displaying text in the JBookman project.

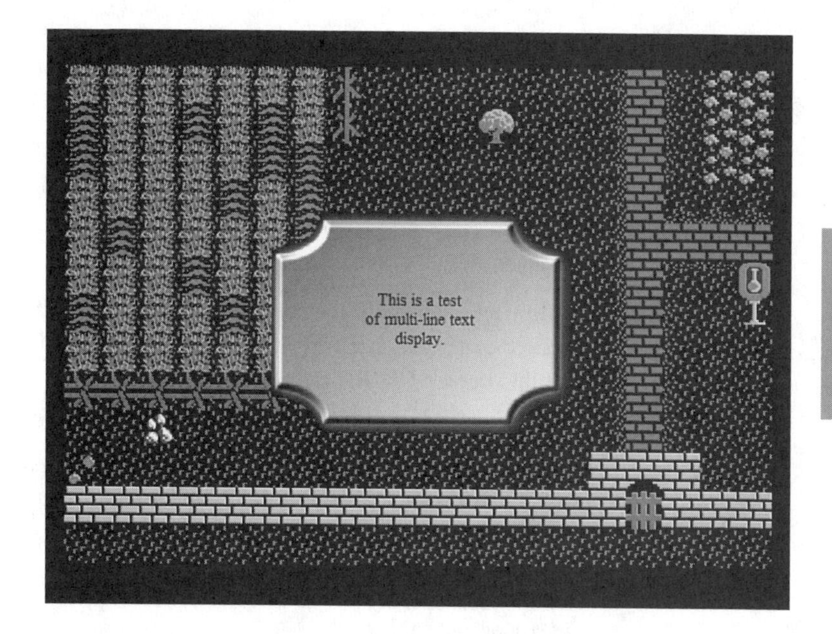

Handling Doors

The doors you'll come across in the many locations in the game have several functions. The first, of course, is to provide access to a building or other new area of the game. For example, as you've already seen, when you want to go into the town's inn, you step through the door.

Doors in *The Adventures of Jasper Bookman*, however, have a few other features you haven't seen yet. The first is that a door can be locked so that the player must have a key in her possession in order to get through the door. If the player doesn't have a key, she'll have to find one before she can get through the locked door.

Doors in the game can also be secret, invisible entrances to other areas. In this way, you can hide parts of the game for which you want the player to search. Unless the player finds the secret entrances to these types of areas, she won't be able to get into the secret areas.

Let's take it one step at a time, though. First, you'll install the source code that handles locked doors. Perform the following steps to add this functionality to the latest version of your JBookman project:

1. In the Engine.h file, add the following lines to the class's private method declarations, right after the line `void HandleFastestAnimation()` that's already there. If you don't want to type this source code, you can copy it from the Code07.txt file in the Chapter16 directory of this book's CD-ROM.

```
int CheckForAndHandleDoor(int iSector);
BOOL HandleDoor(int iSector);
BOOL IsDoor(int iSector);
CDoor* FindDoor(int iSector);
```

2. Add the following methods to the end of the Engine.cpp file. If you don't want to type this source code, you can copy it from the Code08.txt file in the Chapter16 directory of this book's CD-ROM.

```
///////////////////////////////////////////////////////
// CheckForAndHandleDoor()
///////////////////////////////////////////////////////
int CEngine::CheckForAndHandleDoor(int iSector)
{
    if (IsDoor(iSector))
    {
        BOOL bCouldOpenDoor = HandleDoor(iSector);
        if (bCouldOpenDoor)
            return DOORUNLOCKED;
        else
            return DOORLOCKED;
    }
    return NODOOR;
}

///////////////////////////////////////////////////////
// IsDoor()
///////////////////////////////////////////////////////
BOOL CEngine::IsDoor(int iSector)
{
    if (m_Sectors[iSector] == DOOR_EXT && m_byMapType == TOWNEXTERIOR)
        return TRUE;
    else if (m_Sectors[iSector] == DOOR_INT && m_byMapType == TOWNINTERIOR)
        return TRUE;
    return FALSE;
}

///////////////////////////////////////////////////////
// HandleDoor()
///////////////////////////////////////////////////////
BOOL CEngine::HandleDoor(int iSector)
{
    BOOL bCouldEnterDoor = TRUE;
    int door = 0;
    CDoor* pDoor = FindDoor(iSector);
```

```
    if (pDoor->GetLocked() == TRUE)
    {
        if (m_Player.GetKeys() > 0)
        {
            m_Player.SetKeys(m_Player.GetKeys() - 1);
            pDoor->SetLocked(FALSE);
            TurnOnPlaque("You unlock the door.");
            bCouldEnterDoor = TRUE;
        }
        else
        {
            TurnOnPlaque("You need a key.");
            bCouldEnterDoor = FALSE;
        }
    }
    return bCouldEnterDoor;
}

///////////////////////////////////////////////////////
// FindDoor()
///////////////////////////////////////////////////////
CDoor* CEngine::FindDoor(int iSector)
{
    CDoor* pDoor;
    int iDoorNum = 0;
    BOOL bDoorFound = FALSE;
    while (!bDoorFound)
    {
        pDoor = m_Doors.GetDoor(iDoorNum);
        int iDoorSector = pDoor->GetSector();
        if (iDoorSector == iSector)
            bDoorFound = TRUE;
        else
            ++iDoorNum;
    }
    return pDoor;
}
```

These are the methods that check for doors and handle the case of a locked door. You'll examine these methods in greater detail after you finish building this part of the project.

3. Replace the arrow-handling methods with the ones that follow. If you don't want to type this source code, you can copy it from the Code09.txt file in the Chapter16 directory of this book's CD-ROM.

```
///////////////////////////////////////////////////////
// HandleUpArrow()
///////////////////////////////////////////////////////
void CEngine::HandleUpArrow()
{
```

```
    if (IsShowingPlaque()) return;
    int iDoorStatus =
        CheckForAndHandleDoor(m_Player.GetSector() - MAPCOLUMNCOUNT);
    if (iDoorStatus == NODOOR || iDoorStatus == DOORUNLOCKED)
        MovePlayerUp();
}

///////////////////////////////////////////////////////
// HandleDownArrow()
///////////////////////////////////////////////////////
void CEngine::HandleDownArrow()
{
    if (IsShowingPlaque()) return;
    int iDoorStatus =
        CheckForAndHandleDoor(m_Player.GetSector() + MAPCOLUMNCOUNT);
    if (iDoorStatus == NODOOR || iDoorStatus == DOORUNLOCKED)
        MovePlayerDown();
}

///////////////////////////////////////////////////////
// HandleLeftArrow()
///////////////////////////////////////////////////////
void CEngine::HandleLeftArrow()
{
    if (IsShowingPlaque()) return;
    int iDoorStatus =
        CheckForAndHandleDoor(m_Player.GetSector() - 1);
    if (iDoorStatus == NODOOR || iDoorStatus == DOORUNLOCKED)
        MovePlayerLeft();
}

///////////////////////////////////////////////////////
// HandleRightArrow()
///////////////////////////////////////////////////////
void CEngine::HandleRightArrow()
{
    if (IsShowingPlaque()) return;
    int iDoorStatus = CheckForAndHandleDoor(m_Player.GetSector() + 1);
    if (iDoorStatus == NODOOR || iDoorStatus == DOORUNLOCKED)
        MovePlayerRight();
}
```

Every time the player moves, the program must check for a door. The additions to these methods take care of that problem by calling the `CheckForAndHandleDoor()` method.

4. Add the following lines to the end of the Constants.h file:

```
// Door statuses
const NODOOR = 0;
const DOORUNLOCKED = 1;
const DOORLOCKED = 2;
```

5. Add the following lines to the Constants.h file, right after the line `const STREETLIGHT_EXT = 52` that's already there:

```
// Misc. tile IDs for town exterior.
const DOOR_EXT = 15;
```

6. Add the following lines to the Constants.h file, right after the line `const STOVE_INT = 36` that's already there:

```
// Misc. tile IDs for town interior.
const DOOR_INT = 4;
```


You can now compile and run the application. When you do, head to the northeast and find the small house shown in Figure 16.2. When you try to step into the house, the program tells you that you unlocked the door, as shown in Figure 16.3.

When you started the game, you had one key. You've now used it to unlock the door. Step out of the house and again try to go through the door. This time you see the message shown in Figure 16.4. The door is locked again, and you don't have another key!

FIGURE 16.2
A small house with a locked door.

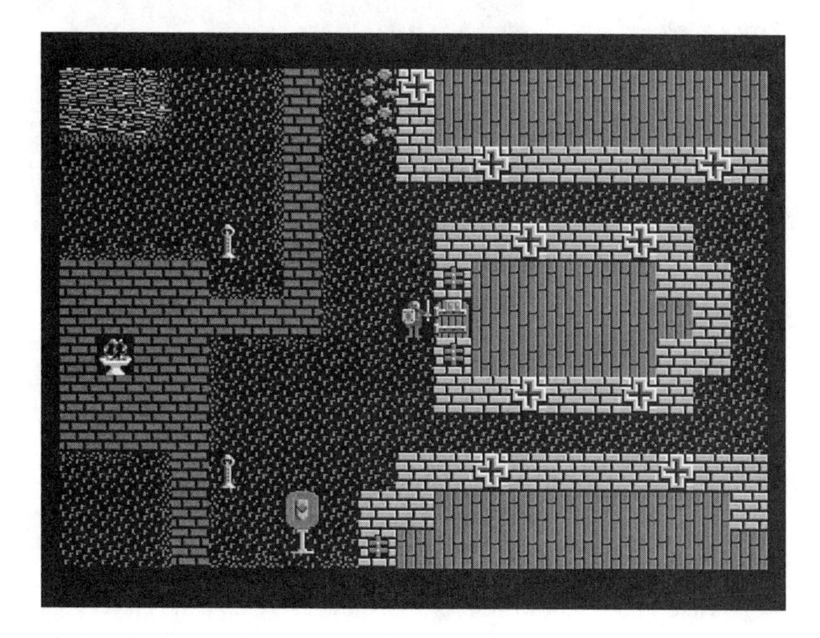

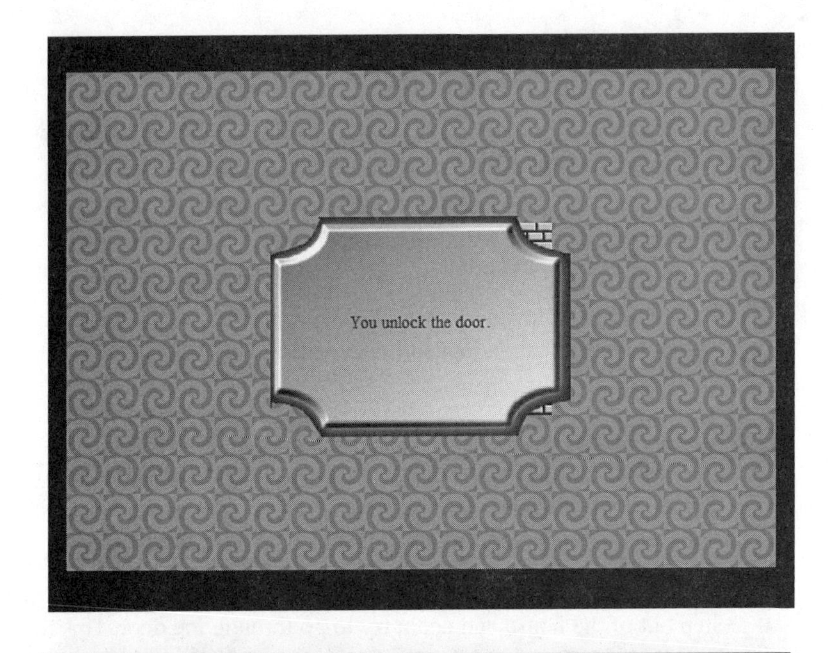

FIGURE 16.3

Unlocking the door.

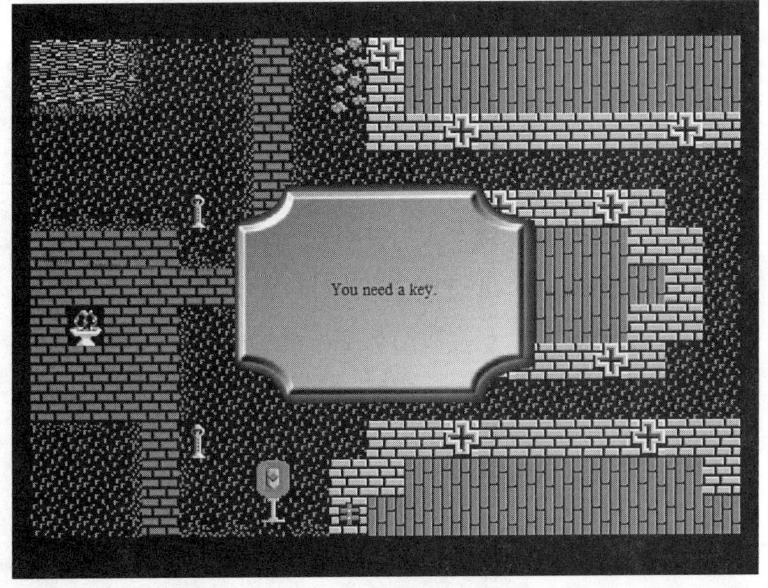

FIGURE 16.4

Trying to get through a locked door without a key.

Here's how it all works. As you know, every time the player presses an arrow key, the program calls one of the arrow-handling functions. There, the program first checks whether the text box (which I call a plaque because of how it looks) is being displayed. If the plaque is on the screen, the arrows method returns immediately:

```
if (IsShowingPlaque()) return;
```

This prevents the player from moving around the screen when the plaque is displayed.

If the plaque isn't on the screen, the method calls the `CheckForAndHandleDoor()` method:

```
int iDoorStatus =
    CheckForAndHandleDoor(m_Player.GetSector() - MAPCOLUMNCOUNT);
```


The `CheckForAndHandleDoor()` method returns one of three values: `DOORLOCKED`, `DOORUNLOCKED`, or `NODOOR`. If the method call returns one of the latter two, the player can move:

```
if (iDoorStatus == NODOOR || iDoorStatus == DOORUNLOCKED)
    MovePlayerUp();
```

Otherwise, the door is still locked (the player didn't have a key), and the move is not allowed.

All the fun really happens in the `CheckForAndHandleDoor()` method and its helper methods. First, the method checks whether the sector to which the player is moving is a door:

```
if (IsDoor(iSector))
{
    .
    .
    .
}
return NODOOR;
```

As you can see, if the target sector isn't a door, the method simply returns `NODOOR`. If there is a door in the target sector, the program calls `HandleDoor()`:

```
BOOL bCouldOpenDoor = HandleDoor(iSector);
```

The `HandleDoor()` method returns `TRUE` if the player can open the door, meaning either the door is unlocked or the door was locked and the player had a key. The program returns the appropriate value depending on what happened with `HandleDoor()`:

```
if (bCouldOpenDoor)
    return DOORUNLOCKED;
else
    return DOORLOCKED;
```

`HandleDoor()` is the method that…well…*handles* the door. First, the method calls the `FindDoor()` method, which returns a pointer to the door object that's located at the given sector:

```
CDoor* pDoor = FindDoor(iSector);
```

The method can then use the pointer to determine whether the door is locked:

```
if (pDoor->GetLocked() == TRUE)
{
    .
    .
    .
}
```

If the door is not locked, there's nothing to do, except return the `bCouldEnterDoor` flag, which the method initialized to `TRUE`. This return value indicates that the player can enter the door:

```
return bCouldEnterDoor;
```

If the door is locked, the program must determine whether the player has a key:

```
if (m_Player.GetKeys() > 0)
{
    .
    .
    .
}
```

If the player does have a key, the program removes the key from the player's inventory, unlocks the door, gives a message to the user, and sets the method's return value to `TRUE`:

```
m_Player.SetKeys(m_Player.GetKeys() - 1);
pDoor->SetLocked(FALSE);
TurnOnPlaque("You unlock the door.");
bCouldEnterDoor = TRUE;
```

If the player doesn't have a key, the program tells the player why he can't go through the door and sets the method's return value to `FALSE`:

```
else
{
    TurnOnPlaque("You need a key.");
    bCouldEnterDoor = FALSE;
}
```

The `FindDoor()` method does nothing more than search through the doors in the `CDoors` object, looking for the one located at the given sector:

```
CDoor* pDoor;
int iDoorNum = 0;
BOOL bDoorFound = FALSE;
while (!bDoorFound)
{
    pDoor = m_Doors.GetDoor(iDoorNum);
    int iDoorSector = pDoor->GetSector();
    if (iDoorSector == iSector)
```

```
            bDoorFound = TRUE;
        else
            ++iDoorNum;
    }
    return pDoor;
```

Don't think I can't hear you C++ experts giggling about the `FindDoor()` method. Yes, I know that this method can be simplified a lot. But that simplification comes at the cost of clarity, and I didn't want to leave anyone in the dark. For all you wise guys, here's a streamlined, but much harder to understand version of the `FindDoor()` method:

```
CDoor* CEngine::FindDoor(int iSector)
{
    int iDoorNum = -1;
    while (m_Doors.GetDoor(++iDoorNum)->GetSector() != iSector);
    return m_Doors.GetDoor(iDoorNum);
}
```

This version of the `FindDoor()` method illustrates how C++ code can be either a miracle or a nightmare depending upon your viewpoint or level of expertise!

Handling Containers

You probably noticed a few objects like treasure chests and barrels laying about the place in *The Adventures of Jasper Bookman*. These objects aren't there just to be pretty. The truth is that the player can search them for valuable items, including gold, keys, weapons, armor, and potions. The only problem is that the current version of the JBookman project doesn't enable the user to search these objects. To add this ability to the program, perform the following steps:

1. In the Engine.h file, add the following lines to the class's private method declarations, right after the line `CDoor* FindDoor(int iSector)` that's already there. If you don't want to type this source code, you can copy it from the Code10.txt file in the Chapter16 directory of this book's CD-ROM.

```
BOOL CheckForAndHandleContainer(int iSector);
BOOL HandleContainer(int iSector);
BOOL ContainerEmpty(CContainer* pContainer);
void RetrieveItemsFromContainer(CContainer* pContainer, char* msg);
void RetrieveGold(CContainer* pContainer, char* msg);
void RetrieveKeys(CContainer* pContainer, char* msg);
void RetrievePotion(CContainer* pContainer, char* msg);
void RetrieveWeapon(CContainer* pContainer, char* msg);
```

```
void RetrieveArmor(CContainer* pContainer, char* msg);
BOOL IsContainer(int iSector);
CContainer* FindContainer(int iSector);
void ShowInventory();
```

2. Add the following methods to the end of the Engine.cpp file. If you don't want to type this source code, you can copy it from the Code11.txt file in the Chapter16 directory of this book's CD-ROM.

```
///////////////////////////////////////////////////////
// CheckForAndHandleContainer()
///////////////////////////////////////////////////////
BOOL CEngine::CheckForAndHandleContainer(int iSector)
{
    BOOL bHandledContainer = FALSE;
    if (IsContainer(iSector))
    {
        HandleContainer(iSector);
        bHandledContainer = TRUE;
    }
    return bHandledContainer;
}

///////////////////////////////////////////////////////
// IsContainer()
///////////////////////////////////////////////////////
BOOL CEngine::IsContainer(int iSector)
{
    if (m_Sectors[iSector] == CHEST_INT && m_byMapType == TOWNINTERIOR)
        return TRUE;
    else if (m_Sectors[iSector] == BARREL_INT && m_byMapType ==
            TOWNINTERIOR)
        return TRUE;
    else if (m_Sectors[iSector] == FOOTLOCKER_INT
            && m_byMapType == TOWNINTERIOR)
        return TRUE;
    return FALSE;
}

///////////////////////////////////////////////////////
// HandleContainer()
///////////////////////////////////////////////////////
BOOL CEngine::HandleContainer(int iSector)
{
    BOOL bCouldOpenContainer = TRUE;
    CContainer* pContainer = FindContainer(iSector);
    if (pContainer->GetLocked() == TRUE)
    {
        if (m_Player.GetKeys() > 0)
        {
            m_Player.SetKeys(m_Player.GetKeys() - 1 );
```

```
            pContainer->SetLocked(FALSE);
            if (ContainerEmpty(pContainer))
                TurnOnPlaque("You unlock it. It's empty.");
            else
                RetrieveItemsFromContainer(pContainer, "You unlock it.");
            bCouldOpenContainer = TRUE;
        }
        else
        {
            TurnOnPlaque("You need a key.");
            bCouldOpenContainer = FALSE;
        }
    }
    else
    {
        if (ContainerEmpty(pContainer))
            TurnOnPlaque("It's empty.");
        else
            RetrieveItemsFromContainer(pContainer, "You open it.");
        bCouldOpenContainer = TRUE;
    }

    return bCouldOpenContainer;
}

///////////////////////////////////////////////////////
// FindContainer()
///////////////////////////////////////////////////////
CContainer* CEngine::FindContainer(int iSector)
{
    CContainer* pContainer;
    int iContainer = 0;
    BOOL bContainerFound = FALSE;
    while (!bContainerFound)
    {
        pContainer = m_Containers.GetContainer(iContainer);
        int iContainerSector = pContainer->GetSector();
        if (iContainerSector == iSector)
            bContainerFound = TRUE;
        else
            ++iContainer;
    }
    return pContainer;
}

///////////////////////////////////////////////////////
// ContainerEmpty()
///////////////////////////////////////////////////////
BOOL CEngine::ContainerEmpty(CContainer* pContainer)
{
```

```
    if (pContainer->GetArmor() == NOARMOR &&
            pContainer->GetWeapon() == NOWEAPON &&
            pContainer->GetGold() == NOGOLD &&
            pContainer->GetKeys() == NOKEYS &&
            pContainer->GetPotion() == NOPOTION)
        return TRUE;
    return FALSE;
}

///////////////////////////////////////////////////////
// RetrieveItemsFromContainer()
///////////////////////////////////////////////////////
void CEngine::RetrieveItemsFromContainer(CContainer* pContainer, char* msg)
{
    char str[1024];
    strcpy(str, msg);
    RetrieveGold(pContainer, str);
    RetrieveKeys(pContainer, str);
    RetrievePotion(pContainer, str);
    RetrieveWeapon(pContainer, str);
    RetrieveArmor(pContainer, str);
    TurnOnPlaque(str);
}

///////////////////////////////////////////////////////
// RetrieveGold()
///////////////////////////////////////////////////////
void CEngine::RetrieveGold(CContainer* pContainer, char* msg)
{
    if (pContainer->GetGold() > 0)
    {
        m_Player.SetGold(m_Player.GetGold() +
            pContainer->GetGold());
        wsprintf(&msg[strlen(msg)], "\nYou find %d gold.",
            pContainer->GetGold());
        pContainer->SetGold(0);
    }
}

///////////////////////////////////////////////////////
// RetrieveKeys()
///////////////////////////////////////////////////////
void CEngine::RetrieveKeys(CContainer* pContainer, char* msg)
{
    if (pContainer->GetKeys() > 0)
    {
        int iNumKeys = pContainer->GetKeys();
        m_Player.SetKeys(m_Player.GetKeys() + iNumKeys);
```

```
        if (iNumKeys = 1)
            wsprintf(&msg[strlen(msg)], "\nYou find %d key.", iNumKeys);
        else
            wsprintf(&msg[strlen(msg)], "\nYou find %d keys.", iNumKeys);
        pContainer->SetKeys(0);
    }
}

///////////////////////////////////////////////////////
// RetrievePotion()
///////////////////////////////////////////////////////
void CEngine::RetrievePotion(CContainer* pContainer, char* msg)
{
    if (pContainer->GetPotion() > 0)
    {
        int iNumPotions = pContainer->GetPotion();
        m_Player.SetPotions(m_Player.GetPotions() + iNumPotions);
        if (iNumPotions = 1)
            wsprintf(&msg[strlen(msg)], "\nYou find %d potion.",
            iNumPotions);
        else
            wsprintf(&msg[strlen(msg)], "\nYou find %d potions.",
            iNumPotions); pContainer->SetPotion(0);
    }
}

///////////////////////////////////////////////////////
// RetrieveWeapon()
///////////////////////////////////////////////////////
void CEngine::RetrieveWeapon(CContainer* pContainer, char* msg)
{
    int iWeaponType = pContainer->GetWeapon();
    if (iWeaponType != NOWEAPON)
    {
        wsprintf(&msg[strlen(msg)], "\nYou find a level %d weapon.",
            iWeaponType);
        if (iWeaponType > m_Player.GetWeapon())
        {
            m_Player.SetWeapon(iWeaponType);
            strcpy(&msg[strlen(msg)], "\nWEAPON EQUIPPED.");
        }
        else
            strcpy(&msg[strlen(msg)], "\nCAN'T USE WEAPON.");
       pContainer->SetWeapon(NOWEAPON);
    }
}
```

```
/////////////////////////////////////////////////////////
// RetrieveArmor()
/////////////////////////////////////////////////////////
void CEngine::RetrieveArmor(CContainer* pContainer, char* msg)
{
    int iArmorType = pContainer->GetArmor();
    if (iArmorType != NOARMOR)
    {
        wsprintf(&msg[strlen(msg)], "\nYou find level %d armor.",
            iArmorType);
        if (iArmorType > m_Player.GetArmor())
        {
            m_Player.SetArmor(iArmorType);
            strcpy(&msg[strlen(msg)], "\nARMOR EQUIPPED.");
        }
        else
            strcpy(&msg[strlen(msg)], "\nCAN'T USE ARMOR.");
        pContainer->SetArmor(NOARMOR);
    }
}
```

These are the many methods required to manage containers in the game, as well as to add to the player's inventory the items found in the containers. You'll explore these methods in greater detail soon.

3. Add the following method to the end of the Engine.cpp file. If you don't want to type this source code, you can copy it from the Code12.txt file in the Chapter16 directory of this book's CD-ROM.

```
/////////////////////////////////////////////////////////
// ShowInventory()
/////////////////////////////////////////////////////////
void CEngine::ShowInventory()
{
    char pstrMsg[256];
    wsprintf(pstrMsg, "Gold: %d\nKeys: %d\nPotions: %d\n\
Level %d Weapon\nLevel %d Armor",
        m_Player.GetGold(), m_Player.GetKeys(),
        m_Player.GetPotions(), m_Player.GetWeapon(),
        m_Player.GetArmor());
    TurnOnPlaque(pstrMsg);
}
```

This method displays the contents of the player's inventory.

4. Replace the arrow-handling methods with the ones that follow. If you don't want to type this source code, you can copy it from the Code13.txt file in the Chapter16 directory of this book's CD-ROM.

```
/////////////////////////////////////////////////////////
```

```
// HandleUpArrow()
/////////////////////////////////////////////////////////
void CEngine::HandleUpArrow()
{
    if (IsShowingPlaque()) return;
    int iTargetSector = m_Player.GetSector() - MAPCOLUMNCOUNT;
    BOOL bHandledContainer =
        CheckForAndHandleContainer(iTargetSector);
    if (bHandledContainer)
        return;
    int iDoorStatus =
        CheckForAndHandleDoor(iTargetSector);
    if (iDoorStatus == NODOOR || iDoorStatus == DOORUNLOCKED)
        MovePlayerUp();
}

/////////////////////////////////////////////////////////
// HandleDownArrow()
/////////////////////////////////////////////////////////
void CEngine::HandleDownArrow()
{
    if (IsShowingPlaque()) return;
    int iTargetSector = m_Player.GetSector() + MAPCOLUMNCOUNT;
    BOOL bHandledContainer =
        CheckForAndHandleContainer(iTargetSector);
    if (bHandledContainer)
        return;
    int iDoorStatus =
        CheckForAndHandleDoor(iTargetSector);
    if (iDoorStatus == NODOOR || iDoorStatus == DOORUNLOCKED)
        MovePlayerDown();
}

/////////////////////////////////////////////////////////
// HandleLeftArrow()
/////////////////////////////////////////////////////////
void CEngine::HandleLeftArrow()
{
    if (IsShowingPlaque()) return;
    int iTargetSector = m_Player.GetSector() - 1;
    BOOL bHandledContainer =
        CheckForAndHandleContainer(iTargetSector);
    if (bHandledContainer)
        return;
    int iDoorStatus =
        CheckForAndHandleDoor(iTargetSector);
    if (iDoorStatus == NODOOR || iDoorStatus == DOORUNLOCKED)
        MovePlayerLeft();
}

/////////////////////////////////////////////////////////
```

```
// HandleRightArrow()
/////////////////////////////////////////////////////////
void CEngine::HandleRightArrow()
{
    if (IsShowingPlaque()) return;
    int iTargetSector = m_Player.GetSector() + 1;
    BOOL bHandledContainer =
        CheckForAndHandleContainer(iTargetSector);
    if (bHandledContainer)
        return;
    int iDoorStatus =
        CheckForAndHandleDoor(iTargetSector);
    if (iDoorStatus == NODOOR || iDoorStatus == DOORUNLOCKED)
        MovePlayerRight();
}
```

These new versions check for containers each time the player moves. You'll examine these methods in greater detail soon.

5. Still in the Engine.cpp file, add the following `case` clause to the `switch` statement in the `HandleKeys()` method:

```
case 73: // I
    ShowInventory();
    break;
```

These lines display the player's inventory in the plaque when the player presses "I" on his keyboard.

6. Add the following lines to the Constants.h file, right after the line `const DOOR_INT = 4` that's already there:

```
const CHEST_INT = 18;
const BARREL_INT = 19;
const FOOTLOCKER_INT = 30;
```

7. Add the following lines to the end of the Constants.h file:

```
// Constants for container items.
const NOWEAPON = 0;
const NOARMOR = 0;
const NOFOOD = 0;
const NOGOLD = 0;
const NOKEYS = 0;
const NOPOTION = 0;
```

You can now compile and run the program. When you do, head over to the armor shop, shown in Figure 16.5. Step through the door, and walk into the treasure chest on the left. As you can see in Figure 16.6, this chest holds a bonanza of goodies. Check out the other chest, too, even though it's empty as shown in Figure 16.7.

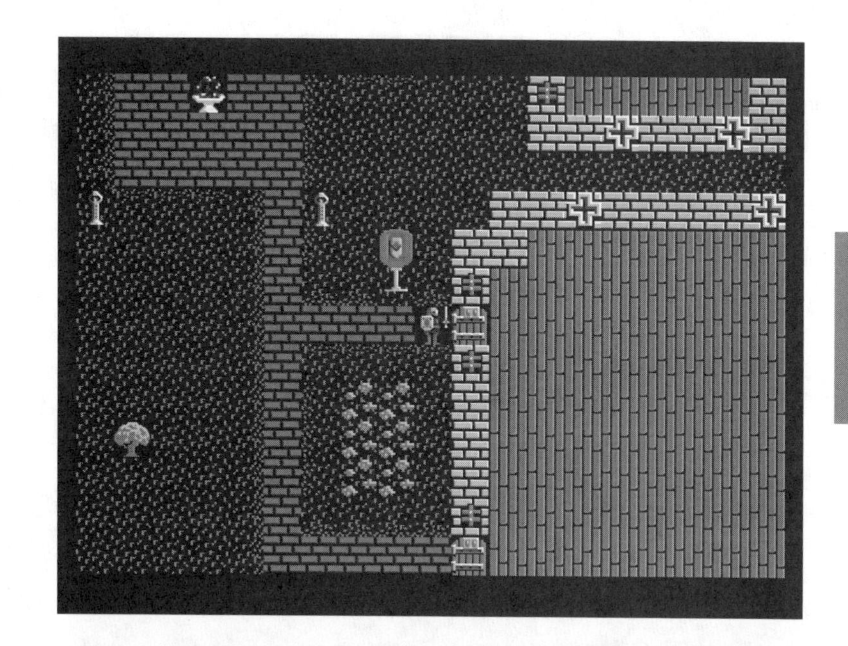

FIGURE 16.5

The player character standing in front of the armor shop.

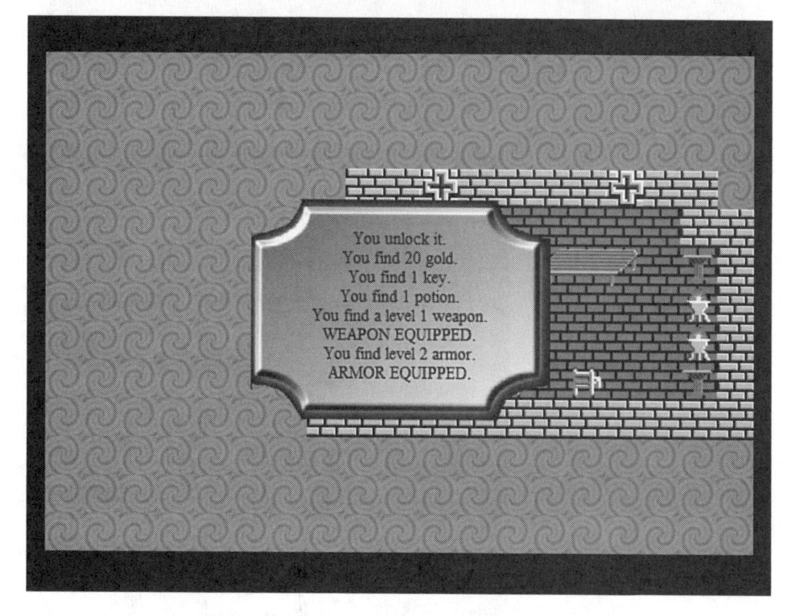

FIGURE 16.6

A treasure chest loaded with great stuff.

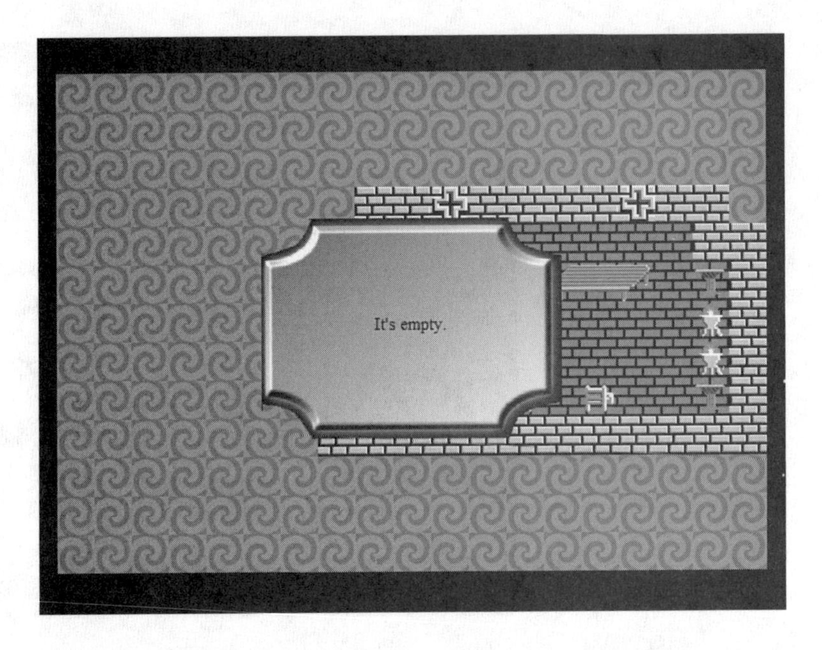

FIGURE 16.7

An empty treasure chest.

You can see what you have in your inventory now. Just press the "I" key on your keyboard, and you'll see a screen something like that shown in Figure 16.8. Of course, what you actually see will depend on what you have in the inventory.

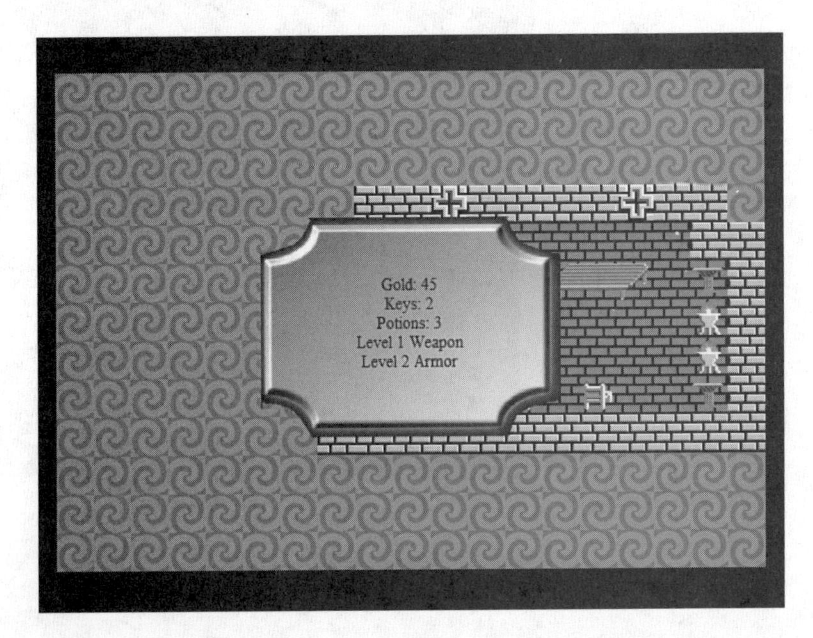

FIGURE 16.8

The inventory display.

When it comes to handling containers in the program, everything starts when the player presses an arrow key to move the player character. In each of the arrow-handling methods, the program calls CheckForAndHandleContainer():

```
BOOL bHandledContainer =
    CheckForAndHandleContainer(iTargetSector);
```

This method returns TRUE if the player manipulated a container and FALSE if the player didn't. In the case of TRUE, the player doesn't need to move, so the arrow method returns right away:


```
if (bHandledContainer)
    return;
```

If the player didn't fool with a container, then maybe there's a door or maybe the player just wants to move:

```
int iDoorStatus =
    CheckForAndHandleDoor(iTargetSector);
if (iDoorStatus == NODOOR || iDoorStatus == DOORUNLOCKED)
    MovePlayerUp();
```

That all seems way too easy, doesn't it? That's because there's a whole lot of programming behind the CheckForAndHandleContainer() method and its helper methods. CheckForAndHandleContainer() itself is pretty straightforward, just checking to see whether a container exists in the target sector and if so handling it:

```
BOOL bHandledContainer = FALSE;
if (IsContainer(iSector))
{
    HandleContainer(iSector);
    bHandledContainer = TRUE;
}
return bHandledContainer;
```

You have to dig deeper to get to the meat of the problem. That digging will first reveal the IsContainer() method, which does nothing more than check the contents of the target sector and the location:

```
if (m_Sectors[iSector] == CHEST_INT && m_byMapType == TOWNINTERIOR)
    return TRUE;
else if (m_Sectors[iSector] == BARREL_INT && m_byMapType == TOWNINTERIOR)
    return TRUE;
else if (m_Sectors[iSector] == FOOTLOCKER_INT && m_byMapType == TOWNINTERIOR)
    return TRUE;
return FALSE;
```

No mysteries there, either. Nope, the real meat is in the HandleContainer() method. This method first defines a flag and gets a pointer to the container that's located in the target sector:

```
BOOL bCouldOpenContainer = TRUE;
CContainer* pContainer = FindContainer(iSector);
```

The `FindContainer()` method works similarly to `FindDoor()`.

With the `CContainer` pointer in hand, the program checks whether the container is locked:

```
if (pContainer->GetLocked() == TRUE)
{
    .
    .
    .
}
```

If the container is locked, the program must check whether the player has one or more keys. If he does, the program takes away a key and unlocks the container. If the container is empty, the player gets a message to that effect. Otherwise, the `RetrieveItemsFromContainer()` method transfers the items from the container to the player's inventory:

```
if (m_Player.GetKeys() > 0)
{
    m_Player.SetKeys(m_Player.GetKeys() - 1 );
    pContainer->SetLocked(FALSE);
    if (ContainerEmpty(pContainer))
        TurnOnPlaque("You unlock it. It's empty.");
    else
        RetrieveItemsFromContainer(pContainer, "You unlock it.");
    bCouldOpenContainer = TRUE;
}
```

If the player doesn't have a key, he's out of luck:

```
else
{
    TurnOnPlaque("You need a key.");
    bCouldOpenContainer = FALSE;
}
```

If the container isn't locked, the player can dig right in. However, the container may or may not have anything in it:

```
else
{
    if (ContainerEmpty(pContainer))
        TurnOnPlaque("It's empty.");
    else
        RetrieveItemsFromContainer(pContainer, "You open it.");
    bCouldOpenContainer = TRUE;
}
```

Finally, `HandleContainer()` returns the results of its efforts in the form of a `TRUE` (the player opened the container) or `FALSE` (the player didn't open the container) value (the program doesn't actually use this return value, but it's there if you want it):

```
return bCouldOpenContainer;
```

Sorry, but you're not done yet. You still have to dig a little deeper. Specifically, you need to look over the `RetrieveItemsFromContainer()` method, which transfers the items from the container and into the player's inventory. All this method really does, though, is call a slew of helper methods, building up a message string as it goes:


```
char str[1024];
strcpy(str, msg);
RetrieveGold(pContainer, str);
RetrieveKeys(pContainer, str);
RetrievePotion(pContainer, str);
RetrieveWeapon(pContainer, str);
RetrieveArmor(pContainer, str);
TurnOnPlaque(str);
```

The helper methods are what you really need to see. Several of them are very similar, so you really need to examine only two. For example, the `RetrieveGold()` method works much like `RetrieveKeys()` and `RetrievePotion()`. `RetrieveGold()` first checks whether the container has any gold:

```
if (pContainer->GetGold() > 0)
{
    .
    .
    .
}
```

If the container has gold, the program gives the gold to the player, adds text to the message string, and empties all gold from the container:

```
m_Player.SetGold(m_Player.GetGold() +
    pContainer->GetGold());
wsprintf(&msg[strlen(msg)], "\nYou find %d gold.",
    pContainer->GetGold());
pContainer->SetGold(0);
```

The `RetrieveWeapon()` and `RetrieveArmor()` methods are similar, so you'll look at only the former. That method first gets the weapon type, which is the weapon level or `NOWEAPON` if there's no weapon in the container:

```
int iWeaponType = pContainer->GetWeapon();
if (iWeaponType != NOWEAPON)
{
    .
```

```
    .
    .
}
```

If there is a weapon in the container, the program first adds text to the message string:

```
wsprintf(&msg[strlen(msg)], "\nYou find a level %d weapon.",
    iWeaponType);
```

Then, the program must determine whether the player can use the new weapon. To use the weapon, it must be a higher level weapon than the one the player already has:

```
if (iWeaponType > m_Player.GetWeapon())
{
    m_Player.SetWeapon(iWeaponType);
    strcpy(&msg[strlen(msg)], "\nWEAPON EQUIPPED.");
}
```

If the player already has a weapon of that level or better, the program adds a message to that effect to the message sting:

```
else
    strcpy(&msg[strlen(msg)], "\nCAN'T USE WEAPON.");
```

Whether the user can use the weapon or not, it is removed from the container:

```
pContainer->SetWeapon(NOWEAPON);
```

The `RetrieveArmor()` method works almost identically.

Adding Secret Doors

A bit earlier in this chapter, I promised that you'd see how to add secret doors to the program. Secret doors work just like any other door with two exceptions: they can't be locked, and, more importantly, they're invisible. To find a secret door, the player must try to walk through the wall. If there's a secret door where the player tries to go, he'll go right through the wall. To add secret doors to the game, perform the following steps:

1. Add the following line to the private method declarations in the Engine.h file, right after the line `void ShowInventory()` that's already there:

   ```
   int CheckForSecretDoor(int TileNumber, int iSector);
   ```

2. Add the following method to the end of the Engine.cpp file. If you don't want to type this source code, you can copy it from the Code14.txt file in the Chapter16 directory of this book's CD-ROM.

```
///////////////////////////////////////////////////////
// CheckForSecretDoor()
///////////////////////////////////////////////////////
int CEngine::CheckForSecretDoor(int TileNumber, int iSector)
{
    int iFinalTile = TileNumber;
    CDoor* pDoor = FindDoor(iSector);
    if (pDoor->GetSecret())
    {
        if (TileNumber == DOOR_INT && m_byMapType == TOWNINTERIOR)
            iFinalTile = BRICKWALL_INT;
        else if (TileNumber == DOOR_EXT && m_byMapType == TOWNEXTERIOR)
            iFinalTile = BRICKWALL_EXT;
    }
    return iFinalTile;
}
```


This method checks for a secret door at the map sector given as the second argument. If it finds a secret door there, the method returns the tile number for a wall, rather than the tile number for a door. This causes secret doors to be passable but invisible.

3. Add the following lines to the `PaintBackground()` method, right after the line `int TileNumber = m_Sectors[iSector]` that's already there:

```
if (IsDoor(iSector))
    TileNumber = CheckForSecretDoor(TileNumber, iSector);
```

When the program tries to display a door, these lines replace the door image with a wall image if the door is secret.

4. In the FirstTown.cpp file, add the following line to the end of the defined constants, right after the line `const GANJEKENTRANCE = 1743` that's already there:

```
const HOUSE02ROOM02ENTRANCE = 831;
```

5. Again in the FirstTown.cpp file, add the following `case` clause to the end of the `switch` statement in the `HandleFirstTownHouse02Room01()` method. If you don't want to type this source code, you can copy it from the Code15.txt file in the Chapter16 directory of this book's CD-ROM.

```
case HOUSE02ROOM02ENTRANCE:
    g_Engine.OpenMapFiles("FirstTownHouse02Room02.map");
    g_Engine.SetCurrentMap(FIRSTTOWNHOUSE02ROOM02);
    g_Engine.ResetAnimation();
    break;
```

These lines load the map for the new room when the player walks through the secret door in House #2's first room.

6. At the end of the FirstTown.cpp file, add the following method definition. If you don't want to type this source code, you can copy it from the Code16.txt file in the Chapter16 directory of this book's CD-ROM.

```
///////////////////////////////////////////////////////////
// HandleFirstTownHouse02Room02()
///////////////////////////////////////////////////////////
void HandleFirstTownHouse02Room02()
{
    switch (g_Engine.GetPlayer()->GetSector())
    {
    case HOUSE02ROOM02ENTRANCE - 2:
        g_Engine.OpenMapFiles("FirstTownHouse02Room01.map");
        g_Engine.SetCurrentMap(FIRSTTOWNHOUSE02ROOM01);
        g_Engine.ResetAnimation();
        break;
    }
}
```

   This method handles the new room, enabling the player to pass through the secret door again and back to the house's first room.

7. In the FirstTown.h file, add the following line to the end of the method declarations, right after the line `void HandleFirstTownPotions()` that's already there.

```
void HandleFirstTownHouse02Room02();
```

8. In the MyEngine.cpp file, add the following `case` clause to the end of the `switch` statement in the `RespondToPlayerLocation()` method:

```
case FIRSTTOWNHOUSE02ROOM02:
    HandleFirstTownHouse02Room02();
    break;
```

9. Copy the following map files from the Chapter16 directory of this book's CD-ROM to your JBookman project's Maps directory.

```
FirstTownHouse02Room01.map
FirstTownHouse02Room01.map.dor
FirstTownHouse02Room01.map.itm
FirstTownHouse02Room01.map.peo
FirstTownHouse02Room02.map
FirstTownHouse02Room02.map.dor
FirstTownHouse02Room02.map.itm
FirstTownHouse02Room02.map.peo
```

Go ahead now and compile and run the program. When you do, head to the small house between the inn and the potion shop. Step through the front door and have a look around. See another door? Nope, but it's there. Explore the back wall, and you'll find the secret door shown in Figure 16.9.

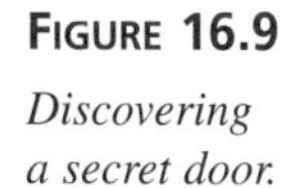

FIGURE 16.9

Discovering a secret door.

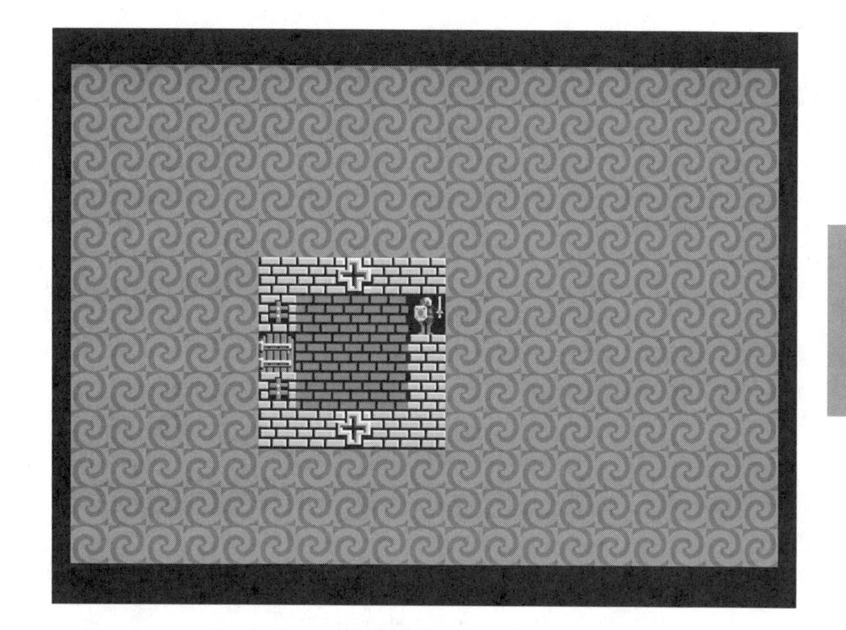

Step through the wall, and you'll find the room shown in Figure 16.10. This mysterious hidden place is actually the entrance to a dungeon that runs underneath the city. The entrance doesn't work yet, but you'll take care of that in the next section. As for the secret door stuff, it's so easy to implement that all the code explanation you need was included with the project steps. Review those steps if you glossed over the explanations.

FIGURE 16.10

The hidden room behind the secret door.

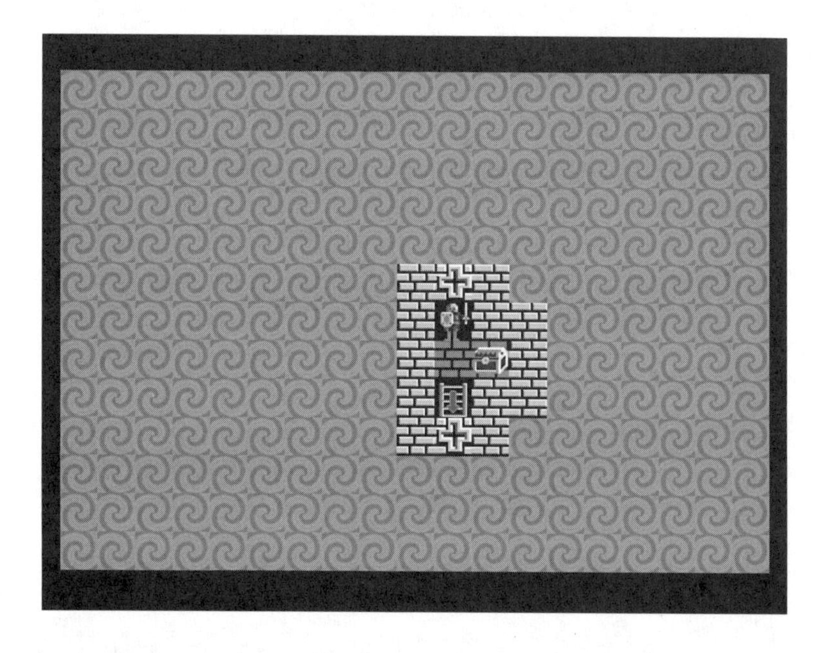

Add the Dungeon

Okay, you're probably dying to know where that hidden entrance in the secret room leads to. I already told you it was a dungeon, but you just gotta see it for yourself, right? No problem. Just complete the following steps to add this new location to the game.

1. In the MyEngine.cpp file, add the following `case` clauses to the end of the `switch` statement in the `RespondToPlayerLocation()` method. If you don't want to type this source code, you can copy it from the Code17.txt file in the Chapter16 directory of this book's CD-ROM.

```
case FIRSTTOWNDUNGEON01ROOM01:
    HandleFirstTownDungeon01Room01();
    break;
case FIRSTTOWNDUNGEON01ROOM02:
    HandleFirstTownDungeon01Room02();
    break;
case FIRSTTOWNDUNGEON01ROOM03:
    HandleFirstTownDungeon01Room03();
    break;
case FIRSTTOWNDUNGEON01ROOM04:
    HandleFirstTownDungeon01Room04();
    break;
case FIRSTTOWNDUNGEON01ROOM05:
    HandleFirstTownDungeon01Room05();
    break;
case FIRSTTOWNDUNGEON01ROOM06:
    HandleFirstTownDungeon01Room06();
    break;
case FIRSTTOWNDUNGEON01ROOM07:
    HandleFirstTownDungeon01Room07();
    break;
case FIRSTTOWNDUNGEON01ROOM08:
    HandleFirstTownDungeon01Room08();
    break;
case FIRSTTOWNDUNGEON01ROOM09:
    HandleFirstTownDungeon01Room09();
    break;
case FIRSTTOWNDUNGEON01ROOM10:
    HandleFirstTownDungeon01Room10();
    break;
case FIRSTTOWNDUNGEON01ROOM11:
    HandleFirstTownDungeon01Room11();
    break;
```

   These lines route program execution to the methods that handle all the new rooms you're adding to the game.

2. In the FirstTown.h file, add the following lines to the end of the method declarations, right after the line `void HandleFirstTownHouse02Room02()` that's already there. If you don't want to type this source code, you can copy it from the Code18.txt file in the Chapter16 directory of this book's CD-ROM.

```
void HandleFirstTownDungeon01Room01();
void HandleFirstTownDungeon01Room02();
void HandleFirstTownDungeon01Room03();
void HandleFirstTownDungeon01Room04();
void HandleFirstTownDungeon01Room05();
void HandleFirstTownDungeon01Room06();
void HandleFirstTownDungeon01Room07();
void HandleFirstTownDungeon01Room08();
void HandleFirstTownDungeon01Room09();
void HandleFirstTownDungeon01Room10();
void HandleFirstTownDungeon01Room11();
```

3. In the FirstTown.cpp file, add the following lines to the defined constants, right after the line `const HOUSE02ROOM02ENTRANCE = 831` that's already there. If you don't want to type this source code, you can copy it from the Code19.txt file in the Chapter16 directory of this book's CD-ROM.

```
const DUNGEON01ENTRANCE = 915;
const DUNGEON01ROOM01ENTRANCE = 1;
const DUNGEON01ROOM02ENTRANCE = 465;
const DUNGEON01ROOM03ENTRANCE = 426;
const DUNGEON01ROOM04ENTRANCE = 556;
const DUNGEON01ROOM05ENTRANCE = 436;
const DUNGEON01ROOM06ENTRANCE = 445;
const DUNGEON01ROOM07ENTRANCE = 249;
const DUNGEON01ROOM08ENTRANCE = 1323;
const DUNGEON01ROOM09ENTRANCE1 = 1094;
const DUNGEON01ROOM09ENTRANCE2 = 1430;
const DUNGEON01ROOM09ENTRANCE3 = 1649;
const DUNGEON01ROOM10ENTRANCE = 1659;
const DUNGEON01ROOM11ENTRANCE1 = 1670;
const DUNGEON01ROOM11ENTRANCE2 = 1467;
const DUNGEON01ROOM11ENTRANCE3 = 1131;
```

4. At the end of the FirstTown.cpp file, add the following method definitions. If you don't want to type this source code, you can copy it from the Code20.txt file in the Chapter16 directory of this book's CD-ROM.

```
///////////////////////////////////////////////////////////
// HandleFirstTownDungeon01Room01()
///////////////////////////////////////////////////////////
void HandleFirstTownDungeon01Room01()
{
    switch (g_Engine.GetPlayer()->GetSector())
    {
```

```
case DUNGEON01ROOM01ENTRANCE:
    g_Engine.GetPlayer()->
        SetSector(DUNGEON01ENTRANCE - MAPCOLUMNCOUNT);
    g_Engine.OpenMapFiles("FirstTownHouse02Room02.map");
    g_Engine.SetCurrentMap(FIRSTTOWNHOUSE02ROOM02);
    g_Engine.GetCDirect3DObj()->SetCurrentTileSurface
        (g_Engine.GetCDirect3DObj()->GetTownIntTileSurface());
    g_Engine.ResetAnimation();
    break;
case DUNGEON01ROOM02ENTRANCE:
    g_Engine.OpenMapFiles("FirstTownDungeon01Room02.map");
    g_Engine.SetCurrentMap(FIRSTTOWNDUNGEON01ROOM02);
    g_Engine.ResetAnimation();
    break;
case DUNGEON01ROOM07ENTRANCE:
    g_Engine.GetPlayer()->
        SetSector(DUNGEON01ROOM07ENTRANCE - 1);
    g_Engine.OpenMapFiles("FirstTownDungeon01Room07.map");
    g_Engine.SetCurrentMap(FIRSTTOWNDUNGEON01ROOM07);
    g_Engine.ResetAnimation();
    break;
case DUNGEON01ROOM09ENTRANCE1:
    g_Engine.GetPlayer()->
        SetSector(DUNGEON01ROOM09ENTRANCE1 + 1);
    g_Engine.OpenMapFiles("FirstTownDungeon01Room09.map");
    g_Engine.SetCurrentMap(FIRSTTOWNDUNGEON01ROOM09);
    g_Engine.ResetAnimation();
    break;
case DUNGEON01ROOM09ENTRANCE2:
    g_Engine.GetPlayer()->
        SetSector(DUNGEON01ROOM09ENTRANCE2 + 1);
    g_Engine.OpenMapFiles("FirstTownDungeon01Room09.map");
    g_Engine.SetCurrentMap(FIRSTTOWNDUNGEON01ROOM09);
    g_Engine.ResetAnimation();
    break;
case DUNGEON01ROOM09ENTRANCE3:
    g_Engine.GetPlayer()->
        SetSector(DUNGEON01ROOM09ENTRANCE3 - MAPCOLUMNCOUNT);
    g_Engine.OpenMapFiles("FirstTownDungeon01Room09.map");
    g_Engine.SetCurrentMap(FIRSTTOWNDUNGEON01ROOM09);
    g_Engine.ResetAnimation();
    break;
case DUNGEON01ROOM10ENTRANCE:
    g_Engine.GetPlayer()->
        SetSector(DUNGEON01ROOM10ENTRANCE - MAPCOLUMNCOUNT);
    g_Engine.OpenMapFiles("FirstTownDungeon01Room10.map");
    g_Engine.SetCurrentMap(FIRSTTOWNDUNGEON01ROOM10);
    g_Engine.ResetAnimation();
    break;
case DUNGEON01ROOM11ENTRANCE1:
    g_Engine.GetPlayer()->
```

```
                SetSector(DUNGEON01ROOM11ENTRANCE1 - MAPCOLUMNCOUNT);
            g_Engine.OpenMapFiles("FirstTownDungeon01Room11.map");
            g_Engine.SetCurrentMap(FIRSTTOWNDUNGEON01ROOM11);
            g_Engine.ResetAnimation();
            break;
        case DUNGEON01ROOM11ENTRANCE2:
            g_Engine.GetPlayer()->
                SetSector(DUNGEON01ROOM11ENTRANCE2 - 1);
            g_Engine.OpenMapFiles("FirstTownDungeon01Room11.map");
            g_Engine.SetCurrentMap(FIRSTTOWNDUNGEON01ROOM11);
            g_Engine.ResetAnimation();
            break;
        case DUNGEON01ROOM11ENTRANCE3:
            g_Engine.GetPlayer()->
                SetSector(DUNGEON01ROOM11ENTRANCE3 - 1);
            g_Engine.OpenMapFiles("FirstTownDungeon01Room11.map");
            g_Engine.SetCurrentMap(FIRSTTOWNDUNGEON01ROOM11);
            g_Engine.ResetAnimation();
            break;
        }
}

//////////////////////////////////////////////////////////
// HandleFirstTownDungeon01Room02()
//////////////////////////////////////////////////////////
void HandleFirstTownDungeon01Room02()
{
    switch (g_Engine.GetPlayer()->GetSector())
    {
    case DUNGEON01ROOM02ENTRANCE - 2:
        g_Engine.OpenMapFiles("FirstTownDungeon01Room01.map");
        g_Engine.SetCurrentMap(FIRSTTOWNDUNGEON01ROOM01);
        g_Engine.ResetAnimation();
        break;
    case DUNGEON01ROOM03ENTRANCE:
        g_Engine.GetPlayer()->
            SetSector(DUNGEON01ROOM03ENTRANCE - MAPCOLUMNCOUNT);
        g_Engine.OpenMapFiles("FirstTownDungeon01Room03.map");
        g_Engine.SetCurrentMap(FIRSTTOWNDUNGEON01ROOM03);
        g_Engine.ResetAnimation();
        break;
    case DUNGEON01ROOM04ENTRANCE:
        g_Engine.GetPlayer()->
            SetSector(DUNGEON01ROOM04ENTRANCE + MAPCOLUMNCOUNT);
        g_Engine.OpenMapFiles("FirstTownDungeon01Room04.map");
        g_Engine.SetCurrentMap(FIRSTTOWNDUNGEON01ROOM04);
        g_Engine.ResetAnimation();
        break;
    case DUNGEON01ROOM05ENTRANCE:
        g_Engine.GetPlayer()->
            SetSector(DUNGEON01ROOM05ENTRANCE - MAPCOLUMNCOUNT);
```

```
        g_Engine.OpenMapFiles("FirstTownDungeon01Room05.map");
        g_Engine.SetCurrentMap(FIRSTTOWNDUNGEON01ROOM05);
        g_Engine.ResetAnimation();
        break;
    case DUNGEON01ROOM06ENTRANCE:
        g_Engine.GetPlayer()->
            SetSector(DUNGEON01ROOM06ENTRANCE - MAPCOLUMNCOUNT);
        g_Engine.OpenMapFiles("FirstTownDungeon01Room06.map");
        g_Engine.SetCurrentMap(FIRSTTOWNDUNGEON01ROOM06);
        g_Engine.ResetAnimation();
        break;
    }
}

///////////////////////////////////////////////////////////
// HandleFirstTownDungeon01Room03()
///////////////////////////////////////////////////////////
void HandleFirstTownDungeon01Room03()
{
    switch (g_Engine.GetPlayer()->GetSector())
    {
    case DUNGEON01ROOM03ENTRANCE:
        g_Engine.GetPlayer()->
            SetSector(DUNGEON01ROOM03ENTRANCE + MAPCOLUMNCOUNT);
        g_Engine.OpenMapFiles("FirstTownDungeon01Room02.map");
        g_Engine.SetCurrentMap(FIRSTTOWNDUNGEON01ROOM02);
        g_Engine.ResetAnimation();
        break;
    }
}

///////////////////////////////////////////////////////////
// HandleFirstTownDungeon01Room04()
///////////////////////////////////////////////////////////
void HandleFirstTownDungeon01Room04()
{
    switch (g_Engine.GetPlayer()->GetSector())
    {
    case DUNGEON01ROOM04ENTRANCE - MAPCOLUMNCOUNT*2:
        g_Engine.OpenMapFiles("FirstTownDungeon01Room02.map");
        g_Engine.SetCurrentMap(FIRSTTOWNDUNGEON01ROOM02);
        g_Engine.ResetAnimation();
        break;
    }
}

///////////////////////////////////////////////////////////
// HandleFirstTownDungeon01Room05()
///////////////////////////////////////////////////////////
```

```
void HandleFirstTownDungeon01Room05()
{
    switch (g_Engine.GetPlayer()->GetSector())
    {
    case DUNGEON01ROOM05ENTRANCE:
        g_Engine.GetPlayer()->
            SetSector(DUNGEON01ROOM05ENTRANCE + MAPCOLUMNCOUNT);
        g_Engine.OpenMapFiles("FirstTownDungeon01Room02.map");
        g_Engine.SetCurrentMap(FIRSTTOWNDUNGEON01ROOM02);
        g_Engine.ResetAnimation();
        break;
    }
}

//////////////////////////////////////////////////////////
// HandleFirstTownDungeon01Room06()
//////////////////////////////////////////////////////////
void HandleFirstTownDungeon01Room06()
{
    switch (g_Engine.GetPlayer()->GetSector())
    {
    case DUNGEON01ROOM06ENTRANCE:
        g_Engine.GetPlayer()->
            SetSector(DUNGEON01ROOM06ENTRANCE + MAPCOLUMNCOUNT);
        g_Engine.OpenMapFiles("FirstTownDungeon01Room02.map");
        g_Engine.SetCurrentMap(FIRSTTOWNDUNGEON01ROOM02);
        g_Engine.ResetAnimation();
        break;
    }
}

//////////////////////////////////////////////////////////
// HandleFirstTownDungeon01Room07()
//////////////////////////////////////////////////////////
void HandleFirstTownDungeon01Room07()
{
    switch (g_Engine.GetPlayer()->GetSector())
    {
    case DUNGEON01ROOM07ENTRANCE:
        g_Engine.GetPlayer()->
            SetSector(DUNGEON01ROOM07ENTRANCE + 1);
        g_Engine.OpenMapFiles("FirstTownDungeon01Room01.map");
        g_Engine.SetCurrentMap(FIRSTTOWNDUNGEON01ROOM01);
        g_Engine.ResetAnimation();
        break;
    }
}
```

```
////////////////////////////////////////////////////////////
// HandleFirstTownDungeon01Room08()
////////////////////////////////////////////////////////////
void HandleFirstTownDungeon01Room08()
{
    switch (g_Engine.GetPlayer()->GetSector())
    {
    case DUNGEON01ROOM08ENTRANCE:
        g_Engine.GetPlayer()->
            SetSector(DUNGEON01ROOM08ENTRANCE + MAPCOLUMNCOUNT);
        g_Engine.OpenMapFiles("FirstTownDungeon01Room10.map");
        g_Engine.SetCurrentMap(FIRSTTOWNDUNGEON01ROOM10);
        g_Engine.ResetAnimation();
        break;
    }
}

////////////////////////////////////////////////////////////
// HandleFirstTownDungeon01Room09()
////////////////////////////////////////////////////////////
void HandleFirstTownDungeon01Room09()
{
    switch (g_Engine.GetPlayer()->GetSector())
    {
    case DUNGEON01ROOM09ENTRANCE1:
        g_Engine.GetPlayer()->
            SetSector(DUNGEON01ROOM09ENTRANCE1 - 1);
        g_Engine.OpenMapFiles("FirstTownDungeon01Room01.map");
        g_Engine.SetCurrentMap(FIRSTTOWNDUNGEON01ROOM01);
        g_Engine.ResetAnimation();
        break;
    case DUNGEON01ROOM09ENTRANCE2:
        g_Engine.GetPlayer()->
            SetSector(DUNGEON01ROOM09ENTRANCE2 - 1);
        g_Engine.OpenMapFiles("FirstTownDungeon01Room01.map");
        g_Engine.SetCurrentMap(FIRSTTOWNDUNGEON01ROOM01);
        g_Engine.ResetAnimation();
        break;
    case DUNGEON01ROOM09ENTRANCE3:
        g_Engine.GetPlayer()->
            SetSector(DUNGEON01ROOM09ENTRANCE3 + MAPCOLUMNCOUNT);
        g_Engine.OpenMapFiles("FirstTownDungeon01Room01.map");
        g_Engine.SetCurrentMap(FIRSTTOWNDUNGEON01ROOM01);
        g_Engine.ResetAnimation();
        break;
    }
}
```

```
///////////////////////////////////////////////////////
// HandleFirstTownDungeon01Room10()
///////////////////////////////////////////////////////
void HandleFirstTownDungeon01Room10()
{
    switch (g_Engine.GetPlayer()->GetSector())
    {
    case DUNGEON01ROOM10ENTRANCE:
        g_Engine.GetPlayer()->
            SetSector(DUNGEON01ROOM10ENTRANCE + MAPCOLUMNCOUNT);
        g_Engine.OpenMapFiles("FirstTownDungeon01Room01.map");
        g_Engine.SetCurrentMap(FIRSTTOWNDUNGEON01ROOM01);
        g_Engine.ResetAnimation();
        break;
    case DUNGEON01ROOM08ENTRANCE:
        g_Engine.GetPlayer()->
            SetSector(DUNGEON01ROOM08ENTRANCE - MAPCOLUMNCOUNT);
        g_Engine.OpenMapFiles("FirstTownDungeon01Room08.map");
        g_Engine.SetCurrentMap(FIRSTTOWNDUNGEON01ROOM08);
        g_Engine.ResetAnimation();
        break;
    }
}

///////////////////////////////////////////////////////
// HandleFirstTownDungeon01Room11()
///////////////////////////////////////////////////////
void HandleFirstTownDungeon01Room11()
{
    switch (g_Engine.GetPlayer()->GetSector())
    {
    case DUNGEON01ROOM11ENTRANCE1:
        g_Engine.GetPlayer()->
            SetSector(DUNGEON01ROOM11ENTRANCE1 + MAPCOLUMNCOUNT);
        g_Engine.OpenMapFiles("FirstTownDungeon01Room01.map");
        g_Engine.SetCurrentMap(FIRSTTOWNDUNGEON01ROOM01);
        g_Engine.ResetAnimation();
        break;
    case DUNGEON01ROOM11ENTRANCE2:
        g_Engine.GetPlayer()->
            SetSector(DUNGEON01ROOM11ENTRANCE2 + 1);
        g_Engine.OpenMapFiles("FirstTownDungeon01Room01.map");
        g_Engine.SetCurrentMap(FIRSTTOWNDUNGEON01ROOM01);
        g_Engine.ResetAnimation();
        break;
    case DUNGEON01ROOM11ENTRANCE3:
        g_Engine.GetPlayer()->
            SetSector(DUNGEON01ROOM11ENTRANCE3 + 1);
```

```
            g_Engine.OpenMapFiles("FirstTownDungeon01Room01.map");
            g_Engine.SetCurrentMap(FIRSTTOWNDUNGEON01ROOM01);
            g_Engine.ResetAnimation();
            break;
        }
    }
```

5. Add the following `case` clause to the `HandleFirstTownHouse02Room02()` method's `switch` statement. If you don't want to type this source code, you can copy it from the Code21.txt file in the Chapter16 directory of this book's CD-ROM.

```
case DUNGEON01ENTRANCE:
    g_Engine.GetPlayer()->
        SetSector(DUNGEON01ROOM01ENTRANCE + MAPCOLUMNCOUNT);
    g_Engine.OpenMapFiles("FirstTownDungeon01Room01.map");
    g_Engine.SetCurrentMap(FIRSTTOWNDUNGEON01ROOM01);
    g_Engine.GetCDirect3DObj()->SetCurrentTileSurface
        (g_Engine.GetCDirect3DObj()->GetDungeonTileSurface());
    g_Engine.ResetAnimation();
    break;
```

6. Add the following lines to the Constants.h file, in the `g_iLocationEnum` enumeration, right after the line `GANJEKWILDS` that's already there. (Don't forget to add a comma after the `GANJEKWILDS` symbol.) If you don't want to type this source code, you can copy it from the Code22.txt file in the Chapter16 directory of this book's CD-ROM.

```
FIRSTTOWNDUNGEON01ROOM01,
FIRSTTOWNDUNGEON01ROOM02,
FIRSTTOWNDUNGEON01ROOM03,
FIRSTTOWNDUNGEON01ROOM04,
FIRSTTOWNDUNGEON01ROOM05,
FIRSTTOWNDUNGEON01ROOM06,
FIRSTTOWNDUNGEON01ROOM07,
FIRSTTOWNDUNGEON01ROOM08,
FIRSTTOWNDUNGEON01ROOM09,
FIRSTTOWNDUNGEON01ROOM10,
FIRSTTOWNDUNGEON01ROOM11
```

7. Add the following method definition to the end of the Direct3D.cpp file. If you don't want to type this source code, you can copy it from the Code23.txt file in the Chapter16 directory of this book's CD-ROM.

```
///////////////////////////////////////////////////////////
// GetDungeonTileSurface()
///////////////////////////////////////////////////////////
IDirect3DSurface8* CDirect3D::GetDungeonTileSurface()
{
    return m_pDungeonTileSurface;
}
```

8. In the Engine.cpp file, add the following `case` clause to the `PlayerBlocked()` method's `switch` statement. If you don't want to type this source code, you can copy it from the Code24.txt file in the Chapter16 directory of this book's CD-ROM.

```
case DUNGEON:
    if (item == BRICKWALL_DUN || item == CUPBOARD_DUN
        || item == TABLE01_DUN || item == TABLE02_DUN
        || item == TABLE03_DUN
        || item == WATER_DUN || item == WATER_DUN + 1
        || item == BED01_DUN || item == BED02_DUN
        || item == BED03_DUN || item == BED04_DUN
        || item == FIREPLACE_DUN || item == FIREPLACE_DUN + 1
        || item == MANINCHAIR01_DUN || item == MANINCHAIR01_DUN + 1
        || item == MANINCHAIR02_DUN || item == MANINCHAIR02_DUN + 1
        || item == MANINCHAIR03_DUN || item == MANINCHAIR03_DUN + 1
        || item == MANINCHAIR04_DUN || item == MANINCHAIR04_DUN + 1
        || item == MANINBED01_DUN || item == MANINBED01_DUN + 1
        || item == MANINBED02_DUN || item == MANINBED02_DUN + 1)
    blocked = TRUE;
    break;
```

9. Add the following lines to the Constants.h file, right after the line `const FOOT-LOCKER_INT = 30` that's already there. If you don't want to type this source code, you can copy it from the Code25.txt file in the Chapter16 directory of this book's CD-ROM.

```
// Impassable Objects in the dungeon.
const BRICKWALL_DUN = 1;
const WINDOW1_DUN = 2;
const WINDOW2_DUN = 3;
const CUPBOARD_DUN = 6;
const TABLE01_DUN = 12;
const TABLE02_DUN = 13;
const TABLE03_DUN = 14;
const BED01_DUN = 24;
const BED02_DUN = 25;
const BED03_DUN = 26;
const BED04_DUN = 27;
const WATER_DUN = 32;
const FIREPLACE_DUN = 38;
const MANINCHAIR01_DUN = 44;
const MANINCHAIR02_DUN = 46;
const MANINCHAIR03_DUN = 48;
const MANINCHAIR04_DUN = 50;
const MANINBED01_DUN = 52;
const MANINBED02_DUN = 54;
```

10. Copy the following map files from the Chapter16 directory of this book's CD-ROM to your JBookman project's Maps directory.

```
FirstTownDungeon01Room01.map
FirstTownDungeon01Room01.map.dor
FirstTownDungeon01Room01.map.itm
FirstTownDungeon01Room01.map.peo
FirstTownDungeon01Room02.map
FirstTownDungeon01Room02.map.dor
FirstTownDungeon01Room02.map.itm
FirstTownDungeon01Room02.map.peo
FirstTownDungeon01Room03.map
FirstTownDungeon01Room03.map.dor
FirstTownDungeon01Room03.map.itm
FirstTownDungeon01Room03.map.peo
FirstTownDungeon01Room04.map
FirstTownDungeon01Room04.map.dor
FirstTownDungeon01Room04.map.itm
FirstTownDungeon01Room04.map.peo
FirstTownDungeon01Room05.map
FirstTownDungeon01Room05.map.dor
FirstTownDungeon01Room05.map.itm
FirstTownDungeon01Room05.map.peo
FirstTownDungeon01Room06.map
FirstTownDungeon01Room06.map.dor
FirstTownDungeon01Room06.map.itm
FirstTownDungeon01Room06.map.peo
FirstTownDungeon01Room07.map
FirstTownDungeon01Room07.map.dor
FirstTownDungeon01Room07.map.itm
FirstTownDungeon01Room07.map.peo
FirstTownDungeon01Room08.map
FirstTownDungeon01Room08.map.dor
FirstTownDungeon01Room08.map.itm
FirstTownDungeon01Room08.map.peo
FirstTownDungeon01Room09.map
FirstTownDungeon01Room09.map.dor
FirstTownDungeon01Room09.map.itm
FirstTownDungeon01Room09.map.peo
FirstTownDungeon01Room10.map
FirstTownDungeon01Room10.map.dor
FirstTownDungeon01Room10.map.itm
FirstTownDungeon01Room10.map.peo
FirstTownDungeon01Room11.map
FirstTownDungeon01Room11.map.dor
FirstTownDungeon01Room11.map.itm
FirstTownDungeon01Room11.map.peo
```

When you compile and run the program, head for that secret room and step onto the ladder heading down to the dungeon. When you do, you'll see the area shown in Figure 16.11. Go ahead and explore the dungeon. You'll see lots of rooms, including those shown in Figures 16.12 and 16.13.

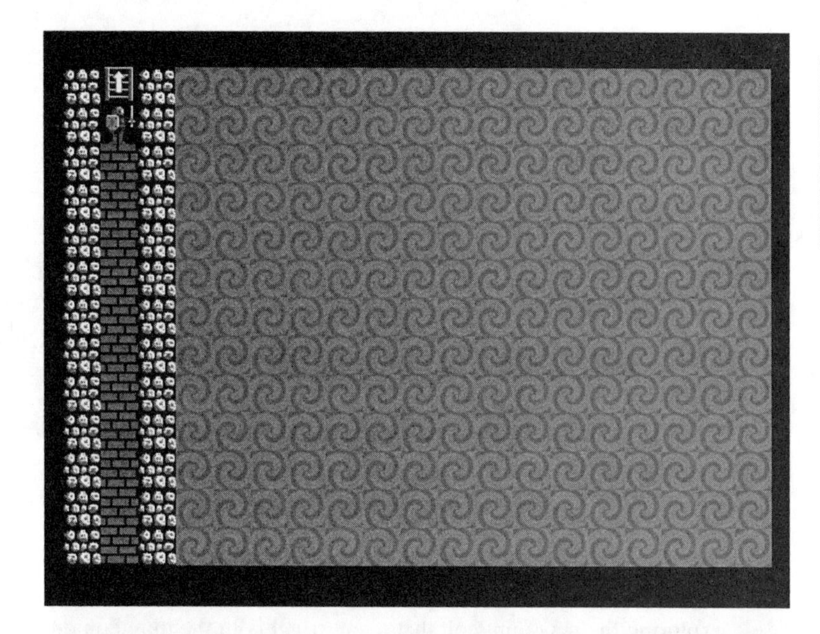

FIGURE 16.11

The player's first step into the dungeon.

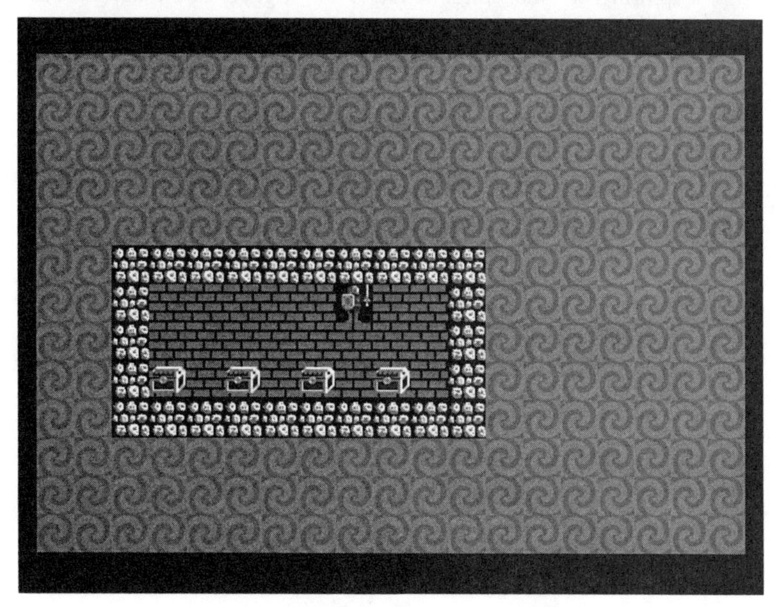

FIGURE 16.12

A treasure room in the dungeon.

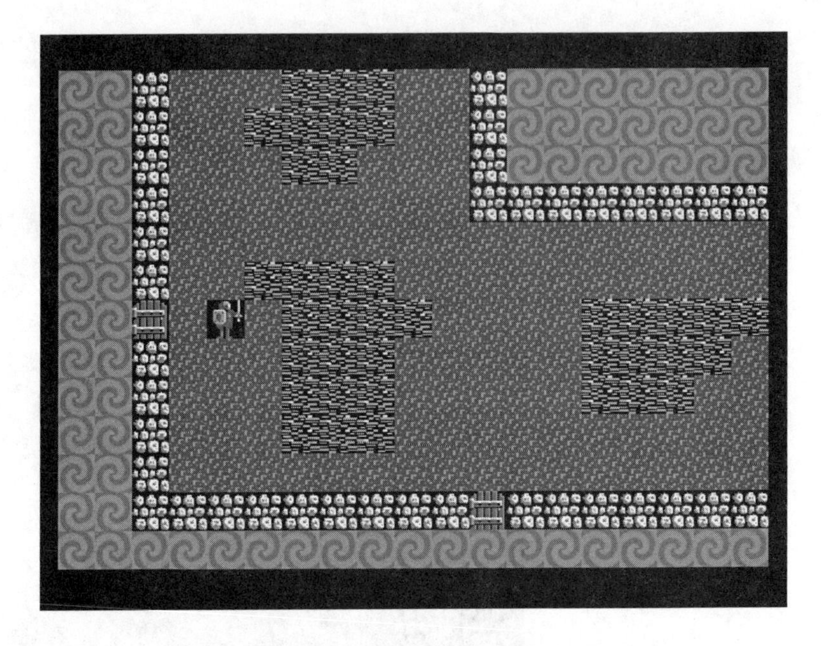

FIGURE 16.13

A mysterious, watery room in the dungeon.

Getting Dungeon Events to Work

This has been a big day, I know. There was a lot of work to do, and there's still one more task to complete—but it will be a short one. You may have noticed when you were exploring the new dungeon that event triggers in the dungeon didn't work. For example, when you step towards a treasure chest, nothing happens. Also, a couple of the doors in the dungeon are supposed to be secret doors and some others are supposed to be locked. To get the dungeon fully working, perform the following steps:

1. In the Engine.cpp, add the following lines to the `IsDoor()` method, right after the second `return TRUE` line:

```
else if (m_Sectors[iSector] == DOOR_DUN && m_byMapType == DUNGEON)
    return TRUE;
```

2. Replace the `IsContainer()` method with the one that follows. If you don't want to type this source code, you can copy it from the Code26.txt file in the Chapter16 directory of this book's CD-ROM.

```
BOOL CEngine::IsContainer(int iSector)
{
    if (m_byMapType == TOWNINTERIOR)
    {
```

```
        if (m_Sectors[iSector] == CHEST_INT ||
              m_Sectors[iSector] == BARREL_INT ||
              m_Sectors[iSector] == FOOTLOCKER_INT)
            return TRUE;
    }
    else if (m_byMapType == DUNGEON)
    {
        if (m_Sectors[iSector] == CHEST_DUN ||
              m_Sectors[iSector] == BARREL_DUN ||
              m_Sectors[iSector] == FOOTLOCKER_DUN)
            return TRUE;
    }
    return FALSE;
}
```


This version of the method is a little better organized, but, more importantly, it adds the source code needed to work with the dungeon maps.

3. Add the following lines to the `CheckForSecretDoor()` method, right before the `if` statement's closing brace.

```
else if (TileNumber == DOOR_DUN && m_byMapType == DUNGEON)
    iFinalTile = BRICKWALL_DUN;
```

4. Add the following lines to the Constants.h file, right after the line `const MAN-INBED02_DUN = 54` that's already there. If you don't want to type this source code, you can copy it from the Code27.txt file in the Chapter16 directory of this book's CD-ROM.

```
// Misc. tile IDs for dungeon.
const DOOR_DUN = 4;
const CHEST_DUN = 18;
const BARREL_DUN = 19;
const FOOTLOCKER_DUN = 30;
```

When you run the program now, everything in the dungeon should be working okay. A couple of the doors you saw previously are now invisible or locked, and you can retrieve items from the treasure chests.

New Members of the `CEngine` Class

Finally, you've nearly reached the end of this day. Pat yourself on the back for a job well done. Over the course of this day's many projects, you added a lot more functionality to the `CEngine` class. Table 16.2 describes the new members you added and summarizes what they do.

TABLE 16.2 New `CEngine` Members

Member	*Type*	*Description*
m_bShowingPlaque	Data	A flag that indicates whether the game engine is currently displaying the plaque image
m_pstrPlaqueMsg	Data	A character array that holds the message being displayed in the plaque
IsShowingPlaque()	Public method	Returns TRUE if the game engine is currently displaying the plaque image
PaintPlaque()	Public method	Paints the plaque image on the screen
TurnOffPlaque()	Public method	Removes the plaque from the display
TurnOnPlaque()	Public method	Displays the plaque image
CheckForAndHandleContainer()	Private method	Calls the helper methods that handle doors
CheckForAndHandleDoor()	Private method	Calls the helper methods that handle doors
CheckForSecretDoor()	Private method	Checks whether there is a secret door at the specified sector and, if there is, returns the ID of the tile to display in place of the door
ContainerEmpty()	Private method	Returns TRUE if the given container is empty
FindContainer()	Private method	Returns a pointer to the container object located in the given sector
FindDoor() in the given sector	Private method	Returns a pointer to the door object located
HandleContainer()	Private method	Handles container objects, including calling the method that transfers a containers contents to the player's inventory
HandleDoor()	Private method	Handles door object, including unlocking a locked door when the player has a key
IsContainer()	Private method	Returns TRUE if the item at the given sector is a container
IsDoor()	Private method	Returns TRUE when the specified sector contains a door
RetrieveArmor() player	Private method	Transfers armor from a container to the
RetrieveGold()	Private method	Transfers gold from a container to the player
RetrieveItemsFromContainer()	Private method	Transfers the contents of a container to the player's inventory

TABLE 16.2 Continued

Member	*Type*	*Description*
RetrieveKeys()	Private method	Transfers keys from a container to the player
RetrievePotion()	Private method	Transfers potions from a container to the player
RetrieveWeapon()	Private method	Transfers a weapon from a container to the player
ShowInventory()	Private method	Displays the player's inventory screen

Summary

This day and the previous one made your burgeoning game a whole lot more interesting by enabling the player to explore and manipulate the game world in various ways. Not only can the player now move from one location to another, but he can also discover fun stuff like hidden doors and valuable treasure. All this treasure will come in handy when you learn to add NPCs, quests, and combat to the game, which you do in the next day.

Q&A

Q. What if the text I want to display won't fit in the text plaque?

A. Currently, the text plaque display in only one size. However, you can make it any size you like, just by changing the vertices used in the `PaintPlaque()` method.

Q. Being able to unlock doors and open containers is pretty cool, but why do the doors lock again and the containers refill themselves with the same objects I just took out of them?

A. Everything in the game gets reset whenever the program reloads a map for an area. To fix this problem, the program must save to disk the changes the player makes in the game world. You'll handle this in Chapter 19, "Saving and Loading Games."

Q. Why are locked doors only locked when you go through them from the front but not from the back?

A. This happens because the door object you manipulate going through a door one way is not the same door object when you're going through the other way. Take the front door of the small house, for example. The door you go through to get into the house is a door object of the First Town area, and so is defined in the FirstTown.map.dor file. However, the door to get out of the house, which appears to be the same door, is actually a door object of the House #2 Room #1 area, and so is defined in the FirstTownHouse02Room01.map.dor file. They are completely different door objects and have their own settings.

Workshop

The workshop includes quiz questions to help gauge your grasp of the material. Even if you feel that you totally understand the concepts presented here, you should work through the quiz anyway.

1. What is a `LOGFONT` structure used for?
2. What relationship is there between a `LOGFONT` structure and an `ID3DXFont` object?
3. What DirectX utility function do you call to create an `ID3DXFont` object?
4. What method do you call to measure or display text?
5. When does the JBookman program look for door objects?
6. Explain the three possible return values from the game engine's `CheckForAndHandleDoor()` method.
7. When does the JBookman program look for container objects?
8. Generally, how does the program transfer an item (such as gold) from the container to the player's inventory?
9. How does the JBookman program hide a secret door from the player?

Answers for Day 16

Quiz

1. What is a `LOGFONT` structure used for?

   It holds the complete description of a Windows font.
2. What relationship is there between a `LOGFONT` structure and an `ID3DXFont` object?

   When you create an `ID3DXFont` object, you pass the `LOGFONT` structure to DirectX. This is the font that the `ID3DXFont` object uses to display text.
3. What DirectX utility function do you call to create an `ID3DXFont` object?

   The `D3DXCreateFontIndirect()` function.
4. What method do you call to measure or display text?

   The `ID3DXFont` object's `DrawText()` method.
5. When does the JBookman program look for door objects?

   Every time the player moves.

6. Explain the three possible return values from the game engine's `CheckForAndHandleDoor()` method.

   The `NODOOR` return value indicates that the target sector is not a door. The `DOOR-LOCKED` return value indicates that the door is locked and the player did not have a key to unlock it. Finally, the `DOORUNLOCKED` return value indicates that the door was locked, but the player had a key and so can move through the door sector.

7. When does the JBookman program look for container objects?

   The same as with the door objects, every time the player moves.

8. Generally, how does the program transfer an item (such as gold) from the container to the player's inventory?

   The program calls one of the `CPlayer` object's "set" functions, such as `SetGold()`, to increase the appropriate item in the player's inventory. The program removes the item from the container similarly, by calling one of the `CContainer` object's set methods.

9. How does the JBookman program hide a secret door from the player?

   By replacing the door image with a wall image.

WEEK 3

DAY 17

Handling Non-Player Characters and Quests

Currently, the starting location of *The Adventures of Jasper Bookman* is a bit of a ghost town. Actually, it's worse than that, because there aren't even any ghosts. Curiously, the town doesn't look very run down for a place that has no one around to take care of it. The truth is that First Town has quite a few people in it. You just haven't yet programmed the part of the game that brings those folks to life.

Once you have a town full of people, you'll want to talk to them, not only to introduce yourself, but also to gather information about the game. Such information usually leads to the quests that make up your game's storyline. It's now time to take care of all these missing game elements. Specifically, in this day you learn how to:

- Draw non-player characters (NPCs) in the town
- Animate the NPC's images
- Add dialog to the game
- Program quests

Populating the Game World

Up until now, the game world of *The Adventures of Jasper Bookman* has been pretty lonely. I mean, there's no one around but the player character, Jasper. If you think back a bit, you'll remember that, in Day 12, "Initializing the Game Data," you loaded all kinds of information from disk and into class objects. Two types of those objects were instances of the `CPerson` and `CPeople` classes. It would be astute of you to think at this point that if there are classes for people, then there must be people somewhere!

You'd be right. There are quite a few people who live and work in First Town. You haven't seen them yet because you haven't written the source code that brings them to life. Load up the latest version of your JBookman project, and perform the following steps to populate First Town with its citizens.

1. Add the following lines to the private method declarations in the Engine.h file, right after the line `int CheckForSecretDoor(int TileNumber, int iSector)` that's already there. If you don't want to type, you can copy the lines from the Code01.txt file in the Chapter17 directory of this book's CD-ROM.

```
BOOL SectorHasPerson(int iSector, int& person);
void MoveNPCs();
void MoveNPCNorth(int person);
void MoveNPCEast(int person);
void MoveNPCSouth(int person);
void MoveNPCWest(int person);
```

2. In the Engine.cpp file, add the following lines to the `PaintBackground()` method, right after the call to `PlaceTile()`. If you don't want to type, you can copy the lines from the Code02.txt file in the Chapter17 directory of this book's CD-ROM.

```
int person;
if (SectorHasPerson(iSector, person))
    PlaceTile(m_Direct3D.GetBackBuffer(),
        m_Direct3D.GetCurrentTileSurface(),
        m_People.GetPerson(person)->GetTile(), DstCol, DstRow,
        COLUMNSINTILEFILE, MAPCOLUMNCOUNT, TILESIZE, XOFFSET, YOFFSET);
```

   These lines draw the NPCs on the screen.

3. Again in Engine.cpp, add the following lines to the `HandleSlowAnimation()` method, right after the `for` loop's closing brace. If you don't want to type, you can copy the lines from the Code03.txt file in the Chapter17 directory of this book's CD-ROM.

```
for (int x=0; x < m_People.GetPersonCount(); ++x)
{
    CPerson* pNPC = m_People.GetPerson(x);
    int r = rand() % 2;
```

```
        if (r == 0)
        {
            int iTile = pNPC->GetTile();
            if (iTile == NPC01 || iTile == NPC02 || iTile == NPC03)
                pNPC->SetTile(iTile + 1);
            else
                pNPC->SetTile(iTile - 1);
        }
    }
```

These lines take care of animating the NPCs.

4. Add the following line to the `ProcessGame()` method, right after the line `RespondToPlayerLocation()` that's already there:

```
MoveNPCs();
```

5. Add the following method implementations to the end of the Engine.cpp file. If you don't want to type, you can copy the lines from the Code04.txt file in the Chapter17 directory of this book's CD-ROM.

```
//////////////////////////////////////////////////////
// SectorHasPerson()
//////////////////////////////////////////////////////
BOOL CEngine::SectorHasPerson(int iSector, int& person)
{
    for (int i=0; i<m_People.GetPersonCount(); ++i)
    {
        if (m_People.GetPerson(i)->GetSector() == iSector)
        {
            person = i;
            return TRUE;
        }
    }
    return FALSE;
}

//////////////////////////////////////////////////////
// MoveNPCs()
//////////////////////////////////////////////////////
void CEngine::MoveNPCs()
{
    static time_t oldTime = time(NULL);
    time_t newTime = time(NULL);
    if (newTime < oldTime+1) return;
    oldTime = newTime;

    for (int person=0; person<m_People.GetPersonCount(); ++person)
    {
        if (m_People.GetPerson(person)->GetCanMove() == TRUE)
        {
            int r = rand() % 2;
```

```
            if (r == 0)
            {
                r = rand() % 4;
                switch(r)
                {
                case 0:
                    MoveNPCNorth(person);
                    break;
                case 1:
                    MoveNPCEast(person);
                    break;
                case 2:
                    MoveNPCSouth(person);
                    break;
                case 3:
                    MoveNPCWest(person);
                }
            }
        }
    }
}

/////////////////////////////////////////////////////////
// MoveNPCNorth()
/////////////////////////////////////////////////////////
void CEngine::MoveNPCNorth(int person)
{
    int iSector = m_People.GetPerson(person)->GetSector() - MAPCOLUMNCOUNT;
    if (m_Sectors[iSector] == DOOR_EXT ||
        m_Sectors[iSector] == DOOR_INT ||
        m_Sectors[iSector] == DOOR_DUN)
        return;

    BOOL canMove = CharacterCanMove(NORTH,
        m_People.GetPerson(person)->GetSector());
    if (canMove && !IsShowingPlaque())
        m_People.GetPerson(person)->SetSector(iSector);
}

/////////////////////////////////////////////////////////
// MoveNPCEast()
/////////////////////////////////////////////////////////
void CEngine::MoveNPCEast(int person)
{
    int iSector = m_People.GetPerson(person)->GetSector() + 1;
    if (m_Sectors[iSector] == DOOR_EXT ||
        m_Sectors[iSector] == DOOR_INT ||
        m_Sectors[iSector] == DOOR_DUN)
        return;

    BOOL canMove = CharacterCanMove(EAST,
```

```
        m_People.GetPerson(person)->GetSector());
    if (canMove && !IsShowingPlaque())
        m_People.GetPerson(person)->SetSector(iSector);
}

///////////////////////////////////////////////////////
// MoveNPCSouth()
///////////////////////////////////////////////////////
void CEngine::MoveNPCSouth(int person)
{
    int iSector = m_People.GetPerson(person)->GetSector() + MAPCOLUMNCOUNT;
    if (m_Sectors[iSector] == DOOR_EXT ||
        m_Sectors[iSector] == DOOR_INT ||
        m_Sectors[iSector] == DOOR_DUN)
        return;

    BOOL canMove = CharacterCanMove(SOUTH,
        m_People.GetPerson(person)->GetSector());
    if (canMove && !IsShowingPlaque())
        m_People.GetPerson(person)->SetSector(iSector);
}

///////////////////////////////////////////////////////
// MoveNPCWest()
///////////////////////////////////////////////////////
void CEngine::MoveNPCWest(int person)
{
    int iSector = m_People.GetPerson(person)->GetSector() - 1;
    if (m_Sectors[iSector] == DOOR_EXT ||
        m_Sectors[iSector] == DOOR_INT ||
        m_Sectors[iSector] == DOOR_DUN)
        return;

    BOOL canMove = CharacterCanMove(WEST,
        m_People.GetPerson(person)->GetSector());
    if (canMove && !IsShowingPlaque())
        m_People.GetPerson(person)->SetSector(iSector);
}
```

These methods move the NPCs around the screen, as well as animate the NPC's images.

6. Add the following lines to the end of the Constants.h file:

```
// NPC tile IDs.
const NPC01 = 58;
const NPC02 = 60;
const NPC03 = 62;
```

And, believe it or not, you're done. Compile and run the program, and First Town will be crawling with folks, all of them moving around the town on their own business. Figure 17.1 shows the town with its new citizens.

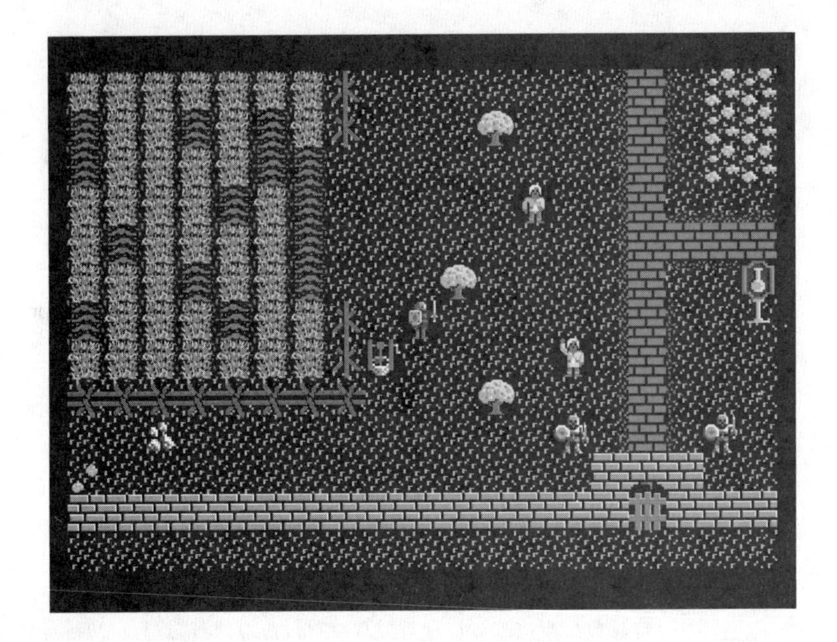

FIGURE 17.1
The now populated First Town.

Processing the NPCs

When dealing with NPCs, the program must perform several tasks. These tasks are as follows:

- Draw the NPCs on the screen
- Move the NPCs around the current area
- Animate the NPCs

The following sections describe each of these important processes.

Drawing the NPCs

The first task the program has with regards to the occupants of First Town is to draw each person's image. This happens in the `PaintBackground()` method, which, up until now, drew only the tiles for the current map. Now, it also draws the NPCs. To do this, the program first checks whether there's an NPC located in the sector currently being processed:

```
if (SectorHasPerson(iSector, person))
```

If there is a person in the sector, the program draws its tile:

```
PlaceTile(m_Direct3D.GetBackBuffer(),
    m_Direct3D.GetCurrentTileSurface(),
    m_People.GetPerson(person)->GetTile(), DstCol, DstRow,
    COLUMNSINTILEFILE, MAPCOLUMNCOUNT, TILESIZE, XOFFSET, YOFFSET);
```

Notice that the ID for the NPC's tile is retrieved from the CPerson object that represents the NPC. This will be important when you see how to animate the NPCs.

The SectorHasPerson() method simply searches through the CPeople object for a person located at the current sector:

```
for (int i=0; i<m_People.GetPersonCount(); ++i)
{
    if (m_People.GetPerson(i)->GetSector() == iSector)
    {
        person = i;
        return TRUE;
    }
}
return FALSE;
```


Moving the NPCs

The next task the program has is to move the NPCs (or at least the ones who are allowed to move) around the town. This process starts in the ProcessGame() method that gets called continuously from the application's message loop. One line does it:

```
MoveNPCs();
```

The MoveNPCs() method is a little tricky, however. This is because, in order to make the people's movement seem more natural, they move at different times. The NPC movement routine also uses a different timing method than the program's main animation routines. The first time MoveNPCs() gets called, it stores the current time in a static variable:

```
static time_t oldTime = time(NULL);
```

As you should know, although this static variable is local to the MoveNPCs() method, it will retain its value even after the method exits.

Every time MoveNPCs() gets called, it gets the current time, compares it with the previously retrieved time, and then saves the current time:

```
time_t newTime = time(NULL);
if (newTime < oldTime+1) return;
oldTime = newTime;
```

The time() function returns the elapsed time in seconds, so you can see in the previous lines that, if a second hasn't passed since the last time the program called MoveNPCs(), the method returns without doing anything. Otherwise, it's time to move some NPCs around. A for loop cycles through each of the CPerson objects:

```
for (int person=0; person<m_People.GetPersonCount(); ++person)
{
    .
    .
```

```
    .
}
```

Inside the loop, the program checks whether the currently accessed person can move:

```
if (m_People.GetPerson(person)->GetCanMove() == TRUE)
{
    .
    .
    .
}
```

If that person can't move, the loop goes on to the next person. If the current person can move, that still doesn't mean he will. In order to keep everyone from moving at the same time, the program gets a random number from 0 to 1. If the number is 0, the person is allowed to move. Otherwise, the loop goes on to the next person:

```
int r = rand() % 2;
if (r == 0)
{
    .
    .
    .
}
```

If the person can move, the program grabs another random number, this time between 0 and 3, and uses that number to determine which direction the NPC will move:

```
r = rand() % 4;
switch(r)
{
case 0:
    MoveNPCNorth(person);
    break;
case 1:
    MoveNPCEast(person);
    break;
case 2:
    MoveNPCSouth(person);
    break;
case 3:
    MoveNPCWest(person);
```

The methods that move the NPCs in a specific direction aren't all that different from the methods that move the player character. However, in the case of an NPC, the program can't allow an NPC to go through a door:

```
int iSector = m_People.GetPerson(person)->GetSector() - MAPCOLUMNCOUNT;
if (m_Sectors[iSector] == DOOR_EXT ||
    m_Sectors[iSector] == DOOR_INT ||
    m_Sectors[iSector] == DOOR_DUN)
    return;
```

Animating the NPCs

Sure, moving the NPCs around the town is a kind of animation, but the program also animates each of the NPC images so that it doesn't seem to be a statue. This type of animation happens in the `HandleSlowAnimation()` method, with which you're already familiar. The new lines start with a `for` loop that searches through each of the NPCs stored in the `CPeople` object:

```
for (int x=0; x < m_People.GetPersonCount(); ++x)
{
    .
    .
    .
}
```


Inside the loop, the program gets a pointer to the next person to process:

```
CPerson* pNPC = m_People.GetPerson(x);
```

The program then gets a random number from 0 to 1:

```
int r = rand() % 2;
```

The random number determines whether to change the tile for the current person. Using a random number in this way accomplishes two things. First, it prevents each of the NPCs from switching to its next animation frame at the same time, which looks very unnatural. Second, the use of the random number makes each NPC's change unpredictable, so even if you're looking at only a single NPC image, it won't keep switching between its animation frames at a steady rate.

If the random number is zero, the program switches the current NPC's image to the next one in the animation sequence:

```
if (r == 0)
{
    int iTile = pNPC->GetTile();
    if (iTile == NPC01 || iTile == NPC02 || iTile == NPC03)
        pNPC->SetTile(iTile + 1);
    else
        pNPC->SetTile(iTile - 1);
}
```

Getting NPCs to Talk

So, the town isn't so lonely anymore, but it sure is quiet, what with no one having a word to say to anyone else. One of the most important features of an RPG is the way the player can talk to people in order to get information and take on quests. This information gathering is, in fact, part of the storytelling process that every RPG must perform. Tackle the following steps to make your NPCs more chatty.

1. Add the following lines to the Engine.h file, after the public method declaration `void PaintPlaque()` that's already there:

```
protected:
    virtual void HandleNPC(int iNPC);
```

2. Add the following line to the class's private method declarations, right after the line `void MoveNPCWest(int person)` that's already there:

```
BOOL CheckForAndHandleNPC(int iSector);
```

3. Add the following method implementations to the end of the Engine.cpp file. If you don't want to type, you can copy the lines from the Code05.txt file in the Chapter17 directory of this book's CD-ROM.

```
/////////////////////////////////////////////////////////
// CheckForAndHandleNPC()
/////////////////////////////////////////////////////////
BOOL CEngine::CheckForAndHandleNPC(int iSector)
{
    BOOL bHandledNPC = FALSE;
    int person;
    if (SectorHasPerson(iSector, person))
    {
        HandleNPC(person);
        bHandledNPC = TRUE;
    }
    return bHandledNPC;
}

/////////////////////////////////////////////////////////
// HandleNPC()
/////////////////////////////////////////////////////////
void CEngine::HandleNPC(int iNPCNum)
{
    CPerson* pNPC = m_People.GetPerson(iNPCNum);
    char msg[128];
    char name[128];
    strcpy(name, m_People.GetPerson(iNPCNum)->GetName());
    strcpy(name, &name[1]);
    name[strlen(name) - 1] = 0;
    wsprintf(msg, "Hi! I'm %s.", name);
    TurnOnPlaque(msg);
}
```

4. Add the following lines to all four of the arrow-handling methods (`HandleLeftArrow()` and so on), right after the line `int iTargetSector = m_Player.GetSector() - 1` that's already there:

```
BOOL bHandledNPC = CheckForAndHandleNPC(iTargetSector);
if (bHandledNPC) return;
```

These lines check for an NPC each time the player moves.

5. Add the following lines to the MyEngine.h file, right before the class's closing brace:

```
protected:
    virtual void HandleNPC(int iNPC);
```

This version of the `HandleNPC()` method overrides the one defined in the `CEngine` class.

6. Add the following lines to the end of the MyEngine.cpp file. If you don't want to type, you can copy the lines from the Code06.txt file in the Chapter17 directory of this book's CD-ROM.

```
///////////////////////////////////////////////////////
// HandleNPC()
///////////////////////////////////////////////////////
void CMyEngine::HandleNPC(int iNPC)
{
    char msg[1024];
    char name[128];
    strcpy(name, m_People.GetPerson(iNPC)->GetName());
    strcpy(name, &name[1]);
    name[strlen(name) - 1] = 0;
    if (strcmp(name, "Fennel Gridrock") == 0)
    {
        wsprintf(msg, "I'm %s, a guard\nhere at First Town. \
I hope you\nenjoy your stay.", name);
        TurnOnPlaque(msg);
    }
    else if (strcmp(name, "Uris Yamdolf") == 0)
    {
        wsprintf(msg, "I'm %s, a guard\nhere at First Town. \
You're Jasper,\nright? You're supposed to talk\nwith Grewell \
Pessle as soon\nas you can.", name);
        TurnOnPlaque(msg);
    }
    else
        CEngine::HandleNPC(iNPC);
}
```

This method, which overrides the `CEngine` version, displays dialog for the NPCs or calls the `CEngine` version for a default response from the NPC.

Another easy project. And you thought it would be hard to get the NPCs to talk. Compile and run the program. When the game screen appears, walk up to anybody in the town and bump into him. (That's the talk command, not a way to push people around!) When you do, the person will either say "Hi!" and give you his name (see Figure 17.2) or will have something more interesting to say. For some interesting talk, try talking with either of the guards (see Figure 17.3).

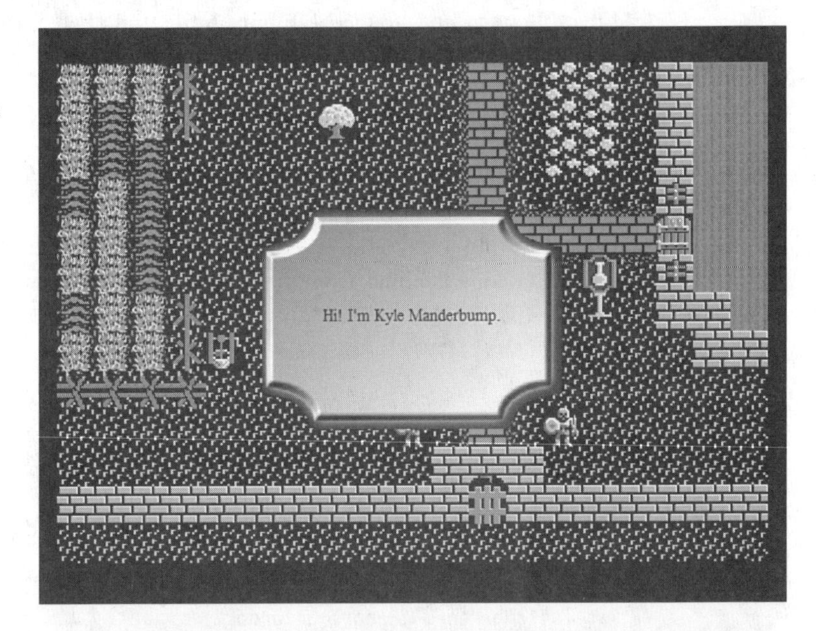

FIGURE 17.2

The player gets the common response from a citizen of First Town.

FIGURE 17.3

The gate guards have a bit more to say.

Understanding How NPCs Talk

How do NPCs talk? With their mouths, just like everyone else! Seriously, though, you already know that you can open a treasure chest by walking into it or that you can unlock a door the same way. If you've played the game as it is so far, you now know that you talk to NPCs the same way again, by walking into them.

The first thing the program needs is a way to respond to the player's movement, if that movement will bring him into an NPC's sector. This is done just as it is with doors and containers, by adding a couple of lines to each of the arrow-handling methods:

```
BOOL bHandledNPC = CheckForAndHandleNPC(iTargetSector);
if (bHandledNPC) return;
```

The `CheckForAndHandleNPC()` method checks whether there's an NPC in the target sector. If there is, the method handles the NPC and then returns `TRUE`:

```
BOOL bHandledNPC = FALSE;
int person;
if (SectorHasPerson(iSector, person))
{
    HandleNPC(person);
    bHandledNPC = TRUE;
}
return bHandledNPC;
```

A `TRUE` return value causes the arrow-handling method to return without bothering with its checks for doors and containers. After all, if there's an NPC in the target sector, there's not a door or container. Also, the player can't move into a sector that contains an NPC. If the player needs to move to that sector, she'll just have to wait until the NPC moves!

If the `CheckForAndHandleNPC()` method finds an NPC, it also handles it. The method does this by calling the `HandleNPC()` method, which is declared in the class like this:

```
protected:
    virtual void HandleNPC(int iNPC);
```

See the `virtual` keyword? This means that you can override the method in your `CMyEngine` class, which you have, in fact, already done. Because of this, program execution goes to the `CMyEngine` class's `HandleNPC()`, rather than the `CEngine` class's version. There, the program can check for special cases before calling `CEngine`'s `HandleNPC()` method for default processing.

The `CMyEngine` version of `HandleNPC()` first gets the NPC's name:

```
char name[128];
strcpy(name, m_People.GetPerson(iNPC)->GetName());
```

```
strcpy(name, &name[1]);
name[strlen(name) - 1] = 0;
```

All the string-handling here just gets rid of the quotation marks that surround the name in the person's name data, as it was loaded from the file.

The method can now compare the NPC's name to names of NPCs that require custom processing:

```
    if (strcmp(name, "Fennel Gridrock") == 0)
    {
        wsprintf(msg, "I'm %s, a guard\nhere at First Town. \
I hope you\nenjoy your stay.", name);
        TurnOnPlaque(msg);
    }
    else if (strcmp(name, "Uris Yamdolf") == 0)
    {
        wsprintf(msg, "I'm %s, a guard\nhere at First Town. \
You're Jasper,\nright? You're supposed to talk\nwith Grewell \
Pessle as soon\nas you can.", name);
        TurnOnPlaque(msg);
    }
```

If the NPC needs only normal processing by the game engine, the program calls `CEngine`'s `HandleNPC()`:

```
    else
        CEngine::HandleNPC(iNPC);
```

The `CEngine` version of `HandleNPC()` does nothing more than display a default message from the NPC:

```
CPerson* pNPC = m_People.GetPerson(iNPCNum);
char msg[128];
char name[128];
strcpy(name, m_People.GetPerson(iNPCNum)->GetName());
strcpy(name, &name[1]);
name[strlen(name) - 1] = 0;
wsprintf(msg, "Hi! I'm %s.", pNPC->GetName());
TurnOnPlaque(msg);
```

Creating a Quest

Now that you have NPCs who can talk, you can start putting together the various quests and story elements that the game will contain. Unfortunately, you can't have much of a story with NPCs who say nothing more than "Hi!" and their name. On the other hand, the details of your particular story are no business of the game engine, which handles only general game tasks, such as supplying the NPCs with their default responses.

Obviously you need some way to hook into the game engine so that *you* can decide what your NPCs have to say rather than the game engine. Again, object-oriented programming (OOP) techniques come to the rescue. Remember how you declared the `HandleNPC()` method as being virtual? You'll now override this virtual method in your `CMyEngine` class, enabling you to provide custom dialog for an NPC or just let the game engine give the default response.

You'll also switch the `HandleContainer()` and `HandleDoor()` methods over to virtual, so that you can choose between handling a container or door in your custom `CMyEngine` class or just let the game engine handle it. Tackle the following steps to add this functionality to the JBookman project.

1. In Engine.h file, move the `HandleContainer()` and `HandleDoor()` method declarations from the private section to below the protected area below the line `virtual void HandleNPC(int iNPC)` that's already there. Change the declarations to virtual, like this:

```
virtual BOOL HandleContainer(int iSector);
virtual BOOL HandleDoor(int iSector);
```

   By changing these to virtual methods, you can override them in the `CMyEngine` class and so provide customized code when needed.

2. In MyEngine.h, add the following lines to the virtual method declarations, right below the line `virtual void HandleNPC(int iNPC)` that's already there:

```
virtual BOOL HandleContainer(int iSector);
virtual BOOL HandleDoor(int iSector);
```

3. In the MyEngine.cpp file, add the following `case` clause to the end of the `switch` statement in the `RespondToPlayerLocation()` method:

```
case FIRSTTOWNDUNGEON02:
    HandleFirstTownDungeon02();
   break;
```

   These lines handle a new location that you'll soon be seeing.

4. Again in the MyEngine.cpp file, replace the current `HandleNPC()` method with the one that follows. If you don't want to type, you can copy the lines from the Code07.txt file in the Chapter17 directory of this book's CD-ROM.

```
/////////////////////////////////////////////////////////
// HandleNPC()
/////////////////////////////////////////////////////////
void CMyEngine::HandleNPC(int iNPC)
{
    char name[128];
    strcpy(name, m_People.GetPerson(iNPC)->GetName());
    strcpy(name, &name[1]);
```

```
        name[strlen(name) - 1] = 0;
        if (strcmp(name, "Fennel Gridrock") == 0)
            HandleFennelGridrock();
        else if (strcmp(name, "Uris Yamdolf") == 0)
            HandleUrisYamdolf();
        else if (strcmp(name, "Grewell Pessle") == 0)
            HandleGrewellPessle();
        else if (strcmp(name, "Willam Groves") == 0)
            HandleWillamGroves();
        else
            CEngine::HandleNPC(iNPC);
    }
```

5. Add the following method implementations to the end of the MyEngine.cpp file. If you don't want to type, you can copy the lines from the Code08.txt file in the Chapter17 directory of this book's CD-ROM.

```
////////////////////////////////////////////////////////
// HandleContainer()
////////////////////////////////////////////////////////
BOOL CMyEngine::HandleContainer(int iSector)
{
    if (m_iCurrentMap == FIRSTTOWNDUNGEON02 &&
            m_Sectors[iSector] == BARREL_DUN)
    {
        FinishWillamQuest();
        return TRUE;
    }
    else
        return CEngine::HandleContainer(iSector);
}

////////////////////////////////////////////////////////
// HandleDoor()
////////////////////////////////////////////////////////
BOOL CMyEngine::HandleDoor(int iSector)
{
    if (m_iCurrentMap == FIRSTTOWN && iSector == HOUSE02FRONTDOOR)
    {
        BOOL bOpen = OpenAbandonedHouse();
        return bOpen;
    }
    return CEngine::HandleDoor(iSector);
}
```

6. Add the following lines to the end of the FirstTown.h file. If you don't want to type, you can copy the lines from the Code09.txt file in the Chapter17 directory of this book's CD-ROM.

```
BOOL OpenAbandonedHouse();
void HandleFirstTownDungeon02();
```

```
void HandleFennelGridrock();
void HandleUrisYamdolf();
void HandleGrewellPessle();
void HandleWillamGroves();
void FinishWillamQuest();
```

7. Add the following lines to the FirstTown.cpp file, right after the line `const DUNGEON01ROOM11ENTRANCE3 = 1131` that's already there. If you don't want to type, you can copy the lines from the Code10.txt file in the Chapter17 directory of this book's CD-ROM.

```
const DUNGEON02ENTRANCE = 87;
const DUNGEON02EXIT = 130;

// Quest flags.
BOOL bSpokeToGrewell = FALSE;
BOOL bSpokeToWillam = FALSE;
BOOL bWillamQuestComplete = FALSE;
BOOL bHasWillamKey = FALSE;
```


8. Add the following `case` clause to the `HandleFirstTown()` method. If you don't want to type, you can copy the lines from the Code11.txt file in the Chapter17 directory of this book's CD-ROM.

```
case DUNGEON02ENTRANCE:
    if (bSpokeToWillam)
    {
        g_Engine.GetPlayer()->SetSector(DUNGEON02EXIT - MAPCOLUMNCOUNT);
        g_Engine.OpenMapFiles("FirstTownDungeon02.map");
        g_Engine.SetCurrentMap(FIRSTTOWNDUNGEON02);
        g_Engine.GetCDirect3DObj()->SetCurrentTileSurface
            (g_Engine.GetCDirect3DObj()->GetDungeonTileSurface());
        g_Engine.ResetAnimation();
    }
    break;
```

9. Add the following methods to the end of the FirstTown.cpp file. If you don't want to type, you can copy the lines from the Code12.txt file in the Chapter17 directory of this book's CD-ROM.

```
//////////////////////////////////////////////////////////
// HandleFirstTownDungeon02()
//////////////////////////////////////////////////////////
void HandleFirstTownDungeon02()
{
    switch (g_Engine.GetPlayer()->GetSector())
    {
    case DUNGEON02EXIT:
        g_Engine.GetPlayer()->
            SetSector(DUNGEON02ENTRANCE - 1);
        g_Engine.GetCDirect3DObj()->SetCurrentTileSurface
```

```
            (g_Engine.GetCDirect3DObj()->GetTownExtTileSurface());
        g_Engine.OpenMapFiles("FirstTown.map");
        g_Engine.SetCurrentMap(FIRSTTOWN);
        g_Engine.ResetAnimation();
        break;
    }
}

//////////////////////////////////////////////////////
// HandleFennelGridrock()
//////////////////////////////////////////////////////
void HandleFennelGridrock()
{
    g_Engine.TurnOnPlaque(
"I'm Fennel Gridrock, a guard\n\
here at First Town. I hope you\n\
enjoy your stay.");
}

//////////////////////////////////////////////////////
// HandleUrisYamdolf()
//////////////////////////////////////////////////////
void HandleUrisYamdolf()
{
    if (bSpokeToGrewell)
        g_Engine.TurnOnPlaque(
"I'm Uris Yamdolf, a guard\n\
here at First Town. It's nice to\n\
have you here helping\n\
the citizens.");
    else
        g_Engine.TurnOnPlaque(
"I'm Uris Yamdolf, a guard\n\
here at First Town. You're Jasper,\n\
right? You're supposed to talk\n\
with Grewell Pessle as soon\n\
as you can.");
}

//////////////////////////////////////////////////////
// HandleGrewellPessle()
//////////////////////////////////////////////////////
void HandleGrewellPessle()
{
    if (!bSpokeToGrewell)
    {
        g_Engine.TurnOnPlaque(
"I'm Grewell Pessle, one of the\n\
town Councilmen. Willam Groves'\n\
son lost his puppy. Find the puppy,\n\
and I'll give you something useful\n\
Speak to Willam for more\n\
```

```
information about the puppy.");
        bSpokeToGrewell = TRUE;
    }
    else if (bSpokeToGrewell && !bWillamQuestComplete)
        g_Engine.TurnOnPlaque(
"You're supposed to be finding\n\
that puppy, remember? Talk to\n\
Willam Groves.");
    else if (bWillamQuestComplete && !bHasWillamKey)
    {
        g_Engine.TurnOnPlaque(
"Great job finding the puppy!\n\
Here's the key you\n\
need to get into the\n\
abandoned house.");
        bHasWillamKey = TRUE;
    }
    else if (bHasWillamKey)
    {
        g_Engine.TurnOnPlaque(
"Thanks for your help\n\
finding the puppy.");
        bHasWillamKey = TRUE;
    }
}

///////////////////////////////////////////////////////
// HandleWillamGroves()
///////////////////////////////////////////////////////
void HandleWillamGroves()
{
    if (bSpokeToWillam && !bWillamQuestComplete)
        g_Engine.TurnOnPlaque(
"My son is very unhappy.\n\
Please find his puppy.");
    else if (bSpokeToGrewell && !bSpokeToWillam)
    {
        g_Engine.TurnOnPlaque(
"Hi, Jasper. Grewell told me\n\
that he spoke to you. I'm Willam\n\
Groves. My son said he last saw\n\
his dog somewhere in the\n\
northwest of the town.");
        bSpokeToWillam = TRUE;
    }
    else if (bWillamQuestComplete)
        g_Engine.TurnOnPlaque(
"Hi again, Jasper! My son is\n\
thrilled to have his puppy back.\n\
Did you see Grewell Passle\n\
about your reward?");
    else
```

```
        g_Engine.TurnOnPlaque(
"Hello, stranger.\n\
I'm Willam Groves.");
}

////////////////////////////////////////////////////////
// FinishWillamQuest()
////////////////////////////////////////////////////////
void FinishWillamQuest()
{
    if (!bWillamQuestComplete)
    {
        g_Engine.TurnOnPlaque("You find a small puppy,\n\
which you tuck safely\nunder your arm.");
        bWillamQuestComplete = TRUE;
    }
    else
        g_Engine.TurnOnPlaque("You find nothing.");
}

////////////////////////////////////////////////////////
// OpenAbandonedHouse()
////////////////////////////////////////////////////////
BOOL OpenAbandonedHouse()
{
    if (bHasWillamKey)
    {
        g_Engine.TurnOnPlaque(
"You use the key you got\n\
from Grewell Pessle to\n\
open the door.");
        return TRUE;
    }
    g_Engine.TurnOnPlaque("You need a special key.");
    return FALSE;
}
```

10. Add the following symbol to the `g_iLocationEnum` enumeration in the Constants.h file:

    ```
    FIRSTTOWNDUNGEON02
    ```

11. Move the constants defined in FirstTown.cpp to the top of FirstTown.h. Also, add the following line right before the constant definitions:

    ```
    #pragma once
    ```

    Other parts of the program now need access to the constants. Putting them into the header file accomplishes that. The `#pragma` prevents the header from being included more than once during a compile of the project.

12. Copy the following files from the Chapter17 directory of this book's CD-ROM to the Maps directory of your JBookman project:

```
FirstTownDungeon02.map
FirstTownDungeon02.map.dor
FirstTownDungeon02.map.itm
FirstTownDungeon02.map.peo
```

The game has gotten to the point now where you can actually play rather than just poke around in the different locations. To see what I mean, compile and run the program. When you do, the game screen appears just as usual, but now you have some new stuff to do. You can just walk around and see who has what to say, and figure out the game's first quest on your own. If you want to do that, stop reading here, and come back when you're done. If you want a guided tour through the first quest, read on.

First, go to the small house with the secret door, as shown in Figure 17.4. Try to go through the door, and you'll get the curious response shown in Figure 17.5.

FIGURE 17.4

The first stop is this small house.

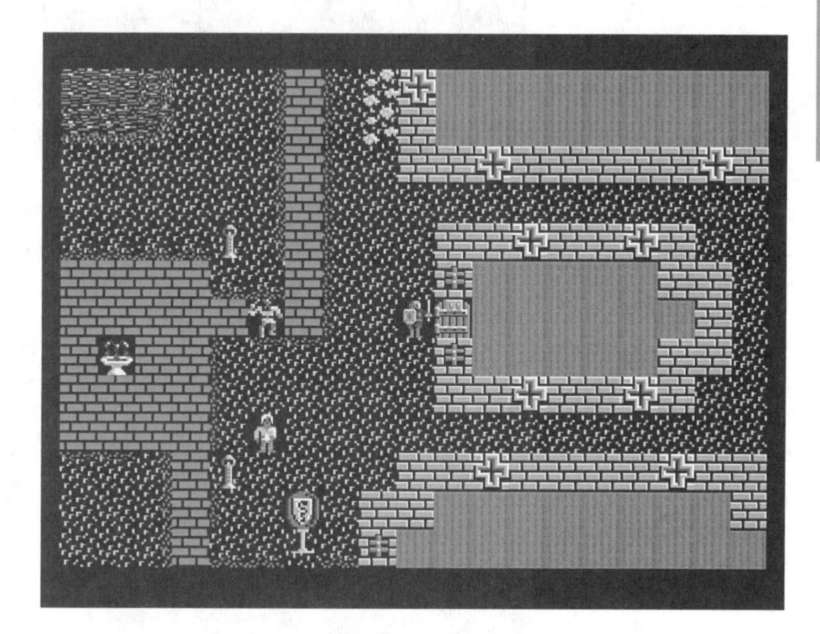

Hmmmm. Used to be you could get into the house just by having any old key in your inventory. Now, it looks like you have to find a different kind of key. Go back to the town gate and talk to the guard on the right. He'll tell you what to do next, as shown in Figure 17.6.

Now, with the name Grewell Pessle, head north until you come across the guy shown in Figure 17.7. When you talk to him, he'll tell you, "I'm Grewell Pessle, one of the town Councilmen. Willam Grove's son lost his puppy. Find the puppy, and I'll give you something useful. Speak to Willam for more information about the puppy."

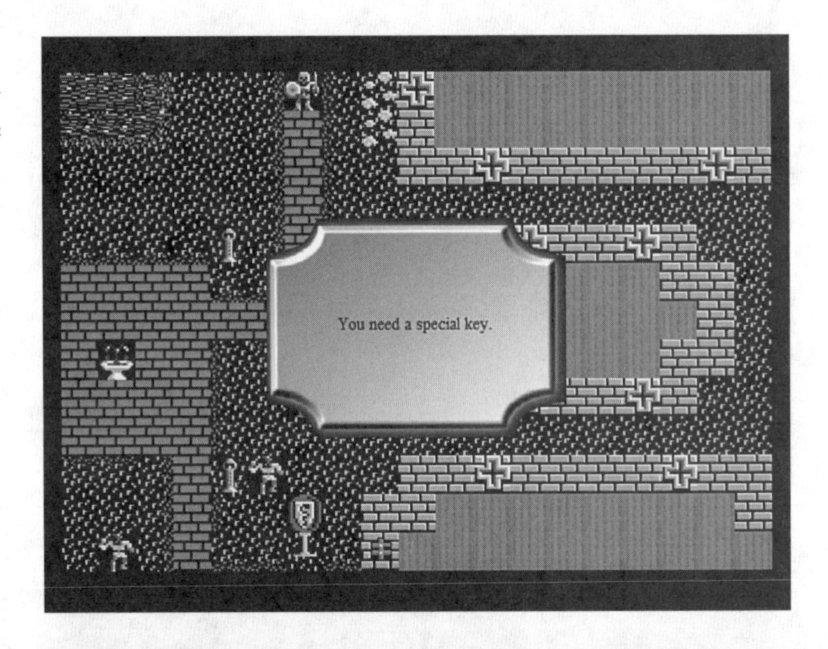

FIGURE 17.5
Now the door isn't just locked; it's locked with a special key.

FIGURE 17.6
One of the gate guards has your first clue.

You can usually find Willam Groves in the western part of the town, but he moves around, so you may have to talk to a few people before you find him. When you do, have a chat, and he'll tell you more about his son's lost pet, as shown in Figure 17.8.

FIGURE 17.7
Grewell Pessle has information and a task for you.

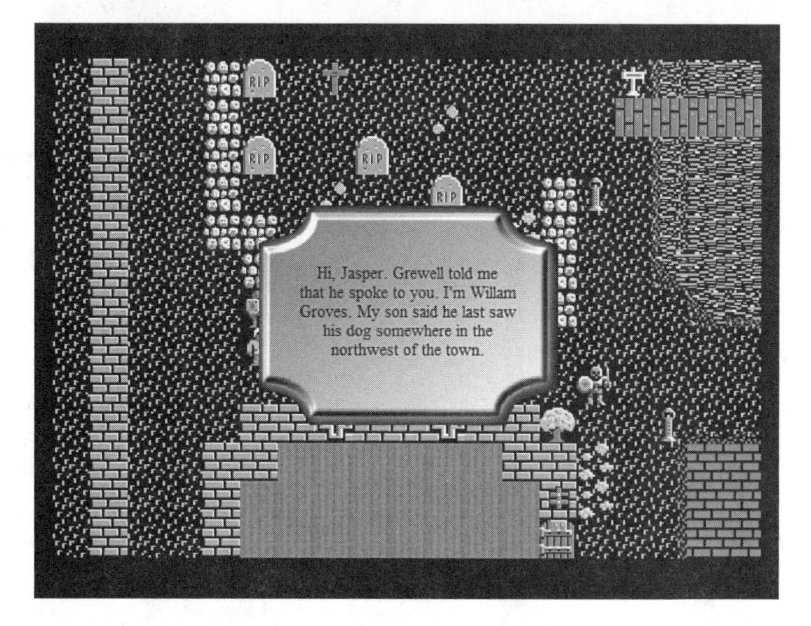

FIGURE 17.8
Willam Groves gives you a hint as to where you might find the missing puppy.

Explore the area next to the wall in the northwest corner of the town, and you'll fall into a hole that leads to a small dungeon, as shown in Figure 17.9.

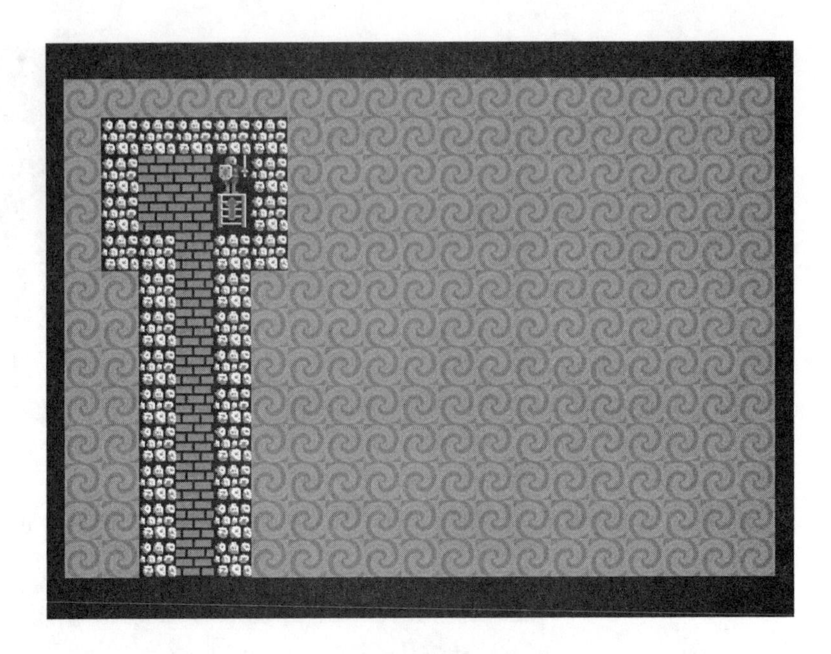

FIGURE 17.9

Another hidden dungeon in the town.

Now, walk south until you get to a room containing a treasure chest and a barrel (see Figure 17.10). You can get some handy stuff from the chest, but when you look into the barrel, you'll find the missing puppy, as shown in Figure 17.11.

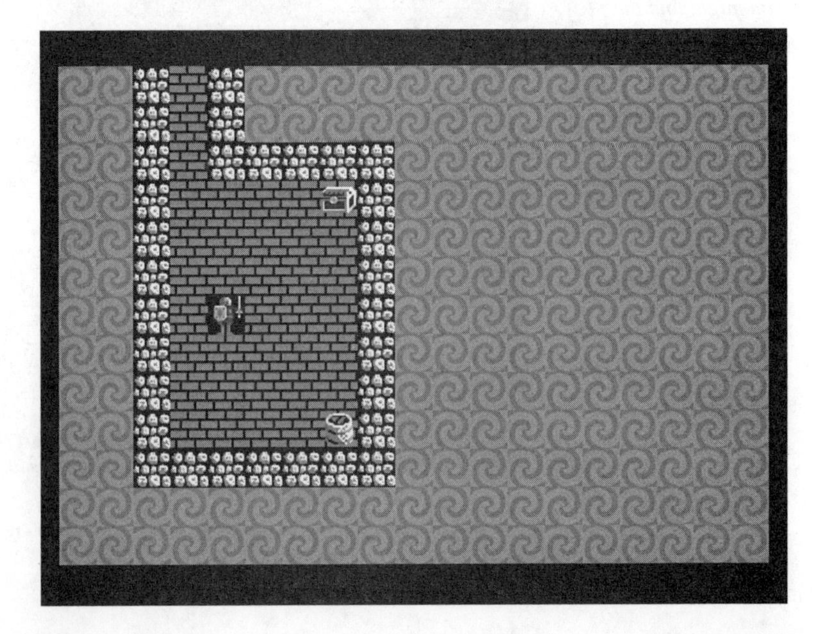

FIGURE 17.10

A special room in the southern part of the dungeon.

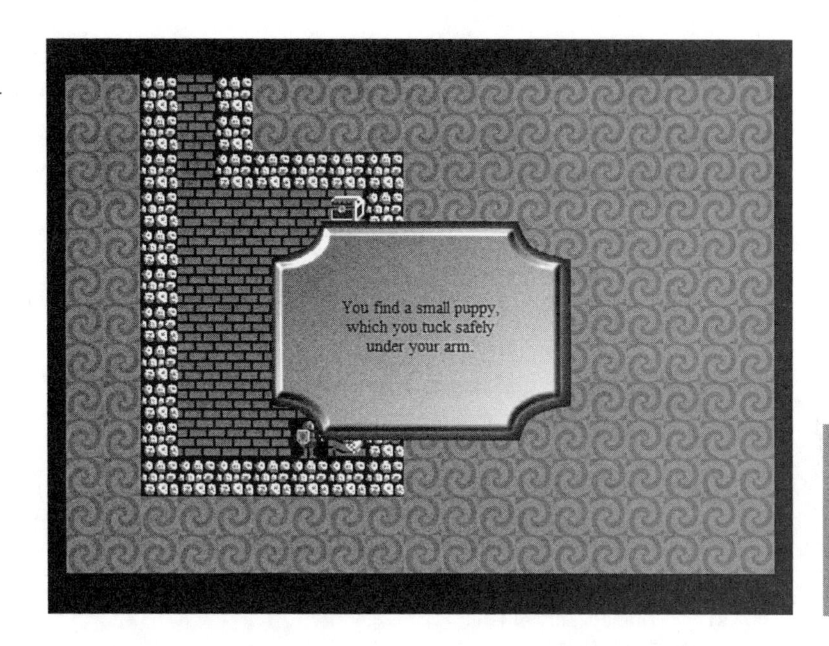

FIGURE 17.11

The pet rescue accomplished.

Head out of the dungeon, and go back to Willam Groves, who will thank you and remind you to check in with Grewell Pessle (see Figure 17.12).

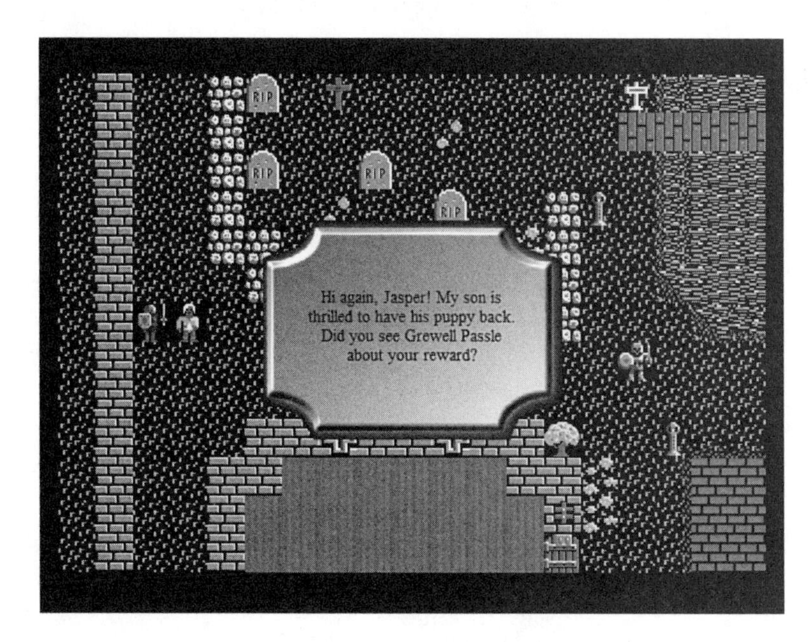

FIGURE 17.12

A grateful father.

Finally, when you talk to Grewell Pessle again, he'll give you the key you need to get into the small house. Head for the house, and in you go! Quest completed.

Digging Into the Quest Programming

Now all you have to do is program about a hundred more quests and the game will be done! Well, not quite. You still have to learn about buying stuff and handling combat. More importantly, you have to study the source code that implements the first quest you just completed.

The quest starts as the player roams around town, talking with its citizens. Bump into an NPC, and he'll have something to say. (Yes, I know there are no female NPCs in the game. This isn't because I'm a chauvinist pig, but rather because the graphics I had to work with turned out to be all male. Sorry about that.) An NPC's response starts with the `HandleNPC()` method. That method first retrieves the NPC's name:

```
char name[128];
strcpy(name, m_People.GetPerson(iNPC)->GetName());
strcpy(name, &name[1]);
name[strlen(name) - 1] = 0;
```

The program can now compare the name with the names of NPCs who have something special to say and call the appropriate method:

```
if (strcmp(name, "Fennel Gridrock") == 0)
    HandleFennelGridrock();
else if (strcmp(name, "Uris Yamdolf") == 0)
    HandleUrisYamdolf();
else if (strcmp(name, "Grewell Pessle") == 0)
    HandleGrewellPessle();
else if (strcmp(name, "Willam Groves") == 0)
    HandleWillamGroves();
```

If the NPC involved in the event has nothing special to say, `HandleNPC()` simply lets the game engine provide the default response:

```
else
    CEngine::HandleNPC(iNPC);
```

Simple, no? The complication comes when you try to keep track of whom the player has spoken with and what the next step in the quest should be. This task requires a set of flags, which the program defines in the FirstTown.cpp file:

```
BOOL bSpokeToGrewell = FALSE;
BOOL bSpokeToWillam = FALSE;
```

```
BOOL bWillamQuestComplete = FALSE;
BOOL bHasWillamKey = FALSE;
```

The flags' names say a lot about how they're used, but you'll get an even better picture as you look through the rest of the source code for the quest. For example, look what happens when the player talks to the gate guard, Uris Yamdolf. In the `HandleUrisYamdolf()` method, the program first checks the `bSpokeToGrewell` flag:

```
if (bSpokeToGrewell)
```

Because the flag can be either `TRUE` or `FALSE`, you can guess that Uris Yamdolf will have two different things to say, depending on the flag's value. If the flag is `TRUE`, the player has already talked with Grewell Pessle, and so the guard doesn't need to tell the player to see Grewell. Instead, the guard has only a polite reply to give:

```
        g_Engine.TurnOnPlaque(
"I'm Uris Yamdolf, a guard\n\
here at First Town. It's nice to\n\
have you here helping\n\
the citizens.");
```


However, if the flag is `FALSE`, the player hasn't yet talked with Grewell Pessle, and so the guard gives this response:

```
    else
        g_Engine.TurnOnPlaque(
"I'm Uris Yamdolf, a guard\n\
here at First Town. You're Jasper,\n\
right? You're supposed to talk\n\
with Grewell Pessle as soon\n\
as you can.");
```

When does the `bSpokeToGrewell` flag get changed from `FALSE` to `TRUE`? When the player talks with Grewell, the program jumps to the `HandleGrewellPessle()` method, which is one of the most complicated in the quest, because it must check the values of three different flags in order to provide the correct responses. If the player has not yet spoken with Grewell, the player is just starting the quest, and the following source code executes:

```
    if (!bSpokeToGrewell)
    {
        g_Engine.TurnOnPlaque(
"I'm Grewell Pessle, one of the\n\
town Councilman. Willam Groves'\n\
son lost his puppy. Find the puppy,\n\
and I'll give you something useful\n\
Speak to Willam for more\n\
```

```
information about the puppy.");
        bSpokeToGrewell = TRUE;
    }
```

Here, not only does the program display the text that explains the player's quest, but it also sets the `bSpokeToGrewell` flag to `TRUE`. This ensures that the player will not get the same speech from Grewell should the player speak to him again. In fact, if the player speaks to Grewell again right away, this source code executes:

```
    if (bSpokeToGrewell && !bWillamQuestComplete)
        g_Engine.TurnOnPlaque(
"You're supposed to be finding\n\
that puppy, remember? Talk to\n\
Willam Groves.");
```

Notice that these lines check not only whether the player has already spoken to Grewell, but also whether the player has yet to complete the quest, an event tracked by the `bWillamQuestComplete` flag.

If the player has completed the quest, but has not yet received the key, the following happens:

```
    else if (bWillamQuestComplete && !bHasWillamKey)
    {
        g_Engine.TurnOnPlaque(
"Great job finding the puppy!\n\
Here's the key you\n\
need to get into the\n\
abandoned house.");
        bHasWillamKey = TRUE;
    }
```

Finally, if the quest is complete and the player has received his reward, Grewell will have only the following to say:

```
    else if (bHasWillamKey)
    {
        g_Engine.TurnOnPlaque(
"Thanks for your help\n\
finding the puppy.");
    }
```

As you can see, the logic can get a little tricky, as you have to make sure you use the flags correctly and that you don't forget to include a required flag for any element of the quest. This complication is coupled with the fact that a quest frequently requires that the player speak with several NPCs and perform several sub-quests in order to be able to complete a major quest.

The method that handles the interaction with Willam Groves works similarly. Look it over on your own to be sure you understand the relationship between the various flags and the NPC's responses.

Another important addition to the program is how the `HandleContainer()` and `HandleDoor()` methods are now declared as virtual and are overridden in your `CMyEngine` class. This change enables you to handle any specific container or door any way you want. For example, when the player looks in the barrel, he finds the puppy:

```
BOOL CMyEngine::HandleContainer(int iSector)
{
    if (m_iCurrentMap == FIRSTTOWNDUNGEON02 &&
            m_Sectors[iSector] == BARREL_DUN)
    {
        FinishWillamQuest();
        return TRUE;
    }
    else
        return CEngine::HandleContainer(iSector);
}
```


Here, you can see how the program routes program execution to the `FinishWillamQuest()` method if the player is trying to open the barrel that contains the puppy. Otherwise, the method simply calls the `CEngine` class's version of the method in order to provide default processing for the container.

In the `FinishWillamQuest()` method, the program first checks to be sure that the player hasn't already rescued the puppy. If he hasn't, the program tells the player that he's found the puppy and sets the appropriate flag. Otherwise, the program tells the player he's found nothing:

```
    if (!bWillamQuestComplete)
    {
        g_Engine.TurnOnPlaque("You find a small puppy,\n\
which you tuck safely\nunder your arm.");
        bWillamQuestComplete = TRUE;
    }
    else
        g_Engine.TurnOnPlaque("You find nothing.");
}
```

The `HandleDoor()` and `OpenAbandonedHouse()` methods work similarly.

New Members of the `CEngine` Class

The `CEngine` class continues to evolve, getting more powerful and flexible. Table 17.1 describes the new members you added to the `CEngine` class in this day.

TABLE 17.1 New CEngine Members

Member	*Type*	*Description*
HandleContainer()	Protected virtual method	Handles the given container, providing the appropriate interaction with the player. Override this method to provide custom interaction with the container.
HandleDoor()	Protected virtual method	Handles the given door, providing the appropriate interaction with the player. Override this method to provide custom interaction with the door.
HandleNPC()	Protected virtual method	Handles the given NPC, providing the appropriate interaction with the player. Override this method to provide custom interaction with the NPC.
CheckForAndHandleNPC()	Private method	Checks for an NPC in the target sector and handles the NPC if one exists.
MoveNPCEast()	Private method	Moves an NPC east one sector.
MoveNPCNorth()	Private method	Moves an NPC north one sector.
MoveNPCs()	Private method	Moves the NPCs around their current location.
MoveNPCSouth()	Private method	Moves an NPC south one sector.
MoveNPCWest()	Private method	Moves an NPC west one sector.
SectorHasPerson()	Private method	Returns TRUE if the target sector contains an NPC.

Summary

You're getting closer and closer to having a full game. Not only can you now move from one location to another and open containers and doors, but you can also have conversations with the many citizens of First Town. You can even tackle a simple quest. Before the game is done, you'll need to add lots of such quests, which is something you'll do after you complete this book. Next, though, you'll learn how to add combat to Jasper's upcoming adventures. This means adding monsters to the game world, as well as manipulating the player character's attributes. Dealing with combat also means—besides swinging a sword—awarding the player with gold and experience points whenever she's successful in combat.

Q&A

Q. How many people can I have in a specific location of the game, such as First Town?

A. The constant `MAXPEOPLE`, currently defined as 100 in the Constants.h file, controls the maximum number of people you can have in one map area. But the truth is that that's probably way too many people to have crammed into a town or other location. Having so many people wandering around makes it difficult for the player to travel through the town. He'll always be bumping into someone in the way, which, just like in real life, can get annoying.

Q. Why do some of the NPCs move around and others just stand in place?

A. If you look back at Day 12, you'll remember that one of the values loaded from an area's people file determines whether the NPC can move or not. In Appendix A, "The JBookman Game Editor," you get a game editor that makes it easy for you to create the game files and determine which NPCs can move and which can't.

Q. What if I want an NPC to say more than will fit in the text plaque?

A. It's common in many RPGs to expect the player to continually talk to an NPC until the NPC stops saying anything new. By presenting a series of text boxes in this way, you can have as long a conversation as you want with an NPC. You just have to have flags, or a counter of some sort, that keeps track of where the NPC is in the conversation. (You know, this sounds like a good topic for an exercise! Hint, hint.)

Workshop

The workshop includes quiz questions to help gauge your grasp of the material. Even if you feel that you totally understand the concepts presented here, you should work through the quiz anyway. The last section is an exercise or two that you might work through to help reinforce your learning.

1. Thinking about the game's data, why is drawing NPCs different from drawing the tiles that represent a game area? That is, why isn't drawing the tiles in the map array (`m_Sectors[]`) enough?
2. Why does the program use random numbers when moving an NPC or performing animation with the NPC?
3. Why does the program use virtual methods for the parts of the code that respond to events like opening doors and containers or talking to NPCs?
4. Why do some NPCs move around the town, while others stand in one place?

5. How does the program know which image in an NPC's two-frame animation sequence to display?
6. In the program, how do you keep track of which elements of a quest the player has completed?

Exercises

1. Make a copy of the JBookman project and modify it so that the guard to the left of the gate can have a three-part conversation with the player. The first part of the conversation is already programmed in the game, so the entire conversation should go like this:

   First Response:

   ```
   I'm Fennel Gridrock, a guard
   here at First Town. I hope you
   enjoy your stay.
   ```

   Second Response:

   ```
   I've been told that
   there are dungeons
   underneath the town.
   ```

   Third Response:

   ```
   Your reputation precedes you,
   Jasper. I hope that you can
   be useful to the townspeople.
   ```

   After the third response, talking to the guard should display the third response continually.

Answers for Day 17

Quiz

1. Thinking about the game's data, why is drawing NPCs different from drawing the tiles that represent a game area? That is, why isn't drawing the tiles in the map array (`m_Sectors[]`) enough?

   The tiles for the game area have their tile IDs stored in the `m_Sectors[]` array. An NPC, however, is an object of the `CPerson` class, and its tile ID does not appear in the `m_Sectors[]` array and so doesn't get drawn when the program draws the background. Instead, an NPC's tile ID is a member of the `CPerson` class, from which the program must retrieve it. The NPC's sector location is also a member of the class.

2. Why does the program use random numbers when moving an NPC or performing animation with the NPC?

   Using random numbers creates more natural movement of the NPCs. That is, not all NPCs end up moving at the same time and they all appear to be more independent of each other.

3. Why does the program use virtual methods for the parts of the code that respond to events like opening doors and containers or talking to NPCs?

   The virtual methods can be overridden in the `CMyEngine` class in order to provide specialized responses to the player's commands.

4. Why do some NPCs move around the town, while others stand in one place?

   Part of the data that gets loaded into an instance of the `CPerson` class is a flag that specifies whether the NPC can move. Although this flag gets set from data in a disk file, you can set the flag (and others) using the game editor, which creates the disk files for you.

5. How does the program know which image in an NPC's two-frame animation sequence to display?

   The tile ID is stored as a data member of the `CPerson` class. The program continually updates the tile ID so that it alternates between the two frames, although it does this using a random-number to keep the animation from being too predictable.

6. In the program, how do you keep track of which elements of the quest the player has completed?

   You define flags for the key events in the quest and use their values to determine what NPCs have to say and how the story progresses.

Exercises

1. Make a copy of the JBookman project and modify it so that the guard to the left of the gate can have a three part conversation with the player. The first part of the conversation is already programmed in the game, so the entire conversation should go like this:

   First Response:

   ```
   I'm Fennel Gridrock, a guard
   here at First Town. I hope you
   enjoy your stay.
   ```

   Second Response:

   ```
   I've been told that
   there are dungeons
   underneath the town.
   ```

Third Response:

```
Your reputation precedes you,
Jasper. I hope that you can
be useful to the townspeople.
```

After the third response, talking to the guard should display the third response continually.

First, you need to add a counter to the FirstTown.cpp file:

```
int iFennelCount = 0;
```

Then, replace the `HandleFennelGridrock()` method with the one that follows:

```
/////////////////////////////////////////////////////////
// HandleFennelGridrock()
/////////////////////////////////////////////////////////
void HandleFennelGridrock()
{
    if (iFennelCount == 0)
        g_Engine.TurnOnPlaque(
"I'm Fennel Gridrock, a guard\n\
here at First Town. I hope you\n\
enjoy your stay.");
    else if (iFennelCount == 1)
        g_Engine.TurnOnPlaque(
"I've been told that\n\
there are dungeons\n\
underneath the town.");
    else
        g_Engine.TurnOnPlaque(
"Your reputation precedes you,\n\
Jasper. I hope that you can\n\
be useful to the townspeople.");
    ++iFennelCount;
    if (iFennelCount > 2)
        iFennelCount = 2;
}
```

WEEK 3

DAY 18

Programming Combat

Wandering around a virtual world and exploring every nook and cranny is great fun, but every game has to present some sort of challenge to the player. Role-playing games usually present two types of challenges: puzzle solving and combat.

You've already learned about adding quests—a form of puzzle solving—to your game. Next, you need to populate the game world with creatures whose sole purpose is to attack the player character at every opportunity. You add that game element to the JBookman project in this day. Specifically, in this day you learn how to:

- Specify where creatures lurk
- Draw creatures on the screen
- Implement battle commands for the player
- Control the battle sequence
- Award the player for defeating a monster

Creating a Class for Monsters

As with such objects as containers and NPCs, the best way to manage the data that represents a monster in the game is to encapsulate that data into a class. This class will not only hold the various variables that control a monster's abilities and status, but also provide the methods needed to access those variables. Perform the following steps to add the `CMonster` class to your JBookman project.

1. Select the Project menu's Add Class command, and create a new generic C++ class named `CMonster`.
2. Replace the code in the Monster.h file with the following. If you don't want to type, you can copy the lines from the Code01.txt file in the Chapter18 directory of this book's CD-ROM.

```
///////////////////////////////////////////////////////
// Monster.h
///////////////////////////////////////////////////////

#pragma once

#include "windows.h"

class CMonster
{
protected:
    char m_pstrName[256];
    int m_iMaxHitPoints;
    int m_iRemainingHitPoints;
    int m_iMaxAttackDamage;
    int m_iExperienceValue;
    int m_iMaxGold;

public:
    CMonster(void);
    ~CMonster(void);

    void SetName(char* n);
    char* GetName();
    void SetMaxHitPoints(int num);
    int GetMaxHitPoints();
    void SetRemainingHitPoints(int num);
    int GetRemainingHitPoints();
    void SetMaxAttackDamage(int num);
    int GetMaxAttackDamage();
    void SetExperienceValue(int num);
    int GetExperienceValue();
    void SetMaxGold(int num);
    int GetMaxGold();
};
```

3. Replace the code in the Monster.cpp file with the following. If you don't want to type, you can copy the lines from the Code02.txt file in the Chapter18 directory of this book's CD-ROM.

```
///////////////////////////////////////////////////////
// Monster.cpp
///////////////////////////////////////////////////////

#include "monster.h"

///////////////////////////////////////////////////////
// CMonster()
///////////////////////////////////////////////////////
CMonster::CMonster(void)
{
}

///////////////////////////////////////////////////////
// ~CMonster()
///////////////////////////////////////////////////////
CMonster::~CMonster(void)
{
}

///////////////////////////////////////////////////////
// SetName()
///////////////////////////////////////////////////////
void CMonster::SetName(char* n)
{
    strcpy(m_pstrName, n);
}

///////////////////////////////////////////////////////
// GetName()
///////////////////////////////////////////////////////
char* CMonster::GetName()
{
    return m_pstrName;
}

///////////////////////////////////////////////////////
// SetMaxHitPoints()
///////////////////////////////////////////////////////
void CMonster::SetMaxHitPoints(int num)
{
    m_iMaxHitPoints = num;
}

///////////////////////////////////////////////////////
// GetMaxHitPoints()
///////////////////////////////////////////////////////
```

```
int CMonster::GetMaxHitPoints()
{
    return m_iMaxHitPoints;
}

//////////////////////////////////////////////////////
// SetRemainingHitPoints()
//////////////////////////////////////////////////////
void CMonster::SetRemainingHitPoints(int num)
{
    m_iRemainingHitPoints = num;
}

//////////////////////////////////////////////////////
// GetRemainingHitPoints()
//////////////////////////////////////////////////////
int CMonster::GetRemainingHitPoints()
{
    return m_iRemainingHitPoints;
}

//////////////////////////////////////////////////////
// SetMaxAttackDamage()
//////////////////////////////////////////////////////
void CMonster::SetMaxAttackDamage(int num)
{
    m_iMaxAttackDamage = num;
}

//////////////////////////////////////////////////////
// GetMaxAttackDamage()
//////////////////////////////////////////////////////
int CMonster::GetMaxAttackDamage()
{
    return m_iMaxAttackDamage;
}

//////////////////////////////////////////////////////
// SetExperienceValue()
//////////////////////////////////////////////////////
void CMonster::SetExperienceValue(int num)
{
    m_iExperienceValue = num;
}

//////////////////////////////////////////////////////
// GetExperienceValue()
//////////////////////////////////////////////////////
int CMonster::GetExperienceValue()
{
    return m_iExperienceValue;
```

```
}

////////////////////////////////////////////////////////
// SetMaxGold()
//////////////////////////////
////////////////////////////////////////////////////////
void CMonster::SetMaxGold(int num)
{
    m_iMaxGold = num;
}

////////////////////////////////////////////////////////
// GetMaxGold()
////////////////////////////////////////////////////////
int CMonster::GetMaxGold()
{
    return m_iMaxGold;
}
```

4. Select the Build menu's Compile option, or just press Ctrl+F7 on your keyboard, to compile the class.

You'll see how to use this new class as you continue to build the JBookman project throughout this day, but a take a couple of minutes now to look over Table 18.1, which describes each of the class's members.

TABLE 18.1 Members of the `CMonster` Class

Member	*Type*	*Description*
m_iExperienceValue	Data	The number of experience awarded to the player for defeating the monster in combat.
m_iMaxAttackDamage	Data	The maximum amount of damage the monster can do to the player. The actual damage to the player is a random value somewhere between 0 and m_iMaxAttackdamage.
m_iMaxGold	Data	The maximum amount of gold awarded to the player for defeating the monster in combat. The actual number awarded to the player is a random value somewhere between 0 and m_iMaxGold.
m_iMaxHitpoints	Data	The monster's maximum available hit points.
m_iRemainingHitPoints	Data	The number of hit points the monster has left. This value goes down each time the player hits the monster with an attack.

TABLE 18.1 continued

Member	*Type*	*Description*
m_pstrName	Data	The monster's name.
GetExperienceValue()	Public method	Gets the m_iExperienceValue data member.
GetMaxAttackDamage()	Public method	Gets the m_iMaxAttackDamage data member.
GetMaxGold()	Public method	Gets the m_iMaxGold data member.
GetMaxHitPoints()	Public method	Gets the m_iMaxHitPoints data member.
GetName()	Public method	Gets the m_pstrName data member.
GetRemainingHitPoints()	Public method	Gets the m_iRemainingHitPoints data member.
SetExperienceValue()	Public method	Sets the m_iExperienceValue data member.
SetMaxAttackDamage()	Public method	Sets the m_iMaxAttackDamage data member.
SetMaxGold()	Public method	Sets the m_iMaxGold data member.
SetMaxHitPoints()	Public method	Sets the m_iMaxHitPoints data member.
SetName()	Public Method	Sets the m_pstrName data member.
SetRemainingHitPoints()	Public method	Sets the m_iRemainingHitPoints data member.

Creating and Displaying the Monster

As the player wanders around the game world, the evil creatures that populate the world make it their business to try and remove our hero from the story. Where these attacks occur is completely up to the game's programmer (that's you), and so the game engine needs to query your `CMyEngine` class for information about monsters and where they lurk. Providing this information is the first step in creating and displaying a monster. Once the game engine has information about the creature, it needs to display the appropriate images on the screen. Perform the following steps to add monsters to your JBookman project:

1. In the Engine.h file, add the following line to the `#include` statements:

```
#include "Monster.h"
```

2. Again in the Engine.h file, add the following lines to the class's protected data members:

```
CMonster* m_pCurrentMonster;
BOOL m_bPlayerTurnToAttack;
BOOL m_bMonsterAttacking;
```

3. Also in the Engine.h file, add the following lines to the class's protected method declarations:

```
virtual BOOL IsMonsterLocation() = 0;
virtual CMonster* GetMonster() = 0;
virtual void ReleaseMonster() = 0;
```

4. Add the following lines to the class's private methods:

```
BOOL CheckForAndHandleMonster();
void PaintMonster();
void PaintBattlePlaque();
```

5. Add the following methods to the end if the Engine.cpp file. If you'd rather not type, you can copy the lines from the Code03.txt file in the Chapter18 directory of this book's CD-ROM.

```
///////////////////////////////////////////////////////
// CheckForAndHandleMonster()
///////////////////////////////////////////////////////
BOOL CEngine::CheckForAndHandleMonster()
{
    if (IsMonsterLocation())
    {
        int r = rand() % 10;
        if (r == 0)
        {
            m_pCurrentMonster = GetMonster();
            m_bMonsterAttacking = TRUE;
            m_bPlayerTurnToAttack = TRUE;
            return TRUE;
        }
    }
    return FALSE;
}

///////////////////////////////////////////////////////
// PaintMonster()
///////////////////////////////////////////////////////
void CEngine::PaintMonster()
{
    unsigned char *vb_vertices;
    IDirect3DVertexBuffer8* pSquare;
    vertex m_square_vertices[] =
    {
      {160.0f, 290.0f, 0.0f, 1.0f, 0.0f, 1.0f }, /* Lower left corner */
      {160.0f, 38.0f,  0.0f, 1.0f, 0.0f, 0.0f }, /* Upper left corner */
      {480.0f, 290.0f, 0.0f, 1.0f, 1.0f, 1.0f }, /* Lower right corner*/
      {480.0f, 38.0f,  0.0f, 1.0f, 1.0f, 0.0f }  /* Upper right corner*/
```

18

```
    };

    // Create and load the vertex buffer.
    HRESULT hResult = m_Direct3D.GetDevice()->
        CreateVertexBuffer(4*sizeof(vertex),D3DUSAGE_WRITEONLY,
        D3D8T_CUSTOMVERTEX, D3DPOOL_MANAGED, &pSquare);
    hResult = pSquare->Lock(0, 0, &vb_vertices, 0);
    memcpy(vb_vertices, m_square_vertices, sizeof(m_square_vertices));
    pSquare->Unlock();

    // Display the texture.
    m_Direct3D.GetDevice()->SetTextureStageState(0,
        D3DTSS_COLOROP, D3DTOP_SELECTARG1);
    m_Direct3D.GetDevice()->SetTextureStageState(0,
        D3DTSS_COLORARG1, D3DTA_TEXTURE);
    m_Direct3D.GetDevice()->SetTextureStageState(0,
        D3DTSS_ALPHAOP, D3DTOP_SELECTARG1);
    m_Direct3D.GetDevice()->SetTextureStageState(0,
        D3DTSS_ALPHAARG1, D3DTA_TEXTURE);
    m_Direct3D.GetDevice()->SetRenderState(D3DRS_SRCBLEND,
        D3DBLEND_SRCALPHA);
    m_Direct3D.GetDevice()->SetRenderState(D3DRS_DESTBLEND,
        D3DBLEND_INVSRCALPHA);
    m_Direct3D.GetDevice()->SetRenderState(D3DRS_ALPHABLENDENABLE, TRUE);
    if(SUCCEEDED(m_Direct3D.GetDevice()->BeginScene()))
    {
        m_Direct3D.GetDevice()->SetVertexShader(D3D8T_CUSTOMVERTEX);
        m_Direct3D.GetDevice()->SetStreamSource(0, pSquare,
          sizeof(vertex));
        m_Direct3D.GetDevice()->SetTexture(0,
            m_Direct3D.GetMonsterTexture(0));
        m_Direct3D.GetDevice()->DrawPrimitive(D3DPT_TRIANGLESTRIP,0,2);
        m_Direct3D.GetDevice()->EndScene();
    }
    pSquare->Release();
}

///////////////////////////////////////////////////////
// PaintBattlePlaque()
///////////////////////////////////////////////////////
void CEngine::PaintBattlePlaque()
{
    unsigned char *vb_vertices;
    IDirect3DVertexBuffer8* pSquare;
    vertex m_square_vertices[] =
    {
      {192.0f, 430.0f, 0.0f, 1.0f, 0.0f, 1.0f }, /* Lower left corner */
      {192.0f, 290.0f, 0.0f, 1.0f, 0.0f, 0.0f }, /* Upper left corner */
```

```
  {448.0f, 430.0f, 0.0f, 1.0f, 1.0f, 1.0f }, /* Lower right corner */
  {448.0f, 290.0f, 0.0f, 1.0f, 1.0f, 0.0f }  /* Upper right corner */
};

// Create a font.
LPD3DXFONT pFont = NULL;
LOGFONT LogFont = {16, 0, 0, 0, FW_NORMAL, false, false, false,
    DEFAULT_CHARSET,OUT_TT_PRECIS, CLIP_DEFAULT_PRECIS,
    PROOF_QUALITY, DEFAULT_PITCH, "Times New Roman"};
D3DXCreateFontIndirect(m_Direct3D.GetDevice(), &LogFont, &pFont);

char msg[1024];
wsprintf(msg, "A %s attacks!\n", m_pCurrentMonster->GetName());
wsprintf(&msg[strlen(msg)], "Monster Hit Points = %d\n",
    m_pCurrentMonster->GetRemainingHitPoints());
if (m_bPlayerTurnToAttack)
    strcpy(&msg[strlen(msg)], "A = Attack\nP = Take Potion\nR = Run");
else
    strcpy(&msg[strlen(msg)], "The creature prepares to attack");

wsprintf(&msg[strlen(msg)], "\nHit Points = %d",
    m_Player.GetHitPoints());

// Calculate the size of a rectangle that can hold the text.
RECT r;
r.left = 0;
r.top = 0;
r.right = 0;
r.bottom = 0;
pFont->DrawText(msg, -1, &r, DT_CALCRECT, 0xff000000);
int iWidth = r.right - r.left;
int iHeight = r.bottom - r.top;
r.left = (640 - iWidth) / 2;
r.right = r.left + iWidth;
r.top = 310;
r.bottom = r.top + iHeight;

// Create and load the vertex buffer.
HRESULT hResult = m_Direct3D.GetDevice()->
    CreateVertexBuffer(4*sizeof(vertex),D3DUSAGE_WRITEONLY,
    D3D8T_CUSTOMVERTEX, D3DPOOL_MANAGED, &pSquare);
hResult = pSquare->Lock(0, 0, &vb_vertices, 0);
memcpy(vb_vertices, m_square_vertices, sizeof(m_square_vertices));
pSquare->Unlock();

// Display the plaque texture.
m_Direct3D.GetDevice()->SetTextureStageState(0,
    D3DTSS_COLOROP, D3DTOP_SELECTARG1);
m_Direct3D.GetDevice()->SetTextureStageState(0,
```

```
        D3DTSS_COLORARG1, D3DTA_TEXTURE);
    m_Direct3D.GetDevice()->SetTextureStageState(0,
        D3DTSS_ALPHAOP, D3DTOP_SELECTARG1);
    m_Direct3D.GetDevice()->SetTextureStageState(0,
        D3DTSS_ALPHAARG1, D3DTA_TEXTURE);
    m_Direct3D.GetDevice()->SetRenderState(D3DRS_SRCBLEND,
        D3DBLEND_SRCALPHA);
    m_Direct3D.GetDevice()->SetRenderState(D3DRS_DESTBLEND,
        D3DBLEND_INVSRCALPHA);
    m_Direct3D.GetDevice()->SetRenderState(D3DRS_ALPHABLENDENABLE, TRUE);
    if(SUCCEEDED(m_Direct3D.GetDevice()->BeginScene()))
    {
        m_Direct3D.GetDevice()->SetVertexShader(D3D8T_CUSTOMVERTEX);
        m_Direct3D.GetDevice()->SetStreamSource(0, pSquare,
          sizeof(vertex));
        m_Direct3D.GetDevice()->SetTexture(0, m_Direct3D.GetTexture());
        m_Direct3D.GetDevice()->DrawPrimitive(D3DPT_TRIANGLESTRIP,0,2);
        pFont->DrawText(msg, -1, &r, DT_CENTER, 0xff000000);
        m_Direct3D.GetDevice()->EndScene();
    }
    pSquare->Release();
    pFont->Release();
}
```

6. Add the following lines to the end of the class's constructor:

```
m_bPlayerTurnToAttack = TRUE;
m_bMonsterAttacking = FALSE;
```

7. Add the following line to the end of the `InitGame()` method:

```
m_Player.SetMaxHitPoints(10);
```

8. Add the following lines to the `PaintBackBuffer()` method, right after the line `PaintPlaque()` that's already there:

```
if (m_bMonsterAttacking)
{
    PaintMonster();
    PaintBattlePlaque();
}
```

9. Add the following line to the beginning of each of the arrow-handling methods:

```
if (m_bMonsterAttacking) return;
```

10. Add the following lines to each of the arrow-handling methods, right after the line that sets the `iTargetSector` variable that's already there:

```
BOOL bFoughtMonster = CheckForAndHandleMonster();
if (bFoughtMonster) return;
```

11. In the Direct3D.h file, add the following line to the class's protected data members:

```
IDirect3DTexture8* m_pMonsterTexture[4];
```

12. Also in the Direct3D.h file, add the following lines to the class's public method declarations. If you'd rather not type, you can copy the lines from Code04.txt file in the Chapter18 directory of this book's CD-ROM.

```
IDirect3DTexture8* GetMonsterTexture(int iFrame);
void CreateMonsterTextures(char* idle1,
    char* idle2, char* attack, char* hit);
void ReleaseMonsterTextures();
```

13. In the Direct3D.cpp file, add the following lines to the end of the class's constructor:

```
for (int x=0; x<4; ++x)
    m_pMonsterTexture[x] = NULL;
```

14. Add the following lines to the beginning of the `CleanUp()` method. If you'd rather not type, you can copy the lines from Code05.txt file in the Chapter18 directory of this book's CD-ROM.

```
for (int x=0; x<4; ++x)
{
    if (m_pMonsterTexture[x])
    {
        m_pMonsterTexture[x]->Release();
        m_pMonsterTexture[x] = NULL;
    }
}
```

15. Add the following methods to the end of the Direct3D.cpp file. If you'd rather not type, you can copy the lines from Code06.txt file in the Chapter18 directory of this book's CD-ROM.

```
///////////////////////////////////////////////////////
// GetMonsterTexture()
///////////////////////////////////////////////////////
IDirect3DTexture8* CDirect3D::GetMonsterTexture(int iFrame)
{
    return m_pMonsterTexture[iFrame];
}

///////////////////////////////////////////////////////
// CreateMonsterTextures()
///////////////////////////////////////////////////////
void CDirect3D::CreateMonsterTextures(char* idle1,
    char* idle2, char* attack, char* hit)
{
    D3DXCreateTextureFromFileEx(m_pD3DDevice, idle1,
        D3DX_DEFAULT, D3DX_DEFAULT, 1, 0, D3DFMT_A8R8G8B8,
```

```
        D3DPOOL_MANAGED, D3DX_DEFAULT, D3DX_DEFAULT, 0xFF000000,
        NULL, NULL, &m_pMonsterTexture[0]);
    D3DXCreateTextureFromFileEx(m_pD3DDevice, idle2,
        D3DX_DEFAULT, D3DX_DEFAULT, 1, 0, D3DFMT_A8R8G8B8,
        D3DPOOL_MANAGED, D3DX_DEFAULT, D3DX_DEFAULT, 0xFF000000,
        NULL, NULL, &m_pMonsterTexture[1]);
    D3DXCreateTextureFromFileEx(m_pD3DDevice, attack,
        D3DX_DEFAULT, D3DX_DEFAULT, 1, 0, D3DFMT_A8R8G8B8,
        D3DPOOL_MANAGED, D3DX_DEFAULT, D3DX_DEFAULT, 0xFF000000,
        NULL, NULL, &m_pMonsterTexture[2]);
    D3DXCreateTextureFromFileEx(m_pD3DDevice, hit,
        D3DX_DEFAULT, D3DX_DEFAULT, 1, 0, D3DFMT_A8R8G8B8,
        D3DPOOL_MANAGED, D3DX_DEFAULT, D3DX_DEFAULT, 0xFF000000,
        NULL, NULL, &m_pMonsterTexture[3]);
}

//////////////////////////////////////////////////////
// ReleaseMonsterTextures()
//////////////////////////////////////////////////////
void CDirect3D::ReleaseMonsterTextures()
{
    for (int x=0; x<4; ++x)
    {
        if (m_pMonsterTexture[x])
        {
            m_pMonsterTexture[x]->Release();
            m_pMonsterTexture[x] = NULL;
        }
    }
}
```

16. In the MyEngine.h file, add the following line to the `#include` statements:

```
#include "Monster.h"
```

17. Add the following lines to the MyEngine.h file, in the public method declarations:

```
BOOL IsMonsterLocation();
CMonster* GetMonster();
void ReleaseMonster();
```

18. Add the following lines to the end of the MyEngine.cpp file. If you'd rather not type, you can copy the lines from Code07.txt file in the Chapter18 directory of this book's CD-ROM.

```
//////////////////////////////////////////////////////
// IsMonsterLocation()
//////////////////////////////////////////////////////
BOOL CMyEngine::IsMonsterLocation()
{
    switch (m_iCurrentMap)
    {
```

```
    case GANJEKWILDS:
        return TRUE;
    }
    return FALSE;
}

//////////////////////////////////////////////////////
// GetMonster()
//////////////////////////////////////////////////////
CMonster* CMyEngine::GetMonster()
{
    CMonster* m_pCurrentMonster = new CMonster();
    m_pCurrentMonster->SetName("Snake");
    m_pCurrentMonster->SetMaxHitPoints(10);
    m_pCurrentMonster->SetRemainingHitPoints(10);
    m_pCurrentMonster->SetMaxAttackDamage(5);
    m_pCurrentMonster->SetExperienceValue(1);
    m_pCurrentMonster->SetMaxGold(5);
    m_Direct3D.CreateMonsterTextures("Graphics\\SnakeA.bmp",
        "Graphics\\SnakeB.bmp", "Graphics\\SnakeC.bmp",
        "Graphics\\SnakeD.bmp");
    return m_pCurrentMonster;
}

//////////////////////////////////////////////////////
// ReleaseMonster()
//////////////////////////////////////////////////////
void CMyEngine::ReleaseMonster()
{
    if (m_pCurrentMonster)
    {
        delete m_pCurrentMonster;
        m_pCurrentMonster = NULL;
        m_Direct3D.ReleaseMonsterTextures();
    }
}
```

19. Copy the following files from the Chapter18 directory of this book's CD-ROM to your JBookman project's Graphics directory:

    ```
    SnakeA.bmp
    SnakeB.bmp
    SnakeC.bmp
    SnakeD.bmp
    ```

Now you can compile and run the program. When you do, head out of town and into the Ganjek Wilds. Wander around the wilds a bit, and it shouldn't take long before you're attacked by a snake, as shown in Figure 18.1.

FIGURE 18.1
The beginning of a battle.

Understanding the New Source Code

So, what's going on here? As you already know, each time the player moves, the arrow-handling methods get called. These methods now not only check for NPCs, doors, and containers, but also for monsters that may be wondering around the area.

```
void CEngine::HandleRightArrow()
{
    if (m_bMonsterAttacking) return;
    if (IsShowingPlaque()) return;
    int iTargetSector = m_Player.GetSector() + 1;
    BOOL bFoughtMonster = CheckForAndHandleMonster();
    if (bFoughtMonster) return;
    BOOL bHandledNPC = CheckForAndHandleNPC(iTargetSector);
    if (bHandledNPC) return;
    BOOL bHandledContainer =
        CheckForAndHandleContainer(iTargetSector);
    if (bHandledContainer)
        return;
    int iDoorStatus =
        CheckForAndHandleDoor(iTargetSector);
    if (iDoorStatus == NODOOR || iDoorStatus == DOORUNLOCKED)
        MovePlayerRight();
}
```

First, if there's already combat in progress, indicated when `m_bMonsterAttacking` is `TRUE`, the arrow methods return immediately, preventing the player from doing anything but fighting the creature at hand:

```
if (m_bMonsterAttacking) return;
```

As with NPCs, doors, and containers, the arrow methods check whether there should be an encounter. If there is an encounter, the return value of `TRUE` from the `CheckForAndHandleMonster()` causes the method to return without bothering to process NPCs, doors, or containers:

```
BOOL bFoughtMonster = CheckForAndHandleMonster();
if (bFoughtMonster) return;
```

The `CheckForAndHandleMonster()` method first calls the `CMyEngine` class's `IsMonsterLocation()` to determine whether the current area contains monsters:

```
if (IsMonsterLocation())
{
    .
    .
    .
}
```


If `IsMonsterLocation()` returns `FALSE`, which specifies that there are no creatures in the player's current location, the `CheckForAndHandleMonster()` method also returns `FALSE`, and that's the end of that. If, however, `IsMonsterLocation()` returns `TRUE`, it's time to check for wandering monsters.

Each time the player moves, there's a one in ten chance that he'll be attacked. The program handles this by generating a random number and using the result to control an `if` statement:

```
int r = rand() % 10;
if (r == 0)
{
    .
    .
    .
}
```

If the random number is 0, the player is to be attacked by a wandering monster. First, the program creates the monster by calling the `CMyEngine` class's `GetMonster()` method, which returns a pointer to a `CMonster` object:

```
m_pCurrentMonster = GetMonster();
```

The program then sets the flags that get the battle sequence underway and returns `TRUE` to prevent the program from checking for other objects in the arrow-handling method from which `CheckForAndHandleMonster()` was called:

```
m_bMonsterAttacking = TRUE;
m_bPlayerTurnToAttack = TRUE;
return TRUE;
```

Some areas of the game are safe from attack, whereas others are chock full of nasty creatures. It's completely up to you where you want your monsters to be and what type of monsters they'll be. This is the reason for the new pure virtual functions, `IsMonsterLocation()` and `GetMonster()`. You must provide these functions in the `CMyEngine` class, because the `CEngine` class expects to be able to call them. In fact, your `CMyEngine` class won't even compile unless you implement these two methods.

The `IsMonsterLocation()` method tells the game engine whether the current location should contain monsters. The location can be any major location in the game or even a single room:

```
BOOL CMyEngine::IsMonsterLocation()
{
    switch (m_iCurrentMap)
    {
    case GANJEKWILDS:
        return TRUE;
    }
    return FALSE;
}
```

The flags that were set in the `CheckForAndHandleMonster()` method have their effect in `PaintBackBuffer()`, where the following lines cause the program to display the battle graphics if the `m_bMonsterAttacking` flag is `TRUE`:

```
if (m_bMonsterAttacking)
{
    PaintMonster();
    PaintBattlePlaque();
}
```

The `PaintMonster()` method displays the texture graphic containing the monster image, and the `PaintBattlePlaque()` method displays the text plaque below the monster's image. In the plaque, the program shows the information the player needs to proceed with the battle. Because these methods are so similar to `PaintPlaque()`, there's no need to go over them in any detail.

The last two pieces of the puzzle are the `GetMonster()` and `ReleaseMonster()` methods that you added to your `CMyEngine` class. The `GetMonster()` method first creates a new `CMonster` object:

```
CMonster* m_pCurrentMonster = new CMonster();
```

It then sets the monster's attributes:

```
m_pCurrentMonster->SetName("Snake");
m_pCurrentMonster->SetMaxHitPoints(10);
m_pCurrentMonster->SetRemainingHitPoints(10);
m_pCurrentMonster->SetMaxAttackDamage(5);
m_pCurrentMonster->SetExperienceValue(1);
m_pCurrentMonster->SetMaxGold(5);
```

Finally, it loads the monster images and returns a pointer to the `CMonster` object:

```
m_Direct3D.CreateMonsterTextures("Graphics\\SnakeA.bmp",
    "Graphics\\SnakeB.bmp", "Graphics\\SnakeC.bmp",
    "Graphics\\SnakeD.bmp");
return m_pCurrentMonster;
```

When the program is finished with the monster, the `ReleaseMonster()` method deletes the monster images and releases the textures (there's actually no call to `ReleaseMonster()` in the program yet):

```
if (m_pCurrentMonster)
{
    delete m_pCurrentMonster;
    m_pCurrentMonster = NULL;
    m_Direct3D.ReleaseMonsterTextures();
}
```


Note that the `GetMonster()` method currently returns only one type of monster. However, this method is where you'll write the program lines that return whatever type of creature is appropriate for the player's current location.

Controlling the Combat Sequence

Thanks to the setting of the flags, the Combat sequence is now under the control of the program's timer. As you know, every tenth of a second, the `HandleTimer()` method gets called. Up until now, that timer handled only the animation sequences for the game. Now, it will also control the battle sequence. Perform the following steps to add the necessary source code to your JBookman project.

1. In the Engine.h file, add the following lines to the class's protected data members. If you'd rather not type, you can copy the lines from Code08.txt file in the Chapter18 directory of this book's CD-ROM.

```
BOOL m_bRunningFromMonster;
int m_iCurrentMonsterFrame;
BOOL m_iMonsterDamage;
int m_iCombatDelayCounter;
```

2. Add the following lines to the class's private methods. If you'd rather not type, you can copy the lines from Code09.txt file in the Chapter18 directory of this book's CD-ROM.

```
void HandleMonsters();
void AttackMonster();
void RunFromMonster();
BOOL CombatDelayOver();
void AnimateIdleMonster();
void AnimateMonsterDamage();
void AttackRunningPlayer();
void AttackPlayer();
void TakePotion();
```

3. Add the following methods to the end if the Engine.cpp file. If you'd rather not type, you can copy the lines from Code10.txt file in the Chapter18 directory of this book's CD-ROM.

```
//////////////////////////////////////////////////////
// AttackMonster()
//////////////////////////////////////////////////////
void CEngine::AttackMonster()
{
    if (m_bPlayerTurnToAttack && m_iCombatDelayCounter == 0)
        m_iMonsterDamage = (rand() % 10) + 2;
    m_bPlayerTurnToAttack = FALSE;
}

//////////////////////////////////////////////////////
// HandleMonsters()
//////////////////////////////////////////////////////
void CEngine::HandleMonsters()
{
    if (!m_bMonsterAttacking) return;
    if (!CombatDelayOver()) return;

    if (m_bPlayerTurnToAttack)
        AnimateIdleMonster();
    else if (m_iMonsterDamage)
        AnimateMonsterDamage();
    else if (m_bRunningFromMonster)
        AttackRunningPlayer();
    else if (!m_bPlayerTurnToAttack)
        AttackPlayer();
}

//////////////////////////////////////////////////////
// CombatDelayOver()
//////////////////////////////////////////////////////
BOOL CEngine::CombatDelayOver()
{
```

```
    if (m_iCombatDelayCounter)
    {
        --m_iCombatDelayCounter;
        if (m_iCombatDelayCounter == 0)
        {
            if (m_bRunningFromMonster)
            {
                m_bRunningFromMonster = FALSE;
                m_bMonsterAttacking = FALSE;
            }
            m_iCurrentMonsterFrame = MONSTERIDLEFRAME1;
            return TRUE;
        }
        return FALSE;
    }
    return TRUE;
}

///////////////////////////////////////////////////////
// AnimateIdleMonster()
///////////////////////////////////////////////////////
void CEngine::AnimateIdleMonster()
{
    int r = rand() % 5;
    if (r == 0)
    {
        if (m_iCurrentMonsterFrame != MONSTERIDLEFRAME2)
            m_iCurrentMonsterFrame = MONSTERIDLEFRAME2;
        else
            m_iCurrentMonsterFrame = MONSTERIDLEFRAME1;
    }
}

///////////////////////////////////////////////////////
// AnimateMonsterDamage()
///////////////////////////////////////////////////////
void CEngine::AnimateMonsterDamage()
{
    m_iCurrentMonsterFrame = MONSTERHITFRAME;
    --m_iMonsterDamage;
    if (m_iMonsterDamage == 0)
    {
        m_iCombatDelayCounter = 15;
        m_iCurrentMonsterFrame = MONSTERIDLEFRAME1;
    }
    int iRemainingHitPoints = m_pCurrentMonster->GetRemainingHitPoints();
    iRemainingHitPoints -= (m_Player.GetExperience() / 100) + 1;
    m_pCurrentMonster->SetRemainingHitPoints(iRemainingHitPoints);
    if (m_pCurrentMonster->GetRemainingHitPoints() < 1)
    {
        m_bMonsterAttacking = FALSE;
```

18

```
        m_iCurrentMonsterFrame = 0;
        m_Player.SetExperience(m_Player.GetExperience() +
            m_pCurrentMonster->GetExperienceValue());
        int iGold = rand() % m_pCurrentMonster->GetMaxGold();
        m_Player.SetGold(m_Player.GetGold() + iGold);
        ReleaseMonster();
    }
}

//////////////////////////////////////////////////////
// AttackRunningPlayer()
//////////////////////////////////////////////////////
void CEngine::AttackRunningPlayer()
{
    m_iCurrentMonsterFrame = MONSTERATTACKFRAME;
    int iDamage = rand() % m_pCurrentMonster->GetMaxAttackDamage();
    m_Player.SetHitPoints(m_Player.GetHitPoints() - iDamage);
    m_iCombatDelayCounter = 15;
}

//////////////////////////////////////////////////////
// AttackPlayer()
//////////////////////////////////////////////////////
void CEngine::AttackPlayer()
{
    m_iCurrentMonsterFrame = MONSTERATTACKFRAME;
    int iDamage = rand() % m_pCurrentMonster->GetMaxAttackDamage();
    m_Player.SetHitPoints(m_Player.GetHitPoints() - iDamage);
    m_bPlayerTurnToAttack = TRUE;
    m_iCombatDelayCounter = 15;
}

//////////////////////////////////////////////////////
// TakePotion()
//////////////////////////////////////////////////////
void CEngine::TakePotion()
{
    if (!m_bPlayerTurnToAttack) return;
    if (m_Player.GetPotions() > 0)
    {
        m_Player.SetPotions(m_Player.GetPotions() - 1);
        int iHealingPoints = ((m_Player.GetExperience() / 100) + 1) * 5;
        m_Player.SetHitPoints(m_Player.GetHitPoints() + iHealingPoints);
        if (m_Player.GetHitPoints() > m_Player.GetMaxHitPoints())
            m_Player.SetHitPoints(m_Player.GetMaxHitPoints());
        m_bPlayerTurnToAttack = FALSE;
    }
}
```

```
//////////////////////////////////////////////////////////
// RunFromMonster()
//////////////////////////////////////////////////////////
void CEngine::RunFromMonster()
{
    m_bRunningFromMonster = TRUE;
    m_bPlayerTurnToAttack = FALSE;
}
```

4. Add the following line to the end of the class's constructor:

```
m_bRunningFromMonster = FALSE;
```

5. Add the following line to the beginning of the `HandleTimer()` method:

```
HandleMonsters();
```

6. Add the following `case` clauses to the `HandleKeys()` method. If you'd rather not type, you can copy the lines from Code11.txt file in the Chapter18 directory of this book's CD-ROM.

```
case 65: // A
    AttackMonster();
    break;
case 80: // P
    TakePotion();
    break;
case 82: // R
    RunFromMonster();
    break;
```


7. In the `PaintMonster()` method, change the call to `SetTexture()` to the following (you're just changing the last 0 to `m_iCurrentMonsterFrame`):

```
m_Direct3D.GetDevice()->SetTexture(0,
     m_Direct3D.GetMonsterTexture(m_iCurrentMonsterFrame));
```

8. Add the following lines to the end of the Constants.h file. If you'd rather not type, you can copy the lines from Code12.txt file in the Chapter18 directory of this book's CD-ROM.

```
// Monster frame IDs.
const MONSTERIDLEFRAME1 = 0;
const MONSTERIDLEFRAME2 = 1;
const MONSTERATTACKFRAME = 2;
const MONSTERHITFRAME = 3;
```

Now you can compile and run the program. When you do, head out of town again and roam around until you get attacked. You always get the first crack at an attacking enemy, so while you decide what to do, the monster waits patiently, displaying its two-frame "idle" animation. In this case, the snake flicks his tail back and forth.

In the text plaque below the creature is a list of commands that you can use to control the battle. Currently, you can press “A” to attack the creature, “R” to run away from the battle, or “P” to take a healing potion. Press “A” for now, and the creature rears back as you strike it, as shown in Figure 18.2. The longer the creature stays in this position, the more damage your attack has done. If you did enough damage, you’ll be able to see the monster’s hit points going down one by one.

FIGURE 18.2
The player attacking a creature.

If the creature survives your attack, it’ll take a swipe at you, as shown in Figure 18.3. You’ll lose a few hit points, but hopefully you’ll survive to attack again. If you get too low on hit points and don’t have any healing potions in your inventory, you’ll need to run for it. When you choose to run, the creature always gets a last attack as you turn your back on it.

Currently, you don’t have any potions, but you can fix that in order to test the program. In the `CEngine` class’s `InitGame()` method, add the following line to start the player character off with a few potions:

```
m_Player.SetPotions(3);
```

Now rerun the program, and get into a couple of fights. When you start to run low on hit points, press “P.” You’ll use one of your potions, and your hit points will go up. Unfortunately, this action counts as your turn, so after you use a potion, it’s the creature’s turn to attack.

FIGURE 18.3

A creature attacking the player.

Animating the Battle

Most of the source code that handles the battle sequence is fairly easy to understand. Each time the `HandleTimer()` method gets called (which is about ten times a second), the program calls `HandleMonsters()`. If there is no battle going on, the `m_bMonsterAttacking` flag will be `FALSE`, and the method returns immediately:

```
if (!m_bMonsterAttacking) return;
```

`HandleMonsters()` also returns immediately if the combat delay timer is running:

```
if (!CombatDelayOver()) return;
```

You'll learn more about this delay a little later, but for now just know that the delay slows the animation sequence enough so that the appropriate creature images stay on screen long enough.

If program execution manages to get past the returns, it's time to do something with the battle sequence. If the program is waiting for the player to enter a command, the `AnimateIdleMonster()` method switches the currently displayed creature image between to two idle images:

```
if (m_bPlayerTurnToAttack)
    AnimateIdleMonster();
```

On the other hand, if the creature has sustained damage from the player's attack, the `AnimateMonsterDamage()` method manages the display:

```
else if (m_iMonsterDamage)
    AnimateMonsterDamage();
```

The third possibility is if the player has chosen to run away. In that case, the `AttackRunningPlayer()` method takes over the battle sequence:

```
else if (m_bRunningFromMonster)
    AttackRunningPlayer();
```

Finally, if none of these cases fit, the only one left is the monster's attack on the player, which the `AttackPlayer()` method handles:

```
else if (!m_bPlayerTurnToAttack)
    AttackPlayer();
```

Now let's dig a little deeper. The `AttackMonster()` method springs into action when the player presses the "A" key. That method first checks whether it's actually the player's turn to attack, and, if it is, determines the amount of damage to the enemy:

```
if (m_bPlayerTurnToAttack && m_iCombatDelayCounter == 0)
    m_iMonsterDamage = (rand() % 10) + 2;
```

After calculating the damage, the method turns off the `m_bPlayerTurnToAttack` flag, which makes it the enemy's turn to attack:

```
m_bPlayerTurnToAttack = FALSE;
```

Setting the `m_iMonsterDamage` variable to a value other than 0, triggers the "monster hit" animation, which is controlled by the `AnimateMonsterDamage()` method. That method first sets the animation frame to the one showing the wounded creature and then deducts 1 from the `m_iMonsterDamage` variable:

```
m_iCurrentMonsterFrame = MONSTERHITFRAME;
--m_iMonsterDamage;
```

If the damage counter is reduced to 0, the animation sequence is over. In this case, the method sets the delay counter so that the current creature image will stay onscreen for a while and sets the current image to one of the idle images:

```
if (m_iMonsterDamage == 0)
{
    m_iCombatDelayCounter = 15;
    m_iCurrentMonsterFrame = MONSTERIDLEFRAME1;
}
```

The next task is to subtract damage from the creature's hit points:

```
int iRemainingHitPoints = m_pCurrentMonster->GetRemainingHitPoints();
iRemainingHitPoints -= (m_Player.GetExperience() / 100) + 1;
m_pCurrentMonster->SetRemainingHitPoints(iRemainingHitPoints);
```

If the creature's hit points are 0 or less, that bugger is dead, which means it's time to end the battle sequence. Doing this requires resetting the appropriate flags, giving the player some experience and gold, and releasing the monster object and its textures:

```
if (m_pCurrentMonster->GetRemainingHitPoints() < 1)
{
    m_bMonsterAttacking = FALSE;
    m_iCurrentMonsterFrame = 0;
    m_Player.SetExperience(m_Player.GetExperience() +
        m_pCurrentMonster->GetExperienceValue());
    int iGold = rand() % m_pCurrentMonster->GetMaxGold();
    m_Player.SetGold(m_Player.GetGold() + iGold);
    ReleaseMonster();
}
```

When the player is deciding what command to enter, the `AnimateIdleMonster()` method keeps the animation sequence going. First it gets a random number and uses the result to determine whether it's time to switch to the next animation frame:

```
int r = rand() % 5;
if (r == 0)
{
    .
    .
    .
}
```


Using a random number this way prevents the animation sequence from falling into an obvious pattern, making the sequence seem a little more realistic.

Switching animation frames is just a matter of setting the data member `m_iCurrentMonsterFrame`:

```
if (m_iCurrentMonsterFrame != MONSTERIDLEFRAME2)
    m_iCurrentMonsterFrame = MONSTERIDLEFRAME2;
else
    m_iCurrentMonsterFrame = MONSTERIDLEFRAME1;
```

The `CombatDelayOver()` method controls how long a creature animation frame stays on screen. The method first checks the `m_iCombatDelayCounter` variable. If this variable is 0, the method returns `TRUE`, indicating either that there's no delay active or that the previous delay is over:

```
if (m_iCombatDelayCounter)
{
    .
    .
    .
}
return TRUE;
```

If there is a delay in progress, the method subtracts 1 from the counter:

```
--m_iCombatDelayCounter;
```

Now, if the counter is not 0, the method returns `FALSE`, indicating that the delay is still active:

```
if (m_iCombatDelayCounter == 0)
{
    .
    .
    .
}
return FALSE;
```

If the delay is over, it's time to reset a couple of flags, set the current animation frame back to the idle creature, and return `TRUE`:

```
if (m_bRunningFromMonster)
{
    m_bRunningFromMonster = FALSE;
    m_bMonsterAttacking = FALSE;
}
m_iCurrentMonsterFrame = MONSTERIDLEFRAME1;
return TRUE;
```

The remaining methods that control the battle sequence should be easy to understand, now that you have some background on how the flags work to control everything.

New Members of the `CEngine` Class

As usual, in this day, you've beefed up the game engine even more. This time around, you've added the ability to create and display monsters, as well as to handle the battle sequence and its animation. As an overview, look over Table 18.2, which describes the new members you added to the `CEngine` class in this day.

TABLE 18.2 New `CEngine` Members

Member	*Type*	*Description*
m_bMonsterAttacking	Data member	A flag that indicates whether the player is currently involved in a battle.
m_bPlayerTurnToAttack	Data member	A flag that indicates whether it's the player's turn to attack.
m_bRunningFromMonster	Data member	A flag that indicates whether the player is currently trying to run from a battle.
m_iCombatDelayCounter	Data member	Holds the remaining ticks for the combat delay timer.

TABLE 18.2 continued

Member	*Type*	*Description*
m_iCurrentMonsterFrame	Data member	Holds the ID of the current monster animation frame.
m_iMonsterDamage	Data member	Holds the current amount of damage being applied to the monster.
m_pCurrentMonster	Data member	Holds a pointer to the current CMonster object.
AnimateIdleMonster()	Private method	Manages the animation sequence for an idle creature.
AnimateMonsterDamage()	Private method	Animates the reduction of a creature's hit points during battle.
AttackMonster()	Private method	Handles the player's attack on a creature.
AttackPlayer()	Private method	Manages a monster's attack on a player.
AttackRunningPlayer()	Private method	Gives the monster one last attack at the fleeing player.
CheckForAndHandleMonster()	Private method	Checks for a wandering monster and handles the monster if one is attacking.
CombatDelayOver()	Private method	Manages the combat delay timer.
GetMonster()	Pure virtual method	Returns a pointer to a CMonster object. Must be implemented in any class derived from CEngine.
HandleMonsters()	Private method	Manages the monster battle sequence.
IsMonsterLocation()	Pure virtual method	Returns TRUE if the current location contains monsters. Must be implemented in any class derived from CEngine.
PaintBattlePlaque()	Private method	Displays the text plaque that holds information for the player about the current battle.
PaintMonster()	Private method	Displays the monster's image.
ReleaseMonster()	Pure virtual method	Destroys the current CMonster object, as well as releases the monster's animation-frame textures. Must be implemented in any class derived from CEngine.
RunFromMonster()	Private method	Handle's the player's retreat from a battle.
TakePotion()	Private method	Increases the player's hit points when he enters the "P" command, assuming that the player has a potion in his inventory.

Summary

Battling creatures adds some tricky source code to the game engine, but nothing that should throw you for a loop at this point. Displaying the creature and the battle plaque works almost exactly like displaying the text plaque that you added earlier in the book. The tricky part is timing everything just right and keeping the various flags updated properly. Still, your battles could be a bit more exciting. What's missing? The all-important sound effects. You'll be adding these effects in Chapter 20, "Creating and Adding Sound." First though, you need to learn to save and load a game in progress. You'll do that in the next day.

Q&A

Q. The snake monster is pretty cool, but I can't have a game with just one creature. What do I do for other monsters?

A. The Monsters folder in the Chapter18 directory of this book's CD ROM contains a bunch of monster textures you can use in your game. Also, you can increase your creature resources by changing the colors of an existing creature. For example, if you take the snake creature and change its basic color from green to gold, you have a new creature. In fact, if you look in the aforementioned Monsters folder, you'll see a set of monster images named GoldenSnake that demonstrate what I mean. Note that it helps a lot to have a paint program with a color replacement function, so you don't have to change the colors "by hand."

Q. Battling creatures in the game is fun, but not much of a challenge considering that the player character never dies. What's up with that?

A. Handling the defeat of the player character is all part of the end-game routines, which you'll program in Day 21, "The Finishing Touches." For now, enjoy your immortality!

Q. What if I need the player to have an interaction with a specific monster in a specific sector of a map?

A. You can implement a feature like this by adding it as an event to the `RespondToPlayerLocation()` method, which lets you take over the game at pretty much any point you want.

Workshop

The workshop includes quiz questions to help gauge your grasp of the material. Even if you feel that you totally understand the concepts presented here, you should work through the quiz anyway. The last section is an exercise or two that you might work through to help reinforce your learning.

1. What are an enemy creature's six attributes?
2. What function does the pure virtual method `IsMonsterLocation()` provide for the program?
3. Why do you think the methods `IsMonsterLocation()`, `GetMonster()`, and `ReleaseMonster()` are implemented as pure virtual methods?
4. How are the `GetMonster()` and `ReleaseMonster()` methods related?
5. Why does the program have only four monster images in memory at one time, regardless of how many creatures there are in the game?
6. Why does each creature need four different images?
7. When does the program check for a wandering monster?
8. Why does the program need the `CombatDelayOver()` method?

Exercises

1. Make a copy of the JBookman project and modify it so that that the dungeon in which the lost puppy is located contains leopards that attack the player. You can find the leopard images in the Monsters folder in the Chapter18 directory of this book's CD-ROM.

Answers for Day 18

Quiz

1. What are an enemy creature's six attributes?

   Name, maximum hit points, remaining hit points, maximum attack damage, experience value, and gold.
2. What function does the pure virtual method `IsMonsterLocation()` provide for the program?

   It notifies the game engine whether there are monsters in the player's current location.
3. Why do you think the methods `IsMonsterLocation()`, `GetMonster()`, and `ReleaseMonster()` are implemented as pure virtual methods?

   The `CEngine` class cannot provide a default implementation for these methods (except maybe empty implementations), because monster locations and monster types are completely up to the game programmer. So, rather than implement

`IsMonsterLocation()`, `GetMonster()`, and `ReleaseMonster()` as normal virtual methods (that is, methods that can be overridden in a derived class), they are implemented as pure virtual methods, forcing the programmer to provide their implementations.

4. How are the `GetMonster()` and `ReleaseMonster()` methods related?

   They are complementary methods in that `GetMonster()` creates a `CMonster` object for the program and `ReleaseMonster()` destroys the object when the program is finished with it.

5. Why does the program have only four monster images in memory at one time, regardless of how many creatures there are in the game?

   The program loads the images as it needs them and releases them when it's done with them.

6. Why does each creature need four different images?

   The first two images comprise the creature's idle animation sequence. The third is the image of the creature attacking the player character, and the fourth is the creature being attacked.

7. When does the program check for a wandering monster?

   Every time the player presses an arrow key to move.

8. Why does the program need the `CombatDelayOver()` method?

   The `CombatDelayOver()` method implements a timer that ensures that frames of the battle animation stay on screen an appropriate length of time.

Exercises

1. Make a copy of the JBookman project and modify it so that that the dungeon in which the lost puppy is located contains leopards that attack the player. You can find the leopard images in the Monsters folder in the Chapter18 directory of this book's CD-ROM.

   There are, of course, many different ways you might complete this exercise. Here's my solution: First, transfer the LeopardA.bmp, LeopardB.bmp, LeopardC.bmp, and LeopardD.bmp files to your JBookman project's Graphics directory. Then, add the following line to the `IsMonsterLocation()` method, located in the MyEngine.cpp file:

   ```
   case FIRSTTOWNDUNGEON02:
   ```

   Next, add the following to the protected method declarations in the MyEngine.h file:

```
CMonster* CreateNewMonster(char* file1, char* file2,
    char* file3, char* file4, char* pstrName, int iMaxHitPoints,
    int iMaxDamage, int iExperience, int iMaxGold);
```

Now, replace the `GetMonster()` method with this new implementation:

```
////////////////////////////////////////////////////////
// GetMonster()
////////////////////////////////////////////////////////
CMonster* CMyEngine::GetMonster()
{
    if (m_iCurrentMap == FIRSTTOWNDUNGEON02)
        return CreateNewMonster("Graphics\\LeopardA.bmp",
            "Graphics\\LeopardB.bmp", "Graphics\\LeopardC.bmp",
            "Graphics\\LeopardD.bmp", "Leopard", 10, 5, 1, 5);
    else
        return CreateNewMonster("Graphics\\SnakeA.bmp",
            "Graphics\\SnakeB.bmp", "Graphics\\SnakeC.bmp",
            "Graphics\\SnakeD.bmp", "Leopard", 10, 5, 1, 5);
}
```

Finally, add the following method implementation to the MyEngine.cpp file:

```
////////////////////////////////////////////////////////
// CreateNewMonster()
////////////////////////////////////////////////////////
CMonster* CMyEngine::CreateNewMonster(char* file1, char* file2,
    char* file3, char* file4, char* pstrName, int iMaxHitPoints,
    int iMaxDamage, int iExperience, int iMaxGold)
{
    CMonster* m_pCurrentMonster = new CMonster();
    m_pCurrentMonster->SetName(pstrName);
    m_pCurrentMonster->SetMaxHitPoints(iMaxHitPoints);
    m_pCurrentMonster->SetRemainingHitPoints(iMaxHitPoints);
    m_pCurrentMonster->SetMaxAttackDamage(iMaxDamage);
    m_pCurrentMonster->SetExperienceValue(iExperience);
    m_pCurrentMonster->SetMaxGold(iMaxGold);
    m_Direct3D.CreateMonsterTextures(file1, file2, file3, file4);
    return m_pCurrentMonster;
}
```

WEEK 3

DAY 19

Saving and Loading Games

Because of the time required to complete a role-playing game, every such game must have a game-save feature. This feature enables the player to quit playing and come back to the game later, without having to repeat the parts of the game he has already completed. Today, you add this important functionality to the JBookman project. Specifically, today you learn how to:

- Decide what values to save
- Maintain the game's data files as the player plays
- Manage game-save files
- Request confirmation for the save, load, and quit commands

Understanding the Game-Save Process

A typical RPG takes a good long time to play to the end. For that reason, it's imperative that such a game have some sort of game-save feature. Your player sure isn't going to want to start from scratch every time he loads up the game! How do you save a game, you ask? You need to write the values of all appropriate variables to disk, so that they can be loaded back into the game at a later date. The tricky part is figuring out which variables need to be saved.

Also adding to the trickiness is that the game needs some sort of temporary game-save feature that works automatically to remember what the player has done. For example, if the player opens a treasure chest and removes its contents, it would be a problem to have the player later return to the treasure chest and find it miraculously refilled.

Choosing Variables to Save

The truth is that only you, the game designer, know exactly which variables need to be saved in order to restore the game correctly. Such variables include flags that specify which tasks the player has completed. The player's current attributes—hit points, gold, potions, and so on—must also be saved. After all, the player isn't going to want to have to start building up the player character all over again.

In the case of the JBookman project, you also need to save the status of all containers and doors. This is because the status of these objects changes in the game. If the player unlocks a door, it should remain unlocked when he reloads the game. If the player opens a treasure chest and removes its contents, the chest should be empty the next time the player opens it.

In the JBookman project (but not necessarily in other RPGs), people in the game (NPCs) have no attribute that's critical to saving a game. The only attribute that changes is the sector in which an NPC is located. You could choose to save that value if you wanted to, but it won't make much difference in the game, even for NPCs who roam around.

Maintaining the Game's Status

In *The Adventures of Jasper Bookman*, whenever the player enters a new area, the program loads the map data for the area, as well as all containers, doors, and people in the area. Currently, the game loads these values from the game's starting files, which means that any changes the player has made—such as emptying a treasure chest or unlocking a door—are lost.

Fixing this problem requires a couple of levels in the game-save mechanism. First, the player must be able to save his progress and restart the game from that point at a later time. This is the level of game saving that most people are familiar with. However, the game also needs a game-save that operates automatically to keep all areas of the game up to date even as the player is playing.

Remember that whenever the player moves from one place to another, all changes in the previous area are lost, because the next time the player enters that area, the game reloads the original data from the start-up files. This is no good. Instead, the game must save the status of an area when the player exits and reload it when the player returns.

When you put all this together with the ability to start a brand-new game, you actually have three types of game data:

- Start-up data—This is the game data that, when loaded, starts a brand-new game. This data, which is located in the Maps directory, never changes.
- Save data—This is the game data that the player explicitly saves in order to begin where he left off at a later date. This data, which is located in the Save directory, changes only when the player chooses the save command.
- Working data—This is the game data that is constantly changing as the player plays. This data, which is located in the Temp directory, changes every time the player manipulates an object or moves from one location to another.

As the player plays the game, the working data needs to be continually updated. Obviously, the program must create a separate set of files for this data. It can't, after all, change the existing start-up files or the player will never be able to start a new game. So, when the working data needs to be updated, the program saves the necessary data into the Temp folder. In the following section, you'll add the source code that takes care of each type of game saving.

Adding the Game-Save Features

Several steps are required to add the game-save features to the JBookman project. To keep the tasks more manageable, the following sections update the different classes and files one at a time. As you'll see, the `CEngine` class will get new methods that handle the default file processing for saving and loading games, whereas the `CMyEngine` class will get methods that handle the data that's unique to your game.

Updating the Game Engine

Almost every time you add a feature to the game, you need to add source code to the game engine. This is no less true of the game-save features. Perform the following steps to update the `CEngine` class:

1. In the `Engine.h` file, add the following lines to the class's protected data members. If you'd rather not type, you can copy the lines from the Code01.txt file in the Chapter19 directory of this book's CD-ROM.

```
char m_pstrCurrentMapFile[MAX_PATH];
BOOL m_bAskingIfSave;
BOOL m_bAskingIfLoad;
BOOL m_bAskingIfQuit;
```

2. Also in `Engine.h`, add the following lines to the class's protected methods. If you'd rather not type, you can copy the lines from the Code02.txt file in the Chapter19 directory of this book's CD-ROM.

```
virtual void SaveGame(BOOL bFullSave) = 0;
virtual void LoadGame() = 0;
void SaveMapFile(BOOL bFullSave);
void DeleteTempFiles();
void DeleteSaveFiles();
void CopyTempToSave();
void CopySaveToTemp();
```

3. Move the following method declaration from the private area to the protected declarations:

```
void GetStringFromFile(std::ifstream& str, char* buf);
```

4. In the public methods, replace the `OpenMapFiles()` declaration with this one:

```
void OpenMapFiles(char* pstrFileName, BOOL bNewGame);
```

5. In the private methods, replace the `ConstructFileName()` declaration with this one:

```
void ConstructFileName(char* fileName, BOOL bNewGame);
```

6. Add the following lines to the class's private method declarations. If you'd rather not type, you can copy the lines from the Code03.txt file in the Chapter19 directory of this book's CD-ROM.

```
void SavePeopleFile(char* pstrFileName);
void SaveContainerFile(char* pstrFileName);
void SaveDoorFile(char* pstrFileName);
void ResetMap();
void HandleS();
void HandleL();
void HandleSpace();
void HandleEscape();
void HandleN();
void HandleY();
```

7. In the `Engine.cpp` file, add the following lines to the end of the class's constructor:

```
m_bAskingIfSave = FALSE;
m_bAskingIfLoad = FALSE;
m_bAskingIfQuit = FALSE;
```

8. In the `HandleKeys()` method, replace the `case` clauses for `VK_ESCAPE` and `VK_SPACE` with the following. If you'd rather not type, you can copy the lines from the Code04.txt file in the Chapter19 directory of this book's CD-ROM.

```
case VK_ESCAPE:
    HandleEscape();
    break;
case VK_SPACE:
    HandleSpace();
    break;
```

9. Again in the `HandleKeys()` method, add the following `case` clauses. If you'd rather not type, you can copy the lines from the Code05.txt file in the Chapter19 directory of this book's CD-ROM.

```
case 83: // S
    HandleS();
    break;
case 76: // L
    HandleL();
    break;
case 78: // N
    HandleN();
    break;
case 89: // Y
    HandleY();
    break;
```

10. Add the following line to the beginning of the `InitGame()` method:

```
DeleteTempFiles();
```

11. Also in the `InitGame()` method, replace the call to `OpenMapFiles()` with the following:

```
OpenMapFiles(m_pstrFirstMap, TRUE);
```

19

12. Replace the `OpenMapFiles()` and `ConstructFileName()` methods with the versions that follow. If you'd rather not type, you can copy the lines from the Code06.txt file in the Chapter19 directory of this book's CD-ROM.

```
////////////////////////////////////////////////////////
// OpenMapFiles()
////////////////////////////////////////////////////////
void CEngine::OpenMapFiles(char* fName, BOOL bNewGame)
{
    char fileName[_MAX_PATH];
    strcpy(m_pstrCurrentMapFile, fName);
    strcpy(fileName, fName);
    ConstructFileName(fileName, bNewGame);
    ReadMapFile(fileName);
    ReadPeopleFile(fileName);
```

```
    ReadContainerFile(fileName);
    ReadDoorFile(fileName);
}

/////////////////////////////////////////////////////////
// ConstructFileName()
/////////////////////////////////////////////////////////
void CEngine::ConstructFileName(char* fileName, BOOL bNewGame)
{
    char NewMapFileName[_MAX_PATH];
    char TempMapFileName[_MAX_PATH];
    strcpy(NewMapFileName, "Maps\\");
    strcpy(&NewMapFileName[5], fileName);
    strcpy(TempMapFileName, "Temp\\");
    strcpy(&TempMapFileName[5], fileName);

    if (bNewGame)
        strcpy(fileName, NewMapFileName);
    else
    {
        std::ifstream testFile(TempMapFileName, std::ios::binary);
        if (testFile.fail())
            strcpy(fileName, NewMapFileName);
        else
            strcpy(fileName, TempMapFileName);
        testFile.close();
    }
}
```

13. Add the following methods to the end of the `Engine.cpp` file. If you'd rather not type, you can copy the lines from the Code07.txt file in the Chapter19 directory of this book's CD-ROM.

```
/////////////////////////////////////////////////////////
// SaveMapFile()
/////////////////////////////////////////////////////////
void CEngine::SaveMapFile(BOOL bFullSave)
{
    ResetMap();
    ResetAnimation();
    char fileName[MAX_PATH];
    wsprintf(fileName, "Temp\\%s", m_pstrCurrentMapFile);
    std::ofstream mapFile(fileName, std::ios::binary);
    mapFile.write((char*)&m_byMapType, 1);
    mapFile.write(m_Sectors, sizeof m_Sectors);
    mapFile.close();
    wsprintf(fileName, "Temp\\%s.peo", m_pstrCurrentMapFile);
    SavePeopleFile(fileName);
    wsprintf(fileName, "Temp\\%s.itm", m_pstrCurrentMapFile);
    SaveContainerFile(fileName);
    wsprintf(fileName, "Temp\\%s.dor", m_pstrCurrentMapFile);
```

```
    SaveDoorFile(fileName);
}

//////////////////////////////////////////////////////
// SavePeopleFile()
//////////////////////////////////////////////////////
void CEngine::SavePeopleFile(char* pstrFileName)
{
    std::ofstream m_peopleFile(pstrFileName);
    m_peopleFile << m_People.GetPersonCount() << '\n';

    for (int person=0; person<m_People.GetPersonCount(); ++person)
    {
        CPerson* pPerson = m_People.GetPerson(person);
        m_peopleFile << pPerson->GetName() << '\n';
        m_peopleFile << pPerson->GetSector() << '\n';
        if (pPerson->GetCanMove())
            m_peopleFile << "#TRUE#\n";
        else
            m_peopleFile << "#FALSE#\n";
        m_peopleFile << pPerson->GetTile() << '\n';
    }
    m_peopleFile.close();
}

//////////////////////////////////////////////////////
// SaveContainerFile()
//////////////////////////////////////////////////////
void CEngine::SaveContainerFile(char* fileName)
{
    std::ofstream ContainerFile(fileName);
    int iCount = m_Containers.GetContainerCount();
    ContainerFile << iCount << '\n';

    for (int container=0; container < iCount; ++container)
    {
        CContainer* pContainer = m_Containers.GetContainer(container);
        ContainerFile << pContainer->GetGold() << '\n';
        ContainerFile << pContainer->GetKeys() << '\n';
        ContainerFile << pContainer->GetPotion() << '\n';
        ContainerFile << pContainer->GetArmor() << '\n';
        ContainerFile << pContainer->GetWeapon() << '\n';
        if (pContainer->GetLocked())
            ContainerFile << "#TRUE#\n";
        else
            ContainerFile << "#FALSE#\n";
        ContainerFile << pContainer->GetSector() << '\n';
        ContainerFile << pContainer->GetTile() << '\n';
    }
    ContainerFile.close();
}
```

```
////////////////////////////////////////////////////////
// SaveDoorFile()
////////////////////////////////////////////////////////
void CEngine::SaveDoorFile(char* pstrFileName)
{
    std::ofstream DoorFile(pstrFileName);
    int iCount = m_Doors.GetDoorCount();
    DoorFile << iCount << '\n';

    for (int door=0; door < iCount; ++door)
    {
        CDoor* pDoor = m_Doors.GetDoor(door);
        if (pDoor->GetSecret())
            DoorFile << "#TRUE#\n";
        else
            DoorFile << "#FALSE#\n";
        if (pDoor->GetLocked())
            DoorFile << "#TRUE#\n";
        else
            DoorFile << "#FALSE#\n";
        DoorFile << pDoor->GetSector() << '\n';
        DoorFile << pDoor->GetTile() << '\n';
    }
    DoorFile.close();
}

////////////////////////////////////////////////////////
// ResetMap()
////////////////////////////////////////////////////////
void CEngine::ResetMap()
{
    for (int x=0; x<MAPSECTORCOUNT; ++x)
    {
        if (m_Sectors[x] > 31)
            m_Sectors[x] -= m_Sectors[x] % 2;
    }
}

////////////////////////////////////////////////////////
// HandleS()
////////////////////////////////////////////////////////
void CEngine::HandleS()
{
    if (m_bMonsterAttacking || m_bAskingIfLoad || m_bAskingIfQuit) return;
    TurnOnPlaque(
"The new save files will\n\
overwrite your previous ones.\n\n\
Are you sure you want\n\
to save the game? (Y/N)");
    m_bAskingIfSave = TRUE;
```

```
}

////////////////////////////////////////////////////
// HandleL()
////////////////////////////////////////////////////
void CEngine::HandleL()
{
    if (m_bMonsterAttacking || m_bAskingIfSave || m_bAskingIfQuit) return;
    TurnOnPlaque(
"Are you sure you want\n\
to load the previously\n\
saved game? (Y/N)");
    m_bAskingIfLoad = TRUE;
}

////////////////////////////////////////////////////
// HandleSpace()
////////////////////////////////////////////////////
void CEngine::HandleSpace()
{
    if (IsShowingPlaque() && !m_bAskingIfSave && !m_bAskingIfLoad)
        TurnOffPlaque();
}

////////////////////////////////////////////////////
// HandleEscape()
////////////////////////////////////////////////////
void CEngine::HandleEscape()
{
    if (m_bMonsterAttacking || m_bAskingIfSave || m_bAskingIfLoad) return;
    TurnOnPlaque(
"Don't forget to save your game.\n\n\
Are you sure you want\n\
to quit? (Y/N)");
    m_bAskingIfQuit = TRUE;
}

////////////////////////////////////////////////////
// HandleN()
////////////////////////////////////////////////////
void CEngine::HandleN()
{
    if (m_bAskingIfSave)
    {
        m_bAskingIfSave = FALSE;
        TurnOnPlaque("Game not saved.");
    }
    else if (m_bAskingIfLoad)
    {
        m_bAskingIfLoad = FALSE;
        TurnOnPlaque("Game not loaded.");
```

```
    }
    else if (m_bAskingIfQuit)
    {
        m_bAskingIfQuit = FALSE;
        TurnOffPlaque();
    }
}

////////////////////////////////////////////////////////
// HandleY()
////////////////////////////////////////////////////////
void CEngine::HandleY()
{
    if (m_bAskingIfSave)
    {
        m_bAskingIfSave = FALSE;
        SaveGame(TRUE);
        TurnOnPlaque("Game Saved");
    }
    else if (m_bAskingIfLoad)
    {
        m_bAskingIfLoad = FALSE;
        LoadGame();
        TurnOnPlaque("Game Loaded");
    }
    else if (m_bAskingIfQuit)
        PostQuitMessage(WM_QUIT);
}

////////////////////////////////////////////////////////
// DeleteTempFiles()
////////////////////////////////////////////////////////
void CEngine::DeleteTempFiles()
{
    char FileName[MAX_PATH];
    WIN32_FIND_DATA fileData;
    HANDLE fHandle = FindFirstFile("Temp\\*.*", &fileData);
    wsprintf(FileName, "Temp\\%s", fileData.cFileName);
    DeleteFile(FileName);
    while(FindNextFile(fHandle, &fileData))
    {
        wsprintf(FileName, "Temp\\%s", fileData.cFileName);
        DeleteFile(FileName);
    }
    FindClose(fHandle);
}

////////////////////////////////////////////////////////
// DeleteSaveFiles()
////////////////////////////////////////////////////////
void CEngine::DeleteSaveFiles()
```

```
{
    char FileName[MAX_PATH];
    WIN32_FIND_DATA fileData;
    HANDLE fHandle = FindFirstFile("Save\\*.*", &fileData);
    wsprintf(FileName, "Save\\%s", fileData.cFileName);
    DeleteFile(FileName);
    while(FindNextFile(fHandle, &fileData))
    {
        wsprintf(FileName, "Save\\%s", fileData.cFileName);
        DeleteFile(FileName);
    }
    FindClose(fHandle);
}

////////////////////////////////////////////////////////
// CopyTempToSave()
////////////////////////////////////////////////////////
void CEngine::CopyTempToSave()
{
    char oldFileName[MAX_PATH];
    char newFileName[MAX_PATH];
    WIN32_FIND_DATA fileData;
    HANDLE fHandle = FindFirstFile("Temp\\*.*", &fileData);
    wsprintf(newFileName, "Save\\%s", fileData.cFileName);
    wsprintf(oldFileName, "Temp\\%s", fileData.cFileName);
    CopyFile(oldFileName, newFileName, FALSE);
    while(FindNextFile(fHandle, &fileData))
    {
        wsprintf(newFileName, "Save\\%s", fileData.cFileName);
        wsprintf(oldFileName, "Temp\\%s", fileData.cFileName);
        CopyFile(oldFileName, newFileName, FALSE);
    }
    FindClose(fHandle);
}

////////////////////////////////////////////////////////
// CopySaveToTemp()
////////////////////////////////////////////////////////
void CEngine::CopySaveToTemp()
{
    char oldFileName[MAX_PATH];
    char newFileName[MAX_PATH];
    WIN32_FIND_DATA fileData;
    HANDLE fHandle = FindFirstFile("Save\\*.*", &fileData);
    wsprintf(newFileName, "Temp\\%s", fileData.cFileName);
    wsprintf(oldFileName, "Save\\%s", fileData.cFileName);
    CopyFile(oldFileName, newFileName, FALSE);
    while(FindNextFile(fHandle, &fileData))
    {
        wsprintf(newFileName, "Temp\\%s", fileData.cFileName);
        wsprintf(oldFileName, "Save\\%s", fileData.cFileName);
```

```
        CopyFile(oldFileName, newFileName, FALSE);
    }
    FindClose(fHandle);
}
```

14. Compile the class (press Ctrl+F7) to be sure everything's all right.

Updating the `CMyEngine` Class

Because much of the data that must be saved in a game-save file depends on your specific game storyline, the main game-engine class has no idea what to save. This means that you also need to add game-save features to your `CMyEngine` class. Perform the following steps to complete this task:

1. Add the following lines near the top of the `MyEngine.h` file, right after the include statements. If you'd rather not type, you can copy the lines from the Code08.txt file in the Chapter19 directory of this book's CD-ROM.

```
// Quest flags defined in FirstTown.cpp.
extern BOOL bSpokeToGrewell;
extern BOOL bSpokeToWillam;
extern BOOL bWillamQuestComplete;
extern BOOL bHasWillamKey;
```

2. Add the following lines to the class's public method declarations.

```
void SaveGame(BOOL bShowMessage);
void LoadGame();
```

3. Add the following method implementations to the end of the `MyEngine.cpp` file. If you'd rather not type, you can copy the lines from the Code09.txt file in the Chapter19 directory of this book's CD-ROM.

```
//////////////////////////////////////////////////////
// SaveGame()
//////////////////////////////////////////////////////
void CMyEngine::SaveGame(BOOL bFullSave)
{
    char dir[10];
    if (bFullSave)
    {
        strcpy(dir, "Save");
        DeleteSaveFiles();
        CopyTempToSave();
    }
    else
        strcpy(dir, "Temp");
    SaveMapFile(bFullSave);
    char fileName[MAX_PATH];
    wsprintf(fileName, "%s\\SaveFile.dat", dir);
    std::ofstream SaveFile(fileName);
```

```
    // Save quest flags.
    SaveFile << bSpokeToGrewell << '\n';
    SaveFile << bSpokeToWillam << '\n';
    SaveFile << bWillamQuestComplete << '\n';
    SaveFile << bHasWillamKey << '\n';

    // save player stats.
    SaveFile << m_Player.GetArmor() << '\n';
    SaveFile << m_Player.GetExperience() << '\n';
    SaveFile << m_Player.GetGold() << '\n';
    SaveFile << m_Player.GetHitPoints() << '\n';
    SaveFile << m_Player.GetKeys() << '\n';
    SaveFile << m_Player.GetMaxHitPoints() << '\n';
    SaveFile << m_Player.GetPotions() << '\n';
    SaveFile << m_Player.GetSector() << '\n';
    SaveFile << m_Player.GetWeapon() << '\n';

    // Save Map info.
    SaveFile << m_pstrCurrentMapFile << '\n';
    SaveFile << GetCurrentMap() << '\n';

    SaveFile.close();
}

///////////////////////////////////////////////////////
// LoadGame()
///////////////////////////////////////////////////////
void CMyEngine::LoadGame()
{
    DeleteTempFiles();
    CopySaveToTemp();

    char buf[128];
    std::ifstream SaveFile("Save\\SaveFile.dat", std::ios::binary);

    // Load quest flags.
    GetStringFromFile(SaveFile, buf);
    bSpokeToGrewell = atoi(buf);
    GetStringFromFile(SaveFile, buf);
    bSpokeToWillam = atoi(buf);
    GetStringFromFile(SaveFile, buf);
    bWillamQuestComplete = atoi(buf);
    GetStringFromFile(SaveFile, buf);
    bHasWillamKey = atoi(buf);

    // Load player stats.
    GetStringFromFile(SaveFile, buf);
    m_Player.SetArmor(atoi(buf));
    GetStringFromFile(SaveFile, buf);
    m_Player.SetExperience(atoi(buf));
```

```
        GetStringFromFile(SaveFile, buf);
        m_Player.SetGold(atoi(buf));
        GetStringFromFile(SaveFile, buf);
        m_Player.SetHitPoints(atoi(buf));
        GetStringFromFile(SaveFile, buf);
        m_Player.SetKeys(atoi(buf));
        GetStringFromFile(SaveFile, buf);
        m_Player.SetMaxHitPoints(atoi(buf));
        GetStringFromFile(SaveFile, buf);
        m_Player.SetPotions(atoi(buf));
        GetStringFromFile(SaveFile, buf);
        m_Player.SetSector(atoi(buf));
        GetStringFromFile(SaveFile, buf);
        m_Player.SetWeapon(atoi(buf));

        // Load map info.
        GetStringFromFile(SaveFile, buf);
        strcpy(m_pstrCurrentMapFile, buf);
        GetStringFromFile(SaveFile, buf);
        SetCurrentMap(atoi(buf));

        SaveFile.close();
        OpenMapFiles(m_pstrCurrentMapFile, FALSE);
        switch (m_byMapType)
        {
        case TOWNEXTERIOR:
            GetCDirect3DObj()->SetCurrentTileSurface
                (GetCDirect3DObj()->GetTownExtTileSurface());
            break;
        case TOWNINTERIOR:
            GetCDirect3DObj()->SetCurrentTileSurface
                (GetCDirect3DObj()->GetTownIntTileSurface());
            break;
        case DUNGEON:
            GetCDirect3DObj()->SetCurrentTileSurface
                (GetCDirect3DObj()->GetDungeonTileSurface());
            break;
        case WILDERNESS:
            GetCDirect3DObj()->SetCurrentTileSurface
                (GetCDirect3DObj()->GetWildernessTileSurface());
            break;
        }

        ResetAnimation();
    }
```

4. Compile the class (press Ctrl+F7) to be sure everything's all right.

Updating the Location Files

As you've learned, every time the player moves from one location to another, the program must save the current location's map files. This means you must update the source-code files for each location. In this section, you take care of that task.

First, add the following after every `case` line in the `FirstTown.cpp` file:

```
g_Engine.SaveGame(FALSE);
```

Here's an example:

```
case DUNGEON01ROOM11ENTRANCE1:
    g_Engine.SaveGame(FALSE);    <------- Here's the new line.
    g_Engine.GetPlayer()->
        SetSector(DUNGEON01ROOM11ENTRANCE1 + MAPCOLUMNCOUNT);
    g_Engine.OpenMapFiles("FirstTownDungeon01Room01.map", FALSE);
    g_Engine.SetCurrentMap(FIRSTTOWNDUNGEON01ROOM01);
    g_Engine.ResetAnimation();
    break;
```

Also add the call to `SaveGame()` to the start of the `if` statement in `HandleFirstTownHouse01Room02()`, like this:

```
void HandleFirstTownHouse01Room02()
{
    if (g_Engine.GetPlayer()->GetSector() == HOUSE01ROOM01DOOR)
    {
        g_Engine.SaveGame(FALSE);    <------- Here's the new line.
        g_Engine.GetPlayer()->SetSector(HOUSE01ROOM01DOOR + 1);
        g_Engine.OpenMapFiles("FirstTownHouse01Room01.map", FALSE);
        g_Engine.SetCurrentMap(FIRSTTOWNHOUSE01ROOM01);
        g_Engine.ResetAnimation();
    }
}
```

Now, you need to do a search and replace on the entire file. Search for this:

```
map");
```

And replace it with this:

```
map", FALSE);
```

There should be a total of 59 replacements.

Finally, make the same changes to the `Ganjek.cpp` file, which should end up looking like this:

```
///////////////////////////////////////////////////////////
// Ganjek.cpp
///////////////////////////////////////////////////////////
```

```
#include <d3d8.h>
#include "constants.h"
#include "MyEngine.h"
#include "Ganjek.h"

extern CMyEngine g_Engine;

const FIRSTTOWNENTRANCE = 860;

//////////////////////////////////////////////////////////////////
// HandleGanjek()
//////////////////////////////////////////////////////////////////
void HandleGanjek()
{
    switch (g_Engine.GetPlayer()->GetSector())
    {
    case FIRSTTOWNENTRANCE:
        g_Engine.SaveGame(FALSE);
        g_Engine.GetPlayer()->SetSector(1701);
        g_Engine.OpenMapFiles("FirstTown.map", FALSE);
        g_Engine.SetCurrentMap(FIRSTTOWN);
        g_Engine.GetCDirect3DObj()->SetCurrentTileSurface
            (g_Engine.GetCDirect3DObj()->GetTownExtTileSurface());
        g_Engine.ResetAnimation();
        break;
    }
}
```

Testing the New Game-Save Features

You're almost ready to compile and run the program. But before you do, create folders named Temp and Save in your JBookman project's main directory. Now, run the program. When the program starts up, it loads all data from the startup data in the Maps folder, placing the player at the very beginning of the game. Head to the Armor shop. Inside, you'll find the two treasure chests shown in Figure 19.1. Open the one on the left, and you'll get a bunch of goodies.

Now, exit the Armor shop, and then turn around and go back in. Check that treasure chest again. Still empty, which proves that the game is now keeping all the areas up to date, even as you play.

Next, press the S key to save your game, and then head out of the Armor shop. Press the L key to load your last game, and *presto!* you're right back where you saved the game.

FIGURE 19.1

A pair of treasure chests.

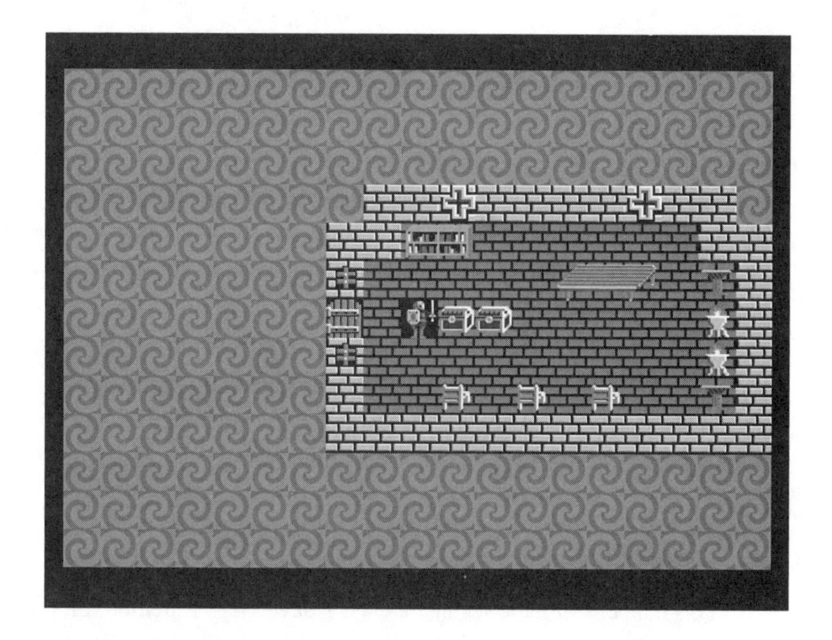

Understanding the Game-Save Feature

There's a lot more going on under the hood than someone might expect when playing the game. Not only can the game now load a previously saved position, but it also continually updates its working files so that it remembers everything that the player does (or at least everything that's important to the game).

As you already know, there are three different sets of data: the startup data, the save data, and the working data. Whenever the player moves to a sector that triggers a move to another area, the game saves the map, door, item, and person files for the area the player is leaving. You can see this happening in one of the case statements in the `FirstTown.cpp` file:

```
case DUNGEON01ROOM11ENTRANCE1:
    g_Engine.SaveGame(FALSE);
    g_Engine.GetPlayer()->
        SetSector(DUNGEON01ROOM11ENTRANCE1 + MAPCOLUMNCOUNT);
    g_Engine.OpenMapFiles("FirstTownDungeon01Room01.map", FALSE);
    g_Engine.SetCurrentMap(FIRSTTOWNDUNGEON01ROOM01);
    g_Engine.ResetAnimation();
    break;
```

Here, before the program changes the player's location, it calls the `SaveGame()` method to save the old location. The `FALSE` argument specifies that this isn't an explicit save by the player, but rather a save to the game's working files.

Also, the case statement calls the OpenMapFiles() method to load the data files for the target location. This new version of the method now requires a Boolean value as its second argument. This value specifies whether the method should load data from the startup files (TRUE) or from the working files (FALSE).

See how easy all this is? You already understand how the game uses the startup and working files. What you haven't figured out yet is the important relationship between the files that result from the player selecting the save command explicitly and the working files.

Think about the working files for a minute. Every time the game needs to keep track of something the player has done with an object in a specific area, it saves the information to the work files. What this means is that the working files are always completely up to date (except for the location in which the player is currently located, which doesn't get saved until the player moves out of the area). So when the player chooses to save a game, all the program has to do is save the current map data and then copy the files from the Temp directory to the Save directory.

This happens in the CMyEngine class's SaveGame() method. First the program must delete the existing save files and copy the temp files into the Save directory:

```
char dir[10];
if (bFullSave)
{
    strcpy(dir, "Save");
    DeleteSaveFiles();
    CopyTempToSave();
}
```

The SaveGame() method then goes on to save the current location:

```
SaveMapFile(bFullSave);
```

Next, the method opens the file to which it will save the quest flags and the player attributes:

```
char fileName[MAX_PATH];
wsprintf(fileName, "%s\\SaveFile.dat", dir);
std::ofstream SaveFile(fileName);
```

With the file ready to go, SaveGame() saves the quest flags:

```
SaveFile << bSpokeToGrewell << '\n';
SaveFile << bSpokeToWillam << '\n';
SaveFile << bWillamQuestComplete << '\n';
SaveFile << bHasWillamKey << '\n';
SaveFile << bGotUniform << '\n';
```

And the method also saves the player attributes:

```
SaveFile << m_Player.GetArmor() << '\n';
SaveFile << m_Player.GetExperience() << '\n';
SaveFile << m_Player.GetGold() << '\n';
SaveFile << m_Player.GetHitPoints() << '\n';
SaveFile << m_Player.GetKeys() << '\n';
SaveFile << m_Player.GetMaxHitPoints() << '\n';
SaveFile << m_Player.GetPotions() << '\n';
SaveFile << m_Player.GetSector() << '\n';
SaveFile << m_Player.GetWeapon() << '\n';
```

Finally, the last bit of information the game needs to save is the current map ID:

```
SaveFile << m_pstrCurrentMapFile << '\n';
SaveFile << GetCurrentMap() << '\n';
```

The last piece of the puzzle is the `CEngine` class's `SaveMapFile()` method, which, as you just saw, gets called from `SaveGame()`.

`SaveMapFile()` must reset any of the maps tiles that may be in their second frame of animation back to the first frame (otherwise, when the animation restarts, it's likely to be all goofed up):

```
ResetMap();
ResetAnimation();
```

Then the program must save all the data for the current area:

```
char fileName[MAX_PATH];
wsprintf(fileName, "Temp\\%s", m_pstrCurrentMapFile);
std::ofstream mapFile(fileName, std::ios::binary);
mapFile.write((char*)&m_byMapType, 1);
mapFile.write(m_Sectors, sizeof m_Sectors);
mapFile.close();
wsprintf(fileName, "Temp\\%s.peo", m_pstrCurrentMapFile);
SavePeopleFile(fileName);
wsprintf(fileName, "Temp\\%s.itm", m_pstrCurrentMapFile);
SaveContainerFile(fileName);
wsprintf(fileName, "Temp\\%s.dor", m_pstrCurrentMapFile);
SaveDoorFile(fileName);
```


Most of the source code you added to the program today is pretty straightforward file handling, and so requires no additional discussion. For example, here are the `DeleteSaveFiles()` and `CopyTempToSave()` methods:

```
///////////////////////////////////////////////////////
// DeleteSaveFiles()
///////////////////////////////////////////////////////
void CEngine::DeleteSaveFiles()
{
```

```
    char FileName[MAX_PATH];
    WIN32_FIND_DATA fileData;
    HANDLE fHandle = FindFirstFile("Save\\*.*", &fileData);
    wsprintf(FileName, "Save\\%s", fileData.cFileName);
    DeleteFile(FileName);
    while(FindNextFile(fHandle, &fileData))
    {
        wsprintf(FileName, "Save\\%s", fileData.cFileName);
        DeleteFile(FileName);
    }
    FindClose(fHandle);
}

///////////////////////////////////////////////////////
// CopyTempToSave()
///////////////////////////////////////////////////////
void CEngine::CopyTempToSave()
{
    char oldFileName[MAX_PATH];
    char newFileName[MAX_PATH];
    WIN32_FIND_DATA fileData;
    HANDLE fHandle = FindFirstFile("Temp\\*.*", &fileData);
    wsprintf(newFileName, "Save\\%s", fileData.cFileName);
    wsprintf(oldFileName, "Temp\\%s", fileData.cFileName);
    CopyFile(oldFileName, newFileName, FALSE);
    while(FindNextFile(fHandle, &fileData))
    {
        wsprintf(newFileName, "Save\\%s", fileData.cFileName);
        wsprintf(oldFileName, "Temp\\%s", fileData.cFileName);
        CopyFile(oldFileName, newFileName, FALSE);
    }
    FindClose(fHandle);
}
```

You should look over the code just to be sure you understand it.

Loading a Saved Game

Loading a saved game is just a matter of retrieving data from the disk and using it to initialize the appropriate variables. All this happens in the `CMyEngine` class's `LoadGame()` method. The first step is to delete all temporary files and copy the current save files to the Temp directory:

```
DeleteTempFiles();
CopySaveToTemp();
```

Then the method opens the file that holds data such as the quest flags and player stats:

```
char buf[128];
std::ifstream SaveFile("Save\\SaveFile.dat", std::ios::binary);
```

Once the file is open, the program reads the quest data from the file and uses it to initialize each of the quest flags:

```
// Load quest flags.
GetStringFromFile(SaveFile, buf);
bSpokeToGrewell = atoi(buf);
GetStringFromFile(SaveFile, buf);
bSpokeToWillam = atoi(buf);
GetStringFromFile(SaveFile, buf);
bWillamQuestComplete = atoi(buf);
GetStringFromFile(SaveFile, buf);
bHasWillamKey = atoi(buf);
GetStringFromFile(SaveFile, buf);
bGotUniform = atoi(buf);
```

Next to get loaded from the file is the player data:

```
// Load player stats.
GetStringFromFile(SaveFile, buf);
m_Player.SetArmor(atoi(buf));
GetStringFromFile(SaveFile, buf);
m_Player.SetExperience(atoi(buf));
GetStringFromFile(SaveFile, buf);
m_Player.SetGold(atoi(buf));
GetStringFromFile(SaveFile, buf);
m_Player.SetHitPoints(atoi(buf));
GetStringFromFile(SaveFile, buf);
m_Player.SetKeys(atoi(buf));
GetStringFromFile(SaveFile, buf);
m_Player.SetMaxHitPoints(atoi(buf));
GetStringFromFile(SaveFile, buf);
m_Player.SetPotions(atoi(buf));
GetStringFromFile(SaveFile, buf);
m_Player.SetSector(atoi(buf));
GetStringFromFile(SaveFile, buf);
m_Player.SetWeapon(atoi(buf));
```


Finally, the program loads the map information and closes the file:

```
// Load map info.
GetStringFromFile(SaveFile, buf);
strcpy(m_pstrCurrentMapFile, buf);
GetStringFromFile(SaveFile, buf);
SetCurrentMap(atoi(buf));

SaveFile.close();
```

Now that the program is finished with the `SaveFile.dat` file, it calls `OpenMapFiles()` to read in the appropriate map data, as well as the associated door, item, and person files:

```
OpenMapFiles(m_pstrCurrentMapFile, FALSE);
```

At this point, the game is fully loaded. However, the program still has to update the screen, which it does by setting the appropriate tile file:

```
switch (m_byMapType)
{
case TOWNEXTERIOR:
    GetCDirect3DObj()->SetCurrentTileSurface
        (GetCDirect3DObj()->GetTownExtTileSurface());
    break;
case TOWNINTERIOR:
    GetCDirect3DObj()->SetCurrentTileSurface
        (GetCDirect3DObj()->GetTownIntTileSurface());
    break;
case DUNGEON:
    GetCDirect3DObj()->SetCurrentTileSurface
        (GetCDirect3DObj()->GetDungeonTileSurface());
    break;
case WILDERNESS:
    GetCDirect3DObj()->SetCurrentTileSurface
        (GetCDirect3DObj()->GetWildernessTileSurface());
    break;
```

Handling the Save, Load, and Quit Commands

One other point of interest is the way the game now handles the quit command, as well as the new load and save commands. When the player enters a command (by pressing the appropriate key on the keyboard), all the program does is ask the player to verify that he really wants to issue the command and set a flag to keep track of the current command mode. For example, here's what happens when the player presses the S key:

```
    if (m_bMonsterAttacking || m_bAskingIfLoad || m_bAskingIfQuit) return;
    TurnOnPlaque(
"The new save files will\n\
overwrite your previous ones.\n\n\
Are you sure you want\n\
to save the game? (Y/N)");
    m_bAskingIfSave = TRUE;
```

Notice that the program first checks other mode flags to be sure the player hasn't entered a previous command or that he is not in the middle of combat.

To finalize a command, the player must press Y to commit to the command or N to abort it. So, it's in the methods that handle these two keys that stuff really gets done. As an example, look over the source code that handles the Y key:

```
if (m_bAskingIfSave)
{
    m_bAskingIfSave = FALSE;
    SaveGame(TRUE);
    TurnOffPlaque();
}
else if (m_bAskingIfLoad)
{
    m_bAskingIfLoad = FALSE;
    LoadGame();
    TurnOffPlaque();
}
else if (m_bAskingIfQuit)
    PostQuitMessage(WM_QUIT);
```

As you can see, it's here that the save, load, or quit commands are carried out.

New Members of the `CEngine` Class

Day by day, the `CEngine` class gets bigger and bigger. Table 19.1 describes the new members you added to the `CEngine` class today.

TABLE 19.1 New `CEngine` Members

Member	*Type*	*Description*
`m_pstrCurrentMapFile[]`	Data member	The name of the currently loaded map file
`m_bAskingIfSave`	Data member	A flag that indicates whether the player needs to enter Y or N in response to the "Are you sure you want to save?" message
`m_bAskingIfLoad`	Data member	A flag that indicates whether the player needs to enter Y or N in response to the "Are you sure you want to load a game?" message
`m_bAskingIfQuit`	Data member	A flag that indicates whether the player needs to enter Y or N in response to the "Are you sure you want to quit?" message
`SaveGame()`	Protected method	Saves all game files
`LoadGame()`	Protected method	Loads the previously saved game
`SaveMapFile()`	Protected method	Saves the map, door, container, and person files
`DeleteSaveFiles()`	Protected method	Deletes all save files
`DeleteTempFiles()`	Protected method	Deletes all working save files
`CopySaveToTemp()`	Protected method	Copies the game-save files to the working files directory

TABLE 19.1 continued

Member	*Type*	*Description*
`CopyTempToSave()`	Protected method	Copies the temporary files to the save files directory
`SavePeopleFile()`	Private method	Saves all person objects to the `.peo` file
`SaveContainerFile()`	Private method	Saves all container objects to the `.itm` file
`SaveDoorFile()`	Private method	Saves all door objects to the `.dor` file
`ResetMap()`	Private method	Resets any animated tiles in a map file to the first tile in the animation sequence
`HandleS()`	Private method	Responds to the S key
`HandleL()`	Private method	Responds to the L key
`HandleY()`	Private method	Responds to the Y key
`HandleN()`	Private method	Responds to the N key

Summary

Because of the amount of time it takes to play a role-playing game from beginning to end, it's imperative that the player be able to save her game and come back to it later. As you've learned, though, the program's game-save features also enable the game to keep all data files up to date as the player plays. This data processing ensures that when a player reenters a location she's been in before the location will be in the same state it was when she left.

In tomorrow's lesson, you add to the game's realism by installing sound effects for several of the game events.

Q&A

Q. It seems to me that with a full-size game, the number of variables that need to be saved will be unwieldy. Is there some way to avoid this?

A. Sure is. Instead of having separate flags for every quest element you need to keep track of, you could create an array of Boolean values. You can write an entire array to a disk file using a single statement. To index such an array in the game, you would use carefully named constants. Here's an example: `GameFlags[TALKEDTOGREWELL]`.

Q. Why do some of the game-save files have such a weird format? For example, why do the door files use values like `#TRUE#` and `#FALSE#`, with those number signs?

A. Because the game editor is written in Visual Basic, it saves data in the Visual Basic format. The number signs surrounding Boolean values is an example of this format, as is the quotation marks surrounding strings. You learn to use the game editor in this book's Appendix A, "Using the JBookman Game Editor."

Workshop

The workshop includes quiz questions to help gauge your grasp of the material. Even if you feel that you totally understand the concepts presented here, you should work through the quiz anyway.

1. How do you know which variables to save to game-save files?
2. What's the difference between the game's startup data files located in the Maps directory and the working files in the Temp directory?
3. How are the game-save files located in the Save folder similar to the working files in the Temp directory?
4. Why doesn't the game need to save data like quest flags in the working data (even though it does)?
5. When the player presses a command key like S for save or L for load, all the program really does is set a couple of flags. Why? Where do the commands actually get carried out?
6. When does the program update the working save files?

Answers for Day 19

Quiz

1. How do you know which variables to save to game-save files?

   You need to save only those variables, such as quest flags and player stats, that are required to enable the player to pick up where he left off in the game. Some variables are obvious, others may be a matter of judgment, others would be pointless to save.

2. What's the difference between the game's startup data files located in the Maps directory and the working files in the Temp directory?

The start-up files represent the game's status at the very start of the game, before the player has done anything. The working files, on the other hand, are continually updated as the player moves through the game, and so represent a kind of snapshot of the changes the player has made to areas he has explored.

3. How are the game-save files located in the Save folder similar to the working files in the Temp directory?

   The game-save files are actually copies of the files in the Temp directory at the time the player issues the save command. The only difference is that the values in the SaveGame.dat file may be more up to date.

4. Why doesn't the game need to save data like quest flags in the working data (even though it does)?

   Because these values don't get wiped out as the player moves from one area of the game to another.

5. When the player presses a command key like S for save or L for load, all the program really does is set a couple of flags. Why? Where do the commands actually get carried out?

   The program needs to wait for the player to confirm that he wants the command executed. The program carries out the command in the `HandleY()` method (which responds to the Y key) and cancels the command in the `HandleN()` method.

6. When does the program update the working save files?

   Whenever the program must load a new map file, which wipes out any changes made to the current location.

WEEK 3

DAY 20

Creating and Adding Sound

No modern game is complete without a bunch of cool sound effects. This is especially true of role-playing games, which try to submerge the player in an intense game world and story. Adding sound to such a game is a big task, one that can't be completed in a book like this. However, what this book can do is get you started with a few sound effects, as well as give you the knowledge you need to add more of your own. Today, you learn to add sound effects to the JBookman project. Specifically, today you learn how to:

- Organize DirectSound source code into a class
- Add the `CWave` class to the game project
- Associate sound effects with game events

Creating the CDirectSound Class

Way back in Day 10, "Creating and Programming Sound," you learned pretty much every thing you need to know to add sound to *The Adventures of Jasper Bookman*. Specifically, you learned to use DirectSound, as well as the Windows multimedia functions, to load and play sound effects. The difference today is that you'll be creating a class to handle the DirectSound stuff, rather than having the sound routines as part of the main program.

So, the first step towards adding sound to *The Adventures of Jasper Bookman* is to add the `CDirectSound` and `CWave` classes to your JBookman project. Load up your JBookman project, and follow these steps to complete that task:

1. Using the Add Class command on the Project menu, add a generic C++ class named `CDirectSound` to the project.
2. Replace the source code in the DirectSound.h file with the following. If you don't want to type the source code, you can copy it from the Code01.txt file in the Chapter20 directory of this book's CD-ROM.

```
///////////////////////////////////////////////////////////
// DirectSound.h
///////////////////////////////////////////////////////////

#pragma once

#include <dsound.h>
#include <D3dx8tex.h>
#include "Wave.h"
#include "Constants.h"

class CDirectSound
{
protected:
    IDirectSound8* m_pDirectSoundObj;
    IDirectSoundBuffer* m_pMonsterDieSound;
    IDirectSoundBuffer* m_pMonsterHitSound;
    IDirectSoundBuffer* m_pPlayerHitSound;
    IDirectSoundBuffer* m_pFootstepSound;
    IDirectSoundBuffer* m_pItemOpenSound;
    HWND m_hWnd;
    char m_szErrorMsg[256];

public:
    CDirectSound(void);
    ~CDirectSound(void);
    void SetWindowHandle(HWND hWnd);
    HRESULT InitDirectSound(void);
```

```
    char* GetErrorString(void);
    HRESULT PlaySound(int iSoundID);

private:
    HRESULT CreateSoundBuffers(void);
    void CleanUp(void);
    HRESULT LoadSoundEffect(char* pstrFileName,
        IDirectSoundBuffer** ppSoundBuf);
};
```

3. Replace the source code in the DirectSound.cpp file with the following. If you don't want to type the source code, you can copy it from the Code02.txt file in the Chapter20 directory of this book's CD-ROM.

```
///////////////////////////////////////////////////////
// DirectSound.cpp
///////////////////////////////////////////////////////

#include "directsound.h"

///////////////////////////////////////////////////////
// CDirectSound()
///////////////////////////////////////////////////////
CDirectSound::CDirectSound(void)
{
    m_pDirectSoundObj = NULL;
    m_pMonsterDieSound = NULL;
    m_pMonsterHitSound = NULL;
    m_pPlayerHitSound = NULL;
    m_pFootstepSound = NULL;
    m_pItemOpenSound = NULL;
}

///////////////////////////////////////////////////////
// ~CDirectSound()
///////////////////////////////////////////////////////
CDirectSound::~CDirectSound(void)
{
    CleanUp();
}

///////////////////////////////////////////////////////
// SetWindowHandle()
///////////////////////////////////////////////////////
void CDirectSound::SetWindowHandle(HWND hWnd)
{
    m_hWnd = hWnd;
}

///////////////////////////////////////////////////////
// CleanUp()
///////////////////////////////////////////////////////
```

```
void CDirectSound::CleanUp()
{
    if (m_pMonsterDieSound)
        m_pMonsterDieSound->Release();
    if (m_pMonsterHitSound)
        m_pMonsterHitSound->Release();
    if (m_pPlayerHitSound)
        m_pPlayerHitSound->Release();
    if (m_pFootstepSound)
        m_pFootstepSound->Release();
    if (m_pItemOpenSound)
        m_pItemOpenSound->Release();
    if (m_pDirectSoundObj)
        m_pDirectSoundObj->Release();
}

//////////////////////////////////////////////////////
// InitDirectSound()
//////////////////////////////////////////////////////
HRESULT CDirectSound::InitDirectSound()
{
    HRESULT hResult = DirectSoundCreate8(NULL, &m_pDirectSoundObj, NULL);
    if (hResult != DS_OK)
        return hResult;

    hResult = m_pDirectSoundObj->SetCooperativeLevel(m_hWnd, DSSCL_NORMAL);
    if (hResult != DS_OK)
        return hResult;

    hResult = CreateSoundBuffers();
    if (hResult != DS_OK)
        return hResult;

    return hResult;
}

//////////////////////////////////////////////////////
// CreateSoundBuffers()
//////////////////////////////////////////////////////
HRESULT CDirectSound::CreateSoundBuffers()
{
    HRESULT hResult = LoadSoundEffect("Sounds\\MonsterDie.wav",
        &m_pMonsterDieSound);
    if (hResult != DS_OK)
        return hResult;
    hResult = LoadSoundEffect("Sounds\\MonsterHit.wav",
&m_pMonsterHitSound);
    if (hResult != DS_OK)
        return hResult;
    hResult = LoadSoundEffect("Sounds\\PlayerHit.wav", &m_pPlayerHitSound);
    if (hResult != DS_OK)
```

```
        return hResult;
    hResult = LoadSoundEffect("Sounds\\Footstep.wav", &m_pFootstepSound);
    if (hResult != DS_OK)
        return hResult;
    hResult = LoadSoundEffect("Sounds\\ItemOpen.wav", &m_pItemOpenSound);
    return hResult;
}

///////////////////////////////////////////////////////
// PlaySound()
///////////////////////////////////////////////////////
HRESULT CDirectSound::PlaySound(int iSoundID)
{
    IDirectSoundBuffer* pBuf;
    switch (iSoundID)
    {
    case PLAYERHIT:
        pBuf = m_pPlayerHitSound;
        break;
    case MONSTERHIT:
        pBuf = m_pMonsterHitSound;
        break;
    case MONSTERDIES:
        pBuf = m_pMonsterDieSound;
        break;
    case FOOTSTEP:
        pBuf = m_pFootstepSound;
        break;
    case ITEMOPEN:
        pBuf = m_pItemOpenSound;
        break;
    }
    HRESULT hResult = pBuf->SetCurrentPosition(0);
    if (hResult != DS_OK)
        return hResult;

    hResult = pBuf->Play(0, 0, 0);
    if (hResult != DS_OK)
        return hResult;

    return hResult;
}

///////////////////////////////////////////////////////
// LoadSoundEffect()
///////////////////////////////////////////////////////
HRESULT CDirectSound::LoadSoundEffect(char* pstrFileName,
    IDirectSoundBuffer** ppSoundBuf)
{
    CWave* pWave = new CWave(pstrFileName);
    if (!pWave->WaveOK())
```

```
    {
        MessageBox(m_hWnd, "Could not load wave file.", "Error", MB_OK);
        PostQuitMessage(WM_QUIT);
        return 0;
    }

    LPWAVEFORMATEX pWaveFormatEx = pWave->GetWaveFormatPtr();
    char* pWaveData = pWave->GetWaveDataPtr();
    DWORD dwWaveSize = pWave->GetWaveSize();

    DSBUFFERDESC dsBufferDesc;
    memset(&dsBufferDesc, 0, sizeof(DSBUFFERDESC));
    dsBufferDesc.dwSize = sizeof(DSBUFFERDESC);
    dsBufferDesc.dwBufferBytes = dwWaveSize;
    dsBufferDesc.lpwfxFormat = (LPWAVEFORMATEX) pWaveFormatEx;

    IDirectSoundBuffer* pDSBuf;
    HRESULT hResult = m_pDirectSoundObj->
        CreateSoundBuffer(&dsBufferDesc, &pDSBuf, NULL);
    if (hResult != DS_OK)
        return hResult;

    LPVOID pSoundBlock1;
    LPVOID pSoundBlock2;
    DWORD dwBytesSoundBlock1;
    DWORD dwBytesSoundBlock2;
    hResult = pDSBuf->Lock(0, dwWaveSize,
        &pSoundBlock1, &dwBytesSoundBlock1,
        &pSoundBlock2, &dwBytesSoundBlock2, 0);
    if (hResult != DS_OK)
        return hResult;

    memcpy((void*)pSoundBlock1, pWaveData, dwWaveSize);

    pDSBuf->Unlock(pSoundBlock1, dwBytesSoundBlock1,
            pSoundBlock2, dwBytesSoundBlock2);

    delete pWave;
    *ppSoundBuf = pDSBuf;
    return hResult;
}
```

4. Add the following lines to the end of the Constants.h file. If you don't want to type the source code, you can copy it from the Code03.txt file in the Chapter20 directory of this book's CD-ROM.

```
// Sound effect IDs
enum g_sounds
{
    PLAYERHIT,
    MONSTERHIT,
```

```
        MONSTERDIES,
        FOOTSTEP,
        ITEMOPEN
    };
```

5. Using the Add Class command on the Project menu, add a generic C++ class named `CWave` to the project.

6. Replace the source code in the Wave.h file with the following. If you don't want to type the source code, you can copy it from the Code04.txt file in the Chapter20 directory of this book's CD-ROM.

```
///////////////////////////////////////////////////////////
// Wave.h
///////////////////////////////////////////////////////////

#pragma once

#include <windows.h>
#include <mmsystem.h>

class CWave
{
protected:
    DWORD m_dwWaveSize;
    BOOL m_bWaveOK;
    char* m_pWave;
    WAVEFORMATEX m_waveFormatEx;

public:
    CWave(char* fileName);
    ~CWave();

    DWORD GetWaveSize();
    LPWAVEFORMATEX GetWaveFormatPtr();
    char* GetWaveDataPtr();
    BOOL WaveOK();

protected:
    BOOL LoadWaveFile(char* fileName);
};
```

7. Replace the source code in the Wave.cpp file with the following. If you don't want to type the source code, you can copy it from the Code05.txt file in the Chapter20 directory of this book's CD-ROM.

```
///////////////////////////////////////////////////////////
// Wave.cpp
///////////////////////////////////////////////////////////

#include "windowsx.h"
```

```
#include "wave.h"

///////////////////////////////////////////////////////////
// CWave::CWave()
///////////////////////////////////////////////////////////
CWave::CWave(char* fileName)
{
    m_dwWaveSize = 0;
    m_bWaveOK = FALSE;
    m_pWave = NULL;
    m_bWaveOK = LoadWaveFile(fileName);
}

///////////////////////////////////////////////////////////
// CWave::~CWave()
///////////////////////////////////////////////////////////
CWave::~CWave()
{
    GlobalFreePtr(m_pWave);
}

///////////////////////////////////////////////////////////
// CWave::LoadWaveFile()
///////////////////////////////////////////////////////////
BOOL CWave::LoadWaveFile(char* fileName)
{
    MMCKINFO mmCkInfoRIFF;
    MMCKINFO mmCkInfoChunk;
    MMRESULT result;
    HMMIO hMMIO;
    long bytesRead;

    // Open the wave file.
    hMMIO = mmioOpen(fileName, NULL, MMIO_READ | MMIO_ALLOCBUF);
    if (hMMIO == NULL)
        return FALSE;

    // Descend into the RIFF chunk.
    mmCkInfoRIFF.fccType = mmioFOURCC('W', 'A', 'V', 'E');
    result = mmioDescend(hMMIO, &mmCkInfoRIFF, NULL, MMIO_FINDRIFF);
    if (result != MMSYSERR_NOERROR)
        return FALSE;

    // Descend into the format chunk.
    mmCkInfoChunk.ckid = mmioFOURCC('f', 'm', 't', ' ');
    result = mmioDescend(hMMIO, &mmCkInfoChunk,
        &mmCkInfoRIFF, MMIO_FINDCHUNK);
    if (result != MMSYSERR_NOERROR)
        return FALSE;

    // Read the format information into the WAVEFORMATEX structure.
```

```
    bytesRead = mmioRead(hMMIO, (char*)&m_waveFormatEx,
        sizeof(WAVEFORMATEX));
    if (bytesRead == -1)
        return FALSE;

    // Ascend out of the format chunk.
    result = mmioAscend(hMMIO, &mmCkInfoChunk, 0);
    if (result != MMSYSERR_NOERROR)
        return FALSE;

    // Descend into the data chunk.
    mmCkInfoChunk.ckid = mmioFOURCC('d', 'a', 't', 'a');
    result = mmioDescend(hMMIO, &mmCkInfoChunk,
        &mmCkInfoRIFF, MMIO_FINDCHUNK);
    if (result != MMSYSERR_NOERROR)
        return FALSE;

    // Save the size of the wave data.
    m_dwWaveSize = mmCkInfoChunk.cksize;

    // Allocate a buffer for the wave data.
    m_pWave = (char*)GlobalAllocPtr(GMEM_MOVEABLE, m_dwWaveSize);
    if (m_pWave == NULL)
        return FALSE;

    // Read the wave data into the buffer.
    bytesRead = mmioRead(hMMIO, (char*)m_pWave, m_dwWaveSize);
    if (bytesRead == -1)
        return FALSE;
    mmioClose(hMMIO, 0);

    return TRUE;
}

///////////////////////////////////////////////////////////
// CWave::GetWaveSize()
///////////////////////////////////////////////////////////
DWORD CWave::GetWaveSize()
{
    return m_dwWaveSize;
}

///////////////////////////////////////////////////////////
// CWave::GetWaveFormatPtr()
///////////////////////////////////////////////////////////
LPWAVEFORMATEX CWave::GetWaveFormatPtr()
{
    return &m_waveFormatEx;
}
```

```
///////////////////////////////////////////////////////////////
// CWave::GetWaveDataPtr()
///////////////////////////////////////////////////////////////
char* CWave::GetWaveDataPtr()
{
    return m_pWave;
}

///////////////////////////////////////////////////////////////
// CWave::WaveOK()
///////////////////////////////////////////////////////////////
BOOL CWave::WaveOK()
{
    return m_bWaveOK;
}
```

8. Right-click the project's name in the Solution Explorer, and select Properties from the menu that appears. The JBookman Property Pages dialog box appears.
9. Click the Linker's Input selection in the left-hand pane.
10. In the Additional Dependencies box in the right-hand pane, enter **dsound.lib** and **winmm.lib**. (Just enter the library names separated by spaces. Don't enter the word "and.")
11. Close the dialog box, and then press Ctrl+Shift+B to build the project to be sure everything's okay with the new classes.

Most of the source code in the `CDirectSound` class comes from the program you created in Day 10, whereas the `CWave` class is virtually identical to the class of the same name from Day 10. For that reason, there's no need to go over the classes in any detail. Instead, just look over Table 20.1, which describes each of the `CDirectSound` class's members. This overview will give you some idea how the class is used in the JBookman project.

TABLE 20.1 Members of the `CDirectSound` Class

Member	*Type*	*Description*
m_hWnd	Data member	The class's copy of the application's window handle
m_pDirectSoundObj	Data member	A pointer to the class's IDirectSound object
m_pFootstepSound	Data member	A pointer to the class's IDirectSoundBuffer object that holds the "footstep" sound effect
m_pItemOpenSound	Data member	A pointer to the class's IDirectSoundBuffer object that holds the "item opening" sound effect

TABLE 20.1 Continued

Member	*Type*	*Description*
m_pMonsterDieSound	Data member	A pointer to the class's IDirectSoundBuffer object that holds the "monster dies" sound effect
m_pMonsterHitSound	Data member	A pointer to the class's IDirectSoundBuffer object that holds the "monster hit" sound effect
m_pPlayerHitSound	Data member	A pointer to the class's IDirectSoundBuffer object that holds the "player hit" sound effect
m_szErrorMsg	Data member	The class's error-description string
GetErrorString()	Public method	Returns the class's error-description string
InitDirectSound() effects	Public method	Starts up DirectSound and loads the game's sound
PlaySound()	Public method	Plays the specified sound effect
SetWindowHandle()	Public method	Sets the class's copy of the application's window handle
CleanUp()	Private method	Releases DirectSound objects created by the class
CreateSoundBuffers()	Private method	Creates sound buffers and loads sound files into them
LoadSoundEffect()	Private method	Loads the specified sound effect from its file into a sound buffer

Using the `CDirectSound` Class in the Game

Now that you have the `CDirectSound` class added to your project, you need to incorporate it into the program. This means not only creating an instance of the class, which happens in the `CEngine` class, but also calling the class's methods to manage and play sound files. Perform the following steps to accomplish this task:

20

1. Add the following line to the include section near the top of the Engine.h file:

   ```
   #include "DirectSound.h"
   ```

2. Also in the Engine.h file, add the following line to the class's protected data members:

   ```
   CDirectSound m_Sound;
   ```

3. Again in the Engine.h file, add the following line to the class's public methods:

   ```
   CDirectSound* GetCDirectSoundObj();
   ```

4. In the Engine.cpp file, add the following line to the end of the `SetWindowHandle()` method:

   ```
   m_Sound.SetWindowHandle(hWnd);
   ```

5. In the Engine.cpp file, replace the current version of the `CheckForAndHandleDoor()` method with the one that follows. If you don't want to type the source code, you can copy it from the Code06.txt file in the Chapter20 directory of this book's CD-ROM.

```
//////////////////////////////////////////////////////
// CheckForAndHandleDoor()
//////////////////////////////////////////////////////
int CEngine::CheckForAndHandleDoor(int iSector)
{
    if (IsDoor(iSector))
    {
        BOOL bCouldOpenDoor = HandleDoor(iSector);
        if (bCouldOpenDoor)
        {
            m_Sound.PlaySound(ITEMOPEN);
            return DOORUNLOCKED;
        }
        else
            return DOORLOCKED;
    }
    return NODOOR;
}
```

6. Replace the current versions of the `MovePlayerUp()`, `MovePlayerDown()`, `MovePlayerRight()`, and `MovePlayerLeft()` methods with the ones that follow. If you don't want to type the source code, you can copy it from the Code07.txt file in the Chapter20 directory of this book's CD-ROM.

```
//////////////////////////////////////////////////////
// MovePlayerUp()
//////////////////////////////////////////////////////
void CEngine::MovePlayerUp()
{
    if (CharacterCanMove(NORTH, m_Player.GetSector()))
    {
        m_Player.SetSector(m_Player.GetSector() - MAPCOLUMNCOUNT);
        m_Sound.PlaySound(FOOTSTEP);
    }
}

//////////////////////////////////////////////////////
// MovePlayerDown()
//////////////////////////////////////////////////////
void CEngine::MovePlayerDown()
{
    if (CharacterCanMove(SOUTH, m_Player.GetSector()))
    {
        m_Player.SetSector(m_Player.GetSector() + MAPCOLUMNCOUNT);
        m_Sound.PlaySound(FOOTSTEP);
```

```
    }
}

/////////////////////////////////////////////////////////////
// MovePlayerLeft()
/////////////////////////////////////////////////////////////
void CEngine::MovePlayerLeft()
{
    if (CharacterCanMove(WEST, m_Player.GetSector()))
    {
        m_Player.SetSector(m_Player.GetSector() - 1);
        m_Sound.PlaySound(FOOTSTEP);
    }
}

/////////////////////////////////////////////////////////////
// MovePlayerRight()
/////////////////////////////////////////////////////////////
void CEngine::MovePlayerRight()
{
    if (CharacterCanMove(EAST, m_Player.GetSector()))
    {
        m_Player.SetSector(m_Player.GetSector() + 1);
        m_Sound.PlaySound(FOOTSTEP);
    }
}
```

7. Again in the Engine.cpp file, replace the current version of the `AttackMonster()` method with the one that follows. If you don't want to type the source code, you can copy it from the Code08.txt file in the Chapter20 directory of this book's CD-ROM.

```
/////////////////////////////////////////////////////////////
// AttackMonster()
/////////////////////////////////////////////////////////////
void CEngine::AttackMonster()
{
    if (m_bPlayerTurnToAttack && m_iCombatDelayCounter == 0)
    {
        m_Sound.PlaySound(MONSTERHIT);
        m_iMonsterDamage = (rand() % 10) + 2;
        m_bPlayerTurnToAttack = FALSE;
    }
}
```

8. In the `AnimateMonsterDamage()` method, add the following line right after the second `if` statement's opening brace:

```
m_Sound.PlaySound(MONSTERDIES);
```

9. In the `AttackRunningPlayer()` method, add the following lines right after the line `int iDamage = rand() % m_pCurrentMonster->GetMaxAttackDamage()` that's already there:

```
if (iDamage > 0)
    m_Sound.PlaySound(PLAYERHIT);
```

10. In the `AttackPlayer()` method, add the following lines right after the line `int iDamage = rand() % m_pCurrentMonster->GetMaxAttackDamage()` that's already there:

```
if (iDamage > 0)
    m_Sound.PlaySound(PLAYERHIT);
```

11. Add the following method to the end of the Engine.cpp file. If you don't want to type the source code, you can copy it from the Code09.txt file in the Chapter20 directory of this book's CD-ROM.

```
//////////////////////////////////////////////////////////
// GetCDirectSoundObj()
//////////////////////////////////////////////////////////
CDirectSound* CEngine::GetCDirectSoundObj()
{
    return &m_Sound;
}
```

12. In the JBookman.cpp file, add the following lines to the `WinMain()` function, right after the line `g_Engine.StartAnimationTimer()` that's already there:

```
HRESULT hResult = g_Engine.GetCDirectSoundObj()->InitDirectSound();
if (hResult == DS_OK)
```

13. In your JBookman project's main directory, create a folder named Sounds.
14. Copy the following files from the Chapter20 directory of this book's CD-ROM to your new Sounds directory:

```
PlayerHit.wav
MonsterDie.wav
ItemOpen.wav
Footstep.wav
MonsterHit.wav
```

You can now compile and run the program. When the game starts, walk around a bit. Each step you take is now accompanied by a sound effect. Walk through a door, and you'll hear a different sound effect. Now, head out of town and into the wilderness. Get into a fight with a roaming creature, and you'll hear the battle sound effects.

New Members of the CEngine Class

In this day, unlike most other days in this last section of the book, you didn't add much to the CEngine class as far as new members go. In fact, you added only two members: the data member m_Sound, which is an object of the CDirectSound class, and GetCDirectSoundObj(), a public method that returns a pointer to the CDirectSound object.

Summary

As mentioned in the introduction to this day, this book provides you with only a few sound effects to get you started. Now that you've completed this day, you can take some time to add even more sound effects to the game, or you can choose to continue on to the next day before worrying about such details.

In any case, a game like this requires many more sound effects than you've added so far. For example, you'll want to add a sound effect for when the player opens a treasure chest. You might also want to add one for when a creature appears on the screen, making that appearance more startling. How about a cool sound for when the player walks through a secret door? There are a lot of possibilities left to explore.

In the next and final day, you'll add the few odds and ends needed to complete the game engine. These additions include enabling the player to purchase items in shops, as well as adding the source code needed to restore the game display properly when the player switches from one running application to another.

Workshop

The workshop includes quiz questions to help gauge your grasp of the material. Even if you feel that you totally understand the concepts presented here, you should work through the quiz anyway.

1. What are the two major functions performed by the CDirectSound class?
2. What does the CDirectSound class's CleanUp() method do?
3. What is the single argument required by the CDirectSound class's PlaySound() method?
4. What class loads the raw audio data into memory from which it can be transferred into a DirectSound buffer?
5. Where does the CDirectSound object get created?

6. What's the name of the library file you need to add to your project in order to have access to DirectSound methods?

Answers for Day 20

Quiz

1. What are the two major functions performed by the `CDirectSound` class?

   Loading and playing sound files.

2. What does the `CDirectSound` class's `CleanUp()` method do?

   It releases the DirectSound objects created in the class.

3. What is the single argument required by the `CDirectSound` class's `PlaySound()` method?

   The ID of the sound effect to play.

4. What class loads the raw audio data into memory from which it can be transferred into a DirectSound buffer?

   The `CWave` class.

5. Where does the `CDirectSound` object get created?

   In the `CEngine` class, where it's defined as a protected data member.

6. What's the name of the library file you need to add to your project in order to have access to DirectSound methods?

   The name of the library is dsound.lib.

WEEK 3

DAY 21

Adding the Finishing Touches

Here you are at last, nearing the end of this book and the building of *The Adventures of Jasper Bookman*. Only a few things need to be added to the program to complete the game engine. Then, it'll be time for you to take what you've learned to fill out the program into a complete Direct3D RPG. That's the really fun part, using the tools you've created to put together a story that your player will be able to play from start to finish. For now, though, it's time to put the last pieces in place. Today you learn how to:

- Program the shopping routines
- Manipulate player-character attributes
- Handle lost devices

Implementing the Shop Routines

One thing to get working in the program is the shopping routines. The location of First Town (and presumably other towns you'll add to the game after you complete this book) has a couple of shops in which the player can buy helpful items. Specifically, First Town has a potion shop, an armor shop, and an inn.

Potions are important to the game because they enable the player to get a boost in hit points during battle. The armor shop, on the other hand, enables the player to upgrade his defensive clothing. Finally, the inn enables the player to get a good night's sleep, during which he regains all his hit points.

Getting these different establishments working isn't too complicated, and, in fact, is just a matter of handling a few new game events. Load up your JBookman project, and perform the following steps to get the town's shops working:

1. In the Engine.h file, change the `HandleKeys()` method declaration to virtual. The declaration will then look like this:

   ```
   virtual void HandleKeys(WPARAM wParam);
   ```

   By making this method virtual, you can override it in your `CMyEngine` class and so handle any keystrokes you like differently from the way the game engine handles them.

2. Also in the Engine.h file, move the `HandleN()` and `HandleY()` declarations from the private section to the protected section and make them virtual, as well. The final declarations will look like this:

   ```
   virtual void HandleN();
   virtual void HandleY();
   ```

3. In the MyEngine.h file, add the following lines to the class, right after the class's opening brace. If you want to avoid typing, you can copy the lines from the Code01.txt file in the Chapter21 directory of this book's CD-ROM.

   ```
   protected:
       // Shop flags.
       BOOL m_bBuyingPotion;
       BOOL m_bBuyingArmor;
       BOOL m_bBuyingWeapon;
       BOOL m_bRentingRoom;
       int m_iPurchasePrice;
       int m_iNewArmorLevel;
       int m_iNewWeaponLevel;
   ```

   Some of these values are mode flags that the program can use to determine whether the player is currently purchasing an item. The other data members here hold values the program needs to process the player's purchase.

4. Also in MyEngine.h, add the following lines to the class's public method declarations. If you want to avoid typing, you can copy the lines from the Code02.txt file in the Chapter21 directory of this book's CD-ROM.

```
virtual void HandleKeys(WPARAM wParam);
void SetPurchasePrice(int iPrice);
void SetNewWeaponLevel(int iLevel);
void SetNewArmorLevel(int iLevel);
```

   These are the new methods that need to be available to parts of the program outside of the class.

5. Add the following lines to the class's protected method declarations. If you want to avoid typing, you can copy the lines from the Code03.txt file in the Chapter21 directory of this book's CD-ROM.

```
virtual void HandleN();
virtual void HandleY();
void HandleBuyingPotion();
void HandleBuyingArmor();
void HandleBuyingWeapon();
void HandleRentingRoom();
```

   These new methods will be used only by the `CEngine` class.

6. In the MyEngine.cpp file, add the following lines to the class's constructor. If you want to avoid typing, you can copy the lines from the Code04.txt file in the Chapter21 directory of this book's CD-ROM.

```
m_bBuyingPotion = FALSE;
m_bBuyingArmor = FALSE;
m_bBuyingWeapon = FALSE;
m_bRentingRoom = FALSE;
```

   Thus code ensures that these important flags start off with a value of `FALSE`.

7. Again in the MyEngine.cpp file, add the following lines to the `if` statement in the `HandleNPC()` method, right before the `else` clause that ends the statement. If you want to avoid typing, you can copy the lines from the Code05.txt file in the Chapter21 directory of this book's CD-ROM.

```
else if (strcmp(name, "Arstin Black") == 0)
{
    HandleArstinBlack();
    m_bBuyingPotion = TRUE;
}
else if (strcmp(name, "Paltum Ganges") == 0)
{
    HandlePaltumGanges();
    m_bBuyingArmor = TRUE;
}
else if (strcmp(name, "Billiam Aberton") == 0)
```

```
{
    HandleBilliamAberton();
    m_bRentingRoom = TRUE;
}
```

These lines route program execution to the methods that handle the shopkeepers.

8. Add the following methods to the end of the MyEngine.cpp file. If you want to avoid typing, you can copy the lines from the Code06.txt file in the Chapter21 directory of this book's CD-ROM.

```
//////////////////////////////////////////////////////
// HandleKeys()
//////////////////////////////////////////////////////
void CMyEngine::HandleKeys(WPARAM wParam)
{
    switch (wParam)
    {
    case VK_ESCAPE:
    case VK_SPACE:
    case 73: //I
        if (!m_bBuyingPotion && !m_bBuyingArmor && !m_bBuyingWeapon)
            CEngine::HandleKeys(wParam);
        break;
    default:
        CEngine::HandleKeys(wParam);
    }
}

//////////////////////////////////////////////////////
// HandleN()
//////////////////////////////////////////////////////
void CMyEngine::HandleN()
{
    if (m_bBuyingPotion)
    {
        m_bBuyingPotion = FALSE;
        TurnOffPlaque();
    }
    else if (m_bBuyingArmor)
    {
        m_bBuyingArmor = FALSE;
        TurnOffPlaque();
    }
    else if (m_bBuyingWeapon)
    {
        m_bBuyingWeapon = FALSE;
        TurnOffPlaque();
    }
```

```
    else if (m_bRentingRoom)
    {
        m_bRentingRoom = FALSE;
        TurnOffPlaque();
    }
    else
        CEngine::HandleN();
}

////////////////////////////////////////////////////////
// HandleY()
////////////////////////////////////////////////////////
void CMyEngine::HandleY()
{
    if (m_bBuyingPotion)
        HandleBuyingPotion();
    else if (m_bBuyingArmor)
        HandleBuyingArmor();
    else if (m_bBuyingWeapon)
        HandleBuyingWeapon();
    else if (m_bRentingRoom)
        HandleRentingRoom();
    else
        CEngine::HandleY();
}

////////////////////////////////////////////////////////
// HandleBuyingPotion()
////////////////////////////////////////////////////////
void CMyEngine::HandleBuyingPotion()
{
    if (m_Player.GetGold() > m_iPurchasePrice)
    {
        m_Player.SetGold(m_Player.GetGold() - m_iPurchasePrice);
        m_Player.SetPotions(m_Player.GetPotions() + 1);
        char msg[80];
        wsprintf(msg, "You buy 1 potion for %d gold.", m_iPurchasePrice);
        TurnOnPlaque(msg);
    }
    else
        TurnOnPlaque("You don't have enough gold.");
    m_bBuyingPotion = FALSE;
}

////////////////////////////////////////////////////////
// HandleBuyingArmor()
////////////////////////////////////////////////////////
void CMyEngine::HandleBuyingArmor()
```

```
{
    if (m_Player.GetGold() > m_iPurchasePrice)
    {
        m_Player.SetGold(m_Player.GetGold() - m_iPurchasePrice);
        m_Player.SetArmor(m_iNewArmorLevel);
        char msg[80];
        wsprintf(msg, "You buy level %d armor for %d gold.",
            m_iNewArmorLevel, m_iPurchasePrice);
        TurnOnPlaque(msg);
    }
    else
        TurnOnPlaque("You don't have enough gold.");
    m_bBuyingArmor = FALSE;
}

//////////////////////////////////////////////////////
// HandleBuyingWeapon()//////////////////////
void CMyEngine::HandleBuyingWeapon()
{
    if (m_Player.GetGold() > m_iPurchasePrice)
    {
        m_Player.SetGold(m_Player.GetGold() - m_iPurchasePrice);
        m_Player.SetWeapon(m_iNewWeaponLevel);
        char msg[80];
        wsprintf(msg, "You buy a level %d weapon for %d gold.",
            m_iNewWeaponLevel, m_iPurchasePrice);
        TurnOnPlaque(msg);
    }
    else
        TurnOnPlaque("You don't have enough gold.");
    m_bBuyingWeapon = FALSE;
}

//////////////////////////////////////////////////////
// HandleRentingRoom()
//////////////////////////////////////////////////////
void CMyEngine::HandleRentingRoom()
{
    if (m_Player.GetGold() > m_iPurchasePrice)
    {
        m_Player.SetGold(m_Player.GetGold() - m_iPurchasePrice);
        m_Player.SetHitPoints(m_Player.GetMaxHitPoints());
        TurnOnPlaque("You have a peaceful night's rest.");
    }
    else
        TurnOnPlaque("You don't have enough gold.");
    m_bRentingRoom = FALSE;
}
```

```
///////////////////////////////////////////////////////
// SetPurchasePrice()
///////////////////////////////////////////////////////
void CMyEngine::SetPurchasePrice(int iPrice)
{
    m_iPurchasePrice = iPrice;
}

///////////////////////////////////////////////////////
// SetNewWeaponLevel()
///////////////////////////////////////////////////////
void CMyEngine::SetNewWeaponLevel(int iLevel)
{
    m_iNewWeaponLevel = iLevel;
}

///////////////////////////////////////////////////////
// SetNewArmorLevel()
///////////////////////////////////////////////////////
void CMyEngine::SetNewArmorLevel(int iLevel)
{
    m_iNewArmorLevel = iLevel;
}
```

9. Add the following lines to the end of the FirstTown.h file:

```
void HandleArstinBlack();
void HandlePaltumGanges();
void HandleBilliamAberton();
```

10. Add the following methods to the end of the FirstTown.cpp file. If you want to avoid typing, you can copy the lines from the Code07.txt file in the Chapter21 directory of this book's CD-ROM.

```
///////////////////////////////////////////////////////
// HandleArstinBlack()
///////////////////////////////////////////////////////
void HandleArstinBlack()
{
    g_Engine.TurnOnPlaque(
"I'm Arstin Black, the\n\
proprietor of this shop.\n\
Would you like to buy a\n\
potion for 8 gold pieces?\n\
(Y/N)");
    g_Engine.SetPurchasePrice(8);
}

///////////////////////////////////////////////////////
// HandlePaltumGanges()
///////////////////////////////////////////////////////
```

```
void HandlePaltumGanges()
{
    g_Engine.TurnOnPlaque(
"I'm Paltum Ganges, the\n\
proprietor of this shop.\n\
Would you like to buy\n\
level 1 armor for 100 gold pieces?\n\
(Y/N)");
    g_Engine.SetPurchasePrice(100);
    g_Engine.SetNewArmorLevel(1);
}

///////////////////////////////////////////////////////
// HandleBilliamAberton()
///////////////////////////////////////////////////////
void HandleBilliamAberton()
{
    g_Engine.TurnOnPlaque(
"I'm Billiam Aberton, the\n\
proprietor of this inn.\n\
Would you like to stay\n\
the night for 6 gold pieces?\n\
(Y/N)");
    g_Engine.SetPurchasePrice(6);
}
```

11. Copy the following new versions of the map files from the CD-ROM's Chapter21 directory to your JBookman project's Maps folder.

```
FirstTownPotions.map
FirstTownPotions.map.dor
FirstTownPotions.map.itm
FirstTownPotions.map.peo
FirstTownArmorer.map
FirstTownArmorer.map.dor
FirstTownArmorer.map.itm
FirstTownArmorer.map.peo
FirstTownInnRoom01.map
FirstTownInnRoom01.map.dor
FirstTownInnRoom01.map.itm
FirstTownInnRoom01.map.peo
```

You can now compile and run the program. When you do, head the player character towards the potion shop. Enter the shop and talk to its proprietor. You'll get the message shown in Figure 21.1. You now have two choices: You can press Y, and buy a potion, or press N, and so exit the conversation without a purchase. If you choose to buy a potion, you'll see the screen shown in Figure 21.2.

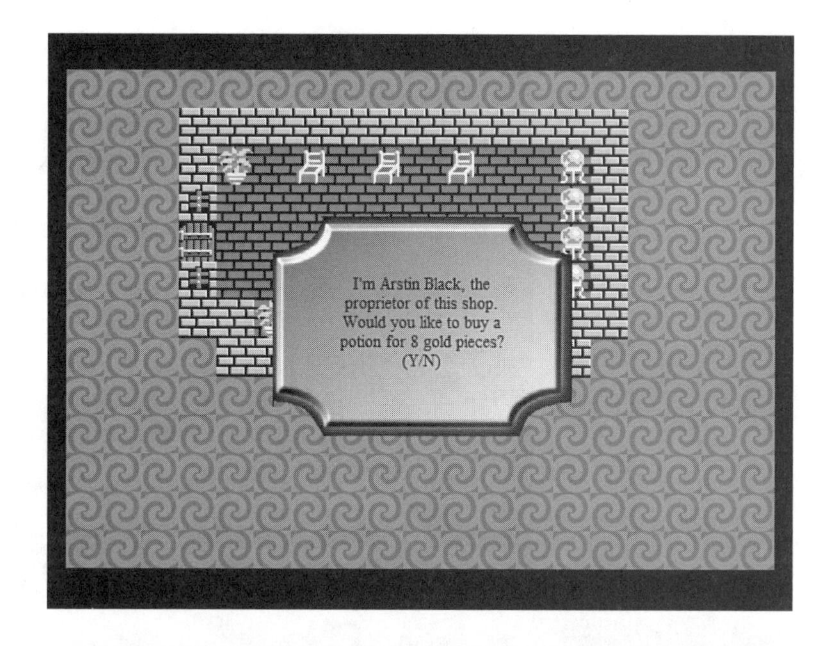

FIGURE 21.1
Talking to the owner of the potion shop.

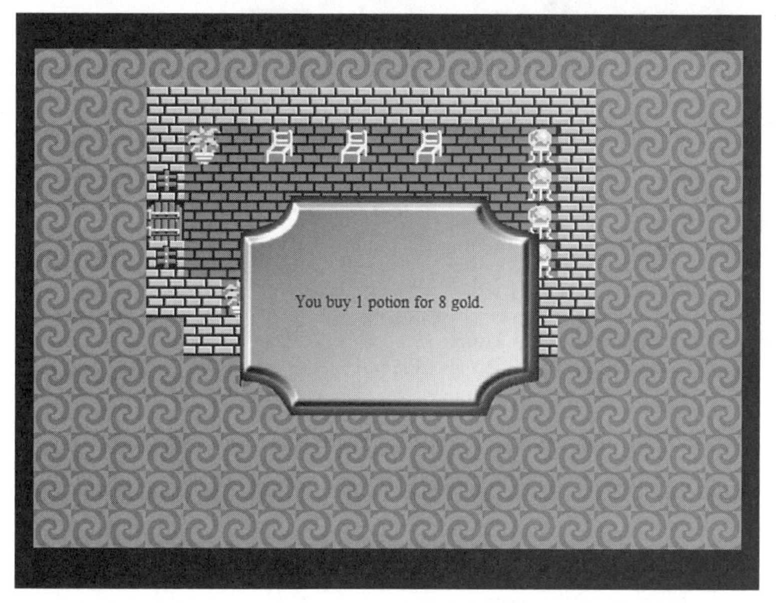

FIGURE 21.2
Buying a potion.

You can now purchase stuff from the armor shop and the inn, too—but only if you have enough gold. If you try to buy new armor, for example, you'll get the message shown in Figure 21.3.

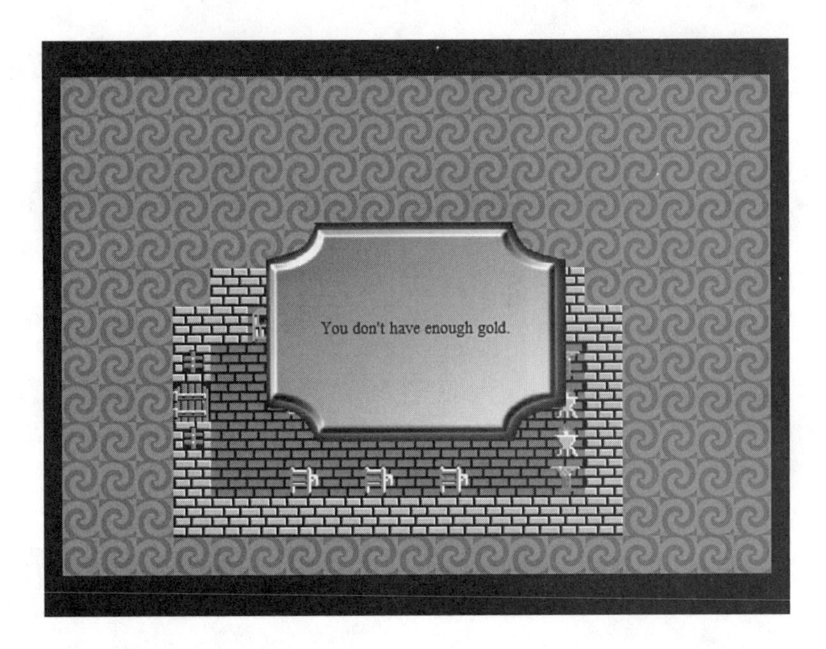

FIGURE 21.3
Trying to buy armor without enough gold.

Examining the Source Code

There's nothing too special about the way the shopping routines work. Let's look at the case of the potion shop as an example. When the player moves toward the potion shop's proprietor, the program routes execution to the proper method for the NPC. This works just as it did with any other NPC in the game, with execution ending up in the `HandleNPC()` method. The part of that method that handles the potion shop looks like this:

```
else if (strcmp(name, "Arstin Black") == 0)
{
    HandleArstinBlack();
    m_bBuyingPotion = TRUE;
}
```

As you can see here, if the player is talking with Arstin Black, the program calls the NPC's specific function and then sets the `m_bBuyingPotion` flag to `TRUE`.

The `HandleArstinBlack()` method, which, like the other NPC methods, is located in the FirstTown.cpp file, looks like this:

```
void HandleArstinBlack()
{
    g_Engine.TurnOnPlaque(
"I'm Arstin Black, the\n\
proprietor of this shop.\n\
```

```
Would you like to buy a\n\
potion for 8 gold pieces?\n\
(Y/N)");
    g_Engine.SetPurchasePrice(8);
}
```

The `HandleArstinBlack()` method does nothing more than display the proprietor's response to the player and set the purchase price for the potion. Having a method like `SetPurchasePrice()` enables you, as the game's programmer, to charge whatever you want for a potion. For example, you may want to charge more in one town and less in another.

At this point, the program waits for the player to press Y or N. If you look at the `CMyEngine` class's overridden `HandleY()` method, you can see how the program uses the various flags to determine what to do with the keypress:

```
void CMyEngine::HandleY()
{
    if (m_bBuyingPotion)
        HandleBuyingPotion();
    else if (m_bBuyingArmor)
        HandleBuyingArmor();
    else if (m_bBuyingWeapon)
        HandleBuyingWeapon();
    else if (m_bRentingRoom)
        HandleRentingRoom();
    else
        CEngine::HandleY();
}
```

The `HandleBuyingPotion()` method handles the actual transaction should the player press the Y key:

```
void CMyEngine::HandleBuyingPotion()
{
    if (m_Player.GetGold() > m_iPurchasePrice)
    {
        m_Player.SetGold(m_Player.GetGold() - m_iPurchasePrice);
        m_Player.SetPotions(m_Player.GetPotions() + 1);
        char msg[80];
        wsprintf(msg, "You buy 1 potion for %d gold.", m_iPurchasePrice);
        TurnOnPlaque(msg);
    }
    else
        TurnOnPlaque("You don't have enough gold.");
    m_bBuyingPotion = FALSE;
}
```

If the player has enough gold, this method simply subtracts the price of the potion from the player's stash, adds one potion to his inventory, and displays a message. Easy enough! The other shopping routines work very similarly.

Battling with Player Attributes

When you created the CPlayer class way back in Day 12, "Initializing Game Data," you saw that the player character possessed several attributes, including hit points, experience points, and so on. Up until now, though, you haven't done much with these attributes. In the previous section, you saw how you can spend gold to buy advantages for the player character. In this section, you'll add the code that incorporates the player's attributes into battles.

1. In the Engine.h file, add the following line to the class's protected data members:

   ```
   BOOL m_bPlayerDead;
   ```

   This important flag will inform the program when the game has ended due to the player character's death in battle.

2. Also in Engine.h, add the following lines to the private method declarations:

   ```
   void EndGame();
   void HandleA();
   void DisplayAttributes();
   ```

   You'll see what these new methods do later in these steps.

3. In the Engine.cpp file, change the `HandleKeys()` method's call to `AttackMonster()` to `HandleA()`. The resulting case statement should look like this:

   ```
   case 65: // A
       HandleA();
       break;
   ```

   Because the A key will now serve two different functions, we don't want to clutter up the `HandleKeys()` method with the details. Instead, the program will handle the key in the new `HandleA()` method.

4. In the Engine.cpp file, add the following lines to the beginning of the `ShowInventory()` method. If you'd rather not type, you can copy the lines from the Code08.txt file in the Chapter21 directory of this book's CD-ROM.

   ```
   if (m_bMonsterAttacking || m_bAskingIfLoad || m_bAskingIfSave ||
       m_bAskingIfQuit || m_bPlayerDead) return;
   ```

   These lines check to ensure that the player isn't already in one of the restricted game modes.

5. Again in the Engine.cpp file, add the following lines to the `AnimateMonsterDamage()` method, right after the call to `m_Player.SetGold()`. If you'd rather not type, you can copy the lines from the Code09.txt file in the Chapter21 directory of this book's CD-ROM.

   ```
           m_Player.SetMaxHitPoints((m_Player.GetExperience()/100)*5+10);
   ```

```
        char msg[80];
        wsprintf(msg, "You defeat the creature and \n\
get %d gold and %d experience.",
            iGold, m_pCurrentMonster->GetExperienceValue());
        TurnOnPlaque(msg);
```

These lines award the player with experience points and gold when he defeats an enemy in battle.

6. Add the following lines to the `AttackRunningPlayer()` method, right after the line `int iDamage = rand() % m_pCurrentMonster->GetMaxAttackDamage()` that's already there:

```
iDamage -= m_Player.GetArmor();
if (iDamage < 0) iDamage = 0;
```

These lines adjust, based on the player's armor, the damage done by a monster attack. The better the armor, the more damage points are absorbed by the armor.

7. Add the following lines to the `AttackRunningPlayer()` method, right after the line `m_Player.SetHitPoints(m_Player.GetHitPoints() - iDamage)` that's already there. If you'd rather not type, you can copy the lines from the Code10.txt file in the Chapter21 directory of this book's CD-ROM.

```
if (m_Player.GetHitPoints() <= 0)
{
    m_bMonsterAttacking = FALSE;
    EndGame();
}
```

These lines end the game if the player character dies in battle.

8. Repeat steps 6 and 7 for the `AttackPlayer()` method.
9. Replace the `if` statement at the beginning of the `HandleS()` method with the following. If you'd rather not type, you can copy the lines from the Code11.txt file in the Chapter21 directory of this book's CD-ROM.

```
if (m_bMonsterAttacking || m_bAskingIfLoad || m_bAskingIfSave ||
    m_bAskingIfQuit || m_bPlayerDead) return;
```

10. Repeat step 9 for the `HandleL()` and `HandleEscape()` methods.
11. Replace the `HandleSpace()` method with the following. If you'd rather not type, you can copy the lines from the Code11.txt file in the Chapter21 directory of this book's CD-ROM.

```
///////////////////////////////////////////////////////
// HandleSpace()
///////////////////////////////////////////////////////
void CEngine::HandleSpace()
{
```

```
    if (m_bPlayerDead)
        PostQuitMessage(WM_QUIT);
    if (IsShowingPlaque() && !m_bAskingIfSave && !m_bAskingIfLoad
            && !m_bAskingIfQuit)
        TurnOffPlaque();
}
```

This method will now end the game when the player dismisses the text plaque that informs him of his death in battle.

12. Add the following methods to the end of the Engine.cpp file. If you'd rather not type, you can copy the lines from the Code12.txt file in the Chapter21 directory of this book's CD-ROM.

```
///////////////////////////////////////////////////////////
// EndGame()
///////////////////////////////////////////////////////////
void CEngine::EndGame()
{
    if (m_Player.GetHitPoints() <= 0)
    {
        m_bPlayerDead = TRUE;
        TurnOnPlaque("Jasper has died in battle.");
    }
}

///////////////////////////////////////////////////////////
// HandleA()
///////////////////////////////////////////////////////////
void CEngine::HandleA()
{
    if (m_bMonsterAttacking)
        AttackMonster();
    else
        DisplayAttributes();
}

///////////////////////////////////////////////////////////
// DisplayAttributes()
///////////////////////////////////////////////////////////
void CEngine::DisplayAttributes()
{
    char msg[256];
    wsprintf(msg,
"Hit Points: %d/%d\nExperience: %d\nLevel: %d\n\
Armor Level: %d\nWeapon Level: %d",
        m_Player.GetHitPoints(), m_Player.GetMaxHitPoints(),
        m_Player.GetExperience(), m_Player.GetExperience()/100 + 1,
        m_Player.GetArmor(), m_Player.GetWeapon());
    TurnOnPlaque(msg);
}
```

You're now ready again to compile and run the program. When you do, take the player character out of town and into the wilds. Get yourself into a fight, and when you win, you'll see a message similar to that shown in Figure 21.4.

Press the A key to bring up your player character's attributes. You should see a screen something like Figure 21.5.

FIGURE 21.4

A reward for a battle well done.

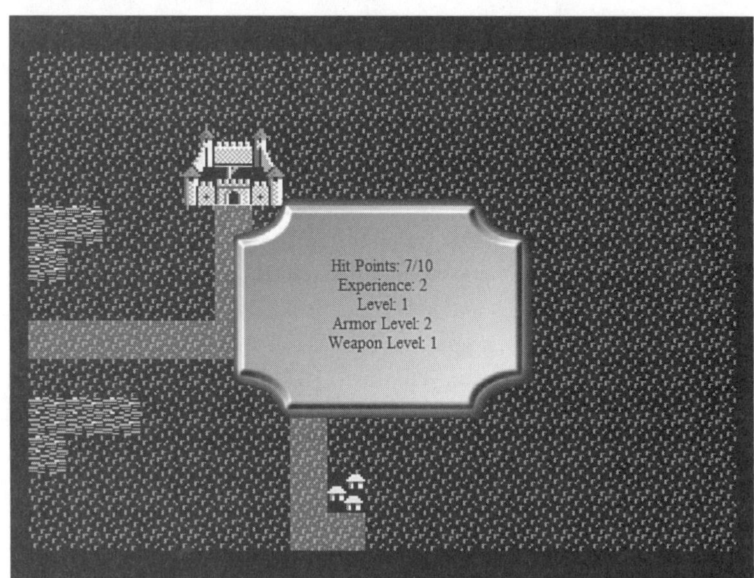

FIGURE 21.5

Displaying the player character's attributes.

Finally, keep fighting creatures until you run out of hit points. The player character dies, and you see the screen shown in Figure 21.6.

FIGURE 21.6
The player character has died during battle.

All the explanations you should need to understand what you've added to the program were included with the project steps. Look them over again to be sure it all makes sense.

Handling Lost Devices

I'm willing to bet that one thing about the JBookman project has been driving you crazy ever since you started putting the program together. Have you noticed how, if you Alt+Tab back to the desktop from *The Adventures of Jasper Bookman*, you can never get the program up and running again—at least, not without shutting it down and restarting?

The truth is that, in this situation, the program really is still running. You can even see its window. The problem is that, after returning to the desktop, the program's window has lost all its graphics and now looks just like any other empty Windows window. This happens because, when you Alt+Tab away from *The Adventures of Jasper Bookman* and back to the desktop, the Windows desktop takes over the video card, throwing away the device object and all the surfaces you worked so hard to get up and running.

This may seem like a huge problem, but it is actually an easy one to fix. First, when your Direct3D program loses its surfaces, even though the program can no longer draw to the screen, all drawing functions continue to work in the sense that they won't crash your program. They simply return the error code `D3DERR_DEVICELOST`. Second, a Direct3D device object provides a method named `TestCooperativeLevel()` that can tell your program at any time whether it still has access to its device and surfaces.

You may recall that the JBookman application continually calls the game engine's `ProcessGame()` method in the application's message loop. As a refresher, take a look at the message loop, which looks like this:

```
MSG msg;
while(1)
{
    if (PeekMessage(&msg, NULL, 0, 0, PM_REMOVE))
    {
        if (msg.message == WM_QUIT)
            break;
        TranslateMessage(&msg);
        DispatchMessage(&msg);
    }
    else
    {
        // Use idle time here.
        g_Engine.ProcessGame();
    }
}
```

The `ProcessGame()` method currently makes calls to three other methods that keep the entire game going:

```
void CEngine::ProcessGame(void)
{
    RespondToPlayerLocation();
    MoveNPCs();
    PaintBackBuffer();
}
```

The `PaintBackBuffer()` method gets called at the end of `ProcessGame()`. It is `PaintBackBuffer()` that does all the drawing (or that calls helper methods that do the drawing). Logic tells you, then, that if you insert a call to `TestCooperativeLevel()` into `ProcessGame()` somewhere, you can check the device status every time the program tries to draw the screen. If `TestCooperativeLevel()` returns `D3DERR_DEVICELOST`, the program can pause until it can get its device back.

But how do you know when the player wants to return to the program? When the Direct3D application's window regains the focus, `TestCooperativeLevel()` stops returning `D3DERR_DEVICELOST` and returns `D3DERR_DEVICENOTRESET` instead. This return code tells the program that it can take the device back and start drawing graphics again.

To get everything going again, you pretty much have to reinitialize Direct3D just as you did when the program first ran, re-creating the device and the surfaces. Your new `ProcessGame()` method ends up looking something like this:

```
void CEngine::ProcessGame(void)
{
    HRESULT hResult = m_Direct3D.GetDevice()->TestCooperativeLevel();
    if (hResult == D3DERR_DEVICELOST)
        m_bGamePaused = TRUE;
    else if (hResult == D3DERR_DEVICENOTRESET)
    {
        ResetDirect3D();
        m_bGamePaused = FALSE;
    }
    else
    {
        RespondToPlayerLocation();
        MoveNPCs();
        PaintBackBuffer();
    }
}
```

Here, you can see that the program has three possible paths of execution. The first is if `TestCooperativeLevel()` returns `D3DERR_DEVICELOST`, in which case `ProcessGame()` sets the `m_bGamePaused` flag to `TRUE` (you can use this flag in the program to stop the program from responding to Windows messages) and exits. The methods that run the game never get called.

The second path of execution occurs when `TestCooperativeLevel()` returns `D3DERR_DEVICENOTRESET`. In this case, `ProcessGame()` calls `ResetDirect3D()`, which gets Direct3D up and running again, and resets the `m_bPaused` flag.

Finally, the third possibility is when `TestCooperativeLevel()` doesn't return `D3DERR_DEVICELOST` or `D3DERR_DEVICENOTRESET`, returning `D3D_OK` instead. In this case, the program simply goes about its normal business with no interruption, processing game data and redrawing the screen.

Ready to see all this stuff in action? Perform the following steps to add lost-device functionality to the JBookman project:

1. In Direct3D.h, move the following from the private method declarations to the public methods:

   ```
   void CleanUp(void);
   ```

   Because the game engine must delete all Direct3D objects before restoring them, it must have access to the `CDirect3D` object's `CleanUp()` method.

2. In the Engine.h file, add the following to the class's protected data members:

   ```
   BOOL m_bGamePaused;
   ```

3. Add the following to the class's private method declarations:

```
void ResetDirect3D();
```

4. Add the following method definition to the Engine.cpp file. If you'd rather not type, you can copy the lines from the Code13.txt file in the Chapter21 directory of this book's CD-ROM.

```
///////////////////////////////////////////////////////
// ResetDirect3D()
///////////////////////////////////////////////////////
void CEngine::ResetDirect3D()
{
    m_Direct3D.CleanUp();
    m_Direct3D.InitD3D();
    if (m_bMonsterAttacking)
    {
        int iHPSave = m_pCurrentMonster->GetRemainingHitPoints();
        m_pCurrentMonster = GetMonster();
        m_pCurrentMonster->SetRemainingHitPoints(iHPSave);
    }
    switch (m_byMapType)
    {
    case TOWNEXTERIOR:
        m_Direct3D.SetCurrentTileSurface
            (m_Direct3D.GetTownExtTileSurface());
        break;
    case TOWNINTERIOR:
        m_Direct3D.SetCurrentTileSurface
            (m_Direct3D.GetTownIntTileSurface());
        break;
    case DUNGEON:
        m_Direct3D.SetCurrentTileSurface
            (m_Direct3D.GetDungeonTileSurface());
        break;
    case WILDERNESS:
        m_Direct3D.SetCurrentTileSurface
            (m_Direct3D.GetWildernessTileSurface());
        break;
    }
}
```

This method not only deletes all Direct3D objects and then restores them, but also ensures that the correct tiles will be used to draw the screen.

5. Replace the `ProcessGame()` method with the following new version. If you'd rather not type, you can copy the lines from the Code14.txt file in the Chapter21 directory of this book's CD-ROM.

```
///////////////////////////////////////////////////////
// ProcessGame()
///////////////////////////////////////////////////////
void CEngine::ProcessGame(void)
```

```
{
    HRESULT hResult = m_Direct3D.GetDevice()->TestCooperativeLevel();
    if (hResult == D3DERR_DEVICELOST)
        m_bGamePaused = TRUE;
    else if (hResult == D3DERR_DEVICENOTRESET)
    {
        ResetDirect3D();
        m_bGamePaused = FALSE;
    }
    else
    {
        RespondToPlayerLocation();
        MoveNPCs();
        PaintBackBuffer();
    }
}
```

6. Add the following line to the beginning of the `HandleTimer()` method:

   ```
   if (m_bGamePaused) return;
   ```

   This line causes the program to ignore all `WM_TIMER` messages, which halts all parts of the game that respond to the timer.

All done! Now you can compile and run the project. When the game comes up on the screen, Alt+Tab back to the desktop. Then, select the game's window, and everything springs back to life.

New Members of the `CEngine` Class

You've now added all you'll be adding to the game engine in this book. That doesn't mean, however, that you can't continue to build more into it on your own. In any case, Table 21.1 describes the new members you added to the class today.

TABLE 21.1 New Members of the `CEngine` Class

Member	*Type*	*Description*
m_bGamePaused	Data member	Indicates whether the game is paused due to having lost its Direct3D device
m_bPlayerDead	Data member	Indicates whether the player character has died in battle
DisplayAttributes()	Private method	Displays the player character's attributes in a text plaque
EndGame()	Private method	Ends the game when the player's hit points drop below 1.
HandleA()	Private method	Handles the A key
ResetDirect3D()	Private method	Restores the Direct3D device and its surfaces

Summary

Well, here you are, all finished with your three weeks of studying 2D game programming with Direct3D. Where did the time go? In this day, you added the last few pieces to the puzzle, leaving you with a fully playable game, albeit one that needs to be extended with your own ideas. Take the time now to work through the last workshop that follows. Then, my friend, you're ready to go off on your own and take *The Adventures of Jasper Bookman* to the places that are unique to your imagination. How cool is that?

Your first steps towards completing the game should be to create some new locations. Flip to Appendix A to learn how to use the JBookman game editor, which will create the location files for you. All you have to do is draw the location on the screen, much as you would with a paint program. Once you have a few new locations, give the NPCs in the location interesting things to say—and especially devise new quests. Try to make the quests like a chain of events that creates a story and leads the player toward the end of the game.

If you have trouble remembering how to perform the common programming tasks needed to add to the game, check out Appendix D for a quick guide to most of the programming techniques you need to complete the game. You'll also want to check out Appendix B, which is a quick reference for the `CEngine` class.

I spent a little time myself, adding some stuff to the game. You can find the results of my efforts in Appendix C, which is a walkthrough of the game up to the point where I stopped working on it. (Actually, I haven't stopped working on it. I'll be working on it long after this book sees print!) There, you can get some hints on how to fine-tune your own game. See you on the software bestseller lists!

Q&A

Q. Okay, we know how to end the game when the player dies, but how about when the player wins the game?

A. You pretty much handle winning the game the same way you do losing the game. One particular event in the game should trigger whatever end-game sequence you have in mind. For example, you might have the player defeat one last horrible creature and then step forward onto the sector the monster once occupied. Moving onto the sector can trigger an event in the same way all other events in the game are triggered.

Q. How long do you think it'll take a programmer like me to finish a game like this, now that I have the game engine to work with?

A. Not to state the obvious, but that all depends on how big of a story you want to create. In any case, to create a game of reasonable length would probably take at least six months if you're working alone.

Q. Now that the game engine is complete, will it do everything I need it to do to finish my game?

A. Like most things associated with creative endeavors, "complete" is a subjective term. Could you write a complete game with the engine just as it is? Yes, I think so. But, as you work on your game, you're likely to have cool ideas that won't work with the engine in its current state. You'll then want to make changes. Just remember that only generalized functionality—that is, things that represent default processing and actions—belongs in the `CEngine` class. The details unique to your story should wind up in your `CMyEngine` class or some other project file, such as the FirstTown.cpp file.

Workshop

The workshop includes quiz questions to help gauge your grasp of the material. Even if you feel that you totally understand the concepts presented here, you should work through the quiz anyway.

Quiz

1. Why did you change the `HandleKeys()` method's declaration to virtual?
2. Where does the program make use of the `m_bBuyingPotion` flag, as well as the other shopping-related flags?
3. What is similar about the way the program handles the shop proprietors and the other NPCs in the game?
4. How does the program manipulate player-character attributes during battle?
5. What happens to a Direct3D full-screen application's device and surfaces when the user Atl+Tabs back to the desktop or to another application?
6. What does the Direct3D application have to do to regain control of the device and its surfaces?
7. What Direct3D method notifies the program when its lost its device and when the device can be restored?

Answers for Day 21

Quiz

1. Why did you change the `HandleKeys()` method's declaration to virtual?

   So that the method can be overridden in the `CMyEngine` class and thus enable that class to handle keystrokes before they get passed on to the `CEngine` class's version of `HandleKeys()`.

2. Where does the program make use of the `m_bBuyingPotion` flag, as well as the other shopping-related flags?

   In the methods that respond to the Y and N keys.

3. What is similar about the way the program handles the shop proprietors and the other NPCs in the game?

   All the NPCs, including shop proprietors, trigger game events that get routed by the `HandleNPC()` method.

4. How does the program manipulate player-character attributes during battle?

   The program calls methods of the `CPlayer` object to add and subtract values from attributes, including hit points, experience, and gold.

5. What happens to a Direct3D full-screen application's device and surfaces when the user Atl+Tabs back to the desktop or to another application?

   The Direct3D application loses its device and its surfaces are destroyed.

6. What does the Direct3D application have to do to regain control of the device and its surfaces?

   The program must release all Direct3D objects and then re-create them.

7. What Direct3D method notifies the program when its lost its device and when the device can be restored?

   The `TestCooperativeLevel()` method.

WEEK 3

In Review

To have an enjoyable RPG, you need to trigger game events that give the player the ability not only to interact with game objects, but also to move from one map to another. When it comes right down to it, the bulk of your game deals with the events that create the game's story. To add events to the game, you must know how to customize the game engine for events and trigger and respond to game events.

The game events are what make your game unique and so cannot be managed by the game engine, which deals only with general game-processing tasks. A good example of such an event is when the player decides to go through a door. The game engine has no idea what you want to have happen when the player goes through that door. It's up to you to tell the game engine what to do.

OOP techniques give you exactly the tools you need to create custom events. All you have to do is create a new class that inherits from the `CEngine` class. Then, you can use the game engine as it is in its current form, and add your own code to the game, without the fear of ruining any of the hard work you've already put into the game.

Many game events can be handled by the main game engine. For example, if you don't need a treasure chest to do anything special, the main game engine can just display its contents to the player. Still, even with objects like treasure chests, you will often need to customize the event handling to handle special occurrences unique to your game. In the JBookman project, this means managing locked, unlocked, and secret doors, as well as enabling the player to interact with containers like treasure chests and barrels.

When you start programming game events, a problem arises. Often, you need to display text that describes the outcome of an event. For example, if the player opens a treasure chest, you have to tell him what he found. Similarly, if the player tries to go through a locked door, you have to tell him he needs a key.

Displaying text in a Direct3D program isn't much more difficult than displaying text in any other Windows program. To accomplish this task, you must create an `ID3DXFont` object, calculate the size of a rectangle that can hold the text, call the Direct3D device's `BeginScene()` method, draw the text, call the Direct3D device's `EndScene()` method, and release the `ID3DXFont` object.

At this point in the project, the starting location of *The Adventures of Jasper Bookman* is a bit of a ghost town. You need to add people to the town. Once you have a town full of people, you'll want to talk to them in order to gather information about the game. Such information usually leads to the quests that make up your game's storyline. To handle the game's people, called non-player characters (NPCs), you must know how to draw NPCs in the town, animate the NPCs' images, and add dialog to the game. You also must understand how to program quests, which are the main tools with which you tell the game's story.

Wandering around a virtual world and exploring every nook and cranny is great fun, but every game has to present some sort of challenge to the player. Role-playing games usually present two types of challenges: puzzle solving and combat. You already learned about adding quests[md]a form of puzzle solving[md]to your game. Next, you need to populate the game world with creatures whose sole purpose is to attack the player character at every opportunity. To do this you must learn to specify where creatures lurk, draw creatures on the screen, implement battle commands for the player, control the battle sequence, and award the player for defeating a monster.

As with such objects as containers and NPCs, the best way to manage the data that represents a monster is to encapsulate that data into a class. This class not only holds the various variables that control a monster's abilities and status, but also provides the methods needed to access those variables.

Because of the time required to complete a role-playing game, the game must have a game-save feature. This feature enables the player to quit playing and come back to the game later, without having to repeat the parts of the game he has already completed. To accomplish this task, you must decide what values to save, maintain the game's data files as the player plays, manage game-save files, and request from the player confirmation for the save, load, and quit commands.

Only you, the game designer, know exactly which variables need to be saved in order to restore the game correctly. Such variables include flags that specify which tasks the player has completed. The player's current attributes—hit points, gold, potions, and so on—must also be saved. In the case of the JBookman project, you also need to save the status of all containers and doors. This is because the status of these objects changes in the game. If the player unlocks a door, it should remain unlocked when he reloads the game. If the player opens a treasure chest and removes its contents, the chest should be empty the next time the player opens it.

The JBookman project uses three types of game-save data. The start-up data, when loaded, starts a brand-new game. This data, which is located in the Maps directory, never changes. Then there's the save data, which is the game data that the player explicitly saves in order to begin where he left off at a later date. This data, which is located in the Save directory, changes only when the player chooses the save command. Finally, the game uses working data, which is the game data that constantly changes as the player plays. This data, which is located in the Temp directory, changes every time the player manipulates an object or moves from one location to another.

No modern game is complete without sound effects. This is especially true of role-playing games, which try to submerge the player in an intense game world and story. Adding sound to such a game is a big task, but basically, to accomplish this task in the JBookman project, you must know how to organize DirectSound source code into a class, add the `CWave` class to the game project, and associate sound effects with game events.

At this point, the game was pretty much complete. Only a few things needed to be added to the program to complete the game engine. In the last day, you learned to program the shopping routines, manipulate player-character attributes, and handle lost Direct3D devices.

The location of First Town (and presumably other towns you'll add to the game after you complete this book) has a couple of shops in which the player can buy helpful items. Specifically, First Town has a potion shop, an Armor shop, and an inn. Potions are important to the game because they enable the player to get a boost in hit points during battle. The armor shop, on the other hand, enables the player to upgrade his defensive clothing. Finally, the inn enables the player to get a good night's sleep, during which he regains all his hit points. Getting these different establishments working isn't too complicated, and, in fact, is just a matter of handling a few new game events.

When the player Alt+Tabs from the game back to Windows, the Windows desktop takes over the video card, throwing away the device object and all the surfaces you worked so hard to get up and running. This may seem like a huge problem, but it is actually an easy one to fix. First, when your Direct3D program loses its surfaces, even though the program can no longer draw to the screen, all drawing functions continue to work in the sense that they won't crash your program. They simply return the error code D3DERR_DEVICELOST. Second, a Direct3D device object provides a method named TestCooperativeLevel() that can tell your program at any time whether it still has access to its device and surfaces.

Appendix A

Using the JBookman Game Editor

One of the biggest jobs in creating an RPG is putting together all the maps that represent the many areas the player can visit and explore. While it's certainly possible to create each map by hand by entering a bunch of numbers into an array, doing the job this way is very difficult. First, you can't see the result until you run the program, and, second, that's a whole lot of numbers!

For these reasons, when most programmers set out to program a new RPG-style game, they start by creating a game editor to generate data files for the game. Luckily for you, I've created just such an editor to develop new locations for *The Adventures of Jasper Bookman*. In this appendix, you learn to use the editor.

Installing and Running the Editor

You can find the JBookman Game Editor in the GameEditor directory of this book's CD-ROM. In that directory, you'll find all the source code for the editor, as well as the editor's executable file. The source code is written in Visual Basic 6.0, so if you own Visual Basic, you can modify the program to fit your needs, if you'd like.

However, if you don't have Visual Basic, you can still use the editor. All you have to do is install the program by running its Setup.exe file (located in the GameEditor\Package directory), and then run the GameEditor program from your Start menu. Note that your screen resolution must be at least 1024×768 to properly fit the editor's main window.

When you run the editor, you see the screen shown in Figure A.1. On the left are four columns of tile buttons, an enlarged image of the currently selected tile, and four buttons to select the type of map—town exterior, town interior, dungeon, or wilderness—that you want to create.

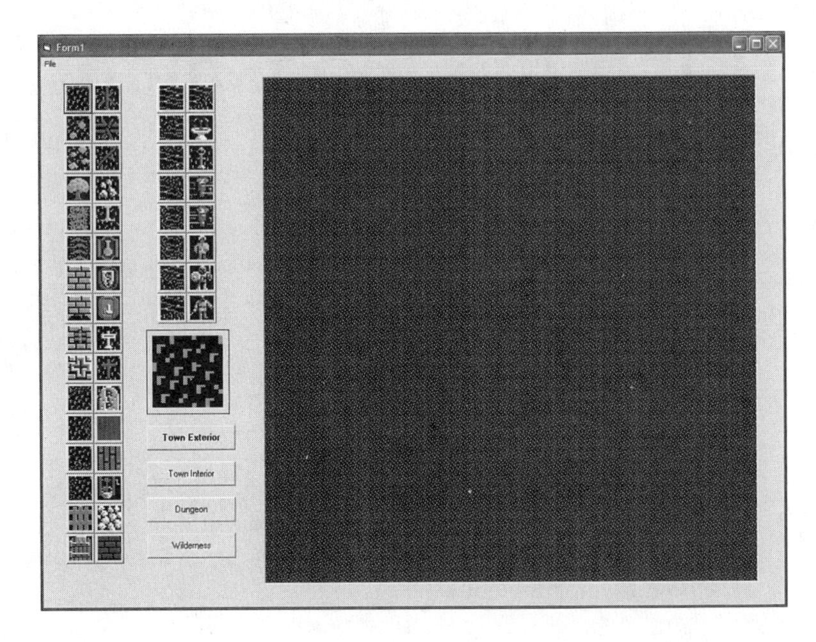

FIGURE A.1

The JBookman Game Editor at start up.

The right side of the window comprises the work area, where you draw your map using any of the available tiles. The work area always starts out filled with the appropriate background tile. For example, a town exterior map starts off filled with grass tiles (as you can see in Figure A.1), whereas a town interior map starts off filled with the purple design that represents an empty area, as shown in Figure A.2.

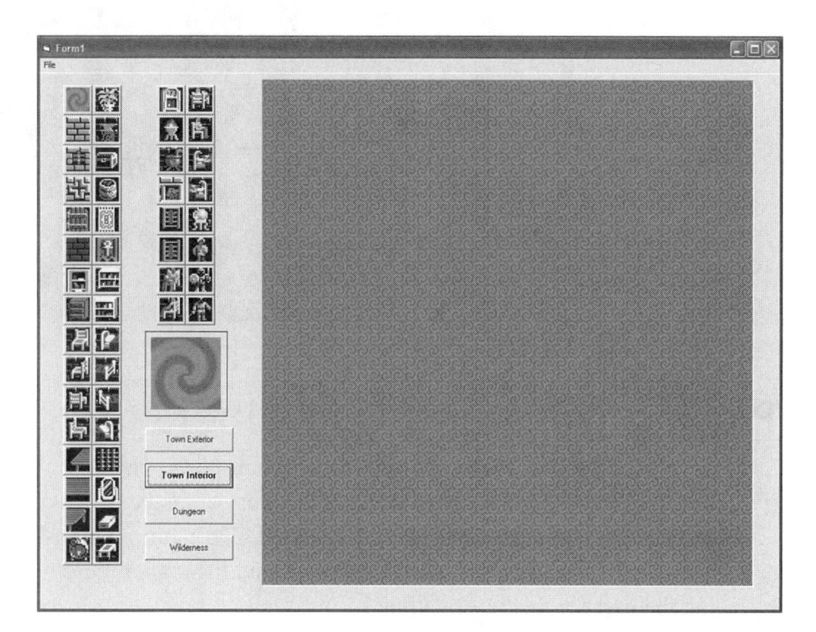

FIGURE A.2

An empty town interior map.

Creating a Map

To create a map, first choose, by clicking the appropriate button, whether you want to create a town exterior, town interior, dungeon, or wilderness map. Then, all you have to do is click the button for the tile you want to use and use that selection to draw in the work area. A single click in the work area places a single tile. If you hold down the left mouse button, you can paint with the tile. Figure A.3 shows the editor after the user has started creating a stone wall.

When placing tiles in the work area, keep in mind that the first two columns of buttons represent non-animated tiles, whereas the second two columns of buttons represent animated tiles. (The editor does not show the animation sequence, but animated tiles will be animated in the game.)

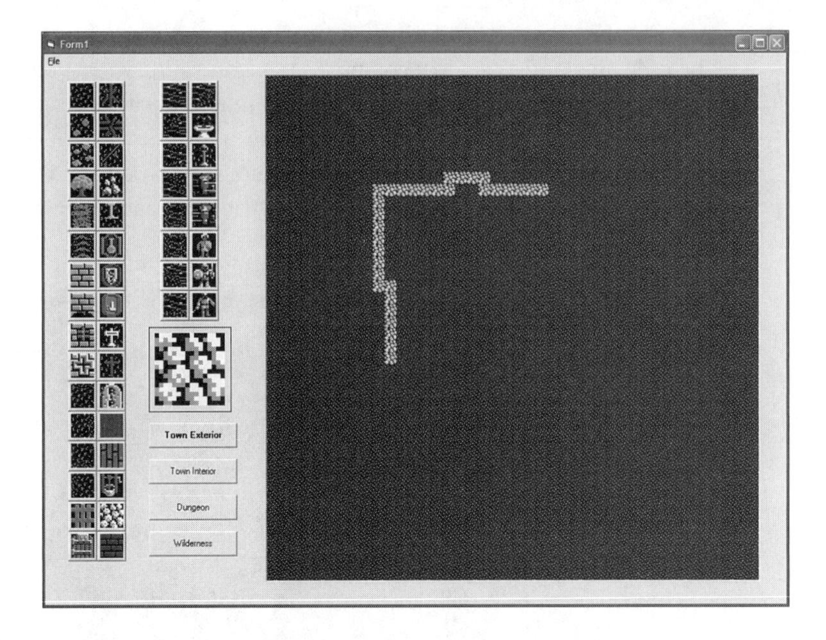

FIGURE A.3

Painting tiles into the work area.

Placing NPCs and Containers

Several of the tiles in the tile set represent non-player characters (NPCs), doors, and containers. When you place such a tile in the work area, the editor requests additional information. For example, when you place an NPC, the editor will ask for the person's name and whether the figure is able to move around the map. Figure A.4 shows the editor asking the user for this information.

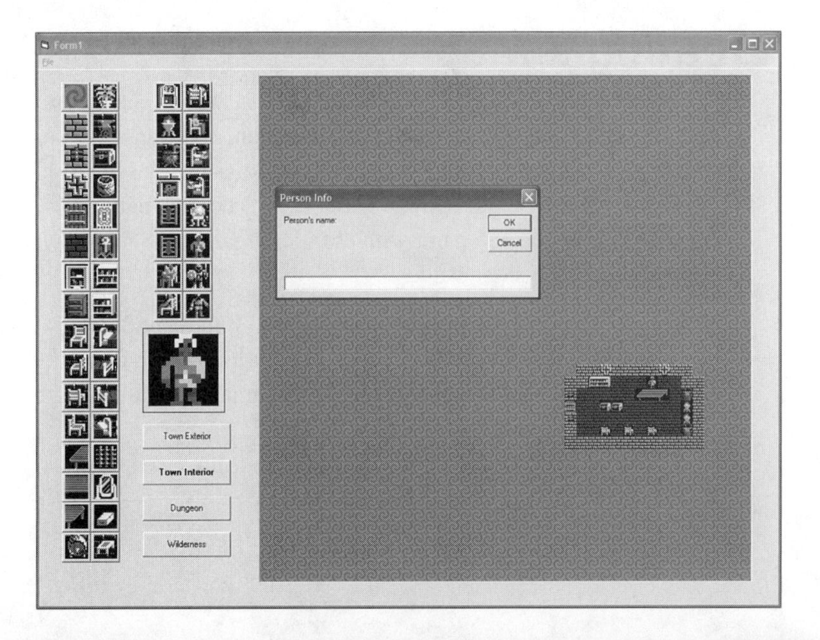

FIGURE A.4

Adding an NPC to the map.

Saving and Loading Maps

When you've finished creating a map, select the File menu's Save or Save As commands to create the data files. The editor creates \.map, .itm, .peo, and .dor files, similar to the ones that you've seen throughout this book. For example, if you created a map for an area called SecondTown, the generated data files will be SecondTown.map, SecondTown.map.dor, SecondTown.map.itm, and SecondTown.map.peo. Figure A.5 shows the user saving a map.

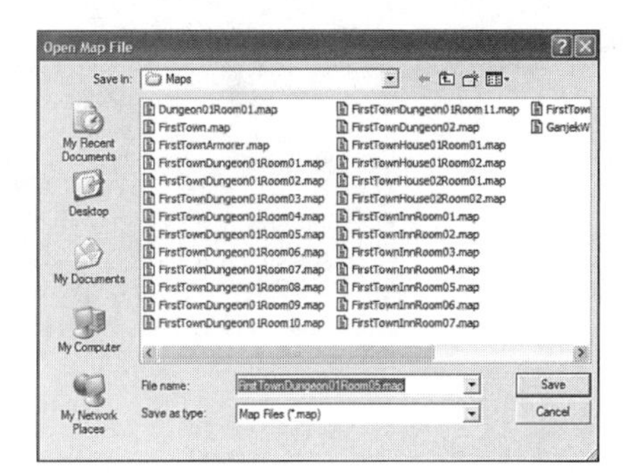

FIGURE A.5

Saving a map.

You can save a map at any time, which means you can save a partial map that you want to finish later. To load the map again, select the File menu's Open command and select the map from the dialog box that appears.

Town Exteriors Versus Town Interiors

As you should already know, the town exterior maps show the outside of a town's buildings, as well as the outside area surrounding these buildings. Almost always, you'll want to start with a town exterior map and use it as the starting point for creating the town interior maps for each building. The JBookman Game Editor provides a quick way to get started on interior maps.

When you have a town exterior map open and then click the Town Interior button, the editor automatically retains the outlines of buildings. For example, Figure A.6 shows the completed exterior map for First Town, an area with which you should already be very familiar. Figure A.7 shows the same area after the user clicks the Town Interior button.

After making the conversion, be sure to save the new map under a different name.

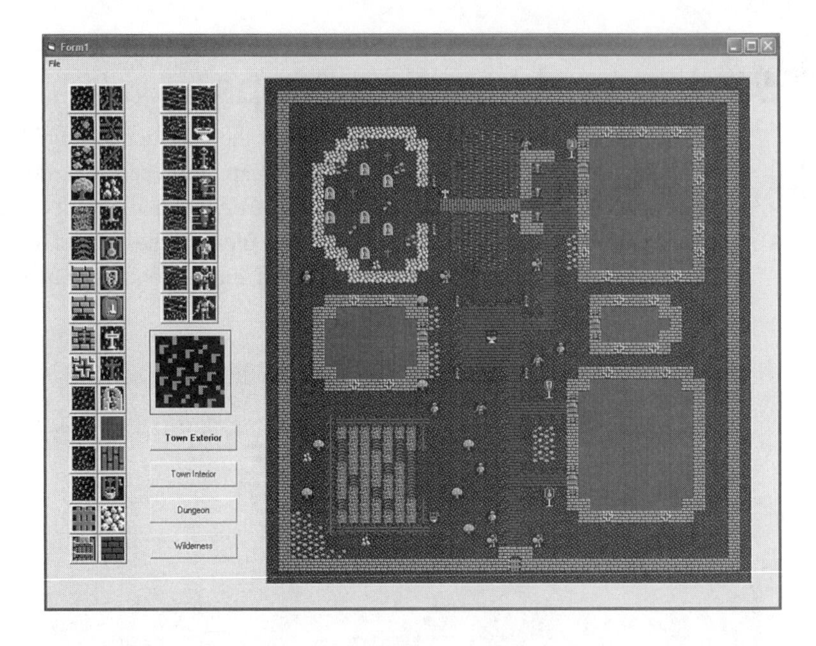

FIGURE A.6

A completed town exterior map.

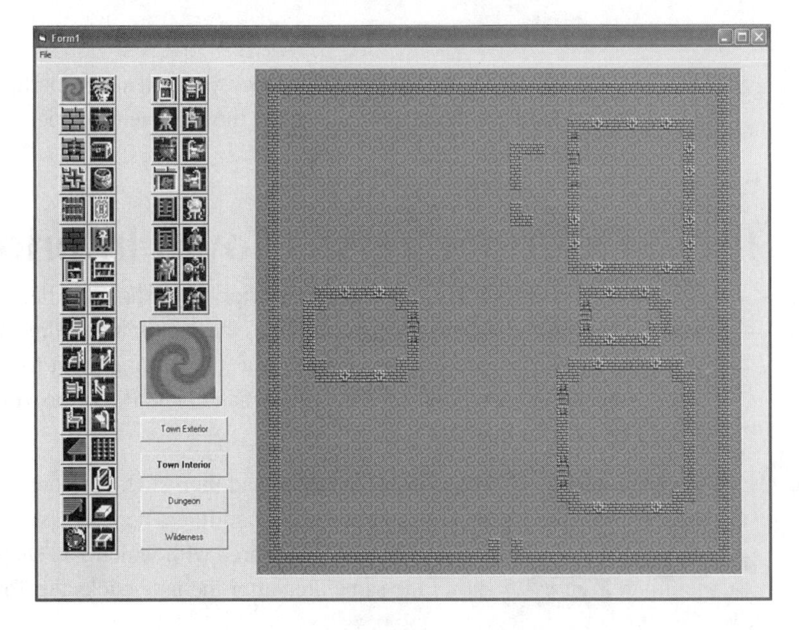

FIGURE A.7

The town exterior map converted to a town interior map.

Viewing Information About a Tile

You can get all the information you need for a specific tile simply by right-clicking it in the work area. For example, Figure A.8 shows the editor displaying information about a wall tile, giving its sector number, column number, row number, and tile number.

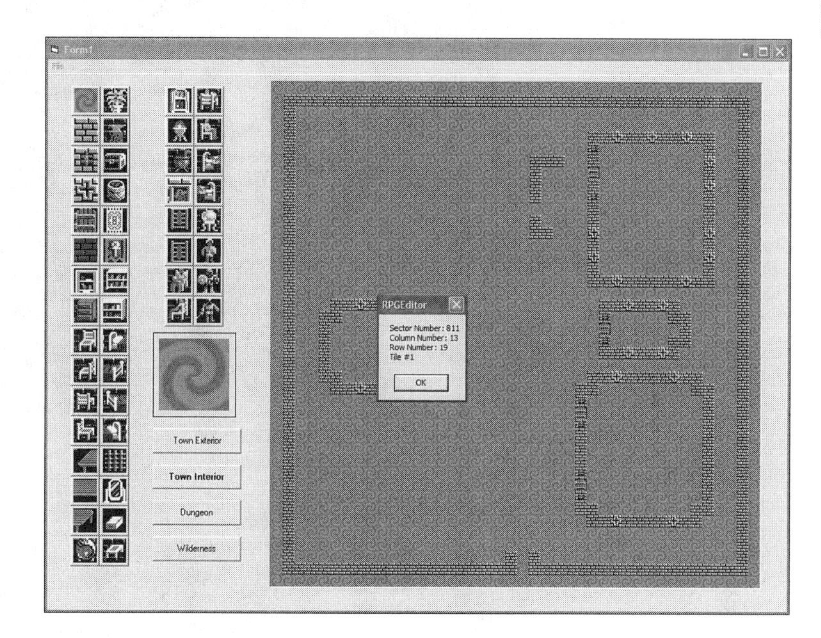

FIGURE A.8
Getting information about a tile in the map.

You can also get information about NPCs, doors, and containers. Again, just right-click the tile in question, and the editor displays all the information you need. Figure A.9, for example, show the results when the user right-clicks a treasure chest.

Deleting NPCs and Containers

To delete a normal tile, all you have to do is paint over it with another. NPCs, doors, and containers, however, work a little differently. When you click on an NPC, door, or container's tile, the editor asks whether you want to delete it, as shown in Figure A.10. Just click the appropriate response.

And that's about it. Please note that this editor is a quickie program that I threw together just to get the job of creating maps done. It's still a bit rough around the edges and undoubtedly has a couple of minor bugs. Still, it works fine for creating the maps you'll need to expand *The Adventures of Jasper Bookman* into a full game. If you're a VB programmer feel free to expand the editor with new features.

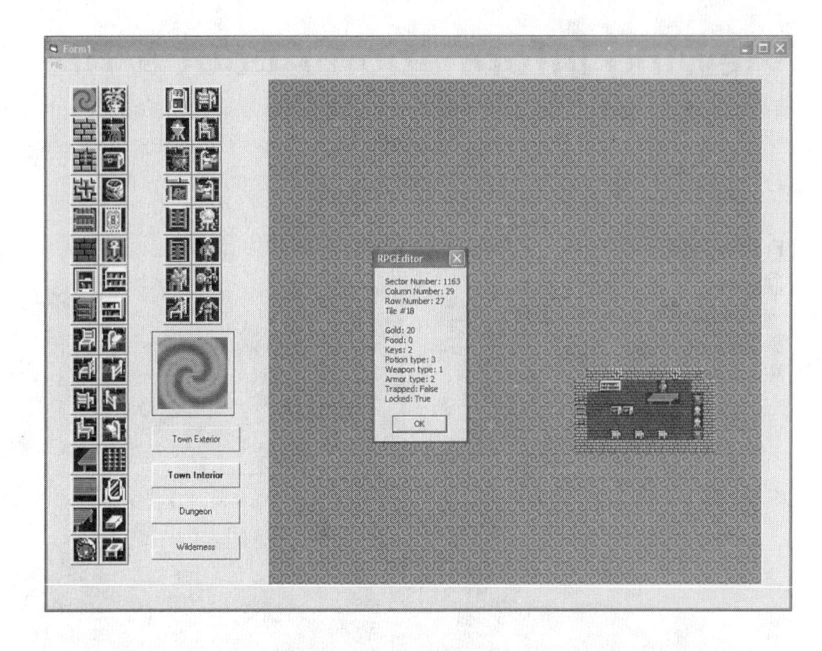

FIGURE A.9

Getting information about a container.

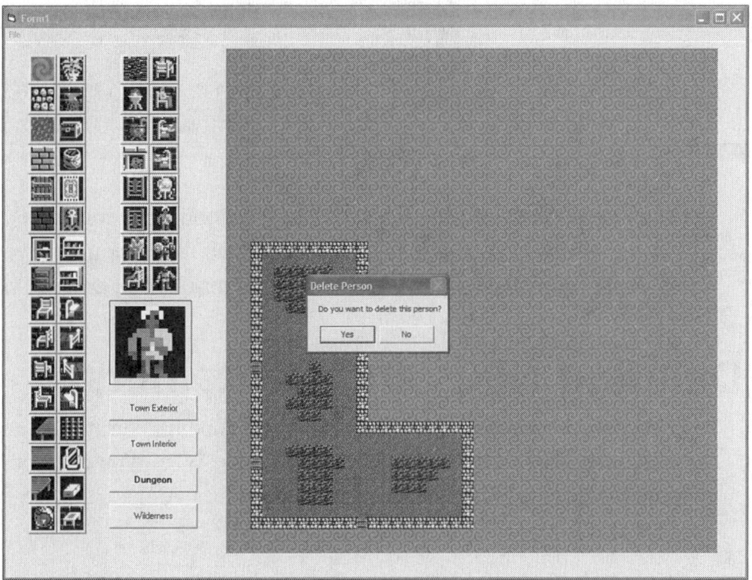

FIGURE A.10

Deleting an NPC.

APPENDIX B

Game Engine Quick Reference

The `CEngine` class is the core of *The Adventures of Jasper Bookman*. For that reason, at the end of each chapter that you added new members to the class, there was a table listing and describing the new members. As you work on adding to the game (or creating your own game from scratch), you'll want to refer to those tables.

Unfortunately, bouncing around from chapter to chapter, looking for the table that contains the class member you want is a real pain in the neck. So, in this appendix, all the tables from those chapters have been combined into two. Table B.1 describes all the class's protected data members, and Table B.2 describes all of the class's methods.

TABLE B.1 Protected Data Members of the `CEngine` Class

Member	*Description*
`m_bAnimationTilesUpdated`	Flag for determining whether slow animation tiles are on their first or second frame.
`m_bAskingIfLoad`	A flag that indicates whether the player needs to enter Y or N in response to "Are you sure you want to load a game?" message.
`m_bAskingIfQuit`	A flag that indicates whether the player needs to enter Y or N in response to "Are you sure you want to quit?" message.
`m_bAskingIfSave`	A flag that indicates whether the player needs to enter Y or N in response to "Are you sure you want to save?" message.
`m_bFastAnimationTilesUpdated`	Flag for determining whether fast animation tiles are on their first or second frame.
`m_bFastestAnimationTilesUpdated`	Flag for determining whether fastest animation tiles are on their first or second frame.
`m_bGamePaused`	Indicates whether the game is paused due to having lost its Direct3D device.
`m_bMonsterAttacking`	A flag that indicates whether the player is currently involved in a battle.
`m_bPlayerDead`	Indicates whether the player character has died in battle.
`m_bPlayerTurnToAttack`	A flag that indicates whether it's the player's turn to attack.
`m_bRunningFromMonster`	A flag that indicates whether the player is currently trying to run from a battle.
`m_bShowingPlaque`	A flag that indicates whether the game engine is currently displaying the plaque image.
`m_byMapType`	The map type ID for the current location.
`m_Containers`	The class's `CContainers` object.
`m_Direct3D`	Holds the class's `CDirect3D` object.
`m_Doors`	The class's CDoors object.
`m_hWnd`	Holds the application's window handle.
`m_iCombatDelayCounter`	Holds the remaining ticks for the combat delay timer.
`m_iCurrentMap`	The map type ID for the current map.
`m_iCurrentMonsterFrame`	Holds the ID of the current monster animation frame.
`m_iFirstMapType`	The map type ID for the starting map.
`m_iMonsterDamage`	Holds the current amount of damage being applied to the monster.

TABLE B.1 Continued

Member	*Description*
`m_iStartSector`	The sector in which the player character begins.
`m_pCurrentMonster`	Holds a pointer to the current `CMonster` object.
`m_People`	The class's `CPeople` object.
`m_Player`	The class's `CPlayer` object.
`m_pstrCurrentMapFile`	The name of the currently loaded map file.
`m_pstrFirstMap`	Name of the first map to display in the game.
`m_pstrPlaqueMsg`	A character array that holds the message being displayed in the plaque.
`m_Sectors`	Array of tile numbers for the current location.
`m_Sound`	An object of the `CDirectSound` class.

TABLE B.2 Methods of the `CEngine` Class

Method	*Type*	*Description*
`AnimateIdleMonster()`	Private Method	Manages the animation sequence for an idle creature.
`AnimateMonsterDamage()`	Private method	Animates the reduction of a creature's hit points during battle.
`AttackMonster()`	Private Method	Handles the player's attack on a creature.
`AttackPlayer()`	Private Method	Manages a monster's attack on a player.
`AttackRunningPlayer()`	Private Method	Gives the monster one last attack at the fleeing player.
`CharacterCanMove()`	Private Method	Checks whether the player character can move to the requested sector.
`CheckForAndHandleContainer()`	Private Method	Calls the helper methods that handle doors.
`CheckForAndHandleDoor()`	Private Method	Calls the helper methods that handle doors.
`CheckForAndHandleMonster()`	Private Method	Checks for a wandering monster and handles the monster if one is attacking.
`CheckForAndHandleNPC()`	Private Method	Checks for an NPC in the target sector and handles the NPC if one exists.

B

TABLE B.2 Continued

Method	*Type*	*Description*
`CheckForSecretDoor()`	Private Method	Checks whether there is a secret door at the specified sector and, if there is, returns the ID of the tile to display in place of the door.
`Column2X()`	Public Method	Returns the pixel X coordinate for a specified sector in a grid.
`ColumnRow2Sector()`	Public Method	Returns the sector number for a specified column and row in a grid.
`CombatDelayOver()`	Private Method	Manages the combat delay timer.
`ConstructFileName()`	Private Method	Creates the path for the file to load.
`ContainerEmpty()`	Private Method	Returns TRUE if the given container is empty.
`CopySaveToTemp()`	Protected Method	Copies the game-save files to the working files directory.
`CopyTempToSave()`	Protected Method	Copies the temporary files to the save files directory.
`DeleteSaveFiles()`	Protected Method	Deletes all save files.
`DeleteTempFiles()`	Protected Method	Deletes all working save files.
`DisplayAttributes()`	Private Method	Displays the player character's attributes in a text plaque.
`EndGame()`	Private Method	Ends the game when the player's hit points drop below 1.
`FindContainer()`	Private Method	Returns a pointer to the container object located in the given sector.
`FindDoor()`	Private Method	Returns a pointer to the door object located in the given sector.
`GetCDirect3DObj()`	Public Method	Returns a pointer to the class's CDirect3D object.
`GetCDirectSoundObj()`	Public Method	Returns a pointer to the class's `CDirectSound` object.
`GetCurrentMap()`	Public Method	Returns the map type ID for the current map.
`GetMonster()`	Pure virtual method	Returns a pointer to a `CMonster` object. Must be implemented in any class derived from `CEngine`.

TABLE B.2 Continued

Method	*Type*	*Description*
`GetPlayer()`	Public Method	Returns a pointer to the class's CPlayer object.
`GetSectors()`	Public Method	Returns a pointer to the tile values for the current map.
`GetStringFromFile()`	Private Method	Reads a string from the current file.
`HandleA()`	Private Method	Handles the A key.
`HandleContainer()`	Private Method	Handles container objects, including calling the method that transfers a containers contents to the player's inventory.
`HandleContainer()`	Protected virtual method	Handles the given container, providing the appropriate interaction with the player. Override this method to provide custom interaction with the container.
`HandleDoor()`	Private Method	Handles door object, including unlocking a locked door when the player has a key.
`HandleDoor()`	Protected virtual method	Handles the given door, providing the appropriate interaction with the player. Override this method to provide custom interaction with the door.
`HandleDownArrow()`	Public Method	Handles the down arrow key.
`HandleFastAnimation()`	Private Method	Performs the fast animation sequences.
`HandleFastestAnimation()`	Private Method	Performs the fastest animation sequences.
`HandleKeys()`	Public Method	Handles keystrokes for the application.
`HandleL()`	Private Method	Responds to the L key.
`HandleLeftArrow()`	Public Method	Handles the left arrow key.
`HandleMonsters()`	Private Method	Manages the monster battle sequence.
`HandleN()`	Private Method	Responds to the N key.
`HandleNPC()`	Private Method	Determines whether the player's requested target location is blocked by an impassable object.
`HandleNPC()`	Protected virtual method	Handles the given NPC, providing the appropriate interaction with the player. Override this method to provide custom interaction with the NPC.

B

TABLE B.2 Continued

Method	*Type*	*Description*
`HandleRightArrow()`	Public Method	Handles the right arrow key.
`HandleS()`	Private Method	Responds to the "S" key.
`HandleSlowAnimation()`	Private Method	Performs the slow animation sequences.
`HandleTimer()`	Public Method	Handles `WM_TIMER` events.
`HandleUpArrow()`	Public Method	Handles the up arrow key.
`HandleY()`	Private Method	Responds to the Y key.
`InitGame()`	Public Method	Initializes all game data at the start of a game.
`IsContainer()`	Private Method	Returns TRUE if the item at the given sector is a container.
`IsDoor()`	Private Method	Returns TRUE when the specified sector contains a door.
`IsFastAnimationTile()`	Private Method	Returns TRUE of the specified tile is a fast animation tile.
`IsFastestAnimationTile()`	Private Method	Returns TRUE of the specified tile is a fastest animation tile.
`IsMonsterLocation()`	Pure virtual method	Returns TRUE if the current location contains monsters. Must be implemented in any class derived from `CEngine`.
`IsShowingPlaque()`	Public Method	Returns TRUE if the game engine is currently displaying the plaque image.
`LoadGame()`	Protected Method	Loads the previously saved game.
`MoveNPCEast()`	Private Method	Moves an NPC east one sector.
`MoveNPCNorth()`	Private Method	Moves an NPC north one sector.
`MoveNPCs()`	Private Method	Moves the NPCs around their current location.
`MoveNPCSouth()`	Private Method	Moves an NPC south one sector.
`MoveNPCWest()`	Private Method	Moves an NPC west one sector.
`MovePlayerDown()`	Private Method	Moves the player character's location down one row in the map grid.
`MovePlayerLeft()`	Private Method	Moves the player character's location left one sector in the map grid.

TABLE B.2 Continued

Method	Type	Description
MovePlayerRight()	Private Method	Moves the player character's location right one sector in the map grid.
MovePlayerUp()	Private Method	Moves the player character's location up one row in the map grid.
OpenMapFiles()	Public Method	Loads all game data from disk.
PaintBackBuffer()	Public Method	Calls the helper functions that render the current scene to the back buffer.
PaintBackground()	Private Method	Draws the tiles that make up the current scene in the viewport.
PaintBattlePlaque()	Private Method	Displays the text plaque that holds information for the player about the current battle.
PaintMonster()	Private Method	Displays the monster's image.
PaintPlaque()	Public Method	Paints the plaque image on the screen.
PaintPlayer()	Private Method	Draws the player character's image in the viewport.
PlaceTile()	Public Method	Draws a single tile onto the back buffer.
PlayerBlocked()	Private Method	Determines whether the player's requested target location is blocked by an impassable object.
ProcessGame	Public Method	Processes game data during the application's idle time.
ReadContainerFile()	Private Method	Reads the item file into the class's `CContainers` object.
ReadDoorFile()	Private Method	Reads the door file into the class's `CDoors` object.
ReadMapFile()	Private Method	Reads the location map into the `m_Sectors[]` array.
ReadPeopleFile()	Private Method	Reads the people file into the class's `CPeople` object.
ReleaseMonster()	Pure virtual method	Destroys the current `CMonster` object, as well as releases the monster's animation-frame textures. Must be implemented in any class derived from `CEngine`.

TABLE B.2 Continued

Method	*Type*	*Description*
`ResetAnimation()`	Public Method	Ensures that the animation sequence remains properly synchronized after the game loads a new area map.
`ResetDirect3D()`	Private Method	Restores the Direct3D device and its surfaces.
`ResetMap()`	Private Method	Resets any animated tiles in a map file to the first tile in the animation sequence.
`RespondToPlayerLocation()`	Pure virtual method	This method, which must be implemented in any class that derives from `CEngine`, continually checks the player's current location for game-event triggers.
`RetrieveArmor()`	Private Method	Transfers armor from a container to the player.
`RetrieveGold()`	Private Method	Transfers gold from a container to the player.
`RetrieveItemsFromContainer()`	Private Method	Transfers the contents of a container to the player's inventory.
`RetrieveKeys()`	Private Method	Transfers keys from a container to the player.
`RetrievePotion()`	Private Method	Transfers potions from a container to the player.
`RetrieveWeapon()`	Private Method	Transfers a weapon from a container to the player.
`Row2Y()`	Public Method	Returns the row in a grid given the pixel Y coordinate.
`RunFromMonster()`	Private Method	Handle's the player's retreat from a battle.
`SaveContainerFile()`	Private Method	Saves all container objects to the .itm file.
`SaveDoorFile()`	Private Method	Saves all door objects to the .dor file.
`SaveGame()`	Protected Method	Saves all game files.
`SaveMapFile()`	Protected Method	Saves the map, door, container, and person files.
`SavePeopleFile()`	Private Method	Saves all person objects to the .peo file.

TABLE B.2 Continued

Method	*Type*	*Description*
`Sector2Column()`	Public Method	Returns the column in a grid given the sector number.
`Sector2Row()`	Public Method	Returns the row in a grid given the sector number.
`SectorHasPerson()`	Private Method	Returns TRUE if the target sector contains an NPC.
`SetCurrentMap()`	Public Method	Sets the map type ID for the current map.
`SetVisibleColsRows()`	Private Method	Calculates the columns and rows of the map grid that need to be drawn in the viewport.
`SetWindowHandle`	Public Method	Sets the class's copy of the window handle.
`ShowInventory()`	Private Method	Displays the player's inventory screen.
`StartAnimationTimer()`	Public Method	Starts the game engine's animation timer.
`TakePotion()`	Private Method	Increases the player's hit points when he enters the P command, assuming that the player has a potion in his inventory.
`TileNumber2SourceX()`	Public Method	Returns the pixel X coordinate of a given tile in the tile's tile file.
`TileNumber2SourceY()`	Public Method	Returns the pixel Y coordinate of a given tile in the tile's tile file.
`TurnOffPlaque()`	Public Method	Removes the plaque from the display.
`TurnOnPlaque()`	Public Method	Displays the plaque image.

APPENDIX C

JBookman—The Latest Version

After completing the writing of a book, there's always a bit of time to add an appendix or two. I took advantage of that time to continue working on the JBookman project. I worked a little on better balancing the game play, but most importantly I added a new town and a new quest.

You can find the latest version of the program in the AppendixC directory of this book's CD-ROM. Feel free to dig in and try to complete the two quests included. If you get stuck, or you just want to see what the new version of the program does, you can use this graphical walk-through of the game. Just follow the figures in order to take a tour of *The Adventures of Jasper Bookman*.

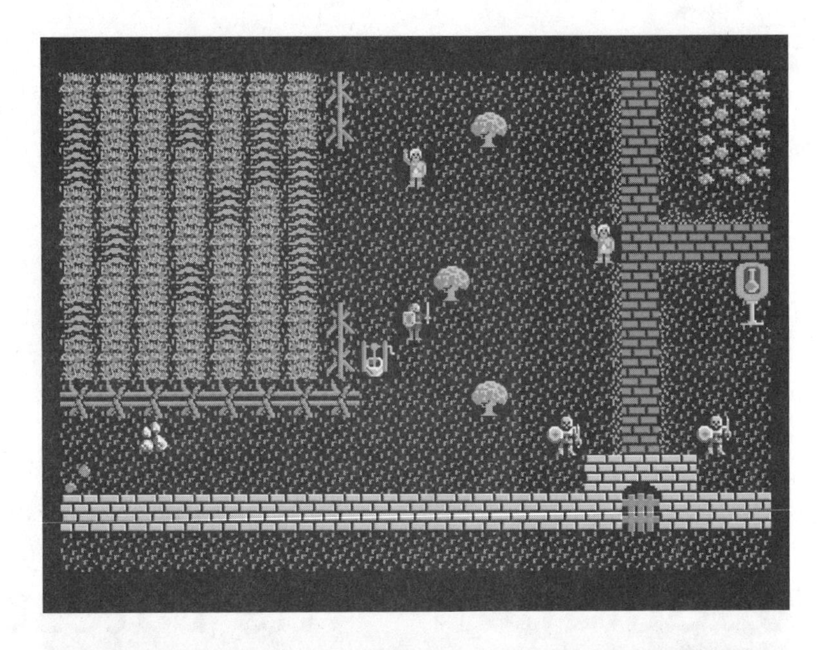

FIGURE C.1

You start off the game near the front gates of First Town.

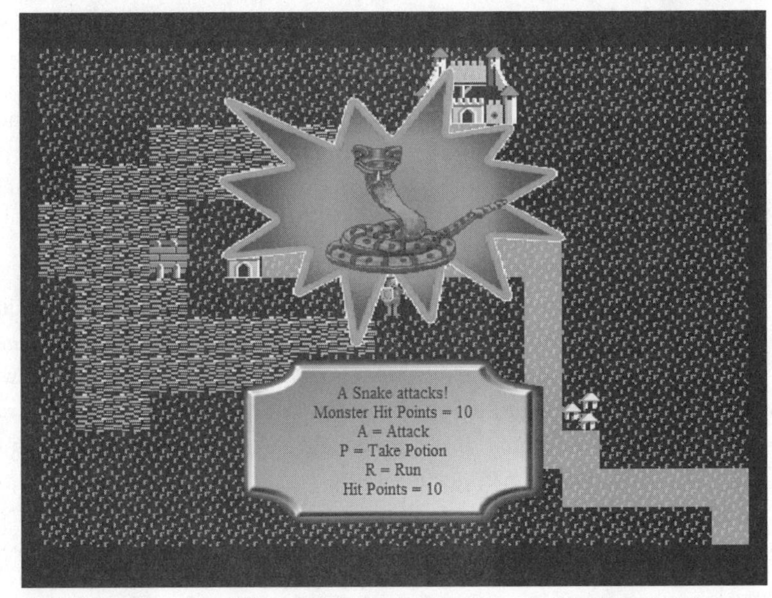

FIGURE C.2

You can head out of town and start battling monsters, but be very careful, because you have no weapon or armor. It'll take you some time to build up some experience and gold.

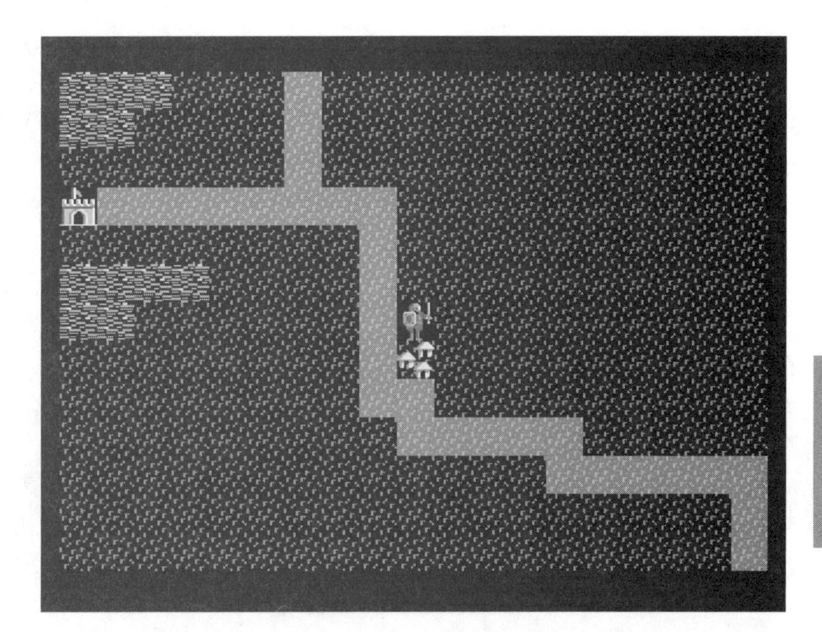

FIGURE C.3

If you happen to survive the creatures long enough to get to Second Town, go ahead and enter the town.

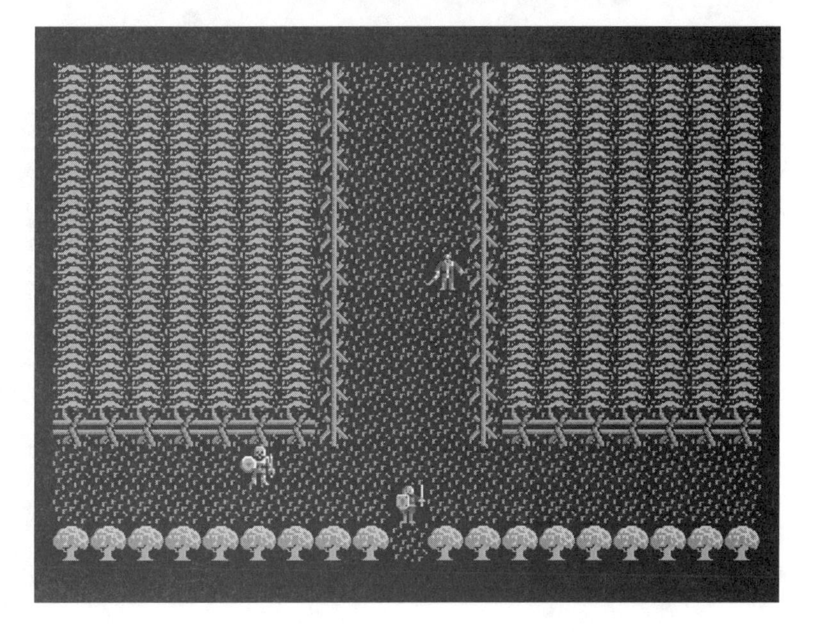

FIGURE C.4

When you enter Second Town, you'll find yourself in a farming village.

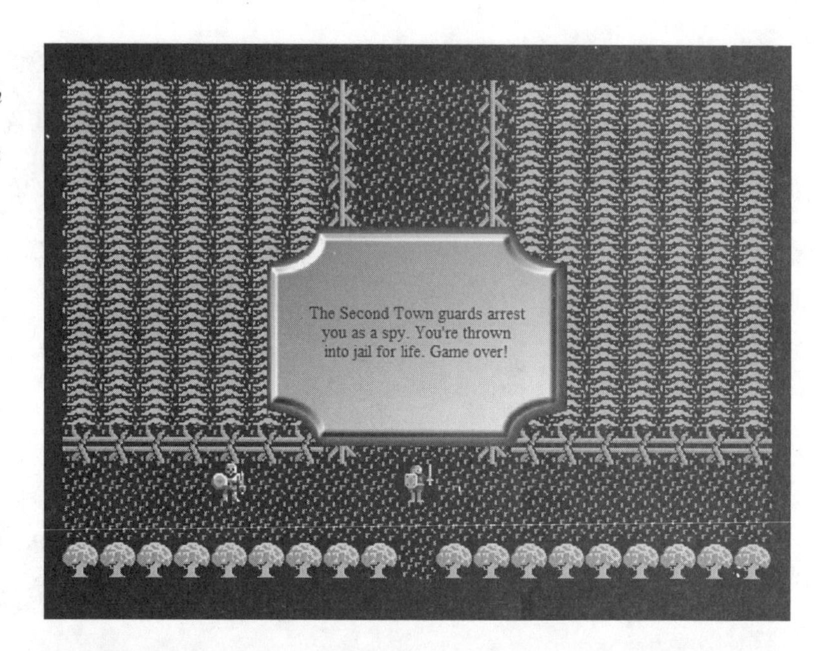

FIGURE C.5

Unfortunately, as soon as you take a step, you'll be arrested as a spy and thrown into jail.

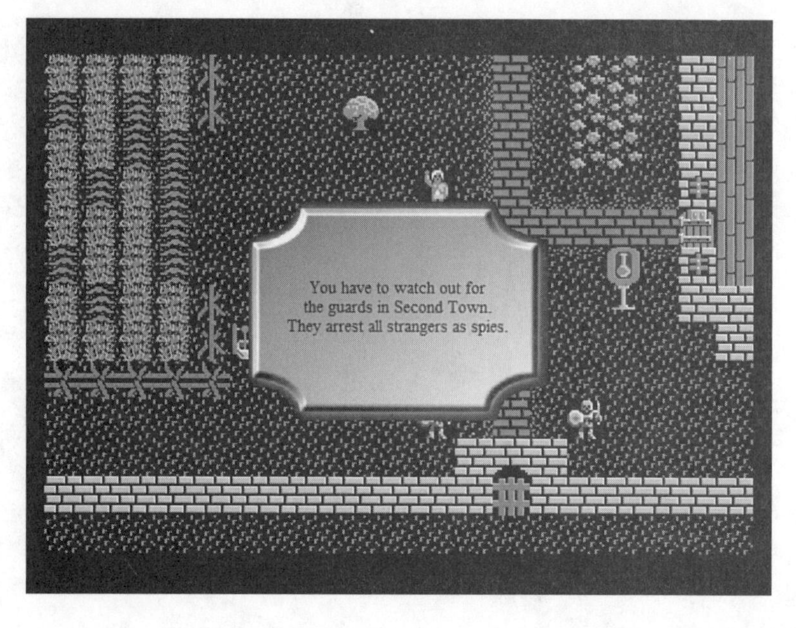

FIGURE C.6

There must be a way to get into Second Town. Maybe you should ask around in First Town. Too bad you didn't talk to this guy before you headed off into trouble.

FIGURE C.7

A little more asking around, and you discover that someone needs to talk to you.

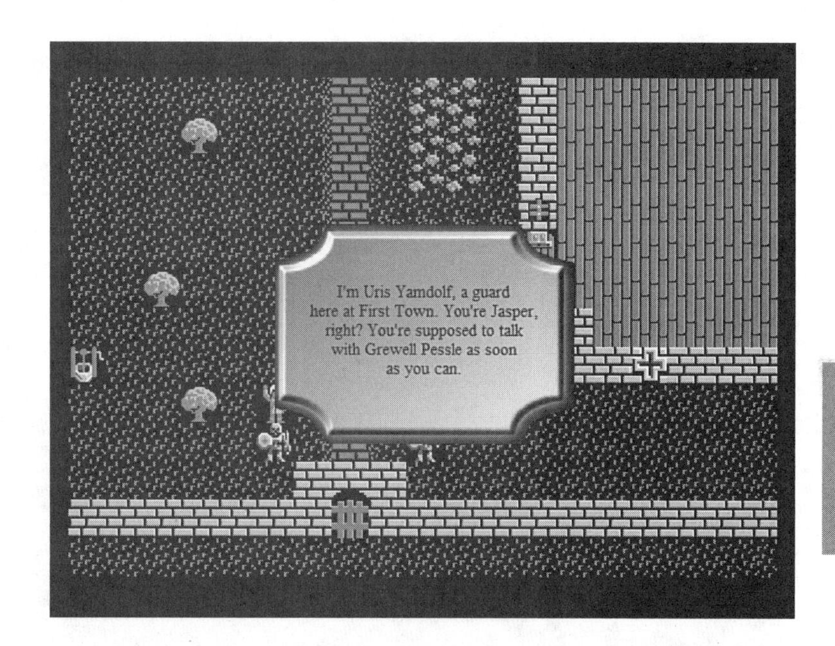

FIGURE C.8

There are quite a few people to talk to in town as you look for Grewell Pessle.

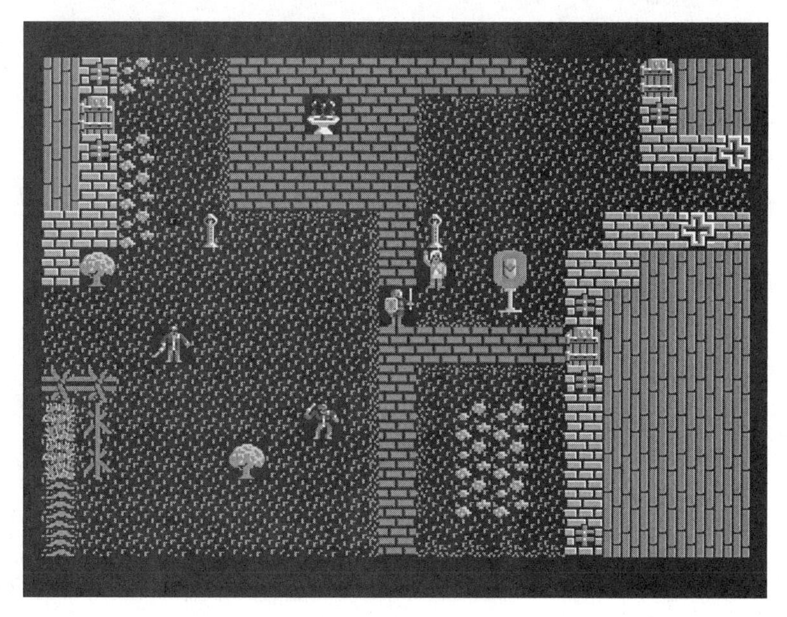

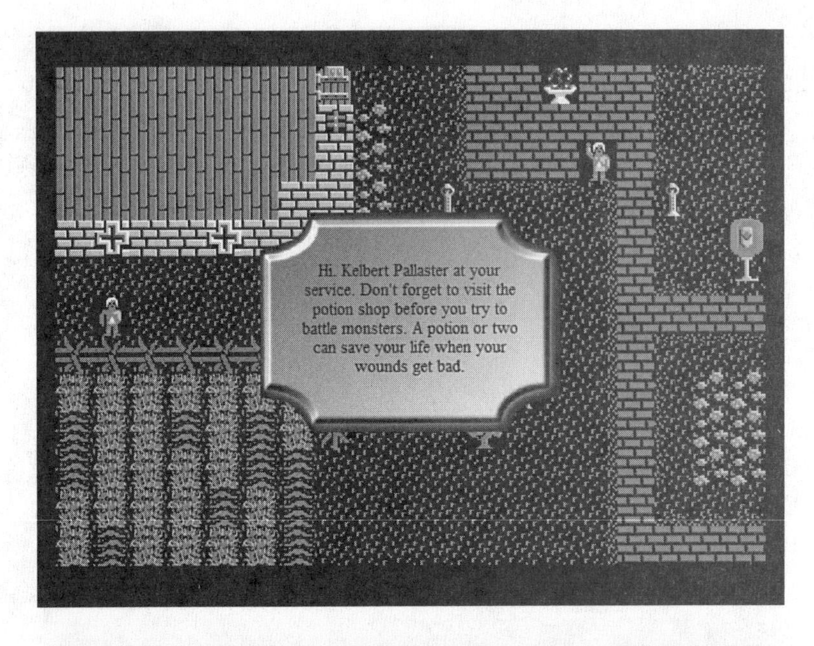

FIGURE C.9

Some information you get helps you to successfully to battle creatures.

FIGURE C.10

You'll also get some hints about what Grewell Pessle wants with you.

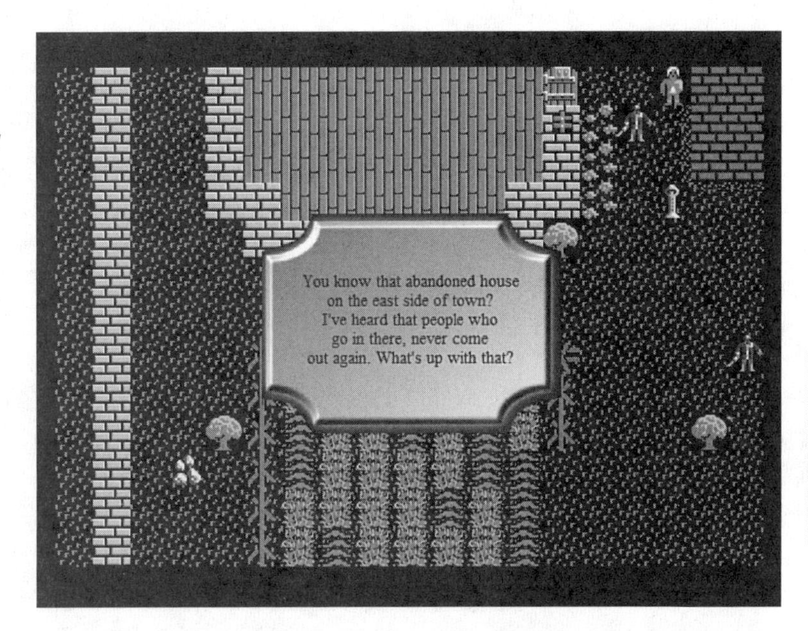

FIGURE C.11

Other town citizens have intriguing information that you'll need to follow up on later.

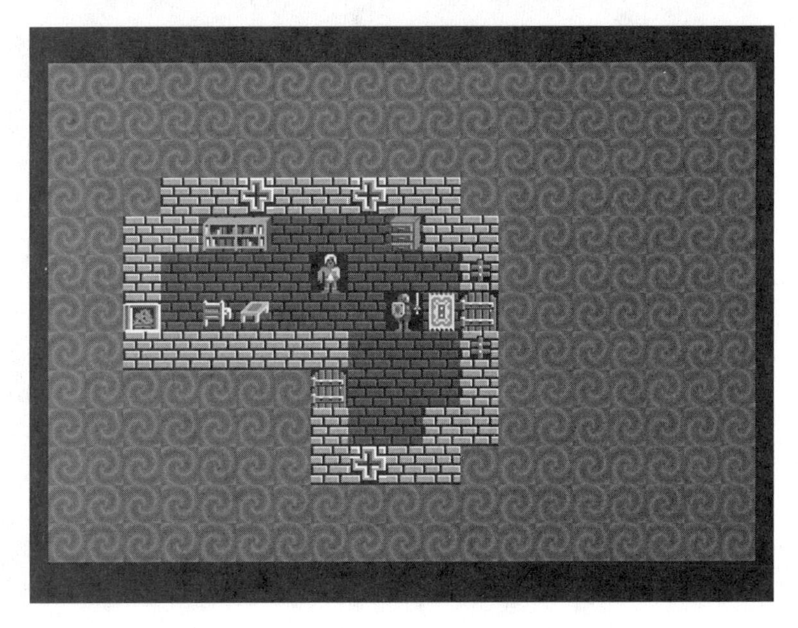

FIGURE C.12

And don't forget to check inside buildings for people who might have something interesting to say.

FIGURE C.13

This homebody has more information about the abandoned house, including exactly where it is.

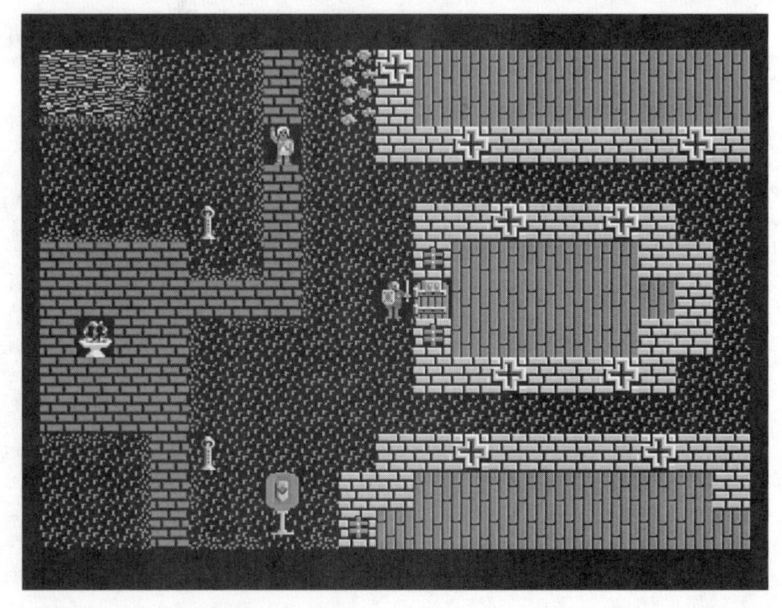

FIGURE C.14

Armed with your new information, you'll probably want to head directly over to the abandoned house...

FIGURE C.15

...only to discover that you can't get in. The only thing left to do is to continue to search for Grewell Pessle.

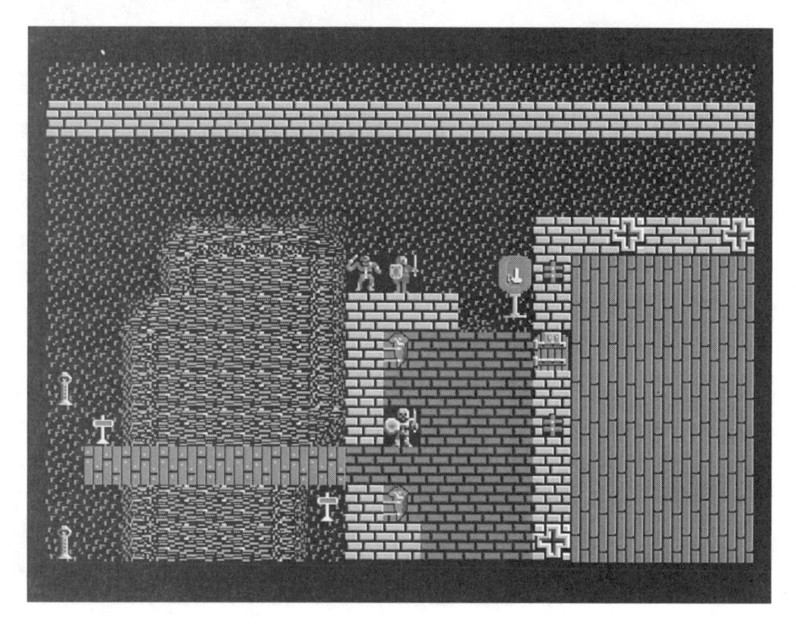

FIGURE C.16

Finally, you'll find this guy hanging around outside of the inn, and...

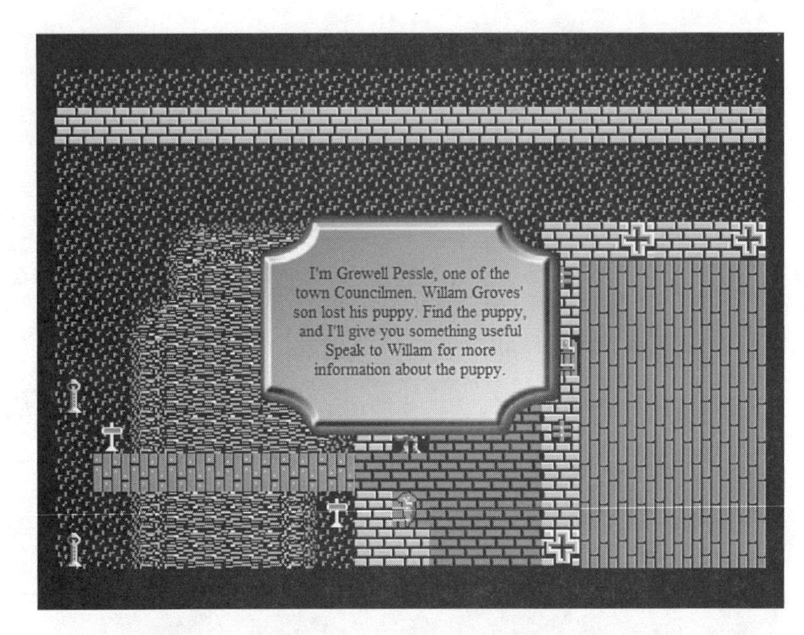

FIGURE C.17

...when you talk to him, you find out he's who you're looking for. You've now got your first quest, to find a boy's puppy, but first you have to search out yet someone else, somebody by the name of Willam Groves.

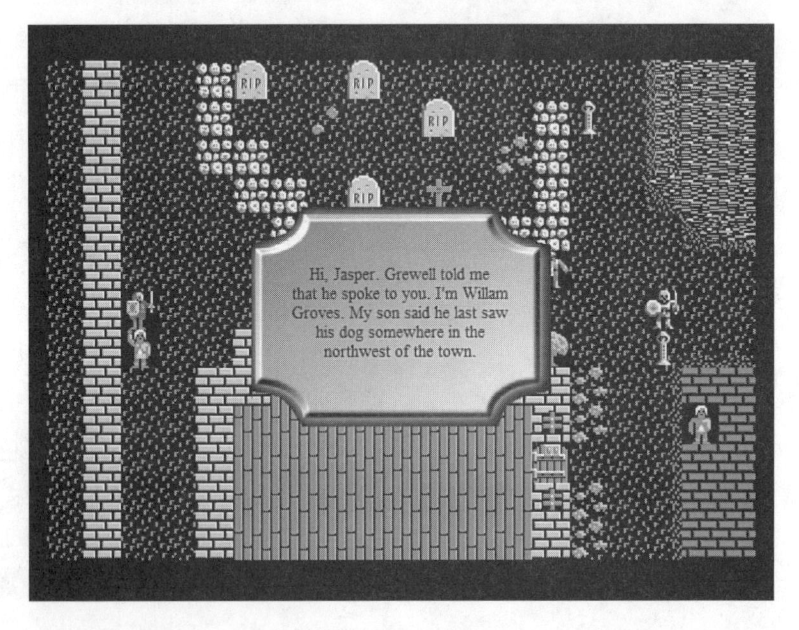

FIGURE C.18

When you find Willam, he'll tell you where to search for the puppy.

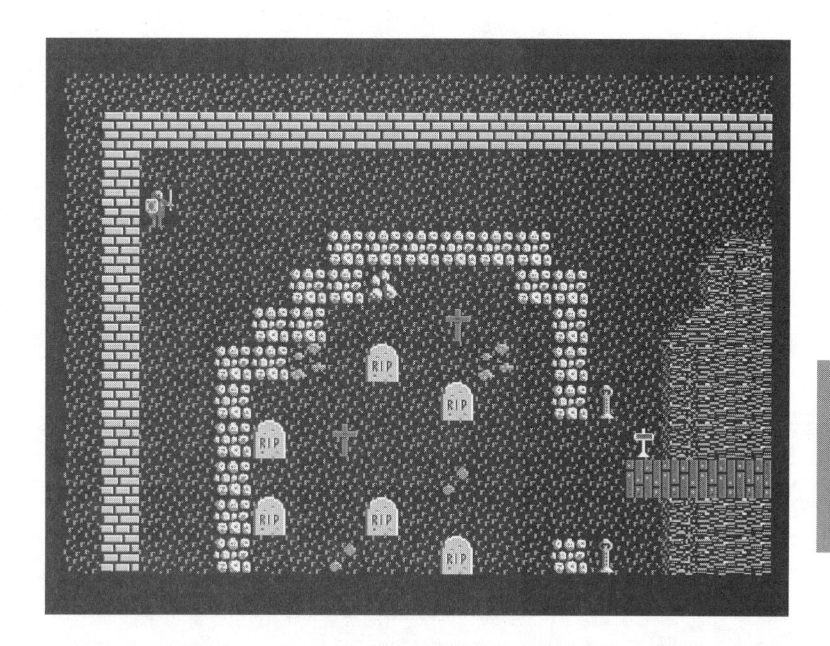

FIGURE C.19

This is the area to search for the puppy.

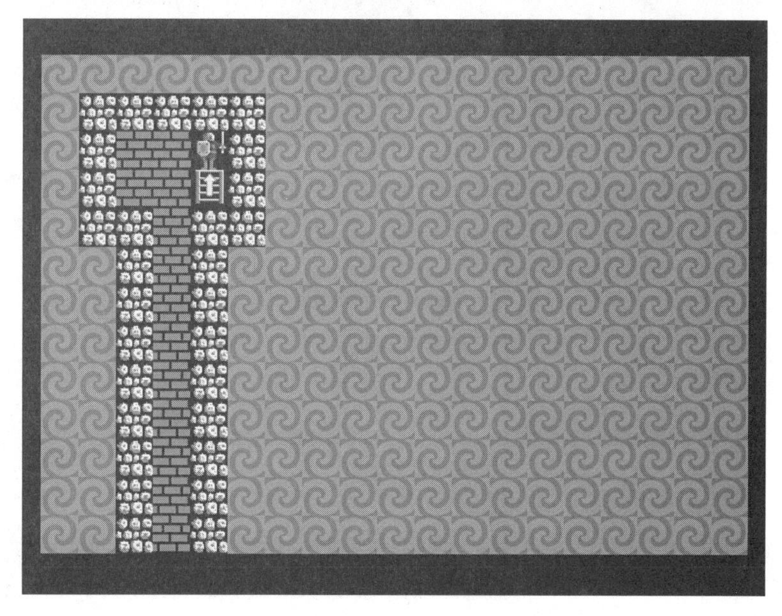

FIGURE C.20

During your search, you'll fall through the ground into a hidden dungeon.

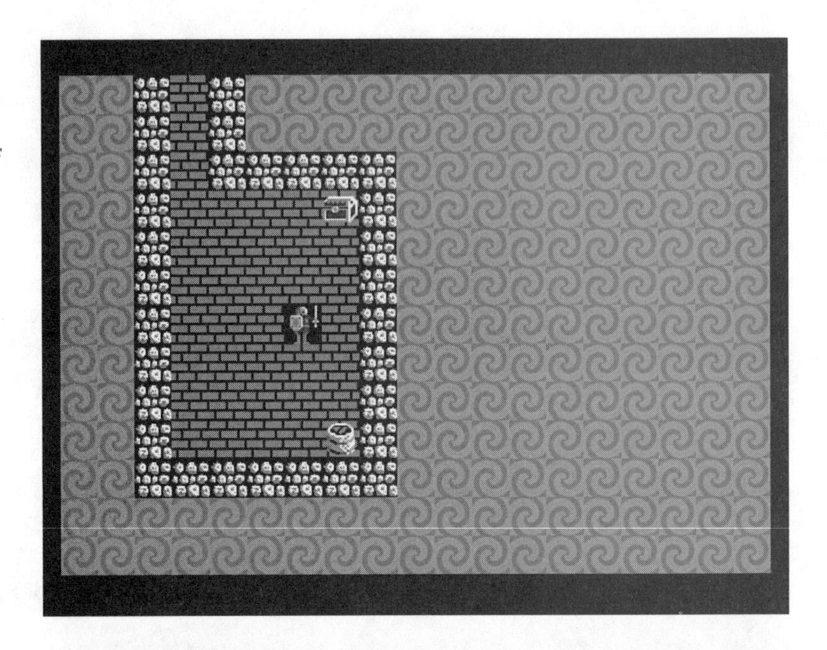

FIGURE C.21

In the dungeon, you'll find this room. The treasure chest contains some useful stuff, but it's the barrel that hides the real prize.

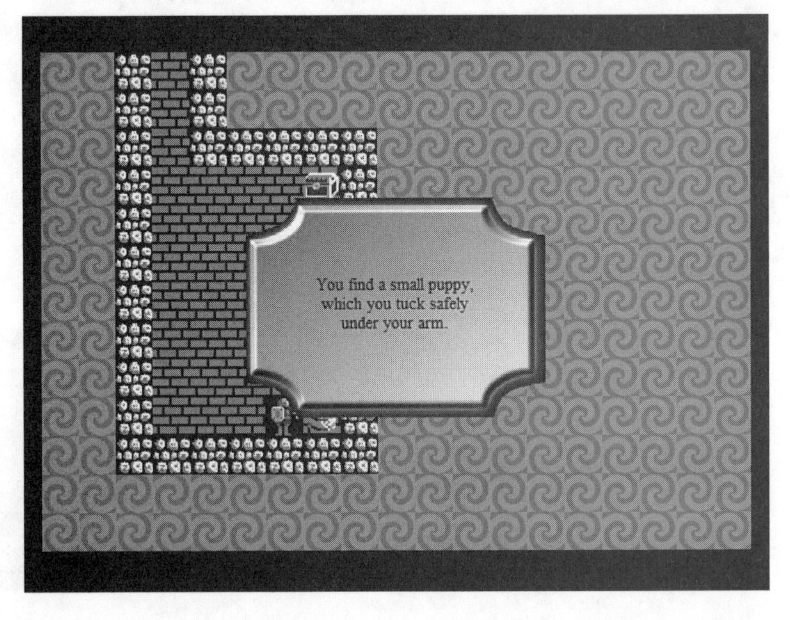

FIGURE C.22

If you search the barrel, you'll find the puppy.

FIGURE C.23

Now, if you head back to Grewell Pessle, he'll give you a reward for your hard work.

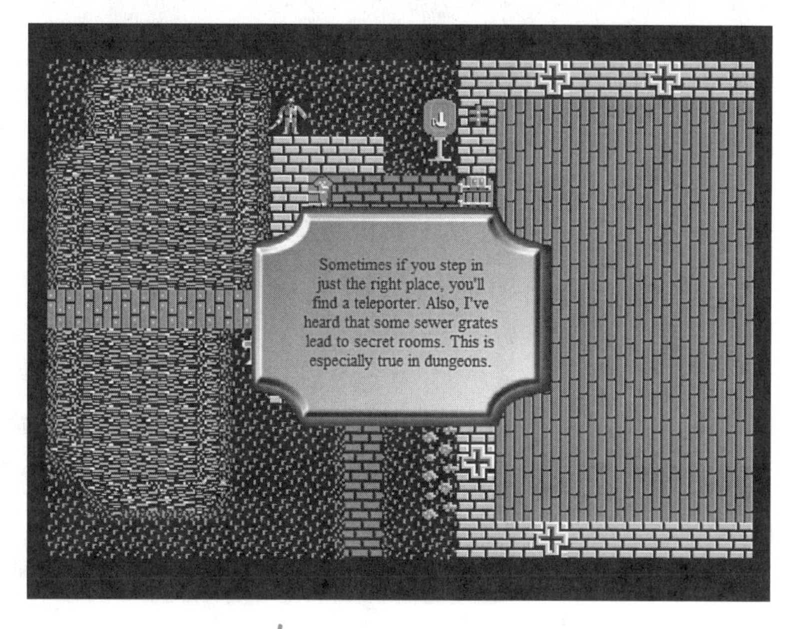

FIGURE C.24

Now that you have the key, you can get into the abandoned house. But before heading off, be sure that you've talked with everyone. You'll get more important hints about the new quest that lies behind the door of the abandoned house.

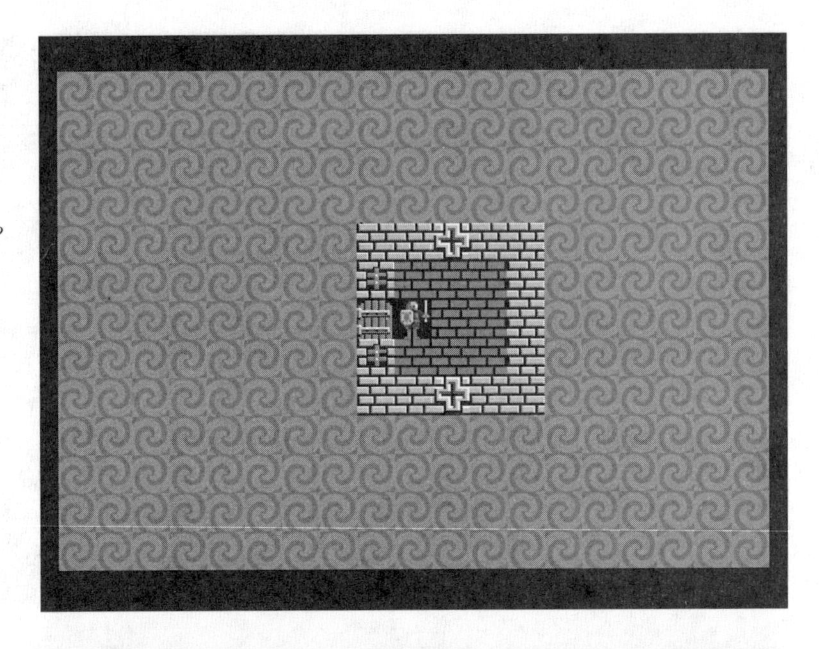

FIGURE C.25
When you enter the house, you'll notice something peculiar. Why is the house smaller inside than it looks from the outside?

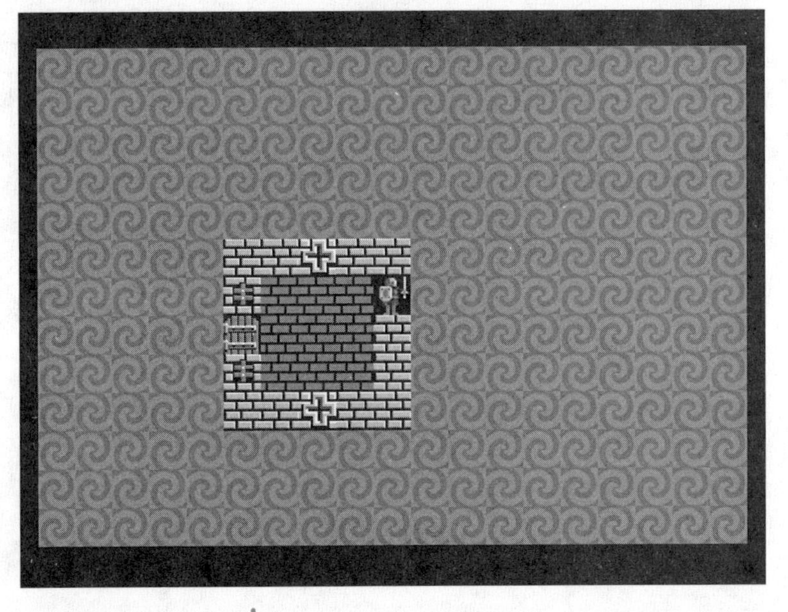

FIGURE C.26
A careful search reveals the answer: a secret door that leads to a hidden room.

FIGURE C.27

The stairs down lead to your first full dungeon.

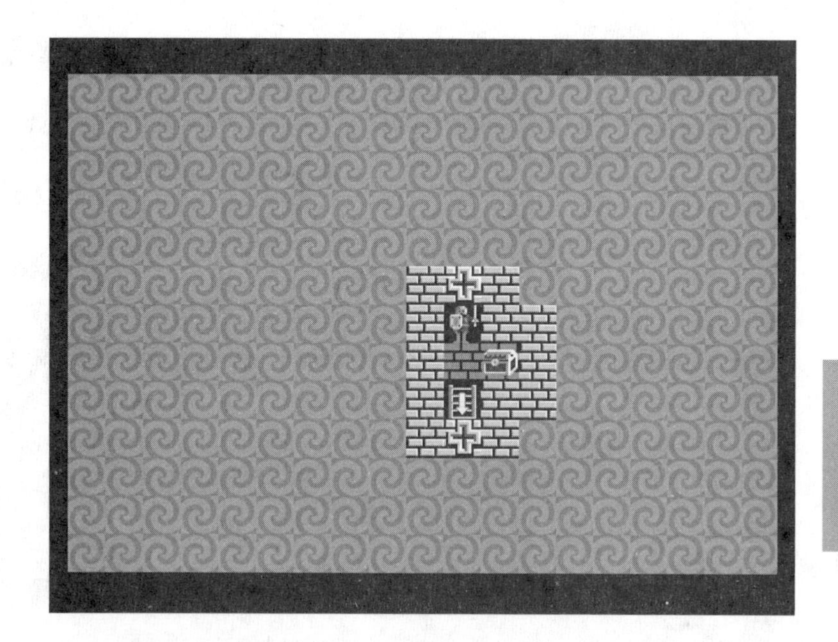

FIGURE C.28

In the dungeon are other hidden rooms, like this one filled with treasure chests.

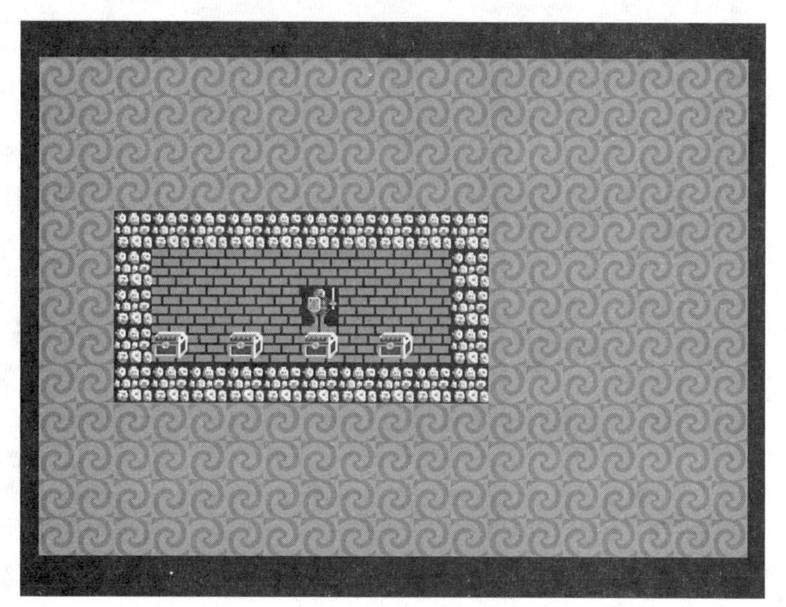

FIGURE C.29

The dungeon is also overrun with monsters, so tread carefully, and make sure you can make it back to the inn to get healed.

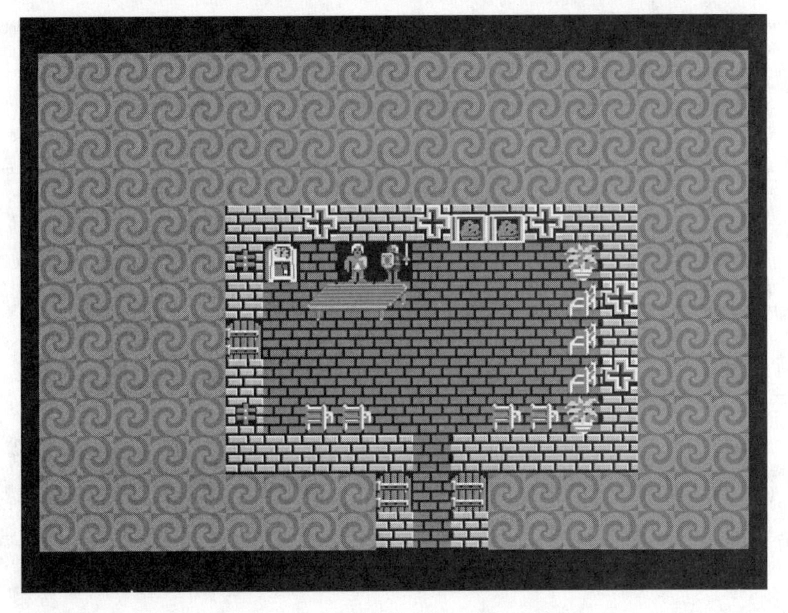

FIGURE C.30

You'll probably need to head back to the inn fairly often, where you should talk to the proprietor, and...

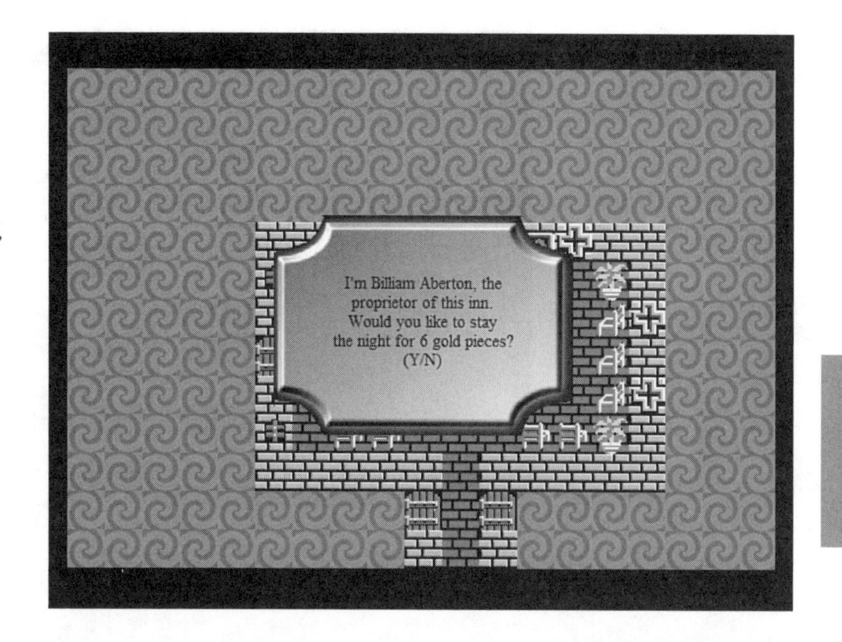

FIGURE C.31
...purchase a bed for the night, which will get you all ready for another trek into the dungeon to take on monsters, gather gold, and earn experience.

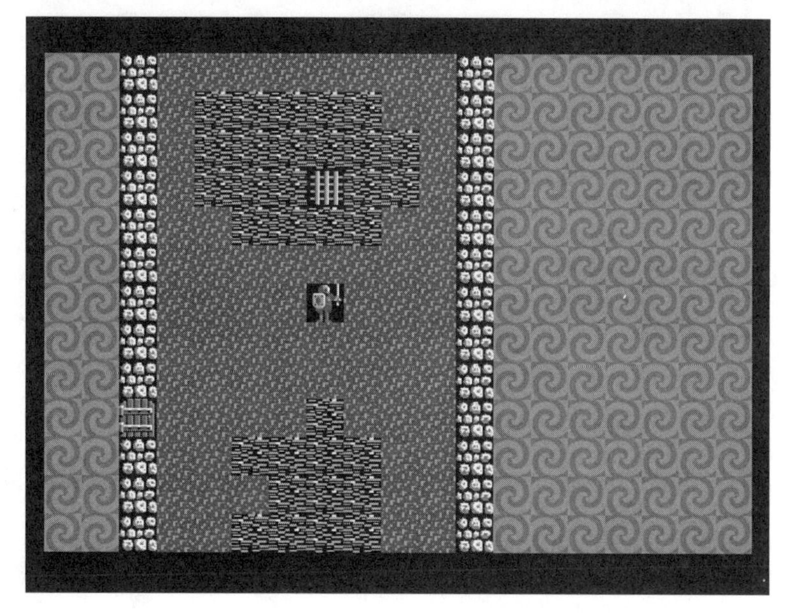

FIGURE C.32
In your search of the dungeon, you'll come across this sewer grate. But you can't cross the water to get to it.

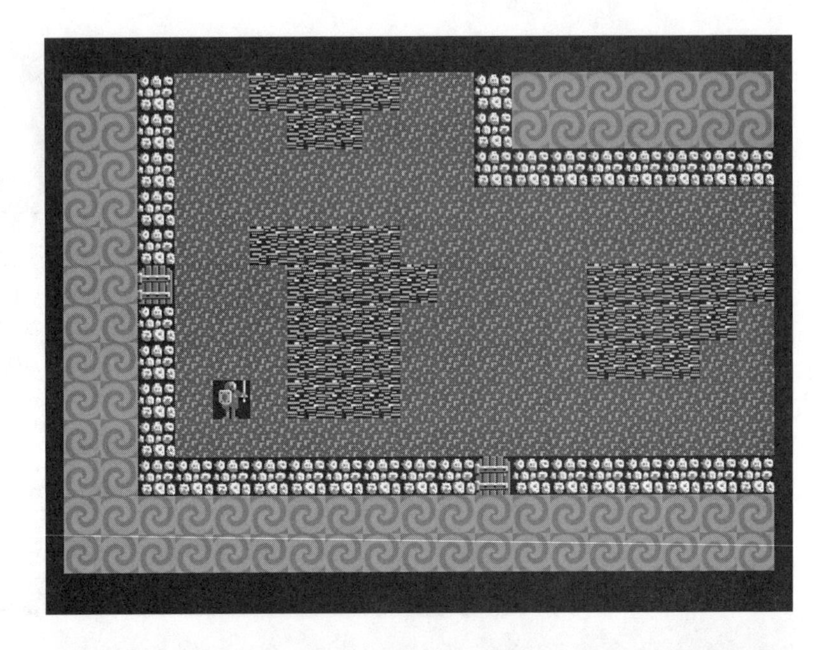

FIGURE C.33

Remember how you learned that dungeons can have teleporters? If you look in this corner of the room with the grate, you'll get a surprise.

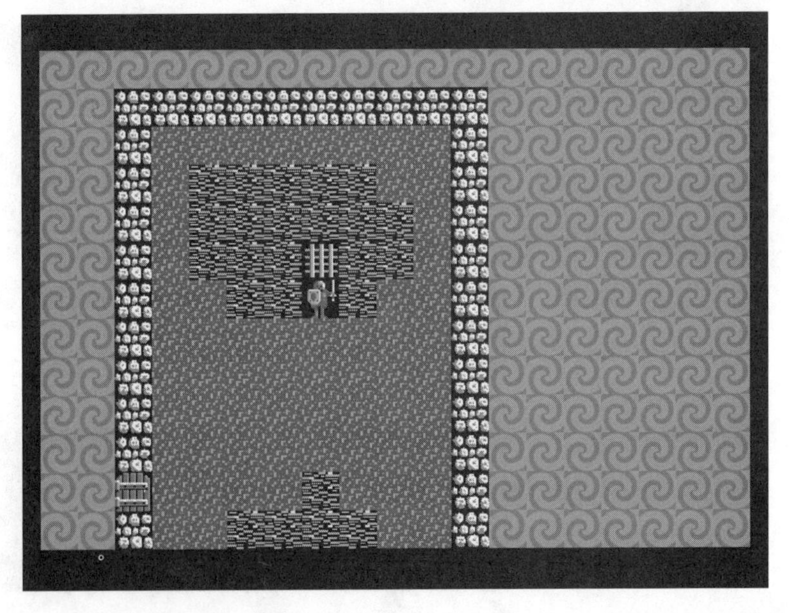

FIGURE C.34

Stepping in the right place gets you teleported right to the grate.

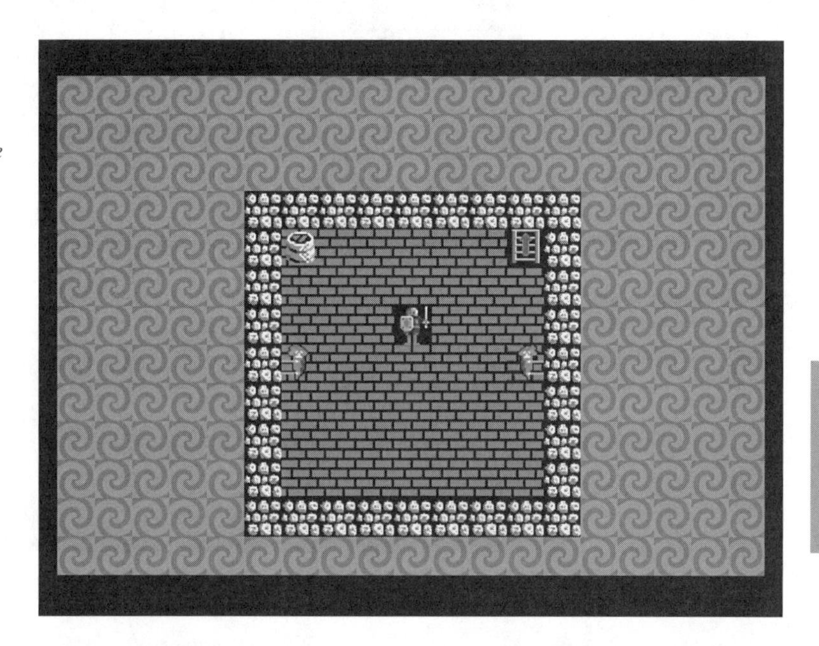

FIGURE C.35

Now you can step onto the sewer grate, which is actually the entrance to this secret room below the dungeon.

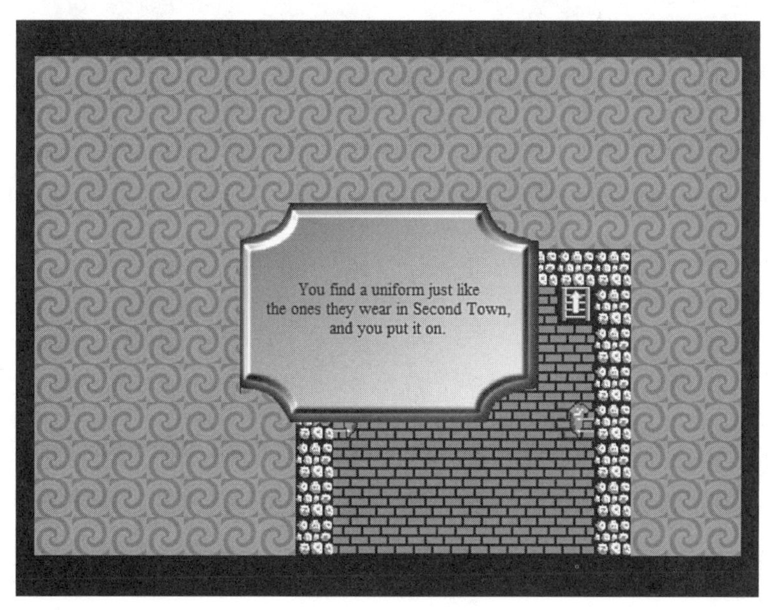

FIGURE C.36

In the barrel, you find an item that should help you out in Second Town.

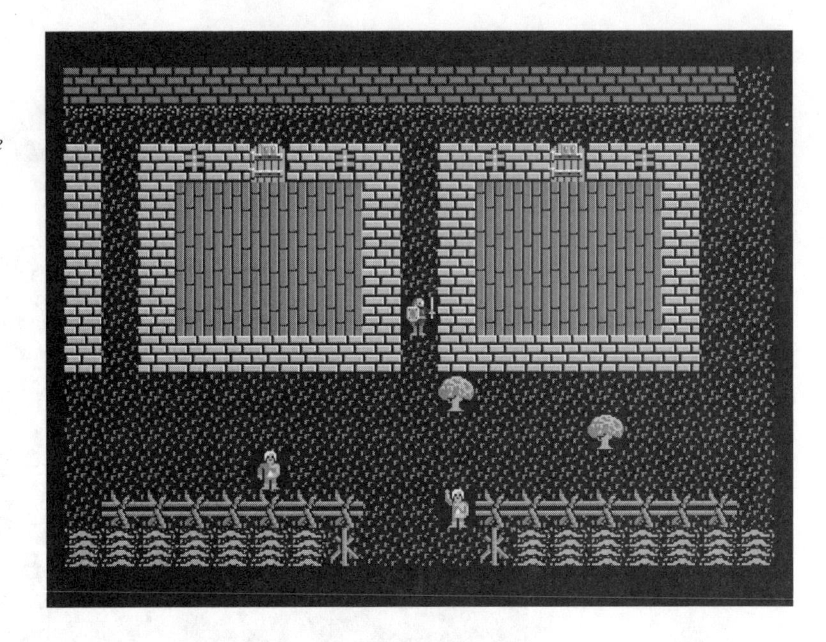

FIGURE C.37

And so you complete the game's second quest. Now that you're wearing the uniform, you can explore Second Town without being arrested as a spy. Note that Second Town is not complete. It's up to you to program the rest of the story!

APPENDIX D

A Quick Guide to Common Programming Tasks for the JBookman Project

As you know, there's still a whole lot of work to be done to turn *The Adventures of Jasper Bookman* into a full-length game. Much of this work involves creating a story line with lots of interesting quests. This type of work you can do in your head, jotting down notes as you go.

However, pretty soon you have to turn all those ideas into program code. Luckily, much of the programming is repetitive. For example, adding a new location to the game is a common task that you'll need to perform again and again. To help you with these common programming tasks, I've put together this quick guide, which will help you easily perform the following tasks:

- Adding a major location to the game
- Adding a minor location to the game

- Adding dialog for a non-player character
- Providing special handling for a container
- Providing special handling for a door
- Adding monsters to a location
- Providing custom processing for a `CEngine` method
- Saving and loading games
- Adding sound effects

Adding a Major Location to the Game

As you continue to work on the JBookman project, you'll need to add many new locations. The game has two kinds of locations. Major locations are things like towns, whereas minor locations are things like buildings and rooms in a town. To keep the game organized, you should create each major location in its own file. Here are the steps:

1. Add a new header file to the program, named for the location. This header file should declare at least one function, named `Handle`*`Name`*`()`, where *`Name`* is the name of the location.

   For example, to add the major location Second town, you'd add a header file named SecondTown.h. This header file should start off looking like this:

```
///////////////////////////////////////////////////////////
// SecondTown.h
///////////////////////////////////////////////////////////

#pragma once

void HandleSecondTown();
```

2. Add a new implementation file to the program, named for the location. This implementation file should define at least one function, named `Handle`*`Name`*`()`, where *`Name`* is the name of the location.

   For example, to continue adding the major location Second town, you'd add an implementation file named SecondTown.cpp. This file should start off looking like this:

```
///////////////////////////////////////////////////////////
// SecondTown.cpp
///////////////////////////////////////////////////////////

#include "constants.h"
#include "MyEngine.h"
#include "SecondTown.h"

extern CMyEngine g_Engine;
```

```
//////////////////////////////////////////////////////////////
// HandleSecondTown()
//////////////////////////////////////////////////////////////
void HandleSecondTown()
{
}
```

3. Add to MyEngine.h an include directive for the new location's header file.

   To continue with the Second Town example, you'd add the following to the include directive in MyEngine.h:

```
#include "SecondTown.h"
```

4. In the Constants.h file, add a constant for the location to the `g_iLocationEnum` enumeration.

   For example, here's the enumeration after a constant named `SECONDTOWN` has been added:

```
enum g_iLocationEnum
{
    FIRSTTOWN,
    FIRSTTOWNHOUSE01ROOM01,
    FIRSTTOWNHOUSE01ROOM02,
    FIRSTTOWNHOUSE02ROOM01,
    FIRSTTOWNHOUSE02ROOM02,
    FIRSTTOWNINNROOM01,
    FIRSTTOWNINNROOM02,
    FIRSTTOWNINNROOM03,
    FIRSTTOWNINNROOM04,
    FIRSTTOWNINNROOM05,
    FIRSTTOWNINNROOM06,
    FIRSTTOWNINNROOM07,
    FIRSTTOWNARMORER,
    FIRSTTOWNPOTIONS,
    GANJEKWILDS,
    FIRSTTOWNDUNGEON01ROOM01,
    FIRSTTOWNDUNGEON01ROOM02,
    FIRSTTOWNDUNGEON01ROOM03,
    FIRSTTOWNDUNGEON01ROOM04,
    FIRSTTOWNDUNGEON01ROOM05,
    FIRSTTOWNDUNGEON01ROOM06,
    FIRSTTOWNDUNGEON01ROOM07,
    FIRSTTOWNDUNGEON01ROOM08,
    FIRSTTOWNDUNGEON01ROOM09,
    FIRSTTOWNDUNGEON01ROOM10,
    FIRSTTOWNDUNGEON01ROOM11,
    FIRSTTOWNDUNGEON01LEVEL02,
    FIRSTTOWNDUNGEON02,
    SECONDTOWN
};
```

D

5. Add a `case` clause for the new location to the `RespondToPlayerLocation()` method in the MyEngine.cpp file.

   For example, in the case of Second Town, you'd add the following:

```
case SECONDTOWN:
    HandleSecondTown();
    break;
```

6. In the header file for the location that contains the entrance to the new location, add a constant for the new location's entrance location.

   For example, if the player enters Second Town from Ganjek Wilds, by stepping on sector #1037, you might add the following constant to the top of the Ganjek.h file:

```
const SECONDTOWNENTRANCE = 1037;
```

7. In the implementation file for the location that contains the entrance to the new location, add a `case` clause to the *`HandleName`*`()` method, where *`Name`* is the name of the location that contains the entrance to the new location.

   For example, if the player enters Second Town from Ganjek Wilds, you might add the following `case` clause to the `HandleGanjek()` method in the Ganjek.cpp file:

```
case SECONDTOWNENTRANCE:
    g_Engine.SaveGame(FALSE);
    // Set the player's starting sector in the new location.
    g_Engine.GetPlayer()->SetSector(1700);
    // Load the map file for the new location.
    g_Engine.OpenMapFiles("SecondTown.map", FALSE);
    // Set the current map to the new location's ID.
    g_Engine.SetCurrentMap(SECONDTOWN);
    // Load the tile set for the new location.
    g_Engine.GetCDirect3DObj()->SetCurrentTileSurface
        (g_Engine.GetCDirect3DObj()->GetTownExtTileSurface());
    g_Engine.ResetAnimation();
    break;
```

8. Copy the map files for the new location (which you created with the JBookman Game Editor) into the Maps folder in your main JBookman directory.

   In the case of Second Town, the files to copy would be as follows (assuming that you used the name SecondTown when you saved the files from the editor):

```
SecondTown.map
SecondTown.map.dor
SecondTown.map.item
SecondTown.map.peo
```

Adding a Minor Location to the Game

After adding a major location to the game, you'll want to fill it out with lots of minor locations. Such locations can include anything from rooms inside buildings to subterranean dungeons. It's all up to you. To add a minor location, just follow these steps:

1. In the Constants.h file, add a constant for the location to the `g_iLocationEnum` enumeration.

   For example, suppose you want to add a house to the Second Town location. Here's the enumeration after a constant named `SECONDTOWNHOUSE01` has been added:

```
enum g_iLocationEnum
{
    FIRSTTOWN,
    FIRSTTOWNHOUSE01ROOM01,
    FIRSTTOWNHOUSE01ROOM02,
    FIRSTTOWNHOUSE02ROOM01,
    FIRSTTOWNHOUSE02ROOM02,
    FIRSTTOWNINNROOM01,
    FIRSTTOWNINNROOM02,
    FIRSTTOWNINNROOM03,
    FIRSTTOWNINNROOM04,
    FIRSTTOWNINNROOM05,
    FIRSTTOWNINNROOM06,
    FIRSTTOWNINNROOM07,
    FIRSTTOWNARMORER,
    FIRSTTOWNPOTIONS,
    GANJEKWILDS,
    FIRSTTOWNDUNGEON01ROOM01,
    FIRSTTOWNDUNGEON01ROOM02,
    FIRSTTOWNDUNGEON01ROOM03,
    FIRSTTOWNDUNGEON01ROOM04,
    FIRSTTOWNDUNGEON01ROOM05,
    FIRSTTOWNDUNGEON01ROOM06,
    FIRSTTOWNDUNGEON01ROOM07,
    FIRSTTOWNDUNGEON01ROOM08,
    FIRSTTOWNDUNGEON01ROOM09,
    FIRSTTOWNDUNGEON01ROOM10,
    FIRSTTOWNDUNGEON01ROOM11,
    FIRSTTOWNDUNGEON01LEVEL02,
    FIRSTTOWNDUNGEON02,
    SECONDTOWN,
    SECONDTOWNHOUSE01
};
```

2. In the major location's header file, add a function declaration named `HandleMajorMinor()`, where *`Major`* is the name of the major location and `Minor` is the name of the minor location.

For example, in the case of Second Town's house, you'd add the following to the SecondTown.h file:

```
void HandleSecondTownHouse01();
```

3. In the major location's implementation file, add a function definition named `HandleMajorMinor()`, where *Major* is the name of the major location and `Minor` is the name of the minor location.

   For example, in the case of Second Town's house, you'd add something like the following to the SecondTown.cpp file:

```
///////////////////////////////////////////////////////////
// HandleSecondTownHouse01()
///////////////////////////////////////////////////////////
void HandleSecondTownHouse01()
{
    switch (g_Engine.GetPlayer()->GetSector())
    {
    case SECONDTOWNHOUSE01ENTRANCE:
        // The following code enables the player to exit the house.
        g_Engine.SaveGame(FALSE);
        g_Engine.GetPlayer()->SetSector(1484);
        g_Engine.OpenMapFiles("SecondTown.map", FALSE);
        g_Engine.SetCurrentMap(SECONDTOWN);
        g_Engine.GetCDirect3DObj()->SetCurrentTileSurface
            (g_Engine.GetCDirect3DObj()->GetTownExtTileSurface());
        g_Engine.ResetAnimation();
        break;
    }
}
```

4. Add a `case` clause for the new location to the `RespondToPlayerLocation()` method in the MyEngine.cpp file.

   For example, in the case of Second Town's house, you'd add the following:

```
case SECONDTOWNHOUSE01:
    HandleSecondTownHouse01();
    break;
```

5. In the header file for the major location that contains the entrance to the new minor location, add a constant for the new minor location's entrance location.

   For example, if the player enters the house in Second Town by stepping on sector #1483 (which probably contains a door), you might add the following constant to the top of the SecondTown.h file:

```
const SECONDTOWNHOUSE01ENTRANCE = 1483;
```

6. In the implementation file for the major location that contains the entrance to the new minor location, add a `case` clause to the `HandleName()` method, where *Name* is

the name of the major location that contains the entrance to the new minor location.

For example, if the player enters the house from Second Town, you might add the following `case` clause to the `HandleSecondTown()` method in the SecondTown.cpp file (you may also have to add the `switch` statement, which is shown here):

```
switch (g_Engine.GetPlayer()->GetSector())
{
case SECONDTOWNHOUSE01ENTRANCE:
    g_Engine.SaveGame(FALSE);
    // Set the player's starting sector in the new location.
    g_Engine.GetPlayer()->SetSector(1482);
    // Load the map file for the new location.
    g_Engine.OpenMapFiles("SecondTownHouse01.map", FALSE);
    // Set the current map to the new location's ID.
    g_Engine.SetCurrentMap(SECONDTOWNHOUSE01);
    // Load the tile set for the new location.
    g_Engine.GetCDirect3DObj()->SetCurrentTileSurface
        (g_Engine.GetCDirect3DObj()->GetTownIntTileSurface());
    g_Engine.ResetAnimation();
    break;
}
```

7. Copy the map files for the new location (which you created with the JBookman Game Editor) into the Maps folder in your main JBookman directory.

   In the case of Second Town's house, the files to copy would be as follows (assuming that you used the name SecondTownHouse01 when you saved the files from the editor):

```
SecondTownHouse01.map
SecondTownHouse01.map.dor
SecondTownHouse01.map.item
SecondTownHouse01.map.peo
```

D

Adding Dialog for a Non-Player Character

One of the most common tasks you'll be faced with as you continue to add to *The Adventures of Jasper Bookman* is getting non-player characters (NPCs) to hold a conversation. Here are the steps you must complete:

1. In the major location's header file, add a `Handle`*`Name`*`()`function, where *`Name`* is the name of the NPC.

   For example, to set up a method for a character named Martal Endwip in First Town, you would add the following to FirstTown.h:

```
void HandleMartalEndwip();
```

2. In the major location's implementation file, add the `HandleName()` function's definition, where *Name* is the name of the NPC.

   For example, to implement the function for Martal Endwip in First Town, you would add something like the following to FirstTown.cpp:

```
////////////////////////////////////////////////////////
// HandleMartalEndwip()
////////////////////////////////////////////////////////
void HandleMartalEndwip()
{
        g_Engine.TurnOnPlaque(
"Sometimes if you step in\n\
just the right place, you'll\n\
find a teleporter. Also, I've\n\
heard that some sewer grates\n\
lead to secret rooms. This is\n\
especially true in dungeons.");
}
```

3. Add an `else` clause for the NPC to the `CMyEngine` class's `HandleNPC()` method.

   To continue with the Martal Endwip example, you'd add the following `else` clause to `HandleNPC()`:

```
else if (strcmp(name, "Martal Endwip") == 0)
    HandleMartalEndwip();
```

Tip

You can cause an NPC to cycle through a series of replies by using a local static variable to keep track of the conversation. Here's an example:

```
////////////////////////////////////////////////////////
// HandleKellersWilopp()
////////////////////////////////////////////////////////
void HandleKellersWilopp()
{
    static int iTalkCount = 0;
    if (iTalkCount == 0)
        g_Engine.TurnOnPlaque(
"What are you doing in\n\
my room? Go away!");
    else if (iTalkCount == 1)
        g_Engine.TurnOnPlaque(
"You again? I thought I\n\
told you to go away!");
    else
        g_Engine.TurnOnPlaque(
"I'm going to call the guards\n\
if you don't leave me alone!");
    ++iTalkCount;
    if (iTalkCount > 2) iTalkCount = 0;
}
```

You can also use quest flags to control a conversation, as shown in the following function:

```
///////////////////////////////////////////////////////
// HandleWillamGroves()
///////////////////////////////////////////////////////
void HandleWillamGroves()
{
    if (bSpokeToWillam && !bWillamQuestComplete)
        g_Engine.TurnOnPlaque(
"My son is very unhappy.\n\
Please find his puppy.");
    else if (bSpokeToGrewell && !bSpokeToWillam)
    {
        g_Engine.TurnOnPlaque(
"Hi, Jasper. Grewell told me\n\
that he spoke to you. I'm Willam\n\
Groves. My son said he last saw\n\
his dog somewhere in the\n\
northwest of the town.");
        bSpokeToWillam = TRUE;
    }
    else if (bWillamQuestComplete)
        g_Engine.TurnOnPlaque(
"Hi again, Jasper! My son is\n\
thrilled to have his puppy back.\n\
Did you see Grewell Passle\n\
about your reward?");
    else
        g_Engine.TurnOnPlaque(
"Hello, stranger.\n\
I'm Willam Groves.");
}
```

D

Providing Special Handling for a Container

Normally, the game engine takes care of containers for you, displaying to the player whether the container is locked and transferring the contents of the container to the player when the player opens the container. However, there will almost certainly be times when you'll want to provide customized handling for a container. To accomplish this task, all you have to do is write a new `else if` clause for the `CMyEngine` class's `HandleContainer()` method (which overrides `CEngine`'s `HandleContainer()`).

For example, suppose you want the player to find a uniform in a barrel. This barrel is located in a level 2 room in First Town's main dungeon. Here's what `HandleContainer()` will look like after adding the required `else if` clause:

```
//////////////////////////////////////////////////////
// HandleContainer()
//////////////////////////////////////////////////////
BOOL CMyEngine::HandleContainer(int iSector)
{
    if (m_iCurrentMap == FIRSTTOWNDUNGEON02 &&
            m_Sectors[iSector] == BARREL_DUN)
    {
        FinishWillamQuest();
        return TRUE;
    }
    else if (m_iCurrentMap == FIRSTTOWNDUNGEON01LEVEL02 &&
            m_Sectors[iSector] == BARREL_DUN)
    {
        FinishUniformQuest();
        return TRUE;
    }
    else
        return CEngine::HandleContainer(iSector);
}

//////////////////////////////////////////////////////
// FinishUniformQuest()
//////////////////////////////////////////////////////
void FinishUniformQuest()
{
    if (!bGotUniform)
    {
        g_Engine.TurnOnPlaque(
"You find a uniform just like\n\
the ones they wear in Second Town,\n\
and you put it on.");
        bGotUniform = TRUE;
    }
    else
        g_Engine.TurnOnPlaque("You find nothing.");
}
```

Here, the `else if` clause in `HandleContainer()` handles the special situation described in the previous paragraph. The function `FinishUniformQuest()`, which is called in the `else if` clause, is also shown here. Always remember to return `TRUE` from the code in `HandleContainer()` so that the game engine knows that the container has been handled.

Providing Special Handling for a Door

Adding special handling for a door isn't much different than doing it for a container. In this case, you need to add code to the `CMyEngine` class's `HandleDoor()` method (which overrides `CEngine`'s `HandleDoor()`).

For example, here's how the game handles the special case of the abandoned house's front door:

```
///////////////////////////////////////////////////////
// HandleDoor()
///////////////////////////////////////////////////////
BOOL CMyEngine::HandleDoor(int iSector)
{
    if (m_iCurrentMap == FIRSTTOWN && iSector == HOUSE02FRONTDOOR)
    {
        BOOL bOpen = OpenAbandonedHouse();
        return bOpen;
    }
    return CEngine::HandleDoor(iSector);
}

///////////////////////////////////////////////////////
// OpenAbandonedHouse()
///////////////////////////////////////////////////////
BOOL OpenAbandonedHouse()
{
    if (bHasWillamKey)
    {
        g_Engine.TurnOnPlaque(
"You use the key you got\n\
from Grewell Pessle to\n\
open the door.");
        return TRUE;
    }
    g_Engine.TurnOnPlaque("You need a special key.");
    return FALSE;
}
```

D

Adding Monsters to a Location

Some areas of the game are safe for the player to travel through—such as in First Town—whereas others, like Ganjek Wilds, are overrun with monsters. However, as the game's programmer, it's completely up to you where monsters show up. Here's how to add monsters to a location in the game:

1. In the MyEngine.cpp file, add a case clause, to the `IsMonsterLocation()` method, for the location in which you want monsters to attack the player.

   For example, suppose you want the player to get attacked in First Town's Dungeon #2, which is where the player finds the lost puppy. You would then add a case clause for the location ID `FIRSTTOWNDUNFEON02`, like this:

   ```
   ///////////////////////////////////////////////////////
   // IsMonsterLocation()
   ```

```
////////////////////////////////////////////////////////
BOOL CMyEngine::IsMonsterLocation()
{
    switch (m_iCurrentMap)
    {
    case GANJEKWILDS:
    case FIRSTTOWNDUNGEON01ROOM01:
    case FIRSTTOWNDUNGEON01ROOM02:
    case FIRSTTOWNDUNGEON01ROOM08:
    case FIRSTTOWNDUNGEON01ROOM09:
    case FIRSTTOWNDUNGEON01ROOM10:
    case FIRSTTOWNDUNGEON01ROOM11:
    case FIRSTTOWNDUNGEON02:
        return TRUE;
    }
    return FALSE;
}
```

2. Add the monster to the `GetMonster()` method in MyEngine.cpp.

   Continuing the Dungeon #2 example, suppose you want the Eye Blob creature to appear in the dungeon, your `GetMonster()` method might end up something like this:

```
////////////////////////////////////////////////////////
// GetMonster()
////////////////////////////////////////////////////////
CMonster* CMyEngine::GetMonster()
{
    CMonster* m_pCurrentMonster = new CMonster();
    switch(GetCurrentMap())
    {
    case GANJEKWILDS:
        m_pCurrentMonster->SetName("Snake");
        m_pCurrentMonster->SetMaxHitPoints(10);
        m_pCurrentMonster->SetRemainingHitPoints(10);
        m_pCurrentMonster->SetMaxAttackDamage(8);
        m_pCurrentMonster->SetExperienceValue(1);
        m_pCurrentMonster->SetMaxGold(10);
        m_Direct3D.CreateMonsterTextures("Graphics\\SnakeA.bmp",
            "Graphics\\SnakeB.bmp", "Graphics\\SnakeC.bmp",
            "Graphics\\SnakeD.bmp");
        break;
    case FIRSTTOWNDUNGEON01ROOM01:
    case FIRSTTOWNDUNGEON01ROOM02:
    case FIRSTTOWNDUNGEON01ROOM08:
    case FIRSTTOWNDUNGEON01ROOM10:
        m_pCurrentMonster->SetName("Eye Blob");
        m_pCurrentMonster->SetMaxHitPoints(5);
        m_pCurrentMonster->SetRemainingHitPoints(5);
        m_pCurrentMonster->SetMaxAttackDamage(5);
```

```
            m_pCurrentMonster->SetExperienceValue(1);
            m_pCurrentMonster->SetMaxGold(5);
            m_Direct3D.CreateMonsterTextures("Graphics\\EyeBlobA.bmp",
                "Graphics\\EyeBlobB.bmp", "Graphics\\EyeBlobC.bmp",
                "Graphics\\EyeBlobD.bmp");
            break;
        case FIRSTTOWNDUNGEON01ROOM09:
        case FIRSTTOWNDUNGEON01ROOM11:
            m_pCurrentMonster->SetName("Green Eye Blob");
            m_pCurrentMonster->SetMaxHitPoints(10);
            m_pCurrentMonster->SetRemainingHitPoints(10);
            m_pCurrentMonster->SetMaxAttackDamage(10);
            m_pCurrentMonster->SetExperienceValue(1);
            m_pCurrentMonster->SetMaxGold(5);
            m_Direct3D.CreateMonsterTextures("Graphics\\GreenEyeBlobA.bmp",
                "Graphics\\GreenEyeBlobB.bmp", "Graphics\\GreenEyeBlobC.bmp",
                "Graphics\\GreenEyeBlobD.bmp");
            break;
        case FIRSTTOWNDUNGEON02:
            m_pCurrentMonster->SetName("Eye Blob");
            m_pCurrentMonster->SetMaxHitPoints(5);
            m_pCurrentMonster->SetRemainingHitPoints(5);
            m_pCurrentMonster->SetMaxAttackDamage(5);
            m_pCurrentMonster->SetExperienceValue(1);
            m_pCurrentMonster->SetMaxGold(5);
            m_Direct3D.CreateMonsterTextures("Graphics\\EyeBlobA.bmp",
                "Graphics\\EyeBlobB.bmp", "Graphics\\EyeBlobC.bmp",
                "Graphics\\EyeBlobD.bmp");
            break;
        }
        return m_pCurrentMonster;
    }
```

Providing Custom Processing for a `CEngine` Method

As you work on your game, you may find that you need to provide additional hooks into the `CEngine` class. For example, you might want to provide special processing for the `PlayerBlocked()` method, which determines when the player is unable to move through an object. To add customized code to the game, you should try not to change the game engine, because the game engine is meant to handle only the default or general aspects of the game. Code that applies only to your specific game story belongs in the `CMyEngine` class. Still, you can change the behavior of the game engine by overriding methods in `CMyEngine`. Here's how:

1. Find the method you want to override in the `CEngine` class and change its declaration to virtual. Also be sure that, if necessary, you move the method from the `CEngine` class's private section to protected or public.

   For example, in the case of wanting to provide special handling for the `CEngine` class's `PlayerBlocked()` method, move `PlayerBlocked()`'s declaration in Engine.h from the class's private area to the protected area, and then add the keyword `virtual` in front of it.

2. In the CMyEngine.h file, add a declaration for the method you want to override.

   Continuing with the `PlayerBlocked()` example, you would add the following line to the protected method declarations in CMyEngine.h:

   ```
   virtual BOOL PlayerBlocked(int g_iPlayerSector, int direction);
   ```

3. In the CMyEngine.cpp file, provide the method's implementation, being sure to call the `CEngine` version of the method whenever special processing is not needed.

   In the case of `PlayerBlocked()`, you might add the following method definition to the CMyEngine.cpp file. This implementation provides all the default processing (by calling `CEngine`'s version of the method), but also prevents the player from stepping into sector #943 in First Town (which is the sector immediately south of the fountain):

   ```
   ///////////////////////////////////////////////////////////
   // PlayerBlocked()
   ///////////////////////////////////////////////////////////
   BOOL CMyEngine::PlayerBlocked(int iPlayerSector, int direction)
   {
       int iSector = iPlayerSector;
       if (direction == NORTH)
           iSector = iSector - MAPCOLUMNCOUNT;
       else if (direction == SOUTH)
           iSector = iSector + MAPCOLUMNCOUNT;
       else if (direction == EAST)
           iSector = iSector + 1;
       else if (direction == WEST)
           iSector = iSector - 1;
       int item = m_Sectors[iSector];

       if (m_iCurrentMap == FIRSTTOWN && iSector == 943)
           return TRUE;
       else
           return CEngine::PlayerBlocked(iPlayerSector, direction);
   }
   ```

Saving and Loading Games

One thing you'll definitely be adding to the game is a ton of quest flags, those Boolean values than keep track of what tasks the player has completed in the story. Every one of these flags (and any other game data you add) needs to be included in the methods that save and load games.

Suppose that you've created a flag named `bGotUniform` that keeps track of whether the player has found a uniform. You'd need to add something like this to the `CMyEngine` class's `SaveGame()` method:

```
SaveFile << bGotUniform << '\n';
```

Of course, anything that gets saved to the save-game file also needs to be loaded. You'd also need to add the following to the `LoadGame()` method:

```
GetStringFromFile(SaveFile, buf);
bGotUniform = atoi(buf);
```

Also, don't forget that the data must be loaded in the same order that it's saved.

Adding Sound Effects

As it currently stands, *The Adventures of Jasper Bookman* can use a few extra sound effects. Adding sound effects to the game is easy, but does require several steps. Here's what to do:

1. In the DirectSound.h file, add an `IDirectSoundBuffer` pointer for the new sound effect.

   For example, suppose you want to add a sound effect for when the player opens a container. You would add something like this to the protected data members of the `CDirectSound` class:

   ```
   IDirectSoundBuffer* m_pContainerOpenSound;
   ```

2. In the DirectSound.cpp file, add to the class's constructor a line that initializes the pointer to `NULL`.

   In the case of the example `m_pContainerOpenSound` pointer, you'd add a line like this to the class's constructor:

   ```
   m_pContainerOpenSound = NULL;
   ```

3. Again in the DirectSound.cpp file, add to the class's `CleanUp()` method the code needed to release the pointer. (Make sure you add the code before the `m_pDirectSoundObj` pointer is released.)

In the case of the example `m_pContainerOpenSound` pointer, you'd add the following to the class's `CleanUp()` method:

```
if (m_pContainerOpenSound)
    m_pContainerOpenSound->Release();
```

4. In the `CreateSoundBuffers()` method, add a call to the `LoadSoundEffect()` method for the sound effect.

   Continuing with the opening-container sound effect example, you'd add something like this to `CreateSoundBuffers()`:

```
hResult = LoadSoundEffect("Sounds\\ContainerOpen.wav",
&m_pContainerOpenSound);
```

5. In the `PlaySound()` method, add a `case` clause for the sound effect. You'll also need to add a constant for the sound to the `g_sounds` enumeration in Constants.h.

   Continuing with the opening-container sound effect example, you'd add a `case` clause something like this to `PlaySound()`:

```
case CONTAINEROPEN:
    pBuf = m_pContainerOpenSound;
    break;
```

6. Find the place where the program should play the sound effect and add a call to the `CDirectSound` object's `PlaySound()` method.

   Continuing with the opening-container sound effect example, you'd probably change the `CEngine` class's `HandleContainer()` method like this:

```
//////////////////////////////////////////////////////
// HandleContainer()
//////////////////////////////////////////////////////
BOOL CEngine::HandleContainer(int iSector)
{
    BOOL bCouldOpenContainer = TRUE;
    CContainer* pContainer = FindContainer(iSector);
    if (pContainer->GetLocked() == TRUE)
    {
        if (m_Player.GetKeys() > 0)
        {
            m_Player.SetKeys(m_Player.GetKeys() - 1 );
            pContainer->SetLocked(FALSE);
            m_Sound.PlaySound(CONTAINEROPEN);
            if (ContainerEmpty(pContainer))
                TurnOnPlaque("You unlock it. It's empty.");
            else
                RetrieveItemsFromContainer(pContainer, "You unlock it.");
            bCouldOpenContainer = TRUE;
        }
        else
        {
```

```
                TurnOnPlaque("You need a key.");
                bCouldOpenContainer = FALSE;
            }
        }
        else
        {
            m_Sound.PlaySound(CONTAINEROPEN);
            if (ContainerEmpty(pContainer))
                TurnOnPlaque("It's empty.");
            else
                RetrieveItemsFromContainer(pContainer, "You open it.");
            bCouldOpenContainer = TRUE;
        }

        return bCouldOpenContainer;
    }
```

7. Copy the sound effect's .wav file into your JBookman project's Sounds directory.

Index

Symbols

A

B

E

F

H

K-L

M

N

O

P

Q

R

T

U

V

W-Z